Forged

in the

Fires

How Providence, Purpose,
and Perseverance Shaped America

E. PAUL YARBRO

ISBN 978-1-0980-2532-8 (paperback)
ISBN 978-1-0980-2533-5 (digital)

Christian Faith Publishing, Inc.
832 Park Avenue
Meadville, PA 16335
www.christianfaithpublishing.com

Printed in the United States of America

To Jennifer, Jake, James, and Eric who believed
in this book—and its author.

Introduction

American history is more than dates or events to be memorized. It is voices from the past calling to our own time, asking us to listen.

American history is the experience of a nation through the actions of its people. A nation is much like an individual with its failures, tragedies, and triumphs adding to its experience. Both make mistakes and can learn from them. Both individuals and nations are shaped by their past and often determine their future in how they perceive it.

Americans share a unique history. It is the story of a people who believed in Christian providence (God's intervening hand in the lives of people and events), the certainty of a greater purpose in a divine plan, and the gritty self-reliance and perseverance to overcome anything. Their stories are the real history of America, not the events themselves.

They were "*forged in the fires of adversity*" and relied on Christian faith to rise above the flames. With the impurities burned away, their character became the sword they carried into history.

They are calling from the past.

It is up to us to listen.

This is their story…

He shall baptize you with the Holy Ghost,
and with fire.

—John the Baptist,
Matthew 3:11

Behold, I have refined thee, but not with silver; I have chosen
thee in the furnace of affliction.

—Isaiah 48:10

God will not have his work made manifest by cowards.

—Ralph Waldo Emerson
"Self-Reliance"

People and nations are forged in the
fires of adversity.

—John Adams

1

The Warrior and the Saint

Jamestown, Virginia, 1609

The short stout man hurried through the forest, shoulders back and head held high. His head was up because he felt alive again.

They had to get back to the colony fast. He needed to explain something to all of them. Coming off one successful outing made him eager to try another.

At five-foot-four, he was two inches shorter than the average Englishman but appeared taller. Sharp-eyed and muscular, he had a full auburn beard, a high forehead, and a Roman nose, but something about his eyes made others uneasy. Why they felt threatened, no one could quite put a finger on, but it was there just the same. He was used to their prejudice and saw much in his twenty-nine years, and though the son of a farmer, he was much more than that.

Captain John Smith restrained his ambition too long and would no longer deny the truth. He had trusted himself and had been victorious once again, and it tasted sweet. Throughout his life, he proved to himself who he was, but for some reason, he felt the need to convince everyone else. Why did others have to validate what he knew to be true? Wasn't it enough that he knew it himself? The gentlemen and their self-righteous claims that birth determined a man's path planted seeds of doubt in the unconscious mind and caused men to question their abilities; though he knew it was a lie, it still controlled society. How many good men would never know their true potential because of this ignorance?

The lives of every man in Jamestown depended on his actions today, and he was ready to shatter the lie. This was why he needed to get there as quickly as possible. He would conquer the darkness of deception with the light of truth. "*To conquer is to live.*" Remembering this motto and the shield it adorned reminded him why. The men of Jamestown didn't know him, but they were about to understand him. With every step, the smile widened as his heart pounded in his chest. They would know who he was soon and be better for it. He had shown the Indians, and now, he would show them as well.[1]

Fifteen other men attempted to keep up with him but to no avail. They were burdened with the baskets of Indian corn, beans, and other staples secured by his gamble. Because of this, they remained vigilant and were startled by every shadow or crack of a branch.

No one could believe what they had witnessed the day before. He was either the bravest or craziest man alive, and they beamed with pride as he urged them to hurry. Some at the settlement said he was arrogant, but his words and actions told these men a different story. His countenance was not arrogance, but confidence in purpose. He wasn't all talk like the others. He had proven his mettle to them.

Turning around, he encouraged them to make haste. The settlement was just past the next rise. He saw their smiles before he resumed his march, and it energized him. They respected courage and leadership, even coming from one of their own. He could depend on them once inside and would need their help enforcing order. Those at the settlement would need a firmer hand to convince. For close to two years, he had tried to tell them they were on the road to destruction, but they scoffed at his warnings.

"Who do you think you are?" they asked. What vanity it was to believe in his own relevance? The gentlemen were their masters. At least, this was what they were told. God's divine plan determined status, not an individual's merit. Gentlemen were born to lead men and

---

[1] Hoobler, Thomas and Dorothy. 2006. *Captain John Smith: Jamestown and the Birth of the American Dream.* Hoboken: John Wiley & Sons, Inc., 37.

nations. All he was qualified to lead were pigs, chickens, and plow horses, they said. How he managed to worm his way onto the council was a mystery. The farmer's son didn't know his place in the English class system. Many reminded him of his lowly birth but failed to convince him of it. They had no idea what he'd been through or all he'd accomplished.

Approaching the stockade, Captain John Smith wiped the perspiration from his forehead with a sleeve and managed another small grin. Calling to the guard, he ordered the gate opened.

Entering the settlement of Jamestown after any period away was like experiencing it for the first time again. Crude shelters of tree branches and decayed cloth lay scattered throughout the camp while the putrid smell of filth, sickness, and human waste invaded the nostrils. Quiet whimpers of pain mingled with hacking coughs rounded out this symphony of despair. The inhabitants didn't seem to care anymore, and hopelessness spread quicker than disease. Some envied the dead and waited to join them while others slept under the shelters. A few sat staring at nothing, lost in memories of better times, but mostly, their minds were as barren as their stomachs; "… they would rather starve and rot with idleness, than be persuaded to do anything for their own relief."[2]

John's grin turned into a grimace. No longer could he sit by and watch as they destroyed themselves and the colony. The English class system produced in the New World what it did in the old—dependency and entitlement.

The settlers would receive minor relief from the baskets of food the expedition carried inside. The common store was rat-infested and moldy from carelessness. The daily ration was reduced to a cup of boiled barley and a cup of worm-infested wheat. The worms weren't so bad; they supplied a bit of the much-needed protein absent from their diets, so no one complained. The water was worse. Parasitic and brackish, it caused dysentery and salt poisoning. It tasted terrible,

---

[2] Smith, John. *A True Relation*. (1608) 37; Price, David A. *Love & Hate in Jamestown: John Smith, Pocahontas and the Start of a New Nation*. (New York: First Vintage Book & Edition, 2003), 55.

yet nobody cared to dig a well. The ground they chose to settle in was surrounded by swamps teeming with mosquitoes, and though an excellent strategic position, it wasn't conducive to health in the seventeenth century. Malnutrition from insufficient diets weakened their immune systems while the typhoid, malaria, and diarrhea weakened their numbers.[3]

Stepping forward, John called for a meeting. It was time to establish this colony on the truth. He was ready to save them with it, even at his own expense. Truth-tellers always made more enemies than liars, because lies were easy to embrace while the truth was a bitter pill. History was full of such examples and he would let posterity judge him by his actions.

Stroking his beard, John's eyes blazed and narrowed. A fire raged inside, and he had no doubt Jamestown would hear him this day. Inhaling, he prepared to breathe life into the colony to reverse its course.

"Who do you think you are?"

He contemplated this question many times before, but now he knew the answer. He had nothing more to prove to himself. The only thing left was to show the rest of them. Maybe truth would conquer their lives in the New World like it helped conquer his own.

"To conquer is to live." They were words to live by for John Smith.

It was all coming back to him now.

* * * * *

Plymouth Colony, Massachusetts, 1630

Sitting at his writing table, Governor William Bradford stared down at the empty page and sighed. How could anyone tell of their journey? Words on a page couldn't convey their story.

---

[3] Williams, Tony. *The Jamestown Experiment.* (Naperville: Sourcebooks, Inc., 2011), 119; John Smith. *The General History of Virginia, New England, and the Summer Isles,* (1624), 208; Price, 108.

He reached over and slid his Bible closer. It was old, and the binding was failing, but he managed a smile when he remembered the countless times he found solace in it. He was somewhat like the old book. He was no longer a naïve boy from Austerfield, England, but his "binding" was starting to fail too. He rubbed the delicate pages between his fingers and saw how fragile they were. God's instruction was the truth which bound it together, making it a steel sword, he decided. This was what bound Plymouth together from the start. The holy book's authors wrote down the sacred words of God himself. He could at least tell their story.

In a way, their journey was the next phase in the Lord's divine plan, he firmly believed.

Squeezing the Bible again, he shut his eyes and prayed for inspiration. How could *he* chronicle their trials? Who was *he* to speak for them?

Faded images invaded the blackness of his mind. He wasn't afraid of the past, but he wasn't eager to visit it either. The past contained many failures, disappointments, and deaths, and he avoided it. Within this pain, he realized, were many lessons. This story must be told. Countless generations, not yet born, deserved to know what they had been through.

He stood and walked over to the door. Stepping out into the sunlight, the weather reminded him of another day.

They had built quite a colony. Gazing across the town, he noticed a bounty of crops gathered near the fields. Children laughed and played while their parents busied about like the beavers whose pelts kept them warm every winter. Ambition was in their faces today, but it hadn't always been this way.

Hazy memories flooded his head, but one flooded his soul. It was one of the most important events of his life. It was a day much like this one when God showed him the way. Seven years had passed since he had to make those two decisions which would determine the future of Plymouth. He saw a younger version of himself and of Plymouth.

It was a day much like this one, he remembered. It was as if he was there again.

* * * * *

Plymouth, 1623

Standing at the edge of the colony, he noticed something odd about the workers in the fields.

The sun was high in the sky, but a gentle breeze made it a pleasant day nonetheless. What was all this commotion about?

One muscular lad threw his hat to the ground and raised his arms in the air, voicing his frustration. Though William couldn't hear what he was saying, he'd witnessed this scene many times before.[4]

He wrestled with this riddle for months, but always without reaching a conclusion. When they decided to establish a colony in the New World, they all agreed to this arrangement, though in hindsight, it was a disaster. All goods produced by the colony went into a common store. Equal shares were distributed among all of them. It seemed logical and fair at first, but over the last few years, they realized misery was all they equally shared.

Why should the young men work harder and receive the same share as those who worked less? How was this fair? He knew he must find a remedy fast. Envy and sloth were infecting the whole settlement and would eventually consume it. This wasn't God's path for them but a path of corruption. All men were corruptible, he knew, and certain things promoted this corruption. They left behind the Old World to shake off this corruption, but it was in their midst again.[5]

The land offered plenty of venison, rabbit, and fowl for meat while the climate and soil were rich in nutrients for crops. Even in the winter, the ocean provided a variety of fish, crab, lobster, and tur-

---

[4] Bradford, William. *Bradford's History of Plimoth Plantation: From the Original Manuscript.* (Boston: Wright & Potter Printing Co, 1898), 163–164.

[5] Ibid.

tle—but still, they starved. All they needed was available, but something wasn't working.

Not only must he find an answer to this pressing internal problem, but another more ominous external threat engulfed the colony.

This threat came from relations with the natives. The first year, the Pokanokets taught them various ways to grow and procure corn, squash, and beans, but this knowledge didn't make them self-sufficient. The will to better themselves seemed to wither while their dependence on trade decreased industry. When trade resumed, they ate better, but when relations soured, they had to fend for themselves. Dependence on trade contributed to less self-reliance. The Indians were unpredictable and halted trade if some chief had second thoughts about them, which they did frequently. William tried to discourage dependence on others for their daily bread, but this contradicted their practices and their adherence to an idea clouded their judgment.

The Indians were also being whipped into a frenzy by two conspirators who wanted to exterminate the English. Chief Massasoit, sick and dying, had warned them of this plot and advised them how to stop it, but William struggled with his advice. What else could he do? If he failed to act decisively or made an error in his decision, the colony faced massacre. This danger, coupled with Plymouth's inner turmoil, placed them at a crossroads, and he had to act.

Self-reliance may fix part of this problem, but the Indians would still see them as weak warriors.

They were farmers, not fighters; William knew this. They came to spread the word of God, not war. As Christians, they knew they must love their neighbor as themselves, but self-preservation took priority. Loving your neighbor as yourself could only be practiced by survivors, not dead men. This paradox caused deep introspection. He was governor and it was his decision.

Both problems required immediate attention. Their fate rested on his shoulders as a curse rested on Plymouth.

William slipped deeper into doubt and wondered if the fiery star he thought was a sign from heaven was really a bad omen after all.

It was too large a burden for any one man to bear, he believed. How could *he* fix it? If only his Dorothy was here. She gave him strength with her assurance. For some purpose, God had chosen him to lead the flock at this very moment, but why him? How could *he* save them from the Indians and themselves? Did he have the wisdom to decide their fate? Or would God show him the way?

Ashamed for doubting, William recovered his resolve.

The answer would come in God's time, not his own. He knew this truth innately, but fear caused amnesia. He must continue to pray and study the scriptures for the answer. Only then a solution could be revealed to deliver them.

It was there; he knew it was there, somewhere. Within creation itself, he would find the answer, but where? Was it inside himself?

If he ignored this truth, they would lose everything.

* * * * *

Plymouth, 1630

How long he stood there daydreaming, he didn't know. These memories reminded him why it was imperative to find the courage to tell their story. His despair was replaced by strength and determination. He remembered what they had sacrificed.

Returning to the house, he sat at his desk and gripped the Bible once again. Within it was all the wisdom of the ages. He had learned much in his own life. He would write their story, but first, he must remember his own. He'd travelled a long way since then.

Setting the withered book down, he dipped the quill, bringing it to the page. He hesitated again, then set his jaw. As he scribbled the first sentence, he remembered a boy with aching feet on a dirt path in England who, against all odds, found his way home.

* * * * *

The future of Plymouth and Jamestown rested in the hands of two men—John Smith and William Bradford. Two men with similar beginnings, who followed different paths, would determine the survival of both settlements. Fourteen years and six hundred miles separated them, but the problems they faced were nearly identical.

In the South, John Smith was Jamestown's only hope.

In the North, William Bradford was Plymouth's.

The fate of the United States of America, at its conception, faced extinction two separate times. Two unlikely misfits were all that stood between life and death of a nation.

Both were the sons of farmers who became outlaws to the society they were born into. Both believed in a greater purpose and the power of the individual.

Two different paths led to similar destinies.

* * * * *

The woods near Willoughby, Lincolnshire County, England, 1600

Under a makeshift shelter of tree branches and brush, John Smith lay comfortably on his back, reading a book. The noise of the woods was like music to his ears. Birds singing and flapping their wings, busy on their daily errands, was peaceful. The emerald leaves of the oaks shimmered from the sunshine penetrating the canopy above. A mild fragrance of violets perfumed the air on a gentle breeze, making him drowsy.

There was no time for sleep. Lost inside the book, he absorbed its wisdom. The relaxing solitude of the forest was the perfect remedy to gather one's thoughts. He would shut out the world to prepare his mind.

Returning from war in the Netherlands, he had to get away from town. Willoughby was short on excitement, and John's war stories were a magnet for the bored townspeople. He wanted to do more than tell stories. He wanted to live them. Soaking up every word of the book, he focused. He wanted more than a small part in a battle. He thirsted for the opportunity to be a great warrior on a field of glory, to reap the rewards of his own merit. Because of his birth, he needed every advantage. Born with a burning desire to break with the class system of England, John believed it was his responsibility to determine his status by his own accomplishments, not his birth. Even though everyone doubted him, he refused to doubt himself.

At twenty, he was bright and courageous with a hunger to learn and achieve. It was the perfect combination for what he was attempting to do. This idea was a radical new concept in the sixteenth and seventeenth centuries. English society based a man's success on birth, not merit. If you were born a farmer's son, you were expected to be a farmer. Only a gentleman's son could be a gentleman. The gentlemen were the upper-class, blessed with money and the right parents. They were the aristocracy of the era but rarely earned their status. They were born into it. The lower classes could do nothing to achieve greater status and accomplishments meant nothing. Who your father happened to be was all that mattered.

John hated this system. Each man should determine their own destiny. His father had nothing to do with his life, other than being his father. Why should a son suffer or benefit from his father's status? Shouldn't each man decide their own status? How many gentlemen had he known who didn't deserve their title? How many commoners had he known with so much potential, but their status kept them from ever trying?[6]

Turning a page, John forced himself to concentrate. He would work harder than the others to even the odds. He would gain the skills of a great soldier before he became one.

Retreating to the woods cut off any other options in his mind. Being a farmer's son was just a matter of one's perception, he thought. Reality was what a man believed he could accomplish, not what a society said he could. If he believed himself a warrior, prepared himself accordingly, by God he would be one. Sir Francis Drake was a sailor and privateer knighted by Queen Elizabeth who had bucked the class system. He was born a farmer's son too and achieved fame,

---

[6] Firstbrook, Peter. *A Man Most Driven: Captain John Smith, Pocahontas, and the Founding of America.* (London: Oneworld Publications, 2014), 32; Hoobler, 19.

fortune, and gentleman status through his own accomplishments. His detractors only wished they garnered such respect. The fear of being judged by your work, instead of family, promulgated snobbery from the nobility. If merit defined the man, then they would lose their status. Drake was an example of what a commoner could accomplish by hard work. John wanted to do the same.[7]

Set on finishing the book, he turned another page; "To know how to recognize an opportunity in war, and take it, benefits you more than anything else. Nature creates few men brave, industry and training makes many."[8]

Such wisdom in few words. *The Art of War* by Niccolo Machiavelli provided simple, concise truths any soldier must learn. Along with *The Golden Book of Marcus Aurelius,* which taught practical advice and virtue, he would strengthen his mind. *The Art of War* showed him how to make various explosives, which might be useful someday.[9] This sojourn in the forest was the first step. It would prepare him mentally and spiritually for the next step. Once his mind was strong, he would train his body. The goals he set for himself were forgone conclusions to the young man. He had no doubt of success. Once he identified his target, he would not avert his eyes until he hit it. It was that simple.

He would finish two more chapters before the hired boy brought his dinner, and though absorbed in the book, he thought of the path he'd travelled thus far.

His father, George Smith, had tried to break him of ambition at an early age. He did this, not to hurt him, but to protect his son from disappointment. John had no chance of becoming a gentleman, his father believed. He was a farmer's son and was expected to remain one. He should be happy with the status that God gave him. There were worse things than being a farmer, George said. One could lead a

---

[7] Smith, John. *The True Travels, Adventures, and Observations of Captain John Smith into Europe, Asia, Africa, and America* 1593–1629. (London, 1704), Ch. 1.

[8] Niccolo Machiavelli. *The Art of War* (1590–1520), trans. Henry Neville 1675, Book 7.

[9] Firstbrook, 31–33; Hoobler, 19–20.

comfortable life and even own a bit of property. The dreams of glory and success would only lead him to the pain of reality.

Born in 1580, John Smith came into the world as a yeoman farmer's son. Yeomen farmers were the middle-class and owned property. George Smith considered himself successful in a practical sense. At least, he wasn't a peasant or tenant farmer. They were at the very bottom of the status system and were basically slaves working for the king and gentlemen for mere scraps. George owned his farm and even made a bit of profit after he paid his taxes to the king, church, and local magistrate.

A moral hardworking man, George lacked the fire in his belly to escape his status. He was just grateful to not be at the bottom.

Status was decided by God, not society, or so they were told. The king and aristocracy, as well as everyone below them, received status by divine right. Divine right meant God determined your parents and your status. To deny this was to deny God's will, and this belief snuffed out ambition. Why dream of greater accomplishments when God chose your lot in life? Most people accepted their place in the world and refused to torment themselves with thoughts of changing it.

John's personality was different from the start. He saw examples of men, like Drake, who advanced themselves by their hard work. This small possibility gave him hope. He liked the idea of deciding his own future.

The hours spent working on his father's farm convinced him it wasn't the life he desired. Seeing the boy restless and bored, George encouraged education. Maybe his son would learn about the real world a bit and see that dreams were not for a farmer's son. If anything, an education and self-discipline may quench some of John's thirst for advancement.

So at six-years-old, the boy walked four miles to and from school to learn the basics: English, Latin, and arithmetic. He showed potential in his studies, and later, George enrolled him at the King Edward VI Grammar School fifteen miles away. This was a boarding school known for strict and vigorous instruction. The distance required him to seek room and board there. Those boys breaking the rules suffered punishment usually in the form of a whipping. John seemed to clash with authority the moment he arrived.

This rebellion to the rules may have come from the influence of his schoolmaster, Reverend Francis Marbury. Marbury was a notorious nonconformist to the Church of England. Years before, he was imprisoned for heresy, for opposing the Catholic rites and traditions that lingered in the English Anglican faith. Marbury's independent mind may have sparked the fire in John. Something ignited his ambition and started him down a path he never retreated from.

At thirteen, he sold his books and carry bag with designs of becoming a sailor. He ran away but was caught and forced back to school and punishment. Realizing John was a hopeless dreamer, George decided to apprentice him to a merchant. If farming or school wasn't enough, then maybe business would provide the passion he sought. It was a minor step up the social ladder, and he would need to learn a trade if farming was not an option.

Still, John dreamed of glory and adventure, but all he got was paperwork and figures. Life became inventory, bills of lading, and numbers. At fifteen, he was bursting at the seams to break from the constraints of society. Then fate stepped in. The following year, George died and John's mother remarried, leaving him, sixteen and alone, to decide his future. He left the apprenticeship and settled his father's estate expeditiously. The teenager heard news of the war raging on the continent and had to join the fight.

England was fighting Catholic Spain to free Protestant Holland. Smith signed up immediately and was in action for two years. Little is known about this period, except that he wasn't thrilled about fighting other Christians and learned basic combat experience as a common soldier. No matter his performance on the battlefield, his status kept him from advancement. Frustrated, he sought important contacts to get his foot in the door but had no luck. On a trip to Scotland, he tried to curry favor with King James of Scotland (the future king of England) but was shipwrecked and became ill instead.[10] John tried to

---

[10] Smith, *The True Travels*, Ch. 1.

purchase his way into status but realized there was only one certain way to gain it—by merit.

Having failed to advance himself through contacts or money, he headed home to Willoughby with his tail between his legs and resolve on his mind.

This is what led him to the woods, under a shelter, engrossed in a Machiavelli book.

He refused to accept status. Others could accept it, but not John. He believed that God gave men freewill, so it was up to each man to choose their own path. Providence would guide them to their purpose. God had created him this way for a reason. With the desire for greatness imprinted on his soul, how could he ignore it? God wouldn't create men to merely exist or just get by. Why would the creator make mediocre men in the first place? Man was born to achieve.

In every page of the Bible, God chose men from lowly backgrounds to work his will. Why did England, a Christian nation, accept the tyranny of status? It was the gentlemen, bishops, and royals who promoted this system. They perpetuated this myth to hold power and dynasties were maintained by the divine right deception. Once common men figured out the truth, there would be hell to pay. The upper-classes knew this and were fearful of revolt. To control the masses, they had to convince them of divine right. John Smith was a man ahead of his time.[11]

Darting his eyes at the clear blue sky, he imagined himself on a field of battle, leading men to victory and conquering his enemies. Envisioning great duels to the death and him, the victor, made his heart race. He had no doubt he would do all this in time, but he had to prepare first.

Smiling, he closed Machiavelli's book and was ready to take the next step.

* * * * *

---

[11] Hoobler, 8,12; Firstbrook, 14–15.

Between Austerfield and Scrooby, England, 1602

Twelve-year-old William Bradford's feet were sore and blistered. Walking seven miles from the village of Austerfield to the town of Scrooby had a way of doing that.[12]

Of course, he wanted to complain, but knew he should deny himself. He knew he must take up his own cross and bare it as the Savior had done for him. So he pushed through the pain and prayed for strength. Thinking of the love and acceptance awaiting him in Scrooby, his pain subsided.

William thought of this and decided that what he focused on became reality. He knew this truth his whole life but often forgot it at moments of adversity. He had to remind himself again and again of this fact. The flesh was weak, but the spirit was strong.

Born March 22, 1590, in Austerfield, England, William Bradford's life was a series of tragedies. At the age of one, his father died, and soon after, his mother followed. Then the boy's grandfather took custody of him and died when William was six. Losing every member of his immediate family, his two uncles, Thomas and Richard, took custody of the orphan. They fed, sheltered, and clothed him but weren't very affectionate. Missing out on the intimate love of a mother and father, the boy escaped into the printed page. Though erudite, William grew into a pale sickly boy who struggled with the labor on his uncles' farm. Recognizing his fondness for books, his uncles allowed him the freedom to study.

The Bible became his family instead. Within its pages, he discovered the intimate relationship he had missed as a child. Christianity filled the hole left by his family. He also sought out others to share it with.[13]

---

[12] Plumb, Albert H. *William Bradford of Plymouth*. (Boston: Gorham Press, 1920), 20.

[13] Philbrick, Nathaniel. *Mayflower: A Story of Courage, Community, and War.* (New York: Viking Penguin, 2006), 7–8; Willison, George F. *Saints and Strangers*. (New York: Reynal & Hitchcock-Kingsport Press, 1945), 45–46; Plumb, 18.

In the village of Scrooby, a group of believers known as Separatists captured his interest. Headed by William Brewster, these religious outlaws chose to worship separately from the Church of England. Since this was illegal, they had to meet in secret and risk arrest. They felt the Church of England had been corrupted by colluding with the king and government. The Separatists believed the Bible was all a follower of Christ needed, and obeying its precepts was all that was required. They considered themselves God's elect or chosen people and spent their days committed to a life of prayer, frugality, and denying the flesh as much as possible. Adhering to the principles of providence, which guided events and faithful servants, the Separatists surrendered to God's will. Providence was God's divine hand of protection and would direct their paths. With the Separatists, William found the family he never had. They welcomed him with open arms and accepted the orphan just as he was.

The Separatists were persecuted relentlessly in England. They were jailed, harassed, and property was confiscated, but this was no deterrent. They continued to worship as they chose, choosing their beliefs over security. The state-sanctioned church demanded obedience, but the Separatists obeyed only God. They followed in the footsteps of a long line of persecution.[14]

William studied history and saw a distinct pattern of corruption endlessly repeated.

The early Christians were persecuted, harassed, and executed by the Romans. Crucified, fed to the lions, and boiled in oil for their beliefs, the early followers died as martyrs and attained sainthood. The indomitable will by the early Christians led Emperor Constantine to co-opt the religion. Though his tale of conversion was accepted, it invited suspicion. Instead of allowing it to overrun the empire, Constantine chose to use it. The Roman Catholic Church was an amalgamation of Christianity, Paganism, and Roman traditions. The Pope, cardinals, and bishops were appointed to create a hierarchy within the church. The empire and church worked together to control its citizens and if either faced opposition, the other provided

---

[14] Bradford, Ch. 1; Philbrick, 10–12; Willison, 43–53.

defense. Heretics were also enemies of the state, and enemies of the state were heretics. This collusion had happened in the past when the Pharisees and Sadducees aided Rome in persecuting Christians.

After the fall of the western empire and Charlemagne's reunification, known as the Holy Roman Empire, this continued corruption inevitably led to the Protestant Reformation. The church controlled through intimidation, imprisonment, torture, and executions as always, but they failed to force compliance. During the Inquisition, one was condemned of heresy simply by disagreeing with a tenet of the church or a practice of the state. Heretics were burned at the stake, beheaded, and tortured various insidious ways for having different interpretations of the Bible. Some victims were singled out simply because they were disliked or an official wanted their property. Even a man's attractive wife could get him charged with heresy by an envious opportunist.

Every citizen paid taxes to the church, and collection was enforced by the government. It wasn't long before most recognized the corruption. Doctrine replaced principle while the church handed out tickets to heaven for compliance and, of course, favors.

Martin Luther and John Calvin tried to return the faith to its simpler past, at first. Breaking away from the Catholic Church, Protestants re-established Christianity on biblical principles, but the pattern repeated, and in time, the Protestants fractured into different denominations and established their own traditions, beliefs, and hierarchies. Eventually, these churches colluded with their individual governments, and the corruption repeated throughout Europe.

The Church of England demanded obedience and revenue from every English citizen. If anyone disagreed with the church or state, they were labelled blasphemers, infidels, cultists, rebels, outlaws, and Separatists. It was the heretic charge all over again. This same tactic was used to ostracize any nonconformists and the bishops were corrupt and flaunted their power without fear of repercussion. Gold jewelry and scarlet robes purchased by many church officials was sacrilegious. Promiscuity, drunkenness, and extravagance became the norm in the clergy, and many looked the other way, ignoring corruption to protect the status quo. Why rock the boat? Why risk losing your property, reputation, freedom, or life to end up labelled a heretic? William knew many who chose property and position over belief.[15]

The Separatists were the next batch of nonconformists who criticized the church for practicing papal traditions and rites, and continuing its materialistic symbolism. The church and its bishops had turned the faith into a business. The clergy controlled the purse strings and hope of reform from within, was wishful thinking. The Archbishop Whitgift had declared, "When they that serve God's altar shall be exposed to poverty, then religion shall be exposed to scorn and become contemptible."[16] The church had no intention of giving up the freeride. What would the nobility think with the representatives of Christ living without luxuries? This corruption only convinced the Separatists that it had gone the way of the Vatican and strengthened their convictions. Anyone who didn't toe the line with the church was ridiculed, marginalized, or destroyed. The church became an enforcement arm of compliance and was proactive in the persecution. The Separatists chose a life of crime rather than desert their faith. They preferred persecution by church and state, rather than damnation by God. This back-to-basics, stripped down Christianity attracted independent-minded believers.[17]

William was one such boy with an independent mind. Reading everything he could about philosophy, theology, history, and faith, he came to conclusions on his own. The church or state wasn't about to tell him what to think or believe. He had his own individual freewill.

Reverend Brewster became an adoptive father to William, and the worship meetings at his house in Scrooby became a second home. Brewster encouraged the boy to seek the truth and find answers himself. William was no automaton member of a cult. He read the Bible diligently and questioned everything until he understood it com-

---

[15] Bradford, Ch. 1; Willison, 18–30; Pirenne, Henri. *A History of Europe*, trans. Bernard Miall. (New York: Doubleday Anchor Books, 1956), Volume 2, Book III, Ch. 2 The Reformation, 270.

[16] Willison, 30.

[17] Willison, 47–54; Plumb, 20.

pletely. He did not accept his faith blindly. He found it by chasing after it.[18]

William's blood relatives and friends felt his association with this strange cult of criminals would ruin the boy's reputation. Why rock the boat? He had an inheritance to protect, why risk it? A few tried to convince him to leave the group. What kind of future would he have with a group of fanatic renegades?[19]

No amount of pressure could change his mind. The Separatists were his family and friends now. He found a home with them, and there he would remain. Replying to his relatives, he showed such loyal dedication at a tender age:

> Were I like[ly] to endanger my life, or consume my estate, by any ungodly courses; your counsels to me were very reasonable. But you know that I have been diligent and provident in my Calling: and not only desirous to augment what I have, but also to enjoy it in your company; to part from which will be as great a cross as can befall me. Nevertheless, to keep a good conscience, and walk in such a Way as God has prescribed in his Word, is a thing which I must prefer before you all, and above life itself. Wherefore, since it is for a good Cause that I am like[ly] to suffer the disasters which you lay before me; you have no cause to be either angry with me, or sorry for me. Yea, I am not only willing to part with everything that is dear to me in this world for this Cause: but I am also thankful that God hath given me a heart so to do; and will accept me so to suffer for him.[20]

---

18 Willison, 46; Plumb, 20.

19 Plumb, 21; Willison, 45.

20 Mather, Cotton. *Magnalia Christi Americana: The Ecclesiastical History of New-England, from Its First Planting, in the Year 1620, Unto the Year of Our Lord 1698, In Seven Volumes*, Volume 1, Book 2 *The New-English History containing*

Absorbed in his thoughts, William knew what he wanted to do and where he was going. He wanted to serve the will of God, and wherever it led, he was ready. Though he had no clue where it would lead him, he put his faith in providence. God had a purpose for him, and providence would lead him there, he was sure.

The air was crisp, and the sun sparkled as he put one foot in front of the other. The smell of burning wood filled his nose, and he knew he was close—the next hill, and there his home would be. Reverend Brewster's home was where he belonged now.

Following the path, William thought of the coming journey. Thinking not of this small walk today, but the journey through life on God's path occupied him. Seeing Reverend Brewster tore him from his thoughts.

Standing in front of his house, Brewster greeted him with a loving smile. He was an average-sized man, but to William, he was a giant.

Joyously he waved back and sprinted the rest of the way down the dirt road. He never once, thought about his sore feet again.

* * * * *

Aboard a ship in the Mediterranean Sea, just off the southeast coast of France, 1601

"It's his fault—the Protestant!"

Sensing the danger, John moved to the other side of the ship but couldn't avoid them. The passengers were angrier than the thunderstorm which rocked the ship violently. The worse the storm got, the worse their anger increased. Somehow, he was the focus of their animosity. The superstitious fools believed his very presence was causing the storm and he was a curse that brought the fury of the sea down on them. The entire ship was occupied by Catholics of different nationalities: French, Spanish, and Italian. They were heading for the holy

---

The Lives of the Governors. (Hartford: Silas Andrus & Son, 1853), 110 Ch. 1; Plumb, 21.

city of Rome on a pilgrimage. They were convinced the infidel was the problem and decided to exact justice on him to calm the sea.[21]

John was on a pilgrimage of his own. He was on his way to join the Christian army fighting in the east. Though this army was mainly Catholic, he saw the war as one of Christian preservation. The Muslim Turks had invaded eastern Europe for the past three hundred years, but recently, they were pushing further west into Hungary and Romania. They were on the doorstep of Rome and John knew if it fell, the rest of western civilization would be next. Putting sectarian prejudice aside, he wanted to fight for all European Christianity, not just England Protestantism.

His motive wasn't purely for unselfish reasons. He wanted in on the fight to experience true combat. The war in Holland had been tough, but against the Turks, he could prove himself.

First, he must survive the trip east. Preparation in the woods outside Willoughby set him in the right direction. Study and exercise helped, but the mental preparation was the real benefit. Sorting his thoughts, he knew what must be done to realize his goal. He built confidence through reflection and putting in the work. His drive and passion was in him by design and he realized he had a destiny. He didn't know the whole story, but he knew there was one out there. All he had to do was go out and create it. To turn the next page, he must make the first move.

Theodore Paleologue, a relative of Constantine XI, the last emperor of the Byzantine Empire who was killed fighting the invasion of the Turks in 1453, became John's teacher. Paleologue was a riding instructor to the Earl of Lincoln at Tattersall Castle at the same time John was busy with his books in the woods nearby. Paleologue took Smith under his wing and invited him to stay at the castle. What were the chances of a real warrior who fought the Turks offering to train him?

Paleologue taught him to be a master horseman and he also instructed him in swordsmanship and jousting. He told John stories about the true nature of the enemy. The warfare he would face was

---

[21] Smith. *True Travels*. Ch 2; Firstbrook, 40–41.

brutal. It was kill or be killed. If outnumbered, there was no surrender. Either fight to the death or torture, slavery, and dishonorable death awaited. He trained intensely, thinking of this. He knew if he didn't have the preparation or skills, all the ambition in the world would only get him killed. Day after day, he trained and honed his skills until he was ready.[22]

Word of fighting in the east and John's self-confidence led him to take the next step. He would find a way to join the Christian army.

First, he travelled through France with four other young men but was robbed of his money and belongings when his baggage left the ship with the others without him. They assured him they would wait while the rowboats returned, but once he was rowed ashore, he found no sign of the others or his belongings. He was left penniless and homeless in an unknown country. Though a broke vagabond, John was blessed with the kindness of strangers wherever he went. Whether they saw something of value in him or just practiced Christian charity, he was always fed, clothed, and sheltered along the way. He never forgot this kindness and it convinced him more than ever that his journey was preordained. Providence would watch over him, he believed.

Eventually, he tracked down the leader of the thieves who had betrayed him. Fighting a duel with the perpetrator, he bested him in a swordfight but spared the man's life when he confessed to the theft and told of his own misfortune of being robbed. Something kept John from exacting revenge on the thief. Maybe it was simply empathy, because he shared the same misfortune, or maybe it was just the kindness of strangers which caused him to exercise mercy. Whatever it was, he allowed the thief to go.

After the duel, he made his way to the southern coast of France where he boarded the ship bound for Rome. He planned on finding some way to get into the Christian force.

This was where he found himself facing the angry passengers who blamed him for the storm. They crowded around him with

---

[22] Smith. *True Travels*. Ch 2; Firstbrook, 34–36; Hoobler, 21–22; Pirenne, (Volume 2, Book II The Turks), 216–217.

ill-intent. One passenger growled as he grabbed John's elbow while others gripped his arms and legs. He never thought they would go this far. Hoisting him overhead, the passengers tossed him over the side of the ship and into the sea below.

Splashing into the frigid water, he surfaced and brushed wet bangs out of his eyes. Being pulled by the waves away from the ship, he could see it wasn't good. He couldn't let his journey end by drowning in the Mediterranean. He still had so much to do. Turning his back to the ship, he just made out a small island in the distance. If he could get there, he would live to fight another day. Dying would have to wait.

Treading water, with the wind and pelting rain working against him, he managed to make it to the island. There he spent a cold and miserable night reminded of his mortality.

Was this his destiny? Was he a castaway on a deserted island? Why was this happening to him? Where had he gone wrong?

He thought his war experience matured him, but the robbery made him doubt it. He thought his time in the woods and training with Paleologue made him wiser, but now he was stranded on an island in the middle of nowhere. He had been naïve and childish, not recognizing the threats. Getting tossed into the sea by crazy religious zealots was his inability to see the obvious. Prejudice within the Christian faith was fresh in the minds of many, and knowing who to trust wasn't easy. The war he fought in Holland was Catholic against Protestant, but this was an old grudge. He should've known that few could forget the mistakes of the past. He didn't live in the past, only the present and future. Changing the past was impossible, and the present and future had such promise. The Christians, Catholics and Protestants alike, had to put aside their interfaith squabbles and unite to defeat the real enemy of them all—the Muslim Turks.

The Turks wanted to kill and enslave them. Christians were fighting each other over disagreements about a verse, prayer, or doctrine. The Turks invaded Europe to spread their religion and stamp out Christianity entirely. It was European stupidity which led them to this impasse, just like it was his own for getting tossed into the sea.

It would be dawn soon. Providence had led him here to this island, he believed. He had to accept and trust it. Exhausted from the laborious swim and icy water, John badly needed sleep. Laying in the sand, he drifted to sleep. He told himself that tomorrow was another opportunity, another day.[23]

Maybe it would be better than today.

* * * * *

Grimsby, England, 1607

Waiting aboard ship, William was excited. They finally decided to find a home elsewhere. Being rowed out to the ship with the other men, he helped load the cargo while the women and children waited on shore. They decided to leave behind England and start anew in Holland. When the civil authorities confiscated property and imprisoned them, they knew it was time to go.

King James announced he intended to prosecute them to the fullest extent of the law. The Bishop of York uncovered the location of their secret meetings at Brewster's house and planned to arrest them at the next gathering. Luckily, Brewster knew the bishop's plan, and they decided to flee. The king and church already made them pariahs in the community. They were ostracized and taken advantage of by their neighbors, and the decision to leave was an easy one. The problem with leaving was that the king and church didn't want them to leave. They wanted their obedience and submission, so they made it a crime to leave England.

The two elders of the Separatists, Brewster and John Robinson, decided to run rather than continue under religious oppression. The escape wasn't going to be easy. If word got out they would all wind up in jail. If they made it out, Holland offered them a new beginning. The right to worship put the Dutch years ahead of every other

---

[23] Smith. *True Travels*. Ch 2.

place on Earth. After securing permission to emigrate, they raised the funds to hire a ship and captain to take them there.[24]

The first captain they hired gladly accepted their money, then reported them to the authorities. After months of confinement and harassment, they raised the funds again. This time, they secured a captain they could trust but accepted the responsibility for the first captain's treachery and their own naiveté. The second time, they were meticulous and shrewd in their choice.

Seventeen-year-old William anticipated the voyage and the beginning of his new life. It was exciting for the teenager, and he had no reservations about going. This was his family, and he never once worried about his inheritance or the relatives he was leaving behind. He would make his own way in the land of windmills and religious freedom. He had no fear of what lay ahead. Providence would guide him where he was supposed to go. Right now, he was meant to go to Holland with his family.

Just then, sounds of horses and shouting brought the young man out of his thoughts. On shore, the women and children waiting to be rowed over began to scream and panic. Coming toward them was a group of armed men on horseback, demanding their surrender. The men onboard ship tried to calm their families, but the captain peered toward shore and frowned. He realized he had to make a split-second decision and called to his crew to prepare to sail. Grabbing the captain by the arm, William pleaded, "Sir, you cannot leave them."

The frustrated captain turned to him and said, "Am I to wait till they capture all of us or shall I save half of us?"

William realized the logic behind the decision. Chances were, the men would suffer persecution more than the women and children if they were captured. Feeling helpless, he looked to Reverend Brewster for guidance, and bowed his head and began to pray. William followed his example.

This was agony on the married fathers who could do nothing but watch the militia roughly abuse their families. On shore,

---

[24] Bradford, 14–15 (Ch. 1); Plumb, 21; Philbrick, 12–13.

the women and children begged the men not to leave them as the ship coasted away. The men could do nothing to stop it. The captain explained he had no choice. They never imagined their families would be trapped ashore while they loaded the baggage and supplies. Such evil never crossed their mind. They were leaving behind a country that didn't want them. Why wouldn't they let them be? Someone must have tipped off the authorities again; but who? Who had such hate for them? They were not worldly and trusted others too much, but they weren't monsters.

William saw men he respected emasculated by the abandonment of their women and children. He couldn't watch anymore. Turning away while the others watched in horror, he closed his eyes and prayed for the safety of those on shore and the strength of the men onboard.

Once the men docked in Amsterdam, Holland, they waited months before receiving word of the fate of their families.

Meanwhile, they raised their heads high and trusted in providence again. They would prepare for the inevitable reunion with their families which God would provide. They would secure jobs and homes in the meantime so they could raise funds to pay the fines and secure transportation for them. They had no guarantee when or if ever they would see their loved ones again, but they leaned on their faith for strength and kept moving forward.

William was amazed by their resilience and character. They never wallowed once in self-pity or doubt. They just left the ship and started to work.[25]

What sort of men were these? he wondered. They weren't physically strong or aggressive toward others, but they possessed an inner strength which dwarfed outer strength. It impressed the seventeen-year-old and made an indelible mark on him.

Smiling, he decided they were the very sort of men he wanted to be like someday.

* * * * *

---

[25] Bradford, 15–21 (Ch 2); Philbrick, 13.

Outside the town of Regall, Transylvania (modern day Romania), 1602

Looking across the plain, John Smith's blazing blue eyes sized up his enemy. The opponent's name was Lord Turbashaw, and rumor had it he was the best fighter in the Turkish army. Supposedly, he had claimed many infidel lives and now was just feet away, sitting proudly on his horse. Both men's armor sparkled in the sun as their horses snorted and whinnied as though they sensed the coming clash. Sweating profusely from the heavy armor, which included full breast plates, gauntlets, and visor helmets, John balanced the forty-pound lance under his arm and waited for the signal. Good old Paleologue taught him the secrets behind this sort of combat.

Jousting pitted two men on horseback in a heavy suit of armor with an eleven-foot wooden lance under one arm, a shield and the reins in the other hand. The object was to hit the opponent with the lance, unseating him from his horse. In this jousting duel, the unseated rider wouldn't just lose the challenge, but also his head. This was a duel to the death, and John believed he drew the lucky lot. He volunteered for this duel. Avoiding danger would never lead him to greatness. He would jump directly into the fire or he would never succeed. He wasn't worried. He had trained for this and was here to prove himself. Confident of his training, the outcome was left up to God now. He was fighting for the right side and felt there was more to do after this. This self-confidence tamed his fear.

Lord Turbashaw entered the field to blaring trumpets with an entourage leading his horse. On his back were two large wings made of "eagle's feathers" and "precious stones." The Christian army returned the trumpet blast in answer to the Turks as John trotted his steed closer to his winged opponent. Both men saluted and took their positions.

Dropping his visor, Smith gripped the lance tighter. The signal to joust would sound in seconds. If Lord Turbashaw was ready to meet Allah with a set of wings already attached, he would oblige.

The signal sounded, and the two men galloped toward each other, every stride increasing the speed. In a few seconds, they would be close enough for impact.[26]

John waited for this moment his whole life.

* * * * *

The only way to beat the Turks was to force them to total surrender by bringing them to their knees with superior force. Strength was the only thing they respected. Machiavelli taught him about combat in the woods of Willoughby, but Paleologue had explained the reality of fighting the Turks. This was nothing like combat in Holland. Beheadings were common practice, and killing the wounded or surrendering Christians was normal here. John remembered Paleologue's stories and took them to heart.

The Ottoman Empire proclaimed itself the Muslim caliphate or the ruling power of all Islam. In the previous three hundred years, the Turks invaded and subjugated the Byzantine Empire and half of eastern Europe. First, they captured Constantinople and renamed it Istanbul. While Catholics and Protestants were busy fighting one another, the Muslims invaded Greece, Bulgaria, Transylvania (Romania), Moldova, Ukraine, and Hungary. Total Islamic domination was the aim, and finishing off Transylvania and Hungary was the final step before starting on Rome and the rest of western Europe. This was a war of aggression, and Christian infighting benefited the Turks. Meanwhile, they were on the march again, and towns fell as they inched closer to Rome. Either the Christians would unite or they would be conquered.

John understood this better than most. Even though a Protestant, he rushed to join the Catholic army. Obviously, he also wanted personal glory, but he realized the threat to western civilization and Christendom. Paleologue instilled in him more than technical skill. He had seared into John's mind what was at stake in this

---

[26] Smith. *True Travels*. Ch 7; Firstbrook, 79–81; Hoobler, 30–32.

global struggle. Joining the Catholic force in Hungary, he was ready to fight.

The Holy Roman Empire had fought the Turks from the beginning, building a chain of fortified towns along strategic points to stop the Muslim advances into central Europe. Instead of stopping them in the east, they waited until the enemy was at the gates. A pivotal fort in Hungary recently fell to the Turks and another was under siege. The town of Olumpagh faced an army of twenty thousand Turks. The Christians were heavily outnumbered, and overwhelming force was not an option this time. Ingenuity and stealth would have to compensate for numbers.

The commanders devised a plan to divide the army into two wings, seven miles apart. The smaller wing would initiate the attack as a feint while the larger wing would deliver the finishing blow. The pincers strategy was calculated to surround the Turks and cause confusion. The weakest part of the plan was communication. The attack would commence after dark, and visibility on the field was not possible. How could they relay messages between the two wings to time the strikes?

In walked John Smith. At twenty-one, he was certain, he was the answer to their prayers. His brashness and arrogance annoyed many, but some of the top brass saw promise in this new strutting gamecock. He had a plan of his own. The solution to the communication problem could be remedied by a system of torches. Seven miles was too far a distance to depend on dispatch riders, but torches could be seen from that distance in the dark. Some commanders doubted it would work, but it was worth a try. They were also worried that once the Turks realized the small force was a feint, they would turn and smash the larger one.

Smith had another idea. They would use deception to make up for lack in numbers. The small arms in 1601 were the matchlock muskets. Using a slow-burning wick or match attached to the trigger, the match would drop into the flashpan and ignite the gunpowder, firing the weapon. In combat, soldiers had a hard time keeping matches lit in wind and rain.

John had another plan involving the use of these matches. By tying three thousand pieces of match to lines of string six hundred feet-long and suspending it between two poles, he would deceive the whole Turkish command. Once lit, these three thousand glowing matches would appear in the darkness as thousands of armed soldiers. The Turks would perceive a larger force with the feinting wing. This would sap their confidence and keep them focused on the smaller feint while ignoring the larger force on their flank. John knew that only perception, not reality, mattered in battle. This boldness and creativity impressed the commanders. He wasn't afraid to take risks.

The signal system worked, and the two wings communicated perfectly. They moved into position and timed the attack with precision. The Turks fell for the ruse and threw their whole army at the feinting force, believing it to be the main army. Because of John's idea, the actual main force surprised the Muslims and pushed them into the water. Smith wrote, "A third part of the Turks…were slain; many of the rest drowned, but all fled." [27]

Olumpagh was rescued by the outnumbered Christians thanks to John's innovative thinking. He was promoted to the rank of captain and received his own 250-man cavalry to command. Because of his fearless certainty, he advanced himself.

During the following summer of 1601, Smith was attached to the Duke of Mercoer's Protestant army which was busy laying siege to the Muslim fortress of Alba Regalis, Hungary. The town was surrounded by a massive wall and several layers of defense before the town. The initial probing attack had already cost many lives. This impregnable bastion was key to halting the Muslim invasion. If they could take this symbol of Islamic strength deep inside Christian Europe, it would cause the caliphate to question their invincibility.

With winter approaching, Mercoer decided to approve the assault. Captain Smith had a reputation for quick thinking and bold tactics from Olumpagh, so Mercoer listened to his proposals. Recalling Machiavelli's *Art of War*, John presented another audacious plan. They would build forty or fifty bombs made of gunpowder,

---

[27] Ibid., Ch 4.

pitch, brimstone, camphor, linseed, and musket balls packed into clay pots. These would then be thrown over the wall just before the attack. These "fiery dragons," as he called them, were primitive hand grenades. These minor explosions would cause enough of a diversion to distract the Turks from the main assault. Once again, he would use distraction to their advantage.

The "fiery dragons" worked just as planned, and Mercoer's main force pushed the Turks back into the town. On September 20, Mercoer's army busted through the main wall of Alba Regalis, and the battle became close-quarter combat. Neither side could gain an advantage. The Turks sent sixty thousand men to counter the Protestant army, and on October 15, one of the bloodiest battles of the war happened. The Christians fought well, though outnumbered. Each side lost six thousand men.[28] With winter closing in and a stalemate on the field, the two sides agreed to a truce. Mercoer divided his army and detached Smith's cavalry to Transylvania (Romania).

That winter was the coldest in six hundred years. Many died from lack of proper food and clothing, but Captain Smith managed to survive, and by spring of 1602, he was ready for action.

After endless hit-and-run raids, the Protestants laid siege to the town of Regall. By summer, another temporary truce was in effect because neither side could gain advantage. As was the custom, and boredom demanded it, each army would offer up a single warrior to fight to the death in a duel. After drawing lots, John won the chance to face his ultimate test. There was no runner-up in this contest. You either won or you died. John never hesitated. He believed it was his destiny.

* * * * *

Forty-pounds of armor and a forty-pound lance while riding a horse was a real workout. Moving faster toward his opponent, John knew exactly what to do. As Paleologue taught him many times, he would hold the lance horizontally. Keeping the weapon level at the

---

[28] Ibid., Ch 5.

moment of impact was the surest way to unseat a rider. What took only seconds seemed minutes to him.

Closer and closer, the two warriors galloped, lances ready, armor blazing in the sun. John concentrated only on his target— Lord Turbashaw. He had to keep the lance straight when they passed or he would miss. He wasn't going to miss, he told himself.

The moment the two riders were within range, John levelled the lance and struck Turbashaw directly in the face. Slowing his horse and turning, he saw the Turk on the ground motionless.

Dismounting, he removed his helmet and drew his sword high in the air. The sun glinted off the razor-sharp steel, he could tell Turbashaw was dead. The tip of the lance had penetrated his face guard and killed him instantly. With one swift slash, John severed the dead man's head. Presenting it to his commander, it was heartily received.

He proved himself as a leader and as a man. Alone in a fight or on the battlefield, he had passed the test. Though most men would count their blessings, he wasn't done.

The Turk commander was livid and wanted revenge for the loss of his best fighter. He challenged the young victor to another duel. Lord Turbashaw had a good friend, Grulago, who relished the honor of avenging him. John didn't hesitate and accepted the challenge. If Turbashaw was the best, Grulago was second best. If for some reason he was better, then he wanted their best. He didn't want anyone to say his win was a fluke. Like many twenty-one-year-olds, he welcomed the duel. Unlike most his age, he had something that couldn't be taught—the absence of fear with the skill to back it up.

During the second duel, both lances shattered on impact, and Grulago pulled his second weapon of choice, the pistol, and fired, hitting John square in the chest. The Turks watching the duel went mad with celebration. The little infidel had played the game of chance too many times. Maybe he would lose his head today.

Looking down at his chest where the ball had struck him, he noticed no penetration. The pistol ball had bounced off the thick armored breastplate. Drawing his own pistol, he took careful aim at Grulago who was dumbstruck that his opponent was still alive. The armor protected him from the pistol ball, and his opponent's armor would do the same. Taking his time, he chose to shoot the man in the arm instead. Unable to hold the reins of his horse, the Turk fell to the ground. Dismounting and drawing his sword, he beheaded Grulago and claimed another victory.

Brimming with confidence, John decided to test the odds and challenged the Turks to a third duel. With another chance to avenge the two losses, the Muslim commander agreed. This time, the new opponent, Bonny Mulgro, chose battle axes and pistols instead of lances. Bonny Mulgro was an expert with the ax and felt confident he could dispatch Smith. As the men passed one another, they fired their pistols and missed. On the second turn, the axes were in play. This time, John was hit so hard by Mulgro's ax, he dropped his own. The Turks cheered uncontrollably again, sure this third duel was theirs. The cocky Englishman pushed his luck too far this time. One win was luck, the second win was miraculous—a third win was nearly impossible.

The Muslim crowd quieted as they waited for Mulgro's finishing strike. Riding toward John, Mulgro swung the ax for a certain hit. Writing of the final moments of the duel, John wrote, "by God's assistance" he "avoided the Turk's violence."[29] Drawing his short sword while dodging Mulgro's ax strike, he maneuvered behind the Turk and stabbed him through the thin back armor. Mulgro fell to the ground, and the Turks who were just cheering couldn't believe it.

John brought his commander a third head that day. Exceeding expectations, the farmer's son was a celebrity of sorts among the army. He was rewarded for his bravery with an excellent horse and a jewel-encrusted sword worth four year's wages. Paraded through camps with all the honors owed, the three heads of his opponents on a pike followed him. He was promoted again but would always identify himself as a captain. It may have been because this was when he outperformed his own expectations. His heroics seemed to inspire the army and showed him the value of leading by example to raise morale.

---

[29] Ibid., Ch. 7.

Fifteen days later, Mercoer's army overran Regall. The Protestants massacred the Turks and went on to capture three more towns. It may have been coincidence, but after John's three duels, the Christian army began to win.

Prince Bathory of Transylvania (Romania) rewarded him the title of gentleman. He received a coat-of-arms with an image of three severed heads and the motto in Latin of "*Vincere est Vivere*," which meant "to conquer is to live." He also received a pension of three hundred ducats per year (four year's wages).

John was officially a member of the gentlemen class. He had title, wealth, and a coat-of-arms to prove it. By merit alone, he accomplished what was supposed to be impossible. He was only twenty-two years-old and had already proved the naysayers wrong. A man could achieve greatness with hard work, no matter his status. A farmer's son could become a gentleman. But John wasn't done yet.

His motto, "to conquer is to live," were words he planned to uphold. Overcoming the challenges that life presented him was the real secret to living.[30]

* * * * *

Aboard the Mayflower off the coast of England, September 16, 1620

The sound of the waves did little to muffle the sound of vomiting. The smell was even worse, but William breathed through his mouth and continued to read his Bible. Years later he would write:

> A great hope and inward zeal they had of laying some good foundation, or at least to make some way thereunto for the propagating and advancing the gospel of the kingdom of Christ, in these remote parts of the world; yea, though

---

[30] Ibid.; Fallows, Noel. *Jousting in Medieval and Renaissance Iberia*, Volume 3: Of Armour and Weapons. (Boydell Press, 2010), Ch. 3–6; Firstbrook, 79–82.

they should be but even as stepping stones unto
others for the performing of so great a work.[31]

Surveying the cramped quarters below decks of the 102 souls,
including himself, he reflected on their predicament. Was this the
instrument which God would use to establish a New Jerusalem?
Would this dark, musty ship full of seasick inexperienced men,
women, and children be the object to carry out his will? Much had
gone terribly wrong from the start, and a big part of it was their
fault, just like the ancient Israelites. Moses led them out of bondage
and into the wilderness and if God felt his people needed to be purified by adversity, then they shouldn't question him. Why did they
believe themselves exempt? After all, Jonah laid in the belly of the
great fish because he refused God's will. Jacob wrestled an angel and
endured fourteen years as an indentured servant before becoming
the patriarch of the twelve tribes. And Christ, God's only begotten
son, suffered the crucifixion for them all. William felt ashamed. They
didn't know suffering yet. Oppression and harassment was nothing
compared to what the early Christians endured.

He was embarrassed for doubting. They had been through
nothing yet.[32]

* * * * *

After the men established themselves, they were reunited with
their families, and Holland became their new home. Amsterdam
already had a Separatist community, but they expected conformity
from the newcomers. The pattern of corruption started once again.
Many rules and traditions had been adopted by the Amsterdam
group and corruption of ministers and man-made dictates created a
new oppression within the Separatist movement. It was further proof
of man's inability to keep God's instructions pure. John Robinson
convinced the others to relocate to the Dutch city of Leiden to create

---

[31] Bradford, 32 (Ch. 4).
[32] Ibid., 90 (Ch. 9).

their own community. After all, they left England to escape corruption of the faith, not to continue in it.

The elders carefully thought out their new community in Leiden. They believed they could create a utopian Christian village apart from Dutch society. They worked from dawn to dark, six days a week, just to survive. Intense labor in the textile industry was a shock to these farmers and craftsmen. The women and children worked as well, and there was little time to enjoy life.[33]

Within a few years, their children started to fall away from the faith and adopted Dutch ways. They became more Dutch than English, and though oppressed by church and state, they still had an affinity for England. This assimilation worried the proud Englanders. Though they appreciated the religious freedom of Holland, they still rejected the laid-back culture and materialism. Holland's economy was booming after its war with Spain (the same war John Smith served in). Prosperity created an environment of excess, which the Separatists never experienced before. This materialism created greed and envy; and these sins they tried to avoid.

Being Bible purists, they promoted frugality and temperance amidst this prosperity. Living a simple life and serving God was their sole purpose. Providence would provide them with all they needed they believed. Materialism was frowned upon, but their children got wrapped up in it just the same. The kids were torn between wanting something better for themselves and despising materialism. It was a two-edged sword. With more wealth, one could give more. Without it, one needed charity. They attempted to balance greed and godly charity with the collective concept of wealth.

Like ancient Israel, they would create a society based on communal wealth, not individual wealth. They thought this equal division would provide happiness for all. This collective view wasn't a new concept. Plato had written about it in his *Republic* as a utopian society. It was an attempt to make the world fair and just. The greed they witnessed from the materialism in Holland convinced them there had to be a better way. Instead of expecting the Dutch to con-

---

[33] Ibid., Chapter 3.

form to them, they sought an alternative. Talk of setting up a New Jerusalem in the New World across the sea by creating their own place became a real possibility. Going to the New World to start over was in everyone's mind.[34]

In 1618, Dr. John Bainbridge, an English physician and astronomer had tracked a mysterious comet streaking across the sky. The blue-green "blazing star" held the world's attention for weeks. Some saw the heavenly sign as a bad omen. In America, the native people are said to have interpreted the comet as a sign of apocalyptic meanings for them and strangely, within the next two years, disease decimated the Indian population. Writing a book on the comet, Bainbridge received critical acclaim and attention from King James. In his book, Bainbridge said the comet was a message from God that the English people would soon receive a great gift of wealth from across the sea. The Separatists looked to this as a sign from God, of course. To them, He was telling them to cross the ocean and establish a land in his name.[35]

While these two motivations helped determine their course, William Bradford was motivated to apply himself in Leiden.

Finishing an apprenticeship to become a master fustian-maker (a durable fabric of cotton and flax), he met Dorothy May in 1613. He also became a full-fledged citizen of Leiden and purchased a house. Then he asked Dorothy to be his wife in 1617. The couple was married and soon had a son they named John. William became a respected elder in the Separatist community. He tried his hand at business but always lost more money than he made. He learned important lessons in those failures that strengthened his character instead of leaving him embittered. If his business sense would've succeeded, he never would've left Holland.

---

[34] Ibid., 31–33 (Ch. 4); Willison, 102-103; Plumb, 2, Chapter 2.
[35] Bunker, Nick. *Making Haste from Babylon: The Mayflower Pilgrims and Their World: A New History.* (New York: Random House, 2010), 17–20; Rex, J & A, MacLean. "King James' Poem on the Great Comet of 1618." *Journal of the British Astronomical Association*, 1987, Volume 97, No. 2/ February, p. 74.

William Brewster and Edward Winslow (two elders of the church) had left the persecution of England behind, but not their grievances. Together, these two started a printing press in Leiden and published pamphlets criticizing King James and the Church of England. Holland was now an ally of England's.

After the successful war against Spain, the two Protestant nations remained cooperative with one another. When King James learned about the pamphlets, he sent officials to Leiden to arrest Brewster. The authorities in Holland aided in the manhunt for the outlaw reverend. Brewster went into hiding, but he couldn't expect to elude arrest for long.

The talk of sailing to the New World turned into action. They petitioned the *Virginia Company* for a tract of land in America. The petition was granted in 1619, and permission to settle near modern-day New York on the Hudson River was official. They decided to use the joint-stock company, the *Merchant Adventurers,* to fund the trip. William sold his house and settled his business interests. He was anxious to continue the path which led him to Scrooby, then to Holland. Now he was ready to follow it to the New World. Referencing Hebrews 11, he wrote, "So they left that goodly and pleasant city, which had been their resting place near 12 years; but they knew they were pilgrims, and looked not much on these things, but lift up their eyes to the heavens, their dearest country, and quieted their spirits."[36]

* * * * *

Now they were on their way. They were on the ship which would take them to "a better country." Finally, a place where they would belong, for God "prepared for them a city."[37] Even though this captain and crew showed disdain for them, they put on a brave front and remained humble. It wasn't right to question the Lord's will, he knew. It was their job to follow, not question his will. They

---

36 Bradford, 72 (Ch. 7).
37 *King James Bible*. (Nelson), Hebrews 11:16 as cited by William Bradford.

were commanded to "trust in the Lord" to "direct" their "paths."[38] They recited this proverb so often, but doubt always sent them back to it time after time. Looking around the cramped hull, he wondered again, *Are these the people to accomplish God's purpose?*

They were brave enough to withstand persecution in England, remain faithful when they were separated from their families, had built a community in Leiden, and took the step to start over in an unknown world to save their children from materialism. When Brewster was threatened with arrest, it was the nail in the coffin. Each stumbling block they faced made them better. When they decided to cross the Atlantic and settle in the wilderness, they accepted that more trials would come.

The representative of the *Merchant Adventurers*, Thomas Weston, was a man who always tried to squeeze every cent out of an investment. Directing the Separatists to sail to the southern coast of England to finish preparing for the three-thousand-mile trip, Weston expected them to return to the nation where they were considered outlaws. Some chose to stay behind, including John Robinson. William and Dorothy's son, John, who was only three, was left behind with Dorothy's family for the boy's safety. The elderly, infirm, and small children were left behind as well. Once they managed to settle the colony, they would send for the others, but leaving them was a heart-wrenching affair. They knew many would've never survived the voyage, and some of them would die before they saw them again; but still, they chose to go.

From the moment they landed in England, everything went wrong. Weston now told them they were a hundred pounds short of funding the voyage. Since they already fulfilled their obligations to the contract, they suspected they were being taken for fools again. Many Separatists questioned Weston's motives. Was he just trying to scam them? Would he turn them in like before? This new problem and the seasickness discouraged many aboard. Some chose to return to Holland or start again in England. The more time they had to think about it, the more some decided the voyage was suicide.

---

[38] Ibid., Proverbs 3:5–6.

Industrious by nature and stubborn to the core, the Separatists sold their butter and some of their leather, guns, and swords to raise the hundred pounds. Even though they needed these in America, they sacrificed these items for a greater purpose but the butter would be greatly missed. Weston now claimed that he needed to replace those who decided to remain behind. There were too many vacancies on the ship and they couldn't sail to the New World with so few people. Seeing an opportunity to make more money, Weston sold passage aboard the ship to anyone willing to sign the contract.

Many who signed on were unemployed and poor. Some would risk what little they had for the promise of something better. At least, in the New World, they might escape the poverty of England. Status determined their success in Europe. In America, they were certain they would start over as equals. These last-minute substitutes were referred to as the Strangers by the Separatists. They called themselves the Saints.

Many Strangers had the same religious convictions as the Saints but were less stringent. Many were loyal to the Church of England; even though they saw the corruption, they chose to remain silent to avoid persecution. The Strangers saw the Saints as holy-rollers who thought themselves God's chosen people. The Saints wondered if their chance to establish a New Jerusalem was compromised now.

Brewster took this in stride. This was just another mystery of God's plan. Providence had put the Strangers among them for some reason. Maybe they were there for conversion or perhaps they would serve a special purpose later. Weston explained that they were needed to fulfill the agreement for the colony.

This agreement said each family or individual must work for seven years, and anything needed to support the colony would go into a common store. Each family or individual received a daily ration based on an equal share. Anything produced above the equal share belonged to the company. At the end of seven years, they would be free to make their own profits.[39]

---

[39] Bradford, 57–58 (Ch. 6).

Their first try at setting sail was a disaster. The first ship they hired, the *Speedwell,* set sail twice but was forced to return because of leaks and structural problems. This caused twenty more Separatists to stay behind, and it seemed the bad luck would continue.

Next, they hired a new captain and ship. The *Mayflower* was commanded by Captain Christopher Jones. Jones, his crew, and the Saints and Strangers set sail on September 16, 1620.

That day on deck, William gazed at the horizon as England faded out of sight. He then turned west and watched the cold blue expanse of the Atlantic. His spirit was joyous, but his flesh was afraid of what lay out there for all of them. After he could no longer see England, he retired to the hull, deep in thought. Opening his Bible again, he noticed Dorothy watching him. He smiled, and she smiled back, but only a little. She was struggling with her own wilderness. Leaving her child behind was like ripping her heart out.

William Bradford

Even though she understood the reason, it did little to ease the pain. "What if we both die?" she asked. John would be an orphan like him. William explained that they all must sacrifice for the will of God. He had left a house and the security of a trade to go wandering in the wilderness. They all left behind security for the unknown. What kind of life would his son have if they remained in Leiden?

They could protect what they had there and settle or they could risk it all for a better life. They were chosen by God to lead the way, he told her. They would be a light for others to see in the darkness.

Turning his head one last time, he saw one of the Strangers, John Alden, eyeing one of the support beams of the ship studying it. He was an experienced carpenter whose skills would certainly be valuable in the New World. He seemed like a good soul, William decided. Maybe Brewster was right. Maybe the Strangers were here for a reason.

Just across from Alden was Captain Miles Standish, another Stranger. He was a short boisterous man who had experience as a soldier and would be handy against the savages if they encountered any.[40]

Maybe all their mishaps weren't accidents. Maybe providence was directing their paths. They would need a carpenter and a soldier in America. Maybe the Strangers were blessings in disguise, "And thus, like Gideon's army, this small number was divided, as if the Lord by this work of providence thought these too many for the great work he had to do."[41]

God knew what he was doing and he had to learn to trust him. William thought of how the husbands and fathers in Leiden had held their heads high, even when they didn't know the fate of their families back in England. What courage and character!

Lifting his own head, he looked across the ship, beaming with pride. Someone up on deck shouted obscenities and shook him out of his good thoughts. It was that wretched sailor on Jones's crew who ridiculed and badgered them about their seasickness. Why would such a horrible creature be allowed to run rampant? Captain Jones never reprimanded this devil once.

William stopped himself from such a sinful thought. God was just. What a man sowed, he would surely reap. He would not allow this man to distract him. His role was to keep the faith and trust in providence. Closing his Bible, he began to pray.

---

[40] Ibid., 83–84 (Ch. 8); Philbrick, 23–29.
[41] Ibid., 85 (Ch. 8).

The *Mayflower* creaked and moaned as the waves smashed into the side of the ship. It appeared a storm was coming.

* * * * *

Battle of Rottenton, Transylvania (Romania), November 19, 1602

The sun rose over the dead mutilated bodies that littered the ground, replacing the darkness. Heads, arms, legs, torsos, bits of flesh, ears, eyes, teeth, and hair covered the landscape. Pools of coagulated blood occupied what ground was visible. As far as one could see, there was death and destruction. Swords, axes, muskets, and arrows had done their job well. The fetid odor of the dead accompanied the sound of the fortunate still breathing. Many begged for help or cried for water. Those discovered alive were dispatched quickly.

The Turks overran the Christian army at Rottenton and those not dead or wounded, retreated. Scavengers collected booty and kills. Any Christian wounded on the field was put to the sword. Caring for the infidels was an added burden to the army, and common soldiers fetched little on the lucrative slave market. Status even determined the value of life on the battlefield.

Captain John Smith had fought bravely, but his good fortune finally ran out. Laying among a pile of his dead comrades and foes, he was severely wounded and unable to flee. Surviving so many perils and achieving much in war, his life was now in the hands of this merciless enemy. He did not expect to live. Maybe they would overlook him among the piles of the dead and not be noticed. The only problem with this was that his wounds were severe and he probably would die whether he was found or not.

Remembering Paleologue's advice that dying in battle was preferable to capture with this enemy, he would play dead and take his chance with the wounds. Closing his eyes, he tried not to breathe as the scavengers approached. One Turk looked down in John's direction and saw movement. Pulling his sword, the Turk smiled and prepared to skewer the infidel. Hearing the sword drawn, John opened his eyes. If he was going to die today, he wanted to see his killer. The man was about to bring the sword down with a look of satisfaction on his face when his expression suddenly changed to curiosity. Stepping closer and peering down, the scavenger smiled.

John was ready to die. He had fought the good fight. He had proven himself and attained gentleman status with hard work and tested courage. The scavenger's smile grew larger, but this time he returned his sword to the scabbard. Confused, John noticed the Turk looking at the ground nearby. Laying there, his shield bearing the image of three severed heads and the motto, "*Vincere est Vivere*," sparkled in the sunlight.

The man was smiling because this infidel was important. He was a gentleman and probably rich. His life was worth something and he would garner a hefty price at the slave market. Either the man would fetch a hefty ransom or his bondage would pay the price. Wealthy men would pay to enslave a gentleman in hopes of collecting a ransom or the pleasure of knowing they had the highest class of Christian as a slave. John's relentless pursuit to achieve status saved his life that day.

After being nursed back to health and on his feet, he was forced to march two hundred miles in chains to be sold at the slave market in Turkey. Once there, potential buyers haggled over the captured infidels as if they were cattle. The slavers forced the prisoners to wrestle and fight one another to exhibit their strength, thus their worth. John was purchased by a wealthy Turk as a gift to his mistress. Taken to Istanbul, the capital of the Ottoman Empire, he served in the house of a young woman named Charatza Tragabigzanda.[42] She treated him humane and found the soldier infidel intriguing. Developing a bit of a crush on him, she found any excuse to be alone with John. He contemplated escape, but being trapped behind enemy lines in a foreign culture left little hope of success. He would bide his time and wait for an opportunity.

Charatza's mother disapproved of her daughter's infatuation with her slave and tried to sell John, but Charatza found out and

---

[42] Smith, *True Travels*, Ch.11.

forbade it. Fearing her mother would try again, Charatza sent him to the home of her brother who owned a huge plantation in southern Russia. There, he would be safe from the schemes of her mother. Eventually, she would join him. Little did she know that her brother and mother conspired to remove the family embarrassment together.

When John arrived in Russia, he realized he was in major trouble. They immediately grabbed and stripped him naked. Then, they shaved his head and face and locked an iron ring around his neck. After that, he was thrown into the grain fields and forced to work from dusk till dawn with only a threshing bat (resembling a cricket bat) to harvest with. This made it impossible to make the quota expected from him. Charatza's brother seemed to take his sister's crush personally and took his rage out on her slave. He would visit John in the field to beat him routinely.

Worked to exhaustion, routinely beaten, and deprived of his freedom, John went from farmer's son to gentleman to slave in a few short years. He flew too close to the sun like Icarus and fell into the sea. Captain John Smith finally obtained gentleman status only to suffer in slavery. Escape seemed impossible. Had he finally gotten himself into a situation he couldn't get out of? John was never one to settle for the *status quo* or willing to accept the impossible. He was an animal now, but he would not be caged for long. Somehow, some way, he would overcome.[43]

* * * * *

Aboard the Mayflower, middle of the Atlantic, October 1620

"Is the little lass a bit queasy?" Grinning, the sailor leered at her.

"Not much longer till you're fish food. Hope I get to throw least half of you overboard 'fore it's through. Chosen people? Chosen for a watery grave!"

Dorothy Bradford backed down the stairs into the hull of the ship on the verge of tears. *What a vile man,* she thought. *Why must*

---

[43] Ibid., Ch.12.

he torment them so? What sort of sick pleasure does he get from mocking sick people? William tried to comfort her, but the cruel man was making a bad situation worse. Searching for the makeshift bedding on the floor of the lower decks, she lay down, burying her face in the blanket. Quiet sobs followed, and William knew it was more than the wretched sailor's words. Poor Dorothy. She missed their baby too much. She was too gentle for all this, too fragile. It was why he loved her so much.

William opened his Bible and tried to read. Thinking of their situation a couple of weeks out at sea, he reflected. If this was the voyage of God's chosen people, he was surely testing them.

Within a few weeks of leaving the English coast, violent storms tossed the *Mayflower* around the sea like a piece of driftwood. Most of its passengers were seasick, some violently. The cramped living space below decks added to the nausea. Bathing was rare and only practiced by few. Drinking water was too precious a commodity to waste, and for weeks, they cooked meals, slept, and sweated in heavy woolen clothes without washing. This level of hygiene was typical in seventeenth century England, and cramped living quarters on a ship permitted few options for fresh air. This combination of odors must have added nausea to the seasickness. Because many were vomiting, the foul smell became unbearable. They saw this journey as a pilgrimage to claim a piece of the New World for a society with its foundation planted firmly in Christian principles. The Strangers were faithful Christians too. The difference between the Saints and Strangers was one of extremes, not beliefs. The Strangers wanted freedom to pursue their happiness just as much as the Saints. The tyranny of king and church opposed freedom of self-determination, and wanted both out of the way.

William Bradford decided even the wretched sailor who upset his wife was part of the plan. His cruelty was there for a specific purpose. The sailors were used to this. They were not. Scared and miserable, they didn't need any added punishment. This man delighted in tormenting them and seemed to find satisfaction in the idea of throwing their dead bodies overboard. The hate within him was projected at them. Captain Jones did nothing. He mistrusted them and their lawless cult. He would take them to America, but that was it. He wasn't there to look after them.

William knew God would have the final say. Maybe not in this world, but certainly in the next. Providence had gotten them this far. He would listen to the advice he gave the others and have faith.[44]

* * * * *

Somewhere near the Black Sea, Ottoman Empire, 1603

Life as a slave was counter to everything John Smith represented. Some of the other slaves seemed to accept their fate. They warned him that escape was futile. Christian slaves had it the worst. Treated like animals, they were at the bottom of the pecking order. The men were starved, beaten, and worked to exhaustion. Any women or children (boys and girls) were turned into prostitutes for the slave master. Life as a slave in Turkey was worse than death.

John Smith received a beating regularly from Charatza's brother and living as a slave was starting to break him down. Having all his energy drained by the backbreaking labor, inadequate diet, and the constant beatings weakened his spirit. By sheer grit, he held to the one thing that kept him going—hope.

The others swore escape was not an option, but he was used to people telling him things weren't possible. They were like the others who said he could never become an officer or change his status. Someone was always telling him what he couldn't do, and he was sick of it. His father, the teachers, everyone—and he proved them all wrong. Their words motivated him.

Charatza's brother was the culmination of all of them, beaten not with a club but by their doubt. They were wrong, and so was this barbarian holding him captive. He would find a way to escape, regardless of the consequence. Death was better than slavery. Paleologue was right. But his hope kept him going because freedom was out there,

---

[44] Bradford, 90–91 (Ch. 9); Philbrick, 30–31; Willison, 136.

if he earned it. So he waited and "God beyond Man's expectation or Imagination helpeth his servants, when they least think of help."[45]

Working one day in an isolated field alone, he contemplated running, but where would he go? No one was around for miles, but a runaway slave on foot would be easy to catch. This wasn't his chance, so he continued to work. Later that same day, Charatza's brother arrived alone on horseback, ready for another dose of the routine beating. Accusing him of laziness, the brother jumped off the horse and began striking John.

Suddenly, the slave's will for freedom and opportunity came together at the perfect moment. If he wanted liberty, he must work for it himself.

Rising with the threshing bat, the slave struck his tormentor, knocking him to the ground. The brother had royally messed up this time. He had showed up alone on horseback in a deserted field. At that moment, all of John's rage and frustration exploded as he beat his tormentor until his brains oozed out of a fractured skull. He was a murderer in a Muslim nation and had to escape.

Taking the dead man's clothes, he mounted the horse and headed north. Russia was there. If captured, he would be tortured and beheaded. It was all or nothing now. Riding day and night, he finally saw a signpost, and it was clear where to go. One arrow with the crescent pointed to Turkey. Another with the holy cross pointed to Russia. He rode for sixteen days until he reached Russia and freedom. He wrote later that "God did direct him." [46]

A good Samaritan woman helped him with clothes, food, and money, and the governor there removed the iron ring from his neck. Eventually, he made his way back to Romania where he was rewarded for all he lost in captivity. He lost a substantial sum, and the prince was glad to help the man who had claimed three heads from the enemy.

John decided to travel Europe and North Africa before returning home in 1604. He was free again and wanted to live a little before he

---

[45] Smith, *True Travels*, Ch.17; Firstbrook, 40.
[46] Ibid; Firstbrook, 107.

went back to work. He had big plans. His search for greatness wasn't over. He wanted to walk in Sir Francis Drake's footsteps. He planned to become an explorer and achieve wealth, fame, and respectability. In his mind, he was just getting started. His time as a slave made him appreciate freedom and self-determination even more.

He wasn't about to waste one more second of it.

* * * * *

Aboard the Mayflower, October/November 1620

The whole trip seemed a blessing from God. His providence was guiding this ship.

Within a few weeks of leaving England, violent storms tossed the *Mayflower* around like a piece of driftwood. Captain Jones had no choice but to resign control of the ship over to the will of the sea. William was certain it was the will of God.

The *Mayflower* was a unique ship. It was built in such a way that it reacted like a buoy. When a wave hit the side of the ship, it would take the brunt and return upright every time. The weight was centered in the lower sections. It made for a wild ride, but the *Mayflower* remained upright. If they would have set out in the *Speedwell,* which was designed differently, they would've sunk. The fact they were on this ship was a miracle.

During these storms, one of the Saints was swept overboard. The young man was on the main deck when a wave struck the ship. Falling over the side, he just happened to grab onto part of the hull before he was swept out into the ocean. "But it pleased God that he caught hold of the topsail halyards…and then with a boat hook and other means got into the ship again and his life saved."[47]

John Howland, the fortunate man, went on to be a productive member of the future colony and fathered ten children and eighty-eight grandchildren.[48]

---

[47] Bradford, 92–93 (Ch. 9).
[48] Ibid, 93 (Ch. 9); Philbrick, 33.

Then there was the wretched sailor who mocked them for their sea-sickness and William had cursed him. Shameful of his behavior, he remembered vengeance was the Lord's, not his, though it seemed vengeance came quickly through. "A special work of God's providence,"[49] he wrote:

> There was a proud and very profane young man, one of the seamen, of a lusty able body, which made him the more haughty: he would always be condemning the poor people in their sickness, and cursing them daily...that he hoped to cast half of them overboard before they came to their journey's end, and to make merry with what they had; and if he were by any gently reproved, he would curse and swear bitterly. But it pleased God before they came half seas over, to smite this young man with a grievous disease, of which he died in a desperate manner, and so was himself the first that was thrown overboard. Thus his curses light on his own head; and it was an astonishment to all his fellows, for they noted it to be the just hand of God upon him.

Providence protected John Howland and delivered justice to the sailor. Some of the passengers were scared and believed the voyage cursed. The "blazing star" was not a holy sign to some, but a curse. William held to his faith in providence and pointed to the two events as proof. Coincidence, many said, then an undeniable event occurred which tested their faith.

The main wooden beam of the ship cracked and bowed from the strain of the storms. If the beam snapped, the ship would come apart and take them to the bottom of the Atlantic. After exhausting all ideas to fix the beam, they surrendered to their fate. They were nowhere near land, and to repair the beam, they would need to lift

---

[49] Bradford, 90 (Ch. 9).

it to hold back the sea. Even if every passenger aboard helped, they couldn't lift it. After the hull started to leak and attempts to patch it failed, all hope slipped away, so the passengers prayed.

What if God didn't save them? What if freewill meant it was up to them to save themselves? Maybe providence was just a coincidence? He strengthened his resolve again. It wasn't luck or coincidence when the cruel sailor died exactly as he condemned all of them. Howland was saved by God's design. Being on the *Mayflower* appeared no accident to him. God had taken care of them all along, and they had to believe he would continue to protect them. Somehow, they would make it. In his prayers, William asked for deliverance. Just feet away, a contraption called a metal screw was the answer to those prayers.

One of the passengers remembered the tool, and a sliver of hope returned. Grabbing the metal screw, they positioned it under the beam. The metal screw was like a large hand jack used to raise house frames. Many considered the purchase a luxury and waste of space, but somehow, the supporters won out and the metal screw remained aboard. Turning the screw, the beam was raised into place and the repairs were made. The Pilgrims, Saints and Strangers alike, believed their prayers were answered. The captain and crew called it a miracle and wondered if these people did have God's ear.

They prayed while the crew despaired, and a miracle happened. William had no doubt that the hand of God protected them on this voyage. What were the chances of having the metal screw on board? No one had the foresight to bring the metal screw for repairing a cracked beam, but it was there nonetheless. God made sure it was there, and it didn't matter if they understood how it got there. It only mattered that it was there. "So they committed themselves to the will of God, and resolved to proceed."[50]

This faith in God's will is what made them so tenacious, even when all appeared lost. It helped define the colony, and later, their nation.

In early November, they sighted land on the horizon. It was the most beautiful thing they ever saw. Only one of them died on the

---

[50] Ibid., 92 (Ch. 9).

voyage, a young boy named William Butten. A baby born on the trip was christened Oceanus. God had protected them, just as William knew he would. Captain Jones explained they were way north of their destination. They weren't near the Hudson River of modern-day New York, but off the coast of Massachusetts instead. Steering the *Mayflower* south, Jones realized the rough sea and shoals were too dangerous, and after a day, he headed back north. It wasn't the right spot, but they had no choice. They found themselves anchored along the isthmus of Cape Cod. William believed they were off course by design. He wrote later that Jones turned back "as by God's providence they did."[51]

This area wasn't unknown either. The famous adventurer, Captain John Smith, had explored and even drew excellent maps of it six years before. Stephen Hopkins, a passenger on board, had been to Jamestown after his own adventure of being shipwrecked on a Caribbean island and told them of the famous captain's exploits. Most of them had read his accounts already and trusted his maps they now used to navigate. It was as if fate had joined the two voyages together. Smith mapped New Jerusalem or New England, so it was available to them.

The coast of Cape Cod was both a vast wilderness and a land of possibilities. From their vantage point, it appeared to be nothing more than a large beach with a backdrop of trees and brush, but they were both exhilarated and frightened by the mystery of the unknown. Were there savages waiting to kill them as soon as they set foot on shore? Would they be able to find food and build adequate shelter before it snowed? It was winter already, and by all accounts, winter was a harsh and brutal master in Cape Cod. The trees had lost their leaves, and the wind cut through the heavy woolen clothes like daggers.

Gazing across the dark blue water at the lonely coast, William smiled. This was where they would build New Jerusalem. He could feel it. Something deep within told him this was their new home. Watching the waves crash into shore, he also wondered what was out

---

[51] Ibid., 93 (Ch. 9).

there. They were already planning a scouting mission to row ashore, and he volunteered. Whatever they found, he wanted to be one of the first to set foot on this sacred ground. He felt a tinge of fear overtake him. They would sacrifice much to be worthy of this blessing—all reward followed a period of struggle.[52]

Just how long or how severe that struggle and sacrifice would be, he didn't know. But he was ready to keep walking this path.

* * * * *

Nevis Island, West Indies, March 28, 1607

Once again, Captain John Smith found himself in a life and death situation. This wasn't a duel or combat on the battlefield but a different kind of warfare. A warfare more treacherous and deceptive than armies could conceive. This warfare was the kind cowards fought, lurking in the shadows; while others did the fighting, they fomented treason.

Accused of conspiring to mutiny aboard the ship bound for the New World, the gallows were erected and waiting for John's neck. The group of men who devised this had every intention of hanging him. One man accused him—Edward Maria Wingfield. This poor excuse of a human, John thought, quarreled with him the entire voyage. Wingfield was a gentleman, born into his status. He despised all beneath his class who thought they could somehow earn their way into his. John represented this more than anyone, and Wingfield looked down his nose at the farmer's son. "Once a dirt farmer, always a dirt farmer" was Wingfield's attitude.

John saw the gentleman as one who never deserved such a status. These two conflicting beliefs represented the Old World and the New World. Wingfield felt that the English class system should simply be transplanted to its settlements while John strongly believed a New World demanded a new way. On the battlefield and in the wilderness, status meant nothing. A man's character and ability meant

---

[52] Ibid., 94–97 (Ch. 9).

everything. John had earned his gentleman status on the battlefield, and he wasn't about to let Wingfield disrespect him. The two hated each other.

Wingfield decided to dispose of the troublemaker by charging him with a crime punishable by death. If he couldn't tame the dirt farmer, he would get rid of him. What if Smith became a leader in the new settlement? What statement would this make of English society? He was filling their heads with revolutionary ideals. If the peasants and merchants believed they could earn their way into the nobility, what would happen to the order of things? This kind of thinking might lead to making a king and queen obsolete. This dangerous thinking had to be snuffed out before it had a chance to grow. Smith's ideals might cause problems for a gentleman in the New World. So Wingfield got his allies angry, convinced them to build gallows, and directed them to hang Captain John Smith.

They were in a tropical paradise surrounded by clear blue water and palm trees, yet all they could see was violence. They needed to get rid of this cancer before it grew and consumed their world. The son of a farmer who thought he was a gentleman was about to be swinging from a rope.[53]

* * * * *

Adventurer Bartholomew Gosnold recruited John to be a partner in his new voyage soon after he returned from Europe and his time as a slave. The Virginian coast of America was an unchartered wilderness of untapped resources and untold wealth. If they organized and led the venture, they would be wealthy men. At least, this was the way Gosnold presented it to John. After his experiences in the war and slavery, he needed something new to conquer. This was exactly the sort of thing he wanted. He signed on and invested some of his own money into the voyage. A venture to set up a colony was no easy task.

---

[53] Smith, *True Travels*, Ch. 27; Hoobler, 87–91; Price, 26.

It would take time and energy to secure investors, recruit settlers, get the king's permission, and purchase supplies. The logistics of this kind of venture were laborious. England still had no successful colony in the New World, and after previous failures, the king hadn't the stomach for another one. The colony of Roanoke Island, off the coast of North Carolina, was the last attempt by England to settle the New World. Sir Walter Raleigh founded and settled the colony only to see it vanish without a trace. Once establishing the settlement and confident it could sustain itself, Raleigh and the colony's new governor, John White, returned to England for provisions. Once there, they were detained by the Spanish Armada which bottled up England and made sea travel impossible.

After the war with Spain, which took three years, Raleigh sent John White back to Roanoke where he found it deserted. All that remained was the word Croatoan carved on a fencepost. All the houses were disassembled as if the settlers had relocated. The colonists were never found. They may have been massacred or enslaved by the Croatoan Indians or voluntarily left with them. No trace was ever found, and it is still a mystery today what fate the settlers met.

This failure and others caused England to drag its feet on authorizing a new colony. Any attempt would need to be unassociated with the government until success could be assured. Another failure would only embarrass them. England badly desired colonies to compete with Spain, Portugal, and France on the world stage. These Catholic nations were dominating the New World and reaping unlimited wealth. Spain had financed its wars with England with the gold and other resources gained from its colonies in the Americas. Wealth was power, and without it, large armies and navies could not be raised. The king wanted colonization, but he needed proof of success before he could publicly support it.

In the meantime, John would do what he always did. He would prepare. This time, he needed to learn cartography to map the ground and would teach himself the known Indian languages of the area. He would learn anything for an advantage in the New World. This took a few years to pull together the money, people, and logistics, and he spent the time honing much needed skills. This venture would be his biggest yet, he firmly believed.

On December 19, 1606, Smith found himself aboard the ship the *Susan Constant*. Two other ships accompanied his, the *GodSpeed* and the *Discovery*. Like Christopher Columbus, John was about to embark on one of the most momentous voyages in history. The *Susan Constant* was commanded by Captain Christopher Newport, Gosnold piloted the *GodSpeed,* and John Ratcliffe was chief of the *Discovery.* Over 140 men and boys were destined for the journey.

The lack of females ensured it was a temporary venture. It was strictly a resource-gathering expedition and not based on permanent colonization. They would first see if it was viable before they could live there and raise families. This was a working settlement which would finance England's future colonies. Gold and other valuable minerals were the goal. If it failed, they could return home without much fanfare. None of the investors cared about permanency. They wanted a return on their investment and nothing else. John intended to explore all possibilities there. If they failed to find the shiny yellow metal, maybe they would find a different resource worth its weight in gold. If they could make it a successful colony, why not try?

For six weeks, the three ships were stuck in the English Channel because of a lack of wind. By the end of January, they finally grabbed a breeze and set sail. By mid-February, they were well out to sea. This is when they all witnessed what they described as a "blazing star" in the sky. Some saw this heavenly sign a bad omen, others a sign of good tidings. Regardless, the comet amazed all aboard ship. The ones who labelled it a bad omen were reassured a few hours later when a massive storm tossed the ships relentlessly about the sea.[54]

By March 23, 1607, the three ships reached the Caribbean island of Martinique. This was where John was accused of conspiring to make himself king of the voyage by Wingfield. Captain Newport had no other choice but to arrest John and confine him onboard.

---

[54] Percy, George. *Observations Gathered out of a Discourse of the Plantation of the Southerne Colonie in Virginia by the English, 1606,* February 12, 1607, (*nationalhumanitiescenter.org*); Willison, George F. *Behold Virginia: The Fifth Crown.* (New York: Harcourt, Brace and Co, 1952), 10; Williams, 43–45; Firstbrook, 145–146, 157.

This was partially to keep the two men away from each other, but Wingfield took pleasure in the arrest.

By the time they arrived in Nevis, Wingfield had plotted to hang John without a trial. There was no need for a trial or even Captain Newport's authority. Wingfield felt he had enough status to be judge, jury, and executioner. John was escorted from the ship while gallows were built. Once the accused saw his accuser's intentions, he pointed out the injustice of it and appealed to men of reason. Luckily, he had friends aboard, and they quickly held off the hangmen. When Newport discovered the plot, he reprimanded Wingfield for overstepping his authority. They had bigger problems to deal with than the feud between two men. The Carib Indians were in the vicinity and were known to be cannibals. Not to mention the unbearable heat had already claimed its first victim. What appeared a tropical paradise was really a tropical hell.

John was again confined for the duration of the voyage, this time to protect Wingfield from him. Newport knew the investors had chosen seven passengers onboard to lead the settlement once they landed in Virginia. These names were concealed from everyone, including the ones chosen. These seven names were locked in a box in Newport's cabin. Until they reached their destination, he was in charge. He made the decisions for now, not Smith or Wingfield.

On April 21, they left the Caribbean behind and headed toward the coast of North Carolina. Another violent storm hit, and they were forced to ride it out below decks.

Many were still afraid of the bad omen the "blazing star" brought. Would they meet the same fate as the people in Roanoke? John saw the storm differently. "God the guider of all good actions, forcing them by an extreme storm to howl all night, did drive them by his providence to their desired port."[55]

* * * * *

---

[55] Smith, John. *The General Historie of Virginia, New England, & the Summer Isles, Volume 1*. (Bedford: Applewood Books, 1629), 87 (Book 3); Willison, *Behold*, 16–17; Williams, 49–50.

Off the coast of Cape Cod, Massachusetts, November 11, 1620

When Captain Jones told them that New England would be their destination and not the Hudson River area, some began to panic. The contract they signed said nothing about New England. Did this mean their patent was now void? A group of Strangers decided they would "use their liberty, for none had the power to command them"[56] when they set foot on shore. William saw all order descend into chaos and their survival depended on cooperation. If anarchy reigned, then they would perish. The cool-headed among both Saints and Strangers recognized the need for cooperation to maintain order among their settlement. In unity, they were strong. With division, they would be picked off one by one.

Gathering together, the men discussed the details of a compact they must agree upon before setting foot on land. They were already preparing to send out a scouting party, so they had to settle on an agreement quickly. After some debate, the Saints and Strangers alike agreed to this compact. Known as the "Mayflower Compact," it stated:

> Having undertaken, for the glory of God and advancement of the Christian faith and honor of our king and country, a voyage to plant the first colony in the northern parts of Virginia, do these present solemnly and mutually in the presence of God and one another, covenant and combine ourselves together into a civil body politic, for our better ordering and preservation, and furtherance of the ends aforesaid; and by virtue hereof to enact, constitute and frame such just and equal laws, ordinances, acts, constitutions and offices, from time to time as shall be thought most meet and convenient for the general good

[56] Bradford, 109 (Bk 2); Philbrick, 39.

of the colony, unto which we promise all due submission and obedience.[57]

This was the first founding document of America and proclaimed the fundamental purpose of their colony. It was an oath to one another to ensure survival of all. The compact also consolidated Saint and Stranger into one people. It also promised "submission and obedience" to all laws once they made some. The "Mayflower Compact" was written to assure law and order. William saw it as another example of providence. The first line said it all. They were creating a whole new world, not for themselves, but for the "glory of God and the advancement of the Christian faith." Saint and Stranger agreed that they must establish Christian liberty in the settlement. Of course, they would bring their English heritage with them, but they would never forget their purpose of creating a New Jerusalem. Writing years later, referencing Deuteronomy 26, William declared, "Our fathers were Englishmen which came over this great ocean and were ready to perish in this wilderness; but they cried unto the Lord, and He heard their voice and looked upon their adversity."[58]

After forty-one men signed the compact, they elected John Carver governor. Though Carver was one of the Saints, they all trusted and respected him. Now they were ready to send out the scouting party. Captain Jones with some of his crew—accompanied by Stephen Hopkins, Captain Miles Standish, and William—made up a party of sixteen men who boarded a shallop (long rowboat) and rowed to shore.

William was breathless at the grandeur of the place. They had made it. This was their wilderness, and once they paid their penance, they would step into the promised land. New Jerusalem was here somewhere among the sand and the brush. He could feel it. Breathing in the cool salty air, he raised his eyes and thanked God.

Once they reached shore, he described their graciousness: "Being thus arrived in a good harbor and brought safe to land, they fell upon

---

[57] Ibid.,109–110 (Bk 2)
[58] Ibid., 96–97 (Ch. 9); *King James Bible,* (Nelson), Deuteronomy 26:7.

their knees and blessed the God of heaven, who had brought them over the vast and furious ocean, and delivered them from all the perils and miseries thereof, again to set their feet on the firm and stable earth, their proper element."[59]

Now they would get to work. Their lives depended on quick action. They needed to scout the area and find ground suitable for supporting a settlement. Any dangers had to be identified and removed. Walking along the shore, they discovered plenty of trees for both fuel and building material. After the first exhaustive day, they returned to the ship and described the bounty awaiting them. They needed more information, so they set out the following day. This time, however, they saw a group of people standing in the distance along the beach. When some of them tried to approach them, they fled. Now they knew they weren't alone. Not knowing whether they were friendly or hostile, they chose to camp that night on the beach and continue exploring the next day. They posted three guards armed with muskets, but nothing happened.

The next morning, they covered more ground. They needed to find a water source and plenty of wildlife for meat. Within the next few days, they found a spring and saw deer, birds, and other small game. Clearly, this place could support a settlement. Staying another night, the next day they found an old cornfield and some strange mounds covered with reed mats. Realizing these were graves, they moved on. Down the beach, they found an area in the sand which appeared smoother than the rest. It seemed out of place and was clear someone had buried something there. Forming a circle, musket in hand, the others dug up the sand.

A few feet down, they found a large basket of seed corn. It was so heavy they barely could pick it up. Their first thought was one of good fortune. Then they decided this must be someone's corn, and if they took it, it would be theft. Contemplating the decision, they rationalized that their survival depended on it. They honestly discussed avoiding angering the natives, but they had families who could benefit from this corn. They had specific instructions from the

---

[59] Ibid., 94 (Ch. 9).

Virginia Company not to make enemies of the Indians and many of the Saints saw them as future converts to the faith.

The English didn't see the Indian as an inferior race but only an inferior civilization. They saw them as savages and primitive pagans who were to be pitied because they never knew the Gospel. Only the good news of the Gospel would civilize them. The Indians could be saved. This was very different from the Spanish view which treated their horses better. If they took the corn, they would start off on the wrong foot and might incite conflict.[60] William described this dilemma: "The corn and beans they brought away, proposing to give them full satisfaction when they should meet with any of them (as about some six months afterward they did, to their good content). And here is to be noted a special providence of God, and a great mercy to this poor people."[61]

He, along with others, believed the corn was found because God had willed it. He provided them with what they needed to get them through winter. A few saw it as theft just the same, most accepted it as necessary. This also put them in debt to the Indians. No one thought the Indians they took the corn from might go hungry. They were convinced God led them to the discovery to sustain them, not to punish the Indians.

Returning to the *Mayflower* with the corn, that night, six inches of snow blanketed the area in what became one of the coldest winters in history. This period was known as the "Little Ice Age" in the northern hemisphere, and Captain Jones was threatening to sail back to England soon, so it was critical they find a place to settle. Sending another scouting party to shore, William volunteered once again. He knew that providence would lead them to the right spot and he, Dorothy, and eventually John would make it their home.[62]

* * * * *

---

[60] Ibid., 98–100 (Ch. 10); Philbrick, 60–65; Willison, 148–151.
[61] Ibid., 100 (Ch. 10).
[62] Ibid., 100–101 (Ch. 10); Philbrick, 65–66.

Chesapeake Bay, Virginia, April 1607

The passengers of all three ships crowded the decks to get a glimpse of the New World. For four months, they anticipated this moment.

On the horizon was land known as Virginia. The thick forest and lush green landscape on the coastline excited the passengers. Surely a plentiful land such as this would provide riches beyond imagination. Most believed food would rain down like manna and gold would shine right through the soil.

John was cynical. Nothing was this easy. If they prospered, it would by the sweat of their brows, not wishful thinking. Once anchored offshore, Newport sent a scouting party ashore to investigate. After some initial exploring, they encountered the Indians. One of the men, George Percy, described what transpired:

> There came the savages creeping upon all fours from the hills like bears, with their bows in their mouths. They charged us very desperately in the faces, hurt Captain Gabriel Archer in both his hands, and a sailor in two places of the body very dangerous. After they had spent their Arrows, and felt the sharpness of our shot, they retired into the Woods with a great noise, and so left us.[63]

To them, this was the behavior of savages. Attacking without provocation or caring if they were friend or foe seemed rash. These natives were the Algonquin of the Powhatan Empire, and their appearance and behavior was frightening to the settlers. They painted their bodies and faces various colors and shaved one side of their heads bald. They also had a curious way of wailing like animals when attacking. Though appearing primitive, John knew they could be cunning and dangerous. They could never discount them.

---

[63] Percy, April 20, 1607 entry; Smith, *General Historie*, 87 (Bk 3), Price, 28–29.

Dealing with the Indians was simple to him. They had to portray strength from the get-go if they expected to survive this place.

After the attack on shore, the scouting party returned to the ships. Newport was ready to unlock the box and reveal the names inside. He read the seven names—Bartholomew Gosnold, John Martin, George Kendall, Edward Wingfield, and Captain Newport. Each named called out was accepted and predicted until he spoke the final name—Captain John Smith.

Wingfield immediately objected. This man was charged with mutiny and under arrest. He couldn't hold a seat on the council. The other members agreed and postponed seating John until the mutiny charge was settled. To add further insult, Wingfield was appointed president of the council. Once again, John was judged by what they thought him to be, not who he was. He came to the New World to lead. He would not be commanded, though he accepted the decision with little objection. Here a man would be judged by what he could offer, not his status. Acquiescing, he decided to lead by example. His accomplishments would define him. An appointment was as meaningless as a name.

The first issue the council faced was where to settle. Sailing up the James River, they assembled on shore for a brief ceremony. After prayers, they erected a large wooden cross and claimed Virginia for England and his Christian majesty, King James. Apprehensive, they continued up the river. To their surprise and delight, they found a friendly tribe of natives who entertained them with a dance. After leaving the amenable village, a few miles further they discovered a swampy isthmus and chose it for their settlement. It had strategic significance, providing easy access to the sea. It was also a military choice, because it would be easier to defend. They named it Jamestown, after the king, and this was the only time Smith and Wingfield agreed.[64]

From the start, President Wingfield denied permission to build a defensive stockade around the settlement or emplace cannon.

---

[64] Ibid., April 29, 1607 entry; Smith, *True Relation*, 34; Smith, *General Historie*, 88 (Bk 3).

Muskets would remain aboard ship except for the few needed for hunting. He believed a show of strength would appear aggressive and incite the Indians. The company made it clear—they must not anger the natives. This was a business venture, and friendly relations with them were of the utmost importance. Wingfield felt a show of peace would get a peaceful reaction. John disagreed adamantly, but he was still not officially on the council and had no power to object.

In the first few days in Jamestown, the settlers noticed Indians spying on them from the surrounding woods. After chasing them away, a chief and a hundred warriors came to the settlement, fully armed. The chief demanded the English lay down their few arms as a sign of peace, but they refused. This encounter nearly escalated when one of the braves tried to steal a hatchet. One settler grabbed the tool from the Indian and pushed him. Another brave raised his war club to strike the settler who pushed his comrade, but both sides calmed their men before this went any further. The Indians left in anger while the English sighed in relief. They were heavily outnumbered and, because of Wingfield's policy, unprepared to defend themselves.

A few days after this initial visit, a smaller band of natives came to the settlement and demanded to be allowed to stay the night. After refusing this bizarre request, some of the settlers decided to show the superiority of their weaponry to the bow and arrow, thinking this would deter their boldness. Setting up a target, they challenged the warriors to prove the penetrating power of their arrows. The arrows penetrated more than a foot into the target to the amazement of the English. One prankster decided to replace the target with a steel one and challenged them to show the first time wasn't a fluke. This time, the arrow shattered on impact with the steel target, and the settlers roared with laughter. The Indians were embarrassed and stormed out of the settlement.

So far, Jamestown's inhabitants weren't making a good impression with the native people. In Native American society, like many societies, weakness was preyed upon, not respected. Slights to personal honor demanded retaliation. Wingfield's policy endangered Jamestown. His eagerness to appear harmless emboldened the Indians. These two meetings were merely opportunities for the

Powhatan to size up their numbers and defenses. John pointed to this mistake but was discounted and ignored. These initial encounters with the natives caused Newport to form an exploratory force to get a sense of the threats around them. He brought twenty-three men, including John on the expedition. The force sailed up the river into an unknown world.

Soon after leaving, they met another friendly tribe who filled them in on the world they had walked into. The Powhatan Empire ruled over all the tribes in the area. It encompassed between 13,000 to 34,000 people. The emperor, Chief Powhatan, ruled by force. An eighty percent tribute from everything produced was paid to him from every tribe. Any tribe who refused to pay tribute either submitted or was eradicated.

Newport realized that anyone this powerful should be made an ally. Arranging a meeting with the chief to discuss some sort of deal, they were told to await his arrival. Upon meeting, Chief Powhatan, Newport suggested a treaty of friendship and showered him with gifts and the promise of more. The chief encouraged them to continue upriver to the Pamunkey village where they would be cordially received and supplied a guide for the journey. Soon after embarking, John felt uneasy about the guide's erratic behavior but couldn't quite put his finger on it. He also felt bothered by the chief's countenance and his gut told him something was wrong, but he couldn't be sure what.[65]

At the Pamunkey village, the English met Chief Opechancanough, Chief Powhatan's younger brother. This man was massive and stood six feet tall and was intimidating. Compared to the English, who averaged five-foot-six, he was a giant. His face and body were painted red and he looked like a demon (this red paint led to the label of "*redskin*"). The big man and his people were rude and hostile toward them and now, Newport and the others began to feel John's unease. It seemed that the Pamunkey were stalling for some reason.

---

[65] Ibid., May 18,20,24, 1607 entries; Smith, *True Relation*, 33; Hoobler, 97–103; Price, 38–42.

John pleaded with Newport to be on guard, and this time, he agreed. Cutting the meeting short, the party boarded their boat and hurried down the river. They all were afraid and concerned for Jamestown and what they would find there.

John's instinct was correct. The same day they left the Pamunkey village, 200 to 400 Indians crept through the long grass surrounding Jamestown. The unsuspecting settlers were busy tilling the fields at the edge of the settlement when suddenly, hundreds of arrows rained down upon them. Those inside Jamestown with a few muskets managed to hold back the onslaught long enough to save most of those caught outside. Some were penned down while the Indians tried to pick them off one at a time. This attack nearly succeeded but for the courage of those who fought back.

Though Wingfield was one of the defenders, it was his policy which had caused it. Cannons from the ships finally chased the Indians away. The casualties were minimal but significant. Seventeen were wounded and one boy was killed. A week later, one of the wounded died as well. One Indian was killed and several wounded, but the psychological effect of the attack was worse than the casualties. They felt vulnerable and naked. Jamestown didn't even have a stockade and the Indians could have overrun them if they had wanted to. For many, this was when reality really hit home.

When John and Newport returned the next day, they understood the purpose of stalling by their disingenuous hosts. They also learned that the chief they met with was not Chief Powhatan but his son. The entire thing was a setup. The Pamunkey kept them busy and away from the settlement to weaken their numbers. Under the guise of friendship, the Indians had played on their goodwill. After this attempt, Wingfield allowed construction of a stockade around Jamestown and ordered muskets, swords, cannons, and gunpowder brought from the ships. Men slept with their muskets ready.

The Indians continued their hit-and-run attacks outside the stockade. The high grass concealed them as they crept up on those unfortunates who ventured out to use the bathroom or hunt. John was livid and stopped biting his tongue. He openly criticized the appeasement policy Wingfield had used and he only called for defensive measures once they were attacked. *What inspiring leadership*, John thought. When word the farmer's son's criticism reached Wingfield, he ordered him back to England.

This time, Newport and others came to Smith's defense. He had been right from the start, and they decided to seat John on the council. He would be a welcomed antithesis to the ignorance of the appeasers. Example and action had won out against status and position, just as he predicted. He would now pursue results.

On June 22, Newport decided it was time to return to England. He sailed for home with the *Susan Constant* and the *GodSpeed* but left the *Discovery* behind for the colony's use. He promised to return within five months loaded with provisions. Jamestown was already low on food, and with Newport's departure, they would lose much of their manpower.

Little was accomplished since their arrival. They still slept in outdoor shelters and had built no houses. Few crops were planted, and the common store was depleted. Not a single well had been dug, and the water they drank was contaminated. Gentlemen like President Wingfield refused to do any manual labor, yet still expected a share of what was produced. He and his supporters appeared unusually healthy and well-fed compared to the rest of Jamestown who were malnourished. Since the president had control over the common store, it wasn't long before word of Wingfield's corruption caused discontent. Those who worked received the same pathetic share as those who did not. This led to less production and dependence on trade with the Indians and Newport's return.

Wingfield's disastrous leadership with the Indians, the common store, and strict adherence to the English status system convinced John that if something didn't change, they wouldn't survive. Just like his escape from slavery, they would face this reality or die.

Standing at the edge of Jamestown, John watched the two ships fade out of sight. They were on their own now. What would become of them? People were sick and hungry. The fear on their faces spoke louder than their words. Some were trying to work, while others sat in their shelters and waited for their share. Maybe Newport would save them in time. Perhaps someone would figure it out. He knew much suffering and pain was on its way. They would learn the awful lessons through trial and error, but many would die before they learned.[66]

If only he could convince them. Touching his forehead, he noticed it was warm and clammy. He didn't have time to get sick now. Yes, the time of suffering for all of them was on its way.

* * * * *

On the shore of Cape Cod, November 1620

William lay restless inside the small barricade erected of logs and branches and tried to take his mind off the day's discovery. What a horrible find it had been.

Stumbling upon another grave, they uncovered a skull with blonde hair buried next to the remains of a small child. Was this an Englishman? Had the Roanoke Colony resettled this far north? Did some other European meet their fate here? Was the child killed by the Indians or did it live among them? Was the child killed with his father? Thinking of his own father, he felt sadness. Then thinking of his own son, he recounted Dorothy's fear something would happen to the child while they were gone, and he felt the same fear.

He didn't like this vein of thought one bit. Maybe this poor man had lived with the natives and had a child with an Indian wife. Though not a common practice yet, it was easier to imagine this than the options he entertained. Had the Indians been so callous they would murder a child? Were they this evil? Were they the savages many called them?

Sleeping on the beach near the fire did nothing to take the chill away. It was total darkness, except near the fire, and the only sounds were the crashing waves and the wind rustling in the trees. Anything or anyone could be lurking out there. The previous night, one of the guards had sounded the alarm. Grabbing their muskets and taking cover, they waited, but nothing happened. The man standing

---

[66] Smith, *True Relation*, 35–36; Smith, *General Historie*, 88–89; Firstbrook, 184–185.

guard spotted several Indians crawling up to their campsite. His alarm scared them away. The whole event put everyone on edge, and now, with the grave discovered earlier, sleeping was difficult, if not impossible. The exploration and the cold exhausted William, and he desperately needed sleep. Clearing his mind, he welcomed the light doze that overtook him.

"*Aaaaaaaaaahhh!*" A maniacal shriek from out of the darkness woke William and the others abruptly.

"*The savages! To arms! To arms!*" Standish yelled.

William clutched the musket and looked for something to shoot. Arrows flew all around, and the wails grew louder as the banshees crept closer. Thinking he saw movement, he fired. The flood of sparks from the explosion illuminated the dark. A cacophony of gunfire, yells, and the crashing surf was distracting. Beginning the long process of reloading, he concentrated on controlling his nerves as the arrows whizzed past him. All he could think of was the blonde skull. Was this the fate the man and child met? Would this be theirs?

The Indians retreated into the trees but continued to send their arrows. They fired a dozen of the razor-tipped missiles for every single shot the English managed. Most of the Pilgrims fired recklessly from adrenaline rushing through their bodies and only frightened the Indians with the noise. Standish had experience in combat and commanded the others, "*Don't waste your shots firing at phantoms!*"

A few of the men had left their muskets at the shallop and ran to retrieve them. The Indians turned their attention on them, trapping several behind the boat with unlit matches unable to fire their muskets. "*Well, well, everyone. Be of good courage!*" Standish called to the trapped men encouraging them, though they had no way to fire back. One brave man sprinted through the gauntlet of arrows back to the campfire and grabbed a burning log. He then retraced his steps back through the danger where his companions lit their matches and returned fire.

The Indians became discouraged with the increased firepower. What sort of men were these English? The leader of the natives tried his own encouragement but to no avail. This Indian avoided being shot multiple times before he realized his men had lost their nerve.

The English muskets inflicted such a terrible wound, and the sound of exploding gunpowder kept the Indians behind cover. The natives finally retreated into the woods. Standish and others chased them for a quarter of a mile before they stopped. Firing their muskets in defiance, they wanted the attackers to know they weren't afraid nor ready to quit.

William was just thankful to be alive. "Thus it pleased God to vanquish their enemies, and give them deliverance: and by his special providence so to dispose that not any one of them were either hurt, or hit, though their arrows came close by them." Though they won the showdown, they all were grateful. "Afterward they gave God solemn thanks and praise for their deliverance."[67]

Leaving the area was a priority in case the Indians returned with larger numbers, so they boarded the shallop and set off down the shore for a new campsite.

On the shallop, the temperature continued to drop as the ocean spray drenched them, freezing their clothes stiff. They lost the rudder and sail after flipping the boat, causing them to head for shore. They couldn't steer but managed to reach a nearby island, which they named Clarke's Island. Building a fire, they warmed themselves and dried their clothes and gave thanks to God again for their rescue.

The next day, they found the perfect spot for New Jerusalem. They named it New Plymouth, and William credited providence with leading them there. The Indian attack and the frigid night on the island guided them to that very spot. By adversity, they were once again delivered. Struggle had blessed them, and God was keeping them safe, he was sure.

He couldn't wait to tell Dorothy the good news. Maybe she would gain hope and strength from this. Now they had their settlement. As fast as they could prepare a home, they could retrieve John and be a family again. The others aboard would be energized as well.

---

[67] *Mourt's or Journal of the Plantation at Plymouth*, ed. Henry Martin Dexter. (Boston: John Kimball Wiggin, 1865), 33-60; Bradford, 102–104 (Ch. 10); Philbrick, 70–74.

After five days of hardship, they returned to the *Mayflower*. As William climbed aboard, he noticed every eye on him. There was sadness and pity in them. Brewster approached him, explaining there had been an accident while he was gone. Dorothy had somehow fallen overboard without notice and drowned the night before. Hearing Brewster's words, he refused to believe. Only after seeing her lifeless face did he accept it. The fear she had of John becoming an orphan was now half true. He would now face life without his wife to comfort and strengthen him and after all their blessings, he couldn't understand why God had let his Dorothy die. Why did he take away the one thing he loved in this world? What purpose did this serve?[68]

Writing of these events years later, William allowed a crack in his usual optimistic persona to show. It revealed an inner turmoil as much as it described the outer turmoil they all felt: "Besides, what could they see but a hideous and desolate wilderness, full of wild beasts and wild men."[69]

Though he said little of Dorothy's death, he internalized the pain and accepted it as the will of God. His flesh was weak, but his spirit carried him through. His wife was in a better place now. It was his task to continue their purpose. She would live in his heart forever. God spared his wife from the suffering they must experience. It was a test and he had to find the fortitude within. The kingdom of heaven was within, and that was exactly where the answer resided.

Reminded of his long walks with sore feet to hear God's word, he would deny himself. He needed to continue his path and ensure the survival of their colony. "What could now sustain them but the spirit of God and his grace?"[70]

William resolved to fulfill his purpose, even if it killed him—and it probably would.

* * * * *

---

[68] Philbrick, 76–77; Willison, 156–157.
[69] Bradford, 95 (Ch. 9).
[70] Ibid., 96 (Ch. 9).

Werowocomoco Village, Virginia, December 30, 1607

Kneeling on the ground with a rock for a pillow, John realized he was in trouble.

Two big Indians held him in place while another raised a war club over his head with the intention of bashing out his brains. What he had done to Charatza's brother was about to happen to him.

He couldn't figure out what had gone so wrong. Chief Powhatan appeared cordial and eager to talk at first, but something went terribly awry. He was about to be executed, and there was no way out of this one. He tried to use status to save his life, but it didn't work. Now his life was in the hands of the "savages," and they were out for blood. In the Powhatan Empire, his gentleman status meant as much as it did to Wingfield. Paleologue had explained about the Turks, and he remembered the sagacious advice that death was preferable to imprisonment by barbarians. Maybe swift execution was a blessing. Compared to what happened to others, this was good fortune.

Closing his eyes, he said one last prayer. This time, he couldn't save himself. It was up to God whether he lived or died and short of a miracle, he was a doomed man.

* * * * *

A few months before John's head ended up on a rock, he faced another deadly challenge. A mysterious illness descended over Jamestown, and he wasn't immune. He wrote, "God (being angry with us) plagued us with such famine and sickness, that the living were scarce able to bury the dead..."[71]

After fighting off Indian attacks, the settlers couldn't fight off disease. Though John recovered, his business partner, Bartholomew Gosnold, did not. Many others died as well. At any one time, there were barely enough settlers on their feet to drag the dead bodies out of the settlement. When they could, they were often attacked by the Indians who crept around in the tall grass outside the settle-

---

[71] Smith, *True Relation*, 36.

ment. With disease ravaging and hostile natives picking off settlers, Jamestown faced extinction. The illness was bad, but the malnutrition which made them more susceptible to it was worse.

The common store divided up an equal share of misery. There was just enough to keep them alive, but it wasn't sufficient. Even if they did very little labor, the calories their bodies required at rest was larger than what they ate. After months of this deprivation, the settlers became apathetic. Under these circumstances, many eventually fell into a state of what behavioral psychologists call "learned helplessness" or the acceptance of suffering because there is no escape from it. They just gave up all hope of improving their situation. Like the status system they accepted in England, they believed themselves helpless to change it but John Smith was different.[72]

From personal experience, he knew men determined their own destinies. In David Price's *Love and Hate in Jamestown: John Smith, Pocahontas, and the Founding of America*, the author points to the concepts Dr. Viktor E. Frankl, a Nazi concentration camp survivor and psychologist, advanced in his book, *Man's Search for Meaning*. If men believed their lives had purpose, they would constantly strive to reach it. Even in a concentration camp, those convinced they had a purpose had a greater chance to survive. Those who understood "there must be a meaning in suffering" found a reason to live. Once apathy affected someone, they eventually reached a state of disillusionment and accepted death.

Dr. Frankl described how many who reached this point soon became sick and died. Many in Jamestown had a similar mental state. John tried to encourage them to get up and work. Though the food was inept, the water poisoned and hope lost, they had to work toward a purpose. Some took his advice, but many refused and died once the illness came and Jamestown would never survive if they continued this course.[73]

---

[72] Price, 48–49; Firstbrook, 189–190.
[73] Price, 55–56; Frankl, Viktor E. *Man's Search for Meaning.* (Boston: Beacon Press, 1959, 2006), 67.

Then miraculously, the Indians decided to make peace and open trade with the English. John attributed this providential event to a higher purpose, "each hour expecting the fury of the Savages; when God the patron of all good endeavors, in that desperate extremity so changed the hearts of the Savages…"[74]

The renewed amity of the Indians brought trade. Trade meant more food and lifted the spirits of the men a bit, but John knew perception wasn't reality. He recruited a crew for an exploratory mission up the river and used this opportunity to find out what was around them. Shortly after leaving, their boat ran aground, and Smith decided to continue up the smaller tributaries with a smaller group. Leaving instructions to the main group not to step foot off the boat, he and two of his crew, Thomas Emry and Jehu Robinson, with the help of two eager Indian guides, boarded a canoe and set off.

Within a few miles, the party decided to take a break and rowed to the riverbank. John felt this was an opportune time to hunt for dinner and told Emry and Robinson to fire warning shots if they encountered any problems. He headed into the woods with one of the guides in search of prey. Little did he know others had found their own prey. Within a short time, John heard shots from the direction of the boat, though it wasn't the agreed upon signal. Perplexed, he soon spotted figures moving from behind trees and brush all around him. There were a few hundred Indians moving toward him.

Arrows filled the space around John, as he pulled his pistol and returned fire. Backing away, he was struck in the leg, and still patiently reloaded (in 1608, it took an experienced soldier twenty to thirty seconds to do this). Grabbing the guide suspected involved in the plot, he used him as a shield. Keeping his eyes on the attackers and backing away, he stepped into a quicksand pit. He was trapped, and the only option was surrender. This would probably mean certain death if he failed to convince his captors of his value. The Indians grabbed him and walked him back to the boat. On the ground, he saw the body of Jehu Robinson riddled with over twenty arrows. Emry was nowhere in sight, and John figured that he had met the same fate.

---

[74] Smith, *General Historie*, 92 (Ch. 1).

Back at the main boat, the crew had their own problems. One of the men, George Cassen, eyed some young native women bathing on shore. Though Captain Smith ordered them to remain on the shallop, Cassen could not resist the allure of the naked females. Jamestown had no women, and months without them was too much for some, including Cassen. Making his way to shore for a better look, his attention on the bathing women, he overlooked the trap he walked into. Watching the glistening nakedness, he never noticed the braves hiding in the surrounding forest.

When he was close enough, the braves surrounded him and dragged the unfortunate man near the fire they built nearby. Stripping him naked, they staked him to the ground and then acted out a grisly ritual. Starting with the Englishman's fingers, they sawed them off one by one and threw them into the fire. Once they finished with his fingers, they removed the skin from his face and head with seashells. Finally, they cut open his abdomen, pulled out his bowels, and tossed them into the flames. Cassen screamed, writhing in agony and pleaded for help. The men in the shallop witnessed this torture but knew they were outnumbered. If they tried to help him, they would meet the same demise, so they were forced to listen to the man's pleas, unable to do anything. Once Cassen died, his body was thrown into the fire and burned.[75]

In the meantime, John was still not out of the woods. His captors seemed ready to execute him, but he thought quickly and pulled a compass from his pocket. Flashing the mysterious device to the Indians, he sparked curiosity to replace their enmity. Chief Opechancanough snatched the compass hypnotized by it. John told them about the planets, moon, stars, and the spherical Earth. Amazed by the white man's knowledge, they seemed convinced he was important. Breathing easier, Smith was certain he had impressed them, but once the novelty wore off, they tied him to a tree, fixed their arrows, and prepared to kill him. Suddenly, Chief Opechancanough raised his hand and stopped the execution. This man would first be

---

[75] Ibid., 94-95 (Ch 2); Price, 59-61; Hoobler, 120-121.

introduced to Chief Powhatan. There might be something valuable about this small man. He would let his brother decide.

So John was sent to the capital city of the Powhatan Empire, Werowocomoco, to meet the chief. Questioned by medicine men and invited to partake in a feast, he was welcomed to Chief Powhatan's longhouse. After a bit of friendly conversation with the big chief, his head was forced onto a rock while men with clubs were ready to execute him again.

* * * * *

Awaiting his fate, John closed his eyes again and prepared to meet his maker.

Then, another miracle happened. A small Indian girl of ten or twelve raced over to John and cradled his head in her arms while shielding him with her own body. She told the executioners to take her life in place of the white man's. *What bravery and compassion from such a young child,* John thought. This brave little girl was Chief Powhatan's favorite daughter, Princess Pocahontas. Why she did this was a mystery to everyone but her father couldn't refuse her and pardoned Smith. Maybe he could use this Englishman to submit his enemies.

Pocahontas seemed impressed with him, so the chief declared John a friend to his people and explained that tribute from Jamestown was expected. He asked for two large cannons and a grindstone for payment. Knowing he could never give arms to his enemies, John agreed to the price with no intention of fulfilling it. He would figure out something on the way back to the settlement.[76]

Describing the journey back to Jamestown, Smith allowed a brief glimpse of his inner fear. "So Jamestown with 12 guides Powhatan sent him. That night they quartered in the woods, he still expecting (as he had done all this long time of his imprisonment) every hour to be put to one death or other: for all their feasting." Though afraid, he also maintained his faith, "But almighty God (by his divine

---

[76] Ibid., 101–102 (Ch. 2).

providence) had mollified the hearts of those stern Barbarians with compassion."[77]

Once back in Jamestown, John heard all about Cassen's fate and some of his old critics blamed him for Emry and Robinson's death. Denying the accusation, his thoughts focused on dealing with Powhatan before he tackled the enemy within. Leading the braves to two massive cannons, he instructed them to deliver both to the chief. The Indians' eyes were as big as the feat which faced them. Each of these cannons weighed thousands of pounds and couldn't be budged, much less pushed back to Werewocomoco.

Explaining this difficulty, the Indians accepted the grindstone and some smaller trifles instead. John then had the cannons fired to demonstrate their power and the Indians fled in terror of the big guns. Though somewhat comical, Smith wanted the braves to return to Werowocomoco with tales of Jamestown's military might. A show of strength would command respect and possibly deter further aggression.

He had cheated death multiple times during this adventure. His quick thinking saved him from Opechancanough's execution while a young girl rescued him from Chief Powhatan's war clubs. John believed the reason he was spared so many times was that he had a purpose to serve. God's providence protected him for this higher purpose, and not until that purpose was fulfilled would he die. Though grateful to Pocahontas, he believed God used her to save him for that purpose.

Just as God hardened the heart of Pharaoh, he sometimes softened them too, John believed. Nothing else could explain it.[78]

* * * * *

---

[77] Ibid., 102–103 (Ch. 2).
[78] Ibid.; Price, 70–71.

Winter, Plymouth, Massachusetts, 1620/21

He was sick, this much he knew. Governor Carver and most of the others were sick or dying. Six Pilgrims were the only ones well enough to care for the rest. Captain Standish and William Brewster were among the fortunate six who appeared immune to the illness. They cared for the sick and kept up spirits. Washing clothes and feeding those who couldn't feed themselves without complaint. William noticed their charity: "And yet the Lord so upheld these persons as in this general calamity they were not at all infected with sickness or lameness…that whilst they had health, yea or any that had need of them. And, I doubt not that their recompense is with the Lord."[79]

Feverish and exhausted, he thought of their circumstances. Many believed the land was cursed, but he believed it to be blessed and they were led to this very spot by the hand of God. Three years before, nearly two thousand Indians perished on this ground from a strange disease. The entire village was wiped out. Evidence of this plague was uncovered as they cleared the ground of Plymouth and the bones of the victims were discovered. Now they were in danger of the same end, and he believed this was merely a trial from God. They would come through this as they always had. They had come so far already.

* * * * *

On December 20, 1620, they began construction on the houses. Frigid temperatures and heavy snow prevented progress. Most were sick, and malnutrition plus hard labor weakened their immune systems and made them susceptible to disease. After a few days, others from the *Mayflower* came to help, and by Christmas, they raised the frame of the first house. Until then, they had been sleeping exposed to the elements with only basic shelters, and the Indians terrorized them with frightening wails from the surrounding woods.

---

[79] Bradford, 112 (Bk 2).

Two more weeks, they finished the ten by ten common house which all of them would occupy until individual houses were completed. Standish designed a layout for the settlement with defense in mind. A stockade was erected around the entire settlement, and cannons were emplaced and always ready. William worked on his own house tirelessly, trying to take his mind off Dorothy, and after one exhaustive day, he collapsed, in severe pain. By evening, he wasn't expected to live.[80] The cold and wear on his body and spirit had finally pierced his armor. He was tired, and his spirit was losing the battle with his body.

Though denying himself, he couldn't seem to overcome the flesh. His precious wife was dead, and his son was motherless, like him. When this sickness claimed him, the boy would be an orphan too. He would live a life of loneliness and feel he never belonged. Lost in his delirium, William wanted to let go. It was too much pain. His parents, his wife and child, his whole life was one of pain. The grief overwhelmed him as the illness ravaged his body. Maybe he should quit fighting. Might he join his loved ones in the afterlife? Thinking of his four-year-old son as an orphan, his grief switched to anger.

What a weak-minded fool he was! How could he allow his son to be orphaned? Would Dorothy approve of her husband giving up so easily? They took this voyage for a purpose and it was greater than any one person. God had watched over him his entire life. He had protected their purpose every step of the way, and he was ashamed of his doubt. Praying for forgiveness, he knew he must continue the path. The Lord had a plan for him, which he had to complete. If the Lord could die for him, the least he could do, William realized, was to live for him.

Miraculously, the next morning, his condition improved and the immediate danger had passed. Within days, he completely recovered, writing that "through God's mercy," he was spared. The crew of the *Mayflower* was stricken by the illness too. William requested beer from Captain Jones to alleviate the sick, but the request was denied. Beer was a sure way to drink uncontaminated water and provided a

---

[80] Ibid., 111–112 (Bk 2); *Mourt's Relation*, 66–73; Philbrick, 81–85.

small quantity of nutrition to boot. Jones said he couldn't spare any, and would need it for the return voyage.

In another strange episode, a belligerent sailor who made fun of them as holy-rollers was on the verge of death and the Pilgrims volunteered to care for him. They treated the man who had mocked them with such compassion that he changed his view. He said one day to them, "Oh, you, I now see, show your love like Christians indeed to one another, but we let one another die like dogs." William knew the man was right about this. The way Standish and Brewster had genuinely cared for the sick was as if there were "angels watching over them." One man was a Saint, the other a Stranger, but both embodied the spirit of their faith. They all became Pilgrims or Plymouthers. They were in this together now, and their common bond was their faith and belief in a divine purpose.

After witnessing the Pilgrim compassion for his sailors, Captain Jones changed his opinion of them as well. He made all his provisions available to Plymouth, including the beer William requested. The power of Christian charity could change any heart, they were convinced. Even Jones and his men felt admiration and respect for these plucky survivors. They were not hypocrites like most. They practiced what they preached.[81]

In the meantime, Captain Standish kept an eye on the Indian threat. Weakened by sickness, the natives could easily finish them off. He tried to train a force of defenders, but many resisted his authority, and others were too sick. Seeing the big picture, Standish knew the Indians were waiting for the plague and starvation to thin their ranks before they attacked. They were primitive but clever and so they waited.

Some weeks, two to three Pilgrims died. By spring of 1622, fifty-two of the original 102 were dead. Whole families were gone. The Indians never attacked, and William credited prayer and God's mercy to their survival. The natives instead decided to pursue friendship with the English. The chiefs saw less danger in making peace. If they eradicated these pitiful whites, more would cross the sea and

---

[81] Ibid., 112–114 (Bk 2); *Mourt's*, 66–73; Philbrick, 85–86.

avenge their deaths. If they made peace, maybe they would be an asset instead of a threat. The land would consume them and until then, they might be useful. An alliance would be made.

By February 1621, the survivors of Plymouth had recovered enough to notice two Indians standing on a hill outside of the settlement. When the settlers tried calling to them, they received no response. Standish and Stephen Hopkins (a Stranger who had been at Jamestown), armed with a single musket, approached the hill cautiously. Laying the musket at the foot of the rise, they proceeded up the hill. Before reaching the top, the two natives fled into the forest. Multiple whoops and wails echoed from the trees, and Hopkins and Standish suspected an ambush.

Returning to Plymouth, they warned the rest to be on guard. Sleeping on their muskets every night, no ambush ever came. By March 16, a single Indian appeared on the hill this time, but didn't stay there. This man strolled confidently down to Plymouth and continued straight into the center of the settlement. One Pilgrim attempted to block his way, but the man simply stopped, raised a single hand, and said, "Welcome, Englishmen!"

Naked but for the piece of leather which covered his groin, the Indian asked for something to eat and beer like an old friend. Many of the settlers were embarrassed by the man's nakedness and kept offering their jackets. The native insisted he wasn't cold. After he ate and took a few swigs of *aqua vitae* (a strong brandy-like liquor), he told them his name was Samoset, explaining that he represented Chief Massasoit who ruled the Pokanoket people who occupied much of the surrounding area. Samoset also spoke of the Nauset, a tribe hostile to the English because over twenty of their tribe were abducted and sold into slavery by an Englishman a few years before.

Now that he broke bread, had a swig of *aqua vitae*, and jawed with the whites, Samoset invited himself to sleep over. This was a common practice among the Indians, but the Pilgrims were immediately paranoid. They tried to dissuade him from staying by offering him a spot on the ship. They thought the fear of abduction would deter him from staying, but they were surprised when the man accepted the invitation. Now believing the native to be trustworthy,

Stephen Hopkins offered the hospitality of his house, and Samoset was bedded down for the night.

The following morning, the Indian promised to bring more of his people on his next visit and left. After Chief Massasoit listened to Samoset's account, his chief advisor, Tisquantum or Squanto, persuaded him to make friends. The chief didn't trust his advisor completely. Squanto had spent years in England after being kidnapped, and Massasoit wasn't sure of his allegiance. Squanto was not a Pokanoket but from the Patuxet tribe, the tribe whose bones the Pilgrims discovered in Plymouth. His education in England caused the chief to question his loyalty, but he trusted the young man's knowledge of the English, so he followed his advice.

Less than a week later, Samoset returned to Plymouth with four others, including Squanto. Squanto warmed quickly to the Pilgrims. His English was flawless, and he reminisced about England. He seemed more English than Indian to them. The natives brought furs to trade, and the visit was genial but this was just the start.

Massasoit, with sixty of his best warriors, appeared on the hill an hour later. His face was painted red and he stood tall and muscular, though he was advanced in years. The Pilgrims weren't sure what this meant. Squanto assured them the chief came in peace. Nervously, they sent Edward Winslow and Squanto to invite the chief and express their message of friendship. Winslow handed the chief and his brother each a knife, a few copper coins, some biscuits, and a bit of the *aqua vitae*. Squanto interpreted the message from the English and their king of peace and friendship. Governor Carver desired trade, but Massasoit sought an alliance.

Impressed with the message, Massasoit decided to visit Plymouth himself. Winslow remained behind as insurance, and Squanto led the chief to the settlement. When Carver met Massasoit, he kissed the Indian's hand to show respect to royalty. This was a European custom, and the chief kissed Carver's hand in return. Sitting on the ground, the two leaders shared a drink and hammered out the details of a treaty of friendship. This alliance agreed to do no harm to one another, punish any who did, return all stolen property, and ensure aid if either was attacked. Massasoit would also spread the word of the treaty to the other tribes. Both men also agreed to leave their weapons behind when they visited each other as a token of goodwill and trust.

Carver was pleased with the agreement and knew that Plymouth's survival depended on it. This would also help promote the Gospel to the Indians. Massasoit was satisfied with the alliance because it provided him with an ally with advanced weaponry to persuade or defeat his enemies. Both leaders wanted the survival and strengthening of their people with the treaty. Before Massasoit left, he instructed Squanto to remain with the English and show them how to survive. To show their gratitude, the Pilgrims sent the chief a large pot of English peas, which he enjoyed.[82]

With a treaty of friendship and the warm weather, Captain Jones decided it was time to sail back to England. On April 5, he prepared to leave but offered space to all who wanted it. After so many deaths and suffering, he was sympathetic. His opinion had changed and he felt obliged to rescue any he could from this brutal place. To his surprise and sadness, not one of the tenacious survivors came forward. In fact, one of his crew decided to remain in Plymouth. John Alden, the carpenter, saw his future in this New World, and her name was Pricilla Mullins. Captain Jones set sail, watching as Plymouth disappeared over the horizon. *Those poor people*, he thought, but if anyone could make a go of that wilderness, he was sure it was these good souls.[83]

Squanto was a godsend, and he and William became friends. He showed them how to manage their crops and the use of dead fish to fertilize the Indian corn he convinced them was the most reliable food source. The barley and peas they brought from England weren't suited for the American climate. Squanto taught them how to use the shade of the cornstalk to protect smaller crops from the heat of the sun. He instructed the men on the proper ways to catch shellfish and where the best spots to hunt certain birds were. In no time, Plymouth had sown fields and full stomachs thanks to Squanto. Massasoit had

---

[82] Ibid., 114–117 (Bk 2); *Mourt's*, 82–94.
[83] Ibid., 120–121 (Bk 2); Philbrick, 100–101; Willison, 180.

sent one of his own to stay with the English, Hobbamock, a loyal warrior who would keep an eye on Squanto. Miles Standish and Hobbamock became close friends and would remain so for the rest of their lives. With hope returning and a spirit of camaraderie among the Indians, it seemed time for another trial.

On an unusually hot day in April for that area, Governor Carver, working in the fields, complained of a headache and collapsed. Many thought he was only overheated but realized it was much worse and he died suddenly. Heatstroke usually occurred in summer months in New England, not the normally mild April. The colony had to elect a new governor to lead the flock and only one man could replace him. He was liked and respected by all in Plymouth and the choice was easy.

William Bradford was elected governor of the Plymouth Colony. He quickly realized what this meant. Before he was elected, he had helped Carver keep up the people's spirits. Now he was responsible for everything himself, and the immense burden was humbling. The future of the colony depended on God's will, but the governor must steer them accordingly. His decisions needed to be right or they all could die.[84]

Providence had placed him in the role, he was sure of it. Not that God killed Carver but only called him home like he had Dorothy. Carver's task was finished and now it was his turn. He did not know why he had been chosen for this, but he knew it was true. He had been spared for this purpose. His whole life had prepared him for this moment. The new treaty of friendship and the blessing of Squanto had filled the common store. Everything was right in the wilderness for God's chosen people for now, and William was grateful.

* * * * *

---

[84] Ibid., 121–122 (Bk 2); Ibid., 102–103.

Opechancanough's Village, Virginia, 1609

The brave was making him nervous and seemed a bit too happy to see him. It reminded him of the time when Jamestown had been attacked and his head was nearly caved in. The Indians had been over-eager to welcome him then. Once again, something told him to be on guard and this time, he was ready. He wanted to trust the natives, but knew he couldn't. Opechancanough had nearly killed him once. If he gave him another chance, the chief wouldn't be impressed by a compass again. He had to be willing to walk into the fire but also be ready to extinguish it too. Puffing out his chest a little more, John asserted his authority.

Suddenly, one of his men ran up and alerted him of the present danger, confirming his suspicions. He had just been told they were surrounded by 600–700 armed warriors. He had been set up again, but this time was different because he was angry, and it gave him courage.

With only sixteen men to fight impossible odds, John was in a serious situation—again.

This was almost getting to be routine. Calming himself, he weighed his options. It was now time to show these treacherous barbarians what the English could do. It was time to show the Powhatan what Captain John Smith was made of.

Hundreds of Indians were closing in on him, ready to strike and he thought of his duels with the Turks. There was one thing barbarians respected.[85] As the warriors came closer, he was ready to joust again.

* * * * *

After his escape from Chief Powhatan's clubs with the intervention of Pocahontas, John faced more challenges to his life from his own people. Accused of causing the deaths of Emry and Robinson, he was charged, tried, and sentenced for execution by those who

---

[85] Smith, *General Historie,* 164; Hoobler, 196.

wanted to remove the farmer's son as a threat to their power. He was slowly gaining support from the settlers, and some factions didn't like it. Many of his supporters looked to him for leadership. The others were men of little action. Unfortunately, now that his plan to win them over by example was succeeding, he was about to be executed. He was certain he was protected from death by God. There was no other explanation and this belief gave him endless confidence and courage. He knew he must serve God's purpose and was protected by divine providence. When he had accomplished this purpose, then his life would be finished. Until that time, he would be fearless.

The very day Smith was to be executed, Captain Newport sailed into Jamestown with more provisions and passengers. Upon learning of John's fate, he immediately ordered his release. Seeing through the plot, he needed Smith to help accomplish the new instructions from the merchant company. Instructed to make peace with the Powhatan by any means, Newport had no experience handling the Indians, but Captain Smith spoke their language and knew Chief Powhatan. His expertise would be invaluable, and Smith commanded the respect that others didn't. He was the best chance Jamestown had for success.

Upon meeting Chief Powhatan, Newport showered him with gifts. He was laying it on thick, and the old chief was pleased. Newport asked for nothing in return, and John saw where this was going. Pulling the sea captain aside, he explained that the Indians would perceive this as submission. If the Indians saw the English from a point of weakness, they would pounce.

Newport disregarded his advice and had orders to win over the natives at any price. If they were expected to find gold or other valuable resources, they needed Powhatan happy, peaceful, and cooperative. After reporting to the merchant company about Indian hostility, Newport was harshly reprimanded and instructed to win them over with goods.

John shook his head. This culture didn't value what another group could provide them if they could gain more by submission. Chief Powhatan saw English appeasement as a sign of fear. If men were this eager to please, they must be incapable of fighting for their own interests. Newport was making the same mistake Wingfield made. Appeasement caused the Indians to lose respect, and fear of the English. John couldn't convince him, but he owed his life to Newport, so he dropped his opposition for now.[86]

As 1608 unfolded, John found himself in another ambush on his way to Werewocomoco. Trade was his intention, but Chief Powhatan preferred their submission. Pocahontas once again, came to the rescue by warning of an attack and put her own life in danger. Chief Powhatan was playing a game of advantage. When friendship gave him an upper hand, he made peace. When Jamestown appeared weak, he made war. John was convinced that a tough posture would remedy this problem, but his words were ignored. After all, he wasn't a gentleman. What did he know? Taking matters in his own hands, he led a small force upriver, burned down a hostile village, and demanded the corn it refused to trade. After this, Powhatan played nice to calm the fiery captain. Smith was the only white man who was a real warrior, the chief thought. He was a worthy adversary.

The colony faced other serious internal problems as well. John tried to show them how to fix these problems, but no one would listen. They simply refused to work. Those few who did work resented carrying the weight of those who would not. The gentlemen expected to be supported by their inferiors as a privilege of status. The settlement's provisions were always depleted either from spoilage, theft, or the Indians refusing to trade. John felt they came to depend on the natives and the return of the supply ship and though Newport brought provisions, he also brought more settlers who depleted the food stores quicker. The settlers seemed to give up on survival of the colony and themselves. They no longer cared to work for prosperity and resigned themselves to make due with a minimum amount. They desperately needed a strong leader to save them.

In a moment of rare good judgment, Jamestown elected John as president. They had enough of the greedy and power-hungry gentlemen leading them to destruction. They needed results, and John never looked back. He worked tirelessly to turn the colony around, and self-preservation was the primary aim. Without it, everything

---

[86] Ibid., 164; Smith, *True Relation*, 52–61; Williams, 115–116.

else was pointless. Jamestown had to deal with the Indian problem first, because it was a clear and present danger. This would help with the food shortage once trade was resumed. Until he dealt with Powhatan, the threats within would wait.[87]

* * * * *

That's what he was dealing with when he found himself surrounded by 600–700 warriors with only sixteen of his own men. He could either accept the inevitable massacre or he could act. He chose action over death.

Could the farmer's son find a way out of the impossible again and save the first English colony in the New World? He thought he could. There was nothing impossible to the man who repeatedly survived death. Personal determination and providence always delivered him, and the fire of ambition was placed in his soul for these pivotal moments. Providence placed him in moments like this for a reason.

Turning, John focused on the massive chief, Opechancanough, and cleared his mind. He would act and not think. This would end one way or another this day. They would think him insane, and maybe he was. Insanity and genius were sometimes the same things. He made his move.

* * * * *

Plymouth Colony, Winter, 1622

Squanto was bleeding from his nose and coughing up blood. Some mysterious illness had taken hold of him, and William was afraid it wouldn't let go until he was dead.

William and Squanto became good friends since their first meeting, and Plymouth was rescued from the brink of extinction by his instruction. The bounty in the autumn of 1621 sustained them through the winter, and the governor called for a celebration. He

---

[87] Ibid., 144–162; Smith, *True Relation*, 52–61; Price, 102–104.

invited the Indians to a feast accompanied by games. This is often cited as the first Thanksgiving but was more likely a harvest festival.

William never mentioned thanksgiving to describe a feast or celebration, and to the Pilgrims, thanksgiving consisted of fasting and prayer, not a celebration. Tradition appears to celebrate this harvest festival rather than a thanksgiving. This bounty was a momentary blessing from the suffering of their first winter. Thanks to Squanto, the next winter was easier. There was another kind of bond between William and Squanto. It may have been their similar lives, both being orphans. As friends, they understood each other.

Now his friend's kind soul lay near death while William tended to his needs. How could he comfort him? If only his friend had converted, he could've done more. Praying for his soul, he wanted to believe God would save his friend. He knew God had sent this unique individual into their midst to deliver them. If God used an infidel for his purpose, surely he would show mercy as well.[88]

Squanto groaned, and the governor wiped his forehead letting him know he wasn't alone. He had grown fond of this man. Squanto had saved them, and William had sacrificed much to return the favor. Now it seemed so senseless.

Bowing his head, the governor of Plymouth prayed for mercy for his friend.

* * * * *

After a minor skirmish at the Nemasket village to rescue Squanto after he was taken hostage for his aid to the Pilgrims, Plymouth enjoyed peace and prosperity for a time. Another shipload of settlers arrived the following spring of 1622 and added seventy more mouths to feed. The Indians were experiencing their own inner turmoil. Some tribes opposed Massasoit's alliance with the English, and this caused deep division within factions. Some wanted peace, while

---

[88] Bradford, 155 (Bk 2); *Mourt's Relation*, 90; Stratton, Eugene Aubrey. *Plymouth Colony: Its History & People 1620–1691.* (Salt Lake City: Ancestry Publishing, 1986), 24–25; Philbrick, 117, 138–139; Willison, 212.

others called for extermination. It was also believed that Squanto himself was conspiring to oust Massasoit for his own power play. Being a Patuxet, not a Pokanoket, he hungered for status too. Under Massasoit, he would never get that chance.

Kidnapped and taken to England, Squanto left behind a thriving village. During his captivity, he had dreamed of escape and after making his way home, he found his village gone. His family was dead and his people were now extinct. It was as if the great spirit had spared him by his captivity. Why had he lived? Was he saved for mediocrity? Upon returning, he realized he must find a tribe to adopt him. He made himself useful to Chief Massasoit and soon found a place, but he never fit in with the Pokanoket. They never trusted him because he spent so long with the white men and learned his ways. Many thought he was one of them. Chiefs achieved their position by wisdom and keen perception. Massasoit was sensitive about potential enemies and friends, and Squanto was suspect. Though he remained loyal until that winter, his plot was uncovered.[89]

Massasoit demanded Plymouth's compliance and demanded Squanto be handed over. William refused to believe the conspiracy and would not comply. The treaty of friendship stipulated that all enemies to either side would be turned over for punishment. This meant death for Squanto, but William couldn't do it. Though he knew he was violating the agreement, he had to protect his friend. He was indebted to this man and had a kinship with him. When Massasoit's men came for their prisoner, William refused to surrender him. Hearing that Plymouth broke the agreement, he no longer felt obligated to hold up his end.

The same year, another group of settlers planted a colony north of Plymouth named Wessagussett. This all-male settlement was like Jamestown. A moneymaking venture was the primary goal of this colony, but caused tension with the Massachusetts Indians. First Plymouth, now this one? The natives saw this threat as competition for hunting ground. Game was scarce, and scavenging was common. The Massachusetts Indians knew if they failed to control the

---

[89] Ibid., 135–137 (Bk 2); *Mourt's*, 91–92; Philbrick, 113–116.

English encroaching on their land, the end of their way of life was just a matter of time. The Massachusetts chiefs agreed, and two of their braves wanted to eradicate both English settlements. Though Massasoit heard of the plot, he had no obligation to Plymouth now that Bradford broke their treaty. Rumor of this reached William's ears, and he told Standish to reinforce the stockade and to prepare for a possible war.

Months passed, but no attack came. Maybe it was all talk? William and Squanto believed Massasoit lost his thirst for revenge or at least wasn't as angry about a plot that never happened, so the two orphans ventured out of Plymouth on a trading mission. This is when Squanto fell ill, and some thought Massasoit had him poisoned, but this was never confirmed.[90] The reason they went on this trading mission was another problem facing the colony.

The common store system the Merchant Adventurers made them use failed to create the harmony it promised. Though each family and individual received equal shares of everything produced, they barely survived. The strained relations with Massasoit and the other tribes caused some of this, but William realized something deeper was to blame. Something caused the Pilgrims to lose motivation for improving their lives. The common store seemed to breed an apathetic attitude among them and William observed:

> For the young men that were most able and fit for labor and service did repine that they should spend their time and strength to work for other men's wives and children, without any recompense. The strong, or man of parts, had no more in division of victuals (food) and clothes, then he that was weak and not able to do a quarter the other could; this was thought injustice. The aged and graver men to be ranked and equalized in labors, and victuals, clothes, and etc., with the meaner and younger sort, thought it some

---

90 Ibid., 155 (Bk 2); Philbrick, 133–137.

indignity and disrespect unto them, and for men's wives to be commanded to do service for other men, as dressing their meat, washing their clothes, and etc., they deemed it a kind of slavery, neither could many husbands well brooke it. Upon the point all being to have alike, and all to do alike, they thought themselves in the like condition, and one as good as another; and so, if it did not cut of those relations that God had set amongst men, yet it did at least much diminish and take of the mutual respects that should be preserved amongst them.[91]

He described their shortage of food and their reliance on faith to show them the way: "All their victuals were spent, and they were only to rest on God's providence; at night not many times knowing where to have a bit of anything the next day...to pray that God would give them their daily bread, above all people in the world."[92]

They needed to find a better way before it destroyed them. The present way simply killed ambition and bred laziness. The young turned on the old, and the strong resented the weak. Hard workers went unrewarded and received the same as the slackers. Thinking he could supplement this by trade, William and Squanto made the trek, but before anything came of this, Squanto was struck down.

* * * * *

As Squanto's breaths became labored, William clenched his teeth. Opening his eyes, the sick Indian tried to talk. Leaning closer, William just made out the words, "Please, Bradford, pray for me so I may go to the English God in heaven."[93]

---

[91] Ibid., 163–164 (Bk 2); Plumb, 49.
[92] Ibid., 164 (Bk 2).
[93] Ibid., 155 (Bk 2).

Touched by this, William assured him he was praying for his salvation. Squanto also wanted him to make sure his friends in Plymouth received his belongings as a token of his affection. Promising again, Bradford bowed his head. Squanto shut his eyes again and struggled to breathe. Then his breathing stopped, and his friend was gone.

Looking up at Squanto's face, he knew it was over. All this good man had done for them had to count for something in God's grace. God had kept him safe in England while his people perished. William was certain this was to ensure his aid to Plymouth. He had been "a special instrument sent of God for their good beyond their expectation."[94] William had saved him from Massasoit only to watch him die this way. The last of the Patuxet was dead.

He had no time to mourn over his friend. The fate of the colony rested on his shoulders. With the common store quandary and the strained relations with the Indians, he knew he had to get back and make some hard decisions.

Shortly after Squanto's death, a messenger came to Plymouth with word of Massasoit's own illness. Convinced he was dying, he asked to speak with the governor, but William sent Edward Winslow in his stead. Winslow and Massasoit were old friends, and Bradford had bigger problems needing his attention. After word of the Massachusetts plot, Squanto's mysterious death, and breaking of the treaty, William suspected it might be a trick. Massasoit was honorable, but those around him may not be.

The fate of the colony hung in the balance, and the governor of Plymouth knew he must act, but how? The Indians were preparing for war, and his only ally among them was sick and dying. Those in the colony were fighting with each other, and the whole experiment was about to fail. It was his responsibility to find answers. As always, he prayed for them.[95]

The orphan from Austerfield had the fate of future generations hanging on his judgment. He had to make the right decisions and make them now. Did he have enough successful experience in mak-

---

[94] Ibid., 116 (Bk 2); Willison, 185.
[95] Ibid., 158 (Bk 2); Philbrick, 142–143.

ing right decisions? No, he thought, all he had managed to do his entire life was make wrong decisions. How could he decide for all of them now?

* * * * *

Village of the Pamunkey Indians, January 1609

Opechancanough's numbers understandably made John's sixteen men panic. Standing in the big chief's longhouse surrounded by two hundred warriors while four hundred more waited with drawn bows outside, the panic and fear of his men irritated him and this irritation made him stronger somehow. He had judged correctly from the start. The only way to deal with a problem was to face it. Stepping closer, John addressed his men: "This is my torment, that if I escape them, our malicious Council with their open mouthed Minions, will make me such a peace-breaker (*in their opinions in England*) as will break my neck. I could wish those here, that make these seem Saints [*referring to the Pamunkey*], and me the oppressor..."[96]

He wanted them to realize the appeasement policy was the cause of their situation. He continued to explain their options: "Should we begin with them and surprise the King [*Opechancanough*], we cannot keep him and well defend ourselves. If we should each kill our man, and so proceed with all in the house; the rest will all fly: then shall we get no more than the bodies that are slain, and so starve for victual."[97]

They could capture Opechancanough and immediately kill those nearby with the hopes that the others would flee in fear from the gunfire. If they did this, the problem of food for Jamestown would still exist. He went on: "As for their fury, it is the least danger, for well you know, being alone assaulted with two or three hundred of them, I made them by the help of God compound to save my life. And we are sixteen and they but seven hundred at the most; and assure yourselves, God will so assist us, that if you dare stand but to

---

[96] Smith, *General Historie*, 165.
[97] Ibid.

discharge your pieces, the very smoke will be sufficient to affright them."

John reminded them of his other escapes from death. He made light of the Indians to encourage his men. "Yet howsoever, let us fight like men, and not die like sheep!" He clenched his jaw and his eyes were aflame. "For by that means you know God hath oft delivered me, and so I trust will now. But first, I will deal with them, to bring it to pass we may fight for something."

Sweeping the sixteen with those burning irises, he now asked for their courage. "If you like this motion, promise me you will be valiant!" His men couldn't believe the complete absence of fear in his face. He was either the most courageous man in the world or the craziest. Either way, this inspired them.

Turning to Chief Opechancanough, John now wanted every Indian within earshot to hear his words. "I see Opechancanough your plot to murder me, but I fear it not. As yet your men and mine have done no harm, but by your direction."[98] He now challenged the chief to a head-to-head duel to settle the standoff personally. Opechancanough had the upper hand; why accept this small scrappy white man's challenge?

Captain John Smith

---

[98] Ibid.

John instructed one of his men to peer outside the longhouse and report on the Pamunkey outside. This man refused his order out of fear, and this act of cowardice was the spark he needed. Calling to the others to secure the house, John made his move for all it was worth. He described himself in the third person: "And in such a rage snatched the King [*Opechancanough*] by his long lock, in the midst of his men, with his pistol ready bent against his breast. Thus he led the trembling King, near dead with fear amongst all his people..." [99]

Grabbing a handful of the chief's hair and shoving a pistol to his chest, John threatened to kill him. "I see (you Pamunkeys) the great desire you have to kill me, and my long suffering your injuries hath emboldened you to this presumption. The cause I have foreborn your insolences, is the promise I made you (before the God I serve) to be your friend, till you give me just cause to be your enemy. If I keep this vow, my God will keep me, you cannot hurt me, if I break it, he will destroy me." Everyone couldn't believe such audacity.

Now he gave them two choices. He first used the stick. "But if you shoot but one Arrow to shed one drop of blood of any of my men, or steal the least of these Beads, or Copper [*referring to the goods they brought to trade*], I spurn here before you with my foot; you shall see I will not cease revenge (if once I begin) so long as I can hear where to find one of your Nation that will not deny the name of Pamunkey."

The second choice was the carrot, though one dangled from strength. "If I be the mark you aim at, here I stand, shoot he that dare. You promised to fraught [*load*] my ship ere I departed, and so you shall, or I mean to lead her with your dead carcasses, yet if as friends you will come and trade, I once more promise not to trouble you." [100] His bravado assured them he was sincere. Their chief's predicament brought it home, and any man so brazen to stand up to these impossible odds earned their respect. He had dared them to kill him and had shown not an ounce of fear. This short, bearded Englishman was a true warrior. John wrote of this success, "All his

[99] Ibid., 166; Firstbrook, 279.
[100] Ibid., 166–167; Hoobler, 194–195.

men (*Opechancanough's*) were easily entreated to cast down their arms."

The Pamunkey decided to trade instead of killing them, and Smith returned to Jamestown with enough food to feed the colony a while longer. John knew Chief Powhatan was behind this ambush and wanted him to understand that a new sheriff was in Jamestown. Leading a raid on Werewocomoco, they burned some houses and crops, but the chief fled after being forewarned. The English were here to stay and would die defending their colony while taking many natives with them. Sure that his message was clear, Smith headed back to Jamestown with a new spirit of certainty in his heart.

He was just getting started.

* * * * *

Jamestown, Virginia, 1609

John stood staring out at the settlement with the memory of his past firmly sorted and packed away. He was about to lead them to the truth, but he had to know the answer to the question he pondered.

Who do you think you are?

This often repeated enquiry somehow made him lose his way. That was the intent of such a question. He had never once thought to answer it. By leaving it unanswered, it sapped his belief in himself. If he answered, it would empower him, but it would also make it final, and the answer might not be what he wanted to hear. This was why the question was used as a weapon because it made one doubt themselves. The gentlemen had used this because they knew he possessed that doubt. Every man had some doubt until they decided to accept this. He was ready and just fine with the answer.

He would show them who he was, just as he had shown the Indians. He was Captain John Smith, son of a farmer, soldier, duelist, slave, mapmaker, colonist, and gentleman. Now he was president of Jamestown. He had been through war, slavery, and doubt but overcame it all. In Virginia, he'd done the same. He jousted with Wingfield, Opechancanough, and Powhatan and gained his status by merit. He earned it all with his own sweat and blood in a society designed to prohibit such a possibility. He wasn't about to let throwbacks of the Old World stop him in the New World. Jamestown would not die on his watch. The people needed someone to tell them the truth. A man should tell himself the truth before he could truly know it. He had to lay the truth on the line and make sure that it was enforced.

The cache of food procured from Opechancanough provided temporary relief, but the common store was infested with rats and the provisions were spoiled. The men were more interested in discovering gold or waiting for the supply ship than feeding themselves. It was time to show them who he was. He was the president of this colony. Providence and merit had made it so, and it was time to show them how a farmer's son managed to become their leader.

Calling an assembly, he spoke in a booming voice, "I speak not this to all of you, for diverse of you I know deserve both honour and reward, better than is yet here to be had. But a greater part must be more industrious, or starve…"

Looking among the settlers, John made eye contact with many of the worst offenders. He made sure they all knew he was in charge. "However you have been heretofore tolerated by the authority of the council. You see now that power resteth wholly in myself: you must obey this now for a law…" Making sure he had everyone's full attention, he laid out his ultimatum "that he that will not work shall not eat (except by sickness he be disabled), for the labors of 30 or 40 honest and industrious men shall not, be consumed to maintain an 150 idle loiterers…There are now no more counsellors to protect you…"[101]

President Smith put the lazy and entitled on notice. Those who worked would no longer pull the weight of those who did not. Of course, he made an exception for the sick, but any able-bodied man who refused to work would not be fed.

With satisfaction, John smiled. Who do you think you are? This question had bothered him before, but now it pleased him, for he

---

[101] Ibid., 174–175; Hoobler, 198–199; Price, 106.

had found the answer. He knew who he was now. He was Captain John Smith—an officer, a gentleman, and a survivor.

* * * * *

Wessagussett Settlement, 1623

When Captain Miles Standish and his ragtag force arrived in Wessagussett, they announced their intentions. Made up of seven Englishmen and one Indian, Hobbamock, Standish's men were there to stomp out the plot against the English colonies. Hobbamock was there as an emissary of Massasoit and one of Captain Standish's friends. The target was two warriors, Wituwamat and Pecksuot, the main conspirators and instigators of the plot. Within a few hours, the two natives strolled nonchalantly into the heart of the colony and approached Standish and his men. They wanted the English to know they were not afraid.

Pecksuot was a tall man who flaunted his bravado over these little white men every chance he could. Unafraid, he had bumped heads with Standish before. In that encounter, the tall Indian mocked and ridiculed him. He would continuously sharpen the knife he wore around his neck trying to intimidate him and Miles couldn't stand him. Pecksuot remembered him from before and arrogantly glared down on the Englishman saying, "You are a great captain, yet you are but a little man." Sneering at the others, he laughed and continued, "Though I am no sachem [chief], yet I am of great strength and courage."[102] Smiling again, he grasped the knife hanging by a string around his neck and began to sharpen it.

Standish was a proud man and took the full brunt of the insult. The knife-sharpening was an attempt to frighten him into submis-

---

[102] Winslow, Edward. *Good News from New England: or A True Relation of things very remarkable at the Plantation of Plymouth in New England.* (London: Bladen & Bellamie, 1624), 17–18; *Good News from New England and Other Writings on the Killings at Weymouth Colony* ed. Jack Dempsey. (Digital Scanning Inc., 2001), 46–48; Philbrick, 150–151.

sion. Pecksuot saw his words found their mark but Miles swallowed his rage for the moment and grinned. Wituwamat laughed at the frightened little white man. Both Indians knew the English weren't men. If any man had insulted their honor that way, the perpetrator would choke on his own blood, but here, this woman just smiled. Disgusted, the two warriors walked away. Hobbamock calmed the red-faced captain, then revealed a hint of a smile. Miles returned a similar expression. After all, perception was everything.

* * * * *

The events which brought Standish and his force to Wessagussett began weeks before. Edward Winslow made his way to Massasoit's bedside, finding the old chief blind and close to death. Winslow wrote about the encounter, "he [*Massasoit*] put forth his hand to me, which I took. Then he said twice, though very inwardly, Keen Winsnow? which is to say, 'Art thou Winslow?'" I answered, Ahhe; that is 'Yes.' Then he doubled his words, Malta neen wockanet namen Winsnow! that is to say, 'Oh Winslow, I shall never see thee again.'"

Whatever message he wanted to convey would have to wait until he recovered, if this was possible. Going to work, Edward tried to get some sustenance into the sick man. While attempting to feed him preserves, he had trouble fitting the knife in Massasoit's mouth, "Then I desired to see his mouth, which was exceedingly furred; and his tongue swelled in such a manner as it was not possible for him to eat...his passage being stopped up."

By scraping this "corruption" from the chief's tongue, he recovered his eyesight within a day. In no time, he was drinking broth and sitting up again. Massasoit was most likely suffering from typhus, and Winslow appeared mystical to the natives when their chief recovered so quickly. The patient was soon well enough to talk to the friend that had saved his life. Massasoit said, "Now I see the English are my friends and love me, and whilst I live, I will never forget this kindness they have shown me."[103]

---

[103] Ibid., 13–15; *Good News from New England*, 32–34; Philbrick, 144–146.

Reminiscent of the dying sailor aboard the *Mayflower*, their Christian compassion blessed them with Jones's charity. Would this bring a blessing too? Massasoit had called for Bradford, but Winslow was better. He had every intention of warning the governor before he died if he could. Now, he cautioned Edward about the coming massacre. Wessagussett was the catalyst, but the extermination of Plymouth was their aim as well. He named the main conspirators and pressed his friend the importance of removing them. If the conspirators were removed, the plot would crumble.

Massasoit promised to use his influence, once they were out of the way, to end future threats to the English. But Winslow had to convince Bradford of this necessity. Knowing the governor's weak stomach for killing after the Squanto affair, the chief hoped his friend could sway him. Sending a message back to Plymouth, Edward prayed he wasn't too late.

When William received the message, he contemplated it only briefly. He knew he had to act. The implications of failure to heed Massasoit's warning would get them all killed. Self-preservation now took precedence over diplomacy and even Christian compassion. If they were dead, God's purpose would never be realized. Spreading the Gospel from New Jerusalem throughout the world would never happen from the grave. They needed to make an example of these conspirators to save themselves and prevent further bloodshed. If it was terrible and swift, the message would be clear. If they didn't act, they would fight one war after another.

Taking Standish aside, William gave him a blank check on his strategy to remove the threat, and called for the prime conspirator's head to be brought to Plymouth and put on display. He would bruise the head of the serpent, even if it bruised his heel. Though taking life was hard for him to accept, he had no alternative. The future of Plymouth rested on his decisions. The Indians respected strength and took advantage of weakness. The entire society revered aggression and domination, and though all of Europe did as well, he saw it his responsibility to preserve New Jerusalem.

William understood that societies and cultures clashed, but there were good and evil men among all civilizations. The king and church had oppressed them, but Massasoit warned them of a threat, even when he hadn't kept his word. Now he had that good chief's instruction to remove the evil among his own people, to save them. Telling Standish the names of the conspirators, William thought he saw a slight smile from his military leader.[104]

Dealing with their own inner problems, the people of Plymouth were slowly sliding into destruction. While Standish prepared to meet the outside threat, he would tackle the inside one.

God did not want His chosen to be dependent on the Indians or provisions from England. They should be independent and self-reliant. God would provide the means; they needed to provide the sweat. The sweat was from the perseverance of the individual and derived from pure faith. God gave man freewill, but he governed the world with his providence. The existence of both meant men were free to make their own path in the world, and God blessed those who walked the one he laid out for them. William decided to follow God's path which was evident in the very nature of the universe he created. The Virginia Company common store system was a contradiction to this, and the governor tossed it out. Meeting with the elders of the colony, he described their decision:

> So they began to think how they might raise as much corn as they could, and obtain a better crop then they had done, that they might not still thus languish in misery. At length, after much debate of things, the Governor (with the advice of the chiefest amongst them) gave way that they should set corn every man for his own particular, and in that regard trust to themselves; in all other things to go on in the general way as before. And so assigned to every family a parcel of land, according to the proportion of their number for that end, only for present use (but

---

[104] Ibid., 13–17; Bradford, 158–159.

made no division for inheritance), and ranged all boys and youth under some family.[105]

William divided the land and told each family or individual that whatever they produced was theirs to keep. The idea of property wasn't new, but the idea of limitless ownership was. In England, status dictated property ownership, not merit. Plymouth became a meritocracy. The seeds of capitalism replaced the socialist system they were told would bring equality and fairness.

As John Smith revealed at Jamestown nearly fifteen years before, William Bradford discovered a purer form of free market ideals which would grow into a mighty force one day. Hard work would be rewarded, and laziness would reap what it sowed. This was a fairer system because it removed the limit on the individual. This created greater independence, and there was an immediate change in the colony, as William explained, "This had very good success; for it made all hands industrious, so as much more corn was planted then otherwise would have been by any means the Governor or any other could use, and saved him a great deal of trouble, and gave for better content."[106]

Plymouth produced more food than needed and the attitude of the people changed drastically. Entire families cared about their property and worked harder for more. "The women now went willingly into the field, and took their little ones with them to set corn, which before would allege weakness, and inability; whom to have compelled would have been thought great tyranny and oppression."[107] Hope and ambition came alive. Individuals determined their limits, not the governing body. Property and the freedom to decide one's fate created a sense of purpose. They were invested in their own futures now. They rose earlier, worked later, and pushed themselves to exhaustion when allowed to keep the profit of their work.

---

[105] Bradford, 162–164.
[106] Ibid.
[107] Ibid.

Seeing the contrast, William criticized the collective concept of the common store:

> The experience that was had in this common cause and condition, tried sundry years, and that amongst godly and sober men, may well evince the vanity of that conceit of Plato's and other ancients [*socialism*], applauded by some of later times—that the taking away of property, and bringing in community into a commonwealth, would make them happy and flourishing; as if they were wiser than God. For this community (so far as it was) was found to breed much confusion and discontent, and retard much employment that would have been to their benefit and comfort.[108]

Referring to Plato's utopian ideal in *Republic*, he realized the deceptions of community property controlled by the state and experienced this on a personal level. Redistribution of property with the goal of leveling the field only led to resentment, laziness, apathy, and mediocrity. This new system appeared closer to creation itself. If birds didn't work for the worm, the other birds didn't share their worms. This truth was in the Bible already, William knew. Reaping what one sowed and bearing one's own burden worked within and without. This was as old as mankind. To enjoy the fruits of your labor meant merit, not status, determined your outcome. A peasant could now rise to prosperity, and a gentleman could choose poverty.

The common store was counter to God's creation. This new way used human nature and motivation to create wealth instead of redistributing it. What seemed so obvious now was often overlooked. The common store was sold to them as fair, equal, and humane, but in practice, it only succeeded in making them all equally poor. Everyone was not equal in property now, but they were equal in acquiring it.

[108] Ibid.

The sick, elderly, and widowed were not forgotten. Because of the overabundance and their Christian values, they contributed more to charity. They did not reward laziness or the unmotivated, but no one starved in Plymouth. William knew he had the power to level everyone by force, but if he left individuals to determine their own course, it benefited all. He simply got out of the way.

Everything wasn't perfect, and more struggles lay ahead, but he discovered the optimum way to manage an economy in the New World, and it would be the envy of millions who would risk everything to participate in it.

* * * * *

Now that Plymouth fixed its interior problems, Standish was working on the Indian threat. After Wituwamat and Pecksuot's insults the previous day, Standish decided to invite the two haughty adversaries to break bread with them and try to find common ground. He figured if they wanted to insult him, he would kill them with kindness. The two braves accepted the invite mainly because winter was lean and a free meal was welcome, but they also knew the little Englishmen would try to please them in hopes of gaining cooperation. They knew who they were up against and these half-starved weaklings were no match for them. The dinner invite was another example of the Englishmen's weakness as warriors.

So the fierce warriors strutted into the cabin where Standish had the food laid out. Being a gracious host, he showed them to their seats. As soon as everyone was seated and eating, Miles had his soldiers close the door to give them privacy to talk. Wituwamat and Pecksuot wondered what manner of gifts they would shower them with as payment to heel.

Catching a glimpse of Pecksuot's knife necklace, the little captain stood and walked up behind him. Having no fear of the "little man," Pecksuot never realized what hit him when Standish snatched the very blade used to instill fear and plunged it into his abdomen repeatedly. The others did the same to Wituwamat, and in seconds, the two fearless warriors were dead.

Hobbamock watched quietly as the conspirators were stabbed to death. Standing, he looked at Standish and said, "Yesterday Pecksuot, bragging of his own strength and stature, said [*that*] though you were a great Captain; yet you were a little man. But today, I see you are big enough to lay him on the ground."[109]

Standish and Hobbamock would remain friends their entire lives. Hobbamock even converted to Christianity and lived in the little captain's home until his death. The bond the two soldiers formed was one of mutual respect and admiration.

Covered in Pecksuot's blood and adrenaline pumping, Standish reached for his helmet and musket. He ordered a raid on the nearby Massachusetts village. Burning it to the ground, they chased its inhabitants into the forest. They had sent the message that Bradford ordered.

Wituwamat's body was retrieved from the cabin and decapitated. The bloody head was wrapped in a white piece of cloth and carried to Plymouth. William instructed them to impale the head on a pole and put it on display at the top of the fort around the colony. He had the white bloodstained cloth flown as a flag. This gory action was meant as a psychological and real warning to anyone. If they meant harm to Plymouth, they may meet the same fate. No more would they practice appeasement. This policy only encouraged aggression, and they would no longer tolerate threats to their colonies. If the Indians weren't prepared to live with them, they had better prepare to pay in blood.

Emissaries from the Massachusetts Indians and nearly every other tribe in the area came to Plymouth bearing gifts and the promise of peace.[110]

Strength had snuffed out the threat. Wituwamat and Pecksuot were the sacrifice for that peace. William was confident they could

---

[109] Winslow, 18; Philbrick, 151–152.
[110] Ibid., 19; Philbrick, 152–155.

live peacefully, but he wanted the message to be understood—they would use war to protect their interests.

* * * * *

William had made the right decisions. Thinking that previous failures would spell future miseries, he never noticed failures shaped his judgment by trial and error. Plymouth was prosperous and strong because of his leadership. Self-reliance made them independent, and a show of military strength made them secure.

After William called for a day of prayer and fasting to give thanks to God for their prosperity and security, clouds appeared and it rained for two weeks. Hobbamock and other natives were amazed by the "the goodness of our God toward us…" After the untold bounty at harvest time that autumn, Bradford called for a day of thanksgiving.[111]

This was the real first Thanksgiving.

* * * * *

Jamestown became a functional colony for the first time under John's leadership. Within three months of his ultimatum, there were twenty-three new houses built, a well was dug supplying fresh water, and nearly forty acres of crops had been sown. The following winter, no one starved, and the Indians didn't harass them once. John Smith had brought peace and prosperity with one simple principle—personal responsibility. The Indians were responsible for their actions and would be held accountable. The settlers were as well. He understood this important principle because he had lived his life guided by it. He was a prime example of making his way by his own actions.[112]

After suffering a serious gunpowder burn that nearly killed him, Smith received word from the stock company that he was relieved from the presidency. Too many complaints by the gentlemen and

---

[111] Ibid., 20; Willison, 240; Plumb, 48.
[112] Smith, *General Historie*, 195–196; Firstbrook, 287; Hoobler, 203–204.

others vying for power had managed to unseat him. Though the colony was finally working, the men in England made their decision based on the complaints about the wannabe gentleman president. Accused of being dictatorial with his ultimatum and cruel in his treatment of the Indians, John fell victim to the status system once again. Family and connections held more sway than results. This class system had no chance in the New World, and if they didn't adapt to the law of nature, they would never survive. If a man wouldn't work, he wouldn't survive, much less succeed. If he wasn't willing to defend his property and rights, he was destined to be fodder for the Indians.

Boarding the next ship, he returned to England and began writing of his adventures to let the world know the story of the farmer's son's rise to greatness through his merit.

In 1614, he sailed to New England and explored and mapped the region the *Mayflower* travelled six years later. He became a celebrity of sorts in the seventeenth century, and his writings made him rich. He even visited Pocahontas when she came to England with her new husband, John Rolfe. The little girl who had saved him twice died shortly after.

When Smith left Jamestown, it returned to its previous state and descended into chaos. Starvation on a scale worse than anything previously experienced swept over the colony. Eventually, it deteriorated into cannibalism and depravity. One man was hanged for murdering his pregnant wife, dismembering her body, and eating it. The Indians saw a weakness again and nearly wiped it out on March 22, 1622. It took another bold leader and a return to John's model to reverse the devastation. Finally, the colony recovered and prospered. More settlements sprang up throughout Virginia, but they all followed Captain John Smith's example of peace through strength and hard work.[113]

By their own merit, they had chipped away at the old status system and would rise from the ashes a new nation. Born out of the flames of hardship and bad judgment, they would change the course of history. Though remnants of status plagued the New World in

---

[113] Ibid., 193–194,

various forms up to the present, the initial mortal wound was made by John Smith.

The United States was conceived on this model. Outward strength and self-reliance were the seeds which grew into the ideals of equality and the right to "life, liberty, and the pursuit of happiness." It started with Captain John Smith.

He dreamed of further adventures but was struck down with an illness in 1631 and died suddenly at the age of fifty-one. He never married or had children but left behind a legacy larger than any name, which is ironic considering he was the last person to put stock in a name. The example he left the world came to embody the American spirit. Even though he was born and died English, he belonged forever to America. He epitomized the idea of self-reliance and proved the English status system was a lie. He believed that empires were built by self-interest and that it was different than self-ishness. Material wealth could serve man instead of man serving it. A self-made man, he credited his success to hard work, perseverance, and providence.[114]

Writing a summation on the purpose of life, John showed a gentler, more reflective side which pointed to the idea that "all men were created equal." "Seeing we are not born for ourselves, but to help each other, and our abilities are much alike at the hour of our birth, and the minute of our death: Seeing our good deeds, or our bad, by faith in Christ's merits is all we have to carry our souls to heaven, or hell."[115] He also wrote, "Virtue only makes men more than men: Vice, worse than brutes."[116]

---

[114] Price, 233

[115] Smith, John. *A Description of New England or, Observations and Discoveries in North America*. (Boston: William Veazie, 1865), 79–80.

[116] Smith, John. *The Complete Works of Captain John Smith (1580–1631) in Three Volumes ed. Philip L. Barbour*, Volume 1, (Chapel Hill: University of North Carolina Press, 1986), 133 (Map of Virginia).

His motto was "*Vincere est Vindice*—to conquer is to live," and he conquered everything he ever faced. Because of this, he lived every day in search of more to overcome.

* * * * *

William Bradford married Alice Southard in 1623 and served as governor five different times over the next thirty years. He served four times as commissioner and two as president of the United Colonies of New England. He was instrumental to this union, which became a precursor to the United States Constitution. The preamble to the constitution of the United Colonies proclaimed:

> Whereas we all came into these parts of America with one and the same end and aim, namely, to advance the kingdom of our Lord Jesus Christ and to enjoy the liberties of the Gospel in purity with peace, and whereas our settling (by a wise providence of God) we further dispersed upon the sea coasts and rivers then was first intended, so that we cannot, according to our desires, communicate in one government and jurisdiction.[117]

Fathering three more children with Alice and adopting an orphan boy, William reunited with his son, John Bradford, in 1627. The boy was eleven when he met his father for the first time and learned about his saintly mother.

Plymouth would see more obstacles with its government and its relations with the Indians, but William set the standard. When future governors veered from this standard, they failed. When they followed it, they found success. Bradford and Massasoit maintained the peace for over fifty years. Only when Massasoit's son, Philip, became chief after his death did the peace end. Known as King Philip's War, this

---

[117] *Preamble to the Constitution of the United Colonies, avalon.law.yale.edu>art1613*; Plumb, 59, 91; Philbrick, 157.

bloody struggle was fought by the sons of Massasoit and Edward Winslow.

William kept his word but never appeared weak as governor. As he grew older, the kindly patriarch was never described as a weakling. Everyone knew he risked much to save Squanto, but they also knew he wasn't afraid to call for Wituwamat's head either. He found the words and finished telling their story in 1651 and *Of Plymouth Plantation* became the best eyewitness account of the Pilgrims' journey.

Falling ill in May of 1657, he spoke his last words on May 18, "The good spirit of God has given me a pledge of my happiness in another world, and the first fruits of eternal glory."[118]

The following day, the orphan boy who denied himself for a greater purpose went home. William's body was dead, but his spirit lived forever in the nation he helped conceive.

* * * * *

William Bradford was a pious man who possessed the warrior spirit. He was the standard of New England which many strived to reach. He and the Pilgrims believed they found that city set upon a hill to be the light to the world from the Sermon on the Mount in Matthew 5:14. Men like Samuel and John Adams, John Hancock, Paul Revere, James Otis, Nathanael Greene, Henry Knox, and Benjamin Franklin grew up in his shadow.

Captain John Smith was the true warrior who never lost his compassion or humanity. He judged everyone on their merit, not their birth. He saw human nature for what it was, not what he wanted it to be. He trusted God created him for a specific purpose and trusted his own ability and providence to see him through.

Smith was the standard for men like George Washington, Thomas Jefferson, Patrick Henry, James Madison, Daniel Boone, Davey Crockett, and Andrew Jackson.

The orphan and the farmer's son; the warrior and the saint— John Smith and William Bradford were both. They had the courage

---

[118] Plumb, 106; Philbrick, 187–189; Willison, 332–338.

and strength of the warrior and the fairness, compassion, and reverence for God, like the saint. These two traits, sometimes opposed, existed in harmony in these two. This union defined the American way. On the National Seal of the United States, an eagle grasps, in one of its talons, a bundle of arrows; in the other, an olive branch. The arrows represent the strength of the warrior, and the olive branch the peace of the saint. At America's conception, two principles defined it—the Christian virtues of justice and peace and the willingness to defend them.

The warrior and the saint reside within every man, but it was stamped upon the heart of every American. Bradford and Smith cleared a path for the millions who came to the New World and made it all possible for those who followed. Much more struggle and growth remained on the path, but they were the first to clear the wilderness.

William Bradford learned a truth about mankind and left it in his writings. Referring to the common store problem, he reflected on man's arrogance and inherent corruption, which was counter to God's natural law of the universe: "Let none object this is men's corruption, and nothing to the course itself. I answer, seeing all men have this corruption in them, God in his wisdom saw another course fitter for them."[119]

Though humanity was corrupt, Captain John Smith provided the answer to overcome this corruption within us and leave our children a better world: "Seeing honor is our life's ambition; and our ambition after death, to have an honorable memory of our life; and seeing by no means we would be abated of the dignities and glories of our predecessors; let us imitate their virtues to be worthily their successors."[120]

We should all strive to be worthy enough to be theirs.

---

[119] Bradford, 164 (Bk 2).
[120] Smith, *Description of New England*, 80.

2

Forged in the Valley

Newburgh, New York, March 15, 1783

As the main door opened into the hall, everyone held their breath. The silence was complete. General George Washington walked through the doorway to everyone's surprise, and pride replaced their anger. The men snapped to attention by habit until the commander gestured with his hand for an at ease.

Surveying the room, he stepped to the front of the assembly as every eye followed him. He commanded the hall. At six-foot-three and nearly 200 pounds, he filled the room with his presence. There was something strange about his bearing tonight. He looked older somehow and perhaps tired. His chestnut hair had turned gray and the blue and gold uniform was faded more than they remembered. His stoic expression told little of his emotions, but it was obvious something was on his mind. They'd all witnessed this look before, many times on the battlefield. They wondered if he was here to take charge and lead the conspiracy. His most trusted lieutenants waited as his blue-gray eyes acknowledged each of them individually. They had been through so much together.

The Revolution was over, but an imminent threat remained. Many in this army planned a revolution of their own. They planned to back a dictator to grab power from Congress. He was the majority's choice to be this strong man.

Washington was fifty-one years old and the most respected man in America. The destiny of the nation sat upon his shoulders. His past would determine the fate of the United States and perhaps the world.

Who was this person who held the course of human history in his hand? What path led him to this moment? What guided him along the way?

George Washington was just a man with faults and flaws like anyone. He was a victim to vanity before. Would he be again? He was guilty of bad judgment before. Would he make the wrong decision this time? How could one man bear such a burden?

He felt like a man trapped on an island, waiting for the dawn.[121]

* * * * *

Ohio Territory, December 1753

To say it was cold was an understatement. To say it was freezing was more accurate. George was chilled to his core. Huddled near Gist, he prayed for daylight. They likely wouldn't live through the night. The temperature plummeted, and the icy wind brought a snowstorm. Visibility was only inches, and the two men were trapped on a barren island with no hope of rescue.

Drenched from tumbling into the river, George's dripping clothes stiffened in the blizzard. Stranded on an island in the middle of a river with no boat, food, or fire made survival seem bleak.

What began as the greatest opportunity of his life turned into the worst experience of it, he thought. Shivering from hypothermia, he knew he was running out of time. If they weren't rescued soon, they couldn't warn Dinwiddie of the French response. Death was not

---

[121] Washington, George. *The Writings of George Washington*, ed. John C. Fitzpatrick. (Washington: US Government Print Office, 1931–1944), Volume 26, 222–227 ("To the Officers of the Army"); Flexner, James Thomas. *George Washington: In the American Revolution (1776–1783)* Volume 1. (Boston: Little, Brown and Company, 1967–8), 505; Chernow, Ron. *Washington: A Life.* (New York: The Penguin Press, 2010), 435–436.

an option. He had to hold on till dawn. If he died, he would never lead men in the war. Dying in glorious battle would be better than dying like this.

Failing to do his duty was a fate worse than death.[122]

* * * * *

The American colonies had grown significantly since the first settlements at Jamestown and Plymouth. For over a century, new colonies sprang up all over the eastern coast and along the inland rivers. British subjects flocked to the New World, and colonies grew into commonwealths. Self-sufficiency and strength transformed tiny settlements into prosperous societies where merit determined success. This hard existence, which chipped these colonies out of wild land, produced a hearty stock of inhabitants who grew independent from the mother country. A new generation of homegrown colonists reaped the benefits of their parents' and grandparents' sacrifices.

In Virginia, the memory of Captain John Smith still garnered respect. Boys were raised to revere him and follow his example of a self-made man, but a few years after Smith's departure from Jamestown, a new institution was introduced to the English colonies—African slavery. The first slaves were brought to America by Spanish ships. Spain was the largest trafficker of slaves in the seventeenth century, but the practice spread quickly to southern tobacco farmers in the New World. Slave labor was free and raised production of crops. The more crops produced with little increase in the cost of labor, the larger the profit. Britain allowed the traffic of human chattel because of this profit. The mother country wouldn't ban slavery until 1833. The growth of plantations created a new nobility, reestablishing the old status system Smith and others tried to disassemble. Once again,

---

[122] *Washington, Writings*, Vol. 1, 30, (December 23, 1753); Gist, Christopher. *Christopher Gist's Journals: with Historical, Geographical, and Ethnological Notes, and Biographies of his Contemporaries*, ed. William M. Darlington. Pittsburgh: J.R. Weldin & Company, 1893), 56.

there were gentlemen, commoners, and indentured servants, but now they added an even lower class—slaves.

The more a plantation grew, the more slaves that were required to work it. Large plantations resided in warm climates of the South, and these areas grew dependent on the institution. Slavery became a norm for southern planters, and slaves were inherited by sons and grandsons for over two generations by the mid-1700s.

From nearly the beginning, a man's value was measured by his property in the American colonies. This represented an individual's merit and sweat. Over time, property became a competition to achieve status. Status meant one could pursue opportunities not accessible to lower classes. When property was passed down to the next succeeding generation, sons entered a society which judged a man's worth by what he owned. Abolition of slaves rarely entered a man's mind when property decided who he could associate with or who he could marry. Status meant power, and continuance of the status quo was defended by those with it. Even if one who inherited slaves wanted to set them free, he had no incentive or option to do so.

This was the world George Washington was born into. Born February 22, 1732, in Westmoreland County, Virginia, to a mildly successful plantation family, George was encouraged to make something of himself. His father, Augustine, was a tall hardworking planter who died suddenly when George was eleven. This left Lawrence, the eldest half-brother (from Augustine's first marriage), the family estate and responsible for family affairs. Under the inheritance tradition continued from the Old World, known as *primogeniture*, a man's estate passed to the oldest son automatically and left the other siblings to fend for themselves. In a society where land and property determined status, this left many siblings without inheritance or status.

Fortunately for the Washington family, Augustine disagreed with *primogeniture* and left the rest of his children minor estates. George received a small tract of land, ten slaves, and a small share of the residual property. His mother, Mary, would administer this estate until he reached the age of twenty-one.

Mary was a domineering woman and intrusive in every aspect of her son's life. If he attempted any ambitious venture outside her control, she put a stop to it immediately. She never acknowledged anything he did without her approval. She didn't even attend his inauguration as president or congratulate him on any other triumphant moment in his life. If she said anything, it was critical. She felt betrayed by his independence, but he never resented her for it. She was his mother, and he never showed disrespect, but her constant meddling pushed him away. A widowed mother in this era was an oddity. Most widows remarried out of necessity, but Mary never married again. George needed manly advice that his mother couldn't provide. Thankfully, his older brother, Lawrence, adopted this role and treated him like a son. Lawrence was the masculine example he strived his whole life to imitate.

When Lawrence left to serve in the British navy, George had no choice but to grow up. He would find his way on his own. From an early age, he longed to escape from home and Mary's grasp. This search for freedom forced him to find satisfaction in simpler things. Exploring the wilderness, working on the farm, and riding a horse gave him a platform to daydream about his future. Though a dreamer, he lacked confidence but was determined to prove to himself that he could achieve greatness. He had more drive than he could handle. The motivation was there, but he needed the opportunity. He decided to work on himself first. When opportunity showed up, he wanted to be ready.[123]

This self-improvement, he concluded, started with one's character. So he made a list of behaviors and labelled them "Rules of Civility and Decent Behavior in Company and Conversation." This became the creed he lived by. These 110 maxims included things such as:

> Show not yourself glad at the misfortune of another, though he were your enemy. Strive not with your superiors in argument, but always sub-

---

[123] Flexner, James Thomas. *George Washington: The Forge of Experience (1732–1775)* Volume 1. (Boston: Little, Brown and Company, 1965), 12–20; Marshall, John. *The Life of George Washington.* (New York: Derbi & Jackson, 1857), 11.

mit your judgment to others with modesty. Labor to keep alive in your breast that little spark of celestial fire called conscience. When you speak of God and his attributes, let it be seriously and with reverence. Honor and obey your natural parents although they be poor.[124]

He developed physical prowess by wrestling with the toughest boys, carrying more than the older boys, and training to be an expert horseman. He expected more of himself than anyone else and refused to aim for mediocrity. He would rely on these simple traits throughout his life.

When George was sixteen, he became an assistant surveyor. Surveying the endless unchartered frontier could fill a young man's pocket faster than most endeavors. He soon developed enough skill to survey projects on his own. Shy and slow to speak, he surveyed much the same. He measured each step or thought before committing to it. Likely, this bashfulness was a reaction to his mother's criticism. Unsure of himself, he lacked confidence in actions and words. This slow-measured thinking was a benefit to a surveyor. The job required meticulous attention to detail and prolonged periods of solitude on the frontier. This added self-discipline and logistical knowledge. These periods alone in the wild left a lot of time to ponder the universe and visualize his future. George dreamed big. At sixteen, nothing was impossible. Just like any typical teenager, the world was his for the taking.

As years passed, he decided he wanted to follow Lawrence's footsteps and join the Royal Navy. Lawrence fought with Admiral Edward Vernon in Britain's war with Spain. Fighting as a marine, Lawrence was a local hero, and his younger brother idolized him. He daydreamed of being a great warrior like the mythic charac-

---

[124] Washington, George. *The Papers of George Washington*, ed. W.W. Abbot. (Charlottesville: University Press of Virginia, 1983), *Colonial Series*, Volume 1, *Rules of Civility and Decent Behavior in Company and Conversation*, Rules: 22, 40, 110, 108.

ters he read about in books. When he told Mary about joining the navy, she disapproved and forbid it. Until he was of legal age, she was his guardian. Though disappointed, he obeyed her wishes. She never understood his ambition, and he never understood her need to control him. From Mary's perspective, she saw her husband die and didn't want to see it happen to her children.

Lawrence, her stepson, had contracted tuberculosis and lost his wife and children to the disease. Lawrence's condition worsened in the humidity of the Virginian climate. Believing a drier climate would help, he decided to sail to the Caribbean. He convinced Mary to let George travel with him. At nineteen, the surveyor travelled to Barbados in September of 1751. He couldn't believe it. He was finally going to see the world outside Virginia. He envisioned a tropical paradise full of adventures, but instead he got sick.

George contracted smallpox while in Barbados and suffered an entire month of high fever and painful oozing blisters but recovered. Tiny scars dotted his cheeks as reminders. The biggest killer in the American Revolution was smallpox, and he was now immune from catching it. Sadly, his brother saw no improvement in his own condition in Barbados, so they returned to Virginia.

Lawrence took a turn for the worse soon after their return and died. George was devastated. No one could ever replace the hole left by his brother's death. Having no surviving members of his immediate family, Lawrence left his estate, Mount Vernon, to his younger brother. He enriched George's life with his example and his property. Though it didn't make him wealthy, it did enhance his status. He now had increased status, which increased his opportunity.

In 1753, George was appointed adjutant general to the district of Virginia responsible for training of the militia. This appointment cemented his interest in becoming an officer in the army. Training the militia was an excellent place to start. He hoped one day to join the British army and lead men in battle, like Lawrence. He took the adjutant general appointment seriously.

In October of 1753, the British crown ordered Virginia's lieutenant governor, Robert Dinwiddie, to send an emissary to the upper Ohio territory to report if the French were settling and building forts on British territory. George was chosen for this mission. Dinwiddie instructed him to seek the help of friendly Indian tribes and guides to locate the French and deliver his ultimatum to evacuate British land or face war.

George wrote of this, "It was deemed by some an extraordinary circumstance that so young and inexperienced a person should have been employed on a negotiation with subjects of the greatest importance were involved."[125]

At twenty-one, with no previous experience, he was thrust into the role of emissary between the two super powers. His decisions and actions could impact the fate of North America. Moving from a surveyor with dreams of military glory to serving the Crown in less than two years was exhilarating but sudden.

Dinwiddie instructed George to enlist the help of Christopher Gist, an experienced guide, tracker, and woodsman. Gist was used to the frontier and could ensure safe passage to the French outpost. With a party of five men, the group headed into the vast unknown. The journey involved treacherous terrain and hostile inhabitants, but the young emissary was ready to prove himself. This was his opportunity to be like Lawrence—to be like his father.

* * * * *

Nothing went right on this trip. The whole expedition was a series of small disasters, and everything took longer than predicted. Leaving for the Ohio Valley on November 15, 1753, with a month's provisions, the expedition took a week to travel seventy-five miles. They encountered rain and snow the entire journey.

After establishing contact with a tribe in the area, the chief, Half-King, assured them he was a friend to the British. He directed his scouts to show George's party the way to the French redoubts. After delivering the message, the French commander left him waiting days for a reply. Clearly, this was a stalling tactic and insulting to the

---

[125] Humphries, David. *The Life of General Washington*. (Athens: University of Georgia Press, 2006), 9-10; Flexner, Vol. 1, 56.

young emissary. The French commander finally replied defiantly that the land they occupied was property of the King of France and they planned to stay.

Knowing this meant war, George realized he must return in a hurry. Getting word to Dinwiddie quickly meant the difference between victory or defeat for Britain. A message to the mother country took three months, and the sooner he got to Dinwiddie, the quicker the response. Eighteenth century armies fought in the spring, and Britain had to prepare. They needed to erect forts, gather supplies, raise arms, and transport soldiers across the sea. George was responsible for raising the alarm, and he had to find the fastest way back. The snow and cold were his obstacles. The provisions were gone, and the horses were exhausted and died carrying men on their backs.

By Christmas, George decided to make better time by continuing alone. Leaving the main party and bringing Gist, he chose to abandon the trail and cut through the forest against the guide's objections. He cared only about the importance of the message, not the logic of how to get it there. This was bad judgment by the inexperienced young man. He refused to take advice from the seasoned Gist.

Cutting through the woods saved little time, so they hired an Indian guide at one of the nearby settlements to take them the rest of the way. Half King's braves got them to the French in faster time than they could themselves. Maybe it would work again.

As they entered the dense forest with the native guide, Gist explained in his journal what happened next:

> We traveled very brisk for eight or ten miles, when the Major's (Washington) feet grew very sore...The Major desired to encamp, to which the Indian asked to carry his gun. But he refused that, and then the Indian grew churlish, and pressed us to keep on, telling us there were Ottawa Indians in these woods, and they would scalp us if we layout; but to go to his cabin, and we should be safe. I thought very ill of the fel-

low, but did not care to let the Major know I distrusted him…we grew uneasy.[126]

Here was Washington, the inexperienced, overconfident, and trusting young buck with no concept of the dangers; and Gist, the experienced woodsman sensing a real threat but unable to convince his superior. The Indian guide made Gist nervous, but George assumed the best. He naively believed he was in control of the situation.

The thick foliage and dark cloudy skies made the day like night, and the forest seemed to suffocate them. Rustling wind and cracking twigs broke the silence too often, making George and Gist nervous. It felt like eyes watched from the shadows.

At a break in the trees, they approached an open meadow and the Indian dashed ahead of them. Confused by the native's behavior, they stopped. Gaining some distance, the Indian halted and turned around, raised his musket, and fired at George.

Missing his target, the native ran and hid behind a tree to reload. Both men raced after the bushwhacker and disarmed him.

Gist was so enraged, he was about to take the Indian's life, but the young major ordered him to stop, explaining that he never saw a man killed before. Sparing his would-be murderer, he ordered him to remain inside an old cabin until they were out of sight or he would let Gist kill him.

Believing the French likely responsible for the attempted assassination, they proceeded with caution. Bounties for their scalps were offered, and every shadow or sound was investigated for possible ambuscades.[127]

Within a few days after nearly being shot, they built a makeshift raft of logs and set off down the river to make time and avoid the scalp-hunters. George was going to get the message to the governor, even if it killed him.

---

[126] Gist, 85–86; Flexner, Vol. 1, 94–95.
[127] Flexner, Vol. 1, 76; Chernow, 36–37

What happened next almost did. He wrote about the incident:

> We expected every moment our raft to sink and
> ourselves to perish. I put out my setting pole to
> try and stop the raft that the ice might pass by,
> when the rapidity of the stream threw it with
> such violence against the pole that it jerked me
> out into ten feet water, but I fortunately saved
> myself by catching hold of one of the raft logs.
> Notwithstanding all our efforts, we could not get
> the raft to either shore: we were obliged, as we
> were near an island, to quit our raft and make
> to it.[128]

George felt the icy needles of the frigid water penetrate to his
bones. Gist was suffering from frostbite, and they had no way to
make a fire. Stuck on an island in the middle of the river with no boat
or raft, the two men faced certain death.

* * * * *

Opening his eyes, George saw the blue-gray streaks of dawn
appear. Maybe if they yelled to shore for help or maybe a passing boat
would hear them. A small hope, but it was all they had. As more light
bled into the sky, they saw what had to be a mirage. They couldn't
trust what their eyes told them.

The river was a single solid sheet of ice from one side to the
other. The temperature dropped dramatically and froze the river.
They hurried across this temporary land bridge and stumbled upon a
lone trading post. Miraculously, the two shaking castaways were soon
dry and warming by a fire, enjoying the hospitality of the owners.

By January 16, 1754, the two survivors reached Virginia, and
George delivered the message to Dinwiddie. Britain had time to send
troops, supplies, and arms by spring.

---

[128] Washington, *Writings* Vol. 1, 129–130; Gist, 86.

Setting out, an ambitious, cocky, and immature young man playing soldier, George returned tougher but humbled and grateful to be alive. Some of this greenness was washed away by the river. The island tested him, and he survived. Much like Captain Smith and William Bradford who both spent time on their own islands, George understood that something other than himself was controlling events. He knew the will of the spirit mattered more than the physical body when it came to adversity, but man's will could not overcome the impossible. Something kept the Indian guide's bullet from killing him, and something froze the river just in time. Something placed them near the trading post and saved their lives.

He also realized that making correct decisions counted as much as courage. Without careful development of both, neither mattered. Without a faith in himself and reliance on divine intervention, he would fail. He decided to succeed by doing.

Governor Dinwiddie, seeing the immediate threat from the belligerent French, ordered the raising of a three-hundred-man force of Virginians. They were the first defense on the frontier, and George was given command.

He was surprised. "I must be impartial enough to confess it is a charge too great for my youth and inexperience to be entrusted with."

He admitted his inexperience now. The near-death experience made him see his limitations and put him in the right frame of mind to overcome them and "in time render myself worthy of promotion."[129]

He was ready to learn from his own mistakes and the wisdom of others. Commanding the Virginian force, he was eager to try again.

* * * * *

In March of 1754, George led the Virginians into the Ohio territory to defend settlements and territorial claims from the French and their Indian allies. On April 18, he and a force of 159 men marched

---

[129] Ibid., 34–35 (To Richard Corbin, March 1754).

into the Three Forks area (Pittsburgh, Pennsylvania). His men lacked proper clothes, supplies, and arms, but he commanded with energy and discipline. He found "a charming field for an encounter"[130] in an area called Great Meadows. Here he prepared to meet the enemy for the first time.

Encountering the French, they only lost one man, but ten enemy soldiers were dead and twenty-two were prisoners. Among the dead was Jumonville, a French aristocrat. They claimed the dead nobleman carried diplomatic credentials and sought peace with Britain when George's troops fired upon them in an unprovoked attack. Papers captured from the enemy showed evidence this wasn't true. The diplomatic credentials instructed the Jumonville expedition to gather information on British positions. Nevertheless, this single encounter triggered the French and Indian War (Seven Years' War). Many on both sides put the responsibility of starting it on George Washington. France and Britain never needed a catalyst like this young Virginian for an excuse to go to war.

Writing to his brother, George described the battle in a short and emotionless letter, except for a telling last sentence: "I fortunately escaped without any wound, for the right wing, where I stood was exposed to and received all the enemy's fire, and it was the part where the man was killed, and the rest wounded. I heard the bullets whistle, and, believe me, there is something charming in the sound."[131]

He possessed courage and better judgment but still maintained some of his youthful immaturity. Writing to Governor Dinwiddie, he portrayed confidence: "For my own part I can answer, I have a constitution hardy enough to encounter and undergo the most severe trials, and, I flatter myself, resolution to face what any man durst, as shall be proved when it comes to the Test, which I believe we are upon the Borders of."[132]

Feeling no fear, George faced battle and survived. Feeling invincible now, his humility was forgotten while a new cockiness replaced

---

[130] Ibid., 54 (To Governor Dinwiddie, May 27, 1754); Flexner, Vol. 1, 87–91.
[131] Ibid., 70 (To John Augustine Washington, May 31, 1754).
[132] Ibid., 60 (To Gov. Dinwiddie, May 29, 1754).

it. He had experience without the humility this time. Lessons would have to be relearned multiple times until they stuck. His confidence was as big as he was, but confidence alone was not enough.

George now ordered his men to build a fortification of logs and dirt on the same ground. Once it was completed, he named it Fort Necessity.

Reinforcements from Britain arrived in their scarlet uniforms commanded by Captain James Mackay. Mackay was commissioned by the Crown and considered George's brevet (temporary) command as colonel unworthy of professional respect. To a British officer, the colonists were not their equals. Mackay told the young colonel that a lower ranking royal officer outranked a colonist with a higher rank. He told the Virginian to step aside. Incensed at the insult, George replied:

> I hope that Captain Mackay will have more sense than to insist upon any unreasonable distinction, though he is and his have commissions from his majesty, let him consider though we are greatly inferior in respect to profitable advantages, yet we have the same spirit to serve our gracious king as they have, and are as ready and willing to sacrifice our lives for our country's as them, and here once more and for the last time, I must say this will be a cancer that will grate some officers of this regiment beyond all measure, to serve upon such different terms, when their lives, their fortunes, and their characters are equally, and I dare say as effectually exposed as those who are happy to have the king's commissions.[133]

When Mackay's men arrived, they set up a separate camp and refused to fraternize with the Virginians. Treated like second-class citizens, they wondered how they were any less British than Mackay's

---

[133] Ibid., 75 (To Gov. Dinwiddie, June 10, 1754).

men. Virginians had risked and sacrificed their lives for king and country but weren't respected as equals. The seeds of rebellion germinated in George's mind from this encounter. His difficulties with supplies and pay further convinced him of the snobbery and prejudice of the home country. To many native-born Brits, colonists were the children of outcasts who couldn't succeed at home, so they chose to live like the Indians. George believed men should be judged by performance, not their place of birth. This belief separated many colonists from their countrymen. This personal experience with the snobbery from the native-born guaranteed George's revulsion of it. Though he was proud to be British, he was proud to be a Virginian too. His desire to become a British Army officer kept his resentment at bay for now. He decided to prove himself worthy of their respect by his actions.

Fort Necessity contained a force of four hundred men, but one hundred were sick. The fort was enlarged and reinforced, but the design was flawed from the start. The woods around it weren't cleared and could be used for concealment by the enemy. This foresight wasn't a part of eighteenth century combat, because armies met out in the open. Concealment was considered dishonorable. Gentlemen stood face-to-face and killed each other. One hundred and fifty years before Fort Necessity, Jamestown, Virginia faced the same problem, but few professional tacticians trained to counter Indian-style warfare.

Fort Necessity was also downhill from the edge of the forest and gave the enemy a strategic advantage of higher ground. George's army was in an unwinnable position.

On July 3, 1754, the French and their Indian allies attacked the fort. No one could target the enemy firing from behind trees and rocks. They meticulously shot down the defenders. George commanded during the assault as his men fell around him, wounded or dead. Then it began to rain. The gunpowder was soaked, and returning fire was impossible. The ground in the fort became a river of mud, blood, and bodies. Some broke into the rum stores in the hope of gaining false courage, but it only quickened their demise. The enemy's gunpowder stayed dry in the shelter of the trees as they continued to pick off George's men. He held out until dark and assessed the situation. Those not dead or wounded were inebriated, and the fort was compromised. He decided to send an emissary with a white flag and ask for terms. More than a third of his men lay dead, dying, or wounded. This disaster was his responsibility, and he had to consider the lives of his men. Holding out would only delay the inevitable.

When the emissary returned, the terms of surrender were generous. If he surrendered the fort, they were free to leave. All he was required to do was sign the surrender. He signed the agreement aided by an interpreter who failed to question why the French commander gave such gracious terms. The preamble of the surrender was a confession. This claimed responsibility for assassinating Jumonville and said France had just cause to avenge the death. Once printed and circulated, the rest of the world accepted that Britain started the war and assassinated an innocent man in peacetime. The international implications proved to many the incompetence of colonials and the superiority of regulars. Washington was the scapegoat. The French simply outsmarted George to blame Britain. Many Brits played into French hands and blamed the war on their hayseed colonists.

George was only guilty of being gullible, overconfident, and unprepared. He allowed courage and a bit of experience to cloud his judgment this time. He thought being a successful leader came simply by acting. Anyone could stand defiant in the face of the enemy, but a great leader must weigh the best options and potential risks. George had done neither, but he learned defeat again, and it was the best taskmaster.

On July 4, 1754, he and his men walked out of the fort, exhausted, hungry, and humiliated. The fort was terribly constructed, and his confidence caused him to act without a plan. This was the opposite of his usual measured judgment acquired as a surveyor. At Fort Necessity, he simply reacted to the situation and assumed a way would appear.

He admitted failure and accepted his bad decisions and vowed to learn from the experience. This time, he made certain he never forgot.

Soon after the defeat at Fort Necessity, the British integrated the colonists with the regular British troops. George's regiment was broken into companies, and colonists were forbidden to attain a rank over captain. He was demoted from colonel to captain, and this insult to his honor demanded resignation. He returned to Mount Vernon disappointed, but was vocal about his willingness to fight in the next campaign as a volunteer. He was embarrassed by the demotion, but the urge to lead men into battle never retreated.

In February of 1755, Major General Edward Braddock arrived from Britain to lead an expedition to the French stronghold of Fort Duquesne. He asked George to join him as an aide. The dream of becoming a British officer became possible again.

He was ready to prove colonists were the equals to the regulars.

* * * * *

Ohio Territory, 1770

The old chief came many miles to see the great warrior of the battle. Sitting around a campfire, the Indian chanted in a ghostly voice. His wrinkled face and gray hair completed the mystery and drama of the supernatural. The flames flickered, revealing his mouth, but darkness concealed his eyes. The white men listened, hypnotized by his words. "I have travelled a long and weary path that I might see the young warrior of the great battle. It was on the day when the white man's blood mixed with the streams of our forest that I first beheld this chief." Dr. James Craik stared at the Indian, then at his friend. George remained stoic, listening to the old man's words, expressionless:

> I called to my young men and said, Mark yon tall and daring warrior? He is not of the red coat tribe-he hath an Indian's wisdom, and his warriors fight as we do--himself is alone exposed. Quick, let your aim be certain, and he dies. Our rifles were leveled, rifles which but for him knew not how to miss—'twas in vain; a power mightier

far than we shielded him from harm. He cannot die in battle.

The fire popped and hissed, startling everyone except George. "I am old, and soon shall be gathered to the great council fire of my fathers in the land of shades; but ere I go there is something that bids me speak in the voice of prophecy."

No one breathed. Though the Indians were known for their superstitions and primitive beliefs, something in this chief's conviction held their concentration. "Listen! The Great Spirit protects that man, and guides his destinies—he will become the chief of nations, and a people yet unborn will hail him as the founder of a mighty empire."[134]

The men around the fire stared at Washington again. Still, he didn't flinch. Lost in his own memories perhaps, George thought of the battle the chief described. He hadn't thought of it in years. His military career was behind him. He was a farmer now and accepted this fact. He had packed away his old uniform with his old ambition, but it still haunted him.

Fifteen years had passed. He was so young and green then. Nearly forty years old now, he accepted the reality that his chance to be a "chief of nations" was in the past.

Though skeptical of the old Indian's prophecy, he did wonder how he had lived when others died around him. He had been in the thick of the carnage but escaped. Others hadn't been so lucky. He should have died there but was spared for some reason.

The embers glowed while he thought about another fire he saw on that fateful day.

* * * * *

[134] Ibid., 121 (To John Augustine Washington, July 18, 1755; Custis, George Washington Parke. *Recollections and Private Memoirs of Washington, by his Adopted Son, George Washington Parke Custis.* (Philadelphia: J.W. Bradley, 1861), 300–307, (Ch. 11, *The Indian Prophecy*); Parry, Jay A. *The Real George Washington.* (National Center for Constitutional Studies, 1991), 48–49; Chernow, 61.

Virginia, 1755

Braddock's plan was bold. He would attack Duquesne with 3,000 regulars and colonists and called for one hundred and fifty wagons but received only twenty-five. The colonies lacked the ability to supply a major campaign like this, and Braddock quickly lost patience, cancelling the operation. George's chance to serve under a British general appeared over, but then, a diplomatic entrepreneur from Philadelphia by the name of Benjamin Franklin offered the means to fund the expedition. Franklin persuaded Braddock to continue his campaign, and fate intervened in George's destiny again.

On June 10, 1755, three hundred men cleared the way for the long train of wagons, horses, artillery, and soldiers. The army was four miles long on a path twelve feet wide and took eighteen days to move thirty miles. Fever and sickness plagued many of the men, and George suffered from dysentery. This caused fever, dehydration, and diarrhea, and made Braddock's young aide miserable. Covering an average of three miles a day, the general needed to make better time and asked George's advice. He told the commander to leave the baggage behind and continue with a smaller detachment of handpicked troops, much like his decision to leave the main party with Gist two years before. Explaining this in a letter to his brother, he wrote:

> ...a prospect that conveyed infinite delight to my mind, though I was excessively ill at the time. But this prospect was soon clouded, and my hopes brought very low indeed when I found that, instead of pushing on with vigor without regarding a little rough road, they were halting to level every mole-hill, and to erect bridges over every brook, by which means were four days in getting twelve miles.[135]

---

[135] Washington, *Writings*, Vol. 1, 115 ("To John A. Washington," June 28, 1755); Parkman, Francis. *Montcalm and Wolfe.* (Boston: Little, Brown and Co.,1884, reprint Viking Press, 1984), 121.

To the ambitious aide's surprise, Braddock ordered him to remain behind with the main force because of the illness. Seeing his disappointment, the general promised to summon him before the action. George spent a week in a sickbed under the camp doctor's orders, and was told he would risk his life if he disobeyed them. Feeling the fever ease a bit, he just had to get to the front. He couldn't tolerate the horse ride there, so he climbed aboard one of the wagons and laid down in it. Neither sickness nor possible death would deter him from the fight. Proving himself mattered more than living.

In the early morning hours of July 9, 1755, he woke to news that Braddock was about to attack. Still sick and in pain, the young aide attached pillows to his saddle and mounted his horse. Nothing was going to keep him from this battle.

An advance party was sent forward to probe for enemy scout patrols. The main force was left in the rear as a reserve. A single shot shattered the stillness, and a skirmish ensued. As the action unfolded, more fire from the trees had Braddock's troops nearly surrounded. George reached the battle only to see the clearing ahead clogged by masses of panicked soldiers fleeing from the fight. He ordered them to stand and fight, but they ignored him. They ran directly into the main force, which Braddock ordered forward as reinforcements. These two formations smashed into each other going opposite directions and this confusion created a traffic jam as the enemy easily picked off the British.

George couldn't believe it. The regular troops were human after all and ran like colonists. The Virginians, ironically, stood their ground that day. Braddock tried forming his men into lines in the open, but the crimson tunics made them easy targets. "We would fight," some yelled, "if we could see anybody to fight with."[136] Braddock was trained as a traditional officer and saw guerrilla tactics not within the rules of civilized warfare. The Indian warfare in the New World changed the rules of traditional warfare. Most American colonists instinctually knew this, but Old World strategists' concepts still reigned supreme in the royal army. The British generals during the French and Indian War refused to adapt to these unorthodox tac-

---

[136] Parkman, 127.

tics. This inability to change with the prevailing winds would eventually lose them their empire.

George sat tall in the saddle and made an obvious target. All around him, men fell dead or wounded. He tried to rally them, but the battle was lost. Indians scalped the dead and wounded as their screams echoed over the musket fire. Braddock's force fired at elusive shadows in the woods if they had anything to fire at. George had a horse shot from beneath him. Mounting another, his hat was shot from his head. Then, the second horse met the same fate.

General Braddock was down, and George had him loaded onto a wagon, then ordered a partial withdrawal back to higher ground. The dying commander ordered a general withdrawal back to the main encampment forty miles away.

On the way back, Braddock died. The experienced regular was a victim of his own inability to break with tradition. This taught George a valuable lesson he would call on in the future. On the battlefield, a commander must adapt to any possibility and improvise accordingly. Strict adherence to any system or idea was a recipe for eventual failure. The young man gained wisdom from Braddock's mistakes and his own.

Washington buried Braddock in the middle of the road and directed wagons to ride over the grave to pack down the dirt and conceal it from the Indians hunting for prize scalps.

The Battle of the Monongahela cost the British 977 killed and 1,373 wounded. It was a disaster in the annals of British military history. Sixty-three out of eighty-three officers were killed or wounded. George was right next to Braddock most of the battle but never received a scratch. Braddock's two other aides were wounded, but not him. He did find four holes in his coat from musket balls later though. Was it luck that a man six-foot-three, in the line of fire, and sick that day didn't receive a mark? Describing this, he wrote, "But by the all-powerful dispensations of Providence, I have been protected beyond all probability and expectation, I had four bullets through my coat, and two horses shot under me, yet escaped unhurt."[137]

---

[137] Washington, *Writings*, Vol. 1, 121 ("To John A. Washington," July 18, 1755).

Returning home, George was appointed commander-in-chief of the Virginia regiment. His fellow Virginians held him in high esteem. For four years, he commanded a threadbare force and did his best to protect the frontier from hostile Indians who continued to raid settlements, killing men, women, and children. He couldn't properly defend such a large area with the troops he had or without money to supply them. The Crown offered no help, and the theater of the war moved to the north. The colonies were on their own.

Frustrated from being ignored and denied promotion again, George resigned his commission in December 1758. "This brings on reflections that fill me with grief and I must strive to forget them."[138] The probability of ever being a military officer looked dimmer to the twenty-six-year-old. He decided to command a farm instead, but the experience of war left a mighty imprint that would serve him again one day.

* * * * *

Ohio Territory, 1770

George kept a somber expression as the old chief finished speaking. Dr. Craik and the others in his party smiled proudly at him as if they thought the old chief's words were true. Craik would repeat this story to soldiers during the American Revolution to keep up morale.

The fire glowed white as embers floated in the breeze. A private man, George never spoke about this incident, but something did protect him that day. The idea of becoming "the chief of nations, and a people yet unborn will hail him as the founder of a mighty empire" was a stretch. He was a farmer now.

He was content with his life and had no desire to lead an empire. His days of military glory were in the past. George Washington was a respected name in Virginia, but nowhere else. If anything, he was the colonist blamed for starting the French and Indian War, losing the

---

[138] Washington, *Papers, Colonial Series*, Vol. 6, 186–187 ("To the Officers of the Virginia Regiment," January 10, 1759); Flexner, Vol. 1, 350 Appendix A.

Battle of Fort Necessity, and being an advisor to the biggest military disaster of that war. He had little chance of redeeming this record now. He was content to be a farmer. A "chief of nations" he wasn't.

* * * * *

After serving in the war, George returned home a hero. Virginians appreciated his experience, even if the British did not. He decided his destiny was with farming, like his father and grandfather, so he decided to be the best farmer he could be.

He turned Mount Vernon into a productive plantation and mastered every facet of agriculture. At first, he attempted to grow tobacco for sale in Britain but turned to milling wheat for Virginians when he experienced the same snobbery from the mother country he did in the army. He traded tobacco with British companies for various goods but received second-rate, subpar, and sometimes damaged products in return. Wine was watered down or missing from crates, china and glassware were broken, and inferior fabrics replaced the finery he ordered. Once again, he was being treated like a second-class citizen. This pushed him to produce his own domestic goods and sell them to Americans instead. By cutting out the middle man, his profits soared, and dependency on British trade evaporated.

George excelled in farming and plantation supervision. Reading diligently on the latest agricultural science, like alternative crop rotations and other experimental techniques, he became an innovator. He invented a special type of plow which dropped seeds in the ground automatically and he read all the contemporary journals on the latest technology. One biographer, wrote, "These were the concerns of a man who intended to remain a planter, grow richer if he could, and enjoy the luxury of a life he had earned for himself."[139] If he was meant to be a farmer, he would make the most of it. This comfortable living was an end to a means—he wanted to stand on his own without Mary or the mother country. Property ownership

---

[139] Freeman, Douglas Southall. *Washington,* One volume abridgement by Richard Harwell. (New York: Charles Scribner & Sons, 1968), 150.

substituted for military glory now. In his search for a purpose, he settled for the material. Even though this never satiated his desire for significance, he retreated to his work.

He acquired much of his wealth and standing from his marriage to Martha Dandridge Custis in 1759. A widow whose late husband left her a substantial estate, Martha was key to his rise in status. Now the failed officer was a gentleman farmer and responsible for more land and slaves.

George inherited a few slaves from his father and brother, but the majority came with Martha. Never a proponent of slavery, he made his opinion of the institution crystal clear. "Were it not then, that I am principled against selling Negroes, as you would cattle in the market, I would not in twelve months from this date be possessed of one as a slave."[140] Making his thoughts known about separating slave families, he wrote, "I have more working Negroes,…than can be employed to any advantage…to sell the overplus. I cannot, because I am principled against this kind of traffic in the human species. To hire them out is almost as bad, because they could not be disposed of in families to any advantage, and to disperse the families I have an aversion."[141] One of the most striking statements he made about slavery was, "There is not a man living who wishes more sincerely than I do to see a plan adopted for the abolition of it…"[142]

His treatment of his own slaves was laid out in instructions to a hired overseer at Mount Vernon:

> It is foremost in my thoughts to desire you will be particularly attentive to my Negroes in their sickness, and to order every Overseer positively to be so likewise; for I am sorry to observe that the generality of them view these poor creatures in scarcely any other light than they do a draft

---

[140] Washington, *Writings*, Vol. 34, 47 (To Alexander Spotswood, November 23, 1794).

[141] Ibid., Vol. 37, 338 (To Robert Lewis, August 18, 1799).

[142] Ibid., Vol. 28, 408 (To Robert Morris, April 12, 1786).

horse or Ox, neglecting them as much when they are unable to work, instead of comforting and nursing them when they lie on a sickbed.[143]

Washington abhorred the institution but didn't know how to abolish it. America would struggle with it for nearly another century and end in civil war. It wasn't as simple as emancipation either. Freeing slaves in most of the South was illegal and cruel. Slaves couldn't read or write and had few ways to make a living on their own.

Many still criticize Washington for his slaves but refuse to tell the other side. He was guilty of inheriting the society of his birth but seemed disturbed by it. His beliefs about slavery were neither prevalent nor popular at the time, even in the North. It should also be remembered that he emancipated his slaves thirty years before Britain and sixty years before the United States. Judging him from the twenty-first century point of view instead of the eighteenth century is a mistake. He was well ahead of his time but not removed from it.

When he wasn't busy running the plantation, he enjoyed his family. His marriage to Martha was based on friendship and enjoying one another's company. This wasn't the youthful lust he experienced as a young man but an enduring foundation of genuine affection. He learned that passion led to fleeting infatuation and emptiness. He put his faith in a mature love, not childish crushes or sexual urges of his youth. In the past, he attempted to win female hearts by flirting and romantic correspondence (like today's social media), but it always ended with wounded confidence and rejection. When it came to the fairer sex, he struggled with his own insecurities. The smallpox scars on his face, bad teeth, and previous rejections made him appear awkward or cold in social situations.

Writing to his step-granddaughter, he counseled her on love and marriage:

Love is said to be an involuntary passion, and it is, therefore, contended that it cannot be resisted.

---

[143] Ibid., Vol. 32, 184 (To Anthony Whiting, October 14, 1792).

This is true in part only, for like all things else, when nourished and supplied plentifully with ailment, it is rapid in its progress, but let these be withdrawn and it may be stifled in its birth or much stinted in its growth. For example, a woman (that same may be said of the other sex) all beautiful and accomplished, will, while her hand and heart are undisposed of, turn the heads and set the circle in which she moves on fire. Let her marry, and what is the consequence? The madness ceases and all is quiet again. Why? Not because there is any diminution in the charms of the lady, but because there is an end of hope.[144]

Explaining that youthful excitement eventually subsides, but real love grows over time, he continued:

Hence it follows, that love may and therefore ought to be under the guidance of reason, for although we cannot avoid first impressions, we may assuredly place them under guard; and my motives for treating on this subject are to show you, while you remain Eleanor Parke Custis, spinster, and retain the resolution to love with moderation, the propriety of adhering to the latter resolution, at least until you have secured your game, and the way by which it may be accomplished.[145]

He wrote to his other step-granddaughter on selecting a husband:

Do not then in your contemplation of the marriage state, look for perfect felicity before you

---

[144] Ibid., Vol. 34, 92 (To Eleanor Parke Custis, January 16, 1795); Flexner, Vol. 1, 200–201.

[145] Ibid.

consent to wed. Nor conceive, from the fine tales the Poets and lovers of old have told us, of the transports of mutual love, that heaven has taken its abode on earth. Nor do not deceive yourself in supposing, that the only mean by which these are to be obtained, is to drink deep of the cup, and revel in an ocean of love. Love is a mighty pretty thing; but like all delicious things, it is cloying; and when the first transports of the passion begins to subside, which it assuredly will do, and yield, oftentimes too late, to more sober reflections, it serves to envince, that love is too dainty a food to live upon alone, and ought not to be considered farther than as a necessary ingredient for that matrimonial happiness which results from a combination of causes: none of which are of greater importance, than that object on whom it is placed, should possess good sense, good dispositions, and the means of supporting you in the way you have been brought up.[146]

Advising her to choose a mate this way, he guaranteed a happy union:

Such qualifications cannot fail to attract (after marriage) your esteem and regard, into which or into disgust, sooner or later, love naturally resolves itself, and who at the same time, has a claim to the respect, and esteem of the circle he moves in. Without these, whatever may be your first impressions of the man, they will end in disappointment; for be assured, and experience will

[146] Washington, *Papers, Presidential Series*, ed. David R. Hoth & Carol S. Ebel (2011), Vol. 16, 682–683 (To Elizabeth Parke Custis, September 14, 1794); Flexner, Vol. 1, 200–201.

> convince you, that there is no truth more cer-
> tain, than that all our enjoyments fall short of
> our expectations; and to none does it apply more
> force, than to the gratification of passions.[147]

This was the same manner George chose Martha, and considered her character, reputation, and compatibility when choosing a wife. He adopted her two children and treated them as his own and she was his best friend. He realized after unsuccessfully chasing romance for so many years he couldn't rely on passion alone. There had to be friendship, loyalty, and comfort for a marriage to work. There was mutual respect between George and Martha, and it worked to strengthen their marriage.

During this period of settling down, Washington matured in his beliefs and convictions. He became a regular church member and community patriarch. Loaning money to needy neighbors, he rarely expected payment. He also took an interest in promising boys and paid for their education. He never had children of his own but knew growing up without a father was difficult, so he tried to be a surrogate of sorts to these boys.

This prestige and newly acquired status led him to a seat in the House of Burgesses (state legislature) where he dealt with the local politics of the day. There he saw the world in a different light. The decisions the Burgesses made affected others, and he wanted to be a man worthy to serve Virginians. So, he courted virtues like humility, charity, and patience, and this prepared him for the dark days ahead.

In 1773, George's twelve-year-old stepdaughter, Patsy, who suffered from epileptic seizures, died from an episode. Witnessing this affected Washington deeply.

Sitting at the dinner table, Patsy fell to the floor, convulsions overwhelming her as the rest of the family watched on in horror, helpless to do anything. Watching her die like that forced George to reflect on the meaning of life and death. Writing to Martha's brother-in-law who recently lost a daughter, he said "the Sweet Innocent Girl

---

[147] Ibid.

entered into a more happy and peaceful abode than any she has met with in the afflicted Path she hitherto has trod."[148]

Though painful, he believed death was part of God's will and divine plan, "but the ways of Providence being inscrutable, and the justice of it not to be scanned by the shallow eye of humanity, nor to be counteracted by the utmost efforts of human power or wisdom, resignation and, as far as the strength of our reason and religion can carry us, a cheerful acquiescence to the Divine Will is what we are to aim."[149] Everything happened for a reason, he was sure. Providence moved people and events to their preordained destinies, and even the death of loved ones was by design. Labelled a deist by some, George believed in a God who intervened in people's lives, and dying led to heavenly rewards. Deists believed neither.

Seventeen years had passed since resigning from the army. Being a farmer, legislator, husband, philanthropist, and father dissolved the immaturity of his early years; "Errors once discovered, are more than half amended."[150]

Awareness of his failures taught him what not to do and the process of elimination led him to realize success was attainable if he kept at it long enough. Imperfection and failure taught important lessons crucial to mastering goals, and the search for self-mastery led one closer to it, even if impossible to obtain. George discovered that the journey toward significance was more important than significance itself. He believed this era in his life was a surrender in his search for purpose, but it was only an incubation period.

Douglas Southall Freeman, who wrote the definitive character study of Washington, summed up this period of his life with precision:

> In larger preparation for the uncertainties of the future, political and personal, he had learned more of law-making, had gained in good will to

---

[148] Ibid., Vol. 3, 138 (To Colonel Burwell Bassett, June 20, 1773).
[149] Ibid., 133 (To Burwell Bassett, April 25, 1773).
[150] Ibid., Vol. 21, 181 (To John Sullivan, In Congress, February 4, 1781).

men, and, facing the vagaries of season and of human nature, was becoming more patient and more willing to bear what he could not cast off. By the thorough performance of commonplace, daily duties he was building slowly the stronger structure of the spirit that men call character.[151]

* * * * *

On April 19, 1775, the Battles of Lexington and Concord ushered in the American Revolution. A handful of militia made up of farmers, artisans, carpenters, fishermen, and merchants had defied the most powerful army the world had ever known and chased it back to Boston, Massachusetts. The cause of this confrontation had its roots in a scheme by the British to confiscate rifles, cannons, and ammunition, but the Massachusetts men were having none of this. Recognizing that an attempt to disarm them was an attempt to enslave them, the colonists fought back. This was the same arrogance the British had shown Washington and his Virginians. The British Parliament passed laws for the colonies without their representation. This was a violation of a basic British right and the colonists recognized it as an arbitrary, despotic power play. Americans considered themselves British, so they couldn't understand why they didn't have the same rights. The king and parliament acted with an elitist attitude toward their American subjects, and a long list of abuses during the decade of debate came to a bloody end.

The Sugar Act in 1764 imposed taxes on molasses, sugar cane, textiles, dye, coffee, and wine.

The Stamp Act, passed in 1765, said that Americans were expected to pay more than citizens of the mother country. This act added taxes to legal documents, magazines, newspapers, and other printed materials.

The Quartering Act in 1765 forced the colonists to provide room and board, at their own expense, to the British forces stationed in America to enforce the despotic laws.

---

[151] Freeman, *Washington*, 150.

The Townshend Acts of 1767 placed duties on paper, paint, lead, glass, and tea. These items were not produced in the colonies and could only be purchased from Great Britain.

In 1768, royal troops first appeared in Massachusetts to enforce the Townshend Acts, because the colonists refused to pay the duties. This created tension in the city of Boston between the troops and the people.

On February 22, 1770, a riotous crowd outside a customs official's house led to the death of an eleven-year-old boy, Christopher Seider (Snyder), when the official fired into the crowd.[152]

On March 5, 1770, the Boston Massacre resulted in the killing of five colonists by British soldiers. Snowballs and rocks thrown by the colonists caused a shaky redcoat to fire into them, signaling his comrades to follow suit. Whether a case of self-defense or not, it really didn't matter to the Americans anymore. The presence of the soldiers in the streets was the real offense to many, and the predictable clash was the fault of the Crown. Samuel Adams and Paul Revere ramped up their resistance with the blood of six Americans to fuel it.

On May 10, 1773, the Tea Act granted a British company a monopoly on all tea sold in the colonies.

On December 16, 1773, Bostonians disguised as Mohawk Indians (to hide their true identities) destroyed three shiploads of tea from Britain by tossing it into the harbor.

In response to the Boston Tea Party, Parliament passed the Coercive Acts, which closed Boston harbor to commerce until the cost of the destroyed tea was paid. The Coercive Acts were the final straw, and Americans convened the First Continental Congress in 1774 to petition the Crown to repeal the acts.

Washington attended the First Continental Congress where representatives from all thirteen colonies met. After drawing up their

---

[152] *Boston Gazette, and Country Journal*, No. 778, March 5, 1770, p. 2, (www.masshist.org/database/viewer.php?old=1&item id=345); Forbes, Esther. *Paul Revere and the World He Lived In.* (Boston: Houghton Mifflin Co., 1942, 172–173; Stoll, Ira. *Samuel Adams: A Life.* (New York: Free Press, 2008), 81–82; Smith, Page. *John Adams*, Vol. 1 (1735–1784), (New York: Doubleday & Co. Inc., 1962), 116.

petition, they set the next meeting for May 1775 to consider any new developments. They were still hopeful about a peaceful solution, and war would be the last option.

The next meeting convened one month after Lexington and Concord. Their attempt to remedy their grievances peacefully turned into a bloody confrontation.

The Second Continental Congress met in Philadelphia and still sought peace but concluded that preparation for war was necessary. If the Crown chose submission to peace, they would need any advantage to resist, and an army needed to be raised.

John Adams and cousin Samuel Adams, in Congress, called for a general to lead this army. George was present that day and wore his old blue and red uniform from the French and Indian War. He never solicited himself, but by wearing the uniform, he announced his availability to serve. After John Adams nominated him to lead the army, the other representatives concurred. No one else had the military experience or the integrity of Washington. Plus, he was from Virginia, and since the war started in the North, his appointment would help unify the colonies.

Though he had grown, his past failures caused him to question his ability. His confidence was low because of the old fear of inadequacy. Was he capable of fighting a British leviathan with a handful of farmers, merchants, carpenters, and woodsmen? He hesitated. Commanding a regiment or even a company was hard enough and an entire nonexistent army would be worse.

The young colonel who gave up his dream of serving in the British army was now the general of the opposing force. Providence had led him back to his original purpose, yet this time, he was different. Writing the first draft of his first inaugural address in 1789, he recalled the mountainous struggle they faced:

> ...the expense in comparison with our circumstances as Colonists must be enormous—the struggle protracted dubious, and severe. It was known that the resources of Britain were, in a manner, inexhaustible, that her fleets covered

the Ocean, and that her troops had harvested laurels in every quarter of the globe. Not then organized as a nation, or known as a people upon the earth—we had no preparation—Money, the nerve of War, was wanting. The sword was to be forged on the anvil of necessity...If we had a secret resource of an nature unknown to our enemy, it was in the unconquerable resolution of our Citizens, the conscious rectitude of our Cause, and the confident trust that we should not be forsaken by Heaven.[153]

On June 16, 1775, he appeared in the uniform he wore sixteen years before, and addressed the Congress:

Mr. President: though I am truly sensible of the high honor done me in this Appointment, yet I feel great distress from a consciousness that my abilities and Military experience may not be equal to the extensive and important Trust: However, as the Congress desires it, I will enter upon the momentous duty, and exert every power I Possess In their Service, for the support of the glorious Cause. I beg they will accept my most cordial thanks for this distinguished testimony of their Approbation.

He continued humbly, "But, lest some unlucky event should happen, unfavorable to my reputation, I beg it may be remembered, by every Gentleman in this room, that I, this day, declare with the

---

[153] Washington, *Papers*, *Presidential Series*, ed. Dorothy Twohig (1987), Vol. 2, 158–173 (Undelivered First Inaugural Address: Fragments, April 30, 1789; Davis, Burke. *George Washington and the American Revolution*. (New York: Random House, 1975), 25–26.

utmost sincerity, I do not think myself equal to the Command I am honored with."

After humility came honor, "As to pay, Sir, I beg leave to Assure Congress that, as no pecuniary consideration could have tempted me to accept this Arduous employment [at the expense of my domestic ease and happiness] I do not wish to make any profit from it: I will keep an exact Account of my expenses; those, I doubt not, they will discharge, and that is all I desire."[154] He wanted no pay, and unsure of himself, he leaned on providence to guide him.

This undertaking was greater than any single person's dream. He hadn't chosen this—it chose him. He was merely a player in the events, and whatever the outcome, it was meant to happen. He believed he served a higher purpose larger than his own ambition or ego. Some accused him of ambitiously seeking this position by wearing the uniform. Even if true, accepting the position was an act of self-sacrifice. If he was captured or lost the war, he would be hanged as a traitor. He accepted no pay, so money wasn't his motivation. If he failed and lived by some miracle, his reputation would be destroyed. If Washington eagerly sought the generalship, he must have been a glutton for punishment. His own private words suggest something else.

In a letter to Martha, soon after his appointment, he explained his feelings:

> You may believe me, my dear Patsy (Martha), when I assure you, in the most solemn manner that, so far from seeking this appointment, I have used every endeavor in my power to avoid it, not only from my unwillingness to part with you and the family, but from a consciousness of its being a trust too great for my capacity...But as it has been a kind of destiny, that has thrown me upon this service, I shall hope that my undertaking it is designed to answer some good purpose... I shall

---

[154] Washington, *Writings*, Vol. 3, 292–293 (Acceptance of Command).

rely, therefore, confidently on that Providence, which has heretofore preserved and been bountiful to me, not doubting but that I shall return safe to you in the fall.[155]

He suffered defeat when he tried to be a British officer. He walked away from his dream and settled for running a plantation. His time as a member of the House of Burgesses prepared him to deal politically with others. He learned the day-to-day operations of a large plantation and increased its productivity. He learned how to ship and place orders, feed and maintain a family, overseers, and slaves, and how to make decisions with consequences. His deeper spiritual beliefs from participating in his parish made him more sensitive to providence, humility, justice, and compassion. These were attributes he would need as general of the army. He had no idea yet that he possessed them.

Writing to a family friend just before leaving for Boston, he described what guided him:

> I am now embarked on a tempestuous Ocean, from whence perhaps, no friendly harbor is to be found… May God grant, therefore, that my acceptance of it, may be attended with some good to the common cause, and without Injury (from want of knowledge) to my own reputation. I can answer but for three things, a firm belief of the justice of our Cause, close attention in the prosecution of it, and the strictest Integrity. If these cannot supply the place of Ability and Experience, the cause will suffer.[156]

---

[155] Ibid., 293–294 (To Martha Washington, June 18, 1775); Middlekauff, Robert. *Washington's Revolution: The Making of America's First Leader.* (New York: Alfred A. Knopf, 2015), 24–25.

[156] Ibid., 296–297 (To Burwell Bassett, June 19, 1775).

Without integrity, his purpose was meaningless. Without adapting to failure, he would have no will to persevere. Without a just cause, providence would not protect him. He still had much to learn, but he had a sturdy foundation from which to build upon. It would see him through the darkest times to come.

* * * * *

Brooklyn Heights, New York, August 30, 1776

Studying the campfires on the heights, Washington saw the soft glow of approaching sunrise paint the night sky. A few hours more was all they needed, he was sure. There were still too many men waiting on the bank, and morning was marching forward, regardless.

British general, William Howe's entire army was just a few hundred yards away and would certainly attack at first light. His scouts would notice the evacuation, and they'd be trapped. Those waiting for the return boats would be captured or killed. He would remain until every man was safely across. This was his doing and he would face the repercussions.

Closing his eyes, Washington knew he urgently needed sleep, but not until it was finished. He hadn't slept for days and was exhausted. His resilience waned while the cause, like him, was on the verge of collapse.

They'd been outfought, outmaneuvered, and outsmarted. He was disappointed in himself. It was Fort Necessity and Fort Duquesne all over again, except in this case, more was at stake than a few acres of wilderness. If the army surrendered, the cause was lost.

Looking back across the river, he thought he heard a distant squeak of oars, but only the black emptiness remained. Where were the boats?

Returning his attention to Howe's lines and the coming sunrise, he noticed fog collecting on the ground. Would the boatmen lose their way to shore now? That fog seemed to symbolize his mood. Why did he not see the flank attack anyway? Those brave souls killed or captured—this was too much burden for any man to bear, he thought. Catching himself, he knew some of this doubt was his lack of sleep. After everything he'd been through, he needed to keep the faith.

As the fog thickened, he heard a slight splash of an oar on the river. This time, he spotted a boat moving toward the bank. Just then, the sun began to rise.[157]

* * * * *

After Lexington and Concord, the British withdrew to Boston. Only an island connected to the mainland by a small land bridge, Boston was an ideal base of operations for the masters of the sea. The Americans fortified north of the city on Breed's Hill (Bunker Hill) and on June 17, 1775, royal troops commanded by General Thomas Gage assaulted the hill until they took it. They suffered over seven hundred casualties for an insignificant hill and showed the measure of their resolve to put down the rebellion.

The Crown had no interest in a peaceful settlement. They were determined to force compliance, and negotiations were over. The Americans on Bunker Hill fought tenaciously until they ran out of ammunition. They resorted to firing stones and nails at the end but were forced to evacuate the fortification.[158]

Washington arrived soon after the Battle of Bunker Hill. Surveying the situation and the condition of the army, he wasn't surprised by what he found. Few men had muskets or ammunition, and there were only a handful of small cannons, but nothing substantial to threaten Boston. The army encampment was filthy, disorganized, and undisciplined. The army had operated in a democratic fashion from the start. Officers often fraternized with enlisted men and garnered little respect. Men refused to recognize rank or salute officers.

---

[157] Ibid., Vol. 5, 508-509 (To the President of Congress, August 31, 1776, "Reasons of Council of War for Evacuating Long Island"); Flexner, Vol. 2, 114–115; McCullough, David. *1776*. (New York: Simon & Schuster, 2005), 186-190; Freeman, *Washington*, 238.

[158] Ketchum, Richard M. *Decisive Day: The Battle of Bunker Hill.* (New York: Anchor Book/Doubleday, 1962, 1974), 172–183.

Everyone was equal, but no one was in charge. In an army, democracy had no place. Order and rank were necessary to fight wars, and mob mentality was chaos.

Soon after his arrival, Washington inspected the camp and witnessed a fight break out among the men. Exasperated by their behavior and the camp's condition, he ran into the midst of the brawl and grabbed two men by their necks in each of his arms, lifting them off the ground. After reprimanding the two surprised men, he released them, then continued his inspection of the camp. He communicated to the troops that he was in charge and expected change. He then mustered out thieves, drunkards, and derelicts and ordered thirty-nine lashes for deserters. Within the first month, he grew more optimistic. "We mend every day and I flatter myself that in a little Time, we shall work up these raw Materials into good Stuff...I endeavor to practice myself, Patience and Perseverance"[159]

General George Washington

When Ethan Allen captured the Canadian stronghold, Fort Ticonderoga, in May 1775, the eighty cannons captured there caught Washington's attention. If he could somehow get those, they'd have

---

[159] Washington, *Writings*, Vol. 3, 374 (To General Philip Schuyler, July 28, 1775); Fischer, David Hackett. *Washington's Crossing*. (New York: Oxford University Press, 2004), 25.

a chance. It would take months to accomplish and require a large force to retrieve the cannons and was through rough wilderness and heavy snow. He desperately needed these guns if he was expected to compete with the enemy in Boston. If he could surround them before they mounted an offensive or their ships returned, he just might force them out of the city. The window of opportunity would close once winter was over, and European armies traditionally fought in spring and summer. If he could get the cannons before then, he had a chance. *But how?* he wondered.

Henry Knox, the chief of artillery, possessed not a shred of military experience. Everything he knew of artillery came from the books he read, but Washington saw promise in the portly bookseller and appointed him to his staff anyway. Judgment of character mattered more to him than experience. As he learned, experience was wisdom only to the man who learned from it. He kept experienced men near him but didn't yet know how deficient in character they were.

Knox devised a plan to transport the cannons back to Boston before the end of winter. His idea sounded implausible to Washington, but Knox convinced him it would work.

A grueling forty-day trip through a frozen hell assisted by ingenious improvisations, and Knox returned to Cambridge (outside Boston) with the cannons. Washington had nearly given up. He called for more militia and began preparations.

Three thousand Americans hauled hundreds of wagons and tools quietly up to Dorchester Heights, a peninsula south of Boston, jutting into the bay and leering down on the city. The wagons contained bundles of sticks or fascines, tight bales of hay, and barrels filled with stones for rolling downhill at the enemy. A thousand men marched back to camp and returned with pre-built portable ramparts and fixed them into the frozen earth. The fortification was erected in about three hours, then workers retired to their tents while 2,400 fresh men arrived to defend it. Four thousand more in reserve awaited the main attack.

The British awoke the next morning to a massive fort threatening Boston. It seemed to have materialized out of the dark. Firing cannons up at the fortification, the redcoat munitions fell short of their target and struck the crest of the hill. Archibald Robertson, the British engineering officer, exclaimed that this, "most astonishing night's work must have been employed from 15,000 and 20,000 men." Another claimed it to be from "the genie belonging to Aladdin's wonderful lamp."[160]

Washington spent the day strengthening the fort and entrenching six massive cannons from Knox's expedition. The royal troops prepared to assault the ramparts on Dorchester Heights, but severe weather interrupted. The storm caused large waves in the bay, suspending amphibious operations, and continued until early the next morning. The British counterattack was abandoned, and the American general considered the storm "a remarkable interposition of Providence" and "is for some wise purpose, I have no doubt."[161] He had risked the entire cause with a bluff of sorts. Short of powder and training, he doubted he had the means to successfully assault the city. He used the perception of strength to threaten the enemy and of course, the storm helped.

On March 27, 1776, the British evacuated Boston by sea, and the American army reclaimed the city. Washington's confidence rose, but with measured humility this time. He knew the enemy would target New York next. Strategically, it made sense. Located in the center of the thirteen colonies, it was ideal as a home base. From there, they intended to split New England from the southern and middle colonies. Manhattan and Long Island were perfect launchpads for the royal navy. The American naval power consisted of a handful of small vessels, and Britain had the largest in the world. New York was also heavy with loyalist sympathizers and would welcome occupation.

Washington advanced troops on foot from Boston to New York. Along the way, they came down with typhus, typhoid fever, dysentery, and smallpox. Less than eight thousand were fit for duty, and

---

[160] Flexner, Vol. 2, 75; McCullough, *1776*, 93; Ward, Christopher. *The War of the Revolution*, Vol. 1. (New York: McMillan Co.,1952), 128.

[161] Washington, *Writings*, Vol. 4, 433 (To Landon Carter, March 25, 1776).

one thousand were down sick as the army marched into Manhattan ahead of the British who were resupplying in Newfoundland.

On July 9, news of the Declaration of Independence reached Washington, and he knew there was no turning back. The colonies officially separated from Britain with the signing of this document, and the men knew what was at stake. In his general orders, Washington wrote, "The blessings and protection of Heaven are at all times necessary but especially so in times of public distress and danger—The General hopes and trusts, that every man, will endeavor to live, and act, as becomes a Christian Soldier."[162]

He was certain if they relied on providence, instead of themselves, they would succeed.

On the twenty-first anniversary of Braddock's defeat, Washington had the Declaration read to the army. He knew the cause was for the independence of a new nation conceived in liberty. If they lost, he would be tried and hanged as a traitor, and millions of unborn would never know freedom. He knew the risk, and the following day, he wrote to Congress, "It is certain, that it is not with us to determine in many instances what consequences will flow from our Councils; but yet it behooves us to adopt such, as, under the smiles of a Gracious and all-kind Providence, will be most likely to promote our happiness."[163]

If they sacrificed for the cause, they would change the world.

In late June 1776, the British fleet sailed into New York's Lower Bay and by July began offloading troops onto Staten Island. The royal fleet overwhelmed the harbor with over 100 ships carrying 30,000 troops. Washington moved the American force into Brooklyn on the northern tip of Long Island. A new commander also arrived with the fleet. General William Howe was a distinguished officer with the confidence of the king behind him. He was there to end the rebellion. With the Americans positioned on Long Island, surrounded by water, he devised just the strategy to accomplish it.

---

[162] Ibid., Vol. 5, 245 (General Orders, July 9, 1776).
[163] Ibid., 247 (To the President of Congress, July 10, 1776).

After six weeks of strengthening his force and unsuccessfully convincing the rebels to capitulate, Howe made his move. On August 22, a British and Hessian force landed on Long Island, south of the American troops entrenched in Brooklyn. Howe learned of a little-known dirt road that could be used to outflank their position. Jamaica Pass would bring the royal force on the left flank of Washington's army. The American commander told the men, "If I see any man turn his back today, I will shoot him through. I have two pistols loaded. But I will not ask any man to go further than I do. I will fight as long as I have a leg or an arm." To others he said, "Quit yourselves like men, like soldiers, for all that is worth living for is at stake."[164]

On August 27, Howe sent his army down Jamaica Pass and surprised the rebels. Instantly, the Americans retreated, except for General Alexander Stirling's small force who eventually surrendered. The Americans pulled back to Brooklyn Heights (the northern bank of Long Island across the East River from Manhattan), and thousands were captured or killed surrendering. Washington was trapped with his back to the river and like the frigid night on the island in 1753, he felt alone. Howe's redcoats with their Hessian mercenaries amassed just beyond musket range and, for some reason, stopped and moved back. Washington couldn't believe it. If Howe attacked, the American army would be crushed, yet the British general halted his troops and ordered them to set up camp. They were fatigued from the day's fighting, and the British general was confident the rebels couldn't escape before morning. He was also squeamish to attack dug-in Americans after the high casualties at Bunker Hill. Howe would rest his force, bring up more reinforcements, gain intelligence, and assess the situation at first light. The American commander stayed awake the entire night to restore order.

The next morning, the British camp was firmly in place, and Howe, choosing caution, decided to chip away at the American defenses until they surrendered. Why force the battle? He had all the time in the world. The British suffered less than 400 casualties in the

---

[164] Flexner, Vol. 2, 109–110; McCullough, *1776*, 176; Ward, Vol. 1, 211–215.

battle while the colonists lost 2,000. Why risk another Bunker Hill when he could starve them out?

Washington had to act fast. He had to evacuate the army across the river without detection. How could anyone move a force so large without notice? He refused to focus on the impossibility of this and instead, simply acted. Adapting and improvising would make it possible.

He ordered the evacuation for the night of August 29 and risked the entire cause. The royal navy was threatening to sail up the East River and trap the Americans on shore, but an unexpected storm kept the ships at Staten Island. Another convenient storm? It was time to move. He had 10,000 men, supplies, wagons, and horses to evacuate across the East River into Manhattan before dawn without being spotted. If the operation was discovered, the enemy would massacre them on the water. It had to be perfect.

A small force was left at the entrenchments to watch the British lines and maintain campfires to create the illusion of a sleeping army. The boats had to load the men, row the entire width of the river to Manhattan, unload, row back to Long Island, and reload. This required multiple trips to evacuate every wagon, cannon, horse, and man without arousing suspicion of the enemy three hundred yards away. The oarsmen wrapped cloth around the oars to muffle the noise of rowing. This regiment of fishermen from Marblehead, Massachusetts, commanded by Colonel John Glover, had to hurry without making a sound, and they had one shot to save the army.

By dawn, the last of the men still weren't across the river.

* * * * *

Brooklyn Heights, Long Island, New York, August 30, 1776

The fog blanketed the entire American camp as the sun rose. Washington and the covering force boarded the boats and crossed the river behind the cover of mist just in time. A few British sentries realized once the fog burned away in the sun what had happened. Alerting the commander and firing on the boats visible in the distance, Howe knew he'd been tricked.

Not one American was left behind, and Washington was last to board a boat. He was convinced providence had saved them. Even with all their effort, time ran out. But then the glorious fog granted them just enough time to complete the evacuation. It was unexplainable.

His mental stamina couldn't contemplate it anymore. He needed to prepare for Howe's next push. Determined to take New York City, the British commander would strike soon, and Washington needed to be ready.

Reaching headquarters that morning, George collapsed from exhaustion. The stress alone was unbearable. "I had hardly been off my horse and had never closed my eyes."[165] He hadn't slept for two days.

A miracle had saved them, but victory would come at a much higher price.

* * * * *

Kip's Bay, New York, September 15, 1776

"*Take the walls!*"

"*Take the cornfield!*"[166] Washington galloped after the retreating men, striking at them with his riding whip and shouting at them to turn and fight, but they continued to run, "I used every means in my power to rally and to get them into some order; but my attempts were fruitless and ineffectual; and on the appearance of a small party of the enemy...their disorder increased, and they ran away in the greatest confusion, without firing a single shot."[167]

---

[165] Washington, *Writings*, Vol. 5, 506 (To the President of Congress, August 31, 1776); Flexner, Vol. 2, 115.

[166] Flexner, Vol. 2, 123; Freeman, *Washington*, 292–293; McCullough, *1776*, 212; Davis, *Washington*, 125–126.

[167] Washington, *Writings*, Vol.6, 58 (To the President of Congress, September 16, 1776).

Losing his temper, he threw his hat to the ground and shouted, *"Good God! Are these the men with whom I am to defend America?"*[168]

Alone, he calmly watched as the enemy charged. His aides grabbed the reins of his horse and led him out of danger. After the debacle on Brooklyn Heights, he was angry, disappointed, and ready to give up. General Nathanael Greene observed "he sought death rather than life."[169]

Howe's amphibious assault was swift and unexpected at Kip's Bay. The British moved up the East River past Washington's position and into his rear again. When he heard the cannons, he raced the four miles to reach the front. A meager force of militia (450 men) manned the defenses at Kip's Bay, and the minute the defenders saw the large bayonets gleaming in the sun, they ran like jackrabbits. The American general now faced an inevitable retreat north through Manhattan Island into Harlem.

At Harlem Heights the following day, Washington sent Captain Thomas Knowlton and over one hundred of his rangers to probe Howe's lines. When Knowlton's men encountered the enemy lines, they fought a minor skirmish using a stone wall for protection. Losing ten men, the rangers pulled back while the British sounded a fox call, mocking them. Insulted, Washington sent a larger force around Howe's right flank. "I am resolved not to be forced from this ground while I have life," he proclaimed.[170]

The redcoats and Hessians were unexpectedly surprised by the rebel fighting spirit and retreated. American casualties were over one hundred, and Captain Knowlton was among the dead. Washington knew men like Knowlton were irreplaceable, but his faith in the army returned for a time. Howe reinforced his retreating line, and Washington had no choice but to retreat again. His army was dwindling away from sickness, desertion, and expiring enlistments, and the British were too numerous.

---

[168] Flexner, Vol. 2, 123; McCullough, *1776*, 212; Fischer, 104; Chernow, 254.
[169] Ibid.; Davis, *Washington*, 126; Chernow, 254.
[170] Washington, *Writings*, Vol. 6, 138 (To Lund Washington, September 30, 1776); Flexner, Vol. 2, 131.

As the last of the American army pulled out of New York City, someone attempted to burn it down. It may have been angry Americans tired of retreating or rogue British soldiers trying to stir up more anti-rebel sentiment. There was no evidence either commander of the rival armies ordered it. Fortunately, the fire only consumed part of the city and the American army remained on the northern tip of Manhattan—once again, with their back against the water.

On October 12, the British landed on Manhattan Island, nine miles away from Washington's position. He knew this was a potential trap and called for a withdrawal to mainland New York state. He left a contingent force at Fort Washington to hold the enemy back while the army pulled back. Howe would have to deal with this before pursuing the main force, and Washington continued a strategy of preserving the army. If the army survived, the cause would. He would keep this in mind throughout the war.

Withdrawing back to White Plains, New York, the Americans constructed entrenchments and prepared to hold the line. On October 28, Howe attacked the fortifications and drove them back. As the British occupied the former redoubts, Washington was amazed again that Howe didn't attack. Instead, his men made camp and settled in just like at Brooklyn Heights. Eight days later, the British general pulled up stakes and headed back to New York City. The weather was getting cooler, and Howe decided to go into winter quarters early. He was done with major operations for 1776, and wanted to enjoy his captured prize now. New York City and another man's wife had him under their spell. He had a small fort to take and could do this from the comfort of the city.

Washington believed Howe had other intentions than Fort Washington. Was it the capital, Philadelphia? The city where the Declaration of Independence was signed and Congress resided would be a nice political victory for the Crown. Howe could capture all the traitors and possibly end the Revolution in a single assault.

Washington raced his army for New Jersey to block any overland invasion to take Philadelphia. He left a force of 7,000 under General Charles Lee at White Plains to cover the Hudson valley and to hit the right flank of a British strike into New Jersey. Standing on the Jersey shore on November 16, the American general was an eyewitness to the Fort Washington surrender. Nearly 3,000 men were captured in that single action. As if this wasn't bad enough, the next day, Massachusetts volunteer enlistments would expire, and on November 30 and December 31, nearly all the remaining enlistments were up.

With desertion, sickness, and expiring enlistments, he faced losing the army without a battle. They were running low on supplies, and returning home was better than starving. Many of them enlisted in the spring and still wore warm weather clothes. Some men's clothing had deteriorated from the elements, and many needed pants, shirts, and shoes. If Congress wasn't going to supply these essentials to the army, then how did they think it could fight a war? Washington pleaded with Congress for provisions, but they were too weak to act. Each state provided its own men and supplies, but many couldn't raise the money to pay for them. Some states failed to do their part while others couldn't provide the difference. Some contractors hired to deliver the supplies were corrupt and sold them instead to the British for real money, not the worthless American currency.

Washington watched the rest of New York fall from the New Jersey shore and contemplated his next move. While the American army sat dwindling in New Jersey, General Charles Lee sat in New York, ignoring Washington's pleas to rejoin the main army. The 7,000 men he commanded were badly needed to replace losses. Lee evaded and delayed complying with Washington's pleas, using excuses that his men were ill-equipped, the routes were obstructed, and he had better "schemes" to discuss with the commander, though he never got around to offering any. He claimed the militia wanted him to stay in New York as if the militia had authority over him. Washington wrote with respect for Lee's rank and experience (Lee was in the British army before the war), pleading again, "I have so frequently mentioned our situation, and the necessity of your aid, that it is painful to me to add a word upon the Subject. Let me once more request and entreat you to march immediately."[171]

---

[171] Ibid., 370 (To Major General Charles Lee, December 14, 1776); Fischer, 148.

Lee continued to ignore his letters. Instead of returning the commanding general's letters, Lee wrote to Washington's adjutant general, Joseph Reed. Reed kept correspondence with the insubordinate general and once added a postscript to Washington's own letter to Lee before sending it. He told Lee that Washington was "indecisive" and Reed was supposed to be one of the commander's trusted advisors.

A courier from General Lee rode into camp one day with a letter addressed to Joseph Reed. Reed was away on an errand that day, so Washington, figuring the message of a military nature, not a personal one, opened it. Inside the note, Lee responded to Reed's postscript agreeing "that fatal indecision of mind which in war is a much greater disqualification than stupidity, or even want of personal courage, accident may put a decisive blunder in the right, but eternal defeat and miscarriage must attend the man of the best parts if cursed with indecision."[172] Washington knew who the accused was but never said a word.

He forwarded the letter to Reed with a written statement in the commander's hand, "The enclosed was put into my hands by an express from White Plains. Having no idea of its being a private letter, much less suspecting the tendency of the correspondence, I opened it."[173] This was all he said and wouldn't discredit himself by wallowing in the mud or fight the will of providence. Lee was scheming for position, and Washington wasn't about to let it undermine the greater cause.

Months later, he wrote Reed his true feelings about it. "I was hurt not because I thought my judgment wronged by the expressions contained in it, but because the same sentiments were not communicated immediately to myself...entitled me, I thought, to your advice upon any point which I appeared to be wanting...withholding that

[172] Flexner, Vol. 2, 154; Freeman, *Washington*, 310.
[173] Washington, *Writings*, Vol. 6, 313 (To Colonel Joseph Reed, November 30, 1776).

advice from me and censuring my conduct to another was such an argument of disingenuity that I was not a little mortified at it."[174]

He wasn't angry about the criticism, but only that Reed did it behind his back. His character told him that criticism was expected, but not a betrayal of trust. From his own self-doubt as an officer, Washington refused to reprimand his experienced generals. He gave respect when respect wasn't deserved because he had developed the trait of humility from his own failures.

This trait would serve him well in the days to come. For now, he had to focus on the struggle ahead.

* * * * *

On December 1, 1776, a large part of the army's enlistments expired. General Charles Cornwallis and his army of over 6,000 men were within six miles of the American camp. Washington tried to persuade the New Jersey militia to stay past their enlistments, but they refused. He was left with only 3,400 effective men to protect Philadelphia.

Lee still refused to comply with his orders, so he moved the army into Pennsylvania and camped on the bank of the Delaware River. The British conquered Rhode Island without a fight and offered amnesty to any who would take an oath of allegiance to the Crown. Congress fled to Baltimore in panic, fearing an invasion of Philadelphia.

To most of the world, the war for independence was over. Even Washington lost confidence in what Thomas Paine called "the black times of Seventy-six."[175] After Reed and Lee's intrigue, many in Congress started to criticize his ability. He also had 3,400 tired, hungry, and ill-supplied amateurs to oppose 6,000 rested, overfed, and oversupplied professionals of the prosperous British military.

---

[174] Ibid., Vol. 8, 247 (To Joseph Reed, June 14, 1777); Flexner, Vol. 2, 160.
[175] *Complete Writings of Thomas Paine, 2 volumes.* (New York: 1945), 80 (To Samuel Adams, January 1, 1803); Fischer, 140.

Writing to his nephew, he was brutally honest: "If every nerve is not strained to recruit a new Army with all possible expedition, I think the game is pretty well up."[176]

His faith and resolve faltered because he couldn't see a way out. On January 1, the army would be reduced to twelve hundred, and he knew Cornwallis would aim for Philadelphia once the Delaware River froze. How was he to fight the most powerful military on Earth with no money, food, or men? It was insanity.

On December 12, Lee finally marched his army. The first night, Lee stayed several miles away from the main army at White Tavern, an inn kept by a widow, with only a dozen guards. Loyalists got wind of Lee's whereabouts and told British patrols. Riding up to White Tavern, they chased away the guards, surrounded the house, and fired through the windows, forcing Lee to surrender. As a prisoner, he was considered a traitor by the British, but Lee was a conniving self-centered eccentric who cozied up to anyone who benefited him. He even sent a message to General Howe offering advice on beating Washington and ending the war. Even the British commander was disgusted by Lee's lack of character but was convinced he captured the only competent general on the American side. If this was the best they had, Howe wasn't worried. With leaders like Lee, it was only a matter of time before the rebellion came crashing down from within.

Word of Lee's capture came like another nail in the coffin. Washington was disappointed by Lee's "folly" but soon accepted it. Writing to his brother John Augustine, December 18, he remained faithful something would deliver them from the abyss:

> You can form no Idea of the perplexity of my Situation. No Man, I believe, ever had a greater choice of difficulties and less means to extricate himself from them. However, under a full per-suasion of the justice of our Cause I cannot [but think the prospect will brighten, although for a

---

[176] Washington, *Writings*, Vol. 6, 398 (To John A. Washington, December 18, 1776); Davis, 155.

wise purpose it is, at present hid under a cloud]
entertain an Idea that it will finally sink tho' it
may remain for some time under a Cloud. [177]

Whether providence acted or not, it freed Washington from a
command problem, and Lee's army was ordered to join the main
force. By December 20, his army had doubled, and it was time to do
something.

Thomas Paine's *The Crisis* was published and read in camp that
December. Paine lived among the men and described their struggles.
He struck a chord when he captured the indomitable spirit of those
who remained even at their lowest point. His words had a resounding
effect on the men:

> These are the times that try men's souls. The
> summer soldier and the sunshine patriot will, in
> this crisis, shrink from the service of his country;
> but he that stands it now, deserves the love and
> thanks of man and woman. Tyranny, like hell,
> is not easily conquered; yet we have this conso-
> lation with us, that the harder the conflict, the
> more glorious the triumph. What we obtain too
> cheap, we esteem too lightly—tis dearness only
> that gives everything its value...By perseverance
> and fortitude we have the prospect of a glori-
> ous issue; by cowardice and submission, the sad
> choice of a variety of evils...[178]

It was the rallying cry for patriots everywhere, and Washington
knew that some decisive action was needed to save the cause and promote enlistments. He believed that providence would lead the way if
he served a higher purpose. His duty was to save the cause and lead it

---

[177] Ibid.
[178] Paine, Thomas. *The Crisis, Part 1*. (New York: Peter Eckler Publishing
Co.,1918), 69, 78.

to victory, but also to instill in the men's minds that it could be done. How could he pull off a miracle in less than two weeks?

General William Howe believed the Americans were beaten and posed no threat. They were nothing more than a nuisance now. His subordinate general, James Grant, controlled the forces in New Jersey and agreed with him. Grant scattered his troops throughout New Jersey because smaller garrisons could forage for food easier than one large force. Stationed at Trenton, New Jersey, directly across the Delaware River from Washington's army, were two to three thousand Hessian soldiers. Hessians, the mercenaries hired from the German states who fought for Britain were indentured servant-soldiers who had no loyalty to the Crown and received little of the money their governments collected for their service. Many deserted during the war and made lives in America. Colonel Johann Rall, the Hessian commander, was convinced from the battles in New York that they could handle any attack from the farmers and young boys who had run from them in Long Island and Kip's Bay.

Washington wrote to General Horatio Gates on December 14 about his suspicion that Howe would attack Philadelphia and they must act soon; "If we can draw our Forces together I trust under the smiles of Providence, we may yet effect an important stroke, or at least, prevent General Howe from executing his Plan."[179]

Ironically, it was Joseph Reed that suggested the bold plan to attack Trenton and the advantages of such an attack. On December 22, Washington called a council of war to plan the operation.

The plan was hashed out in detail. While the main army was crossing the Delaware at McConkey's Ferry, nine miles north of Trenton, General James Ewing and his Pennsylvanian militia were to cross directly over to Trenton. Farther downstream, Colonel John Cadwalader and his troops were to cross below the town. This elaborate plan called for coordination by the three forces and precision timing. Unknown to Washington, a spy was privy to the plan and

---

[179] Washington, *Writings*, Vol. 6, 372 (To Major General Horatio Gates, December 14, 1776).

forwarded it to the enemy. When Colonel Rall received this news, he arrogantly replied, "Let them come."[180]

On Christmas Eve, Dr. Benjamin Rush visited Washington at headquarters on the Delaware. Amidst the depressed state of things, Rush wrote about an incident which gained significance later. "While I was talking to him, I observed him to play with his pen and ink upon several small pieces of paper. One of them by accident fell upon the floor near my feet. I was struck with the inscription upon it. It was 'Victory or Death.'"[181]

It was the only two options he had left.

* * * * *

Christmas night, 1776, Delaware River

Had he done everything possible to ensure the success of this operation? Was there any weakness in the plan?

These thoughts bombarded Washington incessantly while he sat aboard one of the boats ferrying him and the 2,400 other men across the Delaware River. It was nearly midnight and they were still not across.

The ice in the river hindered the long poles the oarsmen used to move the boats across. The same Marblehead Regiment who pulled off the miracle at Brooklyn Heights was attempting to perform another. Loading took too much time. Everything always took too much time. There seemed to always be something in their way.

The river was unbearable because of the frosty gale and swirling snow. His cape was no protection against the piercing wind, and he noticed some of the men were without shoes or winter clothing, yet they remained. The sky was dirty and the hue of mud like the river and not a sliver of moonlight cut the darkness. Only the glow of the

---

[180] Flexner, Vol. 2, 173–174; Fischer, 204; Davis, 161.
[181] Fischer, 220; McCullough, *1776*, 273; Chernow, 272; Ketchum, Richard M. *The Winter Soldiers: The Battles for Trenton and Princeton.* (New York: Doubleday/First Owl Books Edition, 1973/1999), 240–241.

snow on the banks was visible. Horses, equipment, cannons, and men were crammed into the vessels, and the only sound was an occasional snort from the animals or a creak of an oar. The musty odor of horseflesh, river water, and sweat added to the discomfort of falling temperatures.

Washington thought of another December night much like this one over twenty years ago—of he and Gist trapped on an island with no hope of survival. Once again, he felt the same isolation and abandonment. He was on another island, alone this time, and a frozen river wasn't salvation but a curse. Daylight wouldn't bring hope but new problems, and if discovered early, the operation was likely doomed.

They needed to be victorious this time. He had gambled everything on it. Why did everything have to be like this, always a struggle? Maybe it was like Paine said: "The harder the conflict, the more glorious the triumph. What we obtain too cheap, we esteem too lightly—tis dearness only that gives everything its value."

He pondered this for a moment. This was why he chose the password, "Victory or Death." They had to win this or the cause would die. They would not fail. Like the night on the island, he would rely on providence. Whatever happened would be for the best. He knew this, but every time he faced adversity, he would forget again.

Earlier that day, George wrote to Robert Morris, the Philadelphian financier:

> I agree with you, that it is in vain to ruminate upon, or even reflect upon the Authors or Causes of our present Misfortunes, we should rather exert ourselves, and look forward with Hopes, that some lucky Chance may yet turn up in our Favour. Bad as our prospects are, I should not have the least doubt of Success in the End, did not the late Treachery and defection of those who stood foremost in the Opposition, while Fortune smiled upon us, make me fearful that many more

will follow their Example, who by using their Influence with some, and working upon the Fears of others, may extend the Circle so as to take in whole Towns, Counties, nay Provinces. Of this we have a recent Instance in Jersey, and I wish many parts of Pennsylvania may not be ready to receive the Yoke.[182]

Observing the men in his own boat, he saw determination on their faces. It was there, regardless of their suffering. They were malnourished from lack of food, freezing from want of clothing, and tired from want of victories; but they were there, and it empowered him. One victory might spark the spirit of the cause and refill the ranks. One win might convince France to help. It had to work.

His time on the island taught him he must remain faithful. Bowing his head, he prayed.

* * * * *

The boats used to cross the Delaware were flat-bottomed Durham boats. They were forty to sixty-feet-long, eight-feet-wide, and two-feet-deep. Its crew of four used setting poles, two on each side. Pushing the poles against the bottom of the river at the bow, the four men walked along the running boards to the stern and propelled the boat forward approximately the length of the vessel. This was repeated until the opposite shore was reached, but the floating ice made the crossing take longer than anticipated.

Around 11:00 p.m., hail and sleet accompanied by high wind blew out of the northeast. The army was expected to be across the river by midnight with five hours to spare until dawn to cover the nine-mile walk to Trenton. It was 4:00 a.m. before the entire force reached the New Jersey side and were ready to march. They were four hours behind, and Washington's officers began to doubt a surprise

---

[182] Washington, *Writings*, Vol. 6, 436–437 (To Robert Morris, December 25, 1776).

attack. He remained steadfast, though stressed. Writing the next day of this to the president of Congress, he expanded:

> ...the Quantity of Ice, made that Night, impeded the passage of the Boats so much, that it was three O'Clock before the Artillery could all get over, and near four, before the Troops took up their line of march. This made me despair of surprising the Town, as I well knew we could not reach it before the day was fairly broke, but as I was certain there was no making a Retreat without being discovered, and harassed on repassing the River, I determined to push on at all Events.[183]

General Ewing and Colonel Cadwalader were still tied up on the Pennsylvanian side. At their points of crossing, a massive ice jam prevented them from reaching the Jersey side. The American commander wasn't aware of this but still depended on both forces when they entered the town. Little did he know, they were on their own.

A messenger from General Sullivan warned the general the storm was soaking the powder, making the muskets useless. Washington answered him, "Tell General Sullivan to use the bayonet. I am resolved to take Trenton." Nothing would discourage this attack. He was committed to "victory or death" and pushed on.

The nine miles to Trenton was treacherous with an ice-covered ground and a frozen creek to cross with horses and artillery, the cold remained a hindrance. Some soldiers used blankets to cover themselves and tied rags around their feet for shoes. The icy road cut through the rags and left trails of bloody footprints in the snow, but the men never complained. As daylight threatened, Washington feared he had lost the element of surprise. Then, like a guardian angel, the weather shifted to a heavy snowstorm and provided cover.

---

[183] Ibid., 442 (To the President of Congress, December 27, 1776).

Halting the column for a quick breakfast, some of the men fell asleep on the side of the road; two never woke up.[184]

Closing in on Trenton, Washington separated his forces into two columns. One column was commanded by General Sullivan and the other by General Nathanael Greene. The two wings moved down two parallel roads converging on the town. This double envelopment from both ends of Trenton would seal off any escape by the Hessians.

The commander remained with Greene's wing, and as dawn approached, he urged them to, "Press on, men. Press on."[185]

Once Greene's column was moving again, they closed in on the village. Around 8:00 a.m., they encountered a forward picket post and skirmished with the sentries, chasing them away. The storm screened the noise, but other circumstances aided them in surprising the Hessians.

On Christmas night, as Washington loaded into the boats, Colonel Rall, the Hessian commander, sat by a cozy fire playing cards and drinking wine to celebrate the holiday. In the middle of his game, there was a knock at the door. Someone pleaded to speak with him, but his servant refused to interrupt the game. The caller scribbled a note, warning of the American army's coming attack. The servant handed the tipsy German the note, but he simply put it in his pocket, unread, and continued the revelry.[186]

At approximately 8:30 a.m., December 26, the battle of Trenton began. Greene's division divided into three smaller forces under generals—Lord Stirling, Hugh Mercer, and Greene himself—and surrounded the town. General Hugh Mercer coincidentally was General George S. Patton's great-grandfather. General Knox directed cannon fire down the main street into the scrambling Hessians who attempted to form ranks. Two of Knox's guns were commanded by future Secretary of State Alexander Hamilton, a nineteen-year-old captain of artillery.

---

[184] McCullough, *1776*, 277; Flexner, Vol. 2, 175; Davis, *Washington*, 162; Ward, Vol. 1, 295.

[185] Fischer, 228–231; Ketchum, *Winter Soldiers*, 253.

[186] Ibid., 232; Freeman, *Washington*, 320; McCullough, *1776*, 279-280; Ketchum, *Winter Soldiers*, 238–239.

The Hessians fired two volleys, then fell back in disorder. Knox ordered the Virginian regiment with some New England troops to charge forward and capture the enemy battery. Lieutenant James Monroe, future President of the United States, led the Virginians into action. Earlier that morning, Monroe met a young man on the road, John Riker, who mistook the Americans for British and ordered him off his land. Monroe, thinking Riker a loyalist, threatened to arrest him, but Riker realized his mistake and apologized. The young doctor volunteered his newly acquired surgical skills to the army, and the young lieutenant happily accepted.[187]

As the Virginians took the battery, a musket ball severed an artery in Monroe's leg. Dr. Riker clamped the severed artery before he bled to death. Riker had surgical training, a rarity in 1776 and more so in the American army. If Monroe hadn't happened upon the young doctor, he wouldn't have lived to become president.[188]

After the Virginians took the battery, Rall rallied his troops and made a lunge to retake the village. The American infantry sought shelter inside the houses to keep their powder and flints dry and poured an enfilading fire into the Germans. Hamilton's cannon joined in as Sullivan moved to intercept a Hessian retreat south of town. Rall ordered a retreat just as two musket balls struck him in the side, knocking him off his horse. With their commander down, the Hessians surrendered. Washington learned of the surrender when Major James Wilkinson brought him the news. Taking the major's hand and smiling, he said, "This is a glorious day for our country, Major Wilkinson."

Rall died two days later from his wounds. Found on his body in a pocket of his uniform was a note warning of the attack. He never read it.[189]

* * * * *

---

[187] Ibid., 231.
[188] Ibid., 247; McCullough, *1776*, 281; Ward, Vol. 1, 298–300.
[189] McCullough, *1776*, 280–281; Chernow, 276; Ward, Vol. 1, 297–300; Ketchum, *Winter Soldiers*, 239.

The Hessians had twenty-two killed and eighty-three wounded. There were 896 prisoners, six cannons, several muskets, ammunition, powder, and other supplies to add to their total. The American losses were four wounded. The three-part plan to take Trenton had failed, and the crossing and march took longer than expected. The storm which many cursed was actually a blessing by covering their advance. Washington saw the men were exhausted and needed rest, but they were burdened with 896 prisoners now, so he decided to return to the safety of the Pennsylvania side. They followed the trail of bloody footprints the nine miles back to the crossing. Boarding the boats this time, under far worse conditions, the Americans crossed the river again. This time, the river was nearly frozen solid as if to remind him providence was still there.

Though he had a victory, it was short-lived. A big segment of the enlistments would expire on New Year's Eve, and he needed to make another move before then.

On December 29, he ordered the troops back across the Delaware to Trenton for the second time. Even with the victory, it would take time for new recruits to arrive. He had to convince these starving, half-naked, and unpaid men who fought so bravely at Trenton to stay a while longer.

How could he ask them to do more than they already did? Why would they even consider doing more?

* * * * *

Trenton, New Jersey, December 29, 1776

Washington galloped to the front of the men in formation and spoke in a serious tone. A sergeant present remembered his words. "My brave fellows, you have done all I asked you to do, and more than could be reasonably expected." He looked at his army of ragged scarecrows. Some were old men, others just boys. They deserved better than this, but his pleas to Congress fell on deaf ears. He continued, "But your country is at stake, your wives, your houses, and all that you hold dear. You have worn yourselves out with the fatigues and hardships, but we know not how to spare you."

He needed them for one more fight. The opportunity was there, waiting, but he needed an army to take advantage of it. If these men refused, the opportunity would be lost. Appealing to them with genuine emotion, he pleaded, "If you will consent to stay one month longer, you will render service to the cause of liberty, and to your country, which you probably can never do under any other circumstances."

The men remained silent for a few moments before they started talking to each other. "I'll stay if you stay" passed between them. One by one, men stepped forward. Washington's words had found their mark. Nearly every man stepped forward. If their commander was sacrificing for the cause, then they could sacrifice one more month. They knew it might mean death and could have easily gone home, but they stayed for the same reason their commander was still there. Some tried to say they stayed for the money, but it was more than greed that inspired them to risk their lives. Washington inspired a confidence in them. He needed them, and they relied on him for courage.[190]

Now the question was, could he pull off another victory?

* * * * *

While the American general convinced the men to stay, General Charles Cornwallis, commander of British and Hessian troops in New Jersey, twelve miles away at Princeton, received word of the Trenton disaster. Forming a 5,500-man force on January 2, 1777, he marched to retake the town. Impeding Cornwallis's army was the sudden mild weather, which thawed the roads and slowed progress. Regardless, the British made good time to Trenton.

Washington's army was positioned along the south bank of Assunpink Creek. Knowing Trenton was susceptible to attack, he constructed earthworks south of town and waited for Cornwallis.

---

[190] Flexner, Vol. 2, 181; Chernow, 278-279; McCullough, *1776*, 285-286; Fischer, 272-273.

The British arrived in Trenton the same day after a hurried but difficult march; Cornwallis ordered an immediate attack on the Americans across the creek. Attempting to cross a bridge only allowed a limited number of men at a time. Washington concentrated fire on the narrow passage of the bridge and turned the creek red with British blood. After being repulsed three times, the British commander decided to use the artillery. The two sides fired at each other until dark without doing much damage. The redcoats, exhausted from their long march and repeated repulses, retired for the night. Cornwallis saw the American prey trapped on the Jersey side with their backs to the Delaware. Escape would leave them sitting ducks if they crossed the river. They weren't going anywhere, he was sure. It could wait till morning. The Virginian planter had messed up this time. Assuring his officers, Cornwallis said, "We've got the Old Fox now. We'll go over and bag him in the morning."[191]

Washington knew the army was in a bad position, but this was by design. Calling a council of war, he laid out his daring strategy. Drawing on the Brooklyn Heights escape, they would sneak out of Trenton in the night, not across the river into Pennsylvania but into the heart of British territory. The town Cornwallis left weaker when he marched 5,500 men and weapons to Trenton was Washington's target. The same problem of mild weather and miry roads plaguing the British could cause problems for the Americans. Cannon and supply wagons stuck in the mud could wreck the entire plan. Washington considered this possibility, but as the temperature plummeted, an arctic wind hardened the roads. The weather was still on their side, it seemed.

The whole plan hinged on slipping away in the dark. The wagon and cannon wheels were wrapped with cloth to deaden the noise, and the men were ordered to march with unloaded muskets to decrease the chance of an accidental discharge. Only the general officers knew their destination. The army began their march around 1:00 a.m. They left behind a small party to tend the campfires and

[191] Ibid., 183; Fischer, 313; Freeman, *Washington*, 327; Ketchum, *Winter Soldiers*, 291.

keep up appearances. Just like before, Washington was learning from past successes as well as failures. Of course, the British sentries would be expecting him to sneak across the river, not deep into enemy lines.

Once again, everything took longer than expected. The soldiers were six miles from Princeton by seven that morning. Washington detached a smaller force to cover the road back to Trenton, because by daylight, Cornwallis would discover the ruse and realize Princeton was in danger. The surprise would be gone once the sun rose. Everything happened for a divine purpose, and the hand of providence would direct them to the desired outcome.

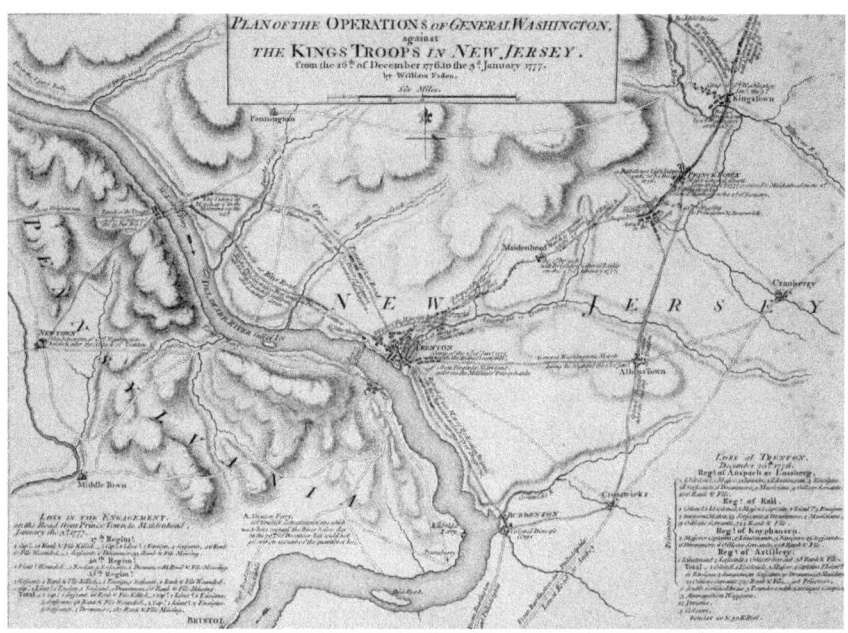

The Battles of Trenton & Princeton, 1776-77

On January 3, 1777, the Battle of Princeton began as chaotic as every other battle in this war. In the early hours of morning, Cornwallis called for more reinforcements from Princeton to aid in the scheduled attack against Washington's army. The American left flank near Princeton who guarded a bridge to block any retreats, were about to run into these reinforcements. Spotting the enemy, Lieutenant Colonel Charles Mawhood quickly formed his redcoats for battle. With only forty yards separating the two lines, the British opened fire.

After a few volleys, Mawhood ordered a bayonet charge, and the Americans, once again, panicked. It looked like another Kip's Bay with all the fleeing soldiers. The officers tried to rally the men but became casualties themselves. General Hugh Mercer was mortally wounded after being surrounded by the enemy and told to surrender (they thought he was General Washington). Mercer drew his saber and slashed away at the British and urged his men to stand their ground. Bludgeoned by a musket and bayoneted seven times, he was left for dead. Laid under a tree, he continued to direct his men. Mawhood's men bayoneted surrendering and wounded Americans in this skirmish. A second wave of Washington's army arrived on the field behind the retreating men and fired two volleys. Fearing the same treatment as Mercer's force, they started to withdraw.

Washington heard the musket fire and galloped toward the action to investigate. Arriving on the field, he took command. Waving his hat and riding at the front of the line, he put himself thirty paces away from the charging enemy without any fear and shouted, "Parade with us, my brave fellows! There is but a handful of the enemy, and we will have them directly."[192]

An American general, six-foot-three, riding a white horse only thirty paces away, made an easy target. One of his officers covered their face with their hat, fearing Washington's death. Mawhood's soldiers were amazed by his courage and never fired at him and the retreating Americans were awestruck. They never witnessed such bravery, and it inspired them to return to the battlefield. If General Washington was willing to risk his life for the cause, why couldn't they? Charging into battle, fearless, they would not retreat again. Some would die that day, but Washington's example reminded them of why they were fighting. This was bigger than any of them. It was the birth of freedom for all mankind, and he was its shining light.

---

[192] Ibid., 185; Fischer, 332–334; Freeman, *Washington*, 329; McCullough, *1776*, 289.

As the Americans attacked with renewed spirit, the British lines broke and retreated. Washington, possibly remembering Harlem Heights, shouted, "It is a fine fox chase my boys!" The "Old Fox" was having a fox chase of his own. After Hamilton's artillery cannonaded a college building, the town of Princeton surrendered.[193]

At Trenton, Cornwallis awoke to a deserted American camp. He realized he'd been duped and quick marched his army back to Princeton. Amazingly, the forward garrison reached the bridge outside the college town as the battle raged. The enemy was checked by Washington's rear guard, and just like at Trenton, the British couldn't get over the bridge.

The Americans had little sleep for two days and needed rest. Washington considered another assault on New Brunswick but, after careful thought, decided to march to Morristown, New Jersey. Hidden among the hills, Morristown would provide protection, rest, and forage for more provisions.

After learning of Princeton's surrender, Cornwallis was convinced that the "Old Fox" would strike again, and New Brunswick was the obvious target. He just missed Washington when he headed in the opposite direction.

Nearly half of the men convinced to reenlist were killed at Princeton or dead by disease that February. Hugh Mercer succumbed to his wounds nine days later.

Trenton and Princeton were major turning points in the war. These two victories convinced the British that Americans could win. These two battles caused Britain to change its strategy and sent a message that Washington was more than a farmer. His army could no longer be thought of as just rabble. The American army was on its feet and fighting, and its commander knew more failure would come, but now they knew how to adapt when it did. He would trust in providence to do the rest. If they were to be a new nation, they couldn't avoid the hard work or sacrifice required to become one.

A new confidence returned to the American people and the cause. Men joined the army and filled the ranks again. Congress

---

[193] Ibid., 185-187; Fischer, 334–336; Davis, *Washington*, 189–190.

trusted Washington enough to give him power to raise battalions, appoint officers, and exercise dictatorial control over the military for six months.

Most Americans believed these two battles were signs of God's blessings. Providence protected the cause and their general. Washington wrote soon after Trenton and Princeton, "In a word, I believe I may with truth add, that I do not think that any officer since the creation ever had such a variety of difficulties and perplexities to encounter as I have. How we shall be able to rub along till the new army is raised, I know not. Providence has heretofore saved us in a remarkable manner, and on this we must principally rely."[194]

He would now have to learn to rely upon himself as well.

* * * * *

Washington retired the army to winter quarters for the rest of the 1776-77 season. Foraging raids were sent out to gather food and necessities. He refused to remain idle and used hit-and-run strikes by smaller groups of regulars and militia to keep the enemy confused and on edge. Ambuscades, snipers, and sabotage exhausted Howe's army, lowering their morale. As long as Howe remained in New Jersey, he would make it a living hell for his army.

While Howe dealt with this, Washington had his own problems. Smallpox spread throughout Morristown and he ordered a risky inoculation method to contain the disease. A doctor would burst an infected patient's pustule and smear the diseased fluid into tiny premade cuts on the healthy man. Ideally, over several days, the patients would contract a mild case of smallpox, recover quickly, and be immune. Unfortunately, a high percentage contracted a severe case, and many died. This was an effective remedy for most, and the disease was eradicated from the camp. Smallpox killed more soldiers during the war than all the battles of the Revolution combined. The American commander providentially had immunity from his time in Barbados with Lawrence.

---

[194] Washington, *Writings*, Vol. 7, 73 (To John Parke Custis, January 22, 1777).

General Howe sat comfortably in New York City, gambling and enjoying the company of another man's wife. His mistress, Elizabeth Loring, was the wife of loyalist Joshua Loring. Apparently, this affair was arranged between the general and Joshua Loring in exchange for a favorable appointment.[195] Howe did, however, devote some of his time to concocting a new strategy to fight the rebels. This time, they would focus on the capital of the rebellion, Philadelphia. The city which wrote the Declaration and housed the rebellion's Congress would be a psychological blow. Howe's spring offensive depended heavily on challenging the Americans on open ground. The guerilla tactics and ambuscades of rebels in New Jersey was less than honorable warfare. Howe knew if he could lure Washington into a head-to-head confrontation, he could end the war. Philadelphia's fall would snuff out their newfound confidence.

Washington wanted to avoid head-to-head battles, because his army wasn't ready to fight professionals on an open field. His objective was to wear down the British and preserve the army. If this meant sacrificing land, he would. The Revolution was an idea inside of each man. If the army survived, the idea would survive. When the enemy occupied land, it was their responsibility to hold it. Maintaining order and supplying troops required resources and manpower diverted from the field. The American aim was to simply harass the occupation and wear them down.

Washington realized subjugating America was nearly impossible, but he would make the enemy pay for every acre they conquered. The Congress and public opinion was a whole different problem. To them, when the British occupied an area, the perception was one of defeat, regardless of reality. If Howe took Philadelphia, it would affect France's possible intervention, discourage loans, and damage the spirit of the cause. Washington had to defend Philadelphia if only to guard against this perception.

In late May 1777, Howe moved 18,000 British and Hessian troops out of Staten Island into New Jersey. He made a feint for Philadelphia, but Washington recognized the ploy. He knew from

---

[195] Fischer, 72; Davis, *Washington*, 201.

gathered intelligence that Howe had no boats or portable bridges to cross the Delaware and he left behind the heavy baggage. Washington kept his army in the mountains and waited.

Howe then tried to lure him out by appearing to retreat. Washington saw an opportunity and sent three brigades to attack the rear of the British column. Daniel Morgan's legendary sharpshooters pursued a detachment of Hessians several miles back to the main army. Angry and frustrated from Morgan's abuse, Howe's army left a path of destruction in their wake. Howe thought the American commander took the bait and turned to meet the attack, but Washington pulled his troops back behind the hills of Morristown as Howe, returned to Staten Island. By June 30, 1777, British troops no longer occupied an inch of New Jersey. Rhode Island and New York City were their only conquests after two years.

A new grand strategy for the colonies came directly from London. An army from Canada commanded by General John "Gentleman Johnny" Burgoyne would march through northern New York state and join up with Howe. This would cut America in half. Howe would attack Philadelphia to keep Washington's army divided and incapable of concentrating in either theater. General Horatio Gates commanded the northern American army, though the men considered the hero of Ticonderoga, Benedict Arnold, their real leader. Washington sent reinforcements to Gates' army at the expense of his own to counter Burgoyne's invasion, and he was hopeful Gates and Arnold could take care of him before Howe attacked Philadelphia.

On July 23, Howe, with over 260 warships, loaded with baggage, horses, cannon, and more than fifteen thousand men, sailed from New York City—destination unknown.

Washington believed Howe was likely heading north to join Burgoyne, but as he prepared to move north, he received word the British armada was sighted off Delaware Bay, heading straight for Philadelphia. Immediately, he moved the army across the Delaware River to protect the city. On August 2, Howe's fleet disappeared once again, and Washington was puzzled. Was Howe making a feint, like in New Jersey, to draw him away from the northern campaign? Or did he intend to strike Philadelphia. The American commander needed better intelligence to make a call. Rash decisions in his past made him apprehensive. Two and a half weeks later, the fleet showed up in Chesapeake Bay, and men were coming ashore. The Chesapeake Bay provided an overland route to Philadelphia thirty-three miles southwest of the city.

He learned from trial and error not to make assumptions based on unreliable information. Every success brought another failure to guard against complacency. He was beginning to see it wasn't about battlefield victories as much as it was about perseverance. They needed to outlast the enemy long enough for providence to lead them to victory.

* * * * *

On September 10, 1777, Washington prepared to defend Philadelphia by placing his army along Brandywine Creek. West of the city, this stream was a natural obstacle in Howe's path. He positioned his main force at a crossing called Chad's Ford, located near the main road that Howe would take into the city. He moved three other divisions on the right to protect the north side of the creek. On his left, the creek's rugged heights presented a natural barrier, making it easy to defend. He put one thousand Pennsylvanian militia there. His right was more secure, because locals assured him the Brandywine had no other crossings for six miles. If the British headed for this crossing, his scouts would alert him. A local militia leader familiar with the terrain, Major Spear, and his men were scouting upstream. Spear or light infantry harassing the enemy advance would alert Washington of any surprises. He had reliable intelligence and a contingency plan this time.

At dawn on September 11, Howe attacked the Americans at Chad's Ford. The British force, under the command of General Knyphausen (the Hessian seeking revenge for Trenton), poured heavy artillery across the creek. Washington rode through the men as they cheered. Riding next to him was a young volunteer from France, the

Marquis de Lafayette. Lafayette became a trusted officer and another son. This would be the Frenchman's baptism of fire.

When the two armies clashed, they were separated by the creek and exchanged artillery fire for a few hours without much effect. A message reached Washington, reporting a large enemy force moving upstream and attempting to cross the creek. He refused to believe Howe would divide his forces, especially when the only crossing was six miles away. This would take entirely too long and leave Knyphausen's force vulnerable. He could smash the Hessians first, then fortify the right and wait for the crossing force to arrive.

Fearing the message might be true, Washington prepared an attack across the creek. Then a message from General Sullivan reassured him the militia upstream had "*heard nothing of the enemy above the forks of the Brandywine.*"[196] Washington trusted the militia's familiarity with the area over his regular scouts, and called off the attack across the creek. He worried he was possibly fighting the entire British force, not a divided one, and decided to wait.

Later that day, a sweating hatless farmer rode into Sullivan's line demanding to speak with General Washington. Sullivan wasn't sure about the stranger at first. This stranger's name was Thomas Cheyney, and Sullivan couldn't ignore the tale he told. Maybe there was something to this, Sullivan brought Cheyney to see Washington. The stranger told his account to the commander. He said he woke up early that morning to do some scouting of his own and was only a hundred yards out when he eyed the scarlet tunics of the enemy. They saw him and fired their muskets as he galloped away. He claimed he avoided capture because of his faster horse.

Washington was frustrated. Here was another report of enemy forces north of his position crossing the creek. He had to first decide whether Cheyney was a loyalist trying to spread false information. This area of Pennsylvania was crawling with British sympathizers. Washington asked Cheyney if he knew spies were hanged to see his reactions. The general's staff smiled and shook their heads. The

---

[196] Flexner, Vol. 2, 222.

farmer saw they didn't believe him and was indignant. "I'd have you know I have this day's work as much at heart as e'[v]er a blood of ye!"

Turning to Washington and dropping on one knee, he drew a map in the dirt of the location of the enemy. "Impossible," Washington barked and waited for the man's response.

"You're mistaken, General," Cheyney insisted. "My life for it you're mistaken. By hell, it's so. Put me under guard till you can find out it's so."[197]

Something made Washington doubt his own judgment. Something in Cheyney's voice made him believe the man. Experience told him he couldn't assume and had to decide between two different uncorroborated claims. He needed to consider Cheyney's story but also the possibility of it being a lie. He calmed his mind and searched for an answer.

Just then, two new messengers brought word the enemy was on their side of the creek and closing in on the American right flank. The second message from Sullivan confirmed the first. Howe learned from a local loyalist of an unknown ford and sent the main army north across the creek. Even many locals hadn't known about this ford. With Cornwallis commanding the British force, Howe ordered him to march to the ford, cross the Brandywine, and head south into the American right. His intention was to push the rebels against the creek while Knyphausen attacked from the other side.

Washington moved quickly and ordered the right wing to turn and face the oncoming assault. He then hurried to the front to hasten reinforcements. The moment they encountered Cornwallis's force, they would be fighting from both sides. Cornwallis was on Washington's right and Knyphausen on his left. Once the battle began, the Hessian commander crossed the creek and attacked the American left flank. Five times, the Americans were driven back, and five times, they regained their position but were outnumbered. Sullivan gave the order for his men to withdraw, but it almost became a rout. General Nathanael Greene's men moved up behind Sullivan's fleeing troops and made a valiant last stand, but it was useless. A

---

[197] Ibid.; Davis, 218; Ward, Vol. 1, 346–347.

general retreat was ordered, but this time, the men withdrew in good order. By nightfall, the battle was over, and Howe held the ground.

Losing Brandywine Creek was a matter of indecision and trusting unverified intelligence. He lost the battle but saved his army again. He also misjudged his adversary. He never believed Howe would divide his army. Washington did force Howe to use men and resources to take Philadelphia and kept the British commander from reinforcing Burgoyne at Saratoga. He had been outmaneuvered but not outgeneraled this time.

On September 26, Howe entered Philadelphia to a warm loyalist reception. Washington moved his army away from the city. He couldn't prevent Howe from taking it. The British general felt he handily whipped the rebels, so he confidently divided his forces. He stationed one force in the Philadelphia and a larger one in the suburb village of Germantown. Washington's army was sixteen miles from Germantown and waiting for an opportunity to strike. Rest and reinforcements were needed, but they'd have them in a few days.

On October 2, intelligence received said Howe had ordered three thousand men to the Chesapeake to escort supplies back to the city. Cornwallis then sent a whole battalion to New Jersey and left 9,000 men in Germantown. To sweeten the pot, Washington just received reinforcements of nearly 11,000 soldiers. Once again, multiple factors created opportunity. Calling a council of war, the American generals drew up a plan.

The village of Germantown consisted of four converging roads bordered by houses with fenced-in yards. The British were camped south of the town. The American plan called for four separate forces to attack down all four roads in a pincers movement. Each column would move to a two-mile starting point at 2:00 a.m. on October 4 and wait. At 4:00 a.m., they would march into Germantown before sunrise and surprise the sleeping enemy with bayonets. Of course, nothing went as planned.

The march took longer than expected, and the main force reached the town at sunrise. An advance force charged the British pickets, but not before they had sounded the alarm. This time, the element of surprise was lost, and the Brits pushed back the advance force. Washington sent two more divisions forward, and the enemy retreated a mile before they stopped. General Howe hurried to the sound of battle. Embarrassed by his retreating men, he tried to rally them. "Form, Form! I never saw you retreat before! It's only a scouting party."[198]

An American cannon struck the tree he stood under and rattled the leaves, making it clear this was more than a scouting party. Six British companies barricaded themselves in a massive stone house, the Chew Mansion. They blocked the first floor and fired their muskets through the second-floor windows down on the Americans. This had success and sent Washington's men reeling back.

Washington asked advice from his staff, and some said to bypass the house but leave a regiment to hold it. But General Knox convinced him he could not leave a castle in the army's rear while moving into occupied ground. So, Washington tried sending an officer with a flag of truce to demand their surrender, but it just ended up getting the officer killed. The artillery couldn't smash the thick stone walls, so they tried to burn it down. They couldn't get close enough to the house to set it afire without being shot. The American commander was stymied by this single obstacle and failed to see the larger battlefield.

Then a dense fog settled over the town and huge clouds of powder smoke made it difficult to see thirty yards. Some Americans became disoriented and fired at each other. Others believed the enemy was attacking from behind because of the action at the Chew Mansion. One column got lost on its way to Germantown while another joined the fight at the Chew Mansion. Most of Washington's men weren't pressing Howe's main force and lost the advantage.

Howe saw the Americans distracted with the Chew Mansion and counterattacked their weakened front. Running low of ammunition and fearing they were surrounded, the Americans began to retreat. Washington tried to energize them, but they showed him their empty ammo boxes, and he knew it was over. He came close to victory, but too many mistakes piled up.

---

[198] Ward, Vol. 1, 365; Davis, *Washington*, 232.

Cornwallis chased the American army for eight miles, keeping his distance. Washington marched them another sixteen miles before he stopped.

There was a lesson with the almost victory at Germantown. The Chew House was a symbol of misdirected focus. While focusing on one distraction, he never saw the opportunity in front of him. The men were getting better with every battle, and even their retreats were more disciplined. They were still unorganized, but they were tough and courageous. By forcing Howe to use his troops to defend Philadelphia, instead of reinforcing Burgoyne, Washington secured the victory at Saratoga. General Gates accepted the surrender of General Burgoyne and his 6,000 men on October 17. Many swore Benedict Arnold won the battle and paid for it with a musket ball in his leg, which left him lame. Saratoga was a sweeping victory and defeated an entire British army and its Iroquois Indian allies. The Brandywine and Germantown defeats were the price paid for Saratoga. The repercussions of this victory would determine the course of the war.

Washington and his army needed more tempering. The raw steel of both the general and his men required the heat in the fires of adversity a bit longer to reach its full strength. Their perseverance and indomitable will would forge them as they wandered in a valley of the shadow of death.

* * * * *

Valley Forge, Pennsylvania, Winter, 1777

General Orders, December 17

The Commander in Chief, with the highest satisfaction, expresses his thanks to Officers and Soldiers for fortitude and patience with which they have sustained the fatigues of the Campaign. Although in some instances we unfortunately failed, yet upon the whole Heaven hath smiled upon our arms and crowned them with signal success; and we may upon the best Grounds conclude, that by a Spirited continuance of the Measures necessary for our defense we shall finally obtain the end of our Warfare, Independence, Liberty, and Peace. These are blessings worth contending for at every hazard... Every motive therefore irresistibly urges us, nay commands us, to a firm and manly perseverance in Opposition to our cruel oppressors...[199]

This was Washington's general orders two days before he marched the army to Valley Forge, Pennsylvania, twenty miles from Philadelphia. They retired to winter quarters, keeping a close eye on Howe.

Congress once again criticized him for the two defeats and his decision to make winter quarters instead of resuming hostilities. He knew the condition of his army—Congress did not:

Without arrogance or the smallest deviation from the truth it may be said that, no history, now extant, can furnish an instance of an army's suffering such uncommon hardships as ours have done, and bearing them with the same patience and Fortitude. To see Men without Clothes to cover their nakedness, without Blankets to lay on, without Shoes,—by which their Marches might be traced by the Blood from their feet,— and almost as often without Provisions as with, Marching through frost and Snow, and at Christmas taking up their Winter Quarters within a day's March from the enemy, without a House or Hut to cover them till they could be built, and submitting to it without a murmur, is

---

[199] Washington, Writings, Vol. 10, 167 (General Orders, December 17, 1777).

a Mark of patience and obedience which in my
opinion can scarce be paralleled.[200]

How Congress, who was responsible for appropriating provisions and pay, could be so callous annoyed him to no end. The armchair generals loved to tell him how to conduct the war but were incapable of recognizing his difficulties. He had 2,898 men unfit for duty from the lack of food, clothes, shoes, and blankets. Writing to Congress, Washington explained the army's predicament in honest terms: "…this army must inevitably be reduced to one or another of these three things: starve, dissolve, or disperse in order to obtain subsistence."[201] To the men, he tried to encourage "the Officers and Soldiers, with one heart and one mind, will Resolve to surmount every difficulty with Fortitude and patience becoming their profession and the Sacred Cause in which they are engaged."[202]

These men remained even without proper food and clothes, yet Congress had the audacity to criticize their performance. They could criticize his performance, but he wouldn't allow them to disparage these men. He would also lead by example and suffer when they suffered. There would be no special treatment for the commander or his officers, and he slept in a cold field tent until every man was in a cabin.

Valley Forge was covered in snow and miserable. The men were hungry and feeble, but still somehow built their own shelters. The cabins were constructed of logs and mud. They were sixteen-feet-long by fourteen-feet-wide with three bunks stacked on top of another in each corner of the room and housed twelve. The roofs leaked from rain or thaw and turned the dirt floors of the cabins to mud. Their diet consisted of flour and water mixed into cakes and cooked over a fire. These "firecakes" provided insufficient vitamins and protein, and the men became more susceptible to disease. Many suffered from pneumonia, dysentery, and typhus. Frostbite was so

---

[200] Ibid., Vol. 11, 291–292 (To John Banister, April 21, 1778).
[201] Ibid., Vol. 10, 192 (To the President of Congress, December 23, 1777).
[202] Ibid., 168 (General Orders, December 17, 1777).

common that many had their limbs, fingers, and toes amputated. The camp hospitals were worse, though Indian meal and rice were available there. Nine out of ten who came down with a fever in one of these germ-infested hospitals, died.

Clothes, food, and provisions arrived infrequently to camp and were always inadequate. One time, a shipment of clothing contained only enough for six hundred men in a camp of four thousand. Contractors who were paid to supply the army were often incompetent and corrupt. They sold the American goods to the enemy, because they were offered top dollar to deprive the rebels of supplies. Washington wrote to General Greene:

> Our Situation, as you justly observe is distressing, from a variety of irremediable causes; but more especially from the impracticability of answering the expectations of the world without running hazards which no military principles can justify, and which, in case of failure, might prove the ruin of our cause; patience, and a steady perseverance in such measures as appear warranted by sound reason and policy, must support us under the censure of the one, and dictate a proper line of conduct for the attainment of the other; that is the great object in view.[203]

As if the problem of supply wasn't enough, Washington also had to fight his own generals and congressmen vying for power. Some wanted to remove him from command and replace him with Horatio Gates. To European-trained officers like Gates, Thomas Conway, and Thomas Mifflin, Washington didn't deserve his position as commander-in-chief. They used their influence to convince many in Congress of his incompetence. Many were envious of his status as an idol representing the cause. Some congressmen were afraid of his popularity and feared he would become a dictator with the

---

[203] Ibid., 106–107 (To General Nathanael Greene, November 26, 1777)

army in his charge. General Thomas Conway wrote a stinging letter to General Gates about the commander, calling for his removal. Thomas Mifflin, an old confidant of Washington's, was working to oust him as well.

The winter of 1777–78 would test the American soldiers and their general, pushing them to the breaking point. Descending into the darkest days of the Revolution, Washington wondered if he'd prepared himself enough. Were past experiences enough to withstand the enemy in Philadelphia and the one within himself?

Watching the soldiers suffer and die while dishonorable men jockeyed for position pushed him to the edge of his patience. This wasn't about any one man. It was about the cause.

* * * * *

Colonel James Wilkinson (aide-de-camp to General Gates), a naïve upstart in 1777, was just learning how to conspire and intrigue. He would resurface many times in American history as a conspirator. At this point, he'd been exposed to the attitudes of superiors who conspired to oust Washington. Wilkinson assumed every officer felt the same about the commander.

On his way to deliver the official report of the Saratoga battle to Congress, Wilkinson stopped over at the American camp and dined with General Lord Stirling, Colonel James Monroe, and Major William McWilliams. After dinner, they enjoyed several drinks and Wilkinson became inebriated and talked openly about General Conway's letter to Gates. Thinking everyone agreed with Conway and Gates, he told them the details of the conspiracy against Washington.

Wilkinson was unaware the men at the table didn't share his views. These loyal officers informed the commander of Conway's plot. At first, Washington ignored the news. Believing he should be above the fray, he remained quiet. When hearing that Congress promoted Conway to major general and inspector general, he could no longer ignore it. Conway had served only a year in the American army. Before this, he had served in the French army. From the moment, he arrived, Conway expected promotion over other deserving officers. Knowing how to grease the wheels, he manipulated Congress to get what he wanted. Why should Conway, with no record of accomplishment, judgment, or bravery, be promoted over senior officers who had proven their worth? Washington knew he might lose his best officers to resignations because of this promotion. He tried to calm his enraged officers and assured them justice would prevail in the end.

Gates was given the credit for the Saratoga victory by Congress, even though many claimed Benedict Arnold the true hero of the battle. "*Granny*" Gates (a nickname his men pinned on him) was the key to the unravelling of the conspiracy. When word of Wilkinson's blabbing reached Gates, he panicked and sent a copy of Conway's letter with an explanation to Congress to save his own neck. When Congress questioned Conway, he denied the existence of such a letter. He offered his resignation as a bluff, but Congress accepted it. Thomas Mifflin also resigned, and Conway claimed to be the victim of a conspiracy, but no one was buying it anymore.

Some months later, General Cadwallader, a loyal Washington supporter, challenged Conway to a duel. He put a bullet through his mouth and neck. Conway, believing he was dying, wrote an apology to Washington. He eventually recovered and returned to France, dying in exile twenty-two years later.[204]

Washington wrote to Lafayette:

> But one Gentleman, whose Name you have mentioned, had, I am confident, far different views. His ambition and great desire of being puffed off as one of the first Officers of the Age, could only be equalled by the means which he used to obtain them; but finding that I was determined not to go beyond the line of my duty to indulge him in the first, nor, to exceed the strictest rules of propriety, to gratify him in the second, he became

---

[204] Flexner, Vol. 2, 269–270.

my inveterate Enemy; and has, I am persuaded, practised every Art to do me an injury, even at the expense of reprobating a measure, which did not succeed, that he himself advised to. How far he may have accomplished his ends, I know not, and, but for considerations of a public Nature, I care not. For it is well known, that neither ambitious, nor lucrative motives led me to accept my present Appointments; in the discharge of which, I have endeavoured to observe one steady and uniform conduct, which I shall invariably pursue, while I have the honour to command, regardless of the Tongue of slander or the powers of detraction.[205]

Determined to continue his course and to keep his principles intact, Washington never lowered himself to the intrigue. Being the general of the army was the will of providence to him, and no one could alter it. If he wasn't meant to be the commander of the army, he could accept it.

Gates wrote to Washington, assuring him of his innocence in the cabal, and asked him to forget the whole ordeal. Washington agreed.

He continued to press Congress for provisions and money. Many times, he sank into an abyss of despair and doubted himself again. He felt alone and powerless to do anything.

One eyewitness account of the general at Valley Forge came from Isaac Potts, the owner of the house Washington occupied that winter:

I was a rank Tory (*loyalist*) once, for I never believed that America could proceed against Great Britain whose fleets and armies covered the

---

[205] Washington, *Writings*, Vol. 10, 236–237 (To Marquis De Lafayette, December 31, 1777).

land and ocean, but something very extraordinary converted me to the Good Faith... It was a most distressing time of the war, and all were for giving up the Ship, but that great and good man. In the woods, I heard a plaintive sound as, of a man at prayer. I tied my horse to a sapling and went quietly into the woods and to my astonishment I saw the great George Washington on his knees alone... He was at Prayer to the God of the Armies, beseeching to interpose with his Divine aid, as it was the Crisis, and the cause of the country, of humanity and of the world. Such a prayer I never heard from the lips of man. I left him alone praying... I turned right about and became a Whig (*patriot*).[206]

Though Potts related this account in his final years and gave his first wife's name instead of his second in 1874, a Potts family history showed writings of Isaac Potts's daughter, Ruth-Anne, corroborating her father's account. George Washington Parke Custis, John Parke Custis's son, wrote of the same event in biographical essays of his adoptive grandfather in 1859. Other accounts of him praying at Valley Forge by Henry Knox, Lafayette, and Peter Muhlenberg are less reliable, but the Potts story was accepted by relatives of both families. A depiction of this event occupies a congressional room at the Capitol to this day. Whether this incident happened or not, Washington gained strength from his faith in moments of adversity.[207]

---

[206] Snowden, Reverend Nathaniel Randolph. *Diary and Remembrances*. (Original Manuscript at Historical Society of Pennsylvania; call number: PA: Am 1561–1568; Johnson, William J. *George Washington: the Christian*. (New York: Abingdon Press, 1919), 102–106.

[207] McGuire, Edward C. *The Religious Opinions and Character of Washington*. (New York: Harper & Bros., 1836), 158-159; Johnson, William J. *George Washington: The Christian*. (New York: Abingdon Press, 1919), 102–107; Parry 273.

Congressional Window at the Capitol

He was still there after others had fallen. His officers still supported him, and Congress realized he was the only man with the character they could trust with so much power. The men at Valley Forge stuck by their general through the dark days and the cabal. With faith in providence, Washington and his men survived the test.

Writing to Lafayette he said:

> It is much to be lamented that things are not now as they formerly were; but we must not, in so great a contest, expect to meet with nothing but Sun shine. I have no doubt but that everything happens so for the best; that we shall triumph over all our misfortunes, and shall, in the end, be ultimately happy; when, My Dear Marquis, if you will give me your Company in Virginia, we will laugh at our past difficulties and the folly of others; where I will endeavour, by every civility

in my power, to shew you how much and how sincerely, I am etc.[208]

George Washington knew the direction of his path but still couldn't see his purpose. He just knew he had to trust God would guide him to it. "A superintending Providence is ordering everything for the best, and that, in due time, all will end well."[209]

* * * * *

That winter at Valley Forge, Washington had held fast to his beliefs. "The determinations of Providence are all ways wise; often inscrutable, and though its decrees appear to bear hard upon us at times is nevertheless meant for gracious purposes..."[210]

With spring, sufficient food, and clothes, a newfound hope arrived. It also brought Baron Friedrich Wilhelm von Steuben. A lieutenant-general under Prussia's Frederick the Great and a master of drill and discipline, he was recommended by Benjamin Franklin who was in Paris negotiating an alliance with France. The baron would serve as a volunteer in the American army, without rank, but was adamant he would serve under no one except General Washington. He spoke little English and required translators to interpret his German to French, then the French to English. He often hosted parties where guests were required to wear ragged breeches. He garnered the admiration of officers, enlisted men, and Washington as well.

He was given the task of molding this motley bunch of citizen soldiers into a professional army. They needed a workable uniform system of drill and maneuver. Von Steuben recognized this raw material from struggle and hardship and believed it would make for a great army. He showed them the correct way to carry and fire a musket, fix bayonets and charge, and deploy and execute battlefield

---

[208] Washington, *Writings*, Vol. 10, 237 (To Marquis De Lafayette, December 31, 1777).

[209] Ibid., Vol. 9, 454 (To Landon Carter, October 27, 1777).

[210] Ibid., Vol. 11, 3 (To Bryan Fairfax, March 1, 1778).

maneuvers. He instilled in them discipline and order. Before long, the men's hygiene and sanitation improved, and clean faces began to appear in formation. With order and discipline and the increased supplies, the men's health improved and their bodies grew stronger.

Washington was aware that Von Steuben was a fake baron. He was a self-made man and claimed the title only to obtain promotion in the European army's aristocratic ranks. Washington wasn't worried about Von Steuben's past or status. He was discriminated against for status, not merit. He saw immediate results in the army, and that was all he cared about. He knew how to delegate authority and employ useful people. It was a characteristic he would use as president. Von Steuben's tenacity and results were what endeared him to the general, not his status.

Von Steuben wrote to a European friend about the Americans. "The genius of this nation is not in the least to be compared with the Prussians, the Austrians, or French. You say to your soldier, 'Do this;' and he doeth it, but I am obliged to say, this is the reason why you ought to do that; and then he does it."[211]

By the end of April 1778, news of France's alliance with America reached Valley Forge. On May 2, Washington's general orders read:

> While we are zealously performing the duties of good Citizens and soldiers we certainly ought not to be inattentive to the higher duties of Religion—To the distinguished Character of Patriot, it should be our highest Glory to add the more distinguished Character of Christian—The signal Instances of providential Goodness which we have experienced and which have now almost crowned our labours with complete Success, demand from us in a peculiar manner the warmest returns of Gratitude & Piety to the Supreme Author of all Good.[212]

---

[211] Flexner, Vol. 2, 287; Chernow, 332–334.
[212] Washington, *Writings*, Vol. 11, 342–343 (General Orders, May 2, 1778).

Washington's faith has been the subject of many interpretations. He was raised an Episcopalian, served as a vestryman in his church, and referred to a creator whose providence intervened in men's affairs. He has been called a deist, but deists didn't believe in a god who intervened in human affairs. Others continue to accuse him of practicing the secret society beliefs of Freemasons or the Illuminati, but a year before his death, he addressed the concern: "I have heard much of the nefarious, and dangerous plan, and doctrines of the Illuminati..." He disavowed his participation in the Masons but felt sure the American lodges hadn't been corrupted yet. "The fact is, I preside over none, nor have I been in one more than once or twice, within the last thirty years. I believe notwithstanding, that none of the Lodges in this Country are contaminated with the principles ascribed to the Society of the Illuminati."[213] He even admitted the Illuminati or Jacobinism of the French Revolution had spread throughout the country and believed Masonic lodges were in danger of being infiltrated by these individuals:

> It was not my intention to doubt that, the Doctrines of the Illuminati, and the principles of Jacobinism had not spread in the United States. On the contrary, no one is more truly satisfied of this fact than I am. The idea that I meant to convey, was, that I did not believe that the Lodges of Free Masons in this Country had, as Societies, endeavored to propagate the diabolical tenets of the first, or pernicious principles of the latter (if they are susceptible of separation). That Individuals of them may have done it, or that the founder, or instrument employed to found, the Democratic Societies in the United States, may have had these objects, and actually had sepa-

---

[213] Ibid., Vol. 37, 453 (To Reverend G. W. Snyder, September 25, 1798); Chernow, 131–132.

ration of the People from their Government in
view, is too evident to be questioned.[214]

Washington was an official member of the Masonic Lodge but
rarely attended meetings. In the turn of the next century, Freemasons
were "contaminated" by Illuminati infiltrators and persist to this day.
Of course, the Masons used Washington's prestige to lend credibility
to their organizations, but evidence points to his Episcopalian affili-
ation more than a Masonic one. He frequented the Christian church
more than the lodges, yet rumors persist. This debate on his faith
continues, though evidence suggests he was a believer of Christian
principles, yet a critic of its church dogma.

Referring to God by titles like "Great Author, Great Architect,
Almighty Being" was a common habit in the colonial period when
taking the name of God in vain was avoided whenever possible.
Providence was a term used by the Pilgrims, and their Christianity
was never questioned. Many times, Washington refers to God and
Christianity in his official documents. In May of 1779, he wrote to
the Delaware Indians, "You do well to wish to learn our arts and ways
of life, and above all, the religion of Jesus Christ. These will make you
a greater and happier people than you are."[215]

Though some historians claim an aide wrote this, Washington
signed and approved it. At this point in his life, he wasn't the type to
let subordinates make military policy.

Some cite one or two examples to support their claims but fail
to recognize the dozens of examples of his Christianity.

In August of 1787, he wrote to Lafayette, "Being no bigot
myself to any mode of worship, I am disposed to indulge the profes-
sors of Christianity in the church with that road to Heaven which to
them seem the most direct, plainest and easiest, and the least liable
to exception."[216]

---

[214] Ibid., 518-519 (To Reverend G. W. Snyder, October 24, 1798); Ibid.
[215] Ibid., Vol. 15, 55 (To the Delaware Chiefs, May 12, 1779); Ibid., 360.
[216] Ibid., Vol. 29, 259 (To Marquis De Lafayette, August 15, 1787).

Chief Justice John Marshall, a confidant of the general, wrote *The Life of George Washington* in the early 1800s and said of him, "Without making ostentatious professions of religion he was a sincere believer of the Christian faith, and a truly devout man."[217] Washington believed one's actions professed more Christian principles than all the church doctrine. He wasn't pious but relied on his faith throughout his life.

The men's health and morale improved at Valley Forge with the coming of spring, and the French alliance injected hope that victory was a real possibility now. France could tie up British ships with their navy, the second most powerful in the world, and their troops could add to the American dwindling numbers. The greatest benefit of the alliance was the prestige and money French intervention would bring. The young nation had been recognized by a world power, and Spain eventually joined the alliance. On May 5, 1778, Washington's general orders proclaimed:

> It having pleased the Almighty Ruler of the Universe propitiously to defend the cause of the United States of America and finally raising us up a powerful friend, among the Princes of the Earth, to Establish our Liberty and Independence upon lasting foundations: It becomes us to Set apart a day, for fully acknowledging the Divine Goodness, and celebrating the important event, which we owe to his Benign interposition.[218]

The following day was a celebration. Extra rum was issued as the commander-in-chief joined the officers in the festivities that night. They had shared common experiences which made them brothers forever, and they were just happy to be alive.

The fires had burned them, but they were stronger from it, and Washington and the cause rose like a phoenix out of the flames.

---

[217] Marshall, 376; Chernow, 131–132.
[218] Washington, *Writings*, Vol. 11, 354 (General Orders, May 5, 1778).

The valley had been crossed, and the ore was forged into the steel of resolve.

* * * * *

Monmouth Courthouse, New Jersey, June 28, 1778

Over the past two years, Washington had gained self-confidence and learned to trust his own judgment but still never trusted himself as a military leader. He respected the experience of professional officers and sought their advice. His own self-doubt contributed to lapses in judgment.

Released from British captivity in 1778, General Charles Lee had been a captive since December of 1776. He arrived in Valley Forge, and Washington received him graciously.

General William Howe had been relieved of duty that spring. Criticized for inaction, Howe was replaced by General Henry Clinton.

Clinton never agreed with Howe's strategy and prepared to evacuate Philadelphia to concentrate his headquarters in New York City. A response to the French declaration of war, the new British commander refused to divide his army while the French navy threatened. Washington received intelligence Clinton was moving supplies and loyalists out of Philadelphia. The British army would travel overland through New Jersey on their way back to New York, and Clinton, in his arrogance, wasn't worried about the Americans. Brandywine and Germantown proved British superiority on the battlefield.

Washington marched the American army to New Jersey, intending to force the British into a major action. He was ready to prove the metal forged during the winter was sharp enough to strike.

The enemy was encamped near Monmouth Courthouse, New Jersey, when Washington called a council of war. Greene and Lafayette pressed for an attack, but Lee strongly opposed action and influenced the others to support him. Lee argued that they couldn't stand up to the British regulars in open battle. He hadn't witnessed the transformation of the army that winter.

Washington saw the men at Brandywine and Germantown and noticed their change at Valley Forge. The farmers, shopkeepers, blacksmiths, and hunters became soldiers under Von Steuben. Just like the journey through his own life, the army was molded by adversity and preparation. Washington believed in their abilities and overruled the council. Lee refused to take command of the advance force, so Washington gave Lafayette his place. Lee reconsidered his decision and asked to be reinstated. Washington granted his request because he still respected the professional and needed his experience. Lafayette was disappointed but quietly deferred to Lee. The plan was to hit the rear of the enemy as they marched toward New York. The advance force would initiate the attack, then the main army would move forward and finish them.

Around noon, Washington was advancing toward the battle when a farmer appeared beside him, claiming that the Americans were retreating. Like a replay of Brandywine, he refused to accept this preposterous claim. Lee had a larger force than the British and no dispatch of a retreat had been sent. Washington demanded to know where the man received his information. Pointing to a soldier, a fifer in the line, the farmer sighed in relief. The fifer validated the civilian's claim, "The Continental troops that had been advanced were retreating." Afraid this rumor would spread, Washington threatened the fifer that if he repeated the rumor, he would have him whipped. He ordered the boy's arrest and raced toward the front to see for himself.

As he advanced, he saw Americans walking back toward him. Just a few at first, then whole regiments began flowing past him and he couldn't believe his eyes. He had misjudged the two eyewitness accounts and failed to see even the possibility of a retreat. Why was Lee retreating for no apparent reason and certainly no order? In the field, an officer reports to the commanding general the situation and requests a retreat. No such protocol occurred, and Lee must have issued a retreat without his approval. He lost his temper when he saw General Lee trotting toward him.

Washington raced toward him and shouted, "What is the meaning of this?"

Lee looked up surprised and said, "Sir? Sir?"

"What is all this confusion for, and retreat?" Washington asked.

Lee began his list of excuses blaming everyone but himself. Washington knew he had made another mistake that could cost them this battle and had to decide quickly. He reprimanded Lee and called him a "damned poltroon." He couldn't believe he had trusted this man to lead the army. His whole life, he admired the professional trained officer and felt inadequate by comparison. His treatment by the British officers in the French and Indian War made him question his own competence. General Lee's actions that day opened his eyes to reality. A capable officer should be judged by his actions and character, not his status. The lesson Captain John Smith left to posterity had to be learned from experience. Washington had learned the lesson and was done with men like Lee.

"My God, General Lee, what are you about? Go to the rear, sir!" Washington rode swiftly toward the fight.[219]

Lafayette described Washington's performance that day. "His presence stopped the retreat; his dispositions fixed the victory; his fine appearance on horseback, his calm courage roused to animation by the vexations of the morning, gave him the air best calculated to execute enthusiasm...I thought then as now that never had I beheld so superb a man."[220]

Washington was angry and fed up with others controlling his outcomes. This was his battle, his responsibility, and his fight. The men cheered as he rode up and down the lines, encouraging them. He inspired them to turn and fight.

This June day was one of the hottest on record, and several soldiers from both sides collapsed from the heat. Mary Ludwig Hayes, wife of a private manning a cannon that day, fetched water from a nearby stream for the thirsty men. Nicknamed "Molly Pitcher," Mary was only twenty-two but a tough woman who chewed tobacco. The soldiers liked her, and when her husband was killed, she took his place firing the gun. When an enemy cannonball flew between

---

[219] Flexner, Vol. 2, 303-305; Ward, Vol. 2, 581; Davis, *Washington*, 289–290.
[220] Ibid., 306; Davis, *Washington*, 291.

her legs and tore away her petticoats, she didn't flinch. She calmly commented how lucky she was the shot wasn't higher.[221]

Von Steuben's bayonet training made the Americans equal to the European soldiers on the field. Their formations were solid and their maneuvers precise. Their intense and disciplined attacks pushed the enemy back several times. Valley Forge had changed them.

After repeated attempts to overtake the Americans, the British retired from the battlefield at sundown. Washington planned to resume hostilities at dawn, but around midnight, Clinton slipped away from Monmouth under the cover of darkness. For the first time, the British were sneaking away.

Many called the Battle of Monmouth Courthouse a tie, but the Americans held the field. They also stood toe-to-toe with British and Hessian regulars and chased them from the field. No one ran, and they pushed the enemy back multiple times. They made a loud statement to the world that day.

Charles Lee was court-martialed for his actions at Monmouth and suspended from the army. He died in 1782, resentful and bitter. His actions at Monmouth likely cost Washington a total victory in the battle, and in the 1930s, evidence of Lee's treasonous behavior as a prisoner came to light. Lee took his place alongside Conway and Mifflin in obscurity and dishonor.

Washington followed the British back to New York City and placed his army at White Plains at the end of July. Describing the previous two years, he wrote:

> After two years Maneuvering and undergoing the strangest vicissitudes, that perhaps ever attended any one contest since the creation, both Armies are brought back to the very point they set out from, and that which was the offending party in the beginning is now reduced to the use of the spade and pick-axe for defense. The hand of

---

[221] Davis, *Washington*, 293; Leckie, Robert. *George Washington's War: The Saga of the American Revolution.* (New York: Harper Perennial, 1993), 486.

Providence has been so conspicuous in all this, that he must be worse than an infidel that lacks faith, and more than wicked, that has not gratitude enough to acknowledge his obligations...[222]

The war had come full circle, and the only British accomplishment was New York City. They had fought and bled for little more than they started with, and the Americans had pushed them out of Boston, New Jersey, upper New York state, and Pennsylvania. Washington was now pressing Clinton.

The rest of 1778 and 1779, Washington watched and waited for Clinton, but he didn't budge. A skirmish in New York, the Battle of Edgar's Lane in the autumn of 1778, was a minor victory by Major Henry "Light-Horse Harry" Lee and his dragoons. Lee had another victory in the Battle of Paulus Hook in New Jersey in 1779, which led Congress to present the horse soldier with a gold medal usually reserved for generals. Washington depended on Lee to keep Clinton on his toes. Eventually, he was promoted to lieutenant-colonel and sent to the Carolinas to harass the enemy. Colonel Lee would go on to become one of Washington's most trusted officer and friend. Thirty years later, Lee would father a famous son, General Robert E. Lee.

Washington used this period of inactivity to work on Congress. Procuring the army's pay and supplies was a separate war itself. Four years was starting to wear on him. His hair was grayer and he had difficulty reading correspondence without eyeglasses but made sure none of his officers saw him wearing them.

After Monmouth, he appeared more aggressive. Gone were the days of second-guessing his ability to lead. He was confident and determined to defeat all enemies, foreign and domestic. When complaining about the selfish interests of some of his countrymen, he wrote:

It is also most devoutly to be wished that faction was at an end and that those to whom everything

---

[222] Washington, *Writings*, Vol. 12, 343 (To General Thomas Nelson Jr., August 20, 1778).

dear and valuable is entrusted would lay aside party views and return to first principles. Happy, happy, thrice happy Country if such was the government of it, but alas! we are not to expect that the path is to be strewed with flowers. That great and good Being who rules the Universe has disposed matters otherwise and for wise purposes I am persuaded.[223]

To the Delaware Indians, he came in peace but made it clear he was tired of being diplomatic. "I am a Warrior. My words are few and plain; but I will make good what I say. Tis my business to destroy all the Enemies of these States and to protect their friends."[224]

As Washington grew bolder, the British decided to turn their attention to the South. The southern states had a large loyalist population, and fomenting civil war there might change the direction of the war. Washington continued to focus on the northern theater because Clinton remained in New York. This new southern strategy was possibly a feint to draw troops from around New York to open an invasion of the Hudson Valley and New England. After General Gates rode seventy miles to the rear after his defeat in the Battle of Camden, South Carolina, Washington sent General Nathanael Greene to defend the South. Greene's objective was the same as Washington's in the North—harass the enemy and keep the army intact.

General Gates, the last of the actors in the Conway Cabal, showed his true colors at Camden. Like the others who plotted against Washington, Gates fell on the sword of his own arrogance.

While Washington breathed easier with the threats from Clinton and the Conway Cabal behind him, another sinister plot within his own circle was underway. The impurities burned away,

---

[223] Ibid., Vol. 13, 348 (To Joseph Reed, November 27, 1778).
[224] Ibid., Vol. 15, 54 (To the Delaware Chiefs, May 12, 1779).

and the sword of the cause, like a sacred fire, would show the way through the darkness to come.

* * * * *

Haverstraw, New York, near West Point, September 1780

"General Arnold, General Clinton will pay 6,000 pounds for the capture of West Point."

"The agreement was for 10,000, not 6,000!" General Benedict Arnold growled.

"I will try to convince General Clinton to pay the price you demand, Sir."

Major John Andre smiled, realizing the capture of West Point may end the rebellion once and for all. Washington was even expected in a few days, and capturing him would be a coup de grace. Luckily, the colonists had plenty of their own happy to betray their cause for money or power.

Arnold wrote out a pass and handed it to Andre. "This pass will get you through the lines. It is personally signed by me. Here are the plans to West Point and the details. Keep them concealed. I will expect you in the morning. Bring the money and my commission. Good evening."

"In the morning, then—Sir." The British major saluted. Arnold returned the gesture and walked to the edge of the trees. Without peering back, he entered the dark woods.

Andre watched him disappear into the forest then shoved the papers into his boot. Now he had to find a way back to his lines without getting captured.

Arnold hurried through the dense foliage, thinking about his actions. Washington had been a second father to him, and now, he was his Judas. For thirty pieces of silver, he had sold his soul.

But he was the one wronged here, not Washington. He had won Saratoga, not Gates, and he had been crippled for his service. They disregarded his accomplishments, and he was accused and reprimanded but received no recompense. *Damn Washington! Damn them all!* They owed him, and they would all pay.

Arnold made his way back to West Point to await General Washington's visit. He was ready to be famous.

Major Andre, now dressed in civilian clothes, made his way through the American lines with evidence of Arnold's treason in his boot.[225]

* * * * *

Washington considered Arnold like a son, just as he did with other promising young officers. Hamilton, Lafayette, and others looked to him as a father figure. The general saw certain qualities in Arnold he himself possessed as a young man. Maybe he was hot-headed and made rash decisions, but Washington remembered his own short temper and bad decisions of the past. He believed the trick was to guide and harness the talent of men like Arnold to realize their greatness. He sympathized with him for being passed over for promotion by Congress but knew he would receive justice in due time. Arnold was energetic and courageous but still had to learn to serve something greater than himself. Washington believed he would learn this in time, and adversity would test him.

After Clinton evacuated Philadelphia in the summer of 1778, Washington gave Arnold the appointment as military governor of the city to reward him for all his sacrifice.

During his time as governor of Philadelphia, Arnold met a vivacious young woman from a well-respected loyalist family, Peggy Shippen. He fell in love with her instantly and coveted the status the marriage could provide, and after a brief courtship, the two married. All he needed now was money to go with the status. Shady deals and suspicious investments led many to accuse him of profiting from the war. Insulted by these accusations, he demanded a court-martial

---

[225] From Andre's account. Flexner, Vol. 2, 383; Freeman, *Washington*, 443–444; Davis, 338; Chernow, 381.

to clear his name. Washington granted him one, if only to satisfy Arnold.

In January of 1780, he was acquitted of two serious charges but found guilty on two minor ones. These minor infractions called for a reprimand from the commander-in-chief. Washington was delighted with the outcome of the court-martial and considered the reprimand as a mere formality. When he wrote the "reprimand," he did in a respectful manner saying, "The Commander-in-chief would have been much happier in an occasion of bestowing commendations on an officer who has rendered such distinguished service to his country as Major General Arnold."[226]

But Arnold took the reprimand personal and resented the commander for it.

On August 1, 1780, Washington offered Arnold command of the left wing of the army. The promotion he felt he deserved since Saratoga was his at last, but he turned it down. Instead, Arnold asked for command of the garrison at West Point, New York, which kept watch over the upper Hudson Valley. West Point was the gateway to upper New York and New England. Washington believed Arnold timid to lead men into battle because of his injured leg but reassured him he would get used to it in time. After he insisted on the command of West Point, Washington, like a patient and understanding father, granted it to Arnold.

Why he insisted on command of a garrison over a field command confused Washington. Arnold had already conspired with the enemy at this point and decided the only way to achieve greatness was to take it. Unlike Washington, he chose the reward of status over character. West Point would be handed over to the British. In turn, they would pay him money and a commission in the royal army. Arnold wasn't content with simple betrayal but wanted vengeance against all those who had wronged him.

In early September, Washington wrote to Arnold at West Point. He planned to visit and asked him to "send down a guard of a captain and fifty at that time, and direct the quartermaster to endeavor

---

[226] Washington, Writings, Vol. 18, 225 (General Orders, April 6, 1780).

to have a night's forage for about forty horses. You will keep this to yourself, as I want to keep my journey a secret."[227]

On September 25, Washington was en route to West Point where he planned to breakfast with the garrison commander. He decided to inspect several fortifications in the area first. He sent word ahead and apologized for his lateness.

Arriving at West Point later that day, Washington was greeted at Arnold's house by an aide who explained the general wasn't there, and Peggy Arnold was still in bed. Assuming Arnold would arrive shortly, the general proceeded to inspect the fort. What he found during his inspection perplexed him. The men, guns, and overall order were in a state of neglect. What had he been doing here all this time?

Returning to Arnold's house for dinner, there was still no sign of him. Peggy was still in her room, and the commander grew suspicious. Deciding to read his dispatches while he waited for an explanation, Washington opened one letter and read it. Then he started to tremble.

"Arnold has betrayed us. Whom can we trust now?"[228] he shouted.

Lieutenant John Jameson in the dispatch, told of three men stopping a man riding past them in civilian clothes the night before. He claimed his name was John Anderson and first said he was a loyalist, then a patriot. The three men stripped this rider and found papers stuffed inside one of his boots. On one paper, there was a pass permitting Anderson to move between the lines. It was signed by General Benedict Arnold. There were other papers in Arnold's handwriting divulging military secrets about West Point. The captured man, John Anderson, turned out to be Major John Andre, adjutant general of the British army.

Washington was furious. How many were involved in this plot? Was the danger over? His priority was to secure West Point and capture Arnold. One eyewitness said the commander was eager to hang him.

---

[227] Ibid., Vol. 20, 48 (To Major General Benedict Arnold, September 14, 1780).
[228] Flexner, Vol. 2, 386; Chernow, 382; Davis, 338.

Unknown to Washington, Arnold had received another dispatch earlier from the same Lieutenant Jameson alerting him to Anderson's capture. Realizing he would be exposed, he fled. Washington questioned Peggy Arnold, but she pretended to be emotionally distraught by her husband's betrayal. He assumed the traitor had abandoned his young wife like he abandoned the cause. This was only a deceptive ploy by Peggy Arnold to appear innocent of her husband's treason. Washington's code of honor saw women as the gentler sex and dependent on men for protection. Women were the epitome of goodness to him. His faith in the goodness of people deceived him once again, but he refused to change because of it.

Arnold escaped to the British lines, and Peggy eventually joined him. He was given a commission in the king's army and led a force to invade Virginia. He was responsible for many of the brutal tactics against Washington's home state and was never captured. Washington tried to negotiate a trade of Andre for Arnold, but Clinton refused. He had no choice but to hang Andre as a spy.

Arnold lived in Britain after the war and died an infamous traitor in debt. He never took responsibility for his own life and placed the blame on everyone but himself and refused to serve something greater. Washington credited Arnold's failure to, "In no instance since the commencement of the war has the interposition of Providence appeared more conspicuous than in the rescue of the post and garrison of West Point from Arnold's villainous perfidy."[229]

* * * * *

The winter of 1780–81 was another dreary time for the American cause. The British invaded the South and captured Georgia, the Carolinas, and were rampaging through the Virginian countryside. American money was worthless, and the men still hadn't been paid. Once again, food, shoes, and provisions were low, so the soldiers sat idly with little to do except grow resentful.

---

[229] Washington, *Writings*, Vol. 20, 173 (To Lieutenant-Colonel John Laurens, October 13, 1780).

The American commander, incensed at those who cornered markets only to sell goods back to the army at outrageous prices, pulled no punches. "I would to God, that one of the most atrocious in each State was hung…No punishment, in my opinion, is too great for the man who can build his greatness upon his country's ruin."[230]

A group of Pennsylvanian soldiers mutinied and marched on Congress to demand their back pay. Washington understood their grievances but knew mutiny could infect the rest of the army. He didn't want to appear soft on mutiny or unfairly punish men with real complaints, so he chose not to act this time after the Pennsylvanians reached a peaceful agreement with Congress. With the mutiny resolved, the country and the commander breathed easier.

Then a group of New Jersey soldiers decided to mutiny, and Washington knew it was spreading. Congress's appeasement of the Pennsylvanians only emboldened others to do the same. Rewarding bad behavior guaranteed more of it.

He sent a force to arrest the mutineers and conducted a swift court-martial. Then he ordered three of the ringleaders shot by firing squad. The executioners would be chosen from the mutineers themselves. These twelve unfortunates fired so close to their comrades that the sparks from the muskets caught fire to the cloth bags that covered their faces. Washington struggled with this decision but knew that order must be preserved. The cause of human liberty was bigger than any single group's grievances, even if justified. What they were fighting for was larger than any injustice. The cause could only survive if the army did. Survival of the army depended on order, and he realized if the army remained idle, it would self-destruct. Only a bold and energetic action could provide direction.

New York City was the obvious target. It was Clinton's main base on the continent, but to attack it, he needed a naval force. The French navy would assist in operations, but it made decisions independently of the Americans. It was in the West Indies at present, so Washington couldn't coordinate a major operation without knowing if they would show up.

---

[230] Ibid., Vol. 13, 383 (To Joseph Reed, December 12, 1778).

General Lord Cornwallis was sent south with a force and had humiliated General Lincoln by demanding unconditional surrender at Charleston, South Carolina, and whipped Gates at Camden. Then he chased Greene all over the Carolinas. Just as Washington maneuvered in the North, Greene engaged the enemy, then withdrew to preserve the army.

Cornwallis's supply lines were overextended, and maintaining them became a headache for the British commander. His men were hungry, isolated, and in need of supplies. General Greene's strategy was to lure Cornwallis further from his supply line in Charleston, South Carolina, and closer to the main army in the North. This clever strategy was why Washington chose Greene to command the southern theater.

The British defeats at the battles of Cowpens and King's Mountain and the disastrous victory at Guilford Courthouse in the spring of 1781 forced Cornwallis further away from his supply lines and into Virginia. He needed to resupply and headed for Chesapeake Bay to await provisioning from New York. Washington sent General Lafayette with a small force to Virginia to keep a close eye on Cornwallis when providence intervened.

On May 22, 1781, Washington received news that the French fleet planned to depart from the West Indies for the American coast and would be available for an operation. The American commander still hoped to move against New York, but the French commander General Rochambeau tried to convince him of the easier target in the Chesapeake. Unconvinced and certain Cornwallis was a feint from Clinton, Washington decided to wait for intelligence before deciding. Reconnaissance of New York reported nearly 17,000 heavily entrenched forces. Hitting Cornwallis's weaker force as a feint might pull some of Clinton's army out of the city and weaken its numbers. Washington remained focused on New York as the grand prize until Rochambeau received word from the French admiral. The French fleet would sail on August 13 with thirty ships, 3,000 men, and siege cannons directly for the Chesapeake. It would remain there until October 15 before returning to the West Indies. They would not engage the British in New York.

This time, providence removed all other options.

Washington knew the when and the where an operation could be put into action and Cornwallis, with the major British force in the South, was in the very same place. All he had to do was get his army there without Clinton noticing. He instructed Lafayette to keep Cornwallis penned up in the seacoast village of Yorktown, Virginia. They had a possible trap, but every part of the plan must be executed with precision. They couldn't risk another Germantown or a tie like Monmouth. He needed an overwhelming victory with no mistakes.

Washington felt the immense pressure, and it was his responsibility to make it happen. He had a powerful French navy and army to back him up this time, and events made it an opportunity.

* * * * *

On August 21, the American and French force headed south. Washington wanted Clinton to believe he was preparing an attack of New York by way of Staten Island. His actual destination was kept secret from all but the top command. As a diversion, he sent a small force to Staten Island, and at the same time, he marched his force toward the city. Once he was sure Clinton took the bait, he turned the army south. If the British commander got wind of the actual destination, he might send reinforcements to Cornwallis or attack West Point and its small garrison of 2,500 men.

Once again, the destiny of the cause depended on a gamble. He must take the risk or the Revolution may be lost from inaction. Americans were growing weary of the war. It was in its seventh year, and many wondered if it would ever end.

Enlistments were down again, because men had to provide for their families. Being away for years at a time without pay was too hard on those left behind. The congress was powerless to collect payment from the states, and the continental currency was of little value. Three years of watching and waiting failed to motivate the people the way Trenton and Monmouth had, and all the high ideals in the world meant nothing if the young country wasn't going to fight for them. Washington had to make a bold move, and Yorktown was it.

General Clinton realized the American commander's intentions once his scouts reported his move south. Sending a fleet of ships to assist Cornwallis, he was optimistic, but on September 5, the British naval force discovered a larger French fleet already in the Chesapeake. A minor engagement failed to save Cornwallis's army. The British ships sailed back to New York, leaving the French fleet in control of the Virginian coast. Cornwallis was trapped with Washington and Rochambeau's armies to his front and a French fleet behind him.

By the time the Americans reached the outskirts of Yorktown, they grew to a force of 8,845 men. The French added another 7,800, making the total, 15,600. Cornwallis had 6,000 men, and for the first time in the war, Washington had numerical advantage, command of the sea, and an army forged in the valley. All the pieces seemed to fall into place.

As the Americans and French marched toward Yorktown, they passed the town of Williamsburg. On their left, across the York River, was the very place where Pocahontas saved Captain John Smith from execution. Directly to their right lay the settlement of Jamestown. General Washington was moving toward his purpose where Captain Smith had found his own nearly two hundred years before.

By October 6, the American and French forces were ready to move. Their heavy guns were in place, and their first parallel (a trench parallel to the fort for moving closer with cannon) was finished. Washington fired the first cannon shot of the Battle of Yorktown.

On October 11, a second parallel about three hundred yards from the British entrenchments was finished. Three days later, two forces—one American under General Lafayette and Colonel Alexander Hamilton and one French—attacked the outer redoubts in the black of night and successfully captured them. The next day, Cornwallis tried a counterattack but failed. Then he attempted to retreat across the bay to the town of Gloucester (much like Washington did at Brooklyn Heights five years earlier), but a violent storm prevented the boats from returning after the first trip across.

On the sixteenth, Washington pounded Yorktown with all his cannon devastating the British entrenchments. Cornwallis's army was low on ammunition, provisions, and morale.

The next day, a British drummer stood on top of the Yorktown fort and played a parley, signaling a meeting to specify terms. Washington received Cornwallis's conditions for surrender but refused them. He demanded unconditional surrender, and Cornwallis had no other choice. His force was exhausted and bottled up in Yorktown. Clinton couldn't even save his army, so he accepted the terms.

At two o'clock on October 19, 1781, the British marched out of Yorktown as their bands played the song "The World Turned Upside Down." They walked between two lines of French and Americans to surrender their muskets in shame. Some showed anger while others cried. Somehow, these farmers, shopkeepers, hunters, and fishermen had beat them. The most powerful empire had lost to a bunch of hicks.

Cornwallis didn't attend the surrender, claiming illness, and gave his sword to a subordinate to relinquish it to the victors. First the subordinate tried to give it to the Rochambeau as an insult to the Americans, but he refused to accept it and pointed to Washington. The British officer reluctantly turned to the American commander and offered the sword. Washington refused to accept it from a subordinate officer and pointed to General Benjamin Lincoln instead. Lincoln had been humiliated by Cornwallis at the surrender of Charlestown, South Carolina, in 1780, and he accepted the sword. This was Washington's way of returning the insult and poetic justice. Lincoln graciously returned the sword back to the Brit. The British could feel superior to the Americans all they wanted, but the Americans chose to take the high road.

Unknown to Washington or Cornwallis, Clinton had planned a rescue of Yorktown with 7,000 men and twenty-five ships, but they set sail on October 19—the very day of the surrender. When news of Cornwallis's surrender reached Clinton, he called the rescue operation back.

As news of the victory reached the rest of the country, celebrations and thanksgivings spread. They had delivered a fatal blow to the British. It was a matter of time before the British realized it. Many denied it at first, but eventually, they saw the inevitable.

Washington sat in his headquarters, humbled by the victory. After all the missteps and treachery, they succeeded in the end. He had many to thank: Lafayette, Von Steuben, Hamilton, Knox, Rochambeau, Colonel "Light-Horse Harry" Lee, and all those who bled, suffered, and died for eight years. He also knew that his life prepared him for this. All the failures were blessings, not curses. His years of self-doubt and regret after failing to become an officer in the British army forged him into the general of the very army that defeated them.

He also knew a greater force guided events in this Revolution and his own personal life. He was a mere implement in a much larger plan, and his own individual purpose served this plan. Selfish motives nearly led him away from this purpose. Years later, he explained, "At disappointments and losses which are the effects of providential acts, I never repine, because I am sure the all wise disposer of events knows better than we do, what is best for us, or what we deserve."[231]

After so many disappointments and losses, he deserved a victory.

* * * * *

Another year passed before the British signed a provisional treaty of peace and nearly another before it was final. During this limbo period, Washington had to keep the army together and on alert in case negotiations broke down and the war resumed. This was no small feat, being that they still hadn't received pay and just wanted to go home to their families. Inactivity and time created an environment for scheming and frustration. Some felt robbed of their glory during the war, and others were resentful of Congress.

Just like Julius Caesar, Napoleon, Cromwell, and Lenin, the army conspired to make him a dictator. Who could turn down the power to create the new nation in their own image? Throughout history, great men had succumbed to the hunger for absolute power. It was believed one could accomplish more with force.

---

[231] Ibid., Vol. 33, 375 (To William Pearce, May 25, 1794).

His whole life had prepared him for this moment. George Washington's finest hour had arrived.

* * * * *

Newburgh, New York, March 15, 1783

Washington stood in front of his officers. They were here tonight to dissolve the congress with the force of the army. Major John Armstrong, aide to General Gates, wrote the correspondence which called for this action and meeting. Washington had read the letters and was there, though uninvited.

He scanned the room. They had been through too much for this:

> If my conduct, heretofore has envinced to you that I have been a faithful friend to the army, my declaration of it at this time would be equally unavailing and improper. But as I was among the first who embarked in the cause of our common country; as I have never left your side one moment, but when called from you on public duty; as I have been the common companion and witness of your distresses, and not among the last to feel and acknowledge your merits; as I have ever considered my own military reputation as inseparably connected with that of the army; as my heart has ever expanded with joy when I have heard its praises, and my indignation has arisen when the mouth of detraction has been opened against it, it can scarcely be supposed, at this late stage of the war, that I am indifferent to its interests.

Washington paused, acknowledging a few in the crowd:

> If peace takes place, never sheath your swords, says he, until you have obtained full and ample justice. This dreadful alternative of either deserting our country in the extremest hour of her distress or turning our arms against it has something so shocking in it, that humanity revolts at the idea.

The officers' eyes widened:

> My God, what can this writer [*addressing Armstrong*] have in view by recommending such measures? Can he be a friend to the army? Can he be a friend to this country? Rather, is he not an insidious foe? Some emissary perhaps from New York [*still occupied by the British*], plotting to ruin both by sowing the seeds of discord and separation between civil and military powers of the continent? There might, gentlemen be an impropriety in my taking notice, in this address to you, of an anonymous production…with respect to the advice given by the author to suspect the man who shall recommend moderate measures and longer forbearance, I spurn it. If men are to be precluded from offering their sentiments on a matter which may involve the most serious and alarming consequences that can invite the consideration of mankind, reason is of no use to us. The freedom of speech may be taken away, and, dumb and silent, we may be led, like sheep, to the slaughter.

Sighing, he continued.

> And let me conjure you, in the name of our common country, as you value your own sacred

honor, as you respect the rights of humanity, and as you regard the military and national character of America to express your utmost horror and detestation of the man who wishes, under any specious pretenses, to overturn the liberties of our country, and who wickedly attempts to open the floodgates of civil discord and deluge our rising empire in blood. By thus determining and thus acting, you will pursue the plain and direct road to the attainment of your wishes. And you will, by the dignity of your conduct, afford occasion for posterity to say, when speaking of the glorious example you have exhibited to mankind, had this day been wanting, the world had never seen the last stage of perfection to which human nature is capable of attaining.[232]

Were they going to shame the righteous cause they had so long fought for? The very same human nature William Bradford encountered at Plymouth threatened again. Would they not even see what could be? History told them the road they were on led to tyranny and destruction. Greece, Rome, and Britain chose this very path, two of which were extinct and one was in decline.

Washington reached into his pocket to retrieve a folded piece of paper. It was a letter from a member of congress explaining the reason for the payment delays and the solutions forthcoming.

Unfolding the letter, he paused as if remembering something. The room stirred. He couldn't make out the blurry words. Thinking of the vanity of his youth, he appeared suddenly aware of something. Reaching into his pocket again, he clumsily searched for something else. The men remained silent and mesmerized by the general's movements. Locating the particular item, Washington pulled out a pair of reading glasses.

---

[232] Ibid., Vol. 26, 222–225 (To the Officers of the Army, March 15, 1783).

He realized the men were staring at him, and with a somber voice, he simply said, "Gentlemen, you will permit me to put on my spectacles...for I have not only grown gray, but almost blind in the service of my country."[233]

Instantly, every eye in the hall glistened with tears of shame. This man who had been the hope and inspiration through the whole struggle in one simple statement saved the United States of America. Though he was still the brave warrior they all knew, he had shown them that he was still a mortal man. The blessings they'd won happened because of selfless sacrifice, not force. The miracles they witnessed were not his doing. By showing his failing eyes to his officers, he reminded them who they were.

He replaced the glasses back in his pocket and walked out of the hall.

The conspiracy was over. He led by example, and his men followed. Washington's own sacrifices meant more to these men than any injustice they faced. Their own sacrifice meant more than this. Ironically, this move toward a dictatorship happened on the Ides of March—the very same day the dictator Julius Caesar was assassinated in 44 BC.

Providence would lead them to the justice and purpose they were owed and guaranteed it. Writing to Reverend John Rodgers a few months later, Washington gave credit where it belonged. "Glorious indeed has been our Contest: glorious, if we consider the Prize for which we have contended, and glorious in its Issue; but in the midst of our Joys, I hope we shall not forget that, to divine Providence is to be ascribed the Glory and the Praise."[234]

Explaining the reasons for American victory later that summer, he wrote, "To say nothing of the invisible workings of Providence, which has conducted us through difficulties where no human foresight could point the way; it will appear evident to a close Examiner,

---

[233] Flexner, Vol. 2, 507; Davis, *Washington*, 451; Freeman, *Washington*, 501; Parry, 385 (From Josiah Quincy, *The Journals of Major Samuel Shaw, with a Life of the Author*. Boston: William Crosby and H. P. Nichols, 1847, p.104); Chernow, 436.

[234] Washington, *Writings*, Vol. 27, 1 (To Reverend John Rodgers, June 11, 1783).

that there has been a concatenation of causes to produce this Event; which in all probability at no time, or under any Circumstances, will combine again."[235]

He understood something was working in the cause of America. God was intervening for his greater good. As long as the nation continued in this purpose, it would continue to have God's favor. Perseverance, while maintaining principles, was key to this favor. A connection to these principles and divine purpose would guarantee the favor of the "beneficent Author of all the good that was, that is, or that will be…"[236]

They endured the humiliating defeats in New York and starvation and disease at Valley Forge. In the dark days, they overcame at Trenton and Princeton.

From an army of scared amateurs, they'd been toughened into the professionals who fought at Monmouth. Betrayal, cabal, conspiracy, mutiny, and idleness, yet they still achieved victory at Yorktown. America was tested in the fires of adversity and would need it for the years ahead. "We shall be guilty of many blunders in treading this boundless theater before we shall have arrived at perfection in this Art."[237] Washington understood the trick to overcoming any obstacle was perseverance, integrity, and reliance on divine providence, and America would emulate his example. Our many "blunders" never stopped us from trying to perfect "this Art."

On September 3, 1783, the final peace treaty was signed. The war for independence was over. On November 25, the British left New York City for home.

Washington joined his officers at Fraunces' Tavern in New York City for a final farewell. With a glass of wine in hand, he said, "With a heart full of love and gratitude, I now take leave of you. I most devoutly wish that your latter days may be as prosperous and happy as your former ones have been glorious and honorable." The other

---

[235] Ibid., 50 (To Reverend William Gordon, July 8, 1783).

[236] Washington, *Papers, Presidential Series*, Vol. 4, 131–132 (Thanksgiving Proclamation, October 3, 1789).

[237] Washington, *Writings*, Vol. 26, 298 (To Marquis De Lafayette, April 5, 1783).

officers grabbed a glass of wine for the toast while he continued, "I cannot come to each of you but shall feel obliged if each of you will come and take me by the hand."

Washington's eyes welled up, and General Knox, without a word, in tears himself, grasped the commander's hand then hugged him. Each of the officers followed Knox's example and embraced the man they had served for eight years. The entire scene unfolded in silence, then Washington departed.[238]

Boarding a barge, which would take him to Philadelphia, a crowd gathered at the shore to get a glimpse of the man to whom they owed so much. His face was tense from holding back tears, and before he drifted out of sight, he removed his hat and waved goodbye.

With one more task to complete, he stood before Congress on December 23 and bowed. The congressmen removed their hats to show their respects. The general was there to relinquish command of the army to the civilian authority. This symbolized all they had fought for—liberty and representation.

In his shaking hand, Washington held a speech he prepared. He was no orator, but he made one more official address as the commander-in-chief:

> Mr. President: The great events on which my resignation depended having at length taken place; I have now the honor of offering my sincere Congratulations to Congress and of presenting myself before them to surrender into their hands the trust committed to me, and to claim the indulgence of retiring from the Service of my Country.
>
> Happy in the confirmation of our Independence and Sovereignty, and pleased with the opportunity afforded the United States of becoming a respectable Nation, I resign with satisfaction the Appointment I accepted with diffi-

---

[238] Tallmadge, Benjamin. *Memoir of Colonel Benjamin Tallmadge.* (New York: Thomas Holman, 1858), 63–64; Chernow, 451–452.

dence. A diffidence in my abilities to accomplish so arduous a task, which however was superseded by a confidence in the rectitude of our Cause, the support of the Supreme Power of the Union, and the patronage of Heaven.

The Successful termination of the War has verified the most sanguine expectations, and my gratitude for the interposition of Providence, and the assistance I have received from my Countrymen, increases with every review of the momentous Contest.

While I repeat my obligations to the Army in general, I should do injustice to my own feelings not to acknowledge in this place the peculiar Services and distinguished merits of the Gentlemen who have been attached to my person during the War. It was impossible the choice of confidential Officers to compose my family should have been more fortunate. Permit me Sir, to recommend in particular those, who have continued in Service to the present moment, as worthy of the favorable notice and patronage of Congress.

I consider it an indispensable duty to close this last solemn act of my Official life, by commending the Interests of our dearest Country to the protection of Almighty God, and those who have the superintendence of them, to his holy keeping.

Having now finished the work assigned me, I retire from the great theatre of Action; and bidding an Affectionate farewell to this August body under whose orders I have so long acted, I here offer my Commission, and take my leave of all the employments of public life.[239]

---

[239] Washington, *Writings*, Vol. 27, 284–285 (Address to Congress on Resigning His Commission, December 23, 1783).

He had done his part and believed he fulfilled his purpose. He left for home and reached Martha's welcoming embrace at Mount Vernon on Christmas Eve. He was ready to live the remainder of his life as a farmer. He was exhausted and satisfied that he'd done his duty.

Little did he know the new and fragile nation he led to independence would call on him again.

* * * * *

He was always on the frontline leading his men. He knew the danger but believed the hand of God determined the outcome, not his fear. Without George Washington, there would be no United States of America. He was the standard bearer for the new nation. No other leader during the Revolution could have filled his shoes. Charles Lee or Horatio Gates would have destroyed the cause with their vanity. He was the right man for the right time and guided the nation on its path.

He wasn't a marble statue or a dusty portrait like we see him today. He was a flesh and blood man with weaknesses and faults like us all, but he chose to rise above them. He lived his life for a greater purpose than himself and acknowledged that God had a hand in it. He also learned to succeed by failing and knew the difference between success and failure was the ability to endure.

In his first inaugural speech as president in 1789, he reminded Americans, "No People can be bound to acknowledge and adore the invisible hand, which conducts the Affairs of men, more than the People of the United States. Every step, by which they have advanced to the character of an independent nation, seems to have been distinguished by some token of providential agency."[240]

He wasn't born a great leader with integrity and character. He wasn't a gifted speaker or ever comfortable in social settings. He had insecurities from smallpox scars, false teeth, and his own self-doubt about his ability to lead, but somehow, he prevailed.

---

[240] Ibid., Vol. 30, 293 (The First Inaugural, April 30, 1789).

He sharpened his character by his experiences. He'd been to the mountaintop and the valley throughout his life. The mountain revealed the divine providence he relied on, and the valley forged him into the kind of man who could recognize it. He knew there was no substitute for experience. Writing to Chief Justice John Marshall in 1797, he said, "Unfortunately, the nature of man is such that the experience of others is not attended to as it ought to be; we must feel ourselves before we can think or perceive the danger which threatens."[241]

Washington was one of a kind. He never had his own biological children but still fathered many offspring; but to most of us, he is the father of his country.

Anyone still searching for a city set on a hill to be the light to the world[242] is his son or daughter. Those who endure the valleys, no matter how long it takes to see the mountains, are his children.

We should visit him often and be proud to call him our own.

---

[241] Ibid., Vol. 36, 93 (To John Marshall, December 4, 1797).
[242] *King James Bible*. (Nelson), (Matthew 5:14 Sermon on the Mount).

3

A Rising Sun

Philadelphia, Pennsylvania, September 17, 1787

The old man's health showed signs he was nearing the end of his journey. All their sacrifice came down to this. It was the best possible they could hope for as they passed the torch to the next generation. What they did with it was up to them now.

Awaiting transportation home, his gout bothering him, he watched the people pass on the street and wondered if they could bear such a responsibility. Leaning on his cane, he grunted and noticed a woman familiar to him approaching. She sternly asked, "Well, Doctor, what have we got? A republic or a monarchy?"

Though worn by age and infirmities, he straightened his arthritic body and puffed out his chest and answered, "A republic madam...if you can keep it."[243]

The woman nodded, smiled, and continued down the street as the old man watched her disappear around the corner. What was her

---

[243] *Papers of Dr. James McHenry on the Federal Convention of 1787, in Charles C. Tansill, compilation, Documents Illustrative of the Formation of the Union of the American States.* (Washington: U.S. Government Print. Off., 1927), 952; Allison, Andrew M. *The Real Benjamin Franklin, Part 1, Benjamin Franklin: Printer, Philosopher, Patriot.* (National Center for Constitutional Studies, 1982/2009), 263; Chernow, 539.

name again? Powel maybe? It would come to him in time, he was sure.

The journey was long but remarkable for Benjamin Franklin. Returning to a memory, like he was known to do, the eighty-one-year-old tried to live every single minute to its fullest. Now he could barely stand or speak.

Staring into the street again, he thought of a young lad. One who could stand all day and often spoke too much, alone in an unknown city, with only the clothes on his back. Chewing on those unusual bread rolls without a care in the world, this was the first meal he had since running away from home. This young man showed little fear and was eager to begin his new life. The city did not possess him; he possessed the city. He vowed to conquer the world and maybe leave it a little bit better than he found it. He had so much to learn still. If he knew then what he did now…no that wouldn't have worked. The journey was worth more than the destination.

Grinning ever so gently the way he was known to do, although his rheumatism pained him some, he peered up at a cool autumn sky. The sun burned bright, like the fire burning inside the young man he remembered so many years ago. Would it remain or would it wear with time—like an old book—like his own body seemed to be doing? His body was fading, but not his spirit. He knew death was merely a rebirth, not the end. Would the country realize this? He wasn't sure.

Returning to the memory of the young man, he thought about a rising sun and all the possibilities on the horizon.

* * * * *

Born in 1706 to a middle-class Boston family, Benjamin Franklin knew early on he was different. He was the fifteenth child born to Josiah and Abiah Franklin who had a total of seventeen children from two different marriages. Such a large family kept the Franklins on a tight budget, and frugality was taught early on.

When he was old enough, he began working in his father's candle-making business, and Ben quickly realized he wanted more than the humdrum life of a wax monger. Josiah couldn't afford to send his precocious son to school, so the boy devoured every book he could find. By the age of twelve, he was apprenticed to his brother James's printing house to learn the trade. A natural at the printing trade, he learned every facet of the business, and excelled in the trade but despised the apprenticeship. James had total control over him, typical of eighteenth century apprenticeships, and often beat him for ridiculous reasons such as simple disagreements. This instilled in the youth an abhorrence of tyranny.

By the age of fourteen, Ben wrote an anonymous article for James's newspaper, the *New England Courant*. Slipping the column under the printing house door before James arrived, the article titled "Silence Dogood" was an immediate hit among Bostonians. Written from the point-of-view of an elderly woman, "Silence Dogood" shared a wealth of homespun wisdom and humor. Ben kept his identity secret, because James told him his writing was subpar. He decided to prove him wrong, and his brother couldn't get enough of "Silence Dogood." Neither could his readers, so Ben outed himself as the author, and James was livid. His kid brother should stick to printing and leave the writing to his elders, but Ben knew his brother was wrong. If he was ever going to realize his purpose, he had to get away from James. By 1723, he ran away from home, determined to chart his own destiny on his own terms.

Leaving Boston, he made his way to New York first but decided to try Philadelphia instead. Arriving in the city of brotherly love, the seventeen-year-old was homeless with just enough money to satiate his hunger. He had no prospects but had his health and ambition and believed in himself. He had to stretch the last of his money until he found work, so he haggled with a baker for "three great puffy rolls."[244] Putting one under each arm for want of any pockets, he devoured the

---

[244] Franklin, Benjamin. *The Works of Benjamin Franklin* ed. John Bigelow, Vol. 1. (New York: G. P. Putnam's Sons, 1904), 65–66 (Autobiography); Van Doren, Carl. *Benjamin Franklin*. (New York: Garden City Publishing Co., Inc., 1941), 39.

third. His future wife, Deborah Read, saw the disheveled vagabond that day and thought he looked ridiculous, but she never forgot him.

Ben leaped into the great unknown, faithful his purpose would be revealed. He applied for a job at a newspaper, but the owner explained he had already hired someone and directed him to another newspaper looking for help. There he met Andrew Keimer.

The job with Keimer led him to another opportunity. Governor William Keith funded a trip to London for establishing a printing house and chose Ben for the venture. Keith turned out to talk more than he came through with the money, and Ben found himself penniless. Stranded in Britain with no way home, he refused to be discouraged and adjusted to his circumstances. First, he needed a job so he could save money for the voyage back to America. Getting a position at a copier, he worked for a year and a half until he saved enough for a passage home. He toiled day and night to master the printing trade, knowing it was key to his success. After a year, he saved enough money for the trip and set sail.

Shortly after returning to Philadelphia, Andrew Keimer decided to leave the printing business and thought of the young upstart. Ben agreed to buy it from him, and the *Pennsylvania Gazette* opened in 1729. It soon became the most successful printing house in Pennsylvania. He published a newspaper, printed books, and was contracted as printer for government papers, which brought in hefty revenues. Now he could support a family, so the following year, he married Deborah Read.

His *Poor Richard's Almanac* was popular and increased sales. *Poor Richard's* proverbs and maxims became standbys in the American vernacular. "Early to bed, early to rise, makes a man healthy, wealthy, and wise" and "God helps them who help themselves"[245] were just a few among dozens. His straight-talking down-home style endeared him to Americans everywhere, and by the age of twenty-three, Ben had carved out a comfortable living and could spend his spare time on other interests.

---

[245] Van Doren, *Benjamin Franklin*, 112; Isaacson, Walter. *Benjamin Franklin: An American Life*. (New York: Simon & Schuster, 2003), 96–99.

He was a sponge studying science, philosophy, and morality, and taught himself six languages. His interest in philosophy led him to create the American Philosophical Society. He read anything: insects, birds, plants, fish, rifles, weather, agriculture, and climate. He invented the lightning rod, the Franklin stove, bifocals, and other inventions which benefited mankind. The lighting rod alone saved countless lives from house fires. He filed no patent on it because he felt it was improper to profit from saving lives. He believed this invention was God's gift to mankind and refused to make money from it.

Independently wealthy, Ben decided to master his own behavior with a set of virtues. He made a list of thirteen morals to govern himself by and each week would try to master: temperance, silence, order, resolution, frugality, industry, sincerity, justice, moderation, cleanliness, tranquility, chastity, and humility. He added humility after a friend told him he was sometimes condescending in debates. On his list, he wrote next to humility, "Imitate Jesus and Socrates."[246] He found after working on this that he had more success persuading others by questioning instead of dominating them with superior knowledge. After several months of trying to master the list of virtues, he concluded it an impossibility. Discovering when he mastered one virtue and tackling the next, he reverted to his old habits with the mastered one. He decided man could improve but not perfect himself and scrapped the idea, though he continued to strive for self-improvement.

Ben's religious beliefs have often been described as deist or even atheist. Though open-minded, his beliefs were more complex than a simple label. Explaining this in his autobiography, he wrote:

> I had been religiously educated as a Presbyterian;
> and tho' some of the dogmas of that persuasion,
> such as eternal decrees of God, election, reproba-
> tion, etc., appeared to me unintelligible, others

---

[246] Franklin, *Works*, Vol. 1, 188–190, 201 (Autobiography); Van Doren, 88; Isaacson, 89–92.

doubtful, and I early absented myself from the public assemblies of the sect, Sunday being my studying day, I never was without some religious principles. I never doubted, for instance, the existence of the Deity; that he made the world, and governed it by his Providence; that the most acceptable service of God was the doing good to man; that our souls are immortal; and that crime will be punished, and virtue rewarded, either here or hereafter.[247]

He also described the God he believed in. "Here is my Creed: I believe in one God, Creator of the Universe. That He governs it by his Providence. That he ought to be worshipped. That the most acceptable Service we are to render him, is doing Good to his other Children. That the Soul of Man is immortal, and will be treated with Justice in another Life respecting its conduct in this."[248] Even though, he never officially joined a church he still spoke on its importance, "Tho' I seldom attended public worship, I still had an opinion of its propriety, and of its utility when rightly conducted, and I regularly paid my annual subscription for the support of the only Presbyterian minister or meeting we had in Philadelphia."[249]

Writing his own epitaph as a young man, Ben said, "The Body of B. Franklin, Printer; Like the Cover of an old Book, Its Contents torn out, And stripped of its Lettering and Gilding, Lies here, Food for Worms. But the Work shall not be wholly lost: For it will, as he believed, appear once more, In a new more perfect Edition, Corrected and Amended By the Author."[250]

His list of virtues idea he credited with a sermon he heard at church on the fourth chapter of Philippians. Writing in the final year

---

[247] Ibid., 185 (Autobiography).
[248] Ibid., Vol. 12, 185 (To Ezra Stiles, March 9, 1790).
[249] Ibid., Vol. 1, 186 (Autobiography).
[250] Franklin, Benjamin. *The Papers of Benjamin Franklin*, Vol. 1, ed. Leonard W. Labaree. (New Haven: Yale University Press, 1959), 109–111 (*Epitaph*, 1728); Van Doren, *Benjamin Franklin*, 124; Allison, 276.

of his life, he said, "As to Jesus of Nazareth…I think the System of Morals and his Religion, as he left them to us, the best the World ever saw, or, is likely to see; but I apprehend it has received various corrupting changes."[251]

He went on to say he had doubts about Christ's divinity but would soon have "an Opportunity of knowing the Truth with less Trouble."[252] He felt actions in this life affected each person in their afterlife. Though not a strict practitioner of dogmatic Christianity, he was a Christian in his actions. He had his doubts and honestly questioned them but was hardly the nonbeliever many frequently apply to him.

Ben's actions told more of his character. He gave generously to charity, not only with money, but also with his time. He also helped to create the first fire and police departments, the first public hospital, first public schools, first public library, first post office, and the first militia.

He believed in helping the destitute but was clearly opposed to a welfare system:

> I am for doing good to the poor; but I differ in opinion about the means. I think the best way of doing good to the poor is, not making them easy in poverty, but leading or driving them out of it. In my youth I traveled much, and I observed in different countries that the more public provisions were made for the poor, the less they provided for themselves, and, of course, became poorer. And, on the contrary, the less was done for them, the more they did for themselves, and became richer.[253]

---

[251] Franklin, *Works*, Vol. 12, 185 (To Ezra Stiles, March 9, 1790).
[252] Ibid., 186.
[253] Ibid., Vol. 4, 347 (*On the Price of Corn, and the Management of the Poor*, 1766).

He was a self-made man who knew both poverty and wealth but also knew there was more to success than simply wealth. Many times, he faced failure and struggle but continued to persevere. Hard work and faith in one's own ability with the help of providence would guide a man to his purpose if he remained virtuous. Nobody was responsible for Ben Franklin but himself. He could have easily blamed his father or brother, James, for any of his missteps but never considered such a path. He could have blamed society or God, but decided instead to take responsibility for his own life and refused to surrender his power to others.

In 1755, Ben raised the Pennsylvania militia to protect the colony from Indian raids during the French and Indian War. He led the militia into the wilderness with the intention of fighting alongside the men. He wasn't the pacifist many claim him to be and though he desired peace, once war began, he was as hawkish as the rest. He knew the quickest way to peace was victory. Like William Bradford of Plymouth who set the example for New Englanders, he knew peace through strength worked.

After the war, Ben became ambassador from the colonies to the mother country, and before the Revolution tried to negotiate a peaceful solution. The king and parliament treated him as they treated all Americans—like second-class citizens. He was invited to attend a session of the British Parliament, so its members could attack and ridicule a representative of the insubordinate colonists. They never allowed him to respond, and Britain's hubris could only be remedied by the coming war for independence. He became a patriot for the cause and returned home. Unfortunately, his own son, William, chose to remain loyal to the Crown during the war, and they were estranged.

Deborah Franklin died in 1774 while he was in Britain, and he never remarried. Rumors of liaisons with French women occurred after her death, making claims of infidelity baseless.

He returned to America in time to be chosen a member of the Second Continental Congress where along with Thomas Jefferson and John Adams, he was chosen to write the Declaration of Independence. These three men were selected and responsible for defining the reason for American independence.

Ben had accomplished so much already, but he was just about to get his second wind.

* * * * *

John Adams already had a distinguished career. He came from a respected family from Massachusetts and attended Harvard College, excelling in the study of law. When he wasn't riding the legal circuit on horseback, representing clients, he was home in Braintree (now Quincy) working on his farm.

In 1770, he made the unpopular decision to defend the British soldiers charged in the Boston Massacre because he believed in justice for all men, including their oppressors. Successful in his defense, he showed the soldiers reacted out of fear for their safety, not malice, when they fired into the crowd. The whole incident was just a terrible accident incited by the policy of king and parliament—not the innocent men in the streets—on both sides.

Adams searched for the truth, not the political agendas involved. He was a scholar in politics, history, and government. He studied the Bible and Greek and Roman classics in the original Hebrew, Greek, and Latin. He read the great thinkers—William Blackstone, Marcus Tullius Cicero, and John Locke. These three philosophers influenced many of his conclusions of the inherent rights of men.[254] From these conclusions, he became a harsh critic of human bondage. "I have through my whole life held the practice of Slavery in such abhor-

---

[254] "1771. Friday. June 7.," *Founders Online*, National Archives, last modified June 13, 2018, http://founders.archives.gov/documents/Adams/01-02-02-0001-0005-0007 [Original source: *The Adams Papers, Diary and Autobiography of John Adams*, Vol. 2, 1771–1781, ed. L. H. Butterfield. Cambridge, MA: Harvard University Press, 1961], pp. 26–28; Letter from John Adams to Abigail Adams, 24 May 1789. [electronic edition]. *Adams Family Papers: An Electronic Archive*. Massachusetts Historical Society http://www.masshist.org/digitaladams/; McCullough, David. *John Adams*. (New York: Simon & Schuster, 2001), 39, 245, 375; Smith, Page. *John Adams*, Vol. 1 (1735–1784) (New York: Doubleday & Co., Inc.,1962), 195, 441.

rence..."[255] His son, John Quincy, would follow in his father's footsteps as a staunch abolitionist in the next generation.

John Adams became an ardent patriot for the cause of independence after seeing firsthand Britain's treatment of Massachusetts. With the first shots at Lexington and Concord, he severed any loyal ties to the mother country. Appointed a representative to the First and Second Continental Congress, he was instrumental in calling for a Declaration of Independence. He served as a war director during the war and had the foresight to nominate Washington as commander-in-chief. Later, he served as minister to France and Holland and procured loans from the Dutch which were pivotal in financing the war. He believed in the sacredness of the cause and understood the price of liberty. There would be much sacrifice and perseverance to attain it:

> The furnace of affliction produces refinement, in states as well as individuals. And the new governments we are assuming, in every part, will require a purification from our vices and an augmentation of our virtues or they will be no blessings. The people will have unbounded power. And the people are extremely addicted to corruption and venality, as well as the great. I am not without apprehensions from this quarter, but I must submit all my hopes and fears to an overruling Providence, in which, unfashionable as the faith may be, I firmly believe.[256]

Adams helped create the Massachusetts constitution and wrote extensively on separation of powers and checks and balances in

---

[255] "From John Adams to Robert J. Evans, 8 June 1819," *Founders Online*, National Archives, last modified June 13, 2018, http://founders.archives.gov/documents/Adams/99-02-02-7148. [Early Access document].

[256] Letter from John Adams to Abigail Adams, 3 July 1776, "Your Favour of June 17..." [electronic edition]. *Adams Family Papers: An Electronic Archive*. Massachusetts Historical Society. http://www.masshist.org/digitaladams/

Thoughts on Government in 1776, "The dignity and stability of government in all its branches, the morals of the people, and every blessing of society depend so much upon an upright and skillful administration of justice, that the judicial power ought to be distinct from both the legislative and executive, and independent upon both, that so it may be a check upon both, and both should be checks upon that."[257]

His scholarly grasp of history and governments was profound. John's observations were fundamental to the American form of government. In his *A Defense of the Constitutions of the United States of America* in 1787, he described what the foundations of an American constitution must contain. He reminded Americans that the sole purpose of government was to protect life, liberty, and property. He cited property as the ultimate end of liberty. Without the protection of individual ownership of property, life and liberty couldn't be sustained:

> Property is surely a right of mankind as really as liberty. Perhaps, at first, prejudice, habit, shame or fear, principle or religion, would restrain the poor from attacking the rich, and the idle from usurping on the industrious; but the time would not be long before courage and enterprise would come, and pretexts be invented by degrees, to countenance the majority in dividing all the property among them, or at least, in sharing it equally with its present possessors. Debts would be abolished first; taxes laid heavy on the rich, and not at all on the others; and at last a downright equal division of everything be demanded, and voted. What would be the consequence of this? The

---

[257] Adams, John. *The Works of John Adams, Second President of the United States with Life by the Author, ed. Charles Francis Adams*, Vol. 6. (Boston: Little and Brown, 1851), 198 (*Thoughts on Government: Applicable to the Present State of the American Colonies*).

idle, the vicious, the intemperate, would rush into the utmost extravagance of debauchery, sell and spend all their share, and then demand a new division of those who purchased from them.[258]

He continued to describe confiscation and redistribution of property the same as theft. "The moment the idea is admitted into society that property is not as sacred as the laws of God, and that there is not a force of law and public justice to protect it, anarchy and tyranny commence. If 'Thou shalt not covet' and 'Thou shalt not steal' were not commandments of Heaven, they must be made inviolable precepts in every society before it can be civilized or made free."[259]

Adams was also a man of simple virtues but complicated beliefs. He made judgments based on his Christian faith and believed in religious freedom. To him, there was right and wrong, but individual opinions were for each person to decide. He promoted Christian morality and the Bible but distrusted the doctrines of churches. He also believed in American exceptionalism. "I always consider the settlement of America with reverence and wonder, as the opening of a grand scene and design in Providence for the illumination of the ignorant and the emancipation of the slavish part of mankind all over the earth."[260]

Though he believed in freedom of conscience, he never wavered in his own convictions. "The Christian religion is, above all the religions that ever prevailed or existed in ancient or modern times, the religion of wisdom, virtue, equity, and humanity…it is resignation to

---

[258] Adams, *Works*, Vol. 6: "A Defence of the Constitutions of the United States of America," 8–9 (Ch. 1: *The Right Constitution of a Commonwealth Examined*).

[259] Ibid., 9.

[260] "[Fragmentary Draft of a Dissertation on Canon and Feudal Law, February 1765]," *Founders Online*, National Archives, last modified June 13, 2018, http://founders.archives.gov/documents/Adams/01-01-02-0009-0002-0001 [Original source: *The Adams Papers*, Diary and Autobiography of John Adams, vol. 1, 1755–1770, ed. L. H. Butterfield. Cambridge, MA: Harvard University Press, 1961, pp. 255–258.]

God, it is goodness itself to man."[261] He believed Christianity was the basis of human liberty. The desire to recognize God-given rights and attribute them to all men came directly from scripture. "One great advantage of the Christian religion is that it brings the great principle of the law of nature and nations—Love your neighbor as yourself, and do unto others as you would that others should do to you—to the knowledge, belief, and veneration of the whole people."[262]

To Adams, Christian morals established the very tolerance and equality required for true liberty. He did, however, recognize many who represented Christian churches corrupted these principles over time and believed all men were created equal but weren't equal in their outcomes:

> That all men are born to equal rights is true. Every being has a right to his own, as clear, as moral, as sacred, as any other being has...But to teach that all men are born with equal powers and faculties, to equal influence in society, to equal property and advantages through life, is as gross a fraud, as glaring an imposition on the credulity of the people, as ever was practiced by monks, by Druids, by Brahmins, by priests of the immortal Lama, or by the self-styled philosophers of the French Revolution.[263]

---

[261] "July 26, 1796. Tuesday," *Founders Online*, National Archives, last modified June 13, 2018, http://founders.archives.gov/documents/Adams/01-03-02-0013-0002-0015 [Original source: *The Adams Papers*, Diary and Autobiography of John Adams, vol. 3, *Autobiography, Part One to October 1776*, ed. L. H. Butterfield. Cambridge, MA: Harvard University Press, 1961, pp. 233–234.]

[262] "August 14, 1796. Sunday.," *Founders Online*, National Archives, last modified June 13, 2018, http://founders.archives.gov/documents/Adams/01-03-02-0013-0003-0014 [Original source: *The Adams Papers*, Diary and Autobiography of John Adams, vol. 3, *Diary, 1782–1804; Autobiography, Part One to October 1776*, ed. L. H. Butterfield. Cambridge, MA: Harvard University Press, 1961, pp. 240–241.]

[263] "From John Adams to John Taylor, 19 April 1814," *Founders Online*, National Archives, last modified June 13, 2018, http://founders.archives.gov/documents/Adams/99-02-02-6282 [Early Access document.]

Sometimes brazen, John rubbed many the wrong way with his certainty. His comments, "Thanks to God that he gave me stubbornness when I know I am right"[264] and "in Politics the Middle Way is none at all"[265] explained his truculence. While in France during the war, the diplomatic skill of Ben Franklin was lost on Adams. He didn't understand why someone wouldn't say what they honestly believed. Franklin's mellow attitude was foreign to him because he didn't understand the French diplomacy. Flattery and elbow rubbing was the surest avenue to bring France into the war, and Ben knew he must play the game to bring them on board. Adams was repulsed by this duplicity and refused to compromise his principles. Moody and often churlish, John was too honest to be a diplomat but was a genius when it came to law and government.

* * * * *

Thomas Jefferson was just beginning a brilliant career in 1776. Attending the College of William and Mary, he studied law and served as a representative in the Virginian House of Burgesses (legislative assembly). There he showed an instant energy and talent for writing. A voracious reader, he studied history, philosophy, agriculture, botany, and biology. His *Notes on Virginia* was an encyclopedia of Virginia. He possessed the largest private library at his home, Monticello, and purchased the latest books on scientific discoveries and theories. He invented the iron plow, which made farming eas-

---

[264] "From John Adams to Edmund Jenings, 27 September 1782," *Founders Online*, National Archives, last modified June 13, 2018, http://founders.archives.gov/documents/Adams/06-13-02-0217 [Original source: *The Adams Papers*, Papers of John Adams, vol. 13, *May–October 1782*, ed. Gregg L. Lint, C. James Taylor, Margaret A. Hogan, Jessie May Rodrique, Mary T. Claffey, and Hobson Woodward. Cambridge, MA: Harvard University Press, 2006, pp. 494–495.]

[265] "From John Adams to Horatio Gates, 23 March 1776," *Founders Online*, National Archives, last modified June 13, 2018, http://founders.archives.gov/documents/Adams/06-04-02-0023 [Original source: *The Adams Papers*, Papers of John Adams, vol. 4, *February-August 1776*, ed. Robert J. Taylor. Cambridge, MA: Harvard University Press, 1979, pp. 58–60.]

ier, and designed the swivel chair, the cipher wheel, and a macaroni maker among other innovations.

Jefferson knew several languages and played the violin. He stood six-feet-two, had red hair, and blue-gray eyes and was considered an enlightened man of the age. In 1776, he was thirty-two with little oratorical skill, but his ability with a quill was admired by his contemporaries. An introvert who expressed himself through the written word combined flowery prose with simple precision few could match.

Jefferson, like Washington, has often been criticized for owning slaves. He, like many Virginians, inherited the system but spent his entire life calling for an end to the institution. In 1785, in his first publication of *Notes on Virginia*, he wrote:

> And can the liberties of a nation be thought secure when we have removed their only firm basis, a conviction in the minds of the people that these liberties are of the gift of God? That they are not to be violated but with his wrath? Indeed, I tremble for my country when I reflect that God is just: that his justice cannot sleep for ever: that considering numbers, nature and natural means only, a revolution of the wheel of fortune, an exchange of situation, is among possible events: that it may become probable by supernatural interference! The Almighty has no attribute which can take side with us in such a context... I think a change already perceptible, since the origin of the present revolution. The spirit of the master is abating, that of the slave rising from the dust, his condition mollifying, the way I hope preparing, under the auspices of heaven, for a total emancipation, and that this is disposed, in the order of events, to be with the consent of the masters, rather than by their extirpation.[266]

---

[266] Jefferson, Thomas. *The Works of Thomas Jefferson*. Vol. 4, (New York: G. P. Putnam's Sons, 1904), 83–84 (Notes on Virginia, Query 18, *Customs and*

He tried ending slavery with the Declaration of Independence, but the section addressing it was removed when deemed divisive. Most abolitionists decided to wait until they won the war before taking on the issue. Without the South, the other colonies couldn't defeat Britain, so they compromised. Jefferson's omitted section indicted the monarch for promoting and allowing it in its colonies:

> He [*George III*] has waged cruel war against human nature itself, violating its most sacred rights of life & liberty in the persons of a distant people who never offended him, captivating & carrying them into slavery in another hemisphere, or to incur miserable death in their transportation thither. This piratical warfare, the opprobrium of infidel powers, is the warfare of the Christian King of Great Britain. Determined to keep open a market where Men should be bought and sold, he has prostituted his negative for suppressing every legislative attempt to prohibit or restrain this execrable commerce.[267]

Later, he succeeded in banning slavery when he drafted the Ordinance of 1784, which determined the future states of Ohio, Indiana, Illinois, Michigan, and Wisconsin. "That after the year 1800 of the Christian era, there shall be neither slavery nor involuntary servitude in any of the said states, otherwise than in punishment of crimes, whereof the party shall have been convicted to have been personally guilty."[268]

Three years later, he praised Edward Rutledge. "I congratulate you, my dear friend, on the law of your state [South Carolina] for

---

Manners).

[267] Jefferson, *Works*, Vol. 2, 210–211 (Reported Draft); Peterson, Merrill D. *Thomas Jefferson and the New Nation.* (New York: Oxford University Press, 1970), 91.

[268] Ibid., Vol. 4, 253 (Draft of Deed of Cession of Northwest Territory, March 1, 1784).

suspending the importation of slaves, and for the glory you have justly acquired by endeavoring to prevent it forever. This abomination must have an end, and there is a superior bench reserved in heaven for those who hasten it."[269]

Even near the end of his life, Jefferson spoke against the great contradiction to "all men are created equal" in 1824. "I shall not live to see it but those who come after us will be wiser than we are, for light is spreading and man improving to that advancement I look, and to the dispensations of an all-wise and all-powerful providence to devise the means of effecting what is right."[270]

Again in 1825, he regretted his own generation's failure to end slavery. "At the age of 82. with one foot in the grave... The march of events has not been such as to render its completion practicable within the limits of time allotted to me; and I leave its accomplishment as the work of another generation... The abolition of the evil is not impossible: it ought never therefore to be despaired of. Every plan should be adopted, every experiment tried, which may do something toward the ultimate object."[271]

In one of the last letters he penned, it was still on his mind in May of 1826 less than two months before his death:

> Persuasion, perseverance, and patience are the best advocates on questions depending on the will of others. The revolution in public opinion which this cause requires, is not to be expected in a day, or perhaps in an age; but time, which outlives all things, will outlive this evil also. My sentiments have been forty years before the public. Had I repeated them forty times, they would only have become the more stale and threadbare.

---

[269] Ibid., Vol. 5, 305 (To Edward Rutledge, July 14, 1787).

[270] "From Thomas Jefferson to Lydia Howard Huntley Sigourney, 18 July 1824," *Founders Online*, National Archives, last modified June 13, 2018, http://founders.archives.gov/documents/Jefferson/98-01-02-4419 [Early Access document from the *Papers of Thomas Jefferson: Retirement Series*.]

[271] Jefferson, *Works*, Vol. 12, 410–411 (To Miss Fanny Wright, August 7, 1825).

Although I shall not live to see them consummated, they will not die with me; but living or dying, they will ever be in my most fervent prayer.[272]

In recent years, Jefferson has been accused of fathering children with one of his slaves—Sally Hemings. Though DNA tests showed evidence Sally's son was fathered by one of the twenty-five males from the Jefferson family in the area, it failed to conclusively identify Thomas Jefferson as the father. There is much more evidence that his brother, Randolph, who was a widower during the years of Sally's pregnancies seems to fit the profile better than his famous older brother. The DNA evidence comes from a descendant of Eston Hemings, born in May of 1808 when Thomas Jefferson was sixty-five and Randolph was fifty-three. Randolph remarried in May of 1808, the same month and year of Sally's last birth.

Randolph was so unlike Thomas in intelligence and judgment. He had no reservations about fraternizing with the slaves at Monticello. Isaac Jefferson, a former slave at Monticello, said in 1847, "Old Master's brother, Mass Randolph, was a mighty simple man. Used to come out among black people, play the fiddle, and dance half the night. Hadn't much more sense than Isaac."[273] Early

---

[272] "From Thomas Jefferson to James Heaton, 20 May 1826." *Founders Online*, National Archives, last modified June 13, 2018, http://founders.archives. gov/documents/Jefferson/98-01-02-6127 [Early Access document from the *Papers of Thomas Jefferson: Retirement Series*.]; Peterson, 1001; Malone, Dumas. *Jefferson and His Time: The Sage of Monticello*, Vol. 6, (Boston: Little, Brown and Company, 1977/1981), 344.

[273] Bear, James A. Jr., ed. *Jefferson at Monticello*. (Charlottesville: University of Virginia Press, 1967), 22 ("Memoirs of a Monticello Slave"); Hyland, William G. Jr. *In Defense of Thomas Jefferson: The Sally Hemings Sex Scandal*. (New York: Thomas Dunne Books, St. Martin's Press, 2009), 30; Burton, Cynthia H. *Jefferson Vindicated: Fallacies, Omissions, and Contradictions in the Hemings Genealogical Search*. (Keswick, VA: Self-published, 2005), 56; Holowchak, M. Andrew. *Framing A Legend: Exposing the Distorted History of Thomas Jefferson and Sally Hemings*. (New York: Prometheus Books, 2013), 117.

accounts by Eston Heming's family claimed Thomas was an uncle, not the father of Sally's children.

Regardless of inconclusive evidence, many claim Thomas is absolutely the father. Even recently, claims of a secret liaison room at Monticello is accepted as truth without a shred of evidence to support it. Popular acceptance of an unproven claim often becomes an "accepted fact." This "accepted fact" is then purported to be an irrefutable truth. The possibility of Randolph being the father of Sally's children serves no purpose to this agenda. Thomas is the intended target, not his brother. Some believe if they tarnish the man, they can tarnish his work. The DNA analysis does not prove nor disprove his paternity, but many point to it as definitive proof, regardless of lack of it.[274]

Jefferson, like Adams, was for the equality of all men, and like Franklin, he despised tyranny. Writing to Dr. Benjamin Rush the famous line "I have sworn upon the altar of god eternal hostility against every form of tyranny over the mind of man."[275] He also believed independence was worth any price. "The last hope of human liberty in this world rests on us. We ought, for so dear a state to sacrifice every attachment and every enmity."[276]

He was a student of Sir Edward Coke, Cicero, Locke, and Edmund Burke and believed men were free by inherent God-given rights. Just like Ben Franklin, he is often labeled everything from a deist to an anti-Christian zealot. In 1774, he wrote, "The God who gave us life, gave us liberty at the same time,"[277] which proved he believed liberty was given by God at birth. Much like Franklin, Jefferson believed in an all-powerful creator who intervened in the

---

[274] Hyland, 166–172; Burton, 168-170; Holowchak, 243–244; Coates, Robert Eyler Sr. *The Jefferson-Hemings Myth: An American Travesty.* (Charlottesville: Thomas Jefferson Heritage Society, 2001), Conclusions; Malone, Dumas. *Jefferson and His Time: Vol. 4, Jefferson the President, First Term 1801–1805.* (Boston: Little, Brown and Co.,1970), 494–498 (Appendix II); Peterson, 706–709.

[275] Jefferson, *Works*, Vol. 9, 148 (To Dr. Benjamin Rush, September 23, 1800).

[276] Ibid., Vol. 11, 193 (To William Duane, March 28, 1811).

[277] Ibid., Vol. 2, 89 (Summary View of Rights of British America, 1774).

world, and to this creator, an individual's actions mattered more than his words.

A private man, Jefferson felt spiritual beliefs were a personal issue between God and each person. "I never told my own religion, nor scrutinized that of another. I never attempted to make a convert, nor wished to change another's creed. I have never judged of the religion of others by their lives..."[278] He also admitted his own beliefs were the:

> ...result of a life of inquiry and reflection, and are very different from the Anti-Christian system attributed to me by those who know nothing of my opinions. To the corruptions of Christianity, I am indeed opposed, but not to the genuine precepts of Jesus himself. I am a Christian, but I am a Christian in the only sense in which I believe Jesus wished anyone to be, sincerely attached to his doctrine in preference to all others; ascribing to him all human excellence, and believing that he never claimed any other.[279]

He believed morality was written on mankind's heart by God and were in the Gospels. "The practice of morality being necessary for the well-being of society, He [*God*] has taken care to impress its precepts so indelibly on our hearts that they shall not be effaced by the subtleties of our brain. We all agree in the obligation of the

---

[278] "Thomas Jefferson to Margaret Bayard Smith, 6 August 1816." *Founders Online*, National Archives, last modified June 13, 2018. http://founders. archives.gov/documents/Jefferson/03-10-02-0186 [Original source: *The Papers of Thomas Jefferson: Retirement Series, vol. 10, May 1816 to 18 January 1817.*, ed. J. Jefferson Looney. Princeton: Princeton University Press, 2013, pp. 300–301.]

[279] "From Thomas Jefferson to Benjamin Rush, 21 April 1803," *Founders Online*, National Archives, last modified June 13, 2018. http://founders.archives. gov/documents/Jefferson/01-40-02-0178-0001 [Original source: *The Papers of Thomas Jefferson, vol. 40, 4 March–10 July 1803*, ed. Barbara B. Oberg. Princeton: Princeton University Press, 2013, pp. 251–253.]; Peterson, 958.

moral principles of Jesus and nowhere will they be found delivered in greater purity than in his discourses."[280]

He believed in Christian principles, though he had his doubts. Like Franklin, he questioned the divinity of Christ because his mind was programmed to doubt what it couldn't see. He seems to have struggled with pure faith, but it isn't known if he eventually accepted it or not. He did, however, believe an all-powerful God who rewarded and punished men by their works, and Christ's teachings were principles which western society depended upon. Whether he was perfect in his faith is open to debate, but he believed individuals should accept spiritual responsibility and only God could judge their soul. His struggle with faith was his own cross to bear.[281]

Established churches directed by men with corruptible natures passing judgments of others was Jefferson's biggest criticism of organized religion. A student of history, he knew the pattern of collusion between governments and churches throughout Europe. Rome and Britain were soaked in the blood of those who refused to conform. Sometimes these nonconformists were called heretics, rebels, and even Separatists. Even the famous, "separation of Church & State" phrase has been revised and misinterpreted. Writing to the Danbury Baptists as President, he said, "I contemplate with sovereign reverence that act of the whole American people which declared that their legislature should "make no law respecting an establishment of religion, or prohibiting the free exercise thereof" thus building a wall of separation between Church & State."[282] The separation is

---

[280] "Thomas Jefferson to James Fishback (Final State), 27 September 1809," *Founders Online*, National Archives, last modified June 13, 2018, http://founders.archives.gov/documents/Jefferson/03-01-02-0437-0003. [Original source: *The Papers of Thomas Jefferson: Retirement Series, vol. 1, 4 March 1809 to 15 November 1809*, ed. J. Jefferson Looney. Princeton: Princeton University Press, 2004, pp. 565–566.]

[281] Malone, Dumas. *Jefferson and His Time: Vol. 1 The Virginian*. (Boston: Little, Brown and Co., 1948), 109; Malone, *Sage of Monticello*, Vol. 6, 490–493; Peterson, 958–961.

[282] "V. To the Danbury Baptist Association, 1 January 1802," *Founders Online*, National Archives, last modified June 13, 2018, http://founders.archives.gov/documents/Jefferson/01-36-02-0152-0006 [Original source: *The Papers*

between church and state, not God and state. Established churches were the intended target, not God. The same man who wrote "we are endowed by our Creator with certain unalienable rights…" wouldn't have contradicted his own words. These were the words the nation based its liberty upon. He ended the same letter with "I reciprocate your kind prayers for the protection and blessing of the common Father and Creator of man, and tender you for yourselves and your religious association, assurances of my respect & esteem."[283]

Though he had his doubts, he was a proponent of Judeo-Christian principles. To deny this is to deny his own words. The wholesale embrace of Jefferson as a deist or atheist by public education, particularly universities, is telling. He once said, "It is error alone which needs the support of the government. Truth can stand by itself."[284]

* * * * *

In June of 1776, a five-man committee was appointed by Congress to write a declaration of separation from Britain. Thomas Jefferson, John Adams, Benjamin Franklin, Robert R. Livingston, and Roger Sherman were instructed to draw up a document for debate. Jefferson was chosen to write it by the others and accepted the task. He knew he must clearly define their reasons for declaring independence and define the concept called natural law to make the case for independence. No country had ever been founded on the idea of natural law, and his job was to put it in writing.

Natural law evolved from thousands of years of human understanding. The Roman statesman, Cicero, referenced often by the founders, spoke of natural law eighteen centuries earlier:

> There is a true law, a right reason, comfortable to
> nature, universal, unchangeable, eternal, whose

---

of *Thomas Jefferson, vol. 36, 1 December 1801–3 March 1802,* ed. Barbara B. Oberg. Princeton: Princeton University Press, 2009, p. 258.]

[283] Ibid.

[284] Jefferson, *Works,* Vol. 4, 79 (*Notes on Virginia,* Query 17, "*Religion*").

commands urge us to duty, and whose prohibitions restrain us from evil...This law cannot be contradicted by any other law, and is not liable either to derogation or abrogation. Neither the senate nor the people can give us any dispensation for not obeying this universal law of justice. It needs no other expositor and interpreter than our conscience. It is not one thing at Rome and another at Athens...this universal law must forever reign, eternal and imperishable. It is sovereign master and emperor of all beings. God himself is its author—its promulgator—its enforcer. He who obeys it not, flies from himself, and does violence to the very nature of man.[285]

William Blackstone's *Commentaries on the Laws of England*, the prime study material for young lawyers, reinforced Cicero's assertion:

...as man depends absolutely on his Maker for everything, it is necessary that he should in all points conform to his Maker's will. This will of his Maker is called the law of nature...This law of nature, being coeval with mankind, and dictated by God, Himself, is of course superior in obligation to any other. It is binding over the globe in all the countries, and at all times: no human laws are of validity, if contrary to this...that man should pursue his own true and substantial happiness...This is the foundation of what we call ethics, or natural law.[286]

---

[285] Cicero, Marcus Tullius. *The Political Works of Marcus Tullius Cicero, Vol. 1, The Treatise on the Republic*, trans. Francis Barham, Esq. (London: Edmund Spettigue, 1841), 270, Book 3.

[286] Blackstone, Sir William. *Commentaries on the Laws of England*, ed. George Sharswood. (Philadelphia: J. B. Lippincott Co.,1893), 39–41 (Intro Sec. 2, "*Of the Nature of Laws in General*").

He continued to point at man's corruption and because of this, the creator used a:

> ...manifold occasion for the benign interposi-
> tion of divine Providence, which, in compassion
> to the frailty, the imperfection, and blindness of
> human reason, hath been pleased, at sundry times
> and diverse manners, to discover and enforce its
> laws by an immediate and direct revelation. The
> doctrines thus delivered we call the revealed or
> divine law...[287]

Blackstone declared there was an eternal law which governed the universe and couldn't be legislated or decreed away. When the creator made man in his own image, he granted him freewill. Thus, freewill made all men equal to determine their own path. This is the foundation of natural law. Only by following this law, there was harmony.

Obeying natural law required one to live a virtuous life because virtue was rooted in natural law. This law was laid out in God's law, which consisted of the Ten Commandments or the two tenets Jesus preached—obey and revere God's law (natural law) and treat your neighbor as yourself (respect of other's inherent rights). Freewill allowed men liberty to obey or refuse to follow this law. Throughout history, governments granted or denied rights. Kings and queens declared they had a divine right to rule. Liberty and equality origi- nated from natural law. Individuals and governments couldn't grant or deny these rights, only the creator of nature could. Jefferson stated in the Declaration:

> When in the course of human events it becomes
> necessary for one people to dissolve the political
> bands which have connected them with another
> and to assume among the powers of the earth, the

---

[287] Ibid.

separate and equal station to which the Laws of Nature and of Nature's God entitle them, a decent respect to the opinions of mankind requires that they should declare the causes which impel them to the separation.

Mosaic and Anglo-Saxon law was the basis for English Common Law, and Jefferson, Adams, and Franklin concurred, but natural law preceded and had supremacy over common law. Many enlightened philosophers and experts on law espoused these beliefs long before 1776. These agitators who denied divine right to rule over man dared say all men were created equal by God. This was a revolutionary idea, nonetheless, and monarchs called it treason, while clergy labeled it heresy. Cicero and Blackstone were cited by Jefferson, Adams, Franklin and nearly all the men who signed the Declaration of Independence.

John Locke, a Scottish philosopher who continued this premise in his *Second Treatise on Civil Government,* had even more influence than Cicero and Blackstone:

> The state of Nature has a law of Nature to govern it, which…teaches all mankind who will but consult it, that being all equal and independent, no one ought to harm another in his life, health, liberty, or possessions; for men being all the workmanship of one omnipotent and infinitely wise maker; all the servants of one sovereign master, sent into the world by his order and about his business; they are his property.[288]

Blackstone dissected natural law into its simplest form. "And these may be reduced to three principle or primary articles; the right

---

[288] Locke, John. *Two Treatises of Civil Government,* ed. Thomas Hollis. (London: A. Millar, et al, 1689), 197 (Bk 2, Ch. 2 "*Of A State of Nature,*" Sec. 6).

of personal security (life), the right of personal liberty, and the right of private property…"[289]

Jefferson wrote six years before the Declaration:

> Under the law of nature, all men are born free, everyone comes into the world with a right to his own person, which includes the liberty of moving and using it at his own will. This is what is called personal liberty, and is given him by the author of nature, because necessary for his own sustenance.[290]

Fellow Virginian George Mason used this same natural law in his Declaration of Rights two weeks earlier:

> That all men are by nature equally free and independent and have certain inherent rights, of which, when they enter into a state of society, they cannot, by any compact, deprive or divest their posterity; namely, the enjoyment of life and liberty, with the means acquiring and possessing property, and pursuing and obtaining happiness and safety.[291]

Jefferson slightly reworded these principles in the Declaration of Independence. "We hold these truths to be sacred and undeniable, that all men are created equal, that they are endowed by their Creator with certain unalienable Rights, that among these are Life, Liberty and Property."

---

[289] Blackstone, 128 (Ch. 1, Bk 1 *Of the Rights of Persons of the Absolute Rights of Individuals*," Sec. 129).

[290] Jefferson, *Works*, Vol. 1, 474 (*Arguments in the Case of Howell vs. Netherland*, April 1770).

[291] Mason, George and Thomas Ludwell Lee. *Virginia Declaration of Rights*, Sec. 1. 1776, Manuscript Division, Library of Congress (33.00.00).

The first was the right to life granted with creation. Protecting life was the primary goal of government, and without the right of self-preservation, all other rights didn't exist. Jefferson wrote:

> A strict observance of the written laws is doubt-less one of the high duties of a good citizen: but it is not the highest. The laws of necessity, of self-preservation, of saving our country when in danger, are of higher obligation. To lose our country by a scrupulous adherence to written law, would be to lose the law itself, with life, liberty, property, and all those who are enjoying them with us; thus, absurdly sacrificing the ends to the means. When in the battle of Germantown, General Washington's army was annoyed from Chew's house, he did not hesitate to plant his cannon against it, although the property of a cit-izen. When he sieged Yorktown, he leveled the suburbs, feeling that the laws of property must be postponed to the safety of the nation.[292]

Jefferson knew the first right had to be protected to ensure the others. Nations, being an assemblage of individuals, were also responsible for protecting the first right. Washington understood this truth and applied it to individuals as well as nations.

The second endowed right was liberty. Once life was secured, the liberty of every individual must be protected. Liberty meant free-will and self-determinism according to natural law. Self-government was liberty for nations.

After Jefferson wrote his first draft, he met with Franklin and Adams to get their input. They changed "sacred and undeniable" to "self-evident" and "Property" to "the Pursuit of Happiness."[293] They

---

[292] Jefferson, *Works*, Vol. 2, 146 (To John B. Colvin, September 20, 1810).

[293] Malone, Vol. 1, 221; Isaacson, 312; Van Doren, *Benjamin Franklin*, 550; Smith, Vol. 1, 272.

realized those without physical property still had the right to pursue happiness like Blackstone declared. This covered real, intellectual, creative, and spiritual property and the pursuit of it. Property was the third endowed right of natural law. Locke pointed to this as the catalyst for government, "the preservation of property being the end of government, and that which men enter into society, it necessarily supposes and requires that the people should have property..."[294]

Failing to do this made government obsolete. It didn't grant the right of property nor take it away. Government which forced its citizens to surrender property for redistribution attempted to level individual pursuits of happiness. A primary reason the colonies declared independence was the Crown's confiscation and disregard of property. The phrase "No taxation without representation" was coined to defend property rights.

Property wasn't a privilege but an inherent right as John Adams clarified, "The moment the idea is admitted into society that property is not as sacred as the laws of God, and that there is not a force of law and public justice to protect it, anarchy and tyranny commence,"[295] and, "Property must be secured or liberty cannot exist."[296] He made the case that without the second right of liberty, the third right collapsed.

All three inherent rights depended on the others and in the precise order listed. Without life, liberty couldn't exist. Without liberty, pursuit of happiness couldn't exist. All rights flowed from these three.

After declaring inherent rights based on natural law and making some minor changes to the Declaration, Jefferson gave the reasons for separation:

> That to secure these rights, Governments are instituted among Men, deriving their just powers from the consent of the governed—that whenever any Form of Government becomes destruc-

---

[294] Locke, 319, Ch. 2, Sec. 138.
[295] Adams, *Works*, Vol. 6, 9 (*A Defence of the Constitutions*).
[296] Ibid., 280 (*Discourses on Davila*, Sec. 13).

tive of these ends, it is the Right of the People
to alter or to abolish it, and to institute new
Government, laying its foundation on such principles and organizing its powers in such form,
as to them shall seem most likely to affect their
Safety and Happiness.

Then he explained why their decision was justified:

Prudence, indeed, will dictate that Governments
long established should not be changed for light
and transient causes; and accordingly, all experience hath shown that mankind are more disposed
to suffer, while evils are sufferable than to right
themselves by abolishing the forms to which they
are accustomed. But when a long train of abuses
and usurpations, pursuing invariably the same
Object evinces a design to reduce them under
absolute Despotism, it is their right, it is their
duty, to throw off such Government, and to provide new Guards for their future security.

Jefferson wrote the Declaration in seventeen days during the
stifling summer of 1776. In 1825, he described his inspiration to
General Henry "Light Horse Harry" Lee:

Not to find out new principles, or new arguments, never before thought of, not merely to
say things which had never been said before;
but to place before mankind the common sense
of the subject, in terms so plain and firm as to
command their assent, and to justify ourselves
in the independent stand we are compelled to
take. Neither aiming at originality of principle or
sentiment, nor yet copied from any particular or
previous writing, it was intended to be an expres-

sion of the American mind, and to give to that expression the proper tone and spirit called for by the occasion. All its authority rests then on harmonizing sentiments of the day…as Aristotle, Cicero, Locke, Sidney, etc.…[297]

The universe, nations, and men were all governed by natural law. This law gave individuals unalienable rights, making them all equal. "Life, liberty, and the pursuit of happiness" were the three pillars of this law. This truth was the rock the United States would be anchored upon in the stormy sea of man-made government. John Adams said, "No man will contend that a nation can be free that is not governed by fixed laws. All other government than that of permanent known laws is government of mere will and pleasure, whether it be exercised by one, a few, or many."[298]

Jefferson ended the Declaration "with a firm reliance on the protection of Divine Providence, we mutually pledge to each other our Lives, our Fortunes, and our sacred Honor." Each man who affirmed this document believed they were acting according to the will of God under his divine protection and signed it with the faith in the rightness of their cause. They were willing to risk their money, reputations, and lives on it.

* * * * *

On August 2, 1776, nearly a month after approving the revolutionary document, the Second Continental Congress convened at the Pennsylvania State House to put their signatures on the final copy.

John Hancock penned his famous mark first, boasting he hoped King George could see it across the Atlantic.

---

[297] Jefferson, *Works*, Vol. 11, 409.
[298] Adams, *Works*, Vol. 4, 403 (*A Defence of the Constitutions*, vol. 1, Ch. 4 "*Opinions of Philosophers*").

"We must be unanimous; there must be no pulling different ways; we must all hang together," he reminded them.

Benjamin Franklin, hearing this, responded, "Yes, we must indeed all hang together...or most assuredly we shall all hang separately."[299]

After the Declaration of Independence, there was no turning back.

* * * * *

Philadelphia, May 13, 1787

The old sage remembered the day they signed the Declaration. It was a glorious moment for the freedom of mankind. Now they had to fulfill the promise of it.

Without a government forceful enough to protect the rights of the people and still separated enough to protect the people from that government, independence would have no teeth.

Sipping his hot tea, Ben winced from the sharp pain radiating from his foot. Keeping it elevated when he could, the attack of gout left him unable to walk but a few steps. Gripping the cane which made possible those few steps, he was grateful the bladder stones weren't brothering him now. He thought of the epitaph he wrote as a youth and sighed. The pages of the old worn book were coming undone, and the gilding had been stripped away all right. Getting old was just an obstacle to the spirit, he reminded himself. Inside, he felt the same as his younger self but had to admit these physical maladies sapped much of his energy. The old book was wearing out, and he knew he hadn't much time left. He had one last chapter to finish.[300]

---

[299] Isaacson, 313; Van Doren, *Benjamin Franklin*, 551.

[300] Van Doren, Carl. *The Great Rehearsal*. (New York: The Viking Press, 1948), 2; Bowen, Catherine Drinker. *Miracle at Philadelphia: The Story of the Constitutional Convention May to September 1787*. (New York: Little, Brown and Co., 1966), 16; Chernow, 527.

Benjamin Franklin

The convention of the states had all the talent of America. Though Jefferson and Adams wouldn't be there, their supporters would uphold their ideas. The men converging on his hometown were the best thinkers on law, government, and liberty. Most had served in government and had firsthand knowledge of its strengths and weaknesses. If they couldn't design a form of government, no one could. When Jefferson saw the list of men coming to the convention, he told Adams, "It is really an assembly of demigods."[301] Mr. Jefferson was a master with the written word, Ben thought. They chose well asking him to write the Declaration.

Sitting in his garden, Franklin decided it was a tad warm for early May. Hopefully, the general wouldn't be uncomfortable on his visit. He was a Virginian and used to muggy conditions at Mount Vernon, but Ben wanted him to have a pleasant visit. Their meeting was more symbolic than anything. The man who won the war and the one who secured the alliance with France would sip tea together and assure their countrymen of unity.

Ben had met Washington before. Once during the French and Indian War and another time in Cambridge, Massachusetts, during

---

[301] "To John Adams from Thomas Jefferson, 30 August 1787," *Founders Online*, National Archives, last modified June 13, 2018, http://founders.archives.gov/documents/Adams/99-02-02-0188 [Early Access document.]

the Revolution. He remembered the young aide to General Braddock eager for action in 1755 and a humble middle-aged man in 1776. He grew rather fond of the general during the Revolution. He had brought the nation to victory, and now, he was here again. He hadn't wanted to come, but he was here nonetheless.

Nearly four years into retirement with his own ailments punishing him, he put the nation first again. An attack of rheumatism had the general in bed for days, but he pushed through the pain and travelled to Philadelphia. James Madison of Virginia nearly begged him to come and reminded Washington his presence meant so much for the unity of the country. If he was there, the people would support it.

Washington knew better than anyone how weak the Articles of Confederation were, and the horrors of Valley Forge, Morristown, and the Newburgh Conspiracy happened because of its impotence. His army starved because of the congress's inability to secure funds and supply them properly. Without a consolidated national government, foreign powers would divide and conquer each state at will. He knew the monarchs of Europe were just waiting to see them fail:

> I am told that even respectable characters speak of a monarchical form of Government without horror. From thinking proceeds speaking, thence to acting is often but a single step. But how irrevocable and tremendous! What a triumph for our enemies to verify their predictions! What a triumph for the advocates of despotism to find that we are incapable of governing ourselves, and that systems founded on the basis of equal liberty are merely ideal and fallacious! Would to God, that wise measures may be taken in time to avert the consequences we have but too much reason to apprehend.[302]

---

[302] Washington, *Writings*, Vol. 11, 55 (To John Jay, August 1, 1786).

The separate states were fighting over boundaries and tariffs. New York charged exorbitant duties on New Jersey exports, and Connecticut's trade was subservient to Massachusetts. Little states feared the power of big states, and every state was out for itself.

An economic depression hit America soon after the war ended. This uncertainty caused many to doubt the future of the United States. The people of Massachusetts wondered why government officials were paid outlandish salaries while they couldn't pay their oppressive taxes. Many wanted forced redistribution of wealth while others wanted freedom from their debt. Tyranny and man's right to pursuit of happiness were the reason they threw off the yoke of Great Britain, and now, their own representatives were reinstating it.

In 1786, the western part of Massachusetts exploded in rebellion. Men under command of war veteran Daniel Shays, armed with pitchforks and clubs, marched on the state supreme court. Their aim was to coerce the judges to forgive their debts and to capture the US Arsenal at Springfield. This open act of war was clearly insurrection. Men couldn't take the law into their own hands when they disagreed with it.

The founders tried time and again to reason and negotiate with Great Britain but were ignored and marginalized. For ten years, they hoped for representation in Parliament. If these men were dissatisfied with their laws and officials, they should elect new representatives who supported their views. Open rebellion could not be condoned. Each nation, like individuals, must practice the first right of self-preservation. The founders understood this and Great Britain fought the rebellion from this principle. All nations must put self-preservation first.

Many throughout the young nation were outraged and worried. A civil war would destroy America before it had a chance to rise. Something had to be done to strengthen the Articles or the country would continue down the same road. Once again, the self-preservation of the nation was the first right and goal of all. If the nation couldn't survive, then all other rights could not be protected. Even though Shay's rebellion ended without major bloodshed, the shadow of it still lingered on the mind of every American.

Shay's rebellion was the catalyst for calling the convention to amend the Articles in Philadelphia the following year. Every state, except Rhode Island, would send its most distinguished statesmen.

The two most revered men in America, by meeting, would show they were on the same page with changing the Articles. While the great legal minds debated the details of a new form of government, Washington and Franklin would try to guide them to the greater purpose.

Ben saw the tall gray-headed warrior strolling toward him and knew instantly it was General Washington. Though he hadn't seen him in over a decade, he recognized him. There was no mistaking his presence. He carried himself like a man with a purpose.

Ben smiled, and gazing up again, he noticed the sun rising high in the sky.[303] It looked like it was going to be one hot summer.

* * * * *

By May 14, 1787, only Virginia and Pennsylvania were present at the State House in Philadelphia. Each day, the Virginians met to discuss a plan for the new government. The convention was originally called to revise the Articles, but the Virginians decided to present an entirely new plan. Virginia sent an A-list for their representation. Along with Washington, Virginia sent the governor of the state Edmund Randolph, esteemed Judge James Blair, George Mason, the writer of the Virginian Declaration of Rights, George Wythe, one of the most scholarly minds of the day, Dr. James McClurg, who served as a surgeon during the Revolution chosen when Patrick Henry refused to attend, and James Madison.

James Madison was a protégé of Thomas Jefferson and stayed in close contact with him over the course of the Convention. They were friends and had nearly identical views. Through Madison, Jefferson *was* at the convention.

Madison was physically small. At five-foot-four, his thin build never had the presence Washington or Jefferson had. He was

---

[303] Bowen, 8–11; McCullough, *John Adams*, 368–371.

soft-spoken and suffered from what was believed to be psychoso-
matic epilepsy, though one recent author suggests he actually had
epilepsy.[304] During his days at Princeton College, he was obsessed
with a fear of premature death and made himself ill from too much
study. He forced himself outside for fresh air and exercise and quickly
recovered.

An ardent patriot during the Revolution, he served as a delegate
from Orange County in the Virginian Convention where he helped
write a Virginian Declaration of Rights and its bill of rights. He
then served in the Virginia Assembly and the Virginian Governor's
Council, first under Patrick Henry, and then Thomas Jefferson. Like
Jefferson, Adams, and Franklin, Madison studied Cicero and Locke
and prescribed to natural law.

In 1779, he served as a representative to the Continental
Congress for a few years but returned to Virginia to make his fortune. Because of his disdain for slavery, he didn't want to continue
the family plantation. He knew he couldn't face life as a lawyer, so he
tried speculating in land with little success. Even though he decided
against a career in the law, his time spent studying it would benefit
him in the future. Choosing instead to be a lawmaker would determine his career and the course of American history.

He served again in the Virginian Assembly and promoted
Jefferson's bill, which proposed the gradual abolition of slavery,
though it was rejected. He also helped defeat a bill which would
make it illegal to free individual slaves.

In 1785, he drafted a "Memorial and Remonstrance against
Religious Assessments" which stated that religious liberty was an
unalienable right. Raised an Episcopalian (Anglican) and son of a
vestryman in the church, James, like Jefferson, Adams, Franklin, and
Washington, had Christian beliefs but was staunchly against church
and government collusion. Like Jefferson, religious beliefs were a personal affair, but evidence of them would surface throughout his life.

---

[304] Cheney, Lynne. *James Madison: A Life Reconsidered.* (New York: Penguin Books,
2014), 2 (*Prologue*).

Before independence, the Church of England was supplemented by taxes in Virginia. If you were a Baptist or Presbyterian, you still had to pay. Many other states after independence tried to support specific churches this same way, but Madison was adamant that freedom of conscience should negate this. It was the only true path to pure liberty. God granted this right when he granted freewill, and it was imperative to protect this right in a nation founded on God-given rights.[305] Madison wrote:

> Because we hold it for a fundamental and undeniable truth "that religion, or the duty we owe our Creator and the manner of discharging it, can be directed only by reason and conviction, not by force or violence." The religion then of every man must be left to the conviction and conscience of every man; and it is the right of every man to exercise it as these may dictate. This right is in its nature an unalienable right.[306]

Some have perverted Madison's words to mean no religious principles in the public forum period. He believed religion was often corrupted by governments like the Catholic Church during the Inquisition, the Church of England's persecution of the Pilgrims, and Muslim clerics today. The conscience of individuals must remain free to decide their own beliefs without any government coercion. Government should not mandate the beliefs of a particular church, but he also knew church-controlled governments were just as dangerous. He understood, however, that without Judeo-Christian principles, there would be no religious freedom, no justice system, and no equality because natural law and tolerance sprang from them.

---

[305] Ketcham, Ralph. *James Madison: A Biography*. (Charlottesville: University Press of Virginia, 1971, 1990), 163–165.

[306] Madison, James. *The Writings of James Madison*, ed. Gillard Hunt, Vol. 2. (New York: G. P. Putnam's Sons, 1901), 184 (Memorial and Remonstrance Against Religious Assessments).

Madison biographer Ralph Ketchum said "he never took an antireligious or even an anti-Christian stance, and he retained the respect and admiration of the devoutly orthodox young men with whom he studied at Princeton. It seems clear he neither embraced fervently nor rejected utterly the Christian base of his education. He accepted its tenets generally and formed his outlook on life within its world view."[307] He was an independent thinker who pursued the truth and questioned everything.

To his friend, William Bradford (no relation to the Plymouth governor), in 1772, he gave advice about living morally. "A watchful eye must be kept on ourselves lest while we are building ideal monuments of Renown and Bliss here we neglect to have our names enrolled in the Annals of Heaven…season [your studies] with a little divinity now and then"[308]

Madison was raised a Christian, but he was not fanatical about his faith. He had his own questions and conclusions about it, but he, like Jefferson, was a far cry from a deist or atheist. By simply opposing church-government collusion, he is often labeled anti-Christian.

He also supported property as an unalienable right. Property was no different than the right to life and liberty and in a speech on government, he said:

> It is sufficiently obvious, that persons now and property are the two great subjects on which Governments are to act; and that the rights of persons, and the rights of property, are the objects, for the protection of which Government was instituted. These rights cannot well be separated. The personal right to acquire property,

---

[307] Ketcham, 47.

[308] Madison, *Writings,* Vol. 1, 10–11 (To William Bradford Jr., November 9, 1772); Ketcham, 52.

which is a natural right, gives to property, when
acquired, a right to protection, as a social right.[309]

Where this seemingly small quiet man lacked in size, he made
up in intellect. He was a giant when it came to ideas of constitutional
history and theory. He knew every ancient and modern form of government, history, and law. His writings were so scholarly and his
demeanor so timid, he lacked social skills. He was, however, exactly
the man needed to help construct a Constitution.

He was also the recorder of every debate of the Convention
and the only reason we know what happened there. Through this
laborious task, he made himself sick once again. He believed future
generations should know the details of such a historic event.

* * * * *

Absolute secrecy was agreed to by the Convention, and guards
were posted outside of the State House. Members were reminded to
keep their words behind closed doors. This level of secrecy was to
ensure they could freely debate without interference or pressure from
their states or constituents. They were free to question, compromise,
and denounce anything without fear of reprisal. They would make
decisions based on the dictates of their own consciences, not their
agendas. To form a government based on God-given rights of life,
liberty, and the pursuit of happiness, they must freely exercise those
rights for themselves. How else could they form a more perfect Union
than by those same rights?

The Virginians devised fifteen resolves known as the Virginia
Plan to replace the Articles. Edmund Randolph presented it to the
Convention on May 28 after a quorum of the states was present.
Virginia wanted more than just a revision of the Articles; they meant
to replace them with an entirely new form of government.

---

[309] Ibid., Vol. 19, 360--361 (Speech in the Virginia Constitutional Convention,
December 2, 1829).

The delegates agreed on a system of debate where each member would present the resolve or issue for discussion and vote. No vote was final, and each issue was merely a rough draft. The Convention could change or reopen an issue at any time. The point of this Convention was to devise a form of government they all would support. Majority would rule in the proceedings, but the minority still had a voice. General Washington was unanimously appointed to preside over the proceedings.

The Virginia Plan suggested three independent branches of government: legislative (where laws are written), executive (where laws are enforced), and the judicial (where laws are interpreted). The legislative branch, or Congress, would be divided into two branches—the House of Representatives and the Senate. Based on the British Parliament with its House of Commons and House of Lords, the House of Representatives (lower house) would represent the people while the Senate (upper house) would represent propertied interests of the states. The intention was to have representatives for each interest of the nation and to keep those interests separate and thus balanced.

The executive branch would be elected by Congress and have a veto power over the legislative. The judicial would consist of a Supreme Court and inferior courts and would give opinions on the constitutionality of laws to check Congress and the executive. Each branch would have checks and balances on the other.

The Virginia Plan was a general outline for a new form of government, but the Convention members were to decide the specifics. It was merely a starting point. Some delegates objected to scrapping the Articles and threatened to leave the Convention. Others feared some of the details of the Virginia Plan but supported parts of it. Most objections were from a state's interest point of view and not a national one. Many states feared losing their power to a federal government. Some objected with concerns of losing too many liberties while others acted in their own interests. This self-interest wasn't necessarily a liability, for it helped moderate the strong central government men, like Alexander Hamilton, and pulled the states' rights men to the ideal of federalism. This faction wanted to keep the Articles intact and spoke of civil war and separate confederacies if they lost their equal representation.[310]

Since representation in the legislature was based on population, small states were asked to sacrifice equal status to large states. The Articles were constructed to even the playing field but only sacrificed large states' share of power to the smaller ones. If New York produced more, it still received an equal vote. No wonder the Articles were ineffective. They attempted to level the individual states without consideration of their populations. Writing in support of the new government, Alexander Hamilton emphasized this weakness. "Why should we do more in proportion than those who are embarked with us in the same political voyage? Why should we consent to bear more than our proper share of the common burden? These were suggestions which human selfishness could not withstand, and which even speculative men, who looked forward to remote consequences, could not, without hesitation, combat."[311]

The same quandary the Pilgrims experienced was now affecting the Articles. This form of socialism attempted to make every state equal, regardless of their contributions to the whole. Why would Virginia or Pennsylvania contribute more if they still counted as one vote each? This early attempt at social justice affected the nation for eleven years and resulted in foreign influence, interstate jealousies, and Shay's rebellion. The Declaration said all men were created equal by their Creator and endowed with unalienable rights, but their pursuit of happiness must be determined by merit. A big state with a large population had a right to more representation. In America's struggle to avoid tyranny, the Articles created anarchy. Every confederation throughout history was either destroyed from foreign threats or domestic decay.

---

[310] Ibid., Vol. 3, 13–21; Ketcham, 196–197; Brant, Irving. *James Madison: Father of the Constitution, 1787-1800.* (Indianapolis: Bobbs-Merrill Co., Inc., 1950), 23–26; Bowen, 32–34.

[311] *The Federalist, on the New Constitution.* (Hallowell: Masters, Smith & Co., 1852), 71 (Federalist Paper 17 "*The Insufficiency of the Present Confederation to Preserve the Union, for the Independent Journal,*" by Alexander Hamilton).

The people were not represented by the Articles, only the states. Connecticut would have the same power as Virginia and Massachusetts. Sections could form alliances to usurp the majority with a simple state count. The Electoral College is often characterized this way but is actually based on population majorities, not state majorities. The Articles relied on state legislature votes instead of the people.

After Edmund Randolph presented the Virginia Plan, the Convention adjourned until the next day to allow reflection. It was discussed in Philadelphia's numerous taverns that evening as the delegates sipped glasses of Madeira while factions coalesced according to interests.

On May 31, the delegates debated and motioned for a vote on the idea of a three-branch government. Massachusetts, Pennsylvania, Delaware, North and South Carolina all voted "aye." Connecticut was opposed, and New York stood divided. New Jersey didn't cast a vote. The majority decided to devise a new form of government instead of a revision of the Articles.

Randolph next presented a resolve suggesting both houses of Congress be comprised of representatives elected by the population. This immediately split the Convention.

The small states wanted to keep representation the same as the Articles—one vote per state. The same issue was raised again. Delaware was forbidden by its legislature to vote for anything else. Madison reasoned that popular representation was the only fair way to derive power. Georgia, sparsely populated, shouldn't get equal representation as Virginia, the most populous state. This matter was debated without reaching a solution and was laid aside for the moment.

The next day, the delegates agreed to a bicameral legislature, but Roger Sherman of Connecticut rose to speak against the first branch (House of Representatives) being popularly elected. He felt the state legislatures should elect the members, not the people. He said the people "should have as little to do as may be about government. They want of information and constantly liable to be misled."[312] In a few

---

[312] Madison, *Writings*, Vol. 3, 46; Bowen, 44; Van Doren, *The Great Rehearsal*, 40–41.

years, the French Revolution would prove him right when it turned into the Reign of Terror. Sherman was the son of a shoemaker and came from the people but was cautious about trusting the people completely.

Elbridge Gerry of Massachusetts was also weary of empowering the people directly. Shay's rebellion left an indelible mark on him and many New Englanders, like Sherman. The mobs rose up out of anger and took the law into their own hands. Democracy in 1787 meant direct democracy, not the representative republic, (often falsely called democracy) functioning today. Democracies in ancient Greece were the examples they meticulously studied. The delegates were believers of republican forms of government, and though some had elements of a more democratic nature, none were purely democrats.

Gerry claimed, "The evils we experience flow from the excess of democracy. The people do not want virtue, but are the dupes of pretended patriots." He continued, "I am still republican, but I have been taught by experience the danger of the leveling spirit."[313] The "leveling spirit" was the same socialism which plagued society throughout history. Making all equal in power and property, regardless of their labor, wasn't fair or congruent with natural law. Gerry believed virtuous leaders should represent the people and these leaders, chosen by the people through good judgment, would represent them. The problem he never predicted was leaders wouldn't always be virtuous.

Then, George Mason of Virginia spoke up. "We ought to attend to the rights of every class of the people."[314] James Wilson of Pennsylvania supported Mason's views and said, "No government could long subsist without the confidence of the people."[315] He felt the state legislatures, not the people, would more likely be obstacles to the national Congress. Madison reminded them the people would support the government if they were included in it. These two views had validity. The people often were misled, and sometimes, leaders

---

[313] Ibid., 47; Bowen, 45.
[314] Ibid.
[315] Ibid., 48; Van Doren, *The Great Rehearsal*, 43.

were corrupt, but how could they find what Aristotle called the perfect mean?

Voting on this point, six states supported popular elections in the House. Only New Jersey and South Carolina were against it.

The next resolve of the Virginia Plan was loudly opposed. It suggested that the second house of the legislature (Senate) would be elected from the first branch (House). This would make the Senate dependent on the House. Seven states voted against the resolve and laid it aside.

The first five days of June were spent debating the veto powers of the executive and judicial branches on the legislative. Most delegates believed in a separation of powers of the three branches with a system of checks and balances. Each branch would have a way to check the other if it overstepped its power. Each should balance the other, and no single branch could consolidate their power. John Adams argued for separation of powers in his *A Defense of the Constitutions of Government of the United States of America* and described the state constitutions and their systems of separate but equal branches with each checking and balancing the other. This would be a safeguard against despotism of any single branch.[316]

Next, the issue of the executive was discussed. Some wanted multiple executives, but the majority favored a single president. Delegates who saw the advantages of a single executive were accused of having monarchist designs. Those who wanted a multiple executive still had a fear of a single strong executive from their experience with a king. Slowly, the two opposing sides defined their differences. Those who favored a strong central government were called *Federalists* and those who wanted a weaker central government with power evenly distributed among the states were called *anti-Federalists*. This problem of the executive was also laid aside for another day.

The election of the executive was discussed next. James Wilson came up with the idea of an Electoral College. Each state would be divided into districts and would select electors to vote for the executive. His motion failed by a vote of eight to two, but by the end of

---

[316] Ibid., 67–72; Ibid., 47–48.

the Convention it was adopted. The Electoral College would ensure large states with huge populations wouldn't garner the executive's attention while the smaller states were ignored. Each state's number of electors were appointed according to population, but only the right combination could elect the executive with the majority of electors. It was a brilliant idea to safeguard the minority (small states) against the power of the majority (large states).

James Wilson was one of the staunchest supporters of the people, yet he knew it was also important to protect minority rights. Today, many call for an end to the Electoral College, calling it outdated and counter to the popular vote, but it is there to ensure the executive branch considers the entire nation for election, not simply New York, California, and Texas.[317]

* * * * *

Pennsylvania State House, June 2, 1787

"Sir, there are two passions which have a powerful influence on the affairs of men. These are ambition and avarice; the love of power, and the love of money. Separately each of these has a great force in prompting men to action; but when united in view of the same object, they have in many minds the most violent effects."[318]

James Wilson read Franklin's comments to the Convention. It was still too painful for him to speak, but the issue was too important not to address. They were discussing executive pay. Some wanted the executive's salary a substantial sum, while others wanted no pay at all. Ben hoped an executive would serve the country for the honor, not the money. He understood the corrupting influence of greed. "And there will always be a party for giving more to the rulers, that the rulers may be able in return to give more to them... I am apprehensive therefore, perhaps too apprehensive, that the Government of

---

[317] Van Doren, *The Great Rehearsal*, 53–56.
[318] Madison, *Writings*, Vol. 3, 68 (June 2, 1787)

these States, may in future times, end in Monarchy."[319] If they made the executive wealthy, future generations would return to despotism.

Wilson continued to read his words, "But this Catastrophe I think may be long delayed, if in our proposed system we do not sow the seeds of contention, faction, and tumult, by making our posts of honor, places of profit." Many were embarrassed with Franklin's assertion, because Washington, who would presumably be the first executive, was present and listening. Wilson read on, "...have we not seen the great and most important of our offices, that of General of our armies executed for eight years together without the smallest salary by a Patriot whom I will not now offend by any other praise..."[320]

Everyone looked at Washington, but he remained detached. There was no doubt to any of the members who would be their first executive.

* * * * *

Once again, the matter of a single or plural executive was discussed. George Mason broke ranks with the Virginians on this point and stated he would never "agree to give up all the rights of the people to a single Magistrate." He supported three executives like Edmund Randolph suggested—one from each section: North, Middle, and South. Most delegates preferred a single president, and history had examples of multiple executives tearing a nation apart in their struggles for power. They felt a strong virtuous leader was easier to embrace. They just needed enough checks and balances to prevent executive tyranny.

After some initial success, the Convention came to a screeching halt. The Virginia Plan was assaulted from those who feared a central government. These men were weary from years of abuse from King and Parliament. The small states felt their power slipping away, and with it the Convention. Franklin reminded the Convention, "The first man put at the helm will be a good one." Heads turned

---

[319] Ibid., 69–70.
[320] Ibid., 70–72 (June 7, 1787).

toward Washington again. "Nobody knows what sort may come afterward."[321]

John Dickenson of Delaware called for members of the Senate to be chosen by state legislatures instead of population. Sherman seconded the motion. Gerry said the Senate should represent the commercial interests of the state, and the House, the landowners. He saw the legislative branch the sole protector of property. The small states were fighting for their power in the new government. If population was the only representation, then the small states they felt, would be impotent. Mason asked what sort of check would protect the states from encroachments by the national government. Wilson warned that using the British model of Lords and Commons was problematic because America had no aristocracy. Mason's supporters felt a meritocracy of property owners would replace the old aristocracy. Every state voted unanimously for the motion.

Gerry and Charles Pinckney then opposed elections by the people. James Wilson countered with, "But I know that all confederations have been destroyed by the growth of ambition of some of their members."[322] He believed that those in power were a larger threat to liberty than the people. The day before, he motioned that the people should elect both houses of Congress. "The government ought to possess not only first the force but secondly the mind or sense of the people at large. The legislature ought to be the most exact transcript of the whole society."[323]

Mason agreed and said the Articles represented the states, not the people of those states, and a new government should have a legislature of the people. George Read of Delaware had said, "Too much attachment is betrayed to the state governments. We must look beyond their continuance. A national government must soon

---

[321] Ibid., 87–88.

[322] *The Records of the Federal Convention of 1787*, ed. Max Farrand, Vol. 1. (New Haven: Yale University Press, 1911), 159 (June 7, 1787, King).

[323] Madison, *Writings*, Vol. 3, 100 (June 6, 1787).

of necessity swallow up all of them. They will soon be reduced to the mere office of electing the national Senate."[324]

Revolutionary veteran, General Charles Cotesworth Pinckney (cousin to the younger Pinckney) of South Carolina, replied to Read, "In South Carolina the inhabitants are so sparse that four or five thousand men cannot be brought together to vote;"[325] explaining that some state's populations were too small for popular elections. The Convention voted eight to two against popular election of the House and adjourned for the day.

On June 8, the delegates considered the resolve dealing with a veto power of Congress over the states. Gerry was opposed to it and believed the power would be abused.

James Wilson stated, "Federal liberty is to states what civil liberty is to individuals." If God-given rights were protected for individuals, then states' rights should be protected by the new Constitution. He reminded the members:

> No sooner were the state governments formed than their jealousy and ambition began to display themselves. Each endeavored to cut a slice from the common loaf to add to its own morsel, till at length the Confederation became frittered down to the impotent condition in which it now stands. Review the progress of the Articles of Confederation through Congress and compare the first and last draught of it! One of its vices is the want of an effectual control in the whole over its parts. What danger is there that the whole will unnecessarily sacrifice a part? But reverse the case, and leave the whole at the mercy of each part, and will not the general interest be continually sacrificed to local interests.[326]

---

[324] Ibid., 106.

[325] *Records of Federal Convention*, Vol. 1, 143 (June 6, 1787, King).

[326] Madison, *Writings*, Vol. 3, 124–125

John Dickenson, Wilson's old law teacher, agreed. Gunning Bedford from Dickenson's state of Delaware shook his fist and disagreed. "Will not the large states crush the small ones whenever they stand in the way of their ambitions or interested views?"[327] Delaware would have little pull in the proposed general government, and he feared the large states would control the Congressional veto. Massachusetts, Pennsylvania, and Virginia (the largest states) voted for the motion, but seven voted against it with Delaware divided. The divisive subject wasn't mentioned again.

The next day, the issue of how states would be represented in Congress was brought up for debate. Would they keep one vote per state like the Articles? Or would they choose them based on population?

William Paterson of New Jersey felt proportional representation would threaten his and other small states with small populations. He asked the members to recite the original reason for calling the Convention in the first place. It was to revise the Articles, not to form a new government. Congress granted no authority to this end. He said passionately, "I will never consent to the present system... Myself or my state will never submit to tyranny or despotism!"

Paterson was digging in and refusing to yield his state's power. The small states' existence was at stake. James Wilson stood and countered Paterson's adamant refusal:

> Shall New Jersey have the same right or council in the nation with Pennsylvania? I say no! It is unjust—I never will confederate on this plan. The gentleman from New Jersey is candid in declaring his opinion. I commend him for it. I am equally so. I say again I never will confederate on his principles. If no state will part with any of its sovereignty it is vain to talk of a national government.[328]

---

[327] Ibid.
[328] *The Records of the Federal Convention*, Vol. 1, 183 (June 9, 1787, Yates).

Judge David Brearley of New Jersey then suggested erasing the state boundaries and redrawing them, but it fell on deaf ears. The large states for population or the small states for equal representation wouldn't budge. The debate became heated and on the verge of collapse as they adjourned for the weekend. The fate of the Constitution hung in the balance.

Madison wrote to Jefferson in France a few days before. "The attendance of General Washington is proof of the light in which he regards it. The whole community is big with expectation; and there can be no doubt but that the result will in some way or other have a powerful effect on our destiny."[329]

In a fragile moment of the Convention, James Madison had faith it would work out for the best while George Washington presided over it.

* * * * *

Pennsylvania State House, June 11, 1787

Sherman proposed a motion for the House members to be elected according to population and the Senate to have one vote each. This compromise was to ensure both large and small states had representation.

John Rutledge and Pierce Butler of South Carolina wanted the House to be apportioned according to the taxes paid to the national government, not population. They wanted wealth and property to count as representation.

At this point, Rufus King of Massachusetts and James Wilson presented the members a motion to agree with an "equitable ratio of representation" without having to decide what this would be for the

---

[329] "To Thomas Jefferson from James Madison, 6 June 1787," Founders Online, National Archives, last modified June 13, 2018, http://founders.archives.gov/documents/Jefferson/01-11-02-0380 [Original source: *The Papers of Thomas Jefferson, vol. 11, 1 January–6 August 1787*, ed. Julian P. Boyd. Princeton: Princeton University Press, 1955, pp. 400–402.]

moment so as to set it aside and move forward until someone had a better idea.

Before the vote on this motion, Benjamin Franklin, sensing a need for calming, handed Wilson another written statement to read:

> It has given me great pleasure to observe that till this point, the proportion of representation, came before us, our debates were carried on with a great coolness and [good] temper. If anything of a contrary kind, has on this occasion appeared, I hope it will not be repeated; for we are sent here to consult not to contend, with each other; and declarations of a fixed opinion, and of determined resolution, never to change it, neither to enlighten nor convince us.

He drew from the wisdom gained with his list of virtues. Number thirteen was humility and said to be more like Socrates and Jesus. He now imparted this truth on the Convention. The delegates must find common ground to save the nation. "Harmony and Union are extremely necessary to give weight to our Councils, and render them effectual in promoting and securing the common good."[330]

He knew if they failed, it would be the end of the idea. Franklin understood this delicate balance and reminded the Convention what was at stake. They had pledged their "Lives, Fortunes, and sacred Honor" eleven years ago for this idea. How could they allow local interests to ruin it?

His words brought a calmness and civility to the room. These sagacious words cooled the tempers of the stifling chamber. He was a master at soothing men's passions and bringing the focus back to the greater purpose. Just as Washington sat quietly at the front, like a beacon in the dark ocean, Ben, like a navigator, kept their discussions on course.

---

[330] Madison, *Writings*, Vol. 3, 136–138 (June 11, 1787).

The delegates voted on King and Wilson's motion, agreeing on equal representation and leaving the specifics to a later date. It was a way out of a heated debate going nowhere and would leave open any possibilities during the future discussions. The vote was seven for and three against.

James Wilson and Charles Pinckney then offered a compromise of counting the "whole number of white and other free citizens…and three fifths of all other persons…" This wasn't an original idea either. The Confederation Congress reached a compromise with this in 1783 for determining how much each state contributed to its coffers.

This infamous "three-fifths" ratio has been purposely misinterpreted to damage the intentions of the Framers and the Constitution itself. This never claimed slaves to be only three-fifths of a person. It was a compromise by the free states to the slave states who originally wanted their slaves to count as a whole person to guarantee more members in Congress, and thus more power. The "three-fifths" ratio was all they received for representational purposes. It measured representation in the legislature, not the value of slave lives to white lives it has often been used to imply. The anti-slavery men realized the slave states were outnumbered and would eventually be outvoted in Congress. The proslavery delegates refused to give ground unless their slaves were counted. To get North Carolina, South Carolina, and Georgia to join the Union, the rest of the Convention compromised on "three-fifths." Ironically, this ratio would cause the South's power to dwindle in the next century and end in an inevitable civil war.

Gerry reminded everyone that slaves were considered property, not human in slave states, and couldn't be counted for representation. In a blatant way of making his point, Gerry asked if the free states could count their cattle and horses since they too were considered property. If slaves were property, they couldn't count for representation. If they were men, they couldn't be slaves. Gerry threw this contradiction back at the proslavery men, but still they persisted. Nine states agreed to the measure while New Jersey and Delaware said no. This wasn't a final vote, and the issue would come up again.[331]

---

[331] Ibid., 143–144.

The Virginia Plan was revised again and now contained nineteen resolutions instead of fifteen. It was no longer the Virginia Plan but became a national plan. Paterson of New Jersey asked for an adjournment until Friday, June 15, so an alternative plan could be offered to the Convention for debate. Nobody suspected a counter strategy to arise, and the delegates assumed revisions would be made on the original, so they agreed to the adjournment. They showed their willingness to hear all sides and confidence in their success.

New Jersey, along with the other small states, would try one last attempt to hold the power they had with the Articles with a long shot. The Convention adjourned until the fifteenth.

* * * * *

On June 15, Paterson presented the New Jersey Plan, a revised version of the Articles of Confederation. The only difference with the New Jersey Plan was that it granted power to collect import duties and regulate trade between states and foreign nations. It also allowed for a multiple executive and federal judiciary. This plan was just the Articles with a little more power over the states. It still left the states with equal representation, regardless of population. The small states were trying to erase the Virginia Plan they had negotiated for more than two weeks. Edmund Randolph said the New Jersey Plan was just the same weak Congress under the Articles, which were beholden to the states and not the people.

Three days later, Alexander Hamilton of New York spoke up in the Convention for the first time. He said he remained silent out of respect for the more experienced members but said he disagreed with both the Virginia Plan and the one from New Jersey. The New Jersey Plan was obviously too weak, but Hamilton rejected the Virginia Plan because it maintained state sovereignty. He thought the states should be done away with and a stronger central authority was needed. He believed the British government was a good example and a single executive and Senate should be chosen for life. The House should be chosen by the people but would be subservient to the Senate. Hamilton said the New Jersey Plan was too democratic and anarchic but admitted his own plan gave less power to the people, "but the people are gradually ripening in their opinions of government—they begin to be tired of an excess of democracy—and what is even the Virginia plan, but pork still, with a little change of the sauce?"[332]

Hamilton was born out of wedlock in the British West Indies. His father abandoned his pregnant mother while Alexander was forced to make it on his own. As a teenager, he worked for a merchant and was often left in charge of the business. Discovered by a clergyman, he was sent to America for an education and excelled in his studies. Shortly after, he enrolled at King's College (Columbia University) and eyed a legal career, but the Revolution interrupted his pursuit. He raised an artillery company and was appointed captain.

He fought during the Battle of New York and caught the notice of General Washington who promoted him to Colonel and appointed him his top aide. He saw action at Trenton and Princeton and after becoming Washington's chief aide, Hamilton took a more administrative role. Writing reports left little opportunity to prove himself on the battlefield, but Washington believed his talent was better served on his staff; Alexander disagreed and resigned. The commander acquiesced, because he saw himself in the young cocksure officer and saw his potential. Washington saw Hamilton as one of his adopted sons and Hamilton saw in the general the father he never had.

He served with distinction at the Battle of Yorktown, and after the war, he resumed a prosperous legal career. He married into one of the most powerful families in New York and was elected a member of the State Assembly and the Continental Congress. When he was picked as a delegate to the Convention, he never imagined he would play a larger role.

Hamilton gained no support for his proposals, and many accused him of being a monarchist. His passionate support of the Constitution after the Convention put in doubt his monarchist views, but he supported a strong national government. Though he was born into poverty, he supported an aristocracy of self-made men

---

[332] *Records of the Federal Convention*, Vol. 1, 301 (June 18, 1787, Yates).

rather than one of birth. He had pulled himself out of illegitimacy and poverty by his bootstraps and had reached the pinnacle of New York society. Hamilton also had trouble controlling his temper and couldn't walk away from a fight. He took political disagreements personal as affronts to his honor and this would lead to his demise.

The following day, James Madison meticulously disassembled the New Jersey Plan. Its supporters were trying to negate the Convention by using the Confederation as a new idea. It had been tried and failed and the small states were willing to dissolve this new Union to maintain the status quo.

Madison asked the delegates if the danger to small states from the large would be worse if they found no middle ground and the Union collapsed. Even smaller confederations had to submit to their strongest members. The amended Virginia Plan was the surest safeguard the small states could ever hope to receive.

The two plans were put to a vote, and the Virginia Plan was chosen by the majority of states, except New Jersey, Delaware, and New York. Maryland remained divided. Now the delegates could work on the construction and framing of the new government. They would hammer out the details of each resolution and vote again.

The summer of 1787 was one of the hottest on record in Philadelphia, and the delegates suffered inside the hall. The call for absolute secrecy required the windows closed so the air was thick and steamy. Day after day, in sweltering heat and humidity, they pushed forward. They knew they must hurry before the news leaked, and the longer it took, the nation would suspect trouble at the Convention. Also, the Articles were still preventing prosperity, and Europe, particularly Britain, was waiting for news of failure from their former colonies. The claim of God-given rights to all men, regardless of birth, was on the chopping block, and the Brits were licking their lips.[333]

The Framers were passionate about the work and knew they were creating a whole new government. Taking the best parts from past and present forms of government and adding checks against any weaknesses, they added their own stamp to represent the tenets they

---

[333] Bowen, 3.

espoused in the Declaration. These unalienable rights would be the anchor their government was chained upon.

* * * * *

The delegates finally settled on a two-year term for House members and a six-year term for the Senate. Then, the issue of representation was once again front and center.

On June 27, Luther Martin of Maryland rose and spoke all day and the next against representation by population. All states should have equal representation, he said, and the purpose for a federal government was to protect the states, not the people individually. He went on to claim the large states wanted popular representation because they intended to use their numbers to force their interests on the small states. Lansing of New York and Dayton of New Jersey moved to go back to one vote per state of the Articles to make it fair.

Madison said the small states would benefit from popular representation, because the people's interests were different throughout the states. The largest states had different interests from one another and common interests with small states. Massachusetts shared interests with many New England states, and some of those states shared interests with New York. Virginia shared interests with North and South Carolina, and they shared interests with Georgia. The fact the people were represented guaranteed security from state interests. The people were so varied in religious denomination, background, and livelihood that the mere numbers of factions kept concentrated power from any particular interest. If the states held too much power, they would always vote for state interests. If Virginia's wealthy planters represented only one percent of the population but had all the power in Congress, then money would rule, not the people. The wealthy should have an equal vote but no more. Popular representation in Congress would keep the wealthy from consolidating power.

Wilson reasoned that equal representation supporters were basically saying that small rural towns should have the same votes as a large city within the state. If the state governments themselves didn't practice this, why should a federal government?

The small state faction tried arguing the same points defeated a few weeks before with little effect. The Convention was called to fix the problems the nation faced from the Articles of Confederation, not hold onto an ineffective system. Some members were willing to sink the whole ship if they didn't get their way, but those who wanted to save the Union knew they must find some common ground.[334]

If they remained deadlocked, then the Convention would fail.

* * * * *

Pennsylvania State House, June 28, 1787

With the Convention at a standstill, Ben Franklin requested a moment to speak, and this time, he spoke himself. Directing his comments to Washington who sat in the presiding chair, he knew they were of the same mind on this point:

> The small progress we have made after four or five weeks close attendance and continual reasonings with each other—our different sentiments on almost every question, several of the last producing as many noes as ayes, is methinks a melancholy proof of the imperfection of the Human Understanding. We indeed seem to feel our own want of political wisdom, since we have been running about in search of it.

He went on to say the Convention had looked at other "models of government" but found none that would fit "to our circumstances." His voice was measured, but confident:

> In this situation of the Assembly, groping as it were in the dark to find political truth, and scarce able to distinguish it when presented to us, how

---

[334] Madison, *Writings*, Vol. 3, 300–308 (June 28, 1787).

has it happened, Sir, that we have not hitherto once thought of humbly applying to the Father of lights to illuminate our understandings? In the beginning of the Contest with Great Britain, when we were sensible of danger we had daily prayer in this room for the divine protection. Our prayers, Sir, were heard, and they were graciously answered. All of us who were engaged in the struggle must have observed frequent instances of a superintending providence in our favor. To that kind of providence, we owe this happy opportunity of consulting in peace on the means of establishing our future national felicity. And now we have forgotten that powerful friend? Or do we imagine we no longer need his assistance?

Ben's words reminded the delegates they were there by the good graces of God and should look to him for guidance. In the early days of the Revolution, the First Continental Congress opened with a three-hour prayer session and relied on it throughout. He continued:

I have lived, Sir, a long time, and the longer I live, the more convincing proofs I see of this truth—that God governs in the affairs of men. And if a sparrow cannot fall to the ground without his notice, is it probable that an empire can rise without his aid? We have been assured, Sir, that 'except the Lord build the House they labor in vain to build it.' I firmly believe this; and I also believe that without his concurring aid we shall succeed in this political building no better than the Builders of Babel: we shall be divided by our little partial local interests; our projects will be confounded, and we ourselves shall become a reproach and bye word down to future ages. And what is worse, mankind may hereafter from this unfortunate instance, despair of establishing Governments by Human Wisdom.

Franklin then called for more. "I therefore beg leave to move—that henceforth prayers imploring the assistance of Heaven, and the blessings on our deliberations be held in this Assembly every morning before we proceed to business…"[335]

He also called on one or more clergymen to lead the Assembly in prayer, and Sherman seconded the motion, though some felt bringing clergy into the proceedings now would cause the public to believe there was serious trouble. A few pointed out, because of the Articles, there was no appropriated money for the Convention to pay clergy, so the motion was never voted on.

Franklin's call to God's providence and favor was a reminder of their answered prayers during the Revolution. Washington must have approved of the motion. No one understood this better than him. Ben was also reminding the members to put away their petty differences and find a solution to God's higher purpose for the nation he blessed with his providence. If they tried to be their own gods and build a tower to heaven, they would see it destroyed. His speech refocused the delegates to the higher purpose they fought the Revolution over.

Something seemed to change in most of the delegates after Franklin's speech. There would be more heated debates and disagreements, but somehow, his words found their target.

Washington's presence instilled confidence, but Ben reminded them of their purpose.

* * * * *

After Franklin's poignant speech, Gunning Bedford of Delaware decided to move in the opposite direction. Aiming his remarks at the large state delegates, he said, "I do not, gentlemen, trust you." He

---

[335] Ibid., 309-312 (June 28, 1787); First Continental Congress Prayer, http://chaplain.house.gov/archive/continental.html

said the small states could never agree to the Virginia Plan, and if the Convention continued to force it on the small states, they would, "Sooner than be ruined, there are foreign powers who will take us by the hand."[336]

The others couldn't believe what they were hearing from Bedford. He threatened collusion with the powers of Europe. Bedford did rephrase his threat after he saw the Convention's outrage, and claimed he was being hypothetical to show the possible consequences if the small states left.

Franklin suggested a solution. The Senate would get equal representation, and the House proportional representation, but only the House could appropriate funds. Then, a few members said the people would never support the Virginia Plan, regardless of compromise. If these few refused to compromise, the Union was impossible.

A few days later, Sherman realized the Convention was "at a full stop" and suggested they force a brokered compromise. General Pinckney suggested a committee of one member from each state to find common ground. After Gouverneur Morris of Pennsylvania stood on his wooden leg and gave a speech for an executive and Senate elected for life, the delegates overwhelmingly voted for the committee idea and adjourned until July 5 in observance of the eleventh anniversary of the independence they were trying to fulfill. A war of blood, treasure, and sacrifice had been their price, and they had to find a way to make it all count. The people expected and deserved as much.[337]

* * * * *

After the holiday break, the committee met, and Franklin's compromise idea was nearly identical to the one the committee put forth. The House would be represented by population, the Senate would have equal votes from each state, but the House would control the financing. The large states were willing to give up popular

[336] *Records of the Federal Convention*, Vol. 1, 500–501 (June 30, 1787, Yates).
[337] Madison, *Writings*, Vol. 3, 344, 350 (June 30, 1787).

representation in the Senate if the House had control over the funds. The people would still control the national property, not the states. There were a few discussions and debates, but the heated rhetoric had disappeared.

The smaller committee had accomplished what the larger Convention failed to do. This was known as the Great Compromise, and the Convention adjourned on July 26 for ten days. Washington went fishing, and Ben went home to rest. They could breathe easier now that the Convention survived the impasse.[338]

* * * * *

August 10, 1787, Pennsylvania State House

> We should remember the character which the Scripture requires in Rulers, that they should be men hating covetousness. This Constitution will be much read and attended to in Europe, and if it should betray a great partiality to the rich— will not only hurt us in the esteem of the most liberal and enlightened men there, but discourage the common people from removing to this country.[339]

Ben winced as he sat down. Those calling for property qualifications for members of the Congress deserved his personal attention. It was the very same issue when Jefferson wrote "property" as the third unalienable right and decided to change it to "pursuit of happiness." Men without physical property still had the protection of this right and should be qualified to serve in the government.

Many believed only representatives who owned property would protect the property rights of the people and was a result of the democratic revolt in Massachusetts. The poor called for an equal share

---

[338] Bowen, 185; Van Doren, *The Great Rehearsal*, 126.
[339] Madison, *Writings*, Vol. 4, 151 (August 10, 1787).

of all the property, and this redistribution attempt frightened many of the delegates. Property ownership was a God-given right. No one had a right to the fruits of another's labor. Franklin detested this leveling attempt as much as anyone, but he knew if only the propertied had representation in the new government, then those in "the pursuit of happiness" would not. A young boy on the streets, just starting out, would have no interest in his country, and some would possess property which had no market value. He knew from his own humble beginnings what an asset a person without property could provide the nation.

The majority sided with Ben on no property qualifications for representatives.

Next, the issue of slave representation resurfaced. The slave states demanded their slaves be counted regarding popular representation in the House. South Carolina had nearly as many slaves as freemen, and this would double their representatives in the House.

Even though slaves couldn't vote or hold elected office, the slave states still expected their representation. They first tried to have slaves counted as a whole person to gain representation by their numbers, but only South Carolina, Georgia, and Delaware voted for it. Two slave states voted to make their slaves count as persons. That contradicts today's argument of the Framers counting slaves as only three-fifths of a person. This was the slave states' attempt to seize power in the House and nothing else. When this failed, the slave states returned to the three-fifths ratio in the Articles.

James Wilson had asked the proslavery delegates back in July, "Are they (*slaves*) admitted as Citizens? Then why are they not admitted on an equality with White Citizens? Are they admitted as property? Then why is not other property admitted into the computation?"[340]

Wilson wondered if slaves were counted, why weren't they considered men and created equal? However, if they were considered property, then why not count all property? He was trying to show their hypocrisy. Wilson was an abolitionist and knew South Carolina's population, slaves included, outnumbered Connecticut's

---

[340] Ibid., Vol. 3, 407 (July 11, 1787).

entire population. For every 30,000 inhabitants, they would receive one member of the House who would vote for the interests of his state.

Gouverneur Morris of New York, another abolitionist, pointed out that if slaves were included in population counts, it would encourage an increase in the slave trade by adding more slaves for more power. He vowed to never compromise in support of slavery, and six states voted against the measure.

The Confederation Congress had just banned slavery in the Northwest Territory with the *Ordinance of 1787*. At least five future states would ban slavery. There were already seven free states and only five slave states. Virginia was the only large state with slavery, and a threat of it spreading was unlikely since the United States was still east of the Mississippi in 1787. Many delegates believed once there was a Union, the free state majority would garner the power, while the proslavery minority would wither.

On the other hand, if the free states wouldn't compromise on representation, the slave states would refuse to join the Union. Without them, the Union would be a weak one. Without the Union, there would never be a debate of the evils of slavery. The principle of self-preservation was in play again. Without life in a person or nation, there was no opportunity to right the wrong. If the slave states refused to join or formed their own separate nation, the Union would be incapable of facing future threats from France, Spain, or Great Britain. Europe would play these separate confederacies off against each other until they destroyed the power of both.

With a Union, they could tackle the problem of slavery as a nation, but without one, there would never be a nation. Some claim the Framers kicked the can down the road for a future generation to deal with slavery, but multiple abolitionists at the Convention believed a Union was the only sure way to abolish it.

The delegates agreed to ban slave importation after 1808 and to tax all slaves imported until the ban went into effect. They finally compromised on the "three-fifths" ratio, believing it guaranteed extinction. This was the only way to ensure the Union without embracing slavery.

George Mason, who owned slaves but opposed slavery, spoke to the Convention. "Every master of slaves is born a petty tyrant. They bring the judgment of heaven on a Country. As nations cannot be rewarded or punished in the next world they must in this. By an inevitable chain of causes and effects providence punishes national sins, by national calamities."[341]

Slavery was a contradiction to the belief that "all men are created equal" and would be settled by a civil war seventy-three years later. This national sin would eventually be washed away in the blood of their grandchildren.

* * * * *

From the middle of August to mid-September, the Convention worked on the remaining details of the new government. There were no more heated debates, and a spirit of respect replaced the animus.

They agreed to a president with veto power over Congress and a four-year term. A vice-president would preside over the Senate and a two-thirds majority of Congress could override a presidential veto. They agreed to a list of specific or enumerated powers for the federal government and an amendment process, which required ratification by three quarters of the states.

A Committee of Style was appointed to write the official document for presentation to the states. Gouverneur Morris was credited with penning it.

On September 12, William Samuel Johnson of Connecticut, read the preamble to the Convention:

> We the people of the United States, in order to form a more perfect Union, establish justice, and insure domestic tranquility, provide for the common defense, promote the general welfare, and secure the blessings of liberty to ourselves

---

[341] Ibid., Vol. 4, 267 (August 22, 1787).

and our posterity, do ordain and establish this
Constitution for the United States of America.[342]

They had done it. They had found a way to compromise and
save the Union. It had been a difficult negotiation, but they somehow came together.

On September 15, the states unanimously voted for the new
Constitution, though every delegate did not. Edmund Randolph of
Virginia and Elbridge Gerry didn't sign the document because they
didn't believe it would be ratified. George Mason didn't sign because
he wanted a bill of rights included, and allowing slave importation
for twenty long years was too much. Madison assured the members this Constitution protected those unalienable rights and were
implied.

The Declaration declared those rights, and this Constitution
was firmly anchored to it, but Madison realized three years later the
need for a bill of rights for protection from the federal government.
The Bill of Rights were attached to the Constitution as the First
Ten Amendments and guaranteed freedom of speech, religion, press,
assembly, the right to bear arms, freedom from unlawful searches
and seizures, and trial by jury. The Tenth Amendment guaranteed
any powers not given to the federal government were reserved to the
states and people. The federal government had enumerated powers
granted in this Constitution as a restraint on its reach—all other
powers were left to the states and local municipalities.

Now all they had to do was get it ratified.

* * * * *

Pennsylvania State House, Monday, September 17, 1787

The Convention convened for the last time to listen to the reading of the Constitution. After this was finished, Benjamin Franklin

---

[342] Ibid., 423 (September 12, 1787).

wanted to address the delegates one final time, but his afflictions forced him to rely on James Wilson to read his words:

> Mr. President, I confess there are several parts of this constitution which I do not at present approve, but I am not sure I shall ever approve them: For having lived long, I have experienced many instances of being obliged by better information or fuller consideration, to change opinions even on important subjects, which I once thought right, but found to be otherwise. It is therefore that the older I grow, the more apt I am to doubt my own judgment, and to pay more respect to the judgment of others.

He admitted he hadn't received everything he wanted, but no one ever did. It was a respectable compromise by a group of gifted men, and he believed they used good judgment:

> For when you assemble a number of men to have the advantage of their joint wisdom, you inevitably assemble with those men, all their prejudices, their passions, their errors of opinion, their local interests, and their selfish views. From such an Assembly can a perfect production be expected? It therefore astonishes me, Sir, to find this system approaching so near to perfection as it does; and I think it will astonish our enemies, who are waiting with confidence to hear that our councils are confounded like those of the Builders of Babel. Thus, I consent, Sir, to this Constitution because I expect no better, and because I am not sure, that it is not the best.

He then called for unanimity of support by signing the document. "I cannot help expressing a wish that every member of the

Convention who may still have objections to it, would with me, on this occasion, doubt a little of his own infallibility—and to make manifest our unanimity, put his name to this instrument." Though Randolph, Gerry, and Mason never signed, he tried again.[343]

Madison recorded that the last words spoken at the Convention were by Ben himself. "Whilst the last members were signing it Doctor Franklin looking toward the President's Chair, at the back of which a rising sun happened to be painted, observed to a few members near him, that Painters had found it difficult to distinguish in their art, a rising from a setting, sun."

Everyone turned their attention to the chair Washington occupied for over three months and stared at the painted sun as Ben continued, "I have, often and often, in the course of the session, and the vicissitudes of my hopes and fears as to its issue, looked at that behind the President, without being able to tell whether it was rising or setting…"

With a slight grin, the old sage stood tall and nodded as he finished his thought, "But now at length, I have the happiness to know, that it is a rising, and not a setting sun."[344]

Ben Franklin saw America as a rising sun with all its brightness for the rest of the world at the dawn of a new age, and he relished it.

* * * * *

The Constitution was sent to the states for ratification. They would appoint ratifying conventions to debate and vote on the new Constitution. Nine states were needed for ratification.

The Virginian ratification convention even witnessed a touch of providence. Some of those in attendance were Patrick Henry, James Monroe, Richard Henry Lee, John Marshall, Henry "Light-Horse Harry" Lee, and James Madison, among others. Patrick Henry's fiery speech said he predicted "dangers" from this new Constitution and warned "the angels on high" were "looking down and reviewing

---

[343] Ibid., 473–475 (September 17, 1787)
[344] Ibid., 482–483 (September 17, 1787); Chernow, 540.

America's future." At that very moment, the sky grew black and a violent storm frightened those in the hall. Had Henry tempted God? Or was it a warning? Within a few days, the Virginians voted to ratify the Constitution.[345]

In Massachusetts, John Hancock and Samuel Adams felt this new federal power threatened liberty itself because it had no bill of rights, but the state ratified the Constitution regardless. Hancock and Adams eventually came around and supported the new government.

When nine states ratified, the nation prepared to inaugurate their new government. Nothing in the world was like the Constitution. It was a revolution by compromise, not bloodshed. The delegates agreed on a federal government to preserve the Union of the states. They surrendered some of their wants and tolerated others for the greater good. Compromising self-interest for a higher purpose was an act of selflessness, and the men at the Constitutional Convention had done just that.[346]

* * * * *

On April 30, 1789, George Washington was inaugurated the first president of the United States. Reluctantly, he accepted the call but still believed he wasn't qualified for such an honored position. He was just an old soldier and farmer, not a politician; but after much convincing that without him at the head of the new government, success was in doubt, he accepted. Providence directed his steps once again, and it always led him on the correct path. It brought him through failure and success in his life and never led him astray. He witnessed its wisdom through the Revolution and the Convention.

He just wanted to live the rest of his life in peace, but he couldn't deny providence. He was the Declaration of Independence in the flesh to most Americans. While he sat at the head of the new government, the people had faith in it. As president, he would set the standard for every president thereafter. He put the executive branch

[345] Bowen, 303; Van Doren, *The Great Rehearsal*, 229–230.
[346] Ibid., 288–291; Ibid., 302.

into practice, and his practical nature and leadership was perfectly suited for the presidency. He won the election unanimously without opposition.

He was sworn into office on the balcony of Federal Hall in New York City, overlooking a huge gathering. John Adams, back from Britain, stood beside him as his vice president. Washington repeated the presidential oath and swore to "preserve, protect and defend the Constitution of the United States." He tacked on his own unique phrase to the end of the oath still used today: "So help me, God." Then he bent down and kissed the Bible he had placed his hand on. Asking God for help and kissing the Judeo-Christian Bible didn't appear to be the actions of a man countless historians claimed was a deist.[347] The crowd erupted in cheers and shouted, "Long Live George Washington!" Without him, this experiment may have failed before it had a chance to work.

He served two terms as the chief executive and left a foundation so impenetrable it still exists today. Washington had the uncanny talent of surrounding himself with gifted people. He delegated authority to cabinet members but listened to different views to make important decisions. This he learned as a general and a farmer.

He appointed Thomas Jefferson as Secretary of State and Alexander Hamilton as Secretary of the Treasury. Jefferson, the small frugal government and states' rights defender, and Hamilton, the strong federal power warrior advised President Washington. Jefferson believed Hamilton was flirting with tyranny, and Hamilton thought Jefferson wanted mob rule and anarchy. They provided Washington with both sides of every issue. Sometimes, the president decided with Hamilton and other times with Jefferson. He tried to find middle ground between the two but always made final decisions. Both men were integral to the formation of the country. Hamilton created the economic system we still use today, and Jefferson warned of the dangers of encroachments by federal power.

---

[347] Flexner, James Thomas. *George Washington: And the New Nation (1783-1793)*, Vol. 3. (Boston: Little, Brown and Co.,1969-70), 187; Freeman, *Washington*, 565; Chernow; 568-569.

These two men would go on to lead the two political parties which formed during Washington's two terms. Hamilton headed the Federalist Party, and Jefferson the Republican Party (different from the modern Republican party and sometimes called the Democratic-Republican Party).

James Madison became a leading member of the House of Representatives, Secretary of State under President Jefferson and the fourth president of the United States. He once reflected on the miracle of this new nation:

> The real wonder is, that so many difficulties should have been surmounted; and surmounted with an unanimity almost as unprecedented as it must have been unexpected. It is impossible for the man of pious reflection not to perceive in it, a finger of that Almighty Hand which has been so frequently and signally extended to our relief in the critical stages of the Revolution.[348]

Alexander Hamilton eventually lost his life in a duel with Jefferson's Vice President, Aaron Burr, in 1804. Hamilton could never walk away from a challenge to his honor.

John Adams was elected the second president of the United States in 1796 and served one term, which he lost to Thomas Jefferson in the election of 1800. The two longtime friends became rivals for the next twenty years until Jefferson sent his regards after Adams's wife, Abigail, died and the two old patriots resumed their friendship. They both would die on the very same day—July 4, 1826—the fiftieth anniversary of the Declaration of Independence. John Adams' final words were, "Thomas Jefferson still survives!" He was unaware the author of the Declaration of Independence died

---

[348] *The Federalist, on the New Constitution*, 166 (Federalist No. 37, James Madison).

earlier the same day. The physical men were gone, but the spirit they left in the Declaration still survives.[349]

George Washington left the presidency in 1797 and retired to Mount Vernon. In his farewell address, he stressed the Union would be preserved, only by adherence to the Constitution, and warned against foreign alliances and political parties. He also reminded Americans how they had prospered thus far:

> Of all the dispositions and habits, which lead to political prosperity, Religion and Morality are indispensable supports. In vain would that man claim the tribute of Patriotism, who should labor to subvert these great pillars of human happiness, these firmest props of the duties of Men and Citizens... Can it be that Providence has not connected the permanent felicity of a nation with its virtue... The experiment, at least is recommended by every sentiment which ennobles human nature. Alas! is it rendered impossible by its vices?[350]

Washington returned home and died two years later on December 14, 1799. At his funeral, General Henry "Light-Horse Harry" Lee, father of General Robert E. Lee, gave the eulogy that defined the essence of his old friend. "First in war, first in peace, first in the hearts of his countrymen, he was second to none in the humble and endearing scenes of private life: Pious, just, humane, temperate, and sincere; uniform, dignified and commanding, his example was edifying to all around him as were the effects."[351]

---

[349] McCullough, *John Adams*, 645-646; Smith, Vol. 2, 1137; Malone, Vol. 6, 498; Peterson, 1008.

[350] Ford, Worthington Chauncey. *George Washington's Farewell Address*. (Boston: Small, Maynard & Co., 1899), 19, 22.

[351] *Eulogies and Orations on the Life and Death of General George Washington, First President of the United States of America*. (Boston: Manning & Loring, 1800), 17 (Henry Lee, Funeral Oration, December 26, 1799); Chernow, 811.

George Washington's journey was over, his purpose achieved. His example would remind every American to persevere against impossible odds and to remember who it was that guided them to their purpose. "Without the beneficent interposition of the Supreme Ruler of the universe, we could not have reached the distinguished situation which we have attained with such unprecedented rapidity. To him, therefore, should we bow with gratitude and reverence, and endeavor to merit a continuance of his special favors."[352]

Until the very end, he never once, accepted the credit himself.

* * * * *

Benjamin Franklin put his name to four documents he helped create—the Declaration of Independence, the French Alliance of 1778, the Peace Treaty ending the Revolution, and the Constitution. He was an inventor, entrepreneur, and successful businessman who embodied the American dream. He died on April 17, 1790, at the age of eighty-four. Ben once wrote, "Well done is better than well said."[353] He had lived life the same, though his words and actions were well-received. He had left the world a far better place. The rising sun he made possible was just peering over the horizon at the sunset of his life, and he would never see all its promise. Would those who inherited the blessings Washington, Jefferson, Adams, and Franklin secured for them continue their work as a rising sun?

The next chapter was about to begin as old enemies prepared to test the young nation. The same fire which purified the last generation in the valley was about to baptize the next one out of the ashes.

The epitaph Ben wrote in his early twenties was a fitting description for the legacy the founding generation left behind. The old worn book was "stripped of its Lettering and Gilding...But the

---

[352] *George Washington Papers, Series 4, General Correspondence*: George Washington to the Rhode Island General Assembly, April 13, 1797. Manuscript/Mixed Material. https://www.loc.gov/item/mgw440604/.

[353] *The Papers of Benjamin Franklin, Vol. 2, January 1, 1735 through December 31, 1744*, ed. Leonard W. Labaree. (New Haven: Yale University Press, 1961), 162–172 (Poor Richard's Almanac, 1737).

Work shall not be wholly lost: For it will, as he believed, appear once more, In a new & more perfect Edition, Corrected and Amended By the Author."[354]

It was up to a new generation to remember the contents of this work and to rely on the Author who would lead them to a more perfect edition.

---

[354] See note 250. Isaacson, 470.

4

Trial by Fire

Waxhaw, South Carolina, 1770s

The boy sat on the ground crying. Why he was weeping was one of those trivial reasons children choose to cry over. Elizabeth Jackson heard her son, Andrew, weeping and raced from her chores to find him. She had to be mother and father now, she had to remember. What was it this time? A fall? A bully? Maybe frustration because he was too small to play with the older boys? Whatever it was, she needed to stop his tears. Andy was so thin, he could blow away in a strong wind, but he had a feisty personality like his mother and could work himself into tears.

Finding him sitting in the dirt with tears trickling down his cheeks, she kneeled and took his chin in her hand. "Don't let me see you crying again!"

Andrew's face contorted, then drooped as he wiped his tears with his shirt sleeves. His eyes were like two shards of blue ice, which seemed to burn right through anyone they focused on.

The woman continued, "Girls were made to cry...not boys." She had to tell him the truth, even if it hurt. It would help him grow to be a man someday.

Andrew's eyes widened by his mother's words, and he asked, "What are boys made for then?"

His mother stared deep into those eyes with her similar piercing gaze. She had to teach him the things his father would have shown him. She needed to raise him to be the kind of man who could survive the frontier, not one of those dandies in the east.

Cracking a grin, her eyes ablaze, she said, "To fight!"

Andrew Jackson would remember his mother's advice the rest of his life.[355]

* * * * *

1807, off the coast of Virginia

Three American sailors lay dead and eighteen were seriously wounded. Black plumes of smoke rose from the wreckage as the scent of charred wood, gunpowder, and blood mixed with the salty air.

Three feet of water filled the hull of the ship as the carnage reached Hampton Roads, Virginia. The sails were shot so many times, they looked like napkins tied to the masts. Moans of agony blended with the rippling waves and crying seagulls.

Three Americans had been kidnapped from the crew of the *Chesapeake.* The skipper, Captain James Barron, was among the wounded.

What caused such a blatant act? Was it rogue pirates or some uncivilized world nation? The United States was not at war, but an act of war was the only way to describe this attack.

On June 22, the *Chesapeake* was off the Virginia coast when the British ship, *H.M.S. Leopard,* pulled alongside and demanded permission to search for deserters. Rumors that they were aboard circulated among the British navy, but Captain Barron knew a for-

---

[355] Remini, Robert V. *Andrew Jackson and the Cause of American Empire 1767–1821,* Volume 1. (New York: Harper & Row, 1977), 10–11; Buell, Augustus. *History of Andrew Jackson: Pioneer, Patriot, Soldier, Politician, President, Vol. 2.* (New York: Charles Scribner's Sons, 1904), 410–411; Rogin, Michael Paul. *Fathers & Children: Andrew Jackson and the Subjugation of the American Indian.* (New York: Alfred Knopf, Inc.,1975,1991), Ch. 3: *"Nature, Property, and Title."*

eign power couldn't demand anything of a sovereign neutral country according to international law, so he refused the request.

Captain of the *Leopard*, S. P. Humphries responded by opening fire on the *Chesapeake* (which was unprepared for a battle so close to shore and during peacetime) and battered it for twenty minutes before she struck her colors.

Humphries then removed three Americans along with one deserter and left the *Chesapeake* disabled in the water. The three kidnapped Americans were impressed after the British fired on the *Chesapeake*. These three Americans were free black men who had been *impressed*—forced to join the royal navy—before but escaped when they returned to American shores. *Impressment* was Britain's answer to grow its maritime power as it fought Napoleon.

The British still regarded the United States as a second-class nation and disregarded the outcome of the Revolution. What could America do to them? The "colonies" couldn't risk another war. General Washington was seven years in his grave, and there was no one to replace him. The British felt the Revolution was an anomaly and it had never really lost the war. Americans were weak and divided without a Washington or a Franklin to inspire them.

President Jefferson was too old and clung to his high ideals of small navies and armies out of fear of an American Napoleon. He hadn't the stomach to fight. He pursued a pacifist foreign policy to stay out of Europe's endless wars. Great Britain saw his timidity as weakness and wasn't worried much about America. Jefferson spent most of his public life as a diplomat and believed in exhausting every possible avenue to peacefully settle disputes. War must be the last option. He wasn't ready to commit to another war with Great Britain.[356]

* * * * *

[356] Roosevelt, Theodore. *The Naval War of 1812.* (New York: Random House Modern Library Edition, 1882,1999), 6; Borneman, Walter R. *1812: The War That Forged a Nation.* (New York: Harper Collins, 2004), 22–24; Howard, Hugh. *Mr. and Mrs. Madison's War.* (New York: Bloomsbury Press, 2012), 3–5;

White House, July 14, 1807

President Thomas Jefferson gazed down at the letter he was writing, attempting to sum up the Chesapeake Affair and options for its recourse:

> Never since the battle of Lexington have I seen this country in such a state of exasperation as at present, and even that did not produce unanimity. The federalists themselves coalesce with us to object. "Reparation for the past, and security for the future," is our motto; but whether they will yield it freely, or will require resort to non-intercourse, or to war, is yet to be seen.

He had hoped non-intercourse would be enough, but he had doubts. Finishing his thought, he scribbled, "We prepare for the last."[357] Though he saw war as a last resort, he feared it was a possibility now.

Twenty-four years had passed since the Revolution, and Britain never really accepted that they had been beaten by a bunch of merchants and farmers. This was an embarrassment to the proud nation and forced many to reevaluate the merits of monarchy.

George III was still on the throne, but in his descent into madness, Parliament grabbed more power from the king. Britain commanded the seas after Lord Nelson's triumph over Napoleon's navy at Trafalgar in 1805, and they were still master of the oceans. Dealing with Napoleon would take another eight years, and Britain believed self-preservation dictated *impressment*. They were willing to use any tactic to achieve victory.

Parliament enacted a law legalizing *impressment* to protect its navy, and America was caught in the middle of the two superpowers.

Malone, Dumas. *Jefferson and His Time, Vol. 5, Jefferson the President Second Term, 1805-1809.* (Boston: Little, Brown & Co., 1974), 420–422.

[357] Jefferson, *Works, Vol. 10,* 460–461 (To Du Pont Nemours, July 14, 1807).

Britain claimed any nation trading with its enemies could be stopped and searched, even a neutral one. They used war as an excuse to kidnap free men and force them into the royal navy, and their massive warships and crews enforced it.

Now American credibility was at risk. Either all men were created equal and endowed with God-given unalienable rights or kings, legislatures, and any bully with the power of force could determine those rights. These two beliefs couldn't coexist. If America backed down, it would send a message to the rest of the world that force was the answer and freedom was a pipe dream. Without the conviction to preserve freedom, it would die by its own hand. If it wouldn't defend its own sovereignty and the rights of its people, the American ideal meant nothing.

Jefferson was nearing the end of his second term and his red hair had grayed. Dressing in plain black and brown suits, he never put on airs at state dinners and had his speeches read to Congress by clerks. He despised ceremony and protocol and once answered the door at the president's mansion (White House) in his bed slippers to a visiting dignitary and thought nothing of the faux pas. Others laughed and called him uncouth, and he had lost his fondness for European traditions. He saw the office of president as a public servant, not a king, and took the responsibility of safeguarding American liberties serious. He was also an idealist and believed in the basic goodness of humanity and felt American ideals would appeal to all men, if they could be reasoned with. He would often change his views, but his core beliefs were nonnegotiable.

The diplomat in Jefferson didn't make him a pacifist, but an all-out war with the world's greatest superpower while America was digging out of the debt of the Revolution seemed reckless to him. He did, however, use force when necessary.

Presidents Washington and Adams dealt with the Barbary pirates by paying tribute, which was nothing but extortion. Another war would have been suicidal for the nation, and it was thought cheaper to pay tribute. The Barbary pirates were Muslim extremists who believed all nonbelievers must convert to Islam or face death and enslavement. The leaders of these North African countries commanded their sailors to capture infidel ships and demand ransoms for the safe return of property and persons. After the ransom was paid, the pirates would find fresh victims. European powers paid tribute to the Barbary States, and Washington and Adams decided to follow suit.

When Jefferson became president in 1801, he already decided not to pay tribute and sent a naval force to the Mediterranean to bloody the bully's nose. Successful, the Barbary States sued for peace in 1805.[358] He understood this enemy and studied the Quran to uncover the enemy's motivation. He concluded:

> ...that it (*Islam*) was founded on the Laws of their Prophet, that it was written in their Koran, that all nations who should not have acknowledged their authority were sinners, that it was their right and duty to make war upon them wherever they could be found, and to make slaves of all they could take as Prisoners, and that every Musselman (*Muslim*) who should be slain in Battle was sure to go to Paradise.[359]

Though victorious in this first war on terror, Jefferson knew France and Britain were different in their capabilities. Their motivation was an act of national self-preservation during war, not religious ideology. Jefferson believed in diplomacy between civilized nations and dealt with violations against American sovereignty with his own country's self-preservation in mind.

---

[358] Malone, Dumas. *Jefferson and His Time*, Volume 4, 96–99; Wheelan, Joseph. *Jefferson's War: America's First War on Terror 1801–1805*. (New York: Carroll & Graf Publishers, 2003, 2004), 5–8.

[359] *The Papers of Thomas Jefferson, Vol. 9, 1 November 1785–22 June 1786*, ed. Julian P. Boyd. (Princeton: Princeton University Press, 1954), 357–359 (American Commissioners to John Jay, March 28, 1786); Founders Online, National Archives, last modified June 13, 2018, http://founders.archives.gov/documents/Jefferson/01-09-02-0315.

The Chesapeake Affair was the Boston Massacre all over again, and Jefferson believed, like the patriots during the Revolution, that peaceful solutions must be pursued first. He was just as outraged as other Americans but knew it took five years from the Boston Massacre to the first shots at Lexington and Concord and was willing to avoid bloodshed if another solution could be found.

If America attempted defiance, while Britain was busy with Napoleon, it might give an advantage to France. If Great Britain sued for peace with the French dictator, it would free them to turn on America. If he allowed these two belligerents to exhaust each other, it may weaken both. In the meantime, the United States had time to prepare. The third president was tough, but he wasn't a fool. The time to strike would come, but not yet.

If Britain could force its will on America, they were still under the same tyranny as before, and the author of the Declaration of Independence would never allow this. He first placed an embargo on British trade to hit them financially, but this embargo failed in its purpose and only hurt New England merchants, causing more anti-administration feeling. When the *Leopard* fired on the *Chesapeake*, it appeared war was inevitable.

Senator Samuel Smith of Maryland spoke for many of his countrymen when he said, "There appeared but one opinion—war—in case that satisfaction is not given."[360]

Lost in his thoughts, Jefferson now recalled his second inaugural address and his own fallibility. He once again turned to God for guidance:

> I fear that any motives of interest may lead me astray; I am sensible of no passion which could seduce me knowingly from the path of justice; but the weakness of human nature, and the limits of my own understanding, will produce errors of judgment...the want of it will not lessen with increasing years. I shall need, too the favor of that

---

[360] Malone, Vol. 5, 425

Being in whose hands we are, who led our forefathers, as Israel of old, from their native land, and
planted them in a country flowing with all the
necessaries and comforts of life; who has covered
our infancy with his providence...[361]

Two years later, he wrote to William Duane about the fragile
state of things. "They [the British] have often enough, God knows,
given us cause of war before; but it has been on points which would
not have united the nation. But now they have touched a chord
which vibrates in every heart."[362]

Still, he hoped for a peaceful solution and the understanding to
choose the correct path.

* * * * *

The Chesapeake Affair came and went with a British apology
and a promise of reparations. This diffused the call for war, but new
outrages continued to spark American anger. Jefferson ended his two
terms avoiding war through diplomacy and handed the reins over to
his successor, Secretary of State Madison, and retired to his home,
Monticello.

James Madison was president for three years when the British
outrages escalated. Familiar with the problems Jefferson faced while
at the State Department, he had his own ideas about dealing with
them. Madison was practical and less chained to abstract ideas as his
predecessor. Where Jefferson believed in diplomacy and embargos,
Madison recognized what was useful and what wasn't and adjusted
accordingly. Where Jefferson was an idealist, Madison was a realist.

If it didn't work, it was time to try something else, and he
micromanaged his administration. Jefferson was laid back and
delegated authority, but Madison learned every facet of his job as
Secretary of State and, as president, was involved in all administra-

---

[361] Jefferson, *Works, Vol. 10,* 136 (Second Inaugural Address, March 4, 1805).
[362] Ibid., 471; Malone, Vol. 5, 425–426.

tive duties. He, like Jefferson, believed in the Constitution he helped author and was key to its formation. Along with Hamilton and Jay, he helped write the *Federalist Papers*, which made the scholarly case for ratification. He believed in limited federal power restricted by the Tenth Amendment and once stated on the floor of the House of Representatives, "The government of the United States is a definite government, confined to specified objects. It is not like the state governments whose powers are more general. Charity is no part of the legislative duty of the government."[363]

He was a scholar and a workaholic, but not much of a talker. When someone attempted conversation, he sometimes left the impression of a cold and stoic man. He was simply shy and introverted, and first impressions told nothing of his personality. Where Washington and Jefferson were tall impressive figures, and Patrick Henry and Ben Franklin were gifted orators, Madison's strength was his intellect and work ethic. He was warm and humorous with those he knew well, though he spent most of his time with his mind on history, politics, and government. He was a scholar on many subjects, but not an astute politician nor very charismatic.

President James Madison

---

[363] *Annals of Congress*, Third Congress, First Session. James Madison Speech in the House of Representatives, debate *"On the Memorial of the Relief Committee of Baltimore, for the Relief of Santo Domingo Refugees,"* January 10, 1794

Luckily, Madison's wife, Dolley, possessed the warmth and charm he lacked, and her popularity benefited his presidency. He was the serious theoretician, and she was the fun and fashionable entertainer. Charismatic, outgoing, and everybody's friend, Dolley was the definition of a socialite, and her frequent dinner parties were the talk of the town by members of both parties. Many thought James too rigid and his young wife too lax, but in reality, they complemented and balanced one another.

He married Dolley when he was forty-three years-old, and she was his first wife. Dolley was seventeen years younger and had been married once before. Her first husband, John Todd, died in 1793 during a yellow fever outbreak, which also claimed her three-month-old son. She was left a widow until she married James a year later, and he welcomed her son and sister like they were his own. He was proud of his new vivacious wife, and most Americans loved her in return.

With all his peccadilloes and slight physical size, Madison possessed an inner strength. Not easily intimidated, his scrawny appearance left many regretting that they underestimated the little president. He came in a small package but possessed a lot of fight.

* * * * *

South Carolina, 1781

"Clean my boots, boy!" The British dragoon demanded of the thirteen-year-old boy as he kicked over a table, spilling articles across the floor.

Andrew glared at the officer as his face flushed red from anger. "Sir, I am a prisoner of war and claim to be treated as such."

The officer scowled, drawing his sword, and slashed at the boy's head. How dare this offspring of traitors disrespect him, the dragoon thought. He would teach the boy a lesson about war he would never forget.

The room was occupied by British horsemen, and there was little space to retreat. Andrew raised his left arm to block the sword and received a deep gash on his hand and head. Badly wounded, the boy turned away as the dragoon commanded his brother, Robert, to clean his boots. Robert refused as well, and the Brit slashed his sword down, severely wounding him.

As Andrew bled profusely, he vowed vengeance on the British, and one day, he would return the scars he would wear his entire life.[364]

* * * * *

Andrew Jackson was born on March 15, 1767. His birth came shortly after his father died and left a family of four. Elizabeth Jackson raised her children alone and was forced to live with the Crawford family, caring for Mrs. Crawford, an invalid, and her eight children. With this arrangement she secured room and board for her fatherless brood.

She wanted her youngest son, Andrew, to be a Presbyterian minister, so she provided him a better education than her two eldest boys, and he learned reading, writing, and arithmetic. It was obvious to everyone early, except his mother, that Andy's personality was ill-suited for the clergy. He swore like a sailor and was always in trouble. Some felt he was bossy because of his relationships with other children, and his temper was erratic and often frightened many. Sometimes, the mere possibility of him losing his temper was enough to get his way, and Andrew learned quick that his temper could gain him advantage.

He continued to use it as an adult but eventually learned the discipline to use it to focus his decisions. Some claim he was acting out the feeling of abandonment by his father and his aggressive behavior was overcompensation for being raised by a single mother. Though he was perceived as pushy, part of him despised bullies, and he was known to protect smaller boys.

---

[364] James, Marquis. *The Life of Andrew Jackson, Complete in One Volume.* (Indianapolis & New York: Bobbs-Merrill Co, 1938), 25–26; Remini, Vol. 1, 21.

Andrew also liked foot races and wrestling, and was always in a fight. Small and skinny, his size didn't hinder him. Though he wasn't the strongest boy, a childhood friend remembered, "I could throw him three times out of four, but he would never stayed throwed. He was dead game, even then, and never would give up."[365]

This rambunctious personality, of course, required the boy to defend his honor in many a street fight. In a day where grown men were shooting at each other on the dueling ground, boys learned the repercussions of disrespecting another's honor. In the South and West, men treaded lightly, because any show of disrespect could get them killed. Some recourse to regain one's honor was a public apology or a duel. It was serious business, and boys learned the honor code from birth. Luckily, fistfights decided the honor of boys, and regardless the outcome of the fight, the honor was defended.

Elizabeth Jackson was a strong-willed woman who understood she must raise three boys and make them men to survive the frontier. To spoil and coddle boys in eighteenth century America would not prepare them for life.

In Andrew, she instilled a sense of self-reliance and personal responsibility. He believed his whole life that men were responsible only to themselves and God. A man should refuse help from others and feel shame if accepted. A man took responsibility for his actions, successes and failures alike. A failure was his alone, and no one else could be blamed.

Of course, with self-reliance came extreme confidence in one's self. Sometimes this turned into arrogance and backfired, but settlers of the frontier idolized rugged, tough, and independent men. Andrew possessed a sense of certainty, which produced the charisma men followed. Something about his manner made them believe they could accomplish anything with him at the helm. Much the way Washington inspired confidence, Andrew possessed this same ability. Though the two personalities were different in action, Washington was reserved and dignified, Andrew was loud, proud, and boisterous—they were similar in presence. Andrew was a scrapper and

---

[365] Remini, Vol. 1, 9.

allowed disrespect from no one. Being fatherless gave him an out of control personality, but Elizabeth's wisdom provided enough character to tame his inner fire.

In 1780, when Andrew was twelve, the American Revolution moved to the southern states. The British commander realized he couldn't crush Washington's army, so he targeted the states of Georgia, South Carolina, North Carolina, and Virginia instead. A large loyalist population could be recruited to fight against their neighbors. A civil war was already ongoing in the South since the start of the Revolution. If the British could conquer the South and separate it from the North, then they would have a military bargaining chip. South Carolina was attacked in May of 1780, and the city of Charleston surrendered.

Loyalist militia raided their patriot neighbors, murdering and looting along the way. They had help from a force of British dragoons commanded by Banastre Tarleton, also known as "Bloody Tarleton" for his brutal tactics. The territory of Waxhaws was raided, and Tarleton lived up to his name by killing Continentals after they surrendered.

Elizabeth, Andrew, and his brother, Robert, helped at the local hospital after the battle and cared for the wounded. Hugh Jackson, the sixteen-year-old brother, died fighting at the Battle of Stono Ferry of heatstroke, and Andrew was only thirteen when he learned of sacrifice. He witnessed his mother's gentle nature and strength when she cared for the wounded.

After the initial invasion, a larger operation of Waxhaw commenced, forcing Elizabeth to take her two sons and flee rather than take an oath of allegiance to the Crown. Refusal to take the oath was as sure as a death sentence, but she could never pledge allegiance to the same nation Hugh had died fighting. She sent Andrew and Robert to find the militia and instructed them to volunteer. She wanted her sons to fight the British, because it was their duty. After all, boys were made to fight.

Andrew saw his first fight the same year, and he rode with Colonel William Richardson Davie at the Battle of Hanging Rock on August 1, 1780. Being only thirteen, Andrew was commissioned to carry messages and run minor errands for the colonel, but this proximity to Colonel Davie had a lasting effect on him. Davie was a courageous but measured leader, and Andrew watched his every move.

In 1781, Andrew and Robert Jackson found themselves in the thick of the fight. Guarding a rebel captain's house, the boys and others were sleeping instead of standing guard when a force of loyalists moved quietly on the house. A British deserter staying at the house realized something was wrong and sounded the alarm. Andrew sprinted out the door and placed his rifle in a tree and waited. He demanded the countersign twice with no response and fired into the dark, just as the enemy attacked, and they held the larger force at bay but were taking casualties.

Suddenly, a bugle blared, and the attackers retreated. A friendly neighbor heard the fighting and employed a ruse he'd used successfully before. By sounding the bugle, the loyalists assumed a cavalry charge was coming, so they retreated out of fear of being cut down. The neighbor was surprised the trick worked and knew it would just buy some time. When a force of British dragoons returned to the house and the militia were overwhelmed, Andrew, Robert, and the others were scattered into the countryside.

Andrew fled with his cousin, Thomas Crawford, as the dragoons nipped at their heels. Chased into a swamp, Thomas's horse got stuck in the mud, and he was captured while Andrew escaped. He found Robert, and the two hid in the brush. At dawn, they went searching for food and decided to leave their rifles and horses behind to avoid suspicion. They found their way to Thomas's house and were discovered by the enemy. Discovery of their rifles and horses alerted the dragoons, and a search of the area led them to the house.

After wrecking the home, the dragoon attacked Andrew and Robert with a sword for refusing to clean his boots. They then transported the two wounded boys to Camden, South Carolina, and were imprisoned.

During the journey, the two wounded boys had nothing to eat or drink for days and often drank from mud puddles to quench their dry tongues. Once they reached the prison, neither received medical attention for their wounds and were forced to sleep on bare cell floors.[366]

The two brothers were separated, and Andrew was alone. Scars forming inside him went deeper than the external ones. He promised himself, then and there, he would die before he bowed down to the British or anyone, and would never be forced to clean another man's boots.

* * * * *

President's House, Washington City, June 1813

Sitting at his bedside, the First Lady listened closely to the president's breathing. Every rise and fall of his chest was labored, but the sound was music to Dolley. Watching him, she realized how much he meant to her, and how much he meant to the nation. She feared it was happening again.

Twenty years before, John, her first husband, had died of yellow fever this very same way. Now James was sick, and she was helpless again. His exhausted frame was wracked by fever, chills, diarrhea, and vomiting—just like John. The doctors assured her it wasn't yellow but bilious fever, whatever that meant. The doctors knew as little as the rest of them and always wanted to bleed the sick, which only made them weaker.

The president had worked too much and wore himself down. The Federalists were criticizing him and undermining the war, but he never once let it affect him. The war wasn't going well, and he was up late, woke too early, and was always reading reports and answering correspondence. The war was always on his mind, and he refused to rest. He wasn't a young man anymore, but he couldn't allow others to carry the load either. He was the president, it was his responsibility, he reminded her when she suggested he take a break, and she admired him for this. He couldn't do it all himself, but he tried. Oh, how he tried.

---

[366] Ibid., 19–22; James, *Jackson*, 18–22.

Dolley felt herself tremble as tears blurred her eyes but fought off the emotion. James expected her to be brave, and the nation must see resolve in their faces or they would doubt the war, he told her. She wanted to be as brave as him, but after all, she was still his wife and a woman. She didn't know if she could be brave, but she would try for him and the country. She wasn't sure she could ever be brave like that, but she was determined to never let fear get in the way of her duty as First Lady. She had fight inside her yet.

Taking a towel from a bowl of cool water, she patted his forehead. His hair was white and had receded to the top of his head. His face was starting to wrinkle, but she could still see the man who asked her to marry him and what he meant to her and the nation.[367]

If it wasn't for this horrible war, he wouldn't be sick.

* * * * *

Impressment was not the only outrage Britain committed. It also incited and armed the Indians to attack settlements on the American frontier, with promises of restoring the land they lost at the end of the Revolution for helping them.

Through trade policy, Britain influenced the northern states to divide the nation. In March of 1812, a plot was uncovered that the British were encouraging New England to secede from the Union. Madison realized the real danger he was facing. If the country split in two and the North became the pawns of Britain, the Union would be broken. Just like the Constitutional Convention, he knew the delegates were deeply divided, but they had to pull together. This war was the same. He couldn't force the Federalists to support the war, but he could try to win them over eventually.

The days of diplomacy with Great Britain were over. The problem wasn't going away, and Madison was used to solving problems. Britain was fighting its toughest struggle against Napoleon, and the president felt the time was right to send another message. The United

---

[367] Ketchum, Ralph. *James Madison: A Biography.* (Charlottesville: University Press of Virginia, 1971,1990), 360–362; Howard, 63–65.

States might be smaller, but where it was deficient in size, it made up in fight.

He must press the seriousness of freedom of the sea and national honor. He had to show Britain and the rest of the world the United States would blacken a bully's eye if pushed too far. New England's refusal to support the administration showed division and encouraged further British arrogance. If America was divided, it was weak and an easy target. Using this division to manipulate the outcome, Britain was emboldened. Madison and his cabinet understood the reasons they refused to respect American sovereignty and why they were so sure of themselves. They were fighting Napoleon for the continent, but they owned the seas, and the former colonies were lucky with the Revolution, but the water was still their domain. They weren't about to give it up.

At the same time, America had to protect its own interests. If Madison backed down, the British would control trade policy in America, and therefore, wealth. A large part of the British strategy was to reclaim its former power. Madison had to show the world the United States was here to stay and wouldn't tolerate violation of its rights.

On June 1, 1812, the president sent a message to Congress, asking for a declaration of war. "Whether the United States shall continue passive under these progressive usurpations and these accumulating wrongs, or, opposing force to force in defense of their national rights, shall commit a just cause into the hands of the Almighty Disposer of Events."[368] He believed the war was justified and trusted "the Almighty Disposer of Events" to settle the dispute according to his will.

Madison didn't know how America would overcome the British war machine. He just believed God's hand would right the wrong. Some say Madison was one of the least religious presidents because of his defense of religious freedoms, but he had faith God was with

---

[368] Madison, *Writings*, Vol. 13, 199–200 (Special Message to Congress, June 1, 1812).

America because it was fighting a just cause. Two weeks later, he proclaimed they were consulting, "the blessing of Divine Providence."[369]

Congress was divided, like the country, and the Federalists opposed war or anything threatening their livelihoods. Madison's party, the Republicans (often called Democratic-Republicans), were led by fiery orators like Henry Clay of Kentucky and John C. Calhoun of South Carolina. This group of pro-war Republicans, labeled the "War Hawks," spoke brazenly and confidently about beating the British and even conquering Canada. Like every war, they had predicted a short one.

Calhoun was a young attorney from South Carolina with a promising career ahead of him as Secretary of War under Madison's successor, James Monroe, and Vice President under Monroe's successors, John Quincy Adams and Andrew Jackson. He also had his own presidential aspirations, but in 1812, Calhoun was a staunch patriot and unionist. Being Scots-Irish, he knew the atrocities the English committed against mankind. He rooted for the underdog and, later in his career, became a sectionalist and defender of slavery, claiming states and minority rights as his justification. He was the prime mover in the 1830s in the nullification crisis, which declared a single state could nullify (refuse to uphold) a federal law if it was determined unconstitutional. His rationale was based on the South's self-preservation of which he represented. This Calhoun would come later, but in 1812, he was a nationalist and committed to the preservation of the Union.

Henry Clay was the flashy young Speaker of the House who drank, gambled, and fought duels to avenge his honor. He wasn't about to let pampered Brits push his country around. He would go on to settle the Missouri Compromise of 1820 and the Compromise of 1850, which twice delayed the Civil War. He would serve as John Quincy Adams's Secretary of State and run unsuccessfully for president three times. He became the icon of the Whig party as a strong unionist, and though a slave-owner, he opposed the spread of slavery. But for now, Clay was a War Hawk, and in 1812, he refused to

---

[369] Ibid., 201 (Proclamation, June 19, 1812).

submit to "debasement, dishonor, and disgrace" from the British and said, "It was not by submission that our fathers achieved our independence." He also asked, "When the burglar is at our door, shall we bravely sally forth and repel his felonious entrance, or meanly skulk within the cells of the castle?" He inflamed congressional fervor by asking, "Shall it be said that…we pusillanimously cling to our seats here rather than boldly vindicate the most inestimable rights of the country?"[370]

Clay also asked all Americans to have faith. "We once triumphed over her, and, if we do not listen to the counsels of timidity and despair, we shall again prevail." With the war a year later, he reminded his countrymen, "In such a cause, with the aid of Providence, we must come out crowned with success; but if we fail, let us fail like men, lash ourselves to our gallant tars, and expire together in one common struggle, fighting for 'seamen's rights and free trade.'"[371] He appealed to their common principles, for it was better to die fighting for something than to live fighting for nothing.

The House voted for war, 79 to 49, and the Senate voted 19 to 13. Nearly every Federalist voted against.

Madison signed the declaration of war on June 18, 1812. Arrogance could be found on both sides, but James Madison knew providence would grant the United States divine justice.

However, on July 28, the city of Baltimore experienced unrest between anti-war and pro-war advocates. Two dozen Federalists were attacked by Republican mobs. After a brief skirmish, the Federalists were arrested for firing on the crowd, but never made it to the jail. The angry mob killed one man and beat and tortured the others for three hours. Among the injured was fifty-six-year-old General Henry "Light-Horse Harry" Lee, horseman of the Revolution and eulogist of George Washington. One of the attackers tried to cut off Lee's nose but disfigured his face successfully. He would never fully recover from his injuries and died six years later, leaving behind

---

[370] Colton, Calvin. *The Life, Correspondence, and Speeches of Henry Clay, Vol. 1.* (New York: A.S. Barnes & Co., 1857), 165-166 (December 31, 1811).
[371] Ibid., (Army Bill, January 1813).

an eleven-year-old son—Robert E. Lee. America was not only fighting the British but each other. The parties Washington warned them about had, for the first time, bitterly divided the nation.[372]

* * * * *

All this had happened one year earlier. The nation was so sure of early success then. What unfolded was a different story altogether. The war wasn't going well so far. In fact, it was a disaster. Secretary of War William Eustis's three-pronged strategy to invade Canada was a farce. The plan had three separate parts: invasion from Detroit in the west, at Niagara, and New York in the center, and an assault on Montreal from the east. These three attacks would be coordinated to simultaneously overwhelm the British in Canada and end the war quickly. The biggest obstacle was communication.

In the early part of the nineteenth century, relaying messages was no easy task. They were delivered by horseback, stagecoach, or boat and took time to get to its destination. There were no locomotives yet, and the telegraph was still years away. The British wouldn't know war had been declared for a month, and in America, it might take weeks for a letter from New York to reach Virginia. How these three theaters would communicate in coordinated movements was anybody's guess. Setting a time and date for the attack was one thing, but what if something went wrong? How could one theater communicate the problem to the other before it was too late?

When war was declared on June 18, the news was sent through the regular mail instead of an express rider to the generals at the front. General William Hull, in Detroit, received notice of war sometime after the British in Canada were alerted to it. This advantage cost Hull control of Lake Erie. British ships approached the unsuspecting American ships on the lake and demanded surrender. They got the drop on them before they even knew what was happening. It

---

[372] Pitch, Anthony S. *The Burning of Washington*. (Annapolis: Naval Institute Press (Blue Jacket Books), 1998), 9–12.

was a problem, which would plague both sides, and would affect the end of the war.

Another problem to the war effort was personnel. Generals were appointed because of seniority and politics, not energy and results. Officers like Winfield Scott and Zebulon Pike were young and willing to take bold actions but were relegated to subordinate roles. Madison and Secretary of War Eustis still feared military power. Napoleon was a prime example of what could happen when a popular military leader used a large army to make himself emperor. It had happened repeatedly throughout history, and Madison and other Republicans were leery about standing armies. They decided to fight a war with political generals instead. Some Federalist officers were passed over for commanding roles because they couldn't be trusted. With New England threatening secession, what would deter an officer with the same views from using his army to overthrow the Republic? This assumption kept incompetent generals in place.

General Hull surrendered Detroit and thus control of the entire northwest (Minnesota, Michigan, Illinois, Ohio, Indiana, and Illinois) without a firing a shot. General Isaac Brock of the Royal Canadian forces told Hull if a battle ensued, he couldn't be responsible for restraining the Indians. Indians used ruthless tactics in battle and fought with no rules or control. Hull knew Brock's threat meant the massacre of men, women, and children, including his own family.

Some have defended Hull's actions and praise him for protecting lives, but his accusers point out that his force outnumbered the British two to one, and for some reason, he decided to surrender without a fight. Hull's surrender angered his own men, and he was removed from service and tried by a military court-martial. He was found guilty of cowardice and sentenced to be shot until President Madison decided to pardon him.

On the Niagara front, General Henry Dearborn wasn't faring better. Dearborn was Thomas Jefferson's former Secretary of War and a veteran of the Revolution but was no commander. Dearborn was one of those generals we see throughout history who think their men are never ready for battle. They must have more training, more supplies, and more numbers. When Dearborn was finally ready, he attacked Montreal with a smaller force, resulting in 950 men being captured.

During this battle, Captain John E. Wool and Lieutenant Colonel Winfield Scott had heroically proved themselves under fire but were abandoned by the New York militia who refused to cross the Canadian border, claiming they had no authorization from their Federalist governor to fight on foreign soil. The rest of the American army retreated in disarray, and by November of 1812, this offensive failed as well.

Replacing William Hull in the northwest was General William Henry Harrison who was planning a spring offensive to regain Lake Erie, Detroit, and all Hull had lost.

In January of 1813, Harrison sent out a small reconnaissance force under General James Winchester, and 850 men were attacked at the River Raisin and decimated by the British and Indians. A third of Winchester's men were killed, and the wounded were slaughtered by the Indians after they surrendered. One witness account of the massacre said, "Many were tomahawked, and many were burned alive in the houses."[373]

Harrison and his men were outraged and eager to exact vengeance. Was there any atrocity the British wouldn't allow? All civilized nations protected prisoners and the wounded, and some revisionists treat British commanders with kid gloves while easily criticizing Americans. The threat to Hull, the River Raisin, and refusal to control the Indians proved otherwise. The British claimed they didn't condone the Indian outrages, but they never restrained them either. Tecumseh, the Shawnee chief, responsible for the call to war, tried to restrain his men more than the British commanders. He may have been the only reason some Americans were spared.

Harrison waited out the winter at Fort Meigs and needed Lake Erie in order to control the area. Erie was the key to the whole

---

[373] Borneman, 70; Hickey, Donald R. *The War of 1812: A Forgotten Conflict.* (Urbana: University of Illinois Press, 1989), 86; Elting, John R. *Amateurs to Arms: A Military History of the War of 1812.* (Chapel Hill: De Capo Press, 1991, 1995), 63.

northwest. Without the lake, he couldn't hold any ground on it. The British ships could freely transport troops and supplies while attacking from the water, and he had to have control of the lake before he could move.

There was a little glimmer of light with the naval victory of the *USS Constitution* over the *HMS (Her Majesty's Ship) Guerriere.* In this famous battle, Captain Isaac Hull, nephew of General Hull, decided to stand and fight and won a minor victory for the United States.

After this first disastrous year of the war, Secretary of War Eustis resigned. Madison appointed New York's John Armstrong as his replacement.

Armstrong had served under Washington as a major and fought at Princeton and Saratoga. He was also suspected as a prime conspirator in the Newburgh Conspiracy, which Washington diffused in 1783. Of course, he explained it away years later as misdirected youth, but many still distrusted him. He was a political asset to the administration because he had powerful connections in New York. The president needed someone who could avoid Dearborn's fate when the New York militia refused to fight. He also needed his military experience. Armstrong was appointed general by his home state and responsible for devising a harbor defense in New York. He also had authored a well-respected military treatise and served as minister to France under Jefferson and Madison and was a logical choice for Secretary of War from a practical political sense.

It appeared to work. The people reelected Madison in the autumn of 1812 against the Federalist candidate, Dewitt Clinton of New York. The electoral result was 128 Madison, 89 Clinton. In his Second Inaugural Address, Madison assured the American people he wouldn't let them down:

> The impressions on me are strengthened by such an evidence that my faithful endeavors to discharge my arduous duties have been favorably estimated, and by a consideration of the momentous period at which the trust has been renewed. From the weight and magnitude now belonging to it I should be

compelled to shrink if I had less reliance on the
support of an enlightened and generous people,
and felt less deeply a conviction that the war with a
powerful nation, which forms so prominent a feature in our situation, is stamped with that justice
which invites the smiles of Heaven on the means
of conducting it to a successful termination.

He vowed to fight the war vigilantly and believed, by the grace
of God, they would end the war with the preservation of their rights.
He went on to stress the reasons for the war. "On the issue of the war
are staked our national sovereignty on the high seas and the security
of an important class of citizens, whose occupations give the proper
value to those of every other class." He explained what failure to prosecute it would mean for them. "Not to contend for such a stake is to
surrender our equality with other powers on the element common to
all and to violate the sacred title which every member of the society
has to its protection." Madison reminded the people this war would
require patience and faith in the justness of their fight. "When the
public voice called for war, all knew, and still know, that without
them it could not be carried on through the period which it might
last, and the patriotism, the good sense, and the manly spirit of our
fellow-citizens are pledges for the cheerfulness with which they will
bear each his share of the common burden."[374]

Americans should be prepared for the long haul, and when
things were bad, they needed to be especially patient. It was how they
reacted under fire which would determine their character.

By June of 1813, Madison had received a ray of light from the
land campaign, but it was bittersweet. In April, Isaac Chauncey's fleet
made an amphibious landing of ground troops near York, Canada,
on Lake Ontario. General Dearborn was still in command, but
Brigadier General Zebulon M. Pike, famed for his explorations and
Pike's Peak, commanded the force on the ground.

---

[374] Madison, *Writings*, Vol. 13, 235–238 (Second Inaugural Address, March 4,
1813).

After a brief skirmish in a wooded area outside York, the Americans pushed the British and Indians back toward the artillery garrison protecting the town. As Pike's force stopped to prepare for an assault and move their cannon up on the garrison, a huge explosion shook the ground. By chance, somebody dropped a match inside the stronghold and ignited the cartridges, killing and wounding dozens of British soldiers. The Americans advanced and found the garrison abandoned. Pike occupied the garrison, and while questioning a British prisoner, an even more powerful explosion shook the ground beneath him. Thirty-eight Americans lay dead, and 221 were wounded by the explosion. Pike was hit by a flying boulder and died later aboard ship.

The uninjured Americans occupied York while the British escaped. Dearborn allowed them to get away and was relieved of command shortly after.

The occupying Americans were blamed for looting and burning of public and private property. The small building used for the local Parliament was torched, and the American army was blamed, though proof was flimsy.

One historian believed this fire was set before the Americans even reached the area, and another claimed a few rogue Americans exacted revenge after finding an American scalp hanging from the speaker's chair in the Parliament building.

Another reason may have been caused by the garrison explosion, which killed Pike. British commander Roger Sheaffe ordered his men to ignite the powder magazine during the retreat. For Americans to be inside the garrison during the explosion, either it was set after they occupied it or a timed-fuse was preset to explode when they did. Either way, it seemed the British were fighting dirty, and it's easy to see how some may have wanted to burn something. After seeing thirty-eight dead and 221 wounded buddies on the ground, the firing of the Parliament house seemed a minor retribution. Some historians feign outrage for this building but don't bat an eye for the dead and wounded Americans who were victims of the British bomb. It is easy to judge them from the comfort of a spectator.

War is violent and brutal, and some morality should govern it, but when one side descends into atrocities, it is only natural to expect a similar retaliation from the other side. Clearly, some of the British had little concern with using brutal tactics. The use of Indians and setting off powder magazines to kill and maim was a bigger offense than the burning of a building. This stands true for both sides. Pretending Americans were barbarians for burning a structure, when it wasn't sanctioned by their commanders or government while ignoring sanctioned barbarity, is hypocritical. This one act of burning the Parliament building at York was an easy excuse given later by the British when they were asked to explain their own future actions.[375]

Even though the war at sea was going well for the much smaller American navy, one tragic event would make it legendary. On June 1, 1813, thirty-two-year-old Captain James Lawrence stared through his spyglass at the British ship speeding toward him and calmly prepared for battle. The *HMS Shannon* fired across his bow, and Lawrence returned fire to signal he was ready to fight. Lawrence's ship, the *USS Chesapeake,* was the same frigate attacked in 1807 off the coast of Virginia.

The American commander moved the *Chesapeake* within fifty yards of the *Shannon* and stood his ground. Cannons roared, and sailors with rifles or pistols fired at each other. Men on both ships were killed and maimed. Heads exploded, and arms and legs were shot off as pools of blood and gore painted the deck. Keeping their footing on deck was difficult, but luckily, they spread sand on it before the battle to help with traction.

Lawrence was struck in the leg by a musket ball, just as the two ships crashed into each other. The British marines jumped aboard the *Chesapeake,* and hand-to-hand combat ensued. Lawrence was hit again by a bullet, this time in the groin, and fell to the deck but continued to command. Even as the *Chesapeake* was overrun, he continued to bark orders. "Don't give up the ship!" he repeated, but it was too late and the American ship surrendered. One hundred

---

[375] Brant, Irving. *James Madison: Commander in Chief.* Vol. 6. (Indianapolis: Bobbs-Merrill, 1961); Borneman, 104–106.

Americans and fifty British were dead or wounded, including both captains. Lawrence held on but died three days later. "Don't give up the ship" would live on to inspire Americans to remember what they were fighting for. The American ship of state was under fire, but like a ghost, Lawrence reminded them from the grave.[376]

By June of 1813, the war was a disaster. The American people were grasping at a handful of naval victories and the taking of York, which turned out to be an empty victory. Support for the war nose-dived, and President Madison appeared to be dying. The Federalists were self-righteously saying they predicted as much.

Deep inside Madison's feverish mind, he still believed they would overcome. This was his cross to bear, and he planned to see it through. He hadn't come this far just to see it disappear. He had to stay the course.

Lesser men would have given up the ship by now.

* * * * *

Camden, South Carolina, 1781

Sick and weakened from exposure, Andrew had been helpless when his jacket and shoes were stolen, and the meager ration of bread wasn't enough, even for his thin frame. Smallpox and dysentery spread throughout the prison, but Andrew somehow avoided contracting these deadly diseases.

Shortly after Andrew arrived at the prison, General Nathanael Greene (George Washington's right-hand man in the southern campaign) and his army were on the outskirts of the prison and planning to take Camden. Andrew and the other captives had renewed hopes of rescue. The prisoners sat by their windows and watched their rescuers in the distance preparing for battle.

The British didn't like this new hope and attitude of the prisoners, so they had the windows boarded up, causing little airflow to reach the Americans. Not one to be denied, Andrew took a little piece

---

[376] Roosevelt, 102–105; Elting, 78; Borneman, 116–117.

of his shaving razor and whittled a knot out of one of the boards so he could watch. Unfortunately, Greene was forced to retreat, and the prisoners were disheartened. Andrew had believed they would be liberated, but when Greene retreated, he gave up. A fourteen-year-old boy—hungry, cold, and exhausted—needed his hope to strengthen his resolve. When this was gone, so was his will. He succumbed to smallpox after his will was shattered by losing hope.

Miraculously, Elizabeth Jackson found her boys and convinced the British commander to release her two sick sons. On seeing Andrew and Robert, Elizabeth realized the urgency of their situation. Robert was in a bad condition suffering from smallpox, dysentery, and an infection caused by the head wound made by the dragoon's sword. He was so sick he had to be placed on one of the horses his mother procured, and she rode with him the whole way to prevent him from falling. Andrew walked beside her, being less sick of the two, the forty-five-mile trek back home. Still without shoes and jacket, he was burning with fever but somehow pushed on.

Two days after they arrived home, Robert died, and Andrew was on the edge of death himself, but Elizabeth nursed him back to health. It took months before he fully recovered; emotionally, he never did.

Once Andrew was well enough and out of danger, Elizabeth felt her nursing was needed at the front. Two of her nephews were aboard the prison ships docked at Charleston, and she felt they and others needed her help. Caring for the sick Americans aboard the diseased ships, she contracted cholera and died shortly after Cornwallis surrendered at Yorktown. She thought nothing of her own health and lost it to care for others.

Fifteen-year-old Andrew was now alone. His entire family was gone. To him, they had been killed by the British. The war was over, but not for him, and he vowed someday to pay them back for the death of his family. Robert was dead because he refused to clean the boots of a dragoon. Hugh died fighting them, and his mother died caring for the prisoners held in filthy diseased conditions because of them. He personally suffered by their hand and would always bear the scars physically from the sword attack, but it would be the scars from the loss of his family which left a lasting impression. He vowed never to allow another man to disrespect him as long as he lived. When Andrew's piercing blue eyes warned other men they were treading on dangerous ground, most knew he was deadly serious.

The memory of his mother's words guided his life. "Her last words have been the law of my life." These last words he often recited:

> Andrew, if I shall not see you again, I wish you to remember and treasure up some things I have said to you: in this world you will have to make your own way. To do that you must have friends. You can make friends by being honest, and you can keep them by being steadfast. You must keep in mind that friends worth having will in the long run expect as much from you as they give to you. To forget an obligation or be ungrateful for a kindness is a base crime—not merely a fault or a sin, but an actual crime. Men guilty of it sooner or later must suffer the penalty. In personal conduct be always polite and never obsequious. None will respect you more than you respect yourself. Avoid quarrels as long as you can without yielding to imposition. But sustain your manhood always. Never bring suit in law for assault and battery or for defamation. The law affords no remedy for such outrages that can satisfy the feelings of a true man. Never wound the feelings of others. Never brook wanton outrage upon your own feelings. If you ever have to vindicate your feelings or defend your honor, do it calmly. If angry at first, wait till your wrath cools before you proceed.

On another account, she told him, "Andy…never tell a lie, nor take what is not your own, nor sue…for slander… Settle them cases yourself."[377]

Americans today could learn something from this eighteenth century woman who taught her son to be a man. If Andrew Jackson's father would have lived, his famous son might have remained unknown. A strong woman acting as mother and father was the only reason Andrew became a legend. Jackson scholar, Robert V. Remini, said of Elizabeth, "She was an extraordinary woman, a woman of courage, high purpose, and incredible interior strength."[378]

Andrew learned about these traits from her, and in a time when men ran the world, Elizabeth was proof that behind every great man, there was a woman. Her courage and strength were her gift to her son and eventually her gift to her nation.

* * * * *

Lake Erie, September 10, 1813

Master Commandant Oliver Hazard Perry looked off his starboard deck across the expanse of Lake Erie. His nine ships were dead in the water.

In the distance, six ships of the Royal Navy were cruising toward the Americans at full sail. The wind was with the British today.

Perry wasn't worried. He had to clear Erie of the enemy before General Harrison could reclaim the ground lost by Hull in 1812. If Detroit was ever going to be part of the United States, he had to rid Erie of the British flotilla.

Thinking of poor Lawrence's death, Perry clenched his jaw and remembered his friend's defiant death. In his hand, he held a recently sewn blue flag requested for this very moment. Stepping onto a carronade carriage, he stood erect as the crew gathered around as he spoke, "My brave lads—this flag contains the last words of the brave

---

[377] Remini, Vol. 1, 11; James, *Jackson*, 28.
[378] Remini, Vol. 1, 24.

Captain Lawrence…" Holding up the flag for them to see, he asked, "Shall I hoist it?"[379]

The crew cheered as Perry smiled. Handing the flag to a crewman, his eyes followed its ascent up the mast. The spirit of the men was right; now, if the wind would cooperate, this would be a fight.

The wind pushing the British ships forward abruptly died away. Perry noticed the change in the wind and decided if the wind wasn't with them, at least, it wouldn't be with the enemy either. Then, as suddenly as the wind stopped, it picked up once more. This time it was with the Americans. Stepping to the front of the *USS Lawrence*, Perry stood tall as they sped toward the enemy flotilla.[380]

The flag flapped in the divine wind as if Lawrence himself directed it. The enemy would hear from his friend today. Emblazoned on the flag in large white letters were the defiant words, "Don't Give Up the Ship."

* * * * *

In July of 1813, President Madison had recovered from the deadly illness which nearly killed him. Though weak, he grew stronger each day and gradually resumed his duties.

The British had occupied Chesapeake Bay and were pushing up the Potomac, burning and looting the Virginian and Maryland countryside, and the president feared the capital city would be next.

In August, a plan to reclaim the lakes on the Canadian border was authorized, and Secretary of the Navy Jones ordered Commodore Isaac Chauncey to proceed. Chauncey sent Perry to Lake Erie to construct two new brigs for service. The *USS Lawrence* and *Niagara* were commissioned and anchored off Put-in Bay, near Sandusky, Ohio. Perry's nine ships were preparing for initiating a fight when the British flotilla appeared on the lake September 10.

---

[379] Howard, 105–106 (Samuel Hambleton Diary, 1813); Altoff, Gerard T. *Oliver Hazard Perry & the Battle of Lake Erie.* (Put-In-Bay: The Perry Group, 1999), 35.
[380] Howard, 106 (David C. Bunnell).

As the two squadrons approached one another, the opening shots broke the crisp afternoon.

The *Lawrence* engaged the *HMS Detroit* but couldn't match the distance of the British long guns. Perry's flagship was shot to pieces and soon out of the fight. Perry boarded the brig *Niagara* to resume the battle, technically giving up the ship, but he wasn't about to give up the fight. As the *Niagara* engaged the *Detroit*, two other British ships collided while the Americans battered the flotilla with endless broadsides. Smelling blood in the water, Perry pushed his ships forward for a finishing blow. The British commander struck his colors and surrendered his squadron.

Perry sent a message to Secretary Jones the same day. "It has pleased the Almighty to give to the arms of the United States a signal victory over their enemies on this Lake."

He sent another dispatch to General Harrison which would be remembered for its pithiness. Harrison waited anxiously for word of the outcome of the battle. The result would determine his campaign in the northwest. Harrison read nine simple words from Perry that described it perfectly: "We have met the enemy…and they are ours."[381]

General Harrison was now free to move forward, and Perry's fleet transported the army across Erie to the Canadian side. Once landing, the Americans chased the unsuspecting British and Indians for miles and caught them near the Thames River. A brutal fight by Kentucky riflemen and cavalry shouting "Remember the Raisin!" overwhelmed the enemy, forcing the Brits and Indians to surrender.

The Shawnee chief, Tecumseh, was killed during the Battle of the Thames. He was the catalyst behind native resistance in the northwest, and when he died, resistance died with him. Only the Creek Indians in the South continued the warpath.

These two American victories and recovery of the territory Hull had lost the year before was the good news the country needed. Only small naval victories and the almost victory in York were all they had until the battles of Lake Erie and the Thames. Madison needed

---

[381] Ibid., 108; Borneman, 132; Altoff, 54.

the news more than anyone. He knew winning a war required diligence and patience. Battles were only a small part of the war. During the Revolution, Madison watched Washington lose time again, but he never gave up, and eventually, the tide turned. Sometimes, Washington enjoyed small victories along the way to give hope to the cause, and Yorktown only happened when all the pieces fell into place.

The Federalists continued to criticize and malign the president. They said he was incompetent and losing the war, and some called for his impeachment and labeled the war, "Madison's War." There were still stirrings in New England of secession, and some weren't simply anti-war but were aiding the enemy. A few New England merchants traded with the British, defying the federal laws. Profit was more important than their rights or nation. Like during the Revolution, these merchants made money with the blood of Americans and likely prolonged the war. Without the ability to divide, Britain probably would've avoided the war entirely and may have negotiated out of necessity. They didn't want to fight Napoleon and a united America, but a divided one with some of its own citizens aiding them was a different story altogether.

By April 11, 1814, Napoleon was defeated, and the British could concentrate all its might in America. Britain had been fighting in North America with a nominal force, because it needed them on the continent, but now it planned to "chastise" the United States with the full force of its might.

Peace negotiations to settle the American war were in the process but broke down when the British decided they had the upper hand. They were delighted at the thought of humiliating the rabble who embarrassed them in 1781. They would finally establish their dominance in the world. The Royal lion had beaten Napoleon, and "little Jemmy" Madison and his amateur army wasn't going to be a problem. A large British fleet was on its way. Secretary of State James Monroe received a letter from one of the negotiators, Albert Gallatin, from London describing the British attitude. "To use their own language, they mean to inflict on America a chastisement that will teach her that war is not to be declared against Great Britain with impunity."[382] They were planning to punish America and instructed Admiral Sir Alexander Cochrane and General of the Army Robert Ross to end the conflict and do it decisively. Rear Admiral George Cockburn had an idea of how to do it once he convinced Cochrane and Ross of its viability. He was certain it would bring "Jemmy Madison" and the United States to its knees.

* * * * *

Harrison's Mills, Kentucky, May 30, 1806

"Gentlemen...are you ready?"

"Ready," Charles Dickinson replied.

"Yes, sir," Andrew Jackson seconded.

The man who asked this question took a breath as Andrew held his own and aimed the pistol at Dickinson who stood twenty-four feet away, pointing his own pistol at him.

Andrew convinced himself to wait for Dickinson to fire first before pulling his own trigger, ensuring he could take time aiming. This meant the possibility of being hit first, maybe even killed, but it was the only way. Some said it was suicide, but Dickinson was the better marksman, and in the heat of battle, most men faltered. Come what may, Andrew could never allow this besmirching of his wife's character. The nerve this man had calling him "a worthless scoundrel, a poltroon, and a coward" as if he could allow this to go unanswered. Strange as it seems today, disrespecting a man's honor in the nineteenth century was a deadly business. What seems to us as simply rudeness today was grounds for killing a man. Dickinson made disparaging comments about Rachel, and any man would have defended his wife's honor from insults. He called her an adulteress and a bigamist. It was this accusation his enemies would use to hurt him, but it hurt Rachel the most. To insult a man's wife was worse than an insult to one's self.

---

[382] Borneman, 229; Lord, Walter. *The Dawn's Early Light.* (New York: Dell Publishing Co., Inc., 1972, 1973), 23.

He always tried to defend a woman's honor. As he saw it, women were the embodiment of virtue, and he would never allow a bully to pick on the fairer sex. Believing all women were innocent and in need of rescue may have originated from a desire to defend his mother. This was also the southern chivalry of the day. Even if a woman was guilty of an impropriety, the honor code dictated her defense. He never liked those who preyed on the weak, and this need to defend them would cause much trouble throughout his life.

This was the real reason Andrew stood ready to kill or be killed on the dueling ground. So he clenched his teeth and prepared to meet his Maker or send Dickinson to the appointment. His blue eyes flashed as he heard the command, "Fire!"[383]

* * * * *

After being orphaned by the Revolution, Andrew left Waxhaws and wandered on his own for a while. He worked a few different jobs and even taught school briefly. He spent most of this time drinking, brawling, and gambling at horseraces and cockfights. He became a connoisseur of horses and an accomplished rider, but soon realized he needed to do something about making a living. He subsisted on the money his grandfather left him, but after a few years of sowing his wild oats, he decided to apply himself. The inheritance was a godsend, but it wouldn't last forever. Four hundred pounds sterling was a good sum, but not a fortune and was nearly gone. So, he chose to study the law.

After passing the bar in North Carolina, which was saturated with lawyers, he heard the fresh territory of Franklin (Tennessee) was a land of opportunity for young lawyers and in need of hard-fighting leaders.

So he went to Tennessee and spent time as an attorney and Indian fighter.

In 1789, the Creek were a constant threat to the new settlers. When they came for vengeance, they went after whoever was avail-

---

[383] Remini, Vol. 1, 140–142; James, *Jackson*, 117

able: men, women, or children. All Americans were fair game and once the war paint was on and their blood was up, they just randomly killed, scalped, tortured, and kidnapped anyone who crossed paths with them. This was a never-ending cycle of terror, and women and children were caught in the middle on both sides.

In one account of the Indian attacks, a Tennessean newspaper wrote "the Indians fell upon the families of the name of Isaac and John Titsworth and killed their wives and children. Killed Evan Shelby and Abednego Lewellyn as they were hunting in the woods."

Another attack was described as "scalped John Blackburn near the spring on the bank of the creek, and left a spear sticking in his body."[384] Jackson biographer Marquis James wrote "On an average of once in ten days throughout 1789 someone was killed within a few miles of Nashville."[385]

The Creek were devastating the countryside and wiping out whole families, and Tennesseans weren't about to sit by and watch. This was the environment many frontiersmen cut their teeth on. It was no surprise why both sides were hostile in Tennessee. Seeing your wife, children, and neighbors killed and mutilated had the tendency to make one want revenge on both sides. Andrew joined the militia soon after arriving and helped defend the frontier against the Indians.

Around this time, Rachel Donelson Robards was planning to flee Tennessee, because her husband Lewis Robards, who was guilty of abuse and abandonment, was on his way back to forcibly take her to Kentucky. She fled to Spanish territory (west of the Mississippi) out of fear, and Andrew, her new suitor, accompanied her there. After hearing that Robards gained a legal divorce, Andrew and Rachel were married. Robards never actually received a divorce and filed a suit against Rachel for living in adultery now that she was a bigamist. Evidence suggests there was never impropriety between Andrew

---

[384] Ramsey, J. G. M. *The Annals of Tennessee to the End of the Eighteenth Century.* (Genealogical Publishing Co., 2009), 484–485; Haywood, John. *The Civil and Political History of the State of Tennessee from its Earliest Settlement Up to the Year 1796, including the Boundaries of the State.* (W. H. Haywood, 1891), 257.

[385] James, *Jackson*, 58.

and Rachel before the marriage and they honestly believed Robards divorced her.

The couple wed sometime in 1790 or 1791 and believed themselves to be man and wife. Robards was, however, granted a divorce in September of 1793. Rachel was embarrassed and humiliated, and Andrew knew the legal ramifications, so he married her again on January 18, 1794 to make it binding. This all seemed an innocent mistake in isolated territorial America in the eighteenth century, but Andrew and Rachel would be haunted endlessly for their mistake.

In 1828, while running for president, his opponents accused him and Rachel of adultery and bigamy. Rachel was extremely religious, and these allegations wounded her gentle soul. Shortly before his inauguration, Rachel passed away, and Andrew always believed she was murdered by his enemies, though he said "but Providence knew what was best for her. For myself, I bow to God's will..."[386] On her tombstone, he inscribed the words, "A being so gentle, so virtuous, slander might wound but could never dishonor,"[387] and later said, "May God Almighty forgive her murderers as I know she forgave them. I never can."[388]

After marriage, Andrew secured a position as attorney general of the Mero district of Tennessee and was elected to the House of Representatives soon after. Then, he was appointed a US Senator and elected judge of the Superior Court of Tennessee. He was a land speculator, ran a couple of businesses, and was elected Major General of the militia. This was an impressive resume for a thirty-nine-year-old with no connections and Andrew was just getting started.

* * * * *

[386] Remini, Robert V. *Andrew Jackson and the Course of American Freedom 1822–1832*, Vol. 2. (New York: Harper & Row, Publishers, 1981), 154.
[387] Ibid., 155.
[388] Buell, 204; Brady, Patricia. *A Being So Gentle: The Frontier Love Story of Rachel and Andrew Jackson*. (New York: St. Martin's Press, 2011), 222; James, *Jackson*, 483.

Harrison's Mills, Kentucky, May 30, 1806

As he waited for Dickinson's .70 caliber slug, he was determined to die like a man if need be. Would the shot miss or kill him?

Andrew felt the slug pierce his chest and couldn't believe the strategy backfired. He squeezed his chest and was convinced the wound was mortal. He wasn't about to die before righting the wrong to his and Rachel's honor.

He slowly raised his pistol again, clutching his breast, and took careful aim.

"My God! Have I missed him?" Dickinson cried and awaited his fate.

Jackson pulled the hammer back and fired. Dickinson fell to the ground with a wound in his abdomen.

Andrew's friends came over to check his wound and noticed his boot was filled with blood. He said, "Oh, I believe that he pincked me, but I don't want those people to know." He was more concerned about how he appeared to Dickinson's people than his dangerous wound.

The doctor who worked on Jackson believed Dickinson had aimed perfectly at his heart, but the baggy overcoat Andrew wore on his tall wiry frame caused him to misjudge his target. Andrew seemed to providentially escape death at every turn.

The slug buried in his breast was too close to the heart and couldn't be removed. He would carry it with him the rest of his life and would experience pain and complications because of it.

The slug would be a reminder of the price of honor. Just like the scars from the British dragoon's sword, he carried the slug like a medal for bravery.

Charles Dickinson would die from his wound that same night. His wife was expecting a child, and Rachel Jackson wept for her and her unborn orphan.[389]

* * * * *

---

[389] James, *Jackson*, 118; Remini, Vol. 1, 142.

Eastern Theater, Summer 1814

Admiral Sir Alexander Cochrane, the recently appointed commander of British forces, was expected to put a quick end to the war. He was a prideful arrogant man who called Americans "a corrupt and depraved race" and a "whining, canting race much like the spaniel and require the same treatment—must be drubbed into good manners."[390] Cochrane was just itching to "drub" the "spaniels," but after an earlier expedition to the South in support of the Creek Indians, he was indecisive as to where to strike next.

Rear Admiral George Cockburn had the answer to Cochrane's problem and promised, "Within forty-eight hours after the arrival in the Patuxent (River) of such a force as you expect, the City of Washington might be possessed without difficulty or opposition of any kind."[391]

Cockburn was a villainous character but practical. He had firsthand knowledge of what took the fight out of Americans. He was responsible for burning towns and confiscating property in the Chesapeake area and was notorious to Americans. His name was synonymous with terror, and this was his aim. He believed that attacking Washington City and burning it would bring America to its knees.

General Robert Ross was doubtful of Cockburn's plan and felt his troop numbers were too low to sack the capital. Surely Americans would bring all possible troops to defend its capital. Ross was an experienced officer in Europe, but Cockburn had regional experience, and had proved the summer before that a small mobile force could raid and devastate towns along the coast successfully. When he attacked and burned a factory miles from the shore without any resistance, Ross was convinced his plan to hit the capital would work. He also assured them that the locals refused to defend their homes and ran when royal soldiers appeared. Cockburn won over Cochrane and Ross, and they approved his plan.

---

[390] Lord, *Dawn's*, 30.
[391] Ibid., 33.

The Americans had no ground troops to defend the capital, and it made no strategic sense the Brits would target it. American leaders never considered the symbolic effect of sacking the seat of government. Some thought Baltimore the likely choice. On August 18, Cochrane ordered Cockburn and Ross to move troops to the coastal town of Benedict, Maryland, and to march overland and take Washington City.

Meanwhile, President Madison was in a cabinet meeting discussing the possibility of such an attack on the capital. He was more concerned about it than Secretary of War John Armstrong, who carelessly dismissed the possibility. "By God they would not come with such a fleet without meaning to strike somewhere, but they certainly will not come here." He flippantly asked, "What the devil will they do here?" His contempt for the president's concerns was remarkable, "No, no Baltimore is the place. Sir: that is of so much more consequence."[392] Armstrong was either incapable of seeing the obvious or deliberately putting the capital at risk. Madison was starting to realize this man's hubris might end in disaster.

Luckily, the president had his own mind, and though he lacked the military experience Armstrong had, he had two attributes the secretary did not—humility and an open mind to all possibilities.

Madison had been a confidant of Washington and saw how the general fought the Revolution. He would rarely reject council and had the character to know he didn't know everything. Many claim Washington was no great intellect, but his brilliance was his character. He surpassed men like Jefferson and Madison when it came to measured judgment, and strict reliance on providence gave him a confidence the intellects lacked. Madison knew this and understood his own limits. As a thinking man, Madison analyzed every aspect of any problem and often encountered indecision. Washington, through experience, learned to take precise actions backed by good judgment. Madison would use the same formula now. He was through letting subordinates make decisions about the war. He drew up a plan to

---

[392] Pitch, 19; Howard, 129.

protect the capital, regardless of Armstrong's opinion, just in case he was wrong about the British target.

He created the tenth military district for the area of Maryland, the capital city, and part of Virginia. He appointed General William Winder of the Maryland militia as its commander. Winder's uncle was Levin Winder, the governor of Maryland and this political appointment would secure Maryland's full cooperation. Politically, it was brilliant. Militarily, it was risky, but it was better than doing nothing as the experts suggested.

When Armstrong discovered Madison's new plan, he shrugged them off as a waste of time and resources. The British would not march twenty miles inland to attack such an insignificant target. The president knew there were endless historical accounts of taking capital cities as a psychological and political objective, but Armstrong ignored them. Washington City had little strategic value other than its capture would send shockwaves through the young country and snuff out the will of the people to prosecute the war. The Federalists could use its loss to pounce on the administration and show proof of its incompetence.

Madison knew his history and Secretary of State James Monroe concurred with his judgment. The president decided to play it safe. To leave the capital defenseless was to ignore reality. If he was anything, James Madison was a realist.

* * * * *

City Hotel, Nashville, Tennessee, September 4, 1813

Jesse and Thomas Hart Benton packed a pair of pistols each and were out for revenge. Waiting at the City Hotel in Nashville, they were eager to see Andrew Jackson. The Benton brothers were out for blood, because Jackson had sided with Jesse's opponent in a duel that ended with a wound in Jesse's pride and his backside. Thomas Hart Benton was one of Jackson's former aides and friends and livid by his betrayal. For some odd reason, he focused on him instead of the man who shot his brother.

Andrew heard they were in town and eager to settle accounts. Never one to walk away from a fight, he walked into town, intending to confront the Benton brothers on his own terms. He gripped a riding whip in his fist and was surrounded by his friends, John Coffee and Stockley Hays.

He spotted Thomas and started toward him, pulling his pistol and brandishing the whip. "Now defend yourself, you damned rascal!" he said.

Thomas Benton reached for his gun, but Jackson beat him to the draw with his own pistol. Benton stepped back from the gun pointed at his chest and noticed Jesse in the doorway behind Jackson, undetected. As Andrew finished his admonishment, Jesse shot him in the back, which caused him to discharge his weapon at Thomas and miss. Thomas then fired his two guns as Andrew fell forward. Jesse ran to finish him off, but a bystander, James Sitler, shielded Andy who was on the floor in a puddle of his own blood.

John Coffee then fired at Thomas and missed as well and chased him down to pistol whip him. Thomas fell backward down a staircase instead as Hays attacked Jesse with a sword cane but broke it on his shirt button. Incensed, Hays threw Jesse to the ground and stabbed him in the arms repeatedly with a knife. Jesse fired his pistol at Hays, but it failed to fire. The gathering crowd pulled them apart and ended the fight.

Andrew was bleeding like a sieve, so he was carried to the hotel across the street and laid on a bed. His left shoulder was shattered, and a slug was lodged in his upper left arm. He soaked two different mattresses as doctors tried to stop the bleeding and told him they needed to amputate. "I'll keep my arm," he said as he lost consciousness.[393]

The doctors weren't about to cut off his arm without permission. They knew the man who killed Charles Dickinson, if he lived, would come after them. So Andrew kept his arm and another souvenir slug. Once again, he had cheated death, and some wondered if this man was human. It was almost as if something protected him

---

[393] James, *Jackson*, 153–154; Remini, Vol. 1, 184–185.

from certain death. For twenty years, he would carry this lead in his body, and it would take three weeks before he could even get out of bed.

This famous street battle was soon overshadowed by the news of the Fort Mims massacre. A hostile segment of the Creek Indians known as Red Sticks (because of the color of their war clubs) had killed 250 men, women, and children at a stockade in Alabama on August 30, 1813. The stockade was the fortified house of Samuel Mims who was a half-Creek merchant who sided with the Americans. The fort was built to protect inhabitants of the area from the Red Stick rampages. Some blacks, mixed-bloods, and friendly Indians sought the protection of the fort as well as the whites. This heinous act wasn't a matter of race but right and wrong.

A thousand Red Sticks rushed the fort, and only a few inside escaped to tell the story. One eyewitness described the brutality. "The children were seized by the legs, and killed by batting their heads against the stockading. The women were scalped, and those who were pregnant were opened, while they were alive, and the embryo infants let out of the womb."[394]

Red Eagle, the Red Stick chief, tried to stop the slaughter but was threatened by his own men with death and backed down. A few blacks inside the fort were spared, only to become slaves to the Red Sticks. To the victor belonged the spoils, but these vanquished were innocent victims.

The Americans on the frontier were outraged by the massacre and refused to sit on their hands any longer while Americans were being murdered.

The Indian problem wasn't new on the frontier, but the war had made it worse. In 1811, William Henry Harrison had crushed the Shawnees at Tippecanoe while their leader, Tecumseh, was on a

---

[394] Pickett, Albert J. *History of Alabama and Incidentally of Georgia and Mississippi from the Earliest Period*. (Robert C. Randolph, 1896), 536–537; Remini, Vol. 1, 190.

diplomatic trip in the South. He was there to form an alliance with the Creeks and told them:

> Accursed be the race that has made women of our warriors, and harlots of our women. Let the white race perish! They seize your land; they corrupt your women; they trample the bones of your dead! Back whence they came, upon a trail of blood, they must be driven. Back aye, back into the great water whose accursed waves brought them to our shores. Burn their dwellings, destroy their stock, slay their wives and children, that the very breed may perish. War now, war always, war on the living, war on the dead. Dig their very corpses from the graves…this is the will of the Great Spirit.[395]

The Red Sticks worked themselves into a frenzy and prepared for a race war to ensure the preservation of their way of life. Encouraged by the British, the Indians in the southern theater were used to drain troops from the northern campaign. As the Brits and northern tribes fought at Detroit, River Raisin, and York, western and southern Americans were busy protecting their families and homes in the South. This divide and conquer strategy by the British promised to return lost territory for their service.

Jackson was still too weak when the committee on public safety asked him to lead an army to protect the frontier and avenge the victims of Fort Mims. Andrew stated, "By the eternal these people must be saved."[396] John Coffee had already raised a twenty-five-hundred-man force, and they were just waiting for Andrew to lead them.

The year before, he led a contingent into the frontier and suffered along with his men, earning the nickname "Old Hickory."

---

[395] Claiborne, J. F. H. *Mississippi, as a Province, Territory and State, with Biographical Notices of Eminent Citizens*, Vol. 1. (Jackson: Power & Barksdale, Publishers, 1880), 317; Remini, Vol. 1, 188.

[396] James, *Jackson*, 154.

Andrew then explained his view on the war and wrote a call to arms. "Who are we? And for what are we going to fight? No—we are the freeborn sons of America; the citizens of the only republic now existing in the world; and the only people on earth who possess rights, liberties, and property which they dare call their own."[397]

Great Britain was his eternal enemy, and he was determined to make them pay for what they did to his family. He wrote to Rachel about a greater force than either one of them controlling their destiny. "I thank you for your prayers. I thank you for your determined resolution to bear our separation with fortitude. We part but for a few days—for a few fleeting weeks when the protecting hand of Providence, if it is His will, will restore us to each other's arms."[398]

He had returned to her safe after the army was disbanded without seeing action, but one year later, providence called him once again. Rachel understood Andrew wasn't just hers to keep and must share him with America. His purpose was larger than their love for each other.

By October of 1813, with an arm in a sling, Andrew mounted his horse and took command of the army of Tennessee. He headed south to meet the next challenge on the road to his destiny.

* * * * *

Near Washington City, August 16, 1814

A British fleet of fifty warships appeared off the coast of Virginia. There was no longer any doubt they meant to end the war. Their destination was unknown.

---

[397] Jackson, *Andrew. Andrew Jackson Papers 1775–1874, Series 1, General Correspondence and Related Items 1775–1885*, 2nd Division Volunteers, March 7, 1812, Manuscript/Mixed Material. https://www.loc.gov/item/maj001411/ Remini, Vol. 1, 169.

[398] Brands, H. W. *Andrew Jackson: His Life and Times.* (New York: Knopf Doubleday, Publishing Group, 2006), 181; Remini, Vol. 1, 174 (Andrew to Rachel Jackson, January 18, 1813).

They could move on Annapolis or Baltimore or they could destroy the naval yard on the Patuxent River and then attack Washington. The naval yard was manned by a small contingent of Marines commanded by Commodore Joshua Barney, but they could only serve as a delaying force. Secretary of State James Monroe told President Madison, "that this city (Washington) was their object," but navy secretary William Jones agreed with Armstrong. This was a feint to draw their attention away from Baltimore, the real target.[399]

Monroe volunteered to go himself to determine British intentions, and the president gave his permission. James Monroe had served under George Washington in the Revolution and came close to losing his life at the Battle of Trenton but for a surgeon being on hand to clamp his severed artery. He was sometimes rash, but nobody questioned his courage. As a protégé and friend of Jefferson, he was an independent thinker and possessed an energy this administration needed. More than twenty dragoons escorted the Secretary of State out of the capital. He was going to find out what the British were doing instead of guessing about it.

When Monroe reached the Patuxent River, he found the highest hill he could and surveyed the area. The enemy were transporting men and provisions to the shore at Benedict, and now it was clear—they were either attacking Washington City or Annapolis, not Baltimore.

The next morning, Monroe returned to his observation post on the hill and now found the British gone. During the night, they had marched north along the bank of the river, and Monroe and his dragoons hurried to find where the enemy had moved. Arriving before the British at the town of Nottingham, the secretary realized this wasn't a raid but an invasion. The infantry moved inland, but there was little time to warn the president.

General Winder was at his headquarters at the Wood Yard twelve miles east of the capital, and Monroe sent word ahead to alert him, then rode to join the fight.

---

[399] Howard, 144; Lord, *Dawn's*, 44.

Winder decided to wait and observe just to make sure the enemy wasn't going to change directions, so he retreated six miles back toward the city. Instead of harassing and obstructing the British to delay them as Madison had instructed, Winder decided to cut the distance between his force and the city in half. To decrease the distance to the objective for the invading army made little sense. Amateur tacticians knew keeping the enemy as far away from the objective was key to protecting it, but not William Winder. Although an honorable man, he should have never been commanding the troops in charge of protecting the capital.

On the river in the distance, Commodore Barney and his marines at the naval yard set fire to their flotilla to keep it out of the hands of the British. Barney and his men evacuated just before they were overrun and joined Winder's army.

On August 22, Madison couldn't stand not knowing any longer and decided to see the situation firsthand. Reports were discouraging, and he felt personal knowledge may assist his decisions. He looked at Dolley and asked if she was willing to stay behind with the possibility of being trapped in the city and separated from him. She was his wife, and even though he knew her character, he still questioned her "courage and firmness" to stay behind.

She probably gave him a look only a woman could that warned him he was treading on dangerous ground. She fired back, "I have no fear but for [you] and the success of the army." The president must have beamed with pride knowing that the First Lady of the United States could take care of herself. He asked her to save the cabinet papers if they had to evacuate and kissed her goodbye, not knowing when they would meet again.[400]

Before departing, he assigned a hundred men to guard the president's house. Though he knew Dolley could handle herself, he was also protecting his most prized possession. President Madison mounted his horse and rode toward the front.

* * * * *

---

[400] Ibid., 154; Pitch, 49; Lord, *Dawn's*, 55–56.

Tallushatchee, Alabama, November 3, 1813

On the morning of November 3, John Coffee with one thousand men was ordered to destroy the town of Tallushatchee. It was inhabited by over two hundred Red Sticks, and Jackson decided to start the Creek War there. Coffee's men surrounded the village and attacked.

With the Fort Mims massacre on their mind, the Tennesseans attacked the town. A young Davey Crockett, after seeing one of his officers killed, described the battle, "We now shot them like dogs."[401] All told, 186 Red Sticks were killed while Jackson lost only five men killed and forty-one wounded. Unlike the Red Sticks at Fort Mims, Jackson's revenge stopped short of intentionally targeting innocent women and children, and eighty-four were captured.

"We have retaliated for the destruction of Fort Mims," Jackson wrote to the governor of Tennessee. It was more than revenge, which motivated the decimation of Tallushatchee. This was a message to those who waged war on women and children—if you indiscriminately murdered innocent Americans, you would be hunted down and wiped out.

After the battle ended, a ten-month-old infant boy was discovered on the battlefield still in his dead mother's embrace. The child was brought to Jackson's attention, which prompted him to ask the native women captives to care for the baby. They answered, "No, all his relations are dead—kill him too."

Andrew couldn't believe their attitude. They believed an orphan was better off dead, and he felt empathy for the boy. What if he would have been discarded when his entire family died? He'd been given a chance, and so would this child, he decided. Taking the baby in his charge, he dissolved brown sugar in some water and enticed the infant to drink it. He then sent him to Huntsville, paying out of his own pocket for the nursing and care. At the end of the war, Jackson brought the boy, Lyncoya, to live in Nashville with his family. He

---

[401] Crockett, David. *A Narrative of the Life of David Crockett, of the State of Tennessee.* (Philadelphia: E. L. Carey & A. Hart, 1834), 88.

and Rachel raised him as their own son and treated him the same as their other adopted son, Andrew Jr. He told Rachel, "He may have been given to me for some valuable purpose… In fact, when I reflect that he as to his relations is so much like myself, I feel an unusual sympathy for him."[402]

What this "valuable purpose," he believed the boy to be was never revealed. Though his treatment of the Indians as president is often criticized, he felt he was protecting them from their eventual extermination. If they would have stayed, in his opinion, they would have eventually been annihilated. Andrew knew whites on the frontier had no sympathy for Indians. They had buried too many loved ones for that. Lyncoya died at seventeen from tuberculosis, but one wonders if he would have lived, would Andrew's Indian policy have been different?

Once word of Tallushatchee's destruction reached the other Indian villages, many decided to side with Jackson. Next, the nearby town of Talladega was singled out by the Red Sticks, and Chief Red Eagle ordered the town destroyed. A force of a thousand angry warriors surrounded Talladega and prepared to wipe it out. If not for the bravery of one friendly Creek in the town who crawled past Red Eagle's men wearing the hide of a pig, Talladega would've been a disaster. Jackson promised protection for all who sided with his army, and Talladega's destruction would have proved his inability to do so. Andrew received word and marched to save the town.

At dawn, on November 9, his force of two thousand formed themselves into a U-shaped curve facing the Red Sticks and proceeded slowly forward. This was the same formation Hannibal of Carthage used to rout the Romans at Cannae centuries before. Jackson was confident Red Eagle didn't know his ancient history.

The Indians reacted as expected. Rushing headlong into the curve of the U, the braves stepped into the trap. Jackson filled the top of the U with men, trapping the Indians in the middle of the circle, surrounding them. The Tennesseans methodically closed the noose,

---

[402] James, *Jackson*, 159; Remini, Vol. 1, 193–194 (Jackson to Governor Blount, November 4, 1813).

killing everything inside the circle. The Creek War may have ended on the outskirts of Talladega, except for an opening in the O caused by a misunderstood order. Through this one mistake, nearly seven hundred Red Sticks escaped to regroup and fight again. Jackson lost fifteen dead and eighty-five wounded. Red Eagle left three hundred dead on the field. It was another victory, but not a complete one.[403]

Two victories in less than a week for an upstart commander wasn't a bad showing, specifically one ignored by Secretary of War Armstrong.

Jackson was determined to end the Red Stick resistance quickly. They were on the run and prime for the picking, but there was one problem—there were no supplies, pay, and the men were hungry. Napoleon's famous maxim that an army marches on its stomach was never more obvious to Jackson. Mutiny was brewing among the militia, and they decided to return home rather than starve. Jackson had to use the regulars to threaten them to return. The following day the regulars attempted to leave, and now the militia blocked their way.

The army was on the verge of anarchy, and the security of the southern United States was in Jackson's hands. Once again, a strong leader had to take decisive action and risk his own hide for a greater idea. He believed he wasn't fighting a simple Indian war but for a larger cause. Like George Washington, he knew an army was forged from experience, and if he could keep it together long enough, they would be victorious. Some say Jackson was arrogant, but his certainty originated in his belief in himself. He suffered along with his men and suffered from dysentery, but he did not let it deter him.

Appealing to the men directly, he pleaded for two more days. If no food and supplies arrived by then, he promised to escort them back home personally. Expecting supplies from Fort Deposit in less than two days, he gambled.

Two days later, the food and supplies still hadn't shown, and the southern campaign was in danger of collapse.

* * * * *

---

[403] Remini, Vol. 1, 196–197.

Near Washington City, August 22, 1814

On the outskirts of the capital, General Winder and Secretary of State Monroe rode at the front of the two-thousand-man force searching for the British army. At the same time, General Ross and Admiral Cockburn were heading straight for them.

The British rushed to its objective while the Americans waited to react. Ross and Cockburn had an easy time thus far. Not one shot was fired at them since they set foot on shore. Many locals put white sheets in their windows to signify submission. Some saw a chance to make money and sold cattle and other supplies to the British as they passed through. While Americans on the distant frontiers starved, others made a profit selling goods to the enemy. This was "Mr. Madison's" war, and any political advantage one could gain was all that mattered to some.

America had come a long way since declaring independence, but it divided into parties as soon as the ink on the Constitution was dry. Bitter partisan power struggles occupied the next twenty years, and division was a way of life. What President Washington warned in his farewell address was disregarded. The second war of independence with Great Britain wasn't enough to unite the nation. Some who opposed the war were Anglophiles still clinging to the mother country while others had no faith in the ability of the new government to protect them. So many just surrendered to the inevitable conquerors of Napoleon. In less than thirty years, many Americans forgot their countrymen had vanquished the most powerful military and believed doing it a second time impossible.

Only those who remembered still believed in the impossible. President Madison, the great individual freedom crusader, kept vigilant faith. He believed like every patriot before that only through struggle did individuals and nations find their purpose. America had lost its way for now, but he had faith it would find it once again.

Winder and Monroe realized whoever controlled the fork in the road controlled the battlefield. The enemy knew their objective, but Winder had no idea where they were heading. The British controlled the initiative, and in war, the one who controls initiative controls the outcome. The other side simply reacts. The one who controls the initiative can decide where and when to strike. Playing to the will of the enemy has never been a winning strategy.

One road led north toward Annapolis and Baltimore, while another road led to Washington City. Winder waited for some hint of where Ross and Cockburn intended to strike, and he was about to find out where.

In the meantime, the capital was in a panic. Monroe sent word the same day warning, "The enemy are in full march for Washington."[404] Anticipating the enemy's target, Monroe chose to act rather than react. Residents of the city rushed to evacuate and left few possessions behind. Some tried to save everything—furniture, bedding, or anything they could load in a wagon. Many had worked their whole lives for their property, and by God, they weren't about to leave it to the British. They knew what they had done on their raids of coastal towns, and they stole what they wanted and burned the rest.

The roads were clogged with people and wagons trying to flee the city. The Declaration of Independence and the Constitution were removed to the countryside as fear gripped the residents.

The president rode out to Winder's camp to inspect the troops. Most of Winder's army consisted of militia called out in emergencies. A small number were regular army, but most were citizen soldiers. Joshua Barney's troops were a handful of sailors and marines made up of free blacks and whites. Barney's confidence in his men was apparent when he told Madison, "They don't know how to run. They will die by their guns first." This integrated force contained seasoned fighters and was ready for battle. Defending their nation, while still half-slave, was a credit to the black fighters. America was their home, and freedom was an idea which belonged to every man, regardless of skin color. It hadn't yet fulfilled the promise of that idea, but it didn't tarnish the idea, only the nation.

Many believed God would eventually right this wrong. God made men free, not governments, and America was the only place

---

[404] Ketcham, Ralph, 577; Lord, *Dawn's*, 54.

founded upon this idea. Many Americans understood slavery was a contradiction to "all men are created equal." Only a change in the hearts of men or civil war could change it. Brother against brother was still too horrible to contemplate, but truth and divine will couldn't be denied forever. These free blacks fought for their inherent rights as well as whites. To deny the contributions of these heroes in our history for a political agenda is a national travesty. It is a lie to say only white men sacrificed for freedom throughout American history. From the Boston Massacre to the Civil War and today, black Americans have given their blood for this country. They fought for this idea, believing one day it would end slavery.

Madison told Winder's officers "to be firm and faithful in their duty." He knew they were tired and hungry from marching all day, but he trusted they would do their best. Whatever the outcome, he believed Americans would do what they always had done—adjust to any hardship, overcome any obstacle, and persevere to victory. With reality staring him in the face, Madison's quiet and calm demeanor caused some to think him aloof, but many saw him confident in the final result.

Secretary of War Armstrong was still in denial. His ego would not allow him to see the truth. While the rest of the countryside was preparing for an attack on Washington City, he continued to say, "They can have no such intention. They are foraging, I suppose; and if an attack is meditated by them upon any place, it is Annapolis."[405]

Armstrong arrived at the front an hour after the intended rendezvous, and Madison reprimanded him. He was supposed to be the experienced military head of the war department, but so far, he had offered no advice or solutions to the situation. Instead, he was angry the president and the Secretary of State were sticking their noses in his department. So Armstrong offered nothing and resented others advice. Madison even asked if he had any advice for General Winder, but he declined and only offered his opinion of the outcome of the impending battle. He said callously if the fight was between American militia and British regulars, the Americans would lose.

---

[405] Howard, 158–160.

Madison couldn't believe it. The Secretary ignored the possibility of an attack on Washington, then had the nerve to predict defeat before the battle even commenced. Either he purposely aided the British or he was a damned fool, Madison thought.

As the midday temperature reached the nineties, the British marched into Bladensburg, Maryland, less than twenty miles from the capital, and few no longer doubted their destination. All standing between the capital and Ross's professionals was Winder's army of mostly amateurs. The president sat on his horse, pondering their chances. If they lost, the capital would fall.

His whole life, he'd helped build the government. All he loved was inside that city, including his wife.

* * * * *

Mississippi Territory, November/December 1813

Two days passed, and still no food or supplies arrived. The men demanded Jackson keep his word and allow them to go home, but he knew the whole Creek campaign and its effects on the entire war were at stake. He stood alone in front of them and stated, "If only two men will remain with me, I will never abandon this post."

His passionate plea resonated with 109 men who agreed to stay. The men who refused to stay still expected him to keep his word. So, he promised to march the rest north, toward Tennessee, on the condition they would return if they met the supply wagons on the way. They agreed.

Twelve miles out, they met the wagons, and Jackson sighed. He had rolled the dice and won. The one hundred and fifty cattle and nine wagons of flour were just what they needed, and the men stuffed their stomachs. With their appetites satiated, one company decided to march home anyways. Jackson, his eyes flashing, rode to the front of the homeward bound company and recruited John Coffee's cavalry to block their way. He ordered them to shoot any man who refused to return and honor their agreement. He had kept his word, and they were going to keep theirs. He had suffered and starved right along with them.

Coffee's men and 109 others back at the camp still suffered, but they were willing to stand with him. How could they think of themselves when their country, their homes, and their brothers-in-arms were in danger? They were the epitome of everything Jackson despised, and he vowed to die before they would leave. As his eyes met theirs, the mutineers knew he was dead serious and decided to return.

When they arrived back at the main army, he found a larger group preparing to leave. He was furious. Men had died from wounds, disease, and starvation, but with full bellies and sufficient supplies now, they dared to leave? Weak from dysentery himself, he still found the fortitude to try and restore order. He'd had it with these mutinies. Grabbing a musket, he took careful aim at them. Still only able to use his right arm from the fight with the Bentons, he braced the rifle on the horse's neck and threatened to put a bullet in the brain of any man who tried to leave. Coffee and Major Reid rode up next to Jackson's horse to show their support. Then slowly, more troops stepped forward to show they were with him. Seeing they were outnumbered, the mutineers decided to stay. Little did they know how good Jackson could bluff—the musket he aimed at them didn't even work. He had held his army together with a broken gun and a stare.

For the moment, he avoided disaster, but now he had to decide what to do before his army's enlistments expired on December 10. This was only a few weeks away, and he wouldn't be able to stop them from leaving this time.

On December 9, one day before the deadline, Jackson rode to the front of the men whose enlistments were up and reminded them of their courage but said he couldn't let them leave until reinforcements arrived. He gave his word again once the new troops showed, they could leave. He asked for their word in return, but no one spoke. They were tired of fighting and starving. They had served their term and just wanted to go home. Jackson realized this, but they had to realize his own problem. Survival of the army was his objective, not deadlines or undisciplined men. They were alone in a hostile forest, surrounded by the enemy, and had to maintain his numbers until reinforcements arrived.

He ordered his artillery to turn the cannons on the men and prepare to fire. Self-preservation dictated his actions. One by one, officers stepped forward and gave their word to stay until reinforcements arrived. No one knows if he would have used the cannons on his own men, but he had no other choice. Whatever his intent, Jackson had saved the army again. Only history could judge whether he was right to do it.

Writing Rachel about this, he said the men were "whining, complaining, seditious, and mutineers" and shared his personal feelings about what he had to do. "This was a grating moment of my life. I felt the pangs of an affectionate parent compelled from duty to chastise his child—to prevent him from destruction and disgrace and it being his duty, he shrunk not from it—even when he knew death might ensue."[406]

Like a father to his army, he used tough love to save them from destruction.

On December 12, the reinforcements arrived, and Jackson honored his word and allowed the men to go home. The new enlistments would expire in a month, and he would be in a similar quandary. It seemed every obstacle possible was in his way. Why did it have to be so hard to accomplish what they expected of him? It was as if his superiors were purposely doing things to cause his failure. Of course, he had many political enemies, but his success was a threat to their power. Armstrong was no help, and Tennessee seemed to ignore his pleas. Like the generation before, he was expected to fight a war without food, supplies, and men. Just as Washington held the army together with tenacity and indomitable will, he would as well. If his enemies were making it harder to weaken him, they were wasting their time. They didn't know him.

---

[406] Remini, Vol. 1, 198–201; James, *Jackson*, 164. *Jackson Papers*, Jackson to Rachel Jackson, December 29, 1813.

Jackson biographer, Robert V. Remini, made an accurate description when he wrote "Jackson seemed to gain interior strength by his many misfortunes. He was one of those extraordinary men who flourish with adversity."[407]

* * * * *

Bladensburg, Maryland, August 24, 1814

Around one o'clock, the British charged across the Eastern Branch Bridge directly at Winder's army. Standing between Washington City and the enemy was an army of civilians and a few Marines. Many were only boys with dreams of glory to be like their fathers in the Revolution.

Winder directed his artillery to fire at the bridge and surprised the British who quickly retreated. The Americans erupted in premature cheers of victory. The enemy regrouped and crossed the bridge under fire. Even with many dead or dying on the bridge, they pushed forward.

Attacking the center of the American line, the British fury frightened the inexperienced shopkeepers and farmers, and they threw down their muskets and ran. A new weapon of terror was used by the British, the Congreve rocket, and it unnerved Winder's men. The Congreve rocket was much like a large bottle rocket which squealed and left a trail of fire in its path. The noise and fireworks were enough to scare those who were already nervous, and the British used it as a psychological weapon, and it worked at Bladensburg.

Winder then ordered his exposed artillery to fall back and take a new position, but faulty communication caused many to assume a general retreat was ordered. The general tried to rally his men, but it was too late. Secretary Monroe put his life in danger when he tried to stop the retreat, but by two o'clock, the battle was over.

Word of the "Bladensburg Races" reached Madison in the rear, and he scribbled a quick note to Dolley, warning her of the situation.

---

[407] Remini, Vol. 1., 203.

Washington City was now undefended, and the British could mop up the remaining opposition at their leisure.

Meanwhile, back at the capital, the First Lady anxiously waited for word from the president. Many tried to convince her to leave, but she continued to deny the worst. Using a spyglass, she peered out a window from the top story of the president's house and searched for some sign of hope. When the message from Madison arrived, she faced the inevitable.

She didn't panic or lose heart. She was the First Lady of the United States and had to set an example for others. She wouldn't show fear or doubt and her usual outgoing and optimistic personality allowed her to react to the crisis with poise. The country had witnessed dark days before and had survived; it would again. She decided, for now, to be practical.

First, she needed to save important items at the president's house. She directed servants to load a wagon with the silver, books, a clock, and the red velvet curtains from the drawing room. The presidential papers were evacuated, and she was delayed by one object, which put her in danger of capture—a full-length portrait of George Washington. She was resolved that in no way were the British going to get this painting. It was more than a picture to her; it was a symbol. They could take their city, but not their spirit. She told the attendants, "Save that picture if possible. If not possible, destroy it. Under no circumstances allow it to fall into the hands of the British."[408]

---

[408] Pitch, 87.

First Lady Dolley Madison

The frame of the portrait was screwed tightly to the wall, and removing it became a chore. After spending too much time trying to remove it, the frame was broken and the canvas was removed. Now she could finally leave the city before she was captured, and boarded a wagon and left the capital. On her way out of the city, she was scared, not for herself, but for the president.

A half an hour later, Madison galloped into the capital and learned he just missed his wife.

Joshua Barney and his marines were the only resistance left on the outskirts of the city, and they made the British pay for every inch of land. Outnumbered and running low on ammunition, Barney's men retreated. Barney himself was wounded but still refused to surrender and was eventually taken prisoner.

After a three-hour rest, Cockburn and Ross resumed their march toward the capital. Excitement filled their ranks because they were about to bring the rebellious child, the United States, to its knees and end the illusion of self-government. They were giddy with confidence and felt they were avenging their fathers who were forced to sue for peace in the Revolution. They also believed they were reclaiming their dominance throughout the world. France's Revolution was a disaster in self-government, and Napoleon was in the dustbin of history.

Now they were certain the last beacon of government by the people was about to join him.

* * * * *

Horseshoe Bend, Alabama, March 27, 1814

After the two battles at Emuckfaw and Enotachopco, Jackson had the Red Sticks on the run and wasn't about to let them get away.

Eight hundred Creek warriors retreated to a fort located at Horseshoe Bend and prepared to fight a siege.

Surrounded by water, except for a small strip of land, Horseshoe Bend looked impregnable, but Jackson saw an opportunity.

Two thousand Americans surrounded the fort and waited for the order. Many Cherokee and friendly Creek fought alongside Jackson's men and saw the Red Sticks siding with the British a lost cause. Jackson placed these friendly warriors on the opposite side of the river to block any possible escape and put his main force in front of the fort. With his men in place, he ordered them to open fire.

Major Coffee sent a small detachment across the river to capture the enemy's canoes but held back his full attack until the Red Stick women and children left the fort. Regardless of biased historians, all of Jackson's decisions weren't heartless. He spared women and children whenever possible.

Jackson was an officer making snap decisions, which could ensure the survival of his army and America or the death of both. This serious responsibility was his and no one else's. The Red Sticks were Britain's allies and would determine the success of a southern invasion. If they kept Jackson's men tied up instead of building naval and land defenses, the British could land in the South unopposed.

At twelve thirty in the afternoon, Jackson ordered the fort taken, and the infantry moved forward. The first man who climbed the fortified wall was immediately shot dead. The next one was a strapping young Tennessean who scaled the wall, slashed his sword, and shouted for his men to follow. Once over the wall, he found himself in a hand-to-hand fight against a horde of Red Sticks with nothing but his sword. Then an arrow pierced his thigh, but rather than falling, he led his men into the fight and forced the Indians to retreat.

This young officer asked a lieutenant nearby to remove the arrow, but after he tried to dislodge it, he was afraid to pull it out for fear of causing it to bleed worse. He suggested a doctor look at it, but the wounded man brandished his sword and said, "Try again, and if you fail this time, Lieutenant, I will smite you to the earth!"[409] So the threatened officer yanked out the arrow and found a surgeon to stem the bleeding.

Jackson witnessed the courage of this young officer and reassured him his fighting was over for the day, but the wounded officer had come here to make his mark, not sit on the sidelines.

As the battle continued throughout the day, Jackson saw the writing on the wall. Getting the Red Sticks to accept this before they were annihilated was a different story.

Sending a flag of truce to the fort, his men encountered a barrage of rifle fire. He realized he couldn't convince the last holdouts to surrender, so he continued the assault. By nightfall, only one breastwork remained defiant inside the fort.

Jackson asked for a volunteer to lead the charge on this last obstacle, but no one stepped forward. The men had fought bravely and were exhausted.

Grabbing a rifle, as he pulled himself off the ground, the brave Tennessean with a bleeding thigh called for volunteers to follow him. Jackson couldn't believe it. Limping, but determined, the young man moved toward the breastwork.

Two slugs pierced his right arm immediately, but he ignored them and called for a charge. He lost so much blood within a few minutes, he had to drag himself to safety before he passed out. The last breastwork was set afire and the final Red Stick defenders abandoned the fort. Jackson was so impressed with the courage of the

---

[409] Houston, Samuel. *The Life of Sam Houston.* Ed. Charles Edwards Lester. (New York: J. C. Derby, 1855), 32; Wisehart, M. K. *Sam Houston: American Giant*, (Washington: Robert B. Luce, Inc., 1962), 18

young volunteer he would never forget. After a surgeon removed one of the slugs, the courageous young officer was given up for dead. The doctors had no idea the toughness of this patient or what the future had in store for him. His name was Sam Houston, and this was just the first test in a long line of challenges that would serve him and his country in the future. He had a much greater purpose for the next generation.

In the morning, Jackson counted his casualties and found forty-nine dead and 157 wounded among his army, and twenty-three killed and forty-seven wounded among his Indian allies. The Red Sticks were decimated with nearly 900 killed, although Red Eagle escaped and could still rally opposition. The stars and stripes were raised over the fort at Horseshoe Bend and renamed Fort Jackson. He demanded the surrender of all the insurgents and future collusion with the British would mean further retaliation.

Chief Red Eagle walked into the American camp and surrendered himself but didn't ask for any terms. Jackson said, "You see my camp—you see my army—you know my object. I would gladly save your nation, but you do not even ask to be saved. If you think you can contend with me in battle, go and head your warriors."

Red Eagle took his time and said, "There was a time when I could have answered you... I could animate my warriors to battle; but I cannot animate the dead."[410]

Red Eagle only asked that his women and children be fed and offered himself up as a sacrifice for their sake. Jackson poured him a brandy and promised food and aid for the women and children. Red Eagle promised he would try to convince any holdouts to surrender. The two men shook hands, and Jackson allowed him to leave the camp. This was an agreement among warriors and an agreement among men.

The Creek War was over, and the British southern campaign of using them was at an end. If the Brits wanted the South, they would have to come and take it themselves.

---

[410] James, *Jackson,* 172; Remini, Vol. 1, 218.

After Horseshoe Bend, Jackson returned home for a short stay. It wouldn't take long before he was called on again to meet an even greater threat.

* * * * *

Washington City, August 24, 1814

"Make ready! *Fire!*"

The sound of shattering glass interrupted the quiet night.

General Ross's men shot out the windows of the Capitol building. This was a statement from King George III. The rebels who betrayed the mother country thirty years ago were finally made to heel.

Breaking down the doors, the soldiers smashed anything they considered unworthy of a souvenir. Ross ordered the building burned, and in moments, the Capitol of the United States was ablaze. Over seven hundred books in the Library of Congress and the law library were consumed.

Ross and Cockburn handpicked 150 men and led them up Pennsylvania Avenue. Cockburn asked one of the city's inhabitants, "Where is your President, Mr. Madison?" The man said he didn't know, so Cockburn excused himself, saying he was on his way to "pay a visit" to the president's house.

When the British detachment entered the White House, they were surprised to see the dining room table set for forty. Dolley had this done in anticipation of the president and his cabinet's return. Ross and Cockburn weren't about to let such amenities go to waste, so they dined on the cold cuts and sipped the Madeira wine. Cockburn drank a toast to "Jemmy," his condescending nickname for the president, and took one of the First Lady's seat cushions to "warmly recall Mrs. Madison's seat." Though disrespectful to Dolley, it was more of an insult to the president's manhood.

After the refreshments, they collected souvenirs, and Ross gave the command to burn it. His soldiers broke out the windows and threw torches inside and marched to the Treasury building and set it ablaze as well. The capital was illuminated by the amber blaze. The winds quickened the fires, and through the cloudy black night, the flames were seen for miles.

For those in the capital, it was disheartening. Some gathered at the Catholic church and prayed for deliverance while others wandered through the countryside, afraid to return. Was it this easy to destroy America? Had the British finally stamped out the beacon of liberty? To many, it seemed so.

To others, anger stirred them. One man, Mordecai Booth, said the sight of the capital in flames was "a sight so repugnant to my feelings, so dishonorable, so degrading to the American character, and at the same time so awful, [it] almost palsied my faculties."[411]

Another man said directly to Cockburn, "If General Washington had been alive, you would not have gotten into this city so easily."

The admiral replied, "No, sir, if General Washington had been president we should never have thought of coming here."[412]

Dolley Madison sat silently at an open window of a friend's home outside the capital and watched the burning city. She was worried about the president. Did he get away in time? Their reunion would have to wait till morning if he hadn't been captured. The thought of an American president being captured by the enemy during war was too horrible to contemplate.

She looked toward the flames on the horizon without a sound.

At that very moment, somewhere in the surrounding countryside, Madison sat on his mount and watched the red fire-lit sky and said nothing.

* * * * *

The following day, Ross and Cockburn continued their destruction of the capital until two coincidences interrupted their fun. Finding over a hundred barrels of gunpowder in the city magazine, they decided to dispose of it by tossing the barrels down a nearby

---

[411] Lord, *Dawn's*, 123–126; Howard, 203.
[412] Borneman, 232; Pitch, 133.

well. In the process of throwing them down the well, a barrel hoop scraped the side of the stone wall, created a spark, and ignited the dry powder. The explosion killed twelve and injured forty-four.

Another episode happened around noon in the form of a powerful thunderstorm. This wasn't any typical storm, but a tornado swept into Washington City. Tornadoes were rare for the area, and many Americans believed the storm was sent by God to expel the invaders. Ross's officers were blown off their horses, and cannons were picked up and thrown as the storm pulled roofs from houses.[413] The intense rain prevented the fires from spreading, and one eyewitness account said Cockburn asked a woman, "Great God, Madam. Is this the kind of storm to which you are accustomed in this infernal country?"

The woman defiantly answered, "No, sir, this is a special interposition of Providence to drive our enemies from our city."[414]

If providence was protecting the nation, then why did it wait until the government buildings burned? Maybe it wanted the buildings to burn, but the storm saved the foundations.

Over two dozen British soldiers were killed in the storm, and Ross marched his army out of the city that night.

* * * * *

Robert V. Remini wrote "good fortune trailed Jackson throughout the War of 1812, some of it earned, most of it entirely accidental." Andrew, he believed was "in the right place at the right time."[415] Few knew Jackson better than Mr. Remini, but "accidental" seems an understatement. Andrew believed he was destined to become a

---

[413] Lord, *Dawn's*, 134–135; Howard, 208; Pitch, 138–140; Ambrose, Kevin and Dan Henry, Andy Weiss. *Washington Weather: The Weather Sourcebook for the D.C. Area.* (Fairfax: Historical Enterprises, 2002), "The Tornado and the Burning of Washington, August 25, 1814." https://www.weatherbook.com/1814.htm; *Smithsonian.com*, Zielinski, Sarah, August 25, 2010, https://www.smithsonianmag.com/science-nature/the_tornado_that_saved_washington-3390121V

[414] Borneman, 232; Pitch, 142.

[415] Remini, Vol. 1, 234.

commanding general to avenge his family against the scourge of the British. Just as Captain John Smith and General Washington trusted in providence—Jackson did as well.

Too many mediocre major generals were gone by this time in the war. The only competent one was William Henry Harrison, but he resigned, frustrated by Secretary Armstrong's treatment. Generals Jacob Brown and Winfield Scott were making improvements in the northern theater, and the army's performance in the battles of Chippewa and Lundy's Lane in July 1814 restored a glimmer of hope that Americans could finally challenge the British on the field. President Madison had a substantial victory in the South with Jackson and promoted him to major general. He put him in charge of defending the southern theater after his willingness to fight and win.

Vice Admiral Alexander Cochrane decided an invasion from the Gulf of Mexico into the southern United States was the key to victory. With a few thousand men, their Indian allies, and help from the Spanish in Florida, he was certain they could conquer the Mississippi Valley and cut it off from the rest of the nation. It could be used to open a two-front war or could be another bargaining chip in a peace settlement. If the British had control of the Mississippi, they would control its commerce.

First, Cochrane sent a force of over one hundred royal marines to Pensacola, Florida. They were charged with arming the Indians and recapturing Mobile, Alabama. Once Mobile was secured, New Orleans would be targeted. New Orleans was the prize. If they captured it, their navy would control the Mississippi all the way to Detroit. The United States would be surrounded by Canada in the north and their ships east, west, and south.

Cochrane's plan was approved and he could expect two thousand reinforcements from Britain for a coordinated invasion of the South by mid-November of 1814. Cochrane sent his marines to Pensacola to take Mobile while he coordinated the invasion of the Chesapeake.

General Jackson with his army arrived in Mobile on August 22, 1814. He entrenched his men at Fort Bowyer on the coast and waited for the attack. He knew about the marines in Pensacola and asked the War Department permission to invade Florida but was denied. He was left to await invasion, instead of using a preemptive strike to discourage them. He warned the enemy if they attempted an invasion, "There will be bloody noses before this happens" and "an Eye for an Eye, Tooth for Tooth, and Scalp for Scalp."[416]

Four British ships were sighted off Mobile on September 12, and three days later, an amphibious assault was launched against Fort Bowyer. In this minor engagement, the British lost one ship, thirty-two dead, and thirty-seven wounded. Jackson lost four dead and five wounded. The Brits accepted this minor defeat and returned to Pensacola.

The first phase of the southern campaign was repelled, and the British realized Jackson was different than the other American generals—he was a fighter. His resolve refused defeat. "The situation of our country require it for who could brook a British tyranny, who would not prefer dying free, struggling for our liberty and religion, than live a British slave?"[417]

Writing to Rachel, he reminded her that their separation was for a greater purpose. "I pray you be calm and Trust to that superintending being who has protected me in the midst of so many dangers and kiss little Andrew for me..."[418]

In November, General Jackson conquered Florida on his own initiative, citing self-preservation as his motivation. He had to remove the threat in his rear before he could ever hope to defend Mobile or New Orleans. News of a New Orleans attack lit a fire under Andrew, and he prepared to march his army to the city. Word that the capital was in ashes added fuel to the fire.

Jackson would choose "dying free...than live a British slave."

* * * * *

[416] Ibid., 237; James, *Jackson*, 182.
[417] Remini, Vol. 1, 239.
[418] James, *Jackson*, 182 (Jackson to Rachel Jackson, October 21, 1814).

Washington City, August 28, 1814

The president, Secretary Monroe, and Attorney General Rush rode into the capital and witnessed the destruction. Madison was described as "tranquil as usual, and though much distressed by the dreadful event...not dispirited." Though he appeared worried, he wasn't about to give up. Seeing the black remnants of the Capitol and the president's house saddened him, but it also strengthened his resolve. The city chosen by Washington, partially designed by Jefferson, and made possible with the compromise he brokered in Congress between Federalists and Republicans was more than buildings or books. Buildings could be rebuilt and books replaced. He was more concerned with the psychological effect on the American people. The enemy had attacked the symbols of their freedom, not mere physical structures. The British intentions were to instill fear that their government could not protect them.

Word from New England wasn't any better. Some were talking secession and planned a meeting in Hartford, Connecticut. If New England left the Union, the whole nation could be conquered at will. Once again, self-preservation became a prime concern. The president decided to trust in the people to do the right thing and they hadn't disappointed him yet.

He did wonder how to instill confidence in the people at one of its darkest hours. Staring up at a wall with the words "James Madison is a rascal, a coward, and a fool"[419] written on it, he never flinched. A mob of irate citizens in the area wanted to hang him while others begged him to surrender and ask for mercy.

He refused to give in to the fear of either side and said, "We will defend the city to the very last."[420] He was the leader of the nation and knew Americans looked to their leaders for reassurance and strength. Washington was the model of this during the Revolution, and now, it was his job to continue. The little bookworm president

---

[419] Howard, 211; Pitch, 163.
[420] Howard, 216 (Thornton in *National Intelligencer*, September 7, 1814).

had made up his mind to fight and was confident of eventual victory. He wasn't about to let British barbarity shake his spirit.

Dolley returned to the city and was overjoyed to see James, but she was saddened by the burning of her lovely house. She was also angry and supported the president's resolve.

Madison knew Secretary Armstrong had to go. The army and the people had lost confidence in him. Armstrong defended himself and said the sack of the capital wasn't his fault, but his refusal to prepare proper defenses after being warned multiple times couldn't be excused. Madison suggested the secretary rejoin his family in New York but didn't ask for his resignation. On September 3, Armstrong officially resigned, and the president appointed Secretary of State Monroe as the new acting Secretary of War. Though Monroe had only his short experience in the Battle of Trenton, he was someone the president could trust. Immediately, Monroe moved to strengthen the Chesapeake defenses.

The British invasion fleet was spotted off the coast on September 6 and looked as if it was planning another strike, and this time, all agreed Baltimore was their aim. After Napoleon was defeated, Britain sent reinforcements to North America. They were now moving to the Canadian border, preparing to cross, and more were gathering in Jamaica for an invasion of the South.

Admiral Cochrane was sure "Baltimore may be destroyed or laid under a severe contribution." He was still optimistic with his razing of the American capital and felt the "spaniels" would roll over and lick the hand of the British lion now.[421]

The American people disagreed with his assessment. Despair and fear quickly morphed into defiance and determination.

The *Niles Weekly Register* said, "War is a new business to us, but we must 'teach our fingers to fight'—and Wellington's invincibles shall be beaten by the sons of those who fought at Saratoga and Yorktown."

---

[421] Lord, *Dawn's*, 167–168.

The *Albany Register*, which previously opposed the war, published, "Let one voice and one spirit animate us all—the voice of our bleeding country and the spirit of our immortal ancestors."

The governor of Vermont, Martin Chittenden, an anti-war leader said:

> The time has now arrived when all degrading party distinctions and animosities, however we may have differed respecting the policy of declaring, or the mode of prosecuting the war, ought to be laid aside; that every heart may be stimulated and every arm nerved for the protection of our common country, our liberty, our altars, and our firesides.

Men swelled the ranks of the army and towns raised troops and money. A recently raised local militia told Monroe, "Conflagration and rapine will never bow the spirit of the American people. Our enemy, we hope, will find that they have miscalculated our resources and spirit."

Jefferson offered his massive collection of books to replace the ones lost at the Library of Congress.

Though there was a new fighting spirit in the people, the nation was nearly out of money to fund the war, and individual citizens raised money for troops, uniforms, and arms. The perseverance and will of Americans had no rival in times of despair. John Jacob Astor, the richest man in America at that time, wrote to Monroe, "Myself with a number of other wealthy citizens are much engaged to form a system for a national bank to relieve the country from its present pressure as respects finance."[422]

The entire country pulled together. Federalist and Democrat-Republican, rich and poor, tradesmen and clergy, men and women came together with a new determination not seen since the Revolution.

---

[422] Ibid., 162–165.

Madison trusted in this spirit and knew what it could accomplish when united in a cause. He witnessed it through the fight for independence and ratification. As Washington believed the hand of providence protected them, Madison never lost faith in it or the country he loved.

As Cochrane sailed toward Baltimore, a squadron of British ships moved into Lake Champlain. Eleven thousand experienced troops from Britain amassed on the Canadian border, ready to invade New York state at the town of Plattsburgh.

The American capital lay in ashes as it faced invasion on three fronts. The might of the British military—who whipped Napoleon—was about to strike its final blow.

How could the United States survive such impossible odds? Would its citizens finally find their will to fight?

* * * * *

New Orleans, Louisiana, December 23, 1814

On the morning of the twenty-third, Major Gabriel Villere rested comfortably in a house on his family's plantation. The rattle of musketry and shouts grabbed his attention, just as British soldiers kicked in the door and announced he was a prisoner of war. The guard he posted to warn him was captured as well.

Though his plantation lay along the route to New Orleans, he never believed the enemy would choose it. It seemed a laborious task to invade through the bayous, but maybe this was why they had chosen it. His misjudgment led to his complacency, and now, the British were only a two-hour march from the city. He was supposed to sound the alarm for General Jackson, but now he was a prisoner instead.

Villere knew the city was vulnerable now, and it was his fault. He had to find some way to warn them. If only he hadn't been so sure. His city would fall because of his stupidity. He needed to find a way to fix this.

Weighing his options, Villere figured he could try to escape and possibly risk his life or he could watch his people lose their city. He made a desperate choice. Jumping through the window, he tumbled into the grass, and once on his feet, he ran into the surrounding brush. The British soldiers were so surprised by his escape, they failed to react in time. Once he reached the brush, it was too late. They were on his land now, and he knew it like an old friend. He had to get word to Jackson fast. Maybe he could rectify his mistake.

By one o'clock, Villere, on his last breath and hungry, reached Jackson's headquarters. As the general listened to the Frenchman's story, his eyes seemed to dance like fiery diamonds.

Slamming his clenched fist into the table, he shouted, "By the eternal, they shall not sleep on our soil!"[423]

* * * * *

Jackson arrived in New Orleans on December 1, and after a quick welcoming ceremony, he went to work preparing to defend the city.

New Orleans was situated on the east bank of the Mississippi River with Lake Pontchartrain to the north and over ten miles of cypress swamps emptying into Lake Borgne to the east. The city was surrounded by water, and an enemy invasion could come from any direction, so defending it would take reliable intelligence and a vigilant citizenry.

Jackson ordered guards stationed at every bayou and asked for volunteers. He sprinkled militia and others throughout the area with orders to watch for the enemy. He received offers of help from pirates Jean Lafitte and Dominique You, Creoles, Indians, Spaniards, and

---

[423] James, *Jackson*, 217; Remini, Vol. 1, 263; Groom, Winston. *Patriotic Fire: Andrew Jackson and Jean Lafitte at the Battle of New Orleans.* (New York: Vintage Books, 2006,2007), 130

free blacks. Some protested when he accepted black men in his ranks, but he replied to the governor of Louisiana:

> Our country has been invaded and threatened with destruction. She wants soldiers to fight her battles. The freemen of color in your city are inured to the Southern climate and would make excellent soldiers. They will not remain quiet spectators of the interesting contest. They must be for, or against us—distrust them, and you make them your enemies, place confidence in them, and you engage them by dear and honorable tie to the interest of the country who extends to them equal rights and privileges with white men.[424]

Jackson also reprimanded a paymaster when the man voiced his opinion of the recruitment of blacks. "Keep to yourself your opinions upon the policy of making payments of the troops…without inquiring whether the troops are white, black, or tea."[425]

He later addressed these men personally in a public proclamation to New Orleans for a call to arms. "I invited you to share in the perils and to divide the glory of your white countrymen. I expected much from you. I knew that you loved the land of your nativity and that like ourselves you had to defend all that is most dear to man—but you surprised my hopes…"[426]

He also shared his confidence in their unique prowess as warriors and appealed to their love of freedom. Though a slave-owner himself, Jackson showed respect to his two black battalions when he reviewed them. The Creole, Indians, Spaniards, blacks, and whites

---

[424] Remini, Vol. 1, 253–254. (Jackson to Governor Claiborne, September 21, 1814).

[425] Ibid., 254 (Jackson to W. Allen, December 23, 1814).

[426] Ibid., 259 (Jackson's Address to the Troops in New Orleans, December 18, 1814).

were simply Americans standing against the invaders of their nation. He had no time for petty prejudices now—the real enemy was at the gates.

Admiral Cochrane's invasion fleet landed on Cat Island on the far side of Lake Borgne, east of New Orleans in early December. He then ordered an attack on American ships on the lake December 14 and easily captured the gunboats. This allowed him easy access over land and removed Jackson's ability to keep an eye on them.

By the sixteenth, Cochrane began transporting men and equipment across the lake to Pea Island. His scouts, with the aid of a local Spaniard, located an unblocked bayou which led to Villere's plantation and ultimately to the Mississippi, eight miles below the city.

After Villere's report, Jackson quickly moved to check the British before they gained momentum. He told his officers, "Gentlemen, the British are below. We must fight them tonight." He ordered the gunboat, *Carolina,* to sail down the Mississippi to the British encampment and lay down a heavy barrage. Then he sent 2,100 men to attack the enemy camp after dark. This night operation would take the enemy by surprise and buy time for them to strengthen the city. Maybe the no-show Kentuckian reinforcements would arrive by then. Old Hickory said, "I will smash them, so help me God!"[427]

The night battle was one of confusion. Soldiers fired on their own men or fired at phantoms. Though it descended into hand-to-hand for a time, the British pushed back the attack, but it bought Jackson more time.

General John Keane was temporarily in charge of the British force until the commanding general arrived and he was cautious. He decided to wait for the rest of the army to be ferried across Lake Borgne before proceeding.

Meanwhile, Jackson pulled his troops back to the Rodriguez Canal, about six miles below New Orleans, and instructed them to start digging. This small ditch was the very place he chose to make their stand. The canal ran east from the Mississippi across the open plain to the cypress swamps and was an ideal place for a defense. The

---

[427] James, *Jackson,* 217; Groom, 130–131; Remini, Vol. 1, 263.

enemy had the river on one side to contend with and the swamp on the other. If they crossed the river, Jackson's gunboats could warn him, but he also positioned an artillery force there, just in case.

The men dug the canal deeper and piled the dirt to its front, forming a wall. The deeper the canal became, the higher the wall grew. In no time, there was artillery on the wall facing the plain, and they continued to make the canal deeper and the wall thicker.

Jackson knew he had bought them the time they needed.

* * * * *

Off the coast of Fort McHenry, Maryland, September 13, 1814

Francis Scott Key, a Georgetown lawyer opposed to the war, was on a British ship in the Chesapeake trying to negotiate a prisoner release when Admiral Cochrane attacked Baltimore.

Key was surprised by the plan and was informed he and his associate, John S. Skinner, would be detained until the attack was over. Aboard the sloop, Key eyed the shore with sudden concern for his country.

Cochrane was about to unleash the largest bombardment of the war on Fort McHenry, Baltimore's star-shaped earthwork, which guarded the bay.

As Key floated miles out in the bay, Major General Samuel Smith was appointed supreme commander for the defense of Baltimore. Smith was Senator Smith of Maryland, the same Sam Smith who called for action after the Chesapeake Affair in 1807. He had served with Washington and was at Long Island, White Plains, Brandywine, and Monmouth. Now sixty-two, Smith's experience matched his toughness. He also possessed an uncanny gift for leading men.

Smith had the citizens of Baltimore digging fortifications while he drilled his forces. Everyone in the city worked from dawn to dusk, but the morale was high. Women and children did their share as well, and the people of Baltimore were determined not to repeat the folly of Bladensburg. Americans from Virginia and other states rushed into the city, hoping to pay back the British for burning their capital.

On Sunday, September 11, British ships were sighted off Annapolis, heading for Baltimore. Smith had one thousand men and fifty-seven cannons inside Fort McHenry under the command of Major George Armistead. The entrance to the bay was obstructed with twenty-four sunken ships and barges in hopes of keeping light enemy vessels out of it.

By eleven thirty, the British fleet was nearing the city, and alarm guns fired throughout Baltimore. Women and children evacuated as men raced to their positions. General Smith sent Brigadier General John Stricker and 3,200 men to stop General Ross and Admiral Cockburn who had landed at North Point with 4,700 troops.

By the next day, the two armies clashed.

The British strategy was to land troops miles down the Patapsco River at North Point and march overland to invest the city, much like they did with the capital. The only problem with their plan was that Stricker's army stood in the way this time, not Winder's. Ross confidently stated, "I'll eat in Baltimore tonight or in hell!"[428]

Shortly after the militia attacked Ross's force, they were driven back easily, and the British commander prepared to bring up his light troops to finish the job. As he barked orders to his men, an American sniper's round found the general, and he fell from his horse. He ordered the men to retrieve Colonel Arthur Brooke to take over the command. It was the last order he ever gave. He bled to death on the field at North Point.

Ross's death shook his army's morale, and although they fought bravely that day, by nightfall, the hostilities ended with little advantage. Brooke planned to regroup and try again the next day.

Meanwhile, back at Fort McHenry, Major Armistead's wife was expecting a baby, but he remained steadfast in his task. He had waited for this day almost as much as the birth of his child.

In the summer of 1813, he wrote to then Senator Smith that the fort was ready, but "it is my desire to have a flag so large the British

---

[428] Pitch, 197; Borneman, 242.

will have no difficulty seeing it from a distance."[429] The flag was sewn by Mary Pickersgill and her thirteen-year-old daughter Caroline in August of 1813, but it wasn't needed until now.

Inside the fort, Armistead had the thirty feet by forty-two feet giant raised up the flagpole for everyone to see.

Miles out at sea, Francis Scott Key saw the giant stars and stripes above the fort and was amazed by the sight.

On September 13, Cochrane ordered an all-out bombardment of the city and the fort. Each of his five gunships could fire fifty to sixty shells an hour. All through the night, hundreds of shells hit the city. The colors illuminated the night sky like fireworks. The flashes and tracers of the shells looked awesome until they landed.

One shell scored a direct hit on the magazine in Fort McHenry but failed to explode. Then a rooster, which seemed to appear out of thin air, jumped up on the wall of the fort and crowed. The troops cheered and saw this as a good omen.

The British tried another landing on the west side of the fort but were pushed back, so Cochrane continued to pound the city.

By 4:00 a.m., the shelling stopped as an eerie silence fell over the bay. Francis Scott Key had no way of knowing if Fort McHenry had fallen. He could only make out a ragged flag flapping in the wind. It was tattered from the shrapnel hitting it. Had the fort and city capitulated? Or was it still defiant? Had the bombardment been too much? Surely, no one could withstand the endless carnage the ships rained down on it.

Scott sighed. He hadn't supported the war, but he never wanted to see his country like this. Would his flag still be there in the morning?

Fearing the worse, he watched and waited for the dawn.

* * * * *

---

[429] Lord, Dawn's, 206; Howard, 236.

Jackson's Headquarters, New Orleans, 1:00 a.m., Sunday, January 8, 1815

In the quiet blackness of slumber, a knock at the door sounded like an explosion to the sleeping officers.

"Who's there?"

In the dark, Jackson heard the door open and sat up. A dispatch at this hour? Placing his feet on the floor, he waited for his eyes to adjust to the dark then stood up.

The carrier then relayed the message to the general. It was General Patterson warning the British were about to attack Morgan's entrenchment on the other side of the river and recommending more troops.

Jackson thought a moment, then replied, "Tell General Morgan that the main attack will be on this side and I have no men to spare. He must maintain his position at all hazards."

After the failed cannon attack on their defenses on New Year's Day, Jackson knew the main British assault was on its way.

Just four days ago, over two thousand Kentucky riflemen finally arrived, raising his numbers, but many were without arms. Jackson shook his head and said, "I don't believe it. I have never seen a Kentuckian without a gun and a pack of cards and a bottle of whisky in my life!"

He now had four thousand men on the frontline and one thousand in reserve, but he was facing the Duke of Wellington's brother-in-law, General Sir Edward Pakenham, considered one of the best in the British military.

Pakenham's plan was to create a diversion across the Mississippi, then use 2,200 men to strike the American left-center and 1,200 to hit the right. Over six thousand royal troops would be in action against Jackson's outnumbered and insufficiently armed men.

Peering at his watch, he noticed it was after 1:00 a.m. and said to his aides, "Gentlemen, we have slept enough."

Mounting his horse, Jackson rode to the canal. Once there, he noticed the aroma of coffee brewing nearby and commented that it smelled better than the usual blend. The pirate, Dominique You, was brewing the coffee and handed a steaming cup to Jackson. The men along the canal watched him as he checked the defenses. It was reassuring that their commander was so calm.

He sipped the coffee and stared into a nearby campfire, thinking of the coming fight. This would be his chance to pay back the British for his mother and brothers. He was ready to fight. His eyes narrowed, and seemed to glow as they flashed across the open plain.[430]

* * * * *

On board a British ship off the coast of Fort McHenry, near dawn, September 14, 1814

Francis Scott Key waited for first light on the deck of the sloop and his ears were ringing from the concussion of the guns. The smoke still floated on the surface of the water obscuring the fort, and he couldn't sleep.

Anticipating the sunrise, he wasn't sure if Fort McHenry was still in American hands or if it had surrendered. Surely, nothing could sustain such a bombardment without capitulating, although he desperately wanted to believe it could.

The sun peeked over the horizon behind him and slowly, the fort started to appear. Looking through a spyglass, he was convinced it was a mirage.

Shutting his eyes, he checked again, exhaling as the goosebumps ran up his back. Another look, and he was certain it was real. Breathing deeply, he tried not to let emotion overtake him, but he couldn't deny it.

The American flag was still waving over the fort, and an intense feeling of patriotism swept over him. The invincible might that beat Napoleon failed to crack Fort McHenry!

Inspired by the sight of the enormous flag waving defiantly, he fumbled for an envelope from his pocket and jotted down a few lines

---

[430] Remini, Robert V. *The Battle of New Orleans*. (New York: Penguin Books, 1999), 137; James, *Jackson*, 240–241; Groom, 175, 187.

of a poem to remember this moment by. "Oh say can you see, by the dawn's early light. What so proudly we hailed, at the twilight's last gleaming" was all he wrote for now, but it was enough to encapsulate the moment.

Admiral Cochrane ordered his ships out to sea, and Baltimore was safe. The British commander would sail south to Jamaica and try New Orleans in December. He couldn't crack Baltimore, but he was confident he could New Orleans.

* * * * *

The defenders of Fort McHenry and Baltimore celebrated their victory that night with parties and revelry. Many went to church and gave thanks for their deliverance.

Their defense seemed to define the entire war somehow. The bully could try all he liked, but when the smoke cleared, they, like their flag, would still be standing there.

In the coming weeks, word of a naval battle on Lake Champlain and a ground operation at Plattsburgh, New York, spread throughout the nation. On September 11, Captain Thomas Macdonough of the American navy soundly beat the British on the lake while General Alexander Macomb's troops fought a decisive land battle. When the British commander was killed, Macomb took advantage of the confusion and pushed the redcoats back across the Canadian border. A message from Macdonough arrived in Washington a few days later. It said simply, "The Almighty has been pleased to Grant us a signal victory on Lake Champlain in the capture of one Frigate, one Brig, and two sloops of war of the Enemy."[431]

President Madison realized the enemy's attempts at invasion were beaten back in the north and east, but he still worried about the south. Hopefully, General Jackson was the right man to defend it. On September 20, Madison addressed Congress on the State of the Union. Describing their victories and the burning of the capital, he focused on the fighting spirit of the nation's citizens. "We see them

---

[431] Borneman, 213; Howard, 251.

rushing with enthusiasm to the scenes where danger and duty call. In offering their blood they give the surest pledge that no other tribute will be withheld." Then he summed up their gritty perseverance, even in defeat:

> The American people will face it with undaunted spirit which in their revolutionary struggle defeated his unrighteous projects. His threats and his barbarities instead of dismay, will kindle in every bosom an indignation not to be extinguished but in the disaster and expulsion of such cruel invaders…They will cheerfully and proudly bear every burden of every kind which the safety and honor of the nation demand.

He then explained his and the nation's feelings about the conflict to the enemy:

> …a sincere desire to arrest the effusion of blood and meet our enemy on the ground of justice and reconciliation, our beloved country, in still opposing to his persevering hostility all its energies, with an undiminished disposition toward peace and friendship on honorable terms, must carry with it the good wishes of the impartial world and the best hopes of support from an omnipotent and kind Providence.[432]

The president put Great Britain and the rest of the world on notice. The United States would no longer tolerate disrespect to their sovereignty. Like the revolutionary generation before them, they would pay any price for their liberty.

---

[432] Madison, *Writings*, Vol. 13, 311–312 (Sixth Annual Message, September 20, 1814).

Like Captain John Smith of Jamestown and Governor William Bradford of Plymouth, Madison desired the peace of a saint but demanded the respect of a warrior, and like Washington, he trusted in divine providence.

Back home in Baltimore, Francis Scott Key finished his poem, and it eventually became the American national anthem, "The Star-Spangled Banner."

The final verse defined the nation:

> Oh, thus be it ever, when freemen shall stand
> Between their loved home and the war's desolation!
> Blessed with victory and peace, may the heav-
> en-rescued land
> Praise the Power that hath made and preserved
> us a nation
> Then conquer we must, when our cause it is just,
> And this be our motto: "In God is our trust."
> And the star-spangled banner in triumph shall
> wave
> O'er the land of the free and the home of the
> brave![433]

* * * * *

New Orleans, January 8, 1815

At 4:00 a.m., the initial British assault moved forward. Once they realized they had left the fascines and ladders for scaling the wall behind, their battle plan collapsed, and the attack turned into a confused melee. One British officer sent troops to retrieve the ladders, but it was too late. The battle didn't wait for them.

Jackson ordered all available men to the wall. As massive lines of British marched within range, the wall seemed to erupt in flames.

---

[433] National Park Service. *The Star-Spangled Banner,* last updated February 26, 2015. https://www.nps.gov/stsp/learn/historyculture/starspbanner.htm.

Every cannon and rifle fired into the sea of redcoats, wounding and killing dozens. As one line of Americans would fire and move to the back to reload, the next line moved up and fired.

"Stand to your guns, don't waste your ammunition—see that every shot tells," Jackson shouted. Seeing the Congreve rockets unnerving some, he assured them these "toys" were loud and showy but lacked any punch.

General Andrew Jackson

"Give it to them, my boys!" His eyes flashed again. "Let us finish the business today!"[434]

The grapeshot from the American cannons devastated the British lines as rifles picked off officers. Commanders were down all over the field as hundreds of dead and wounded piled in front of the wall. General Pakenham tried to take personal charge of the attack when it seemed to be faltering but was wounded in the thigh and fell from his horse. His men carried him from the field when he was struck in the groin and passed out, so they laid him under an oak tree. Pakenham never regained consciousness and died. With few officers to lead them, the attack lost any order that remained.

---

[434] Remini, Vol. 1, 277.

Jackson encouraged the men as they poured continuous fire on the enemy. Unable to withstand such carnage, the British retreated.

Americans—white, black, Creole, Indian, Spanish, and French—cheered their general and the retreating enemy. Jackson acknowledged their joy, but experience taught him to confirm victory before celebrating. Staring across the battlefield, he waited for the smoke to clear and saw their victory. They had won; miraculously, it seemed. The odds were against this motley collection of misfits and their backwoods general, but they had done it nonetheless. The British had underestimated them once again and paid dearly for it.

General Jackson understood the extent of this victory when he saw the endless ocean of dead and wounded enemy on the field. "I never had so grand and awful an idea of the resurrection as...I saw... more than five hundred Britons emerging from the heaps of their dead comrades, all over the plain rising up..."[435]

The British casualties totaled 2,037 dead and wounded while the Americans had only seventy-one. Jackson credited the lopsided victory not to his generalship, but said, "It appears that the unerring hand of providence shielded my men from the shower of balls, bombs, and rockets, when every ball and bomb from our guns carried with them the mission of death."[436] In his report to Secretary Monroe he said, "Heaven, to be sure, has interposed most wonderfully in our behalf, and I am filled with gratitude when I look back to what we have escaped."[437]

Jackson was confident and always quick to remind others of his leadership qualities, but the Battle of New Orleans humbled even him. This unexplained miracle was more than any one man's doing. Their success over the enemy came from, "The signal interposition of heaven." The general suggested a day of thanksgiving to the Abbe Dubourg when the army returned to the city:

> ...while it must excite in every bosom attached
> to happy Government under which we live,

---

[435] James, *Jackson*, 247; Remini, Vol. 1, 284.
[436] Remini, Vol. 1, 286; James, *Jackson*, 247 (Jackson to John Hays, January 26, 1815).
[437] Ibid., 287 (Jackson to James Monroe, February 17, 1815).

emotions of the liveliest gratitude, requires at the same time some manifestation of those feelings. Permit me therefore to entreat that you will cause the service of public thanksgiving to be performed…in token at once of the great assistance we have received from the ruler of all Events and our humble sense of it.[438]

On January 25, 1815, the British invasion fleet sailed away and the threat to New Orleans, the South, and the nation was over.

* * * * *

By February 4, news of the victory at New Orleans reached Washington, and celebrations spread up the east coast, igniting festivities throughout the nation. Americans felt a new sense of self. They had defended their rights again and won at Baltimore, Plattsburgh, and New Orleans. The navy had exceeded their expectations. The Hartford Convention failed to gain support for secession, and after the capital was burned and the gallant defense of Baltimore, even the staunchest Federalist abandoned such traitorous talk. The Federalist Party had gambled in opposing the war and would disappear by the next presidential election. A new amalgamated party of united Americans would govern the nation into the next decade.

In Ghent, Belgium, Henry Clay, John Quincy Adams, and others finally negotiated a peace treaty with Great Britain. It was finalized on December 24, 1814, so the Battle of New Orleans had no effect on the final draft. This would cause many to disregard its importance. If it had been considered, the negotiations probably would've turned out different. However, the final agreement between both nations was a return to the boundaries before the war began. Neither side gained any more land than they started with, causing many to label the War of 1812 a draw. Because of sluggish commu-

---

[438] Ibid., 290 (Jackson to James Monroe, January 19, 1815); James, *Jackson*, 247.

nications in 1814, it took another month and a half before word of the treaty reached America, and both sides knew the war was over.

On February 13, the news reached the capital, and once again, celebrations erupted across the nation. Madison sent a message five days later, reminding Americans "and while we accord in grateful acknowledgments for the protection which Providence has bestowed upon us, let us never cease to inculcate obedience to the laws, and the fidelity to the Union, as constituting the palladium of the national independence and prosperity."[439]

In his seventh annual message on December 5, 1815, he said:

> I ought not to repress a sensibility, in which you will unite, to the happy lot of our country and to the goodness of a superintending Providence, to which we are indebted for it. Whilst other portions of mankind are laboring under the distresses of war or struggling with adversity in other forms, the United States are in the tranquil enjoyment of prosperous and honorable peace. In reviewing the scenes through which it has been attained we can rejoice, in the proofs given that our political institutions, founded in human rights and framed for their preservation, are equal to the severest trials of war as well as adapted to the ordinary periods of repose. As fruits of this experience and of the reputation acquired by the American arms on land and on water, the nation finds itself possessed of a growing respect abroad and of a just confidence in itself, which are among the best pledges for its peaceful career.

---

[439] , *The Papers of James Madison, Presidential Series Vol. 8, July 1814–18*, ed. Angela Kreider, J.C.A. Stagg, et al. (Charlottesville: University of Virginia Press, 2015), 599–601; *Founders Online. National Archives.* http://founders.archives.gov/documents/Madison/03-08-02-0523

The president then predicted the future of the nation. "Under other aspects of our country the strongest features of its flourishing condition are seen in a population rapidly increasing on a territory as productive as it is extensive in a general industry and fertile ingenuity which find their ample rewards..."[440]

The United States had faced its first real challenge since the Revolution and came out of it purified. There was a new national confidence and purpose. No longer did it see itself as a nation of British heritage, but it had its own identity. It was about to enter a new period of peace, prosperity, and growth not experienced, and would become a major power on the world stage.

James Monroe would succeed Madison as president and served two terms. This "Era of Good Feelings" would unite the nation like never before, and the Monroe Doctrine would warn Europe to keep its influence out of the western hemisphere. Monroe's Secretary of State, John Quincy Adams (son of the second president and main author of the Monroe Doctrine) succeeded him but only served one term like his father.

James Madison left the presidency in 1817, retiring to his home at Montpelier, Virginia, and died on June 28, 1836. Dolley Madison outlived her husband by thirteen years and lived in Washington City her last years after Montpelier was sold. A lifetime of service to the nation left James and Dolley deeply in debt.

Madison's fighting spirit and reliance on providence made "Little Jemmy" great in the eyes of the nation. Though his previous accomplishments often outshined his presidency and historians would describe his management of the war as a failure, he honored his pledge to defend the Constitution. "Mr. Madison's War" served a larger purpose in the end for the country, and the smallest president to ever occupy the office overcame the naysayers and stood like a giant.

General Andrew Jackson would go on to command in the Seminole War, be elected a United States Senator, and narrowly lose the presidency in 1824 to John Quincy Adams by one vote in the

---

[440] Madison, *Writings*, Vol. 13, 343 (Seventh Annual Message, December 5, 1815).

House of Representatives after winning the plurality of popular and electoral votes. He was elected the seventh president in 1828 and served two terms.

His life was one of struggle and success. The young orphan who blamed the British for the loss of his family avenged them at New Orleans. The most unlikely personality came to define the ideal American. He was brash but brave, and though he talked big, he backed it up with actions. There was nothing disingenuous about him. He was the same man in public as he was in private.

The war tested the country to its breaking point and made it stronger. With the capital burned, Americans for the first time faced the reality of losing everything.

Jackson and Madison led America through its darkest period since Valley Forge. America's second trial by fire is often forgotten, but it should be remembered.

Through the fires of adversity, America rose out of the ashes of the War of 1812. Out of these ashes, a stronger nation rose like the sun Benjamin Franklin envisioned and shone brighter.

Elizabeth Jackson's advice to her young son long ago became the rallying cry for every American.

"What were Americans made for, then?" the young nation asked.

"To fight!"

James Madison, Andrew Jackson, and the other heroes of the War of 1812 showed the rest of the world that to fight was to never give up.

5

Make Your Mark

San Jacinto, Texas, General Houston's Headquarters,
April 20, 1836

Sam Houston looked out across the prairie. The enemy's camp was so close he could smell them cooking dinner. He thought about what was at stake and what had been sacrificed. Men had died for this purpose. They had lost their lives to secure it.

Three days ago, he told his army the man responsible for the deaths of their fellow Texans at the Alamo was across the way. Some of them had family and friends who died by this man's sword, and they were itching to fight.[441]

Houston had tasted success before and knew it was only temporary. He had been governor of Tennessee and a war hero, and had married into an influential southern family. He was a confidant of President Andrew Jackson, and now he was General of the Army of the People of Texas. He'd experienced the soaring heights of success and reaching the top, but he also knew what falling from the heights felt like.

Some would say he made a career out of failure, and every time he had the golden ring in his grasp, he dropped it in a well and fell

---

[441] Houston, Sam. *Life of Sam Houston (The Only Authentic Memoir of him ever published)*, ed. Charles Edwards Lester. (New York: J.C. Derby, 1855), 123.

flat on his face. He had tasted failure more than success, and it was a wise teacher.

A drunk and a slacker, he had known humiliation. He knew failure was fleeting if you picked yourself up and kept going. Just like the landscape of his new home, Texas, life was an endless succession of hills and valleys from deserts to lush green riverbeds. Through this, he learned discipline.

He was a flawed man tired of repeatedly picking up the pieces of his life and wondered if he would ever make his mark in the world.

Houston thought of his time at Horseshoe Bend with Andrew Jackson as a young officer. He was tough and could overcome any enemy. Looking around at the men retiring for the night, he regretted some of them must die the next day. He also knew the kind of men that made up his army. He fought with this sort before and knew what happened to those who underestimated them. They had no uniforms or supplies, and their pay was still forthcoming. They were a scattered, unorganized, dirty, and unshaven mob, but they were still there.

Men like these didn't come in pretty packages. They were good men and ready for a fight. Many wanted to strike earlier and wanted revenge, but Sam knew they weren't ready until now.

Like Thomas Paine said, sixty years before in the dark days of the Revolution, "These are the times that try men's souls" and the "summer soldiers and sunshine patriots" had fallen away. Those left were fighting for something greater than mere selfish gain, and they knew death was possible. They recognized tyranny when it showed itself. Raised on American ideals, many of their fathers and grandfathers served with Washington or in the War of 1812. The American spirit was in their blood, and no one had to tell them about freedom or tyranny. This Mexican king was no different than King George, and tyranny came in every nationality. This was their moment to either submit or stand up against it, and they already knew anything "easily conquered we attain too cheap we esteem too lightly."

Juan Seguin, the leader of two dozen Texan Mexicans (Tejanos) in Houston's army understood what they were fighting for as well. Mexicans siding with Santa Anna tried to make it a race and religious war, but some knew it was about tyranny. Seguin saw what good men, white and brown, had sacrificed for freedom.

Other Texans felt the same. Some married and befriended Tejanos. This struggle wasn't about race but right and wrong.[442] It was the American story all over again, and there were ideas which meant more than race, church, or politics. Some were willing to sacrifice their lives for "life, liberty, and the pursuit of happiness."

General Antonio Lopez de Santa Anna was across the way with 1,800 battle-hardened men and was eager to end this rebellion once and for all. A bunch of farmers and hicks were no match for the Napoleon of the West (a nickname he gave himself). It would end right here on this plain. The world would know he ruled Texas, not these rejects from America. They were trespassing foreigners Mexico allowed to colonize its northern province, and they repaid her generosity by trying to claim it as their own. Half of them were illegal aliens who ignored Mexico's immigration laws and paid no taxes. They refused to convert to Catholicism as the immigration agreement required. They wouldn't assimilate and still held their allegiance to the United States. They prospered off the resources of Mexico and had the audacity to defy his authority.

He enacted laws, banning Americans from immigrating, but still they kept coming. He had predicted the Americans would try to claim independence and steal Mexico's land. Some of them even said Texas was part of America, having been sold in the Louisiana Purchase in 1803. What nonsense! It had always been Mexico's. He had fought the Spanish for the independence of Mexico a few short years ago and knew Texas was theirs. Mexican national interest was at stake, not to mention his authority and reputation.

Santa Anna was not about to let this happen. He had ended this uprising a month ago, but these hillbillies and their drunkard general thought they could continue to defy him. This would be a hard lesson for them to learn.

---

[442] Donovan, James. *The Blood of Heroes: The 13 Day Struggle for the Alamo—and the Sacrifice that Forged a Nation.* (New York: Little, Brown and Co./Back Bay Books, 2012), 252–254, 331.

The Americans believed they came from a special nation blessed by God. Their God-given rights went with them everywhere they went. What arrogance! Their self-proclaimed God-given rights were the rights their leaders in America had agreed to, not Mexico. She had her own government with its own rights. People required a strong disciplinarian sometimes for this exact reason. Freedom sounded nice in theory to Santa Anna, but in the real world, force was king. He already proved this to those who dared to stand against him. These Anglos were about to get another lesson in force.

Houston trotted out in front of the men on a smoke-colored horse as his army of over 930 followed him toward Santa Anna's camp. When they were within two hundred yards, the Texans started to sprint and shouted their battle cry so loud, the Napoleon of the West could hear it: *"Remember the Alamo! Remember Goliad!"*[443]

* * * * *

A new breed of pioneer came to the western frontier in search of a new beginning. Like the Pilgrims before them, they were searching for a second chance. The chance to start a new life in a new land was all they asked.

They were raised to believe in the Declaration of Independence and the Constitution, and most grew up in Christian homes where the Bible was the only book they owned. Some lived in brutal conditions where their daily thoughts and actions revolved around survival. Others grew up in affluent environments and received the benefit of a classical education, becoming lawyers, newspapermen, and merchants.

They came from the North and South, rich and poor, politicians and trappers—these men came west searching for a place to make their mark.

---

[443] Houston, *Life*, 128; James, Marquis. *The Raven*. (New York: Paperback Library, Inc.,1929,1966), 209; Wisehart, M. K. *Sam Houston: American Giant*. (Washington: Robert B. Luce, Inc.,1962), 240.

A new attitude took hold of the people who settled the western lands of Indiana, Ohio, Illinois, Kentucky, Tennessee, Alabama, and Missouri. A different style of dressing and talking identified this generation. Different from New Englanders and the upper east, they weren't quite the southerners of the Old South of Virginia, Georgia, and the Carolinas either. They possessed their own distinct culture and called themselves Westerners.

After the War of 1812, Americans no longer identified themselves as ex-British citizens but as Americans with their own unique culture. American slang and manners were different from Europe, and those who came to the United States left their nationalities behind. Though they retained their distinct heritages, they used what was useful and discarded what wasn't. This assimilation strengthened the American culture with every generation. America became the powerhouse who overcame the British Empire twice and proved those wrong who said a republic couldn't last. People with God-given rights and the power to vote for their leaders was absurd to most of the world. They simply pointed to the French Revolution and the bloodshed it ushered in, only to end with Napoleon who tried to conquer the world. To them, America was on borrowed time and had been lucky so far. Unlike the French Revolution, Americans had George Washington and a government founded upon the principle that rights came from God, not the state.

This difference meant success and failure, and Americans were proud of this. They learned the stories firsthand about Washington's army being saved time again and how the nation was pulled from the brink of ruin by the hand of providence in the War of 1812. This was the beginning of American *exceptionalism* or the belief the United States was God's chosen nation. There was little question about this in most nineteenth-century American minds.

After Thomas Jefferson was elected to the presidency in 1800, the people began to see their nation in a different light. Because of his tendency to trust the people to govern themselves, Americans started to believe in themselves as individuals. The common man was now celebrated, and men like Daniel Boone and Andrew Jackson were the rock stars of their day. No longer was it only possible for the well-born and well-bred to succeed, but anyone who was determined enough could pursue their own happiness. More and more, merit decided status, and the aristocracy of property lost prestige. A man's character and actions took precedence, and self-reliance and courage measured his value.

There was proof of this in the election of 1828 when the frontier orphan, Andrew Jackson, became president. His election said to every American anyone with the gumption could be president. He was considered the first commoner Chief Magistrate, because the last five presidents came from prestigious families and were highly educated. Andrew Jackson came from neither and owed his success to hard work, toughness, and ambition. To most Americans, he single-handedly won the War of 1812 and kicked the British out of America. He epitomized the western American and made it all the way to the White House. If Andy Jackson could make it in America, then anyone could. Washington and Jefferson embodied the ideals of the Declaration and the Constitution, but Jackson represented how those ideals applied to the common man—and westerners followed his lead.

The founders promised a nation where all men were born equal and had the freedom to determine their own destiny. The snobbery of Europe's class system was relegated to the dynastic families in the North and the plantations in the South. A new understanding in America seeped into the minds of young men from all backgrounds. They were ambitious and rough men who believed in individual destiny and purpose. Something deep inside themselves pushed them forward, and an insatiable desire for meaning made them restless, unable to settle down or accept mediocrity. They searched for their own greatness, and wanted to make their mark.

Of course, this new attitude developed a strain of hard drinking and hard fighting men, who lived off the land and told tall tales of their adventures. Some of these accounts were true, but many were embellishments, exaggerations, and lies. The ideal of a frontiersman was as important as the ideal of Washington and Jefferson in the new American identity. This new American represented a tough, confident, and self-reliant individual who could accomplish the impossible if they had a mind to and *was* the American dream to the average man—and it was dynamite.

A flood of these new Americans rushed into the fresh territory of the Louisiana Purchase and found opportunities and land not available in the states. Hundreds of brave men, women, and children went west in search of their fortune and fame.

The Mexican territory bordering the American frontier was an even wilder frontier. Dealing with its own instabilities, Mexico couldn't police all this vast territory, and anarchy was rampant in Texas, California, and the other southwestern areas.

Comanche in the north and the Apaches in the west raided settlements in Texas, and Comancheros (bandits who ran guns, whisky, and other contraband to the Indians) made fortunes and paid hush money to Mexican officials to look the other way. Settlers on the frontier also faced Mexican bandits who usually killed any men and sold females as sex slaves to the Indians or the highest bidder. The law of the jungle ruled Mexico's northern territories and it either was incapable or refused to police them. It was preoccupied trying to keep one government in power long enough to govern, much less deal with its territories or foreign policy.

Though this caused problems for the United States, Mexico decided to protect its own interests first with the establishment of colonies in Texas to act as a buffer zone. In the late 1820s, Mexico promoted immigration to Texas to bring order to its northern province. The idea was to settle the area with colonists and use them to tame the land. They could collect taxes from the colonists and not waste their own people protecting its border. Let someone else do the work, and Mexico could simply sit back and reap the rewards.

Many Americans saw their future in Texas. They saw a second chance to own land, start a business, or make their fortune. Some had burned their bridges and abandoned their previous lives for the promise of this Shangri-La. They wanted to wipe the slate clean and leave their pasts behind.

The inherent human desire to be born again was the real motivator. Americans were looking for a second chance, and Mexico opened its welcoming arms.

These Americans were people of action and stewards of their God-given rights. Though a requirement for immigrating to Texas was becoming a Mexican citizen, they still cherished their American ideals. They took these ideals with them to Texas in their hearts and minds, for they knew God made all men equal, not governments.

Mexico was about to find out you can take the man out of America, but the idea of God-given liberty he carried with him, no matter the land he made his home.

* * * * *

San Antonio, Texas, Inside the Alamo, March 6, 1836

For the first time in his life, Davey Crockett couldn't overcome a challenge just by sheer will. Surrounded and down to a handful of men, the Texans were fighting a losing battle. It was now hand-to-hand and personal.

The odds weren't in their favor, but Davey was determined to take some with him. He never quit fighting before and wasn't about to now. If those bastards wanted to kill him, they were going to pay for it. Nobody had ever bested him in a fight, and even if they killed him, they were going to remember him.

Davey Crockett was where he wanted to be, even as he saw the inevitable. This was his greatest moment, and if he died today, he would do it on his own terms.[444]

* * * * *

David Crockett was born into struggle and hardship in 1786, east of Knoxville, Tennessee. His grandparents were killed by Creek Indians, and his Uncle James was abducted and forced to live with them for twenty years before he was rescued. Life on the frontier was one of constant fear and vigilance. You never knew when your

---

[444] Lord, Walter. *A Time to Stand: The Epic of the Alamo.* (Lincoln: University of Nebraska Press, 1961), 161–162; Donovan, 292.

number might be up, and if the weather didn't get you, the Indians or the wild animals would. These frontier families lived at the mercy of nature. If the rain would keep their crops growing or the hunt would provide meat, each day was a battle with the elements and the land just to survive. The Crocketts, like most settlers, leaned on their faith and God's providence. Believing he would provide gave them strength to continue. Just like the Pilgrims, these settlers trusted in providence and their own determination. To this wild country, more came to test their mettle and faith.

Out of this environment, Davey Crockett was born. His father, John, had a history of failure and poverty sprinkled with small periods of prosperity. Debt was often the reason for his failures, and he struggled to provide for his family. Though he struggled, John was a hero of the Revolution, and everyone agreed he was honest and steadfast. He had many ideas to make money, but they never paid off. When these ideas failed, he had little to show for it, except loans building interest. This cycle was repeated in attempts to pay the loans but only added to his debt. Added to this debt problem eleven children, and he was pretty much fighting a losing battle.

The Crocketts were a nomadic people. They would reside in an area until they could no longer make ends meet, then pull up stakes and move to the next opportunity. John finally opened a roadside tavern in the front of his house to accommodate the influx of new settlers and traveling businessmen, lawyers, and workmen. David certainly picked up some of the influence of this environment and the rowdy big-talking travelers.

At the age of twelve, his father hired him out to a teamster, driving a herd of cattle 225 miles to the east. This arrangement was to pay off some of John's debt. In early America, sons by law were expected to help pay their father's debt until they reached the age of twenty-one.

On the return trip, the cattleman tried to force David into indentured servitude and had no intention of taking him home. After pretending to agree to the cattleman's new arrangement, the boy ran away one wintry night and found his way home.

Once back home, David started school, but after fighting with a classmate, John chased his son, brandishing a stick in a drunken rage, but failed to catch him. He ran because of his father's Scots-Irish temper, his appetite for whiskey, and his ability to hold a grudge longer than most men. He decided to keep running this time. Making it on his own would be the answer to his father's tyranny.

He had some experience working for the teamster, so he secured another job. After realizing the life of a teamster wasn't for him, he decided to be a sailor instead. Once his boss heard his new plans for the high seas, he threatened to beat him if he quit. Once again, David was held against his will and he resented it. His boss was probably trying to keep the young man from making an unwise decision, but David saw it differently. He was a free man, in charge of his own life. He ran away from home to keep his father from treating him like a child. He certainly wasn't about to let someone do it. His experience with the teamster his father hired him out to was the reason he had such an independent attitude at an early age. He saw he could determine his own path. So he ran away again. This was a pattern he would repeat throughout his life. When things became difficult or boring, he would just run away. Knowing there were opportunities out there, he felt if he just kept moving, he would find one.

This time, he was penniless and had to rough it. Sleeping outside and scrounging for food, he grew lonely and homesick. Not knowing what to do or where to go, he said, "I was determined to throw myself on Providence, and see how that would use me."[445]

Eventually, a good Samaritan felt sorry for him and convinced others to take up a collection for the homeless boy. He supported himself with this long enough to find a job. Hired as a hatter's apprentice for a four-year commitment, he only worked for a year and a half when the hatter, drowning in debt, disappeared, leaving him without a dime.

He decided depending on others was no way to live. The only way to make it in this world was to depend only on himself. So he worked odd jobs and saved until he had enough to get him back

---

[445] Crockett, 37.

home. He had something still to do there. On the way, he nearly froze to death crossing a river in a canoe but fortunately found a hospitable home where more kindly souls gave him whisky and a fire, which probably saved his life.

When he returned home, his family didn't recognize him. He had grown so much since leaving and looked more like a young man than the boy who left. He waited to see how long it would take for them to identify him, so he pretended to be a traveler and ate dinner with them. His sister finally realized it was him and announced to the others that her brother was home. Like the prodigal son, he was glad to be home after experiencing the outside world, and John's anger was now happiness.

The one thing David felt he must do was to help his father. This sense of responsibility was likely guilt he felt for running out on him. John Crockett, after all, was a decent man, even if he was short-tempered when he drank. So David agreed to work off John's debt in exchange for releasing him from any further responsibility. It seemed this way, he could help his father and gain his blessing.

David worked for a year to pay all of John's debt. After this, he was free to pursue his own life. He quit his job and bargained with another employer to work in exchange for an education. He learned reading, writing, and basic arithmetic. At the same time, he also learned to be his own man. As a boy, he thought simply wanting success was enough to get it. As a man, he realized he would have to go out and earn it himself. To do this, he knew he must become a person who could succeed first. Paying off his father's debt was the first step, and getting an education was the next, but taking personal responsibility was a leap in the right direction.

He was growing up, and at nineteen, he knew if he wanted to succeed, he needed respectability. He had his eye on marriage, and nothing motivated a young testosterone-driven man to attain status in society better than the allure of a woman. After an initial engagement and a messy break-up, David fell in love. In August of 1806, Davey Crockett got married.

Over the next two years, the young couple had two sons—John and William. David moved his family farther west so he could make his fortune. Like his father, he tried several moneymaking schemes without success. In the meantime, he used his natural talent for hunting to feed his family and waited for the next opportunity.

During this time, he believed he was preparing for "future greatness"[446] but wasn't sure how it would all play out.

* * * * *

San Antonio, Texas, Inside the Alamo, March 6, 1836

Lying on a cot inside the chapel and holding two loaded pistols, James Bowie was feverish and weakened by the tuberculosis ravaging his body. Hearing the battle raging outside the walls of his room, he knew it would soon find him and he had to be ready.

Making sure his famous knife was within reach, he was determined to make it a fight. Knowing the reality of the situation between bouts of delirium, he hadn't come to Texas to lay down and die. But this was exactly where he found himself at the most pivotal moment of his life. If he could at least take one with him if only to feel useful, he would feel better.

Mexican soldiers shouted outside the door of the chapel and were breaking it in. Jim Bowie resolved to be himself again, if just for a moment.

The door crashed in. Two Mexican soldiers entered the doorway with their muskets raised and bayonets smeared scarlet with his friends' blood. The murder on their faces was all he needed to know.

Raising his dual pistols, Jim Bowie took careful aim. If he was destined to die today, he was ready to die like a man.[447]

* * * * *

---

[446] Ibid., 69.

[447] Lord, *Stand*, 165; Tinkle, Lon. *The Alamo: 13 Days to Glory*. (New York: Signet/ New American Library, 1958), 146.

Born in Kentucky in 1796 and raised in Missouri and Louisiana, James Bowie was an original. He grew up idolizing his older brothers, John and Rezin. The Bowie brothers were always vying for the newest angle or the latest scheme to achieve fortune and status. The Bowies were nomads like the Crockett clan and went wherever circumstances led them in search of a better opportunity which seemed to be just out of their grasp. They finally settled in Louisiana and started a lucrative business in timber-cutting.

Elve Bowie was the matriarch and kept her children inside long enough to teach them to read and write and some basic arithmetic. She also tried to teach them a reverence for the word of God and even invited a traveling preacher into her home to teach them the scriptures. She prayed these principles would stick with her rambunctious boys, but they were always getting into fights and finding trouble everywhere they went. John, Rezin, and James were always looking for the bigger better deal, and they often found it.

When the British were about to invade New Orleans in 1814, Jim and Rezin eagerly volunteered to defend the city under General Jackson, but they enlisted on the very day of the battle January 8, 1815. This opportunity was a once in a lifetime event, and they had missed it. Jim dreamed of glory and destiny and believed he was meant to see a great battle someday. The experience of drilling and preparing for war did, however, prepare him for the future.[448]

Soon after the war ended, Jim decided to make a living on his own. He bought land on credit with the intention of paying for it with the timber on it. This made him realize the talent he had for making deals, so he started speculating in land too. He purchased it with no money down and would sell it by the time the payment was due. This would eventually get him into trouble, but he managed to make it work for a while. Always thinking of new ways to make a fortune without struggling like his father, he chose to use his mind instead of his muscles to make a living. His plans often led to illegal

---

[448] Bowie, Walter Worthington. *The Bowies and their Kindred: A Genealogical and Biographical History*. (Washington: Press of Cromwell Brothers, 1899), 272.

or unethical ways of making money, but he was young and willing to break the rules if he could get away with it.

After the land speculation went sour, James came up with an idea to make a fortune by using a technicality in the slave-trade law. With the help of his brothers, James began importing slaves into the US. Since the importation of slaves was made illegal by the Constitution after 1808, they found a way to corner the market and skirt the law at the same time. Buying slaves for one dollar per pound from the pirate Jean Lafitte in Mexico, they would smuggle them into Louisiana, then report the illegal slaves to the local sheriff who would then, by law, sell them at a public auction. The Bowies were rewarded for reporting the slaves with a half price discount if they chose to buy the slaves.

Now a slave purchased for $150 would sell for $1,000. They would pay $500 and have a legal slave worth $1,000. When they sold the slave at regular price, they made a profit of $350, over double their original investment. Jim was laundering slaves. How he figured out this complicated ruse with a basic education was due to an inner shrewdness, though the moral ramification never seemed to enter his mind. The law could only make something illegal and couldn't force men to obey it.

They often found inventive ways to get around these laws, and it was why the founders insisted on character and morality as pre-requisites for safeguarding liberty. If the people lost their morals, laws wouldn't matter. Liberty required a moral populace to function. If Americans lost their morality, they wouldn't hold their leaders accountable. With an immoral people, more crime would surface, and immoral leaders would pass new laws legalizing the old crimes and restrict freedoms. These would be more effectively enforced by the government with the loss of more freedoms. Importing slaves was already illegal, and the slave-trade was a problem of morality, not law.[449]

---

[449] Davis, William C. *Three Roads to the Alamo: The Lives and Fortunes of David Crockett, James Bowie, and William Barret Travis.* (New York: Harper Collins/ Harper Perennial, 1998), 58–60.

To Jim Bowie, slavery was just a way of life. He inherited the culture which promoted it. Young ambitious men from the South still searched for status through their wealth, and land and slaves promised wealth.

In Jim Bowie's world, the slave interests rationalized loyalty to the Constitution (the law of the land) because it didn't prohibit slavery but ignored the Declaration of Independence (the foundation of the law), which declared all men equal by their creator.

With the independent and wealthy profiting from this contradiction, it was no wonder young firebrands like the Bowies saw slave laws as a suggestion. In their minds, they were using the system to make money. The right and wrong of the system wasn't a concern to them. Much like today, when morality is skewed by society, the young follow it accordingly. When adults disregard morality, their children do as well. Part of America disregarded the wrong of slavery, so their kids assumed it was right.

By the age of twenty-one, Jim Bowie had grown into a local legend. He was an expert woodsman and hunter and one of the toughest fighters around. Known for his fist and knife fights, Bowie was the equivalent of a mixed-martial arts fighter, a seasoned bar room brawler, and a pinch of Green Beret all in one.

Locals warned others to avoid Bowie on a drinking binge. He was a dangerous man, especially when he was in the mood and you added alcohol to the fire. In this state, he had a short temper and hunted for trouble. Staying clear of him was good advice. Alcohol disagreed with Bowie's normal personality. He was usually polite but confident and wouldn't disrespect another man who hadn't offended him, and expected the same treatment from others.

He had grown to six feet and a muscular 180 pounds. He was the real rugged American with true grit. Women found him attractive, and men respected him for his toughness. He symbolized the new American on the frontier, and his reputation was about to grow. A big part of Jim Bowie's legend was true.[450]

---

[450] Bowie, 271.

James Bowie

Known as the Sandbar Fight, Bowie gained national prestige and immortalized his self-designed knife. In 1827, a thirty-year-old Bowie got into an altercation that wasn't initially his fight. A duel between his friend Samuel Wells and Dr. Thomas Maddox took a turn for the worse.

Two groups of men rode to the Mississippi River and paddled boats to the state of Mississippi from the Louisiana side. Dueling was illegal in Louisiana, but not Mississippi. They just changed venues to avoid prosecution.

Each man brought their friends to ensure the duel was fair and orderly. Wells brought Bowie and four others to back him up, and Maddox had over a dozen with him. By chance or on purpose, one of Maddox's men was Major Norris Wright, an enemy of Jim Bowie.

A year before, Bowie and Wright had bumped heads at a card game. Jim heard Wright was lying about him, and when he confronted him, Wright pulled a pistol and fired, intending to kill him. Miraculously, the bullet hit a pocket knife and only bruised him. Incensed, Jim beat Wright almost to death before he was restrained.

Having Wright across from him at the duel was just asking for trouble. Several of the individuals in the opposing groups were long-time enemies, and this duel was meant to settle their differences.

Wells and Maddox stood facing each other with pistols loaded. Upon firing, they missed each other, and a second attempt had comparable results, so their honor was restored by the bravery displayed and they shook hands. Maddox invited both sides to a drink to end the day when one of Well's friends, Samuel Cuny, saw his old enemy, Colonel Robert Crain. Pulling his pistol, Cuny said to Crain, "We might as well settle our troubles here and now." Cuny's brother stepped between the two and tried to get his brother to put the gun away. While this was unfolding, Bowie saw the drawn pistol and assumed an ambush was underway. As soon as Crain saw Jim, he fired but missed.

"Crain, you have shot at me and I will kill you if I can!" Jim yelled, firing at Crain but missed as well. Crain attempted to run and fired at Cuny, striking him in the leg. Jim saw Cuny was shot and pulled his knife, running for Crain. The Bowie knife wasn't any regular knife. It was nine inches long, nearly two inches wide, and ended in a razor-sharp point. It was an intimidating weapon for any man to be on the other side of, and Crain probably came close to releasing his bowels when he saw it. Crain threw his empty pistol as a last resort and managed to hit him in the head with it. Seeing stars, Bowie recovered and started forward again.

Dr. Maddox grabbed Jim to hold him back, but his adrenaline gave him untold strength. Bowie kept moving toward Crain, and Norris Wright realized he had an opportunity to avenge the beating he took by Bowie. Along with two others, Wright slowly eased up on Jim and aimed his pistol.

Bowie noticed his old enemy taking advantage of the situation and found a nearby tree jutting out of the sand to use as a shield.

"You damned rascal, don't you shoot!" Bowie warned.

One of Jim's friends handed him a pistol. Now the fight was fair again, and the two men fired at each other but missed. Bowie's friend fired at Wright but only nicked him. Wright overreacted to this flesh wound and thought he was dying. "The damn rascal has killed me!"

Another of Jim's friends grabbed him by his shirt and said, "This must be stopped sir, this must be stopped."

Just then, Wright shot Bowie in the chest and blew away the friend's finger at the same time. The bullet punctured a lung and made breathing difficult. This caused him to cringe but in no way deterred him from seeking retribution. By sheer toughness, Bowie charged the shooter but was shot again by one of Wright's accomplices. Hit in the leg this time, he fell to the sand, unable to rise. Wright and his two helpers proceeded to stab him with their cane swords.

Jim used his knife and free hand to fight off the blades coming from three directions. One cane sword bent when it hit his breastbone, but he somehow grabbed Wright's sword and pulled himself up. Staring into Wright's eyes, Jim said, "Now, Major, you die." He plunged the knife into the man's chest and twisted the blade, killing him instantly. Wright fell on top of Bowie, trapping him to the ground. One of the dead man's cohorts saw a chance to avenge his friend and moved in to finish Bowie. Thomas Wells (Samuel's brother) shot the attacker in the arm, and Jim slashed the man's side with his knife, chasing him away.

Shot twice and repeatedly stabbed, Bowie was in bad shape. The doctors didn't give him much of a chance to make it. Both Wright and Cuny died that day. Cuny's femoral artery was severed when he was shot in the leg and bled to death. Crain helped tend to Jim's wounds. They had no quarrel. Crain was merely defending himself, and Bowie thought he was defending his friends. Crain killed Cuny by accident, and Wright was killed in self-defense. Within the year, the two adversaries, Crain and Bowie became old friends. Going through battle led men to understand and respect each other on the frontier.[451]

The Sandbar Fight was reported by the newspapers across the nation, and Americans knew of Jim Bowie and his infamous knife. He became a folk hero of sorts, and his reputation grew bigger than the man himself. He was a nineteenth century celebrity of sorts.

One of his friends described him as fearless. Another said, "When unexcited there was a calm seriousness shadowing his coun-

---

[451] Davis, W, *Three Roads*, 212–216; Bowie, 273–274; Donovan, 42–45.

tenance which gave assurance of great will power, unbending firmness of purpose, and unflinching courage."[452]

James never talked tough and found no need to brag. He knew he could handle himself, but the Sandbar Fight let everybody else know it too.

* * * * *

Sam Houston's family was like many who left Virginia in search of a new beginning. Their hopes and expectations were like the innocence of children heading out into the world for the first time. Adventure and unlimited possibilities were on the minds of Americans who headed into the wilderness. Like the Crocketts and Bowies, the Houstons were looking for a second chance.

While preparing for the journey west, Sam's father died suddenly, forcing the boy to become man of the house. He was fourteen that year of 1807, the very same year the British fired on the *Chesapeake.*

The Houstons moved west to the state of Tennessee that year, and even though he tried to be a man, Sam was only a boy. He'd rather get lost in a book like the *Iliad* by Homer, which told of mythological heroes and quests for glory. This was preferable than doing chores or learning a trade. He wasn't a lazy boy but was easily distracted by his own imagination or exploring. He felt compelled to drift with the wind and see where he ended up instead of following any routine. The very moment a boy needed a father to discipline and guide him, Sam was in control of his own path. He grew into a wild, spontaneous, and unpredictable young man who made his own decisions. When it was suggested he be apprenticed at a gristmill to bring some order to his life, he ran away instead.[453]

Intrigued by Indians, Sam figured he would live with the Cherokee in the area. He just showed up at their settlement and

---

[452] Davis, W, *Three Roads*, 94.
[453] Houston, *Life*, 20–22; James, *Raven*, 19-22; Wisehart, 7–9.

made himself at home. Once he met the leader of the tribe, Chief Jolly, he won him over, and they welcomed the young man.

Indians then were considered barbarians and heathens by most whites. They mistrusted or despised them, and fear by both sides often led to hostility. Even the peaceful tribes who many times allied with Americans were lumped in with the rest.

Sam was an anomaly for that time. Why would an American boy from a civilized Christian family want to go live with "savages?" His decision to run away and live with the Cherokee was teenage rebellion against the society, which produced mediocrity, not greatness in his opinion. He didn't want to simply exist but wanted to make his mark in the world. Something drew him to the Cherokee, and he followed.

Chief Jolly became a surrogate father to Sam. Naming him the Raven, a Cherokee symbol for good fortune and destiny, they taught him how to hunt and track, live in the wild, and the universal sign language. He occasionally returned home to let his mother know he was fine, and she used these occasions to ask him his intentions. Did he plan to live as an Indian his whole life or return to society? He often asked himself this same question, but being average was not an option, so he decided to take the first step. Saying goodbye to his Cherokee family, he returned to his home to make his mark.[454]

His first idea was to be a teacher, though he had little education. This was the start of his belief that one must see the finish line before running the race. All the skills would come during the doing, he believed. It was a habit he would repeat many times in his life. If he wanted to achieve anything, he would simply do it. He wouldn't wonder how to do it or talk himself out of it—he simply did it.

He opened a log cabin school, teaching the basics and, of course, the *Iliad*. He charged eight dollars per term and printed a large sign to advertise. Eventually, he built a respectable business. Recollecting his time as a teacher in old age, Sam said, "I experienced a higher

---

[454] Houston, *Life*, 22–24.

feeling of dignity and self-satisfaction than from any office or honor which I have since held."[455]

One place couldn't keep him tied down no matter how much it satisfied him, and in 1813, at the age of twenty, he joined the army to fight the British. After hearing his decision, his mother handed him a musket and said, "There, my son, this musket, and never disgrace it: for remember, I had rather all my sons should fill one honorable grave, than that one should turn his back to save his life." She wanted it understood what she expected from him and finished with "the door to my cottage is open to brave men, it is eternally shut to cowards."[456]

Though his mother was content her son be courageous, his brothers and friends were horrified when he decided to enlist as a regular soldier due to his father's service as an officer during the Revolution. This meant Sam would disparage the family name, and under the southern code of honor, it was blasphemy. He was determined to advance himself through his own achievements, not his father's reputation, and the tradition was elitist. He would become an officer by merit, not tradition, and it was important to start at the bottom and work his way up. He neither felt he deserved nor wanted entitlement. This was the sure way to prove his own worth and imagine the ending rather than the beginning of his journey. He answered his brothers and friends' criticism with a stern proclamation. "You don't know me now, but you shall hear of me!"[457] They laughed at such bravado, but they didn't know him yet.

In a matter of weeks, Sam was promoted to sergeant because of his integrity and actions. He was described by Senator Thomas Hart Benton as "generous, brave and ready to do or to suffer" and "always prompt to answer the call of honor, patriotism, and friendship." In very little time, Sergeant Houston was Lieutenant Houston, and he saw action with Major General Andrew Jackson's army at the Battle of Horseshoe Bend. He fought with a bravery to make his

---

[455] Wisehart, 14; James, *Raven*, 28; Houston, *Life*, 26.
[456] Houston, *Life*, 27; James, *Raven*, 29–30.
[457] James, *Raven*, 30; Wisehart, 15.

mother proud and was seriously wounded. He nearly died as surgeons removed one musket ball from his shoulder and opted to leave the other inside, fearing removing it would likely kill him. Many wrote him off as a dead man, but some fellow Tennesseans supplied him with whisky for the pain and carried him the entire trek to his mother's house so he could die with family.

This journey took two months, and when he arrived home, his mother barely recognized the sickly scarecrow who was once her son, but she beamed with pride. Though he was weak at present, he was certain he would overcome his condition.[458]

After Horseshoe Bend, General Jackson and Sam became lifelong friends. Jackson admired the young man's grit and courage and felt kinship for the fellow Tennessean. He probably saw himself in Sam, and the son he never had. Becoming a mentor, Houston idolized him as the example of what a man should be.

Although Sam wanted to return to the war, his condition was still questionable. His recovery was slow, and the doctors in Tennessee were limited in what they could do for him. The army sent him to Washington for better care, but the capital was in shambles because the British had burned it in August of 1814, just before he arrived. After the Battle of New Orleans, a peace treaty ended the War of 1812, but veterans like Sam still suffered from their wounds.

The second musket ball inside his body was the problem to his recovery, and if it wasn't removed immediately, he would risk losing his arm, and possibly, his life. Sam took a shot of whisky and gripped the back of a chair while the surgeon reopened the wound. It took some time searching for the slug, and he lost a lot of blood before it was extracted. Because of this, he spent the next few months reading a Bible his mother gave him and regained his strength. It would take him over two years to fully recover and return to the army, but he overcame it.[459]

---

[458] Houston, *Life*, 31–33; James, *Raven*, 32–34.
[459] Ibid., 34–35; Wisehart, 19–20.

Upon returning to the army, he was promoted to first lieutenant, and Jackson sent him on a special mission only providence could have designed.

The Cherokee were on the verge of war after a few tribes signed treaties, giving away land. The officials convinced a few chiefs to sign the treaties to claim legality, but the Cherokee saw through the scam.

Jackson was busy fighting the Seminole Indians in the Florida territory at the time and needed someone he trusted to calm the uprising brewing. So he sent Sam who had a special relationship with the Cherokee. He returned to Chief Jolly's camp, this time as a representative of the very government who cheated his Indian father's people. Houston was torn over his loyalties to both sides but knew the Cherokee had been tricked, but if the Indians went to war, it would mean their extermination.

Land was set aside for the Cherokee in the Arkansas territory to recompense their loss. When this territory became the border of the expanding nation, speculators and some in the government found new ways to break the treaty. This was the reason tribes attacked settlers. To the American Indian, land meant survival, but to some Americans, land was the path to wealth. The minerals and natural resources alone were coveted by many. By signing the first treaty, the American government agreed to prohibit its citizens from encroaching on Indian land. In turn, the Indians agreed to prohibit their people from attacking settlements. Both sides were unsuccessful with their promises.

In the case of the Cherokee, self-preservation and greed were the motivators for breaking the treaty. Sam Houston's task was to convince Chief Jolly to agree to a new treaty, and he did this to protect them. He knew Americans were still angry because many tribes had sided with the British during the Revolution and War of 1812. If the Cherokee went to war, they would pay for the sins of the Red Sticks and Shawnees. Though he understood their reluctance, he pleaded with the chief to accept the treaty.[460]

---

[460] Ibid., 40–41; James, *Raven*, 37–40.

The next year, he grew discontented with army life and resigned. Needing a new challenge, he decided to try the civilian world again in hopes of achieving status and raising a family. Both were reasons to leave the army, but an inner drive pushed him to strive for more. Where the next step led on his journey to the good fortune the Cherokee envisioned was anybody's guess.

Only the Raven could determine his destiny by spreading his wings and seeing how high he could fly.

* * * * *

In 1813, Fort Mims was attacked by the Red Sticks, and five hundred Americans were massacred. This happened in Davey Crockett's backyard, and was an immediate threat to his home and family. So he decided to join the Tennessee volunteers to avenge Fort Mims and protect his home. His wife, Polly, was against his decision to go to war. He was their sole provider, and she couldn't hunt and fish. How would she feed the family while he was off playing soldier? What if he was killed? What would she do then?

Davey told her, "If every man would wait till his wife got willing for him to go to war, there would be no fighting done, until we would all be killed in our own houses."

Polly didn't like it but eventually accepted her husband's decision, and Davey left to join up with General Jackson's army. Davey said his "dander was up" and he was itching for a fight and about to scratch. He was ready to defend his country and knew he could lose his life. It was his duty to the country and maybe a little personal against the Indians. His grandparents were killed by Indians on the frontier, and Davey wanted revenge. He was also motivated by his need to do something important and said, "I instantly felt like going, and I had none of the dread of dying that I expected to feel."[461]

During the Creek War, he experienced the snobbery of officers much as George Washington experienced in his early days. The American army had a similar problem, and many officers looked

---

[461] Crockett, 72–73.

down on enlisted men as their inferiors. They disregarded the wisdom of the hunters, trackers, and woodsmen because they saw them as uneducated hicks. Davey would never forget the mistakes made because the officers wouldn't take their advice.

He saw the problems with the inadequate supplies and food. The soldiers were malnourished and on the verge of mutiny, and Crockett's solution was to hunt. Wild pigs, birds, rabbits, or anything available, he provided his division with his skills. If they needed anything, his answer was to simply get it. Complaining about the problem didn't solve it.

Davey participated in the Battles of Tallushatchee and Talladega, but was humbled by the slaughter at Tallushatchee. The men were out for vengeance for the Fort Mims massacre.

The day after the battle, Davey and a group of men returned to the village, hungry and foraging for any scraps the Indians may have left behind. In a cellar of one of the burned-out houses, they found a few potatoes, and the ravenous men began to eat them. Davey was sickened by the event. "The oil of the Indians we had burned up on the day before had run down on them, and they looked like they had been stewed with fat meat." This inhumanity seared into his memory the horror of war and how starving men turned into animals. "Hunger compelled us to eat them, though I had little rather not, if I could have helped it…"[462]

He served another year in the war and once avoided starvation by trading bullets to friendly Indians for two hats full of corn. His ingenuity saved him and others from needless suffering, but he was glad to be going home.

In no time, Davey and Polly welcomed a new baby girl—Margaret. It was a time of reunion and new beginnings after a long separation. Shortly after giving birth, Polly became ill and died. Davey was devastated and said, "The doing of the Almighty, whose ways are always right, though we sometimes think they fall heavily on us."[463]

---

[462] Ibid., 89–90.
[463] Ibid., 125.

Putting his trust in providence, he realized God's purpose was a difficult pill to swallow.

Feeling Polly's loss was two-fold, not only did he lose his partner in life, he lost the mother of his children—one a newborn. In a day where men participated little with child-rearing, providing and caring for them alone would be too much, so he found a local woman whose husband was killed at Fort Mims. She had some money, a farm, and two kids of her own, and Davey proposed to her immediately. The obvious advantage of this arrangement would benefit both families, and she accepted. Elizabeth Crockett got his affairs in order and was a trustworthy partner and mother. She brought structure to the children's lives and was a grounding influence on Davey and his wild ways.

But no one could tame him completely, and shortly after the marriage, Davey and some friends set out on a trip in search of better land. After a few days in the wilderness, their horses wandered away from camp, leaving them stranded on foot. Davey left the group to track his horse, but after walking nearly fifty miles with no success, he found himself alone and exhausted. At a nearby home, he asked for a place to stay the night, and they welcomed the tired stranger.

The next morning, his legs ached and he could barely walk. He knew he must get back to camp and weakly limped back in that direction, but by noon, he was sweating profusely and realized this was something more than fatigue. He was seriously sick, and thinking a rest might help, he lay down on the ground and slept. Fortunately, some amiable Creek Indians stumbled upon him and carried him to another homestead. There, a generous woman attempted to care for the stricken man, but he was suffering from the symptoms of malaria.

After another try to make it home on a borrowed horse, he was delirious and near death. He then found his way to another home and lay in a coma for two weeks. The good Samaritan woman there decided to feed him an entire bottle of frontier medicine containing mostly alcohol and figured it couldn't hurt. Miraculously, he woke from the coma the next day and slowly began to recover. Along with alcohol, the medicine contained Peruvian bark, also called quinine, which helped reduce the severity of malaria. How the woman had the medicine containing quinine and knew he needed the whole bottle was beyond logical explanation, though Davey had relapses of the disease throughout his life he believed he was spared for a greater purpose.[464]

Making his way back home, he was elected lieutenant colonel of the county militia, town commissioner, and state representative. His veteran status and personality was perfect for politics, and his genuine charm made him a natural. Never phony, Davey was the same, running for office or telling a story to a group of friends. He never avoided issues and spoke directly to the people. He told them the way things really were, whether it was popular or uncomfortable, and never pretended to have all the answers. He was funny and simple in a down home way but shrewd. He shared drinks and stories with his constituents and was never afraid to laugh at himself.

Davey was comfortable in his skin and confident he could solve real problems. He believed in serving his constituents and not the party's interests. Building his reputation and experience, he decided it was also time to get his financial house in order, so Elizabeth and Davey began construction on a gristmill, distillery, and a gunpowder mill. He hoped to make them profitable, but while serving his first session in the legislature, a flash flood washed his moneymaking dreams away.

Unsure why God allowed the water to carry away his future, he refused to entertain disappointments. He simply packed his family and moved them 150 miles to western Tennessee and built a new house. Once again, the pattern of changing location and starting over was repeated. Instead of wringing his hands and complaining, he just started over fresh in another place. Not a characteristic distinctly his own, but a common one among western Americans, Davey never whined or gave up. When he was down, he got back up and tried again.

Though resilient, Davey resigned himself to a life of hunting, farming, and wandering. He was changing, and his former self was

---

[464] Ibid., 128–131.

washed away with his business dreams. A new Davey Crockett was about to rise out of the flood.

After losing his first attempt, he was elected to the United States Congress in 1828. He lost his seat in a close race in 1831 and won it back two years later. He benefited from Andrew Jackson's presidential victories which promoted the theme that the common man could serve the people better than career politicians. Jackson represented the frontier soldier who saved the nation during the War of 1812 and never sugarcoated the truth. Davey fit this mold better than anyone.

At the Capitol, he championed a bill which would allow poor farmers and homesteaders in Tennessee to buy the land they occupied at an inexpensive price. Facing the forces of special interests, Congressman Crockett refused to play the Washington game. He would rather lose an election than compromise a belief or disregard the people for personal gain. He wasn't a politician as some have portrayed him and was quite terrible at winning support from powerful interests. He voted for what he believed was right, not what the Democrats told him to support. Led by President Jackson and Vice President Martin Van Buren, the party decided to force Davey out of Congress when he wouldn't toe the line because independent minds weren't tolerated in Washington.

Davey was worried the old general he admired was slowly becoming a dictator. He had revered Andrew Jackson, and it was not easy to oppose the most popular man in the country. Crockett saw President Jackson as his example of the ideal man, but now he saw what politics could do to even the best of men. Executive tyranny was a serious threat with the Jackson administration, and he regularly ignored Congress and the Supreme Court.

The national bank of the United States was the first Federal Reserve of its day, and President Jackson saw it as an institution benefitting the rich and holding the common man in debt. Alexander Hamilton set the bank up in 1791, but it expired in 1811. Congress and Madison decided to recharter it in 1816 in the aftermath of the War of 1812 to prop up the national debt. This new charter would expire in 1836, but Congress passed a bill to renew it, and Jackson vetoed the bill and won reelection. He then removed the nation's money and distributed it among state banks.

President Jackson's overreach may be justified, but his treatment of Congressman Crockett wasn't. Davey opposed the anti-bank policy because it was unconstitutional for the president to make law, and Jackson's new animosity toward states' rights seemed more Federalist than the party of Jefferson and Madison. Crockett also opposed the president's Indian Removal Act of 1830, calling it unfair to force people from land they were promised by treaty. He may have opposed it because he felt a certain kinship with them for saving his life once, but he always sided with the underdog.

Regardless of his motivations, Davey became a pariah in his own party, and his district was gerrymandered, so he lost his reelection in 1835. Feeling betrayed by his country, he realized when greedy men controlled anything, they invariably ruined it.

Before the results of the election, Davey said if he lost, they "might all go to hell—I would go to Texas!"[465]

He saw a new beginning in Texas and could wipe the slate clean there. He tried to succeed by the current rules but was smeared, ridiculed, and marginalized. In Texas, he could purchase cheap land and renew his reputation. They were recreating the spirit of 1776 in Texas and maybe they would appreciate him. Many said Texas was another lost cause, but Davey knew it was where he belonged.

His restless spirit would never allow him to stop searching for future greatness. His maxim, *"Be sure you're right—then go ahead."* wouldn't allow him to ever give up. A man like him knew nothing else.

* * * * *

San Antonio, Texas, Inside the Alamo, March 6, 1836

William Barret Travis scanned the ground around the fort and, through the darkness, saw thousands of Mexican soldiers. It came

[465] Davis, W, *Three Roads*, 408; Levy, Buddy. *American Legend: The Real-Life Adventures of David Crockett.* (New York: G.P. Putnam's Sons, 2005), 229.

down to this moment, and he had prepared the men the best he could. It was in God's hands now, and the outcome was foreordained now that reinforcements hadn't arrived. If they were to die tonight, then let them die gloriously like men. They would take as many of Santa Anna's soldiers with them.

Maybe they could kill enough to force a retreat or maybe the Texan army would show up any minute and save them like a scene in *Ivanhoe*. He didn't really believe this, but he had always believed everything happened for a reason, and if they died today, maybe it was to save Texas and make their mark.

For William Barret Travis, fighting and dying for Texas independence was an honor. Bravado, bravery, and adrenaline coursed through his body as he grabbed his shotgun and ran to the front of the fortress wall. Overtaken by emotion, he yelled, "Come on, boys, the Mexicans are upon us—and we'll *give them hell!*"[466]

* * * * *

William Barret Travis was only twenty-six when he found himself in command at the Alamo. Born in South Carolina in 1809, the Travis clan moved to Alabama when he was only nine. Attending school, he studied Greek, Latin, philosophy, ancient history, mathematics, speaking, composition, writing, and religion. He had a talent for public speaking and became an effective writer. He also discovered a love of books and became a voracious reader.

Heroic warriors of the past, real and fictional, were his favorites. William Wallace, the brave Scotsman who defied England and died for Scottish independence and Sir Walter Scott's *Ivanhoe* told of a time when chivalry, honor, and courage guided men. Most boys were raised on stories of the American Revolution and the War of 1812, where the underdog Americans overcame the mighty British Empire not once, but twice, through heroic sacrifices. None of the harsh realities of war were ever described in these accounts, only the glories

---

[466] Davis, W, *Three Roads*, 560; Lord, *Stand*, 155.

of battle. Young men felt compelled to find glory for themselves, and William Travis was one such boy.

As he grew into a young man, he taught school while studying law. Being immature himself, he fell for one of his older students and married her. Soon the youngsters started a family with the arrival of a son, Charles, but Travis still struggled to make ends meet working as a lawyer with the new addition. His area was overrun by a surplus of attorneys, and it was a daily miracle to find work.

Trying the newspaper business was one possible avenue. The print news had little competition in Alabama in those days. Buying his own printing press and doing all the work himself, he drummed up advertisers and managed to stay afloat for a while. In time, the newspaper failed, and Travis was desperate. After passing the bar, he couldn't find work in the law either and became discouraged. He heard a calling to greatness and that God had a bigger plan for his life, but he felt like everything he tried ended in failure.[467]

He was motivated and a man of action. Many saw an arrogance in the confidence of the self-reliant young man in his twenties, but he held himself to a higher standard than most. When he failed, he was crushed. When he succeeded, he was proud but expected more from himself. Coming off as snobbish and stuffy, many believed he looked down on them. They saw a brash and cocky young cub who thought he was smarter than everyone else. He was none of those things, but because he expected a higher standard of himself, he expected it of others.

If Travis was in his forties, rather than his twenties, it wouldn't have been much of an issue, but because of his youth, he came off as arrogant. The problem was not with his personality as much as it was with his style of leadership. When people decided they didn't like you, it was hard to get them to listen. Travis believed leading by example caused others to follow. He read of flawless leaders who led from the front and wanted to emulate them. Others misunderstood his aims. Whether he was likeable or not, people respected him.

---

[467] Davis, W, *Three Roads*, 196–199; Lord, *Stand*, 52–53; Donovan, 10.

Travis wasn't only having problems in his career, but his marriage was no different. The couple started having issues over possible infidelity on his wife's part, and Travis decided to walk away from the marriage along with the debt and uncertainty. Texas was the land of second chances, and he desperately needed one.

Leaving his life behind, Travis moved to Stephen Austin's Texas colony and set up a legal practice. There was no surplus of lawyers to compete for business in Austin's colony. Eventually, he had more business than he could handle and finally found a place he belonged.

Stephen Austin settled nearly three hundred families in Texas in 1825. His father, Moses, dreamed up the idea but died before he saw the reality. Stephen was erudite, principled, calm, and not a natural leader like his father, but he possessed the steady patience Ben Franklin and James Madison provided to the arena of fighters and naysayers in their own time. When Mexico enacted a new law promoting colonization, thousands flocked to Texas. Hoping to establish settlers in Texas to deal with the Indians, Mexico saw an advantage.

Once the Texans created a flourishing settlement and became self-sufficient, the government of Mexico realized they couldn't control them. The Texans enjoyed semi-autonomy, and Mexico gained little by the arrangement. When a coup brought Anastasio Bustamante to power, he decided to enforce Mexico's laws in Texas. After executing the ousted president, Bustamante placed the Mexican military in control of the colony. Custom houses were established to enforce tax collection, and further immigration to Texas was banned. Illegals would be prosecuted. This wielding of power and intimidation by the new Mexican regime caused the freedom-loving Texans to resist. They were accustomed to a hands-off government in Mexico City. Now the government was in their pockets and in their business, and they resented it. They had built Texas by their sweat and ambition. After creating a garden out of the wilderness, the Mexican government decided to come and take a piece of it.[468]

Even though further immigration was prohibited, thousands of Americans still entered Texas illegally. Slavery was banned in Mexico

---

[468] Lord, *Stand*, 30–32; Donovan, 36.

but was never enforced in Texas. Only ten percent owned any slaves, and most Texans were from the southern United States, so this was a small number. Mexico made righteous denouncements against it but did nothing with its own oppressive social structure. The *peonage* system continued as Spain had left it, dividing the people into two distinct classes. The wealthy landowners possessed all the power and land while the "peons" or peasants labored to scratch out an existence.

Purposely put in debt by their employers, the peons were slaves to the landowners. By giving advances on pay and forcing purchases from company stores, which charged just enough to ensure the peon's indebtedness, it was impossible to ever get out of debt. This guaranteed their servitude. Many were treated as poorly as the slaves, only they called them by another name. It took until the mid-twentieth century for Mexico to stop using the peonage system. Though it officially banned slavery, it used the peonage system to enslave blacks as well as its own people, and Texas was no exception to the tyranny of Mexico.[469]

Travis recognized the tyranny of the Mexican government and despised it. Growing into a tall, good-looking, blue-eyed, and auburn-haired gentleman, he was considered by the rugged frontiersmen as a sort of a dandy or pretty boy who enjoyed loud expensive clothes and good hygiene. In a world of buckskin breeches, coonskin caps, and homespun shirts, Travis appeared to be a soft city slicker to many.

His age didn't help any with his image, and many sneered at him. A twenty-three-year-old dandy commanded no respect in Texas. William Barrett Travis would, in time, show Texans why they shouldn't judge a book by its cover or discount the courage of the young.

* * * * *

[469] Knight, Alan. *Journal of Latin American Studies Vol. 18, No. 1 (May 1986). Mexican Peonage: What Was It and Why Was It?* pp. 41–74, retrieved from http://www.jstor.org./stable/157204; Donovan, 34–35.

After leaving the army, Sam Houston decided to relocate to Nashville, Tennessee, and pursue a career in law. Contacting a relative in town, Judge James Trumble, he asked for help to pass the bar. Impressed by Sam's determination, intelligence, and energy, the judge instructed him on the requirements to pass the exam, and in six months, he was officially a lawyer. Normally, this took a year and a half to pass the bar exam, but Sam was no ordinary person. When he set his mind on a goal, he focused completely on it. All else was unimportant, and he never questioned his ability to accomplish it or doubt the result. Just as he told his brothers, everyone would soon "hear of me."

Over the next few years, he was appointed prosecuting attorney of the county, colonel and adjutant general of the militia, and eventually major general of the militia. He kept rising in society and seemed to be blessed in every attempt, and whatever he wanted seemed to fall into his lap. Sam also visited General Jackson at his home, the Hermitage, in Nashville regularly. His reputation as a lawyer, leader, and a heavy drinker developed relationships he kept his entire life.

Elected to Congress in 1823, he met the giants of the era: Henry Clay, Daniel Webster, John C. Calhoun, and the elderly sage of Monticello, Thomas Jefferson. He stumped for General Jackson in his unsuccessful bid for presidency in 1824 and even briefly courted Mary Custis, granddaughter of George Washington and future wife of General Robert E. Lee.[470] At the Capitol, Houston became involved with a Jackson opponent when he insulted Congressman John P. Erwin on the House floor. Erwin's friend, General William White, came to his defense by challenging Houston to a duel, and Jackson coached him on how to successfully fight one. Honor made it impossible to refuse a duel, even though he never fought one before. Instructing Sam to bite down on a bullet to steady his aim, Andrew Jackson was one to listen to when it came to intimate combat. He'd killed a man once, and his street fight with the Benton brothers was legendary.

---

[470] James, *Raven*, 50.

At the duel, Houston took Jackson's advice and bit the bullet, literally. After White missed with his first shot, Sam clenched the musket ball in his mouth, steadied his aim, and shot him in the groin. Realizing what he'd done, he ran to the downed man and asked White to forgive him. The wounded man calmed his opponent and forgave him. White recovered from his wound, but Sam was embarrassed by the incident and came to despise dueling. He even talked Jackson out of another near confrontation. Though Sam was not a man to trifle with, he hated injustice, and dueling was simply two alpha-males attempting to gain respect by killing their opponent. He saw no justice in it.[471]

Though ashamed, the duel only enhanced his reputation in Tennessee and was considered a badge of honor. When Sam ran for governor, he won easily. Soon after the election, General Jackson was elected the seventh president of the United States, and Democrats controlled Tennessee and the nation.

Houston succeeded beyond all expectations, but he was still lonely. He wanted a wife and a family, like everyone else, and needed a woman's grounding influence in his life. Eliza Allen was the young vivacious daughter of a distinguished family in Tennessee society, and Sam asked her father for her hand and received it. Eliza didn't quite feel the same about Sam, but her father pressured her into the union. The status of the governor's wife would be worth it to her father, but she had feelings for someone else, though she bowed to paternal wishes. Sam and Eliza were married on January 22, 1829.

Everything appeared perfect in Houston's world. He rose to Governor of Tennessee and was President Jackson's confidant and now had a beautiful wife. Eliza was nineteen, and Sam was thirty-six, but Eliza's immaturity affected the marriage more than her age, and she still pined for her lost love. Returning home one evening, he found her burning love letters and weeping uncontrollably. This caused an argument, and Eliza told him she wasn't in love with him. Her reluctance in the bedroom the previous three months was over another man, not the fear, she told him. He lost his temper

---

[471] Ibid., 57–59.

and accused her of infidelity, which she denied, and he stormed out incensed by her aloofness.

Once he calmed down, he returned home, only to find her no longer there. She went back to her parents with no intention to return. Going to the Allen residence, the governor begged her to return home and promised to work something out, but she refused. Her parents weren't helping the matter, and news of the spat between the governor and his wife spread rapidly. All of Nashville gossiped about the scandal and its effect on his reelection. Word of mouth was the social media of its day, and it travelled far and fast throughout Tennessee.[472]

Not only was his marriage in shambles, but he was also embarrassed publicly. His opponent in the race trashed him over the incident, but Sam refused to respond to the accusations and caused many to believe them. Mobs burned him in effigy and called him a coward and, of course, the drunk label resurfaced. When he appealed to Eliza's father for help, he was ignored.

His perfect life turned on him in a flash. Marital problems in the nineteenth century were immediate grounds for dismissal from public office. A man holding an important office was expected to keep his family in order, and failure would cause humiliation to befall the whole state. How could he run the state if he couldn't keep his wife in line? The governor of Tennessee, the home state of President Jackson, was particularly responsible for protecting his state's reputation. The people in Tennessee believed Sam's star had fallen and his rise in the history of America was over. The shine of his reputation had burned out.

His brothers and friends wrote him off when he joined the army as a private, but providence intervened. He was now heading in the wrong direction. His purpose wasn't to get comfortable or settle down in life yet or being governor. Even being married to Eliza wasn't his destiny.

Instead of fighting the inevitable, he resigned as governor on April 16, 1829. It was the only solution he could muster in his weak-

[472] Wisehart, 41–44; James, *Raven*, 65–68.

ened condition. Broken, he believed his spirit would never be the same and, in his eyes, his life and career were over, destroyed by a nineteen-year-old child who thought marriage was merely a suggestion. The war couldn't beat him, but Eliza did, and his downfall came from an enemy he never suspected—a woman. He had to get away to think and needed a place to figure it all out—but where? When he was a boy, he found shelter with the Cherokee, and now as a grown man, where could he go? The answer was an obvious one.

A week later, he stepped aboard a steamship heading west. Along the route, he was introduced to James Bowie but could never fathom how their paths would converge again one day. For now, he just wanted to escape. There was only one place he wouldn't feel the shame or pain and could forget the past and pick up the shattered pieces of his dignity. The place to find peace was the only home he could count on.[473] There, he believed all his problems would disappear.

* * * * *

After running fraudulent land deals, Jim Bowie was forced to leave Louisiana, and going to prison was a real possibility. The scam had finally run its course, and he was facing time. Texas was the place to go when someone needed to start over. Jim decided to try his luck in the booming silver mines, hoping to make his fortune. Buried treasure was in line with his "get rich quick" ideas, and he liked the adventure it promised. There was also opportunity to get cheap land in Texas. Cheap land would soar in value once the colony prospered, and others settled, looking for a homestead. Jim's eyes were dollar signs. Seeing an opportunity to reinvent himself, he felt it was never too late to start over.

Jim Bowie had grown into a tall, muscular, and attractive man who caught the eyes of Texan women and the senoritas as well. When he arrived in Texas, he caught the attention of Don Juan Martin de Veramendi, a wealthy landowner and respected citizen of the area. He

---

[473] James, *Raven*, 77=78.

also grabbed the attention of Veramendi's beautiful nineteen-year-old daughter, Ursula. Her father saw potential in Bowie's ambition, and Ursula saw an attractive, confident man love-struck with her. Jim fell in love with Ursula, and her father's money and connections only sweetened the deal. He had other women before, but Ursula was his first real love. Becoming a Mexican citizen, he converted to Catholicism and learned Spanish. He purchased millions of acres of land and helped Ursula's father in several ventures. He was in Texas to stay.

In 1831, Ursula and Jim married, but he was determined to make it on his own without her father, so he immediately set out to find the silver that would make him rich. This time, Bowie would solidify his reputation in Texas.[474]

Along the San Saba River, Jim and nine others, including his brother, Rezin, and a thirteen-year-old mulatto boy named Charles found themselves surrounded by 124 Tawakoni Indians with very little cover or ammunition. Bowie's group kept the Tawakoni at bay for ten hours and killed thirty braves and wounded forty. Their group lost one killed and three wounded, and was a miraculous feat for even Jim Bowie to accomplish. Keeping a level head, he told the others to aim for the leader of the Indians. When the Tawakoni attempted to rescue their wounded commander, Bowie's men could pick them off one at a time. Working just as he expected, the Indians losses mounted and they abandoned the siege the next morning.

The San Saba battle was significant because it cemented James Bowie's tough guy image in Texas. The Sandbar made him dangerous in a street fight, but the San Saba galvanized him as a leader. Facing ten to one odds, he had led men under fire and won.[475]

In the summer of 1833, Jim contracted either malaria or yellow fever when on a visit to Louisiana. Just like Crockett, it put him on his back and convalescing for weeks. Recuperating at a friend's home in Louisiana, he received news which nearly killed him.

---

[474] Davis, W, *Three Roads*, 292–296; Donovan, 48-49; Bowie, 270.
[475] Donovan, 49–50; Davis, W, *Three Roads*, 300–304; Bowie, 272.

Ursula was dead, and her entire family was gone, wiped out by the worldwide cholera outbreak that year, which started in Asia, Africa, and Europe, then spread west to New York, Kentucky and, finally, Texas. The epidemic killed millions, and the Veramendis left San Antonio for a family retreat to escape, but the disease found them anyway. Some accounts claim Jim lost two children along with Ursula, both her parents, and her adopted brother. He was crushed, losing everything he held dear in a single moment, and still weak from his sickness, Jim sank into a depression. He started drinking, going on binges, and picking fights. Losing his family caused him to lose direction. What would he do now? He had put all his faith into this new life and wasn't sure how to pick up the pieces.[476]

Eventually, the old Bowie knew he had to push forward. Where, he didn't know, but he picked himself up and moved in another direction. His path had led him to a fork going two different directions. Down one, he could wallow in self-pity and drink himself to death, and down the other, he could take a chance with the unknown again. He would trust it would lead him to his purpose.

When it rains, it pours, and the dictator of Mexico, Santa Anna, had Bowie arrested and jailed for his land grabs and annulled land he owned. He stripped him of any wealth he acquired in Texas, so he lost his family, property, and freedom in an instant. Jim and a friend escaped from jail, and he vowed vengeance on the man responsible for taking his fortune. He had sacrificed his family for Texas, and confiscating his property and arrest was the reward.[477]

After Santa Anna's strong-arm tactics throughout Texas, the town of Nacogdoches elected Jim Bowie, colonel of the militia. After raiding an armory, he tried to convince Texans to resist, but they weren't ready to go this far yet. Jim decided to visit home (Louisiana) one more time to tie up some loose ends, and while there, he heard rumors of a coming revolution in Texas. The people were finally pushed to the limit and were ready to make their stand.

---

[476] Davis, W, *Three Roads*, 361–362; Bowie, 277.
[477] Ibid., 425.

In the summer of 1835, he heard about an uprising in Gonzales, Texas, where townsmen were preparing to fight Santa Anna's tyranny. Colonel Bowie suddenly realized where his unknown path led and quickly returned to Texas to render his services.[478] Texas needed fighters, and that was the one thing Jim Bowie knew how to do well.

* * * * *

Anahuac, Texas, 1832

When Mexico sent troops to William Barret Travis's town of Anahuac and started bullying the Texans, he decided to make his own stand.

Militia captain Patrick Jack and Travis threatened the Mexican colonel in charge of the garrison at Anahuac with retaliation. Colonel John Bradburn was an American mercenary who fought for Mexican independence, received a commission in the army, and was now following orders to enforce the dictator's will on his fellow Americans. Jack and Travis were bluffing, and Bradburn called them on it. He arrested the two men and confined them in the garrison jail to await their fate.

The Texans had had enough and formed a militia of one hundred and fifty men to march on the garrison and rescue Travis and Jack. When word of the approaching attack reached the garrison, the two prisoners were tied to the ground and had rifles trained on them. Bradburn warned the militia if they attempted a breech, he would order their execution. Travis shouted to the militia not to worry about him and Jack. He would rather die a thousand deaths than let Bradburn's tyrannical treatment go unpunished.

Luckily and providentially, cooler heads prevailed. Bradburn was recalled from Anahuac and the prisoners were released. But Travis had proved himself to the others with his bravery. Under the threat of death, the young dandy had impressed the men. No longer

---

[478] Donovan, 51–53; Bowie, 272; Davis, W, *Three Roads*, 429–431.

did they look at him as less than a man and his toughness or courage was no longer in question.[479]

* * * * *

Two years later, Santa Anna took power in Mexico and promised a return to republican principles. Many Texans put their hopes in his words but soon realized the emptiness of those words. He ushered in something much worse, they soon realized. Strapped for cash, the dictator sent an armed force to Anahuac in 1835 and ordered them to collect duties by force. If the Texans didn't pay, they were arrested. After a prominent businessman, Andrew Briscoe, was arrested on a bogus charge, some Texans planned a reprisal like the one in 1832. Reminded of that encounter, they picked Travis to lead them. Devising a secret password for the operation, Travis picked the same one George Washington used at Trenton—"Victory or Death."

The Texan force of two dozen men fired a warning shot from a cannon outside the Mexican compound, and Travis met with the garrison's captain and demanded unconditional surrender. Sensing a possible catastrophe, the captain surrendered his forty-four men to Travis's Texans. After promising to leave Texas, the Mexicans were released.

Many in Texas saw Travis's attack in Anahuac as irresponsible and said he had committed an act of war on Mexico while many were still hoping for a peaceful settlement with Santa Anna. This loose cannon had risked all their livelihoods for personal glory, and they quickly distanced themselves from his actions.

Some Texans supported Travis and were relieved someone had finally stood up to the tyrant who trampled on their liberties. Travis's actions spoke for the feelings of many and were a spark of the fire to come. Writing to Jim Bowie after the Nacogdoches skirmish, Travis said, "God knows what we are to do. I am determined, for one, to

---

[479] Davis, W, *Three Roads*, 270–272.

go with my countrymen; right or wrong, sink or swim, live or die, survive or perish, I am with them."[480]

In August 1835, Santa Anna ordered William Barret Travis and other hotheads arrested. Texans knew he and the others would likely be executed as examples to discourage the rebels, and they saw the writing on the wall. Tyrants understood only one thing—force. The Texans were outnumbered, outgunned, and out of money. After negotiations failed, they felt it was their generation's turn to preserve the freedom their forefathers bled and died for. Every generation owed its freedom to previous ones and were expected to repay the debt by being watchmen of their own. If it meant death, so be it. After all, the Texans were still Americans at heart, and God-given rights couldn't be erased by any tin-pot dictator. It was time to make their stand.[481]

So Texas raised an army and gave Travis command. He wrote his response to inspire freedom-loving people everywhere to join the fight. "Let us be men and Texas will triumph…let us resist until our bodies and our property lie in one common ruin, ere we submit to tyranny." He was willing to lose everything for the greater cause.[482]

William B. Travis

---

[480] Ibid., 455.
[481] Lord, *Time*, 37; Davis, W, *Three Roads*, 453–455.
[482] Davis, W, *Three Roads*, 458.

In February of 1836, Travis was on his way to San Antonio to take charge of an old Spanish mission called the Alamo. He was certain he had found his purpose.

* * * * *

The underlying cause of the coming conflict didn't happen because Texans coveted more slave land as some historians like to claim. It took an unalloyed tyrant to push them to their breaking point before they resorted to armed conflict. The actions of the Mexican government under Santa Anna's dictatorship spoke for themselves.

Mexico began its war for independence from Spain in 1810. Inspired by the American Revolution, they wanted to establish a second republic in the western hemisphere. Just as the French, they started with genuine intentions but allowed their revolution to be co-opted by devious and corrupt men with darker agendas. There was no George Washington in Mexico to refuse the power of a dictator. Mexican leaders often accepted it when offered or killed for it. Eleven more years of bloodshed was required before they declared their independence.

In 1813, at the Battle of Medina (coincidentally located outside San Antonio, Texas), the Spanish fought a group of rebels who had been victorious in a previous battle and declared independence. These rebels were made up of Mexican, American, and British, and Spain wanted Medina to be a warning to revolutionaries. Exercising the full power of Spain, they sent General Joaquin de Arredondo and nearly two thousand troops to squash the uprising. Arredondo had success stomping out revolts in other towns before and could be relied on for the job.

Arredondo easily defeated the rebels and killed six hundred. He then ordered the three hundred prisoners executed and put their heads on display in San Antonio. Like a horde of Huns or Mongols, they terrorized the town for two months, raping the women, confiscating property, and summarily executing suspected enemies.

A young lieutenant serving under Arredondo at Medina won acclaim for valor. His name was Antonio Lopez de Santa Anna, and Medina was his first taste of battle. He learned that swift violent action was the only way to stop a revolution, and showing no mercy guaranteed submission. He also gained a perception of Americans at Medina as weak fighters. He saw them as invaders and should be crushed like bugs underfoot. At the Battle of Medina, the young lieutenant saw what true brutality could do and never forgot.

Santa Anna was, above all else, an opportunist, and when the Mexican revolutionaries started to win the war, he simply switched sides. After independence, he became a general and survived every succeeding coup because he waited to see who had the advantage before choosing sides. He was instrumental in overthrowing President Pedraza and won hero status in 1829 when he defeated a Spanish force trying to reclaim its lost colony.

Elected President in 1833, he promised peace and prosperity for all and claimed to be a fighter for individual rights and equal representation. Even Texans saw Santa Anna as a better choice and believed he would fix Mexico once and for all.

Santa Anna didn't much enjoy the administration of government, so he let Vice President Valentin Gomez Farias, a reformer, do the day-to-day work. He retired to his lavish estate and commanded from afar while Farias implemented laws to weaken the Church and the military influence, making Mexico more republican. This, of course, created two powerful enemies at the same time, and the Catholic Church and the Mexican military convinced Santa Anna that Farias must go, so he was removed. More than likely, the dictator saw an advantage cozying up with the two factions in 1834 and his statement, "I swear to you that I oppose all efforts aimed at destruction of the constitution and that I would rather die before accepting any other power that that designated by it" wasn't set in stone. So he scrapped the Mexican constitution and suspended the legislature. Mexico wasn't ready for freedom, he said, and she needed a strong man to lead the way. Explaining these views to a former American minister, he said, "A hundred years to come my people will not be fit for liberty. They do not know what it is, unenlightened as they are, under the influence of a Catholic clergy, a despotism is the proper government for them."[483]

According to him, Mexico needed a dictator to control it, so he simply became one. He disbanded state militias, gained control of local officials, and warned of repercussions to any opposition. He needed money to enforce his will, so he imposed large duties on imports.

Backlashes to his actions erupted in the Texas and Zacatecas provinces in the north soon after. Zacatecas was easily snuffed out by taking a page from Arredondo's example at Medina. The rebels there were led by Francisco Garcia, an ex-governor, and his force of 1,200 Mexicans were routed and killed. Then Santa Anna's men were rewarded with their victory with free reign over its citizens. Once again, rape, theft, and execution were the order of the day.

The dictator returned to Mexico City to a hero's welcome, and the exalted leader was celebrated after he sanctioned murder and rape of his fellow citizens. History tends to ignore the Zacatecas event, because it gets in the way of the revisionist claim that the Texas Revolution was motivated by race and greed. Santa Anna thirsted for power and domination, and it was irrelevant who his enemies were. Anyone of any race or creed who got in his way was made to pay. Texas was the next bug to crush, and he relished the thought.

In 1834, Stephen Austin was hopeful he could negotiate a peaceful solution and travelled to Mexico City. Upon his arrival, he was immediately arrested and imprisoned without a trial. The founder of Texas who preached peace was now a victim of Santa Anna's assault on freedom. Austin wasn't released until the middle of 1835, and his treatment convinced Texans resistance was the only option. This was a tipping point for many who believed the dictator would stop at nothing to bring them to heel.[484]

In September of 1835, Mexican soldiers entered the town of Gonzales, Texas. Confiscating a business for a headquarters and beating a young man, they demanded the town surrender its cannon.

---

[483] Donovan, 30, 120–123; Lord, *Stand*, 62–63.
[484] Donovan, 38–40.

The little gun was no threat to Mexico or its army and was merely used to scatter Indian raids. It was more for show than anything, but Santa Anna ordered it confiscated to enforce his power. They had no Second Amendment in Santa Anna's Mexico, and Gonzales was a fabricated event to gain popular support in subduing Texas.

Surrendering arms was a foreign concept to Americans. This God-given right of self-preservation was the first of the sacred rights granted to all men. It also represented the first step toward total tyranny in Texas, and taking the cannon was a test. If they surrendered the cannon, he would be back for their rifles. This was the pattern of history, and the first shots at Lexington were fired by their fathers and grandfathers when the King's soldiers came for their cannon. They had refused to surrender it, and Concord was the price the British paid for the attempt.

Though Texans were no longer in the United States, they had heard these stories their whole life, and they were imprinted on their hearts. The Declaration of Independence was a universal declaration of rights which must be protected. Life, liberty, and pursuit of happiness wasn't just an ideal existing in a single country, and Americans exported it to the world.

Santa Anna cared nothing for the self-evident truths of Americans. Just because they thought they took their rights wherever they went didn't make it true. Where was God and his rights when Medina and Zacatecas were disciplined? Government denied and granted rights with force and nothing more.

The men of Gonzales refused to turn over the cannon and took the Mexicans rifles instead. Santa Anna's soldiers returned a few days later with a force of one hundred cavalry demanding the cannon again. Stalling to round up more men, the Texans grabbed their rifles and ran to the battle. They designed a flag to wave at the cavalry with the phrase, "Come and take it" scrawled over an image of a cannon. Texans had taken as much as they could, and now they were ready to fight.[485]

---

[485] Ibid., 57–60.

Firing of the cannon prompted the Mexican horsemen to attack, but they retreated when a larger force of rebels arrived. This was just the excuse Santa Anna wanted, and it lit the fuse of the Texas Revolution.

Empowered by their success at Gonzales on December 5, 1835, Texans assaulted the force at San Antonio (San Antonio de Bexar) under the command of Major General Martin Perfecto de Cos, Santa Anna's brother-in-law. Intent on showing the dictator in Mexico City their resolve, they moved in force. After a bloody fight for the town, General Cos retreated into the old Spanish mission, the Alamo, which he transformed into a fort. Barricading the front gate, Cos prepared for a siege, and Texans surrounded the town and waited. Juan Sequin and the Tejano cavalry were key to stopping the Mexican mounted soldiers. Wounded with no provisions, Cos surrendered a few days later. By December 14, the Mexican army left town after being paroled.

There were no Mexican forces in Texas after Cos left, and the people were euphoric by their victory. In the United States, Texas was the talk all over the country, and President Jackson made no public comment, but privately, he paid close attention. What courage and fortitude! Hundreds of Americans soon headed for Texas, hoping to get there before all the fighting was done. To them, it felt like 1776 and 1812 all over again.[486]

When Santa Anna learned of his brother-in-law's defeat and humiliating surrender, he was enraged. How could a professional force of trained soldiers lose to a bunch of rabble? The "Napoleon of the West" would teach them a lesson they would never forget. He had always held Americans in contempt and once threatened the US directly during a speech, saying he didn't fear the United States. Like the British commander in 1814, he promised to "chastise" them for instigating revolution in Texas. He said, "I will march to the Capital, I will lay Washington City in Ashes as it has already been done" to stir up dark memories of defeat in the War of 1812.[487]

---

[486] Lord, *Stand*, 67–60; Donovan, 60–61.
[487] Donovan, 125.

He wouldn't allow the "foreigners" to get away with this behavior. He instructed his army to treat them accordingly:

> The foreigners who wage war against the Mexican nation have violated all laws and do not deserve any consideration, and for that reason, no quarter will be given them… They have audaciously declared a war of extermination to the Mexicans and should be treated in the same manner.[488]

A war of extermination? Exactly where was evidence of Texans killing Mexicans? Even in battles, Mexican prisoners were given quarter and released. Santa Anna told lies to work the Mexican people into a frenzy, and just as every tyrant in history had done, he created a false justification to attack those who opposed him. He learned well from Arredondo all those years ago, and Santa Anna's accusations against Texas were his own crimes. A Mexican newspaper called on their countrymen to "wipe out the stain in blood of those perfidious foreigners." Whether their fear of "foreigners" populating parts of Mexico and forming their own independent governments was a real concern or not, it seemed to him a justification for "exterminating" them.[489]

Juan Seguin was the leader of a Tejano force of nearly forty men fighting with the Texans, and many were married to Mexican women and had children. Some Mexicans supported them in silence, because there was a price to pay for sympathizers and collaborators. Some in Mexico resented Texas and Zacatecas for creating prosperity in their provinces while the rest of Mexico was struggling under the peonage system.[490]

Santa Anna was on his way to end the uprising, and Texas would soon know his resolve. He assured his officers, "The superiority of the Mexican soldier over the mountaineers of Kentucky and the hunters

---

[488] Ibid., 130–131.
[489] Lord, *Stand*, 62.
[490] Donovan, 252–254; Lord, *Stand*, 87.

of Missouri is well-known. Veterans seasoned by twenty years of war can't be intimidated by the presence of an army ignorant of the art of war, incapable of discipline renowned for insubordination."[491]

What Texas needed now wasn't men who would follow a dictator off a cliff but those self-reliant unique individuals who were willing to sacrifice their lives for something greater than themselves.

Davey Crockett, Jim Bowie, and William Barrett Travis were on their way to San Antonio de Bexar, the Alamo, and history.

* * * * *

The Alamo, Travis's Headquarters, February 24, 1836

He braced as the room shook from the artillery shell slamming into the outer wall, and he knew it was just a matter of time. What choice did he have now? Santa Anna promised no quarter for them, and surrender wasn't considered. They would all be put to the sword if he overran them.

There really was no choice between surrender or fighting. They could try to fight their way out, but where would they go? The Mexicans could pick them off one by one in the desert and would have an open highway to subjugate the rest of Texas.

Travis knew they were the last obstacle in Santa Anna's way and may buy some time for the people to organize an army. This might make all the difference. Not that these men would agree to surrender if they received quarter. They intended to whip the enemy soundly.

He had sent messages to the town of Goliad where Colonel James Fannin and his army were defending against a second Mexican force heading their direction, but there was still no word after repeated attempts. Houston told Bowie to leave the Alamo and blow it up because it had no strategic value. Defense from a fort was a fool's errand, and trapping an army in a fort was suicide.

Travis disagreed with Houston's assessment and believed the Alamo had military value. He and Bowie agreed that San Antonio

---

[491] Lord, *Stand,* 68.

was crucial to Texas, and if they made a stand here, it might stop Santa Anna from steamrolling over the rest. It had worked at Bunker Hill, and the British lost seven hundred men, making their generals weary of attacking entrenched Americans throughout the war. This gave Washington time to save his army on many occasions. During the War of 1812, Jackson and his outnumbered army held off the British at New Orleans from behind ramparts. Travis knew these examples of heroic stands and knew defending the Alamo wasn't impossible.

Travis must appeal to every Texan and American to rush to their rescue and join the fight for freedom. Essentially trapped on an island in a sea of a hostile enemy, they had little ammunition, food, one hundred and forty-six men, and a dozen or so women and children. Santa Anna had a force of over fifteen hundred soldiers, and he was now shelling them. Soon he would send his infantry to raze the fort.

Sitting at his table, Travis knew his message would be his final bid for aid. As the fort trembled from another shell, he scribbled:

> To the People of Texas & all Americans in the world—
>
> Fellow citizens and compatriots—
> I am besieged by a thousand or more of the Mexicans under Santa Anna—I have sustained a continual Bombardment & cannonade for 24 hours & have not lost a man—The enemy has demanded a surrender at discretion, otherwise, the garrison all will be put to the sword, if the fort is taken—I have answered the demand with a cannon shot, & our flag still waves proudly from the walls—<u>I shall never surrender or retreat.</u> <u>Then,</u> I call on you in the name of Liberty, of patriotism & everything dear to the American character, to come to our aid, with all dispatch— The enemy is receiving reinforcements daily & will no doubt increase to three or four thousand

in four or five days. If this call is neglected, I am determined to sustain myself as long as possible & die like a soldier who never forgets what is due to his own honor & that of his country—Victory or Death.

William Barret Travis

He underlined "Victory or Death" a total of three times to push the point home. They would either win or die in the defense of freedom. He also saw a divine message and added a postscript:

P.S. The Lord is on our side—when the enemy appeared in sight we had not three bushels of corn—we have since found in deserted houses 80 or 90 bushels & got into the walls 20 or 30 head of Beeves—

Travis[492]

He saw God's hand provide food for them just as they were nearly out. They were destined to stay, no matter the outcome. Sealing the letter, he handed it to Juan Seguin with orders to ride to Goliad. Travis was still distracted by the cannonade, though it didn't unnerve him but only emboldened him.

Across the way, in the Mexican camp, the green flag of no quarter fluttered high above San Antonio, and the smell of gunpowder mixed with the warm breeze. Santa Anna looked on and waited.

* * * * *

---

[492] Davis, W, *Three Roads*, 457; Tinkle, 75.

The Alamo, February 27, 1836

He had him in his sights. Recognizing the target was a man of importance, he slowed his breathing and aligned his sights. Taking one final breath and holding it, he applied slow pressure to the trigger, and if the wind was just right, he would take down his prey.

Davey Crockett had a bead on Santa Anna and was a hair from ending the life of the cause of this mess in one single shot.[493]

* * * * *

The previous few days went from celebration to reflection. He arrived at the Alamo, a celebrity of sorts, and many genuinely felt Crockett and his men were the cavalry coming to save them. Davey, the fierce hunter in buckskins and a coonskin cap, wrestled bears and could whip a hundred men with one arm tied behind his back. He had brought only a dozen Tennesseans with him. A dozen Davey Crocketts could beat Santa Anna's entire army alone, some thought. Many in the Alamo saw the larger than life legend as the answer to their prayers, and his presence could turn the tide. Speaking to the defenders on his arrival, he said, "I have come to your country, though not, I hope, through any selfish motive whatever. I have come to aid you all that I can in your noble cause. I shall identify myself with your interests, and all the honor that I desire is that of defending as a high private, in common with my fellow citizens, the liberties of your common country."[494]

The crowd cheered and quickly warmed to him. He was one of them and was officially welcomed as a Texan. Two days later, on February 22, the Alamo celebrated George Washington's birthday with a celebration of music, dancing, and drinks. Of course, Davey and his Tennesseans were the rowdiest of the bunch, and they enjoyed blowing off steam, anticipating the days ahead. They sensed

[493] Tinkle, 77; Donovan, 241.
[494] Lord, *Stand,* 82–83; Donovan, 178–179.

it might be their last shindig, and that night, word of Santa Anna's army entering San Antonio put a damper on the festivities.[495]

Five days later, Davey stood behind the outer wall of the Alamo firing his rifle at the Mexicans occupying the town. Encouraging the defenders to stand fast and inspiring confidence, he was invaluable moving up and down the ranks when someone needed assurance. He helped get their minds straight with some good old-fashioned Crockett wisdom from his yarns.

The Mexicans were slowly digging trenches closer to the fort, and Davey saw the reality of their situation. He also believed in the possibilities of his fellow Americans and never counted them out.

The Alamo was a massive area for one hundred and fifty defenders to handle. It was built for defending Indian attacks, not for artillery, and even though the walls were three feet thick, they were nothing more than dried adobe (sun-dried mud and straw).

The interior of the Alamo was a large common area, and along the walls, there were various rooms including a chapel, kitchen, and jail. There were two corrals for horses and cattle with four-foot high walls on one side, and the main gate was the strongest point. General Cos briefed Santa Anna on these details, and he knew not to focus their main attack there. Cos would be responsible for leading the main attack and knew the compound was vulnerable because it was too large to defend with one hundred and fifty men. Thousands of Mexican soldiers would attack at every point, and no matter how determined the Alamo's defenders fought, it would be impossible to defend every point. Decreasing the size of the defense would have increased their chances like the Spartans at the Thermopylae pass, and even if they were overwhelmed by sheer numbers, a smaller area could be deadly for an attacker. The odds were against the men in the Alamo, and many saw the impending disaster approaching, but like the three hundred Spartans, they refused to back down.

Crockett wrote to his wife and children soon after he entered Texas and assured them, "I am rejoiced at my fate. I had rather be in my present situation than to be elected to a seat in Congress for life.

---

[495] Davis, W, *Three Roads*, 528.

I am in great hopes of making a fortune for myself and family bad as has been my prospects." In typical Crockett fashion, he looked at the situation for the possible opportunities and never dwelled on the problems. He sought solutions instead and ended his letter with advice for his children. "I hope you will do the best you can and I will do the same, do not be uneasy about me for I am with my friends."[496]

David Crockett

He was with friends, and those in the Alamo were his kind of people. They were a mixed batch of backwoodsmen, tradesmen, farmers, young, old, and fugitives, and some came from Missouri, Arkansas, Alabama, Kentucky, Tennessee, New York, Connecticut, and even Great Britain. The majority were white, but some were Tejanos who were fighting against tyranny, not skin color. Like those at Trenton, Valley Forge, and New Orleans, this hodgepodge of humanity was fighting for the rights of all men. Tired from lack of sleep and insufficient rations, many in the fort suffered from dysentery from the poor water sources, but something kept them there regardless.

* * * * *

---

[496] Lord, *Stand*, 54; Levy, 251; Davis, W, *Three Roads*, 417.

Davey spotted Santa Anna riding defiantly in the open and decided to take a shot. The dictator's arrogance was his weakness. Pulling the trigger, the usual dead shot Crockett was too high. Flustered, the "Napoleon of the West" ran for cover, never realizing how close he came to death. Davey never knew how close he came to preventing many future deaths, but it was not meant to be, and the events unfolding were destined to play out. This stand had a much deeper significance.

Sending off another message, Travis pleaded again for reinforcements and ended with "God and Texas!" and "Victory or Death." He also sent a note to his son, Charles—if he should die, he had died for his country and he should be proud of his father.[497]

Travis and Crockett had come to terms with their purpose. Saved or destroyed, it was in God's hands now.

* * * * *

The Alamo, Sundown, March 5, 1836

Jim Bowie felt terrible. Racked by fever, chills, and a hacking cough from either typhoid or tuberculosis, he lay on a cot in a room near the main gate, delirious. In and out of consciousness, he had heard the earlier barrages and skirmishes and badly wanted in on the fight but couldn't even stand up. After everything, it seemed he would miss the biggest fight of all.

After his ninety men routed four hundred Mexicans at the town of Concepcion in October of the previous year, he had nothing more to prove to himself or others. They killed fifty of the enemy and only lost two men, and it seemed to revive the Texan fighting spirit. They believed they could best superior numbers with superior fighters because their marksmanship and courage were the best in the world.

Jim had successfully led the revolution, only to be stranded on his back, sick. This forced him to hand his command over to Travis, and although this young firebrand's ego was greater than his expe-

---

[497] Donovan, 249–250; Levy, 274–275; Lord, *Stand*, 143.

rience, he could be trusted. But, hell, who didn't have a huge ego at that age? Jim remembered his own early days and all the mistakes he had made. Travis was brave and a true patriot, but it still annoyed him that he wouldn't be in the fight. To a man like Bowie, this was unbearable, and beaten by an illness was humiliating to him. He couldn't accept it but had little choice in the matter. His mind wanted to fight, but his body refused.

At first, drinking kept him functional, but then Travis accused him of being a drunk, and maybe he was one. After all, the inner pain was something he couldn't overcome, and alcohol seemed to numb him to the emotional and physical pain, though it never left him. He still missed Ursula and the promise of what might have been.

For the last few days, the Alamo had been bombarded with artillery relentlessly, and the Mexican snipers kept the men guarding the walls awake. Exhausted, the defenders finally realized that Fannin or Houston weren't coming, and a somber humility occupied the fort.

Travis called a meeting in the courtyard later that night, and as the sun set, the sky turned from blue to grey; the men sensed the desperation. Bowie, on his cot, was carried into the courtyard. Sick or not, this concerned him as well. The Mexican cannons had grown silent, and Travis's voice was crystal clear. "I have deceived you by the promise of help," he said with regret. Standing at the center of the gathering, he told them what they already knew. They were on their own, and the reality of this floated on the air for a moment. His despair quickly changed to certainty. "Our fate is sealed. Within a very few days...perhaps a very few hours...we must all be in eternity. This is our destiny and we cannot avoid it. This is our certain doom."

He told the truth, because they deserved nothing less, and now they all had to decide. "All that remains is to die in the fort and fight to the last moment... We must sell our lives as dearly as possible." Making eye contact with every man, he checked for understanding, and it was there.

Assuring them he personally would stay and make a final stand, he told them it was up to each to decide their own fate. If they could hold out just long enough, they might give Texas time to form its army.

Stepping back with defiance on his face, Travis drew his sword and scratched a line on the ground. This line in the sand was deep enough for those in the back to see.

"I now want every man who is determined to stay here and die with me to come across this line." Pausing, he inhaled, held it just a second, then asked, "Who will be the first?"

Tapley Holland was the first to step forward. He was only twenty-five, but his courage inspired the others. He had a whole life ahead of him but was willing to sacrifice it for an idea. It wasn't about what they had to lose if they stayed but what losing the idea would mean if they did not.

Davey Crockett stepped forward and others followed. Within seconds, only Bowie on his cot and another man remained on the other side of the line.

Jim tried to pull himself up but couldn't manage the strength he found inside. "Boys, I am not able to go to you, but I wish some of you would be so kind as to remove my cot over there." They all smiled, and his cot was carried across the line by his brothers-in-arms. This single act of courage caused them to let out a hearty cheer.

The last man, Louis Moses Rose, never stepped over the line, and Bowie asked him, "You seem not to be willing to die with us, Rose."

"No, I am not prepared to die, and I shall not do so if I can avoid it," Rose replied.

Crockett added, "You may as well die with us, old fellow, for you cannot escape."[498]

Rose decided to make a try, climbed over the wall, and made it through the lines. Until the day of his death, he told the story of Travis's line in the sand. Some refuse to accept this eyewitness account, but Rose's confession of being the lone man who wouldn't cross the line seems out of character for a liar. Why didn't he embellish the story to make himself appear more important or heroic? Why tell a lie that gives you a reputation of a coward? Though many in

---

[498] Donovan, 357–358; Tinkle, 117–120; Bowie, 272, 276; Lord, *Stand*, 146–147.

modernity will argue his good sense, in nineteenth-century America, it would be perceived as cowardice.

Most tall tales elevate the storyteller, but Rose's story tells of a man afraid to die and chose to run. Why would he ever admit being a coward, only to make heroes of those who stayed behind unless he was honest? He branded himself in history as the man who refused to cross the line and never recanted.[499]

Rose was the only man who chose to leave, and those who stayed behind steeled themselves for the battle to come. The time for inner reflection was at an end, and it was time to make Santa Anna pay dearly if he wanted the Alamo.

Crockett handed Bowie two loaded pistols. He just had to fight, somehow, and anything less was unacceptable. If he could stay conscious, he would make his stand.[500]

William Barret Travis, James Bowie, and Davey Crockett were ready. It seemed as if their entire lives were preparation for this very moment. After years of bouncing around, searching for their places in the world, there would be no more running away for these three men and over a hundred Texans inside the Alamo. It was time to make their mark.

* * * * *

Santa Anna's Headquarters, San Antonio, Dawn, March 6, 1836

Santa Anna had enjoyed his time in San Antonio waiting for the rest of the army to show up. On February 23, part of his army entered San Antonio and observed the situation. For thirteen days, he waited for the right time to strike.

After a small skirmish between the Texans and some of his men, he looked elsewhere for excitement. Hearing of a Mexican woman with an attractive daughter who lost a husband in the action, he

---

[499] Donovan, (*See Afterword*, 331–374); Bowie, 276.
[500] Tinkle, 130.

decided to help. Though he expected more from the girl than her gratefulness as payment, her mother said no man but her husband could receive this kind of thanks. Santa Anna wanted the girl, so he devised a way to get her.

Having an officer dress in a priest's clothing to impersonate one, Santa Anna pleaded for the daughter's hand. The mother agreed to let her daughter marry the president of Mexico, and the fake priest performed the mock wedding. The dictator claimed his new bride, and on their wedding night, the couple consecrated their nuptials. Even as a womanizer, Santa Anna was willing to lie and hurt others to get what he wanted. Already married, he couldn't marry the young girl anyway. Bigamy was illegal, so he had to fake the marriage to add the pretty girl to his conquests. It was good to be a dictator, he reasoned.

Santa Anna's brother-in-law, General Cos, who lost the Battle of Bexar, still felt the sting of the defeat. It bothered Santa Anna more than Cos, and he took the insult personally. He couldn't accept that these "lawless foreigners" whipped his professional soldiers, and he would right this wrong.

He called off his artillery on the afternoon of March 5 to give the Texans a false moment of peace. The exhausted garrison would be given a chance to relax and lower its guard before he crushed them.

Planning to assault the fort before sunrise, he served his troops rations of liquor to give them courage. He reiterated that no quarter was the order of the day—not a suggestion.

Sometime after 5:00 a.m. on Sunday, March 6, Santa Anna's soldiers formed outside the Alamo. Shouting, "Viva Santa Anna!" and "Viva la republica!" the element of surprise was lost as fifteen-hundred Mexicans charged the fort defended by one-hundred and fifty Texans. It was ten to one odds for the Texans who chose to cross the line.

* * * * *

Inside the Alamo, Dawn, March 6, 1836

Travis heard the *deguello* music playing in the distance for some time. *Deguello*, or slit throat, meant no quarter, and Santa Anna borrowed this tradition from the Spanish who borrowed it from the Moors, the Muslims who invaded Spain in 711. He then heard the Mexicans shout something as his men fired from the walls, and he knew the Alamo was under attack.

Carrying a shotgun in one hand and his sword in the other, Travis ran to the north wall to see for himself. From the top of the north wall, he saw the flames from eight hundred Mexican muskets in the dark of the morning and knew this was his moment.

"Come on, boys, the Mexicans are upon us, and we'll *give them hell!*" he shouted. Running to the front of the wall and firing the shotgun, Travis showed them all he was no young dandy and was born for this moment of glory, just like *Ivanhoe* and William Wallace as he stared into the jaws of death.

Santa Anna's troops returned fire, and Travis toppled onto a nearby cannon; he had been hit. Joe, his slave, wasn't sure how bad he was hurt until he got a closer look.

The slug had hit Travis directly in the forehead, killing him instantly. In his hands, he still clutched the shotgun. Just like the heroes he idolized as a boy, his name would be memorialized. "Victory or Death" were the words he lived and died by.

Believing that some things were worth dying for, Travis had made his final stand.[501]

* * * * *

Though the Texans made Santa Anna's men pay dearly for the Alamo, the sheer numbers were against them. Once the Mexicans compromised one wall, they overran the fort and broke into the hospital in the chapel, shooting and bayoneting the sick and wounded Texans.

Jim Bowie sat up in his cot and fired Crockett's two pistols at the approaching enemy. Pouring into the room, Santa Anna's soldiers bayoneted him multiple times and shot him twice in the head.[502]

---

[501] Lord, *Stand*, 155–156; Davis, W, *Three Roads*, 560; Tinkle, 129,136.
[502] Tinkle, 140, 146; Lord, *Stand*, 165; Donovan, 288–291.

He died as he had lived—like a man.

Though he didn't die standing the way he would have preferred, this last moment was all classic Bowie. He managed to die fighting, regardless of his condition. His whole life had been a life of fighting. Now he was with his beloved Ursula and was no longer restless or searching for his place in the world.

* * * * *

The Alamo defenders put up one hell of a fight, but with ten to one odds, they faced the impossible. Some defenders tried to fight outside the fort but were quickly killed by Santa Anna's cavalry.

One Texan, Almeron Dickinson, located his wife, Susanna, and told her, "If they spare you, save my child," referring to his young daughter, Angelina. One last hug, and he ran out, and Susanna never saw him alive again.

Gregorio Esparza died in that final fight outside the chapel where Almeron Dickinson fell. Mrs. Esparza and her children witnessed his death and wept near his body until she was forced to leave. Gregorio's brother was a soldier for Santa Anna, so out of respect for one of his men, the dictator had the brother buried, though Gregorio chose to die a Texan. Galba Fuqua, who was only sixteen, was one of the defenders who fell near Dickinson, and Tejano died alongside white. In death, they were now immortal brothers.[503]

The last survivors of the Alamo attempted to use the chapel to make a last stand but were killed within its walls. Crockett and his Tennesseans fought hand-to-hand until the very end. Muskets were used for clubs, knives, hands, teeth—anything they could use as a weapon, they used. It was brutal, and they refused to give up until sheer numbers overwhelmed them.

Davey Crockett's body was found with his men, and several dead Mexicans lay nearby. His chest was covered with blood from the mortal wound.[504] Did he die with a big crocodile smile on his face?

---

[503] Lord, *Stand*, 160–162; Tinkle, 286.
[504] Donovan, 290–292; Tinkle, 138–139; Lord, *Stand*, 161–162.

There's no report of this, but as he told his wife and children, "Do not be uneasy about me, for I am with my friends."

He ran away from failure his entire life but chose to run no more. Davey had died with his friends, and this was where he wanted to be.

The women, children, and slaves were spared inside the Alamo, and they were the eyewitnesses of its defenders' last moments. Susanna Dickinson and her daughter gave accounts and never changed their story. Joe, Travis's slave, was another reliable witness.

Mexican General Castrillon tried to take prisoners and asked Santa Anna for mercy, but the dictator reprimanded him and ordered the execution of all those captured. The few survivors were bayoneted to death, and that was the extent of his mercy. One Alamo survivor by the name of Warnell tried to hide among the dead but was found and summarily shot.

Then, Santa Anna ordered the Alamo dead burned in a massive funeral pyre to desecrate their remains. No mercy, even after death.[505]

The men who died at the Alamo did buy some time for the Texas army. Four days before its fall on March 2, Texas declared independence from Mexico.

* * * * *

Word of the Alamo's fall reached Texas, prompting many to join the army. The loss of Travis, Bowie, and Crockett sent shock waves throughout Texas and the US.

Colonel James Fannin at Goliad was the next to face Santa Anna's wrath. General Urrea defeated the Goliad garrison on March 19, and Fannin asked for terms of surrender. Urrea said he would try to protect his men from execution and disagreed with Santa Anna's brutal treatment of surrendering prisoners, but he was powerless.

Colonel Fannin surrendered as his men were packed like sardines into a church to await their fate. On March 26, a dispatch from Santa Anna said "foreigners" captured were to be executed with

---

[505] Lord, *Stand*, 174–175; Donovan, 293–294.

no exceptions. Colonel Jose De La Portilla received the order, and though he and Urrea were disgusted by the atrocity, they had to follow orders or face execution themselves.

On March 27, Palm Sunday, Fannin's men were marched down four separate roads and shot. The fifty wounded and sick in the church were murdered in their beds. Many were stacked on top of each other and shot two at a time. Colonel Fannin was permitted to sit in a chair before he was shot in the face. Nearly four hundred Texans were slaughtered at Goliad, and once again, their bodies were burned in a mass funeral pyre.[506]

Santa Anna's brutality shocked the world and only caused more support for Texas. What kind of animal would murder prisoners or the wounded and sick? Americans everywhere sympathized with their ex-countrymen and money, materiel, and men poured into the Texas cause.

* * * * *

Battle of San Jacinto, Texas, April 21, 1836

Sam Houston trotted toward the Mexican camp, reflecting on the past few years. The path which led him to the plain of San Jacinto, leading the Army of Texas into battle, was one of struggle. He had reached the bottom, and it looked like he would never rise again after he left Tennessee.

Retreating to his adoptive family, the Cherokee, he tried to escape from the world where he didn't belong. Living among the Indians, he was welcomed once again as an official member of the tribe. Dressing in deerskins and feather headdresses, he grew a goatee and took a Cherokee wife. He also remained intoxicated the entire time and kept nine barrels of liquor in his cabin for personal use.

The Osages called him "Big Drunk," and he described his own alcoholic despair in third person. "He buried his sorrows in the flowing bowl" and "gave himself up to the fatal enchantress..."

---

[506] Donovan, 315–317.

The Cherokee loved their white brother when he was sober, but Chief Jolly said to him with the tough love of a father, "A man who is drunk is only half a man."

Once, in a drunken rage, Sam struck Chief Jolly and was beaten unconscious by the others. Inebriated, unconscious, and assaulting the man who treated him as his son, Sam had hit bottom and realized he must go back. He knew he could stay drunk, hidden away from the world and wrapped in self-pity, or he could pick himself up and try again. He left the Cherokee, determined to find his place in the world.[507]

Returning to civilization, he first had to find a way to make a living. On a business venture in Washington DC, he made a rash decision which would change his life forever.

A rival congressman called him a crook, and he lost his temper, severely beating the man in the street. Congress, in an unprecedented move, called Houston to answer for his actions, but holding a trial for an American citizen who hadn't committed a federal crime was unconstitutional. Sam defended himself with such an impressive showing, he was acquitted of all the charges and only reprimanded. President Jackson and the rest of the city applauded his speech, and he became the old Sam Houston again, but this time, he was wiser. All his anger and disappointment left him with the trial, and Jackson offered the reborn maverick a job, but he declined. His destiny was somewhere else, he told him. Settling for security and predictability had only led him to failure. His path had to follow the will of providence and lead him to his destiny.[508]

It led him straight to Texas.

Three years later, he was leading the Army of Texas into battle. He learned of the Alamo's fall soon after he returned from Indian Territory. This trip, he was hashing out a treaty with the Cherokees to ensure Texas wouldn't have to worry about them while they were fighting Santa Anna. He tried to convince Bowie to leave the fort,

---

[507] Wisehart, 62–63; James, *Raven*, 132–133.
[508] James, *Raven*, 136–138.

but his stubborn courage wouldn't consider it. Sam now promised these men that their sacrifice wouldn't be in vain.

After the provisional Texas government made its declaration of independence on March 2 (Sam's forty-third birthday), he began organizing and drilling the Army of Texas. He was appointed commander-in-chief of the ragtag group of frontiersmen, shopkeepers, and farmers. He'd come a long way since his humiliation and resignation as governor of Tennessee and felt like a new man. That's what Texas was to him—a place for a new beginning.

Retreating for over a month, he finally felt they were ready to fight. Disciplined and strengthened with more recruits, he now had Santa Anna where he wanted him. Like Washington at Yorktown fifty-five years before, Houston faced a similar opportunity. The enemy were trapped with its back to a river.

On April 19, the anniversary of Lexington and Concord, Houston addressed the people of Texas. "We view ourselves on the eve of battle. We are nerved for the contest, and must conquer or perish. It is in vain to look for present aid: none is at hand. We must now act or abandon all hope! Rally to the standard, and be no longer the scoff of mercenary tongues." Appealing to them in a way most of them understood, he continued, "Be men…be freemen…that your children may bless their fathers' names!"[509]

He promised if these men would fight for something greater than themselves, the world would soon hear of them. This he understood from his own life and knew the pivotal moment in this struggle was now, "I leave the result in the hands of an all wise God, and I rely confidently upon His Providence. My country will do justice to those who serve her. The right for which we fight will be secured, and Texas shall be free."[510]

---

[509] Houston, Sam. *Writings of Sam Houston, Vol. 2, ed. Amelia W. Williams and Eugene C. Barker*. (Austin: University of Texas Press, 1939), 24 (To the People of Texas, April 19, 1836).

[510] Houston, *Life*, 114 (To Colonel Rus in the Field, April 19, 1836).

His steady confidence had returned, and he was no longer a broken vessel. As men followed him into battle, he would "trust in God and fear not."[511]

Sam Houston 1850s

On April 21, 1836, Sam Houston and the Army of Texas fought an eighteen-minute battle which destroyed Santa Anna's army. Many Mexican soldiers seeing the thirst for vengeance in the Texans' eyes tried to surrender. They threw up their hands and cried, "Me no Alamo!" and "Me no Goliad!" but many received the same "no quarter" their fellow Texans did. Many of Houston's officers restored order and ordered their men to give surrendering Mexicans quarter.

Sam had two horses shot out from under him and was wounded by a musket ball in his leg. Bleeding heavily, he chose to stay in the fight. When it was all over, the Texans had lost two killed and twenty-three wounded. Santa Anna lost 630 killed, and 730 of his men were now prisoners.[512]

Like Andrew Jackson's victory at New Orleans, this was a miraculous and total victory. One problem remained at the end of the Battle of San Jacinto. The "Napoleon of the West" was missing. He

---

[511] James, *Raven*, 203.
[512] Houston, *Life*, 128–130.

was last observed running away, and Houston ordered him captured alive. It was imperative he talk to the dictator, so he needed to be kept alive.

The next day, a Texan sergeant out deer hunting discovered a Mexican soldier in a thicket. The man swore he was a private in Santa Anna's army. With tears in his eyes, he finally admitted he was an aide to the dictator, and the Texan marched his prize catch into camp. Passing the other Mexican prisoners, the sergeant noticed them coming to attention and saluting the aide. "El Presidente!" they shouted and his captor was dumbstruck. His catch was more than an aide to the tyrant. He had bagged Santa Anna himself.

He was rushed to Houston's headquarters. Sam was drowsy from the effects of opium he needed for his shattered leg, and he stared up at the dictator as he sat under the shade of a tree. Santa Anna admitted his identity and said Houston was no ordinary man for conquering the "Napoleon of the West," but he was obligated to treat him as a prisoner.

Sam said, "You should have remembered that at the Alamo."

"You must be aware that I was justified in my course by the usages of war," Santa Anna declared. "I had summoned a surrender, and they refused…the usages of war justified the slaughter of the vanquished."

Sam explained to the pompous man that civilized nations didn't fight wars this way. The dictator excused his actions. He said he was only following the orders of his government. Houston couldn't believe what he was hearing and shot back, "Why, *you* are the Government of Mexico!"

"I have orders in my possession commanding me to act!" Santa Anna replied.

"A dictator, sir, has no superior," Sam countered.

The tyrant came back quickly with another excuse. "I have orders, General Houston, from my government, commanding me to exterminate every man found in arms in the province of Texas and treat all as such as pirates." He blamed his government for his murderous actions.

Houston made clear that Texas had been independent for over a month and went on to school the dictator:

> *But if you feel excused for your conduct in San Antonio, you have not the same excuse for the massacre of Colonel Fannin's command. They had capitulated on terms proffered by your general. And yet after capitulation, they were all perfidiously massacred, without the privilege of even dying with arms in their hands.*[513]

Sam was angry but controlled. Santa Anna said he knew nothing about the Goliad affair and General Urrea was the real perpetrator. He said he would execute Urrea for this heinous act.

Houston was a bit nervous because his men wanted the man's head. Calling for a hanging, he ordered the men to disperse. Santa Anna was visibly scared. Sam knew if anyone deserved execution, it was this animal in front of him, but he realized he had leverage to achieve the greater good. Revenge, though justified, wouldn't do anything for Texas.

He convinced Santa Anna to sign a treaty of surrender, ending the war. Then he had him order all Mexican troops out of Texas immediately.

The Treaty of Velasco in May 1836 recognized the Rio Grande as the southern Texas border. Santa Anna remained a prisoner until Mexico honored the terms of the treaty. By taking the high road, Sam used the leverage for Texas.[514] He also proved he would never be like Santa Anna.

*　*　*　*　*

Mexico refused to recognize Santa Anna's authority to sign the treaty but would elect him president again. Two more times, he

---

[513] Wisehart, 247–249; Houston, *Life*, 144–147.
[514] Wisehart, 267–268.

would send armies back to San Antonio, but was repelled both times. In 1845, after losing another battle, he was exiled to Cuba.[515]

Mexico and the US were on the verge of war after Texas became the twenty-eighth state in 1845 and Mexico refused to recognize it. Britain showed interest in Texas, and their designs on California didn't help the situation. California was still part of Mexico, but the British threatened to violate the Monroe Doctrine, and the United States would oppose them with force, if necessary. Mexico itself benefited from this doctrine when it separated from Spain. America supported their Revolution, but since the Texas Revolution, relations had chilled.

British aims to colonize the southwest and California were a threat to American interests, these sparsely populated unchartered lands, where violent Indian tribes roamed and bandits had no respect for life or property. Mexico didn't have the money or stability to govern these northern territories, and anarchy still reigned. This lawlessness clashed with the trade routes between the US and Texas.

During this period, twenty-two Americans were executed without trial, and Americans in California and New Mexico were mistreated, arrested, and handled with no regard to individual rights by Mexico.

President James Knox Polk, a protégé of Andrew Jackson, offered to buy California from Mexico, but was turned down. In Cuba, Santa Anna promised to negotiate peace with the United States if they helped him return, and Polk naively saw his offer as an opportunity to avoid a war. Mexico owed two million dollars to the United States for outrages against American citizens. They were still delinquent, so Polk offered a solution to pay their debt and make extra on the deal, but they refused.

In December 1845, Mexico refused to accept the United States minister John Slidell. He was authorized to offer up to $40 million for the territory. Mexico saw this as a grasp for power and refused to be pushed around by America. If they sold their territory, they would relinquish their right to it.

---

[515] Donovan, 339.

In January 1846, President Polk sent General Zachary Taylor and his force of 3,500 American troops to Corpus Christi, Texas. In March, they moved to the Rio Grande to defend the border from seven thousand Mexican forces across the river in Matamoros. This force had moved there when Texas was annexed, and Mexico wouldn't accept the Rio Grande as the Texas southern border. They claimed the official border was farther north on the Nueces River and accused the United States of invading Mexico. Those who claim the US stole Texas from Mexico conveniently forget the Battle of San Jacinto and the Treaty of Velasco that Santa Anna, the leader of Mexico, signed.

On April 9, 1846, Colonel Truman Cross failed to return from his scouting mission. General Pedro de Ampudia just arrived in Matamoros to command the Mexican troops and was excited about the war with America. Ampudia was from the same stock as Santa Anna, and he once fried a victim's head in oil to maintain its freshness as he put it on public display. He sent Taylor an ultimatum, demanding his withdrawal to the Nueces in twenty-four hours or risk war.

Taylor was not one scared of puffed-up threats. He had fought in the War of 1812 and successfully defended a fort with a tiny force against a superior Indian attack. He fought the Seminole and the Blackhawk War and was a tough experienced warrior who never cowered from a challenge. His orders were to defend the Texas border, and he planned to follow them.

Still concerned about Cross, he sent a patrol in search of him. This patrol was ambushed by Mexicans, and Lieutenant David Porter was killed and Truman Cross's body was discovered soon after.

On April 23, 1846, Mexican cavalry crossed the Rio Grande. Taylor ordered Captain Seth Thornton and sixty-three horsemen to find out their intentions. Once again, this force under Thornton was ambushed and eleven men killed, five wounded, and the rest were taken prisoner.

Taylor interpreted these actions as war and prepared to retaliate. He sent President Polk the news. Polk received the message weeks later and asked Congress for a declaration of war. On May 11, 1846, Congress voted for war with Mexico. Divided along party lines,

Democrats voted for it, and Whigs (a new political party) opposed it. A newly elected congressman from Illinois made a fiery speech in opposition and claimed Polk caused the war by moving troops to the border. Years later, he would regret this speech and lost elections over this stand. It was one of the many lessons Abraham Lincoln would learn before he found his own purpose.[516]

Three days before the vote to declare war, Taylor fought the first battle of the Mexican-American War. For two years, the two countries fought a one-sided war, and the Mexican military was no match for the new American army. Modern cannons and a whole slew of talented young officers were responsible for this lopsided victory. Many future warriors cut their teeth in this war: Robert E. Lee, Ulysses S. Grant, Thomas J. "Stonewall" Jackson, George Meade, and Albert Sidney Johnston, to name a few. Every single major battle ended in an American victory.

When Polk accepted Santa Anna's promise of peace and helped him return to Mexico, he regretted it and should have remembered what Santa Anna had done to Texas. Polk thought he could end the war but inadvertently made Santa Anna general of the Mexican army, thus creating a more formidable foe.

Regardless of the president's misstep, General Winfield Scott and the American army occupied Mexico City in 1847, ending hostilities.

On February 2, 1848, Mexico signed the Treaty of Guadalupe-Hidalgo, officially bringing the war to a close. The treaty stipulated the Rio Grande as the southern border of Texas. California, New Mexico, Colorado, Nevada, and Arizona were to be ceded to the United States for $15 million dollars and remission of two million in Mexican debt. Ratified by both countries, the treaty ended this twelve-year-long ordeal with Mexico. The United States lost 13,780 killed, and tens of thousands more died from disease. Thousands were wounded and maimed, and it cost nearly $100 million, the equivalent of billions today.

---

[516] Bill, Alfred Hoyt. *Rehearsal for Conflict: The Story of our War with Mexico.* (New York: Alfred A. Knopf, 1947), 90–92.

The southwest, California and Texas were paid for with the blood of soldiers and the hard-earned tax dollars of the American worker. Some claim a stronger country preyed upon a weaker one, but evidence shows both sides own some of the blame. Do the victors in a war always get the blame? And do the defeated always claim victim status, regardless of actions?[517]

The struggle in Texas is remembered today in books, movies, and reenactments and strikes a nerve in many American hearts. The Alamo's defenders are the quintessential example of laying one's life down for another. Some regard this sacrifice as a waste of lives, but like a soldier jumping on a grenade, the Alamo represents the ultimate sacrifice to Texans and Americans still today.

Andrew Jackson died in June of 1845, but not before he saw Texas join the Union. The frontier that he ensured with the Battle of New Orleans now stretched to the Pacific, and the fighting spirit he inspired in Americans now became their creed.

Sam Houston went on to become the first president of the Republic of Texas, then US Senator, and finally Governor of Texas. He remarried in 1840 and conceived eight children after he was fifty years old. His wife, Margaret, eventually helped him overcome his drinking, and he finally found his place in the world.

The Raven could rest his wings, but his flight wasn't quite over yet. His last act would be a courageous attempt to save the nation he loved.

* * * * *

The Alamo, February 25, 1837

Less than a year after the Alamo's fall, Texas cavalry officer, Juan Seguin, ordered a coffin built, and the ashes of the dead defenders

---

[517] Van Deusen, Glyndon G. *The Jacksonian Era 1828–1848*. (New York: Harper & Brothers, 1959), 239; McCormac, Eugene Irving. *James K. Polk: A Political Biography, Vol. 2: To the End of a Career, 1845-1849*. (Newtown: American Political Biography Press, 1922, 2000), 537; Hoyt, *Rehearsal*, 318, 324.

were laid inside. A full military funeral was held in honor of the garrison's heroes.

Seguin had survived but often wondered why. By fate, he was chosen by Travis to deliver a message, and he continued to fight with Houston at San Jacinto. Maybe this was the reason he was spared and the Alamo's defenders had not died in vain. He would go on to be a Texas senator and a mayor, and his contributions to independence and defense of liberty are cherished by Texans today.

At the funeral eulogy, he reminded the crowd, "There are your brothers Travis, Bowie, and Crockett and others whose valor places them in the rank of my heroes." Carved into the lid of the coffin were the names William Barret Travis, James Bowie, and David Crockett.[518]

They would always be remembered for their selfless sacrifice and would come to define the heroic and self-reliant American. They were among the first of these rugged individuals who tamed the west. No matter what mistakes they made, their moments at the Alamo, seemed to wash them away. Though they never seemed to find their own place in the world, each followed a path that led them to their final purpose.

It seemed they belonged there at the doomed mission, forever drifting on a warm breeze and making their final stand. They had made their mark and could rest assured their restless spirits finally found a place to call home.

---

[518] Donovan, 345; Davis, W, *Three Roads*, 570–571.

6

Six Shades of Blue and Gray

Prologue

Virginia, April 19, 1861

How could he decide such a life-defining decision? How does one choose between his country and his home? His family and friends were his home. Pacing back and forth in his upstairs bedroom, he agonized over the choice. Kneeling, he asked God for guidance. If he chose the Union, he would be promoted to General of the Army of the United States. If he turned it down and chose his home, Virginia, his military career would likely be over, and he would see the destruction of his country. It was on this very day, eighty-five years ago, when his countrymen fired the first shots at Lexington and Concord.

Some would find this choice an easy one. Promotion, more money, and status or failure, poverty, and obscurity were usually an easy choice. For Robert E. Lee, it was the hardest decision of his life. He knew that to rely on his own understanding would be wrong, and he asked God to guide him. Throughout his life, God had directed him and had never let him down. He knew that he would, once again, and would search for the answer in prayer. He'd trust that God's will would move him toward the right one.

Robert E. Lee was fifty-three, handsome, and many believed more so now than when he was younger. At five foot eleven and one hundred and seventy pounds, he was an impressive figure, but his size wasn't what impressed people. His presence and the way he carried himself was almost majestic, not in a snobbish way, but confident.

He had mahogany brown hair peppered with gray, and a mustache accented his dignified face. His coffee-colored brown eyes that were almost black reflected both calm and the storm that resided within. When others saw him, they saw integrity and stability.

Virginia was his home. Her Blue Ridge Mountains, endless rivers, and the Chesapeake Bay was in his blood. This lush green landscape was where he had played as a boy, and it was America to him. Its founder, Captain John Smith, Washington, Jefferson, Madison, Monroe, Patrick Henry, George Mason, Edmund Randolph—they were all Virginians, and he was proud to be one.

His home, Arlington, looked across the Potomac and saw the half-constructed Capitol dome in the city named after his idol, George Washington, the most revered Virginian.

Washington was his role model, and his father, Henry Lee, was one of General Washington's most trusted cavalry officers and a trusted friend. Called "Light Horse Harry" for his command of horses, he uttered the famous phrase, "First in war, first in peace, first in the hearts of his countrymen" at Washington's funeral in 1799.

Robert also had an intimate connection to Washington when he married Mary Anne Randolph Custis, the daughter of George Washington Parke Custis, George Washington's step grandson and keeper of his memory.

Washington was always a presence and reminder to Robert. His was the standard to live by, and he saw many similarities between himself and the general. Both had lost their fathers young and were excellent with horses.

He now faced the same fateful decision Washington faced in 1775—choose your mother country over your home. Robert faced staying with the United States, which his idol helped form, or going with Virginia, which Washington called home. He could see the same crisis forming. It was either submit to the will of the federal government or break away and form another. The decision was the same.

What if Washington would have lost? What if he would have been tried for treason and hanged? He was Robert E. Lee, not George Washington and couldn't expect to fill those shoes. To Robert, it wasn't about being Washington but following his example. Washington had set the standard. He had trusted in God's providence to guide him through it all. Now he must do the same.

The next day, Robert Edward Lee sat at his desk and wrote without pause. He had made the decision and God revealed the answer through his prayer.

Where it led now, he would rely on God's providence as guidance to his purpose.[519]

* * * * *

Chancellorsville, Virginia, May 2, 1863

Colonel A. L. Long of General Lee's staff shivered from the chill of the spring night. It was still a few hours till daylight and the coming battle.

Long noticed General Jackson shaking by the campfire. Good old "Stonewall" looked like he needed a cup of coffee to warm his insides. Known as "Stonewall" to the world, he was simply "Old Jack" to his men.

Long handed the general a steaming cup, and Jackson responded with gratitude through his body language. The clang of metal sounded nearby, and the surge of adrenaline sharpened their senses. A sword leaning against a tree had tumbled to the ground, and Long said it was a bad omen. This had been a common belief of knights in the past, and it just so happened to be General Jackson's sword. Long retrieved it and handed it to his bearded commander who returned

---

[519] Freeman, Douglas Southall. *Lee: An Abridgement in one volume by Richard Harwell, of the four-volume Robert E. Lee.* (New York: Collier Book MacMillan Publishing Co., 1961, 1991), 111; Davis, Burke. *Gray Fox: Robert E. Lee and the Civil War.* (New York: Wings Books/Random House, 1956), 15.

it to his waist without a word. He had to talk to General Lee immediately about his plan.

Sitting on cracker boxes near the fire, Lee and Jackson were
deep in animated conversation by 3:30 a.m. Jackson explained that
his men found a path to sneak around General Hooker and the entire
Union right flank. Hooker's army was 70,000 strong and ready to
crush Lee's army and end the rebellion once and for all.

Looking across the campfire, Lee asked, "General Jackson, what
do you propose to do?"

Pointing at the map between them, Jackson said, "Go around
here."

"What do you propose to make this movement with?" Lee
asked.

"With my whole corps," he answered.

Lee was shocked by his words. He wanted to take 28,000 on a
long march around Hooker's army and leave him with a mere 14,000
to defend Richmond. It was the first rule of war—never divide your
troops—but Lee knew bold action often defied the rules in combat.

"What will you leave me?" Lee asked.

"The divisions of Anderson and McLaws."

Astounded by his audacity, Lee furrowed his brow. Over
100,000 bluecoats were Jackson's intended target. Two to one odds,
and he wasn't even sure what exactly his lieutenant planned to do.

Lee twirled his pencil and stared into the fire, thinking of the
risk. Jackson was a risk-taker, but his aggressiveness and the ability
to think fast made him dangerous, and if anyone could pull it off, it
was him.

Lee looked at him again. The tall strange man with piercing
blue eyes peered back with a divine confidence many of his generals
lacked, waiting for permission. He might be a little unorthodox, but
he was a fighter, and that is what won battles.

"Well...go on," Lee finally said.[520]

---

[520] Jackson, Mary Anna. *Life and Letters of General Thomas J. Jackson (Stonewall Jackson).* (New York: Harper & Bros, 1892), 434–435; Robertson, James I. Stonewall *Jackson: The Man, The Soldier, The Legend.* (New York: MacMillan

Jackson mounted and rode off into the night. He had an army to move. Around 5:00 a.m. he marched his 28,000 men on a twelve-mile route around Hooker's right. Keeping this plan secret, Jackson refused to even tell his officers their objective. It appeared, at first, they were retreating away from the frontlines, and Hooker's scouts reported this. The Union commander boasted of victory the next day. If Lee ordered his best general back, then he was not prepared to fight.

At 3:00 p.m., Jackson wrote Lee of his progress. "General, the enemy had made a stand at Chancellor's which is about 2 miles from Chancellorsville. I hope as soon as practicable to attack. I trust that an Ever Kind Providence will bless us with success. Respectfully, TJ Jackson, Lt. Genl."[521]

After reporting his location, Jackson continued the march, and by five that afternoon, he attacked Hooker's right flank. It was the greatest flanking attack of the war, and Jackson just seemed to get better with each battle. His judgment and daring had peaked, and his genius as a military tactician was because of his eccentricities. With him at the front, the South couldn't lose, it seemed.

Around 9:00 p.m., the battle continued in a pitch-black wilderness. This forested area was aptly named the Wilderness. Battle lines weren't obvious, confused skirmishes erupted, and troops fired on each other in the melee.

Galloping in the darkness, "Old Jack" saw General A. P. Hill and stopped to ask him how soon he would be ready to attack. These two men never liked one another since they met. Jackson even had Hill arrested and charged for disobeying orders and insubordination. Hill attempted vindication by going to trial, but Jackson never followed up for unknown reasons. It might have been he changed his mind after Hill's performance at Antietam or Lee's smoothing of

Publishing, USA/Simon &Schuster, 1997), 713–714; Davis, Burke. *They Called Him Stonewall: A Life of Lt. General T. J. Jackson, C.S.A.* (New York: Fairfax Press/Crown Publishing, 1954,1988), 409–411; Lee, Robert E. Jr. *Recollections and Letters of General Robert E. Lee.* (New York: Doubleday Page & Co. 1909), 258.

[521] Jackson, 436; Robertson, 720; Davis, Burke, *Stonewall*, 417.

wounded egos and reinstating Hill for his bravery. Jackson concurred with Lee's actions, and the squabble was resolved, it appeared. Both respected courage.

After conferring with Hill, Jackson rode ahead. Someone fired in their direction, making Jackson and his staff's horses skittish. A North Carolina regiment kept firing at every sound in the belief that Union cavalry was near.

Jackson reared back in the saddle, and his horse ran forward, smacking his face into a tree branch, nearly unseating him.

Two of his staff snatched the reins and got the animal under control. The general appeared to be in pain, and upon asking him if he was hit, he responded by gritting his teeth and saying, "I fear my arm is broken."

"Where are you struck?" an officer asked.

"About halfway between the elbow and the shoulder," Jackson grimaced.

Three bullets had struck him. Two in the left arm and one in his right hand, but no vital areas appeared hit, though his left arm was shattered. Four of his officers were dead and three were wounded by the friendly fire, but at least their chief was only wounded in his arms. He escaped death as if by some miracle.

Placed against a tree while a litter was constructed and a medic was sought, Jackson showed discipline by his calm demeanor. General Hill rode up and jumped off his horse near him.

"General Jackson, I am sorry to see you wounded and hope you are not hurt much."

"My arm is broken," he replied.

Checking his wounds, Hill propped the wounded man's head on his leg for support.

"I will try and keep your accident from the knowledge of the troops," Hill assured him.

"Thank you," Jackson said quietly. Somehow the animosity between the two was gone and reflected their character.

Jackson thought he could walk but realized he was weakened from the loss of blood. He was placed on a litter and carried through the woods under enemy fire. After being dropped twice, he finally reached a field hospital and underwent emergency surgery to remove the shattered left arm. Even though he lost a lot of blood, he was relatively young and fit and should make a full recovery in no time.[522]

Jackson was the single most important general in Lee's army and was indispensable. Since the war began, "Stonewall" had steamrolled over the Union army, and the South was winning the war. Now they were once again threatening the Union capital, and victory seemed within grasp.

After learning that Jackson was wounded, Lee stated, "Any victory is dearly bought that deprives us of the services of General Jackson even for a short time." Informed on the extent of these wounds, he sighed. "Oh, don't talk about it. Thank God, it is no worse."[523]

* * * * *

President Lincoln's Second National Fast-Day Proclamation, March 30, 1863

> Whereas, the Senate of the United States, devoutly recognizing the supreme authority and just government of Almighty God in the affairs of men and of nations, has by a resolution requested the President to designate and set apart a day for national prayer and humiliation: And whereas, it is the duty of nations as well as men to own their dependence upon the overruling power of God; to confess their sins and transgressions in humble sorrow, yet with assured hope that genuine repentance will lead to mercy and pardon; and to recognize the sublime truth, announced in the Holy Scriptures and proven by all history that those nations only are blessed whose God

---

[522] Ibid., 441–444; Ibid., 729–731; Ibid., 426–428.
[523] Freeman, *Lee*, 295; Davis, Burke, *Gray Fox*, 197.

is the Lord: And in so much as we know that by His divine law nations, like individuals, are subject to punishments and chastisements in this world, and may we not justly fear that the awful calamity of civil war which now desolates the land may be but a punishment inflicted upon us for our presumptuous sins to the needful end of our national reformation as a whole people? We have been the recipients of the choicest bounties of Heaven. We have preserved these many years in peace and prosperity. We have grown in numbers, wealth, and power as no other nation has ever grown; but we have forgotten the gracious hand which preserved us in peace, and multiplied and enriched and strengthened us; and we have vainly imagined, in the deceitfulness of our hearts, that all these blessings were produced by some superior wisdom and virtue of our own. Intoxicated with unbroken success, we have become too self-sufficient to feel the necessity of redeeming and preserving grace, too proud to pray to the God who made us. It behooves us, then, to humble ourselves before the offended Power, and confess our national sins, and pray for clemency and forgiveness: Now, therefore, in compliance with the request and fully concerning in the views of the Senate, I do by this my proclamation designate and set apart Thursday, the 30th day of April 1863 as a day of national humiliation, fasting, and prayer. And I do hereby request all the people to abstain on that day from their ordinary secular pursuits, and, to unite at their several places of public worship and their respective homes in keeping the day holy to the Lord, and devoted to the humble discharge of the religious duties proper to that solemn occasion. All this being done in sincerity and truth, let us then rest humbly in the hope authorized by divine teachings, that the united cry of the nation will be heard on high, and answered with blessings no less than the pardon of our national sins, and the restoration of our now divided and suffering country to its former happy condition of unity and place.[524]

* * * * *

A month later, Lincoln sat at his desk with the president of the Illinois Wesleyan University, Oliver S. Munsell, and worried about the war. Still, the Confederate army was making the Union army look like amateurs. The Battle of Chancellorsville had just opened the spring offensive for the Union and ended in a crushing defeat. General Lee and General Jackson had whipped Union General Hooker, causing him to retreat, and it looked like 1863 would be just like 1862 and 1861. Lee would keep winning, and Union generals would keep running, it seemed. Jackson had been wounded, so maybe his loss for a while would help.

The South's greatest tactician would be out of commission for a while, and at least General Grant was making some promising headway in the west at Vicksburg, Mississippi. He had the city under siege and expected their capitulation soon. Vicksburg was the key to the opening the back door to the Confederacy. Grant was optimistic, but the people of Vicksburg held out with a stubborn determination. Confederate Joseph E. Johnston had an army in the vicinity to possibly help Vicksburg, but he refused to move, claiming his help would be in vain.

While Lincoln sat there listening to Munsell, he thought about Mary. She had never recovered since the tragedy last year, and was

---

[524] Lincoln, Abraham. *Complete Works of Abraham Lincoln ed. John G. Nicolay and John Hay*, Vol. 8. (New York: Francis D. Tandy Co., 1894/1905), 235–237 (Proclamation Appointing A National Fast-Day, March 30, 1863).

still deeply depressed and often moody, just like she was after the first time. Who could blame her? He barely came out of it himself. If it wasn't for the comfort he found in his faith, he would have fallen apart too. Mary was faithful, but she couldn't find the solace in it like he had, even though he was feeling a little lonely this night with Mary and Tad in New York. He had come a long way since Springfield, Illinois, career-wise as well as spiritually. His journey was almost complete.

Munsell asked Lincoln a serious question. "Will our country come through safe and live?"

The president contemplated his question. Stroking his beard, he anxiously tried to speak, but his lips trembled as tears rolled down his face. After a second failed attempt, he finally found his voice:

> I do not doubt...I never have doubted...that our country would finally come through safe and undivided. But do not misunderstand me; I do not know how it can be. I do not rely on the patriotism of our people though no people have rallied around their king as ours have rallied around me. I do not trust in the bravery and devotion of the boys in blue; God bless them though. God never gave a prince or conqueror such an army as He has given to me. Nor yet do I rely on the loyalty and skill of our generals; though I believe we have the best generals in the world at the head of our armies.

Munsell wasn't sure where the president was going, but he was amazed with the intensity in which he spoke. Lincoln paused to emphasize his next words, leaning toward the university president, his eyes ablaze with certainty. "But the God of our fathers, who raised up this country to be the refuge and asylum of the oppressed and downtrodden of all nations, will not let it perish now. I may not live to see it."

Reflecting a moment as if accepting as fact, he continued, "I do not expect to live to see it...but God will bring us through safe."

The silence in the room was eerie. Munsell's eyes blurred with tears. He couldn't comprehend the faith Lincoln felt that God would protect the United States. He was touched by the president's acquiescence of his own death and his reliance on God's will. His unshakable trust in the country's survival brought tears to Munsell's eyes, and the humbled university professor couldn't believe such "sublime faith" existed and felt ashamed by his own doubts and fears. "And from that hour my faith in the ultimate triumph of our country never again faltered, and I bade Mr. Lincoln, as it proved, a final farewell, thanking God, as I had never before thanked Him, for such a leader in our country's deadly hour of peril."

The Union was on the verge of defeat. The congressional elections the year before were a landslide against him. He was pushed and pulled from two sides of his own political party, the Republicans, and he was also being maligned by the pro-Union Democrats.[525]

The radical Republicans were for a harsher war and thought Lincoln was too soft on the South. The conservative Republicans thought he was making a mistake changing the war from one of Union to one of slavery. Both agreed Lincoln made bad decisions. The northern Democrats wanted to end the war and to sue for peace, and felt granting the South its independence was the answer.

The radicals were treating the war as a holy war against slavery, and Christian pulpits were cursing the abomination as turning from God. They believed that it had to be eradicated from America, by the sword, if necessary.

Being pulled from every side, Lincoln maintained his newfound faith.

In early July, one of the most pivotal moments of the whole war was about to happen in a small Pennsylvanian town called Gettysburg. Lee's army had invaded the North again, and Lincoln

---

[525] Collis, Charles H.T. *The Religion of Abraham Lincoln.* (New York: G.W. Dillingham Co., 1900), 22–23 (The Story of Mr. Munsell); Johnson, William J. *Abraham Lincoln, the Christian.* (New York: The Abingdon Press, 1913), 109–111.

knew that if the Union lost again here, they might lose the whole war. He went to his bedroom and locked the door.

Dropping to his knees, he prayed harder than he had ever prayed before. He hadn't always made the right decisions and had many regrets, but he was asking God for guidance.[526]

* * * * *

The war was in its third year, and so many things had gone wrong. When Lee had invaded Maryland the year before and retreated, there was a glimmer of hope. After the harsh winter of little activity by both sides, the Battle of Chancellorsville opened the New Year with another defeat for the Union. Lincoln could change the generals, but nothing seemed to change the fact that Robert E. Lee's Army of Northern Virginia was winning. The North had better equipment, more men, factories, and money, but couldn't beat the southern army. He even tried to read books on military strategy to gain any advantage but realized he wasn't a general. One thing he knew was his top generals were too cautious and too quick to retreat.

In the beginning, he had made the war about Union, not slavery. In his first inaugural address, he said, "I have no purpose, directly or indirectly, to interfere with the institution of slavery in the States where it exists. I believe I have no lawful right to do so, and I have no inclination to do so."[527]

He also claimed:

My paramount object in this struggle is to save the Union, and is not either to save or to destroy slavery. If I could save the Union without freeing any slave I would do it, and if I could save it by freeing all the slaves I would do it; and if I could

---

[526] Ibid., 18–19 (General Sickles Memorable Interview with Lincoln); Rusling, James F. *Men and Things I Saw in Civil War Days.* (New York: Eaton & Mains Press, 1899), 15.

[527] Lincoln, *Works*, Vol. 6, 170 (First Inaugural Address, March 4, 1861).

save it by freeing some and leaving others alone I
would also do that. What I do about slavery and
the colored race, I do because I believe it helps
to save the Union; and what I forbear, I forbear
because I do not believe it would help to save
the Union. I shall do less whenever I shall believe
what I am doing hurts the cause, and I shall do
more whenever I shall believe doing more will
help the cause. I shall try to correct errors when
shown to be errors; and I shall adopt new views
so fast as they appear to be true views.

He ended by explaining this was his "purpose according to my
view of official duty" and did not modify his "oft-expressed personal
wish that all men everywhere could be free."[528]

Even though he personally despised slavery, as president, his
job was to enforce the law of the land, not to make it. He began his
presidency with the purpose of preserving the Union and upholding
the law, even if he believed some laws unjust. He never intended to
end slavery by force. Many in the North wanted this, but Lincoln
thought, much like Jefferson and other founding fathers, that slavery
would eventually die by its own hand. Northern industrialization
was slowly turning slavery into an obsolete practice. He believed in
another generation, it would no longer exist. It was the spread of
slavery he was most concerned about.

Many wanted to legalize slavery in the new territories to ensure
the spread of it, and if the free states gained more states in Congress,
it would be the end of slave power. Secession was the final attempt at
survival for the South.

The war had been about slavery all along. Whether the South
saw it or not, slavery was the root of the problem. Even the North's
unjust tariffs on southern goods was an attempt to punish it. Trying
to spread slavery to the territories was the South's attempt to even
the odds in the states by changing their majority in Congress, and

---

[528] Ibid., Vol. 8, 16 (To Horace Greeley, August 22, 1862).

the North knew if they kept slavery out of the territories, it would eventually disappear.

Lincoln had already changed the direction of the war to what he felt was God's real purpose for it.

* * * * *

Outside Petersburg, Virginia, June 18, 1864

"Attention! Trail arms! Double-quick march!"

The young officer drew his sword. Sprinting with his brigade over the rise, bullets sang past his head, and his men had bayonets ready for hand-to-hand fighting up close.

Cannon shot, grape, and canister (multiple smaller balls for killing massed troops) rocketed through the air like a biblical swarm of locusts, and the smoke from the cannon obscured eyesight, but its acrid odor stung the nose.

Men in blue fell all around him, yet he urged on his men. His presence kept them moving forward. Attacking fortified positions was never child's play. The surrounding terrain was crucial to success and if it took too long to close the space, many more would be killed.

The colonel spotted some bushes and small trees to their front and signaled for a left turn to bypass the foliage. This detour would mean many more casualties, but there was little alternative.[529]

Colonel Joshua Lawrence Chamberlain of Maine led this hopeless charge because he believed men should be willing to fight for their convictions. Now he was staring down certain death.

A professor of foreign languages at Bowdoin College in Maine, he had joined the Union army in 1862 when President Lincoln called for 300,000 more volunteers. He explained why he answered the call. "I fear, this war, so costly of blood and treasure, will not cease until the men of the North are willing to leave good positions and sacrifice

---

[529] Trulock, Alice Rains. *In the Hands of Providence: Joshua Chamberlain and the American Civil War.* (Chapel Hill: University of North Carolina Press, 1992), 208–209.

the dearest personal interests, to rescue our Country from desolation, and defend the National existence against treachery at home and jealousy abroad."[530]

His wife didn't want him to join the fight. They had two children and a comfortable life, and if he went to war, she would barely get by on his army pay, if at all. Chamberlain felt his wife needed to make sacrifices for the cause, and if only single, childless, and unemployed men were willing to sacrifice for it, evil would win.

There had been a Chamberlain in the Revolution and the War of 1812, and he knew it was his turn. His father was an ex-soldier himself and dreamed of his son going to West Point, but his mother wanted her gifted boy to be a preacher. Neither choices appealed to Joshua, but his mother's wish meant college, and he wanted an education.

So he attended Bowdoin College and discovered a talent for foreign languages, public speaking, and teaching. Learning nine languages in just a few years, it was easy for him to move from student to professor. Yet, he still felt unfulfilled.

Growing up a Christian, Chamberlain held the common belief in divine providence. The nation was founded in "a firm reliance" on it, and to him, it was God's divine plan and purpose for each of his children. Devout Christians and freethinkers believed in providence, and this became the American creed. Chamberlain decided that providence guided him to this very moment.

He wasn't created to be a professor. This was simply preparation to teach him patience and sound judgment to be used in battle. From Antietam to Gettysburg, he had served this purpose. Now at Petersburg, in the last months of the war, he was there to witness the triumph. The Lord had truly blessed him.

Standing before his troops, he urged them to the left of the brush in front of the fortification. If they couldn't get there the shortest way, they would improvise. Suddenly, he stumbled. A sharp pain in his back nearly dropped him. A bullet had entered his hip and

---

[530] Ibid., 7–8.

damaged everything in its path, and his only thoughts were of his poor mother. What would she think of him being shot in the back?

Bleeding profusely, he remained calm. If he went down, his men might lose their fight. If he could show courage now while wounded, it would inspire them. Using his sword as a crutch, he stayed in the fight. His men couldn't believe it. This man was superhuman it seemed, and they fought harder.

Chamberlain was seriously wounded, and blood loss weakened him. Going to his knees first, he finally fell over and was moved to the rear. While lying among the wounded bullets whizzed overhead, and he thought of his mother again.

A stretcher arrived, but he told the bearers to attend to others. Convincing him they had orders, he relented.

The Union attack on Petersburg failed that day, and General Grant ordered a halt. When the doctors attended to Joshua, they assured his brother, Tom, he wouldn't survive. Blood vessels were severed, his groin area was damaged, and he would likely bleed to death before they could repair the damage. He couldn't believe after all he had survived that this was the way he would die.

The surgeons decided to try. Who knew? They needed a miracle but were willing to give the young colonel a chance to live. They operated while he was conscious without anesthetic, and at one point, they considered ending the attempt to relieve his agony. The intense pain inflicted seemed inhumane for a lost cause, but Chamberlain demanded they continue. His steely determination convinced them to keep trying. Finally, they extracted the bullet and repaired what was possible. Maybe it would give this heroic officer a little more time.

The next morning, Joshua was delirious and barely clinging to life, but he knew he had to say goodbye to Fannie and his children somehow. Writing out a letter in excruciating pain and weak from loss of blood, he spoke from the heart:

> My darling wife, I am lying mortally wounded
> the doctors think, but my mind & heart are at
> peace Jesus Christ is my all-sufficient savior. I go

to him. God bless & keep & comfort you, precious one, you have been a precious wife to me. To know & love you makes life & death beautiful. Cherish the darlings & give my love to all the dear ones Do not grieve too much for me. We shall all soon meet Live for the children Give my dearest love to Father, mother & Sallie & John Oh how happy to feel yourself forgiven God bless you ever more precious precious one Ever yours.

A few days later, General Grant promoted Joshua Chamberlain to brigadier general for "meritorious and efficient services in the field of battle." It was Grant's first field promotion of the war.[531]

* * * * *

Two miles east of Appomattox Courthouse, Virginia April 9, 1865

His headache was back, and the pain was too strong to ignore this time. The enemy was surrounded, but he knew he had to convince Lee to surrender. He was the key to everything. Unable to sleep, he paced back and forth clenching his head.

With the first touch of daylight, he went to General Meade's headquarters and poured a cup of coffee. The caffeine took the edge off his migraine and allowed thought.

The Union army was in Lee's way, and they had more soldiers, more food, and more cannons. It was up to General Lee now. He could fight it out or order his troops to disperse and commence a guerrilla war which would continue the war for years. Maybe he would choose to surrender and end this now.

Grant had sent a message to Lee, asking for his surrender, and Lee requested a meeting today to hear the terms. Known as Unconditional Surrender Grant, Lee didn't expect favorable terms.

---

[531] Ibid., 210, 214–215.

483

Puffing on his cigar, Grant wrote to Lee:

> General: Your note of yesterday is received. As I have no authority to treat on the subject of peace, the meeting proposed for 10 a.m. today could lead to no good. I will state, however, General, that I am equally anxious for peace with yourself, and the whole North entertains the same feeling. The terms upon which peace can be had are well understood. By the South laying down their arms they will hasten that most desirable event, save thousands of human lives, and hundreds of millions of property not yet destroyed. Sincerely hoping that all our difficulties may be settled without the loss of another life, I subscribe myself, etc. U.S. Grant Lieutenant General[532]

Grant knew Lee was a man of integrity, and hoped that he could see the futility of the continuance of the war. Many would die senselessly on both sides if he chose to fight.

When Grant accepted the rank of lieutenant-general and commander of all the Union armies, he was humbled, and saw the challenge he faced. President Lincoln said to him on the day of their meeting:

> General Grant, the nation's appreciation of what you have done, and its reliance upon you for what remains to be done in the existing great struggle, are now presented, with this commission…With this high honor, devolves upon you, also, a corresponding responsibility. As the country herein trusts you, so, under God, it will sustain you I scarcely need to add, that, with what I here speak for the nation, goes my own hearty personal concurrence.

---

[532] Grant, Ulysses S. *Personal Memoir of U.S. Grant*, Vol. 2. (New York: Charles L. Webster & Co., 1886), 484.

Replying to the president and the large audience at the White House that day, Grant said:

> Mr. President, I accept the commission, with gratitude for the high honor conferred. With the aid of noble armies that have fought in so many fields for our common country, it will be my earnest endeavor not to disappoint your expectations. I feel the full weight of the responsibilities now devolving on me; and I know that if they are met, it will be due to those armies, and above all, to the favor of that Providence which leads both nations and men.[533]

General Grant had faced many hardships before with determination and perseverance, but this was his greatest challenge. Because of his tenacity, he was given command of the Union army. Lincoln had handed over the responsibility that had weighed on his shoulders from the beginning. Now it was Grant's burden.

General Ulysses S. Grant

---

[533] Ibid., 115–116.

Tens of thousands had died since then, and still he could not get Lee to surrender. He had stubbornly pressed his army, and still, no surrender. Another puff of his cigar, he mounted his horse and headed to the front.

Later that day, he received Lee's reply to his letter. Dismounting and sitting on a little hill in the grass, he read:

> General: I received your note of this morning on the picket line, whither I had come to meet you and, ascertain definitely what terms were embraced in your proposal of yesterday with reference to the surrender of this army. I now ask an interview in accordance with the offer contained in your letter of yesterday for that purpose. R.E. Lee, General

He had asked specifically for an interview for surrender. Could it be possible? Grant quickly wrote a reply, asking for a place to conduct the interview and had it delivered. Sighing, Grant wondered if it was real. Would Lee surrender and not continue the slaughter?

Standing up, he remounted his horse. Being steady in sensibility, Grant held back his excitement. Funny—his headache was finally gone.[534]

* * * * *

Fort Monroe, Virginia, Autumn 1865

Jefferson Davis missed his wife and children. He was tired but couldn't sleep. They captured him in Georgia soon after the surrender. Marching him through a line of Union soldiers, he was called names—"traitor" was the most popular, but "Hang the damn rebel" came in a close second. To them, he was the scapegoat for starting the war.

---

[534] Ibid., 485.

He was transported to the fortress Fort Monroe in Virginia and put in chains. He fought them when they tried to put them on, but four big guards restrained him while the blacksmith fastened them to his legs. They put a guard in his cell to watch him twenty-four hours a day, and couldn't even use the bathroom without an audience.[535]

Davis was the sacrifice for the South, and he knew it. The North needed someone to blame for all the carnage that gripped the nation for four years. Some suggested hanging him on the Fourth of July for an extra celebration, but others wanted him to get life in prison at hard labor for defending slavery.

He was guilty. Guilty of supporting the Constitution and secession, but he was no traitor. Treason was an attempt to overthrow the existing government or betraying it. He upheld secession because the federal government became oppressive to the South. Just like the thirteen colonies when Great Britain violated their rights, they separated. That was all the South had done. Now the victors could call them traitors, but if Great Britain would've won, the founders would now be known as traitors. He was in the company of Washington, Jefferson, and Franklin. It just turned out differently for the Confederacy.

Slavery wasn't the core issue with him, though he believed it was his constitutional right to own slaves. It wasn't even the main argument from the North at first. Whether slavery was immoral or not, it wasn't the real issue that had caused the war. Being denied rights that the law guaranteed was.

There was a constitutional process to end slavery, and even though the Constitution did not grant the right to meddle with slavery, a new amendment could be voted on. If this amendment passed the House, Senate, and the President, it was sent to the states for ratification. If three-quarters ratified it, it was the law of the land. It was not easy to do, but it was designed by the founders that way. It was an attempt to regulate the federal government from changing the Constitution at will, and gave the states and people a say in the

---

[535] Cooper, William J. *Jefferson Davis, American*. (New York: Vintage Books/ Random House, 2000,2001), 577–579.

process. The politicians in the North were restrained from making any law that restricted anything not mentioned in the Constitution without amending it, yet they did anyway.

The Constitution already settled the slavery issue. It was written into the document as a compromise. The Union itself was only possible by that compromise and the Supreme Court ruled in 1857 that Congress had no power to regulate slavery. It also defined slaves as property and not citizens of the United States. Chief Justice Roger B. Taney himself wrote the opinion, and the Dred Scott decision was the law of the land and settled.

The North had stated that the law didn't matter. Thirty years before, the firebrand John C. Calhoun tried to promote the concept of nullification, the ability of a state to nullify an unjust law, and was called a traitor and vilified by those same northerners. The issue then was a punitive tariff that hurt the South and benefited the North, but now the tables were turned and they magically agreed with Calhoun's view. The rule of law was the only thing standing between civilization and the jungle. It kept men from anarchy. Without the law, there was chaos.

He and others knew this was tyranny. The majority could not skirt the law, neither could Congress or the president. When they denied the South their rights by skirting the law, it was time for secession. The founding fathers exercised this right when the mother country did the same. The very document that proclaimed independence from Great Britain and founded the United States stated the doctrine of secession.

The North and their president denied this very right by an imaginary concept of the Union being perpetual. They claimed the Union could not be broken. It was unbreakable, because the people, not the states, had made it. The states were the people, and the states had to ratify the Union. It was a weak argument that many used to say the right to secede was illegal. The Declaration of Independence, the very foundation of the Union, said, "That whenever any form of Government becomes destructive to these ends (life, liberty, and pursuit of happiness), it is the right of the People to alter or abolish it, and institute new Government…"

What did this mean if it was illegal? The very existence of the United States was, by their logic, illegal. The Union was an agreement between states if the government did not become destructive to their rights. Without the restraint of law, all rights could be overturned.[536]

Even Lincoln once stated on the House floor in his defense of the Texas Revolution:

> Any people anywhere, being inclined and having the power, have the right to rise up, and shake off the existing government, and form a new one that suits them better. This is a most valuable—most sacred right—a right, which we hope and believe, is to liberate the world. Nor is this right confined to cases in which the whole people of an existing government, may choose to exercise it. Any portion of such people that can, may revolutionize, and make their own, of so much of the territory as they inhabit... It is the quality of revolutions not to go by old lines, or old laws; but to break up both, and make new ones.[537]

He couldn't uphold the founders' secession from Great Britain and stand against the South's secession from the Union without contradicting himself.

How could a nation founded on secession from a tyrannical government tell its own states that they couldn't legally do the same if they felt the government had become tyrannical? Lincoln contradicted himself, and realized this when he changed the war aim to slavery.

---

[536] Davis, Jefferson. *The Rise and Fall of the Confederate Government*, Vol. 1. (New York: D. Appleton & Co.,1881), Chapters 11–12; DiLorenzo, Thomas J. *The Real Lincoln: A New Look at Abraham Lincoln, His Agenda, and an Unnecessary War*. (New York: Three Rivers Press, 2002, 2003), 85–88.

[537] Lincoln, *Works*, Vol. 1, 338–339 (Speech in the US House of Representatives, January 12, 1848).

The Confederacy was justified with secession, but they lost the war, and now the victors wanted vengeance. Davis was to be the scapegoat for the entire war, and later that fall, accepting this circumstance, he said, "I have not sunk under my trials," and "I would rather be a sacrifice for the country, than it should be a sacrifice for me."

He spent his time imprisoned, reading the Bible and the *Book of Common Prayer and Scripture*. Praying several times a day, he accepted his situation as God's will and told Varina "all things are set in order by infinite wisdom and goodness."[538] If he was to be hanged, it was God's will and he would trust it.

Many in the North wanted him to pay for the war, and many were calling for his execution to wash away the suffering of the dead. His poor wife and children would be left to fend for themselves. He had served the United States for most of his life, in public service and war, and had given more to the nation than those now calling him a traitor.

Every civil war in history ended with executions and retaliation from the victors to the defeated. What would make the American Civil War any different?

* * * * *

I.
The Forge

Springfield, Illinois, November 1860

Though he knew he'd won, the closer inauguration day came, the closer the immensity of the burden he would inherit dawned upon him. Exhausted from endless job-seekers and the added stress, he plodded home and stretched out on the couch for a nap.

General Scott, commander of the army, warned of nefarious people who wanted him dead, and his safety must be priority. He'd

---

[538] Cooper, 590–591.

received several threatening letters calling for his execution, and Mary was frightened, but he knew the intent of the threats were to cause fear. He wouldn't give them the satisfaction of success.

Why was his election so polarizing? He never ran to change anything and was rather conservative when it came to the new Republican Party. Some in both parties were radicals, but he intended to govern all the people, not just the party. He was not elected dictator, and Congress made law. The president merely enforced that law, and they acted as if he was the next Napoleon.

The only military training he had was drilling in the militia during the Black Hawk War in 1832. Unfortunately, he did stumble upon some dead comrades once and immediately knew war was cruelty. He even lost his taste for hunting after he shot a turkey once when he was eight. It never appealed to his nature. In fact, he was quite passive most his life, except in debate, and would have to lead this nation nevertheless. He could be firm when matters of principle were under fire, though, but he wasn't looking to destroy the Union. He certainly wasn't a military man, but he started thinking he might need to be soon.

He believed the founders were the wisest men in history and the Declaration of Independence was the greatest document ever penned. Some had other interpretations of it, but he was confident he understood their meaning. He never avoided debate and studied the issues and contemplated every possibility while maintaining a firm anchor in truth. Why were so many afraid of him as their president?

Lying on the couch, he thought of the problems facing him and couldn't sleep. Eying a bureau mirror across the room, he stared at his reflection for a moment. His face seemed to be a double image. One side of his face was normal, but the other side appeared pale and lifeless. Springing from the couch to get a closer look, the image faded, and his face was normal again, though he never thought of his own face as normal. Maybe he was just tired or overstressed or crazy. He needed a break from thinking about the break-up of the Union.

Lying back down, he inspected the mirror again. Just as before, the two Lincoln faces glared back at him—one alive, one dead. He shivered.

When he told Mary about the experience, she said it was an ominous warning. She believed in the supernatural since Eddie's death, and now she had to worry about him. She thought this sign meant he would survive his first presidential term, but not his second, and that this was a premonition of his own death.

It bothered him too and it was a gnawing "pang" always in the back of his mind, reminding him of his own mortality. He didn't need to be reminded of death—he knew it all too well.[539]

* * * * *

Born in Kentucky on February 12, 1809, Abraham Lincoln inherited one thing from his parents—poverty. His was a life destined for the plow and illiteracy.

His father, Thomas, was the son of one of the first settlers in that unchartered wilderness that Daniel Boone and others called the "dark and bloody ground." In the mid-eighteenth century, Kentucky, Ohio, Indiana, Illinois, and Tennessee were unsettled forests where the law of the jungle determined who survived. You either adapted to the environment or you died.

Thomas Lincoln was a nomad by necessity. When he failed in one place, he moved on. When Abraham was seven, Thomas pulled up stakes and settled the family in Indiana in 1816, and it took him nearly a year to build their crude log cabin with a dirt floor and a loft for Abe to sleep in.

Though he was only eight-years-old by the time the cabin was finished, the boy went to work for his father. He chopped wood, split fence rails, and plowed the field, and Thomas was a strict overseer with Abraham. Sometimes he whipped the boy for simply disagreeing or butting into conversations. It was a hard life where there was no time for debate. Every minute of work might mean more food on

[539] Lamon, Ward Hill. *Recollections of Abraham Lincoln,* ed. Dorothy Lamon Teillard. (Washington: Published by the Editor, 1911), 112–113; Oates, Stephen B. *With Malice Toward None: The Life of Abraham Lincoln.* (New York: Harper & Row/Mentor, 1977,1978), 212.

the table, and one started the day in the dark and ended it that way. The specter of death was always there, waiting to pounce.

Thomas knew about death, and in 1786, at the age of six, he saw his father, Abraham, murdered by Indians. A Virginian and friend of Daniel Boone, Thomas' father heard stories from the famous adventurer of the opportunities in the Cumberland Valley and moved his family there. Within a few years, he was dead at forty-two. As the boy bent over his father to help, the Indian approached him with the intention of either killing or kidnapping him. Suddenly, the native fell dead from a gunshot through the heart. From a knothole in the cabin, his brother, Mordecai, fired his musket and saved the life of the future president's father. When Thomas had his own children, he honored his slain father by naming his son after him.

Abe's mother, Nancy Hanks Lincoln, came from the ultimate dysfunctional family. Lincoln often referred to his maternal grandmother as a "halfway prostitute" because of Nancy's illegitimacy. Several of the Hanks family were illegitimate, and the rumor was that Nancy was promiscuous. This caused Abe embarrassment, even though he once said, "Did you ever notice that bastards are generally smarter, shrewder, and more intellectual than others?"[540]

His mother's reputation embarrassed him as a boy, but he eventually came to terms with it later.

In 1818, Nancy Lincoln contracted the milk sickness (a disease caused by ingesting contaminated milk or beef from a cow that has eaten the white snakeroot plant). She died at the age of thirty-four after succumbing to the ailment. Abe was nine and shared the cabin with his dead mother for days while Thomas fashioned her coffin. The effect this had on him one can only speculate, but it was likely the seed of sadness that affected him most his life.

Abe's twelve-year-old sister, Sarah, tried to fill their mother's shoes as the woman of the house, but Thomas soon saw that he

---

[540] Burlingame, Michael. *Abraham Lincoln: A Life*, Vol. 1. (Baltimore: Johns Hopkins University Press, 2008), 13–14; Sandburg, Carl. *Abraham Lincoln: The Prairie Years and the War Years, One Volume Edition.* (New York: Harcourt, Brace and Co., 1954), 3.

needed another mother and wife for his home. Travelling back to Kentucky, he returned with Sarah Bush Johnston and her three children. This Brady Bunch of sorts combined her fatherless children with Thomas' motherless ones.

Sarah Lincoln became the shot in the arm the Lincoln cabin needed. She filled the emptiness left by Nancy and treated Abraham and Sarah like her own. She never played favorites and equally showed affection to them all. Sarah brought stability and kindness where Thomas could not, and Abe considered her his new mother and she was to be one of the biggest influences in his life.

Abe was described as quiet and bashful but mannerly. He was a loner, and one account complimented him as "clean," which was an oddity for the poor on the Indiana frontier. He was often called a peacemaker, though he was a good wrestler and fought only when he had no choice. Fighting on the frontier was like hunting, a rite of passage and a useful skill. One time, Abe was kicked in the head by a horse and claimed to have died and come back. He spent most of his time, when he wasn't working, fishing with his dog or had with his nose in a book. He also soaked up the frontier culture of folklore and superstition and listened to Thomas and others tell fascinating tales and funny stories.

Abe loved to learn and ponder things. Thomas thought he needed to toughen his son up to face the realities of life by the arduous work and skills of a farmer, but the boy hungered for knowledge of the world, not the plow. He was a hard worker but hated farming and preferred to use his mind to decide his course. Thomas would make fun of his son's passion for books and call it a waste of time. Once, he even threw out Abe's books when he felt the boy wasn't attending to his work. This did not deter Abe in the least, and he devised ways to combine work and reading or found any spare moment an opportunity to learn.[541]

He read anything he could find: *The Bible, Aesop's Fables,* John Bunyan's *The Pilgrim's Progress, The Life of George Washington,* and any books he could borrow. He learned to read, write, and do arith-

---

[541] Ibid., 10–11; Sandburg, 11–12; Oates, 9.

metic at fifteen by teaching himself from mostly borrowed books. He memorized whole passages by reading them multiple times or would write them, sometimes using a stick to scratch it in the dirt or on tree bark. If he didn't have a way, he found a substitute, and his ingenuity and self-reliance created avenues when there weren't any.

He knew the Bible well and grew to respect the wisdom within its pages, but he felt the handful of preachers he encountered on the frontier twisted those words to fit their own agendas. These few representatives of Christianity made him cynical and caused him to question his own faith as a young man.

He was intrigued by the miracles the founders experienced, and Washington and Jefferson were his idols. His favorite book was *The Life of George Washington,* and he particularly enjoyed the Battle of Trenton when the Americans overcame every obstacle to cross the Delaware and beat the Hessians, turning the tide of the Revolution.[542]

All this learning caused him to question everything, even his situation. How could it be his purpose to work himself to death for scraps like his father? All that would get him was misery and poverty. Was this all life had to offer? He was often hired out as a laborer to pay his father's debts and once said he felt like a slave. This made him despise anyone who would force another to do their own work and made him a proponent of the free market and self-determination. He once explained this:

> As labor is the common burden of our race, so the effort of some to shift their share of the burden onto the shoulders of others is the great durable curse of the race... Free labor has the inspiration of hope; pure slavery has no hope. The power of human exertion and happiness is wonderful. The slave master himself has a conception of it... The slave whom you cannot drive with the lash to break twenty-five pounds of hemp in a day, if you will task him to break a hundred, and prom-

---

[542] Oates, 9–12; Sandburg, 13–14.

ise to pay for all he does over, he will break you a hundred and fifty. You have substituted hope for the rod. And yet perhaps it does not occur to you that the extent of your gain in the case, you have given up the slave system and adopted the free system of labor.[543]

He once teased a young Virginian about southern dependence on slavery and explained the sharp contrast of the free states. "It is different with us. Here it is every fellow for himself, or he doesn't get there."[544] He concluded much as Captain John Smith, William Bradford, and most of the founders did that the "hope" of individual merit in a "free labor system" or free market was the only panacea for the corruption of man and his urge to enslave others. Benefiting from the fruits of others' labor was anathema to America. The first settlers starved because they wouldn't work for their own bread, and the Pilgrims starved because the lazy received the same equal shares as the productive. At its root, slavery was simply the symptom of this "curse" of mankind. Freedom was the answer for universal "happiness," and humans were created for self-government as individuals and nations.

The more he learned, the more he knew there was to offer. He didn't merely read information and accept it as truth but tossed it around in his mind until he understood every single aspect. Only then would he accept it as truth until something new surfaced to challenge it. This independent-minded youth from the backwoods outpaced others with a college education and social and monetary advantages. This helped him stand apart and made him an original.

He did learn some things from Thomas like working hard, which taught him ambition. He also imitated his father's knack for telling stories, and this became a unique part of his personality the rest of his life. Thomas couldn't read, much like most farmers, and telling stories was the venue to circulate news, tradition, and gossip.

---

[543] Lincoln, *Works*, Vol. 2, 185 (Fragment on Slavery, July 1, 1854?).
[544] Hill, 15; Burlingame, Vol. 1, 380.

Abe also soaked up the frontier culture in folklore, and superstition and anecdotes and fables were first-class entertainment of that era. Men like Davey Crockett, Mark Twain, and Lincoln defined western Americans.

As he grew into a young man, Abe started to think about making his own mark in the world. At seventeen, he tried his hand at working on a ferry boat but quickly found he couldn't make it profitable.

Around this time, his sister, Sarah, married a man he didn't approve of, and within two years, she died at the age of twenty-one. Abe had lost another person he loved, and his animosity to her husband was likely an insecurity of her abandoning him with her nuptials. The ingrained sadness manifested from the death of his mother intensified with Sarah's death.

Thomas Lincoln saw his father killed, lost his second son at birth in 1813, lost Nancy in 1818, and ten years later, his daughter. His pessimism probably rubbed off on his son. "Everything I ever touched either died, got killed, or was lost." Though fatalistic, Thomas said, "It's the hand of Providence laid upon me."[545]

After Sarah's death and bad luck in Indiana, Thomas moved his family to greener pastures in Illinois. The Lincolns settled in Decatur and endured the brutal winter of 1830–31. Illinois seemed a better fit and was the fresh start they needed.

Abe, his cousin, and one of Sarah Bush Lincoln's sons, John Johnston, dreamed up a moneymaking venture of transporting cargo down the Mississippi on a flatboat. Optimistic, the young men set out, but twenty miles downriver, the boat became stuck on a dam and started filling with water. Using the same ingenuity that used dirt as paper, Abe figured a way to get out of the fix they were in, and removed half the cargo and placed it on shore, then distributed the remaining cargo around to balance the boat. After this, Abe drilled a hole in the front to drain the water, and when he sealed up the hole, the boat moved easily across the dam.

This practical savvy caused many people on shore and in towns along the river in Illinois to recognize Lincoln as a man who used his

---

[545] Burlingame, Vol. 1, 6.

mind and could get things done others couldn't. After the flatboat business went bust, he was immediately offered a job as clerk for a general store. Sensing another opportunity, he accepted the position.

Working at the general store, he gained friends with his brand of humor and peculiar skill at wrestling. Challenged by the best wrestler in the region, he accepted, and just as he was about to win, several of his opponent's friends jumped in to assist and overpowered him. This didn't scare Abe but only energized him, and he challenged each of them to a match one at a time. The original opponent, Jack Armstrong, liked the spunk of the lanky clerk and declared the fight a draw.

After this, Armstrong and his gang became friends with Lincoln and admired his toughness, wit, and honesty. They called themselves the Clary Grove Boys and were a rowdy bunch who liked to fight, drink, and raise hell. Abe fit right into the group, because he was tough but not a braggart. He became the leader of the gang, and they respected him, and even though he didn't drink, he was one of them. He tried drinking some years before but hated the way it controlled his mind. This mental "slavery" didn't appeal to him, but he never judged others who drank and was frequently among them, telling stories, enjoying the camaraderie.

During this period, he also discovered an interest in reading the law. He read books on statutes, common law, and studied the Declaration of Independence and Constitution. He gobbled up anything having to do with court proceedings and immersed himself in the study of law.[546]

When it came to women, Abe was shy and awkward, and because of his appearance, he had little confidence about females. He possibly feared their rejection because he felt unattractive. His face was long and asymmetrical, and one eye was not the same as the other (a result from the horse kick). He was tall and gangly and looked like he had no idea what to do with his arms. Physically, he was a mess but possessed other traits that made one forget his looks

[546] Oates, 17–20; Donald, David Herbert. *Lincoln.* (New York: Simon & Schuster,1995), 39; Burlingame, Vol. 1, 60–62.

like humor, intelligence, and charm. Lincoln wasn't like most men on the frontier, because he had sensitive eyes that reflected a compassion inside, and his charisma drew others to him, removing the focus on his looks.

Nineteen-year-old Anne Rutledge was a different story altogether. This pretty young girl captured Abe's heart, and she enjoyed his conversation and attention. Her father owned a small library where Abe studied and organized a debate club where he learned to speak in public. Though nervous, he was learning to be persuasive in debate. Lincoln courted Anne, and in no time, some believe, the two were engaged.

Looking for more security and promise, he ran for the Illinois state legislature in 1832 but lost the election. Later the same year, he volunteered to fight in the Black Hawk War and was elected captain of his hometown militia, but after drilling and marching through the wilderness to reach the fight, the war ended. He explained later the only blood lost by his men was from the swarms of mosquitoes, though they did discover some dead Americans scalped once, and it made an impression on him. He gladly retired his career in the art of war.

Returning, he bought an interest in a general store and formed a partnership with William F. Berry. Lincoln permitted too much credit and was terrible at demanding payment, so they were soon in debt. When Berry died suddenly, he was held responsible for the entire debt and accepted responsibility. Bankrupt and sued, it took him fifteen years to pay off the debt. This was a prime example of where he got the nickname "Honest Abe."

After the store went belly up, he got a job as postmaster of New Salem, Illinois, and was directly appointed by President Andrew Jackson. Though not a Jackson supporter, he still accepted the job and honor. It didn't pay much, so he supplemented his income by doing odd jobs and a bit of surveying he taught himself from books.

In 1834, he once again ran for the state legislature, but this time he was victorious. He was no longer just a store clerk but a respectable citizen in his community.

Inspired by another candidate and seeing the next natural step, Abe decided to study the law as a career. He borrowed the necessary law books and passed the bar in 1836. His future looked promising, and now he could get married.

In 1835, Ann Rutledge died suddenly of typhoid fever, and Abe was devastated. Once again, a woman he cared for died, abandoning him. Death seemed to follow him, and he wondered if he was the reason. A few speculate Lincoln's lifelong depression became chronic with Ann's death. Some believe his ambition reflected his feelings about himself, and his quest for success was really a quest for the approval of others. "I have no other [ambition] so great as that of being truly esteemed of my fellow citizens." Every woman who returned his love left him, and most ignored him. He believed he was unlovable, and his shyness around women was his expectation of rejection. When a woman returned his love like his mother, sister, or Ann, he was truly surprised and cherished them higher than all others. When he lost them, he lost that which gave him value, and so he expected to lose before he did. When they died, it was simply fate's way of rejecting him.[547] His need for affection led to an engagement with a woman he didn't love.

He was engaged to Mary Owens long before he ever met her. Another woman played matchmaker and after meeting her, Abe knew there were no sparks but still felt obligated to marry her. He mentioned that she was free to back out if she chose, and Mary must have sensed his true feelings because she soon called off the engagement. Now he felt rejected by someone he didn't want to marry as well as the sting of abandonment.

Once again, he channeled the loss of Ann and even the rejection of Mary Owens into his ambition and continued his law career. He jumped into the political debates of the time and, in 1839, met Mary Todd at a party. By the next year, they were courting, and before the year was out, they were engaged.

Mary's sister and brother-in-law were against the engagement from the start. The Todd family was a firmly established, well-edu-

---

[547] Donald, 45, 57–58; Burlingame, Vol. 1, 67–68, 173.

cated, and highly respected family of Kentucky. Mary's father, Robert, was a prominent banker and landholder, and here was this uncouth nobody from a broken home, asking for a Todd girl's hand. *Is he a gold digger? Or does Mary want to live a life of poverty?* they wondered.

After everything he had accomplished from his meagre beginnings, he still could not outrun his past and was judged by his family and status, not his character or merit. In the land where all men were created equal, some still thought themselves superior. The status system of early Jamestown was still in play over two hundred years later. To top off a run of bad luck, he also lost his bid to the state legislature in 1841.

Convinced Mary would be better off without him, he ended their engagement. Sinking into deep depression, he had lost another woman he loved. Throwing himself into his work again, he formed a law partnership and was soon busy working cases.

After helping a friend, Joshua Speed, over fear of marriage, Lincoln convinced himself of the wisdom he offered Speed and hurried to Mary and reconciled. They were married in 1842, and nine months later, Mary gave birth to their first son, Robert Todd Lincoln.

Living in a tavern while Abe worked off his general store debt, the newlyweds had a rough going. Working cases by travelling the circuit, he paid off his debt and purchased a house. Mary and Robert were often home alone for six months out of the year.

The Todd family finally accepted Abe as an equal, but their marriage was tumultuous at times. Mary had many insecurities, and her new husband's absence did nothing to ease her worries. He was busy running for Congress again but came up short.

In 1846, their second son, Edward, was born, and Lincoln managed to win election to the United States House of Representatives. Opposed to the war with Mexico, the freshman representative accused President Polk of starting it to extend slavery, but the stance was unpopular with the Illinois constituency, and politically, a misstep.

Four years later, another compromise in Congress was brokered in 1850 over the land acquired from the Mexican War. Henry Clay, Daniel Webster, and Stephen Douglas of Illinois orchestrated the Compromise of 1850, leaving it for the next generation. This compromise allowed Texas to enter as a slave state, California and New Mexico were free to determine their own course, and the Fugitive Slave Law made it a federal crime for free states to refuse to return runaway slaves in their midst. This last one was hard for the North to swallow, but the South accepted this concession, and many in the North resolved to never follow it. For now, the tinderbox cooled.

In 1850, four-year-old Eddie Lincoln died from what many believe to be pulmonary tuberculosis, and Abe and Mary were shattered. Mary was inconsolable for weeks while Abe again threw himself into his work to distract from the inner pain. The depression he suffered most his life returned, and the feeling of a cursed existence made him pull away from others. Mary suffered from mood swings and severe depression and feared she would lose Abe and Robert too.

She sought aid in the church of Pastor Dr. James Smith, who comforted both grieving parents, reassuring them that Eddie was in heaven. Abe befriended Dr. Smith, even reading the pastor's book against skepticism in the Christian faith. Lincoln read the Bible but still had doubts and questions his analytical mind couldn't sort. Eddie's death was a tragedy which led him to seek the truth, and to pretend he was an atheist or even a deist is absurd. As a thinking person, he had to understand a concept before accepting it. Blind faith did nothing for someone like him who asked questions. True faith had to be sought, pondered, and even doubted before it had any chance of acceptance. This tragedy, providentially brought Lincoln closer to God, and Dr. Smith believed he became a true Christian during this period.[548] His brother-in-law, Ninian Edwards, claimed Abe said to him one day around this time, "I have been reading a work by Dr. Smith on the evidences of Christianity, and have heard him preach and converse on the subject, and I am convinced of the truth of the Christian religion."[549]

By the end of the year, Abe and Mary had another son, William Wallace Lincoln, named for the Scottish hero who led a rebellion

---

[548] Oates, 101; Burlingame, Vol. 1, 359-360; Johnson, *Lincoln*, 50–57.

[549] Johnson, *Lincoln*, 53 (Ninian Edwards to Rev. James A. Reed, December 24, 1872).

against the English. Willie helped heal the emptiness of losing Eddie, and they fawned over the baby, cherishing him even more because of the painful loss.

A month later, Abe received a letter notifying him his father was dying. Though Abe and his father were never close, he regretted not being able to be by his side, but Mary was sick, and he had obligations with work and couldn't leave. He did ask his stepbrother in a letter to relay a message to him:

> I sincerely hope Father may recover his health but, at all events, tell him to remember to call upon and confide in our great and good and merciful Maker, who will not turn away from him in any extremity. He notes the fall of a sparrow and numbers the hairs of our heads, and He will not forget the dying man who puts his trust in Him. Say to him that if we could meet now it is doubtful whether it would be more painful than pleasant, but that if it be his lot to go now, he will soon have a joyous meeting with many loved ones gone before, and where the rest of us, through the help of God, hope ere long to join them.[550]

Thomas Lincoln died soon after, and some historians claim Lincoln didn't believe in an afterlife around this time, but these words of comfort to his dying father seem to refute this. Maybe it was just compassion to ease his father's fear, but why would he lie to him? This seems counter to the character of a man who was known for his honesty. It is clear what he meant when he said "loved ones gone before" and "a joyous meeting." Where exactly would this happen without an afterlife?

Lincoln believed in an intervening providence as well. When American icon Henry Clay died in June of 1852, he eulogized him by

---

[550] Lincoln, *Works*, Vol. 2, 148–149 (To John D. Johnston, January 12, 1851).

saying, "Such a man the times have demanded, and such, in the providence of God, was given us. But he is gone. Let us strive to deserve, as far as mortals may, the continued care of Divine Providence, trusting that in future national emergencies He will not fail to provide us the instruments of safety and security."[551] This transformation in Lincoln's beliefs would prepare him for the trials ahead.

Henry Clay, Daniel Webster, John Quincy Adams, and other peacemakers were dead. The giants who avoided civil war for thirty years were no longer among them, and this new generation didn't understand compromise. Both sides were angry because for far too long, representatives had compromised their core principles too often, and each side became more polarized over these differences.

* * * * *

Brierfield, Davis Bend, Mississippi, February 10, 1861

Looking at the roses in his garden, he stared in wonder. Roses were such perfect reminders of God's creation. This world contained so much beauty like a rose, but also so many thorns.

His blessed Union was the same. It had brought the nation to such a beautiful existence, but the thorns of disunion would inevitably draw blood, he could see.

What the founders left for them had been squandered and the new abolition party and their inexperienced president would shred the Constitution to further an agenda.

Varina was like a rose too. Beautiful and feminine, but she could also draw blood when he was in the wrong.

Clipping the rose bush, he felt at peace. He had not felt this peaceful in so long. The fate of the nation no longer depended on him, yet he prayed they would be allowed to leave the Union peacefully.

---

[551] Ibid., 177 (Eulogy of Henry Clay, delivered in the House at Springfield, Illinois, July 16, 1852).

Smiling at Varina, he remembered when they were first married, how young she had been, and how she helped him forget the pain from his first marriage. She was truly his rose in this life of thorns, and he had enjoyed it all.

The rosebush, the clear blue sky, and his beautiful wife—what more could he ask for?

"Telegram, sir," the messenger said, startling him from his daydreams. He took the paper and opened it.

Quietly reading the message, his face sunk under the force of the words:

> Sir: We are directed to inform you that you are this day unanimously elected President of the Provisional Government of the Confederate States of America and request you come to Montgomery immediately.

One moment, he was at peace, clipping his roses, and now the greatest burden was thrust upon him. They expected him to lead this new nation; but how?

Excusing himself from the garden, he had to pack and be on the next train in the morning. Just as God banished Adam and Eve from Eden, he and Varina would never see their beautiful garden again. His path was no longer rose-colored, but of course, his life had never been all roses either.[552]

* * * * *

Jefferson Davis was born in Kentucky in 1808. His birthplace was only a hundred miles from Lincoln's and he was born seven months earlier.

---

[552] Foote, Shelby. *The Civil War: A Narrative, Vol. 1, Fort Sumter to Perryville*. (New York: Vintage Books, 1958, 1986), 17; Cooper, 352.

His father, Samuel, named him after his hero, Thomas Jefferson, but christened him with the middle name of Finis, ensuring he was the last child of ten.

Just like Lincoln, Davis was born in a log cabin and poverty, but his sojourn there was short-lived.

Samuel soon relocated to Louisiana, then Mississippi, and found something lucrative to earn a living from—cotton. Cotton was a gold mine if someone could produce enough of it and be competitive. For this, slaves were essential, and Samuel built a farm and some wealth with shrewdness and slave labor.

Jefferson was told to go to school when it was time but refused. His father sent him to work in the cotton fields to show the boy what real work was, and within two days, Jeff gladly returned to school. He realized that backbreaking labor was crazy and chose to use his mind instead. Though it was a minor event, it changed his direction, and a lesson he remembered in every pursuit.

By the age of fourteen, he travelled back to Kentucky to attend Transylvania University. Samuel died while he was there, and his eldest brother Joseph became his guardian. Joseph suggested West Point, but Jeff never had any interest in the military. Securing the appointment, his older brother urged him to attend.

During his West Point stay, Jeff was an average student because he liked to fight and drink too much, but managed to graduate in 1828. He spent the next seven years as an officer in the United States Army. His commanding officer was Colonel Zachary Taylor, future commanding general in the Mexican War and twelfth president of the United States. Taylor saw potential in the young officer and became a mentor of sorts. When Davis met Taylor's sixteen-year-old daughter, Knox, he quickly began a passionate courtship with her. Taylor was a career soldier and rarely spent time with his family when he wasn't serving on some battlefield or protecting the frontier from Indians. His children had grown up without him and he certainly didn't wish this for his daughter, so he disapproved of Davis for a future son-in-law. This stubborn stand of the commanding officer just drew Knox closer to Davis.

Jeff refused to dishonor himself and resigned from the army. He eloped with Knox and took her to his home in Mississippi without her father's consent. There he received an eight-hundred-acre planta-tion with fourteen slaves from Joseph as a wedding gift and became a cotton farmer to support his new wife.

He was ready to build a future for them, but within three months, they both contracted malaria. Kept in separate rooms to quarantine the disease and the emotional pain, they suffered from fever, chills, and delirium. After a few days, Jeff's fever broke, but he could hear Knox in the other room singing from her delirium. Still fatigued, he struggled to her bedside, and could not believe the ema-ciated figure was his wife. Staying by her side, she died soon after.[553]

Davis took another month just to recover from the malaria him-self, but it would take years before he recovered from Knox's death. He became withdrawn, depressed, and all his plans crumbled.

When pain was all-consuming, distraction often worked, so he immersed himself into building the plantation. Little reminders would keep Knox's death on his mind, but work would help him forget for a while. His belief in God carried him through this pain-ful time. He believed providence had other designs for him, and God's will couldn't be thwarted, so he pushed forward. This tragedy matured him both emotionally and spiritually.

Where Lincoln was a thinker of great ideas and slow to act, Davis would act quickly and think about it later. It was his nature to act from conviction and trust his heart he was right rather than pondering the issue. This was why he went to West Point, resigned his commission, and ran away with Knox. He believed action was his duty, and God would direct it through providence. Of course, some of this can be attributed to youth and inexperience, but there was purpose to his actions.

While he built his plantation, Brierfield, he also studied law and planned for the future.

Davis also had a unique way in how he managed his slaves. His overseer, James Pemberton, was a slave. He trusted him like family, and when he was away, he knew James would manage the plantation. Jeff's policy was to never punish the slaves unless an all-slave jury

---

[553] Foote, Vol. 1, 5–8.

convicted them, and he saw his slaves as valuable, not expendable. Without healthy, well-behaved slaves, he would not prosper. The way he ran his plantation didn't justify slavery, but this fact did remove the façade that all southern slave owners were monsters. It's as important to know this as it is to learn about its horrors. Of course, as in all walks of life, there were psychopaths who enjoyed the power they had over their slaves and mistreated them.[554]

Depending on sources, between 3–8 percent of families owned slaves in the United States in 1860. Some claim the higher number if factoring in all family members as owners, including children. Regardless the precise percentage, this was a small minority of the population. This doesn't imply only slave owners supported the institution, but it cannot indict each individual family member as a slave owner either. Some children of slave owners fought for the North and supported abolition, and the issue tore families apart, both North and South.

Some slave owners were black men, and the largest number cited from the 1830 Census reported over 3,000 families owned slaves. This, of course, uses families collectively, not individually, and points to more than race for being the catalyst for slavery. Many blacks bought family members themselves without legally being able to free them, but some used slaves on their plantations and even fought for the Confederacy. Though only a small minority of blacks owned slaves, it is important not to judge an entire race for the actions of a few.

Though race had little to do with human bondage, you can bet many white slave owners used race to justify slavery in many cases. Slavery throughout world history has rarely ever been about color, race, or religion as many claim. Nearly every group of human beings have been slaves or slave owners. Some lessened it to indentured servitude or the feudal system, but it was all the same in practice.

European and Asian feudal systems enslaved those of their own race as did African tribal hierarchies. As Lincoln discovered, real slavery has been a scourge to the world since the beginning and was about

---

[554] Ibid., 9-10; Cooper, 83–85.

man's desire to benefit from another's labor. The Jews were enslaved by the Egyptians, Assyrians, Babylonians, and certain Indian tribes in America kept other tribes as slaves. The English kept the Scots and Irish under their boot of despotism, and Rome had slaves of all races and creeds. The African slave trade existed because hostile tribes sold the subjugated ones to slave traders to bring to the New World. This tyranny enslaved mankind from the beginning and has been propped up with every excuse in the world, including race. The claim of superiority over another has little to do with skin color or any other difference, and was a fundamental difference in beliefs. Most Americans didn't own slaves, and many were working to end it. It was an ugly stain left over from the British Empire, and events were about to wash it away.

With this reality, some did try to justify slavery with white supremacy, but others blamed the North of using slavery to force its will on them when the law was on their side. Some saw this conflict between God's law and man's.[555]

Jeff Davis never thought much of these deeper moral questions yet. He was preoccupied with the law and a new love.

Varina Howell was seventeen, and Jeff was thirty-four when they met. After their initial encounter, Varina wrote her mother:

> He impresses me as a remarkable kind of man, but of uncertain temper, and has a way of taking for granted that everybody agrees with him when he expresses an opinion, which offends me; yet he is most agreeable and has a peculiarly sweet voice and a winning manner of asserting himself.

---

[555] Census Bureau: Census of 1860. https://www.census.gov//history/www/reference/maps/distribution_of_slaves_in_1860.html; http://www.civilwar.net/pages/1860-census.html; Woodson, Carter G. *Free Negro Owners of Slaves in the United States in 1830.* (Washington: Association for the Study of Negro Life and History, 1924), Full Report; Sowell, Thomas. *Black Rednecks and White Liberals.* (New York: Encounter Books, 2005, 2006), 120, 127–28, 261,

Varina was taken by Jeff Davis because of his rugged confidence, but it was a bit overbearing, though she saw a gentler side in him others never saw. "The fact is, he is the kind of person I should expect to rescue one from a mad dog at any risk, but to insist upon a stoical indifference to the fright afterward." She fought this admiration by inserting, "I do not think I shall ever like him as I do not think I shall ever like him as I do his brother Joe. Would you believe it, he is refined and cultivated, and yet he is a Democrat?"[556] Coming from a Federalist and Whig family, calling him a Democrat was the worst she could call him. He was a scoundrel and a miscreant, and she didn't like him.

Determined not to like him, Varina and Jeff were engaged the following year, married the year after, and shortly after returning from their honeymoon, he was elected to the state legislature.

Soon after learning of his election and just settling down with a new wife, war broke out with Mexico, and Jeff volunteered for the Mississippi Rifles.

His old colonel and father-in-law, General Zachary Taylor, was now in command of the army in Mexico. Using the potential he recognized in Jeff years before, he saw it come to fruition on the field.

Jeff fought bravely in the Battle of Monterey and was crucial at the Battle of Buena Vista where he threw back Santa Anna's cavalry charge, which guaranteed the victory. He was shot in the foot during the fight but stayed in the battle and only sought help when the fighting ended. Taylor told him, "My daughter, sir, was a better judge of men than I was."[557]

On crutches, he returned home to a hero's welcome, and the governor of Mississippi appointed him to the US Senate. After that, Jeff Davis never looked back. A stint in the Senate led to a sterling

---

[556] Davis, Jefferson. *The Papers of Jefferson Davis, Vol. 2, June 1841–July 1846*, ed. James T. McIntosh. (Baton Rouge: Louisiana State University Press, 1974, 1987), 20 (Varina Howell to Margaret Howell, December 19, 1843); Tate, Allen. *Jefferson Davis: His Rise and Fall*. (Nashville: J. S. Sanders & Co.,1998), 71; Cooper, 98.

[557] Foote, Vol. 1, 12; Cooper, 161–164.

performance as Secretary of War under President Franklin Pierce and a return to the Senate in 1857.

President Jefferson Davis

As his career gained momentum, Varina and Jeff lived a turbulent life, and their marriage suffered. Much of the time, she stayed at Brierfield alone, but when they were together, they had some heated arguments. Jeff tended to treat Varina like his daughter, rather than his wife. He tried to teach her how to be a good wife instead of letting her learn it herself, and she resented him because he disregarded her opinion. She was a naïve girl in his eyes, but Varina had become her own person while Jeff was gone. She finally convinced Jeff to show her respect, and he finally saw her as his better half.[558] Having resolved the issues in his marriage, he had a harder time resolving the ones in the nation.

At the end of the Mexican War, the territory acquired caused a major split in the country over what rights these new states would be granted.

Presidential hopeful, William H. Seward from New York made a speech in Congress in 1850 and said, "We cannot, in our judgment, be either true Christians or real freemen if we impose on another a

---

[558] Cooper, 173–174, 198–199.

chain that we defy all human power to fasten on ourselves. He alone who ordained the conscience of man and its law of action can judge us."[559] He then ruffled the hair of every southerner when he stated:

> But there is a higher law than the Constitution, which regulates our authority over the domain, and devotes it to the same noble purposes. The territory is a part—no inconsiderable part—of the common heritage of mankind, bestowed upon the Creator of the universe. We are his stewards and must so discharge our trust as to secure in the highest attainable degree their happiness... Sir, our forefathers would not have hesitated an hour. They found slavery existing here, and they left it only because they could not remove it.

Seward went on to use the Northwest Territory Ordinance of 1787 as an example of how the founders intended on "establishing an organic law" for the new states formed out of it. Slavery was prohibited in any future states there, and this was their repudiation of the institution.[560]

The "higher law" claim was Seward's reference to God's law or natural law. He claimed men corrupted the law, but there was right and wrong, regardless of man's law. Like the founders who formed the Union, natural law trumped man's law. Many in both parties were appalled by this claim, and they argued the law was the only solution to combat the law of the jungle. America was a nation of laws, not men, and without the law, society would collapse.

Those opposed to slavery or its extension believed there were bad immoral laws, and it was every man's obligation to fight them. Slavery was not part of "certain unalienable rights" endowed by the

---

[559] Seward, William H. *The Works of William H. Seward, Vol. 1*, ed. George E. Baker. (Boston: Houghton, Mifflin, and Co., 1884), 67 (Freedom in the New Territories, March 11, 1850).

[560] Ibid., 74–75.

Creator, clearly; but how could someone defy the laws written by representatives elected by the governed? The founders compromised with the slave states to form the Union, not to uphold slavery.

Jefferson Davis countered Seward's assertion and stated that the spread of slavery wasn't an issue. The Constitution granted the states power to determine their own course regarding this. The only problem now was those in Congress trying to force their opinions through federal intervention on the states. The federal government was an agreement between the states to form a national government, but the states never surrendered their own rights in doing so. The Tenth Amendment guaranteed these rights by delegating all powers not specified in the Constitution for the federal government, to the states and people.

What a slave owner did with his slaves was not the federal government's business, and if he wanted to take his property into a new state, he had every right. The right of property was one of the three unalienable rights named in the Declaration and the Constitution was the law of the land and upheld the right to property. It also didn't forbid slavery, so the law of the land was on their side.[561]

Jeff understood the law and vowed to be its defender.

* * * * *

New Haven, Virginia, December 1831

"Mama," the timid boy with dark features asked gently.

"Thomas," an ill woman with the same dark hair called.

The seven-year-old was scared his mother was about to die; this much he knew—she'd been sick for a long time and was exhausted.

Calling to his sister, Laura, she asked them to come nearer. They had been whisked away from their uncle's home where she had sent them five months earlier. It had been a traumatic day for young

---

[561] Davis, Jefferson, *Rise*, Vol. 1., 127–157 (Pt. 2: Ch. 6–9); McPherson, James M. *Battle Cry Freedom: The Civil War Era*. (New York: Oxford University Press, 1988), 23.

Thomas when his mother sent him away. She was all he had left in the world.

When he was two, his six-year-old sister caught typhoid and died. His father was so distraught and fatigued from work, he contracted it as well and died. Leaving Thomas, brother Warren, the newborn, Laura, and his mother to fend for themselves, she was all he had ever known.

When it was time to leave that day she first sent them away, he had sprinted from the house and hid in the woods. He was determined to stay, even if he had to live outside forever.

When darkness and an empty stomach came, he turned himself in, and within a few hours of his mother's convincing, he agreed to go. She cried when they were preparing to leave the next day, and at the last minute, she ran to him, hugging him once more. He would always remember that his whole life with tears in his eyes.

Now she was saying goodbye for the last time, and he ran and hugged her.

Pale and emaciated, she could barely speak. "Goodbye, Thomas. You have all the blessings I can give you."

Wiping his eyes with his sleeves, he said, "Don't leave me again, Mama. Please don't go."

But she died at thirty-three and he was now on his own, an orphan at seven.[562] Thirty years later, he would name his daughter Julia in honor of her. "My mother was mindful of, when I was a helpless, fatherless child, and I wish to commemorate her now."[563]

Julia's death determined the boy's course early. With this single tragic event, blessings followed which instilled in him a sense of self-reliance, but it also kept him distant from others because of the pain of loss.

His father, Jonathan, was a well-meaning but irresponsible man. Admitted to the bar in 1810, he was destined for a bright future but had no talent for the law. A compulsive gambler, he was in perpetual

[562] Jackson, 16–17; Robertson, 7–10.
[563] Ibid., 19; Robertson, 649.

debt, and the endless stress of providing for his family made him susceptible to illness, eventually killing him.

Julia and her three children were left penniless, so she taught school to keep a roof over their heads, but they were just scraping by. When Blake Woodson proposed to her, she jumped at his offer, and by 1831, she was pregnant again and sick. Sending the children to their relatives, she could no longer care for them, and after the birth, her condition worsened. Aware she was dying, she called for the children.

Thomas Jonathan Jackson was born in 1824 in Virginia. After Julia's death, he moved to Jackson's Mill, Virginia, with his uncle Cummins Jackson who became Thomas's father figure and taught the boy how to fish, hunt, farm, and how to ride and handle horses.

As a youth, Thomas loved to play war and was insistent about being the commander. Playing with white and slave children, he led armies into imaginary battles, and his sister was always his favorite playmate. His older brother, Warren, wasn't as close, but Laura and Tom had a connection which only orphaned siblings near in age possessed. Often they would spend hours playing in secret places along the river under the shade of a tree, creating imaginary worlds free from dying mothers.

Around the age of nine, Thomas began to contemplate his future in this world and started his own business. He struck a deal with a merchant who agreed to pay him fifty cents for every fish over a foot in length he caught. He managed to earn a hefty sum from this venture, and once, when he caught a three-foot pike, he refused offers from others to pay double the price the merchant paid. A man of his word, he took the fish to his associate and refused to accept any more than the agreed amount of fifty cents. "No, sir, this is your pike at fifty cents, and I will not take more for it. Besides, you have bought a good many from me that were pretty short."[564]

When Tom was twelve, his sixteen-year-old brother, Warren, agreed to take him on a moneymaking venture. The journey eventually led them hundreds of miles down the Kentucky and Mississippi

---

[564] Ibid., 27–29; Robertson, 15.

Rivers where they spent the summer chopping wood on an island for passing steamboats. After six months of this backbreaking existence, the weary boys came down with malaria. Hitching a free ride on a steamboat, they returned to Virginia, seasoned by the experience.

In 1837, at thirteen, Thomas learned surveying and worked on construction of a turnpike being built in Lewis County. The next year, he met his good friend, Joseph Lightburn, whose family introduced him to the world of reading. Tom threw himself into his studies and learned everything he could. Arithmetic was his strongest subject, but he liked reading about the American Revolution. His favorite book was Parson Weems's biography of Francis Marion, the American guerrilla fighter in South Carolina. He wasn't a quick learner but would immerse himself in one subject until he mastered it, no matter how long it took. A childhood friend said of him, "Brilliant, but was one of those untiring, plain, matter-of-fact persons who would never give up…until he accomplished his object."

Joe Lightburn also introduced him to the study of the Bible and invited him to his church. Julia had been a Presbyterian, but religion was never studied, only accepted, so Tom began searching for a deeper understanding of his faith and praying every night. He began to speak of "an all-wise Providence."[565]

At sixteen, Tom became a school teacher for a period and was appointed constable of West Fork County at the age of seventeen.

In 1841, he was at the deathbed again of his brother, Warren, when he died of tuberculosis at the age of twenty. He'd lost both parents, his older sister, and now Warren. Laura was the only surviving sibling, but she was away living with other relatives, and he was alone again. He accepted Warren's death from a new interpretation of his faith.

In 1842, Thomas applied for an opening to West Point. Even though he lacked the classical education for the military academy, he knew if given the chance, he would strive harder than anyone to achieve success.

---

[565] Robertson, 17–19.

Losing the chance appointment to another, Tom held to his faith in God's will and that everything happened for a reason. This was just another stumbling block to test him.

Providentially, the young man who got the appointment decided after one day, that the military life wasn't for him and quit. Tom saw this as an obvious reward for passing the test of his faith and crammed for the entrance exam. He procured a reputable citizen to write a letter of introduction to the congressman of his district by walking through a rainstorm.

Late in the evening, answering his door, this influential attorney saw the young man soaked from head to foot, pleading for a chance to attend West Point. He asked Tom if he believed he could maintain the academic standard if he got the chance, and the drenched youth lifted his head and said, "I know I shall have the application necessary to succeed. I hope that I have the capacity. At least I am determined to try, and I wish you to help me to do this."[566]

The attorney was impressed with his ambition and sense of purpose, so he wrote the letter and knew there was more to success than just formal education. Motivation mattered greatly, and this unknown young man had the makings of greatness. He received the appointment.

Tom struggled the four years at the academy but demanded more of himself than any other cadet. He studied by candlelight after lights out, and slowly, he raised his grades.

The other cadets saw him as strange, awkward, and a little crazy. His countenance was stern, and he rarely smiled, though he was extremely shy; these first impressions decided for many that he was cold. This reserve was simply a defense mechanism from his fear of loss, and his distance protected him from it. Besides, he was way too busy studying and drilling to make friendships to compensate for his educational deficiencies.

He was also a hypochondriac and believed in odd remedies and cures. This most likely developed from the fear of an early death. After all, his whole family, except Laura, had died young, and com-

---

[566] Jackson, 31; Robertson, 25.

mon sense told him he might as well. Complaining of digestive problems, he believed certain foods caused these symptoms while others healed them. He possibly had irritable bowel syndrome because he often claimed a bland diet had kept it in check and ate very little, because food was nothing but necessity. He never ate for enjoyment and disciplined his mind to control any urges. Refusing to indulge in tobacco, gambling, or drinking alcohol he devised a list of axioms to govern his behavior:

> Sacrifice your life rather than your word. Spare no effort to suppress selfishness. Temperance: Eat not to dullness, drink not to elevation. Resolve to perform what you ought: perform without fail what you resolve. It is man's highest interest not to violate, or attempt, to violate, the rules which Infinite Wisdom has laid down. It is not desirable to have a large number of intimate friends.[567]

This was a code of discipline he used to reach the top third of his graduating class of 1846. It was believed by many if he had one more year, he would have made it to the top five easily.

The year of his graduation, the war with Mexico was heating up and he was ready to prove himself in action. In charge of an artillery company, the young lieutenant arrived in Mexico in 1847, and after a bombardment of the town of Vera Cruz and its capitulation, he proved himself at the Battle of Cerro Gordo. Under the command of General Winfield Scott, he showed a propensity for getting the job accomplished with few complaints. The victory at Cerro Gordo taught him about swift flanking movements, pursuit of the enemy, and crushing opposition before it had time to react.

Right before the attack on Mexico City, Tom was ordered to the rear, and the possibility of missing battle was disheartening. Once again, he felt God was trying to teach him something, so he accepted his will. "I throw myself into the hands of an all wise God and hope

---

[567] Ibid., 35–38; Robertson, 36, 154–155.

that it may yet be for the better. It may have been one of his means of diminishing my excessive ambition and after having accomplished his purpose, whatever it may be, he then in his infinite wisdom may gratify my desire."[568]

His faith paid off again. A month later, Santa Anna and 30,000 Mexicans blocked General Scott's path into Mexico City, requiring all available forces back to the front. At the Battle of Contreras, Tom was pivotal to victory and refused to give up his ground. He received a promotion to captain and was commended for bravery.

The new captain's real test came in the Battle of Chapultepec, where advancing infantry under fire by Mexican artillery needed this removed, and Tom's company was called on.

Out in the open, under continuous fire, his men had a grim time as the shells exploded and bullets whirred past heads, unnerving his troops.

Walking back and forth in front of the cowering soldiers was Captain Jackson, yelling, "There is no danger. See? I am not hit!"

Just as he said this, an artillery shell careened between his open legs, barely missing him. This act of unbelievable courage inspired one man who came forward to help. Together they moved the cannon into place and held back the Mexican army long enough for General William J. Worth to call his retreat. Tom suggested to the general that pulling back would be a larger risk than staying and fighting, and Worth saw the logic of the young captain's words and reconsidered. Just then, the entire army artillery moved forward to support them, and Worth moved his infantry forward, pushing the enemy back.

This seemingly insignificant action became the turning point in the battle, and General Worth said of Tom's performance, "The gallant Lieutenant Jackson...continued dangerously at his post, combating with noble courage."

After the fall of Mexico City, General Scott invited all his officers to a victory reception and greeted his guests as they arrived.

---

[568] Robertson, 57–59.

When Tom was introduced to him, he said, "I don't know if I will shake hands with Mr. Jackson."

The room became silent, and all eyes were on the young officer. Lowering his head and blushing, he felt like retreating now.

Speaking again, the commander jovially said, "If you can forgive yourself for the way in which you slaughtered those poor Mexicans with your guns, I am not sure that I can!" Reaching out his hand and smiling, Scott waited for his hand, and Tom grabbed the big man's paw, smiling as the room erupted in applause.

Promoted to brevet major soon after battle, he earned the most promotions of any officer throughout the Mexican War. Years later, Tom recounted his actions at the Battle of Chapultepec, saying, "It would have been no disgrace to have died there, but to have failed to gain my point it would."[569]

After the war, Major Thomas Jackson returned to peacetime service and realized it wasn't the same as combat duty. After a lengthy feud with one of his commanders, he resigned his commission and accepted an offer as a professor of natural and experimental philosophy at the Virginia Military Institute in Lexington. The cadet who had to work harder than the others to overcome his lack of an education was now teaching. Though a true tactician, teaching wasn't his gift. Memorizing sections from books, he taught word for word to his students and expected them to do the same. His pupils found him dull and strict but, in time, came to respect the eccentric teacher regardless.

Soon after taking the teaching job, he fell in love and was married in August 1853. Ellie Junkin Jackson was Tom's world and helped fill the empty space he lost when his mother died, and his fear of losing someone he loved weakened and he was content.

She became pregnant in 1854, but the pregnancy was not routine. Though Tom beamed with pride at his young wife, he was concerned when she went into labor. Ellie had complications, and the baby was born stillbirth. He fought back the tears for now, because his wife wasn't out of danger yet. He prayed to God to spare his wife,

---

[569] Jackson, 41–43; Robertson, 66–70.

and at first, she seemed to recover, but she soon took a turn for the worse. She hemorrhaged and died, and much like before, he lost everything he loved.

After her burial, he stayed at the grave long after the others left and was haunted by the memory of her holding their young son in her arms for all eternity. Why did everyone he loved die? he wondered. Writing to Laura, he held firm to his faith. "I have been called to pass through the deep waters of affliction… It is his will that my Dearest wife and child should no longer abide with me…I can willingly submit to anything if God strengthens me." He did not curse God but depended on him even more to assuage the pain. Writing in his book of maxims, he said, "Objects to be affected by Ellie's Death: to eradicate ambition, to eradicate resentment, to produce humility. If you desire to be more heavenly minded, think more of the things of Heaven and less of things of Earth."[570]

His favorite Bible verses were Romans 8:28, "And we know that all things work together for good to them that love God, to them who are the called according to his purpose," and Philippians 4:13, "I can do all things through Christ which strengthens me." He relied upon them and repeated these throughout his life. They provided comfort, but his grief overwhelmed him at times, and he said to a friend, "I do not see the Purpose of God in this, the most bitter, trying affliction of my life, but I will try to be submissive though it breaks my heart." He needed to grieve, even though he believed too much grief was disobedience to God. It was a matter of faith to him, but his inability to rejoice that Ellie and his son were the lucky ones in heaven made him doubt the strength of that faith. What he failed to understand was that he was flesh and blood and needed to grieve to move forward. He would never find happiness for those in heaven without first grieving for his loss and turned inward thinking of his own death, exclaiming, "Ah, if I might only please God to let me go now!"[571]

---

[570] Ibid., 85; Robertson, 157–159.
[571] Ibid., 61, 73, 248; Robertson, 160.

He would eventually pry himself from despair and wrote to Ellie's brother George, "I cannot realize that Ellie is gone, that my wife will no more cheer the rugged and dark way of life. The thought rushes upon me that it is insupportable—insupportable! But one upward glance of the eye of faith, gives a return, that all is well, and that I can do all things through Christ that strengthens me."[572]

Leaning on his faith, he decided to tell others about it. This was his purpose, and doing God's will healed his pain. "I am where God would have me be..." He helped spread the good news of the gospel to the slaves in Lexington. "My Heavenly Father has condescended to use me as an instrument in getting up a large Sabbath-school for the negroes here." Blacks weren't taught the Bible, but he felt it was his duty to "redeem them from the slavery of sin."

Virginia law made it illegal to teach reading and writing to slaves, but Tom felt the slaves were God's children and needed his blessings and salvation like everyone. He didn't believe in slavery but accepted it as God's will or it wouldn't be so, and believed if it be his will, they would be freed. His classes had nearly a hundred students, and he was highly respected by blacks as well as whites in Lexington.[573]

* * * * *

St. Louis, Missouri, December 23, 1857

It had to be done. He couldn't let his family down now. They were depending on him. Reaching into a coat pocket, he touched the cold metal one last time. It wasn't what respectable men did, but it must be done.

Walking along the street, he searched for the name of the shop, J. S. Freligh. This was the place. Feeling the cherished object again, he resolved to continue and just went in without thinking. He'd think about it tomorrow.

---

[572] Robertson, 163.
[573] Ibid., 168–169; Jackson, 60.

A few minutes later, he exited the establishment. Apprehensive, he glanced at the paper in his hand again. "One gold hunting detached lever watch and gold chain, $22.00." Below was an agreement to pay back the twenty-two dollars by January 23, 1858—make a new loan or forfeit the watch.

His gold watch was gone, and if he couldn't raise the money in a month, it may be gone permanently. That watch meant the world to him, but Julia and the children meant more. They had to have presents for Christmas, and they were expecting a new baby in a few weeks. She didn't need to worry.

Pocketing the receipt, he smiled. This was the price for failure. His wheat, oats, and corn were worthless in this depression, and the Panic of 1857 hit the country hard and nearly destroyed the farm. Failing multiple times at moneymaking ventures, including farming, he finally felt like he had it this time. It was time for something to succeed. But no, the timing was off, and the wheat production was too low. You couldn't sell crops to those who couldn't buy them.

Oh, well, pawning the watch was just another adjustment. He adjusted and adapted to circumstances his whole life, and this time was no different. He may have to depend on his father after all, but he wanted to prove himself without his help.

In fact, it seemed everything Ulysses Simpson Grant tried failed. For the last few years, he had been cutting trees on his land and hauling it over a dozen miles to St. Louis to sell on the street. Whatever he had to do to support his family, he would do—even swallowing his pride.

Losing the watch would be worth it when he saw the smiles on his family's faces Christmas morning. He thought of his return from the Mexican War so penniless, he had to borrow money from Simon Bolivar Buckner to get home. That was humiliating enough, but asking a passerby if they wanted to buy firewood felt like hitting bottom.

Scratching his auburn whiskers, he removed his floppy black hat, and the frosty air cooled his head.

At five foot seven, he was skinny and didn't possess a commanding bearing, but he never cared about his size or demeanor and simply wanted to make a living. This was all he asked from life, yet he walked into a disaster every time, and no matter what he tried, he could not make it work. He tried the army, but it led him to drink from the boredom and missing his family. He'd failed so many times, he stopped counting, but somehow, he kept trying because giving up was not in him.

What was an old washed-up army officer-turned-farmer going to accomplish now? He was nearly forty and way past his prime, and it was too late for him. Maybe he should hope for one of the boys to find success. Maybe he'd wasted his chance with bad decisions, and this was it.

Oh, well, he thought, he'd work on it tomorrow.[574]

* * * * *

Ulysses S. Grant was born in Ohio in 1822, and as a boy was gifted when it came to handling horses. His father, Jesse, owned a tannery, but the smell of blood and rotting carcasses made Ulysses physically sick, and he vowed to never work there. He had a delicate relationship with Jesse and could never live up to the expectations of the aspiring businessman. Where his father was energetic and ambitious, Ulysses was slow to decide, but knew he didn't want to follow in his father's footsteps, yet he still wanted to please him.

By the time he was a teenager, the tannery was quite successful. Knowing the boy wanted no part of the tannery, Jesse believed the army would be perfect for his restless son with no direction. He just needed some discipline to set him right, and with Jesse's clout in the community, he managed to get Ulysses appointed to West Point in 1838 at the age of sixteen.

Arriving the following year at the academy, he started off on the wrong foot. His actual birth name was Hiram Ulysses Grant, and many warned him he would receive the nickname HUG, so

---

[574] Lewis, Lloyd. *Captain Sam Grant, 1822–1861.* (Boston: Little, Brown and Co., 1950), 354, 358; Smith, Jean Edward. *Grant.* (New York: Simon & Schuster, 2001), 92.

he changed his name to Ulysses Hiram Grant. When he reported for duty, he found the wrong name on his application because the academy registered him as Ulysses Simpson Grant. The senator who appointed him thought his middle name was his mother's maiden name and inadvertently renamed him. With West Point's strict adherence to the rules, Ulysses accepted the new name and never bothered to changed it back. A paperwork mistake was responsible for one of the most famous names in history.

Grant entered the academy smaller and younger than the average cadet. Only five-foot-one and one hundred and fifteen pounds, everyone treated him like a kid. His new name earned him the nickname of Sam because his initials happened to be US, like Uncle Sam, so the name stuck.

Sam wanted to go home from the start and wasn't fond of the army. He would never purposely get expelled but planned on leaving when his enlistment was up. He figured he would do his best since the United States government was footing the bill for his education and felt he owed his country this much.

After graduating, he was stationed at Jefferson Barracks near St. Louis, Missouri and there met Julia Dent. This romance was interrupted by the Mexican War in 1846, when he was ordered to report for duty.[575] He then found himself in Texas with General Zachary Taylor, and the young lieutenant was impressed with the general's countenance and style of dress. He also liked the way Taylor gave orders and left it up to the officers to get it done. Wearing a simple black tunic and a straw hat with no epaulets, braid, or pomp, Taylor was plain spoken and acted like one of them. He never demanded loyalty by his rank but depended on his results for earning respect. Sam never forgot Taylor's style of leading and would model it in the future.[576]

Participating in the opening battles of the war, Sam's talent for organization and transport landed him in the quartermaster department. He was responsible for supplying the troops with ammuni-

---

[575] Grant, Vol. 1, 43–46; Lewis, 61–63.
[576] Ibid., 100–102; Smith, Jean, 40.

tion, food, horses, wagons, canteens, and shoes. To some, this position would be a relief to acquire a safer role in the war, but Sam
made sure to personally deliver wagons to the frontline and join in
the fighting. At the Battle of Monterey, he charged with the leading
regiment. He was there to fight, not sit safely in the rear. Once a
colonel warned the spunky young lieutenant, "Remember we are in
an enemy's country, that enemy alert and enterprising. Be careful to
always temper bravery with prudence and caution."

Grant replied, "Yes, caution I will observe, but when there's not
more than two of him to one of me, we'll have a fight. That's what
we are here for."[577]

Though he later wrote he was opposed to the Mexican War,
Grant was first and foremost a soldier, and no matter his views of it
later in life, he held very different views when he wrote Julia about it.
"If these Mexicans were any kind of people they would have given us
a chance to whip them enough some time ago and now the difficulty
would be over; but I believe they think they will outdo us by keeping
us running over the country after them."[578]

He realized that occupying territory mattered little if an enemy
force was still there, and conquering land was pointless if you failed
to crush the enemy's army.

With this inner toughness and eagerness for combat, he also
recognized the horrific nature of war. He was once observed tending
to his wounded comrades on the field instead of joining the fight.
Playing quartermaster, infantryman, and medic, he multitasked and
learned much others did not.

His bravery during battle was never suspect, and at the Battle
of Monterey, Sam was in the middle of the house to house fighting
inside the city. The Americans became separated from their lines with
ammunition running low, and Sam volunteered to ride through the
withering fire to get help. Mounting a horse and riding it Indian style
(hanging off one side of the horse and using it as a shield), he made
it through the lines, and his comrades were rescued. Later, Grant

---

[577] Lewis, 185.
[578] Ibid., 170 (To Julia Dent, September 6, 1846).

downplayed the event, but many remembered the brave scrappy lieutenant who saved them.[579]

Much of the time, American forces waited for the Mexicans to appear instead of spending energy chasing them, and this meant way too much idleness and boredom for the young men far from home. It was a predictable recipe for trouble.

Drinking was a problem which led to a myriad of bigger problems. Prostitutes were rampant in every town, and lonely, young, and intoxicated men frequented them. Drinking and gambling were the most popular way to pass time, and Sam wasn't an exception. There were a few incidences of crimes against the Mexican people, but offenders were usually punished, though Taylor often relied on his underlings, and some crimes were swept under the rug. Taylor made clear to the troops that the army's policy in Mexico was one of respect for persons, private property, and their Catholic faith. The idea of winning hearts and minds of a conquered foe was an old one, and just like any demographic, there were those who broke the law. Every time an American committed a rape, theft, or murder, the entire army was blamed by Mexico and many anti-war advocates. Real criminals were usually prosecuted, but war with a hostile populace made it impossible to verify every accusation.

This was the environment where Sam developed his famous drinking problem. He wasn't a daily drinker but a binger, though a little went a long way, and his low tolerance for alcohol contributed to his easy inebriation. Knowing he had a low tolerance may have kept him from drinking more often, but when he did, it made him an obvious drunk.

After Taylor conquered half of Mexico, President Polk sent Major General Winfield Scott to finish the rest. Grant was ordered to join Scott's force for the rest of the war but always preferred General Taylor's style to the flashy Scott. Sam's adoration for Taylor didn't blind him to Scott's brilliant strategies and risky maneuvers, and learning both generals' styles of leading gave him an advantage over men who only learned one. These lessons seemed inconsequential to

---

[579] Grant, Vol. 1, 116–118; Smith, Jean, 56; Lewis, 177–179.

him at the time, but they would pay dividends later.[580] During this time with Scott, he met fellow officers P. G. T. Beauregard, Robert E. Lee, George B. McClellan, and others who would command armies during the Civil War.

Grant had a vital role in the battle which finally took Mexico City in 1847, essentially ending the war, and his experience taught him many lessons he would never forget. Just before returning home, he wrote Julia his views on Mexico:

> I pity Mexico. With a soil and climate scarcely equaled in the world she has more poor and starving subjects who are willing and able to work than any country in the world. The rich keep down the poor with hardness of heart that is incredible. Walk through the streets of Mexico for one day and you will see hundreds of beggars, but you never see them ask alms of their own people, it is always from the Americans that they expect to receive.[581]

In June of 1848, the American Army boarded ships and headed for home. Sam remarked that the Mexican people seemed sad to see them go. "As the Army passed out of their towns, crowds of these poor people surrounded our troops and threw bouquets of fruit to the soldiers and many of them wept most piteously, crying out that they had lost their only friends."[582]

His later opposition to the war may possibly be rooted in this view because he sympathized with the common people who suffered by the war, not the Mexican government and the system which oppressed them. He later developed a political bias against President Polk, a southern slave owner, and believed he started the war with Mexico for the acquisition of new slave states. Jesse had always been

---

[580] Ibid., 138–139.
[581] Lewis, 276; Smith, Jean, 71.
[582] Ibid., 278.

a staunch antislavery man, and his family concurred. Illinois and Ohio held strong antislavery views, and Sam was no different. He did, however, see it as a regretful reality protected by law, and those who wanted civil war to end it had little comprehension of the horror a civil war would bring.

In the summer of 1848, Grant rode up to Julia's house in St. Louis a different man. On August 22, they were married, and after a short honeymoon, Sam was ordered to report to Sackett's Harbor, New York. Julia joined him and even managed to get him to stop drinking, which was a habit by this time, and these were happy days for the young couple but short-lived. Julia gave birth to a boy, Fred, and Sam's life seemed complete, but soon after, he was ordered to the Pacific Coast, and Julia and Fred remained behind. There was no family housing in San Francisco, and California was still an untamed place of hostile Indians, outlaws, and disease. Their safety and his lack of funds for their passage made it impossible to bring his new family along. He was furious but duty-bound and boarded a steamship headed for Panama.[583]

With a canal still years away, the trip to California by ship was anything but routine. The steamer left the east coast bound for Panama, and once there, the passengers continued overland until they reached the west coast. There they boarded another ship for the rest of the journey up the coast to San Francisco. The treacherous part of this trip was the country of Panama which was riddled with disease. Its humid jungles were ideal for outbreaks of malaria and cholera, and Sam found himself in the middle of an epidemic.

Men, women, and children were dying all around him, and he was thankful Julia and the baby had remained behind. They both likely would have died. One of his good friends, Major John Gore, collapsed right in front of him, dying a few days later.

Sam lent money to Gore's widow after all her valuables were stolen by Indians a few days later, and he helped the sick by lending them money to return home and pay for their care. He tended to them himself, making sure they safely made it to their return trans-

---

[583] Grant, Vol. 1, 193; Lewis, 287.

port. Likened to "a ministering angel" by one of the passengers, he learned then that disease was a greater threat to an army than bullets and shrapnel.[584]

Arriving in San Francisco in September of 1854, Grant settled in for the worst period of his life so far. His second son, Ulysses S. Grant Jr., was born, and he wasn't there. Missing the boys growing up, caused him to slide into a depression. Homesick, bored, and depressed, he quickly turned to alcohol.

This period of finding company in a bottle would haunt Grant his whole life, and he could never live down the label of drunk. Like Sam Houston, he would wear the label forever.

This was also the period where he learned about failure and attempted several business ventures. First, he tried raising crops to sell, but a flood wiped them out. Next, he tried again while selling firewood to steamboats down river but never made any money. He even tried to transport chickens (a rare find in California at the time) to sell, but they died before they reached him. Everything he tried ended in failure, and military living was making him miserable.[585] Writing to Julia, he said, "So anxious to see you and our little boys, that I am almost tempted to resign, and trust to Providence, and my own exertions for a living where I can have you and them with me."[586]

After two years of separation from his family, he resigned from the army. Some accounts point to drinking as the reason. One story states that his commander gave him the option to resign or face a court-martial for being drunk on duty, but Grant chose resignation and left no evidence of the charge. This unofficial claim was a thorn in his flesh which he carried the rest of his life. When he made a mistake in the future, it would always be because of his drunkenness, regardless of the truth.

---

[584] Ibid., 197–199; Lewis, 301–303; Smith, Jean, 79.
[585] Lewis, 318–319, 324; Smith, Jean, 83–85.
[586] Smith, Jean, 86.

His resignation was accepted by Secretary of War Jefferson Davis, future President of the Confederacy, and he returned to St. Louis, Julia, his sons, and his future.[587]

* * * * *

A mountain pass near Rio del Plan, Mexico, April 15, 1847

The Mexican soldiers enjoyed the cool water from the ravine and knew the Yankees were nearby. He understood this much Spanish, but concentrating under the circumstances was difficult. He had been frozen there for some time, and it seemed like they would never leave. Even worse, he was so close—he could reach out and touch them.

Luckily for Robert E. Lee, they had no idea he was right behind them. Laying in the grass behind a log with the enemy all around was one thing, but when the two Mexicans sat down on that same log, it was too much. Would they ever go or would they discover him? Lying motionless for hours and barely breathing, they simply needed to turn around to see him. They had to discover him, and it was insane to think they wouldn't, but maybe the audacity of it all would blind them. The fact it was so unthinkable is what made it possible, and who would think an enemy soldier would hide behind the very log they chose to rest on way behind their own lines?

General Winfield Scott wanted to know if Santa Anna's 12,000-man army could be turned on its flank. For this information, Scott needed a scout to locate the enemy position and find the best route for a surprise attack, Captain Lee was just the man for this important task.

He'd recently been appointed to Scott's staff of advisors, and after his notable service with General Wool and his previous reconnaissance of the enemy near Vera Cruz, the commander was too

---

[587] Ibid., 86–89; Lewis, 330–332.

impressed not to grab him for himself. Up until then, Lee had missed out on most of the action of the war and was vocal about serving.

Now a trusted member of the commanding general's inner circle, the current information he had to report was going to affect the next battle and maybe the entire war, if he could remain undiscovered.

Close calls were becoming a common occurrence lately, but he didn't mind. A month before, he had nearly been killed when a frightened American sentry mistook him as an enemy soldier and fired his pistol at him. The shot flew between his arm and torso, burning his jacket and missing him by a hair. By the grace of God, he believed he was spared.

A few days after this close call, he saw his first action. As an engineer, he was responsible for construction of fortifications and ramparts, but the day he saw action, he commanded the cannons which brought the city of Vera Cruz to surrender.

It had all happened so fast, and now he was stuck here, inches from the enemy, and it might all be over with the twist of a head and a willingness to see reality. He had so much to do in this war still, but if it was God's will he be captured, he would accept it.

As the darkness thickened, the two enemy soldiers rose and left the stream. Waiting some time to be sure they were gone, he slowly stood and was stiff from laying in a frozen position for so long. He had trouble at first, and his joints didn't forgive as much as they used to. He had just turned forty and noticed the difference. Refusing to wait for the blood to work its way into his extremities, he rushed to get back to headquarters with this information.

Quickly but quietly, he started back. Behind enemy lines with crucial intel on the Mexican army, anxiously he proceeded. The path near the stream led right to Santa Anna's left flank and could end this war if he could get back fast enough.

On the way down the pass, Lee struck a tree and slipped, tumbling down a ravine. Pulling himself up, shaken but unhurt, he continued. With sore joints and the rugged terrain, he refused to focus on the pain for even a moment. He had to get back. There was more at stake here than just his hide. He understood the meaning of sacrifice and denying his own wants. His whole life had been an example of it.[588]

* * * * *

Robert Edward Lee was born on January 19, 1807, in the same county in Virginia where George Washington was born—Westmoreland County.

Not only was he born in the same area, but his father was General Washington's most trusted cavalry leader and friend, General "Light Horse Harry" Lee. Returning from the war, Harry Lee had some minor success but lost everything in the Panic of 1797 and ended up in a debtor's prison. During the War of 1812, Harry Lee was a staunch Federalist and was victim of a brutal attack during the Baltimore Riot. He was beaten so severely, some said he was never the same and began drinking, gambling, and living beyond his means. He died in 1818 after an absence from home for five years, leaving his wife and children to fend for themselves.

His mother, Anne Hill Carter, was the anchor in Robert's life and taught him self-discipline, perseverance, and frugality. She was worried about her son following his father's path, and she made certain he had a proper education with a foundation in Christian principles. His mother and sister Ann were invalids, and by the age of eleven, Robert had assumed the sole responsibility for their care. To him, this was a son's duty to his family, not a burden, and he never neglected them or complained. This self-discipline and compassion trained the young man for patience and empathy for others and would serve him well throughout his life.

Most young boys in America, especially in Virginia, idolized the example of George Washington. Robert's own father knew him, and he felt somehow connected to the icon. Washington was his standard of what one should strive to emulate in character and actions. His

---

[588] Freeman, *Lee*, 58–60.

own father was a great fighter, but George Washington's integrity and accomplishments were everything Henry Lee was not.[589]

He was forced to become an adult early with care of his family, but he would swim and fish like other boys. He was always considerate, responsible, and a model son and serious about following in Washington's footsteps.

In July of 1825, he received an appointment to West Point and graduated second in his class of forty-six cadets. He received no demerits the entire four years and chose to be an engineer. His mother died the same year he graduated, and he returned home to settle her estate. While there, he met Mary Anne Randolph Custis who helped fill the void left by his mother. She was also related to his idol, Washington. Her father, George Washington Parke Custis, was the step-grandson of the general. His father was John Parke Custis, Martha's son who the first president adopted as his own.

Mary Custis's father was the official keeper of Washington's memory, and Robert held in his own hands objects his hero held. His courtship with Mary seemed to be predestined. Luckily, the young officer was stationed nearby, not some faraway frontier, so he and Mary had opportunity to court and, in 1831, were married. In personality, the two were complete opposites. Robert was organized, disciplined, and focused, and Mary was forgetful, unpunctual, and unstructured. These two different personalities created harmony in the relationship. He taught her the value of responsibility, and she showed him the value of taking life less seriously. He adored Mary, and she was proud of her dashing husband.[590]

After a short honeymoon, he was ordered to Fort Monroe, Virginia, and was stationed in Virginia for ten years as an engineer stranded in an office most of the time busy with paperwork. It was easy duty, but he wanted to be in the field.

His next station was Jefferson Barracks, near St. Louis, Missouri. The Mississippi River was obstructing river traffic and threatening to make St. Louis an obsolete city. He was chosen for his talent to over-

---

[589] Ibid., 9–11.
[590] Ibid., 14–15, 27–28.

see the cutting of a channel to divert the river and relieve the city. After successfully redirecting the river, he was moved to Iowa and New York to help with their river problems.

Mary and Robert had seven children—three sons: Custis, Rooney, and Robert Jr.; and four daughters: Mary, Anne, Eleanor, and Mildred. His large brood was dear to him, and though he was a strict patriarch, he was always fair. He did expect his children to live up to their potential and adhere to Christian ethics but knew when to play and show affection too. He was remembered as a playful and loving father by his children.[591]

His career was a different matter, and the army offered little opportunity for advancement. He'd spent fifteen years in service and was still only a captain. With only two promotions in all those years and no active duty, he began to believe his hope to be like Washington was slipping away. He was a bureaucrat instead of a warrior, and this frustration and his commitment to family pushed him to consider leaving the army. An engineer could make decent money in civilian life, and the army appeared a dead-end job unless there was a war.

Just as his dreams seemed to be lost, the Mexican War intervened, and in August of 1846, he was ordered to report to General John E. Wool in Mexico, and he left immediately determined to make his mark.

* * * * *

Returning to headquarters after running down the ravine, Lee reported to Scott that Santa Anna's left flank could be turned, and the general ordered the attack, making Robert the guide to lead the army around it.

On April 17, 1847, the Battle of Cerro Gordo commenced, and for two days, Captain Lee was everywhere, directing troops around the flank and leading the force which cut off the Mexican retreat.

---

[591] Lee, Robert E. Jr. *Recollections and Letters of General Robert E. Lee.* (New York: Doubleday, Page and Co., 1909), 8–10; Freeman, *Lee,* 37–39.

The Americans routed Santa Anna's army and captured nearly every cannon along with three thousand prisoners.

Scott praised Lee's service and promoted him to the rank of brevet major (a temporary battlefield promotion). He was then given the responsibility for scouting enemy positions and finding routes around enemy flanks at the Battles of Contreras, Churubusco, Molina del Rey, and Chapultepec. Chapultepec was the decisive battle which bagged Mexico City and ended the war. Lee assisted Scott on the plan of the final attack on the city and commanded troops in the field. Working to exhaustion for nearly forty hours without sleep, he passed out, and after a couple of hours of rest, he returned to his post. His spirit was willing, even when his body wasn't.

For his service, he was promoted two more times to brevet colonel. The general formed a high opinion of Lee and expected a bright future of the brilliant officer. His work and perseverance changed his path, and he was closer to following in Washington's footsteps.[592]

A few days after the final attack on Mexico City, he said, "I endeavored to give thanks to our Heavenly Father for all His mercies to me, for His preservation of me through all the dangers I have passed, and all the blessings which He has bestowed upon, for I know I fall short of my obligations."

After humbling himself and thanking God, he made clear what guided him. "We must trust to an overruling Providence by whom we will be governed for the best, and to our own resources."[593]

After the Mexican War, Robert returned to engineering duty in Baltimore, Maryland. Being close to home was a blessing, and though he loved his family, he soon felt the frustration of inaction again.

In 1852, he was appointed superintendent of West Point. This appointment was a reward for his performance in Mexico, but Lee wasn't happy with the post and as always, he took it in stride and did his duty. He tried to save problem cadets who faced dismissal and to

---

[592] Freeman, *Lee*, 61–63.
[593] Jones, J. William. *Life and Letters of Robert Edward Lee, Soldier and Man.* (New York: The Neale Publishing Co., 1906), 52 (Perote, April 25, 1847).

be fair and merciful when he could. Troubled cadets were priority, and he visited any who were sick or struggling. Sometimes he wrote to parents to give encouragement and assure them it was not a matter of character when one was dismissed.

Though compassionate, he was also a disciplinarian in much the same way he raised his children. There wasn't any yelling or harsh punishment, but standards must be met. He used mutual respect to guide the cadets, and if God could guide his own children with doses of grace and judgment, then he would try as well. His son, Robert Jr., explained that once his father told him to do something, it was never doubted that he wouldn't be obeyed. He was fair, but once he said something, he meant it.[594]

Mary's mother died in 1853, and Lee tried to comfort her by sharing a belief he would rely on many times. "May God give you strength to enable you to bear and say, "His will be done." She has gone from all trouble, care, and sorrow to a holy immortality, there to rejoice and praise forever the God and Saviour she so long truly served. Let that be our comfort and that our consolation. May our death be like hers, and may we meet in happiness in Heaven."[595]

Even though he submitted to God's will, he still longed for a field command. The Indian uprisings in Texas made it necessary for Secretary of War, Jefferson Davis, to form four new regiments for duty in Texas. In March of 1855, Lee left his easy superintendent job at West Point and joined the Second Cavalry as a lieutenant-colonel, serving under Colonel Albert Sidney Johnston.

After three years of service on the frontier, he headed home to settle the estate of George Washington Parke Custis, Mary's father, who recently died. Mary was now suffering from a debilitating arthritis and had a tough time caring for herself.

---

[594] Lee, 9, 12–13; Freeman, *Lee*, 86.
[595] Lee, 18–19.

Much like his mother and sister, Robert again accepted the care-giver role without complaint. He would serve God in whatever way he willed.

* * * * *

Brewer, Maine, 1840s

"Clear that wheel!" the grizzled man shouted.

The wagon wheel was stuck between two tree stumps, and to make matters worse, there was an entire load of hay on it.

"How am I going to do it?" the boy asked his father, assuming he didn't understand the impossibility of the command.

"Do it, that's how!" he stoically replied.

Do it—this was all he had to say? What did he think his young son was? A miracle worker? Seeing his father's expression told him the old man was dead serious and expected his son to accomplish the task at hand.

Agitated, he sprang from the wagon, gripped the wheel, and rocked it back and forth. This jerking surprised the oxen pulling the wagon and caused them to lunge forward, lifting the wheel clear of the stump.

Joshua Chamberlain couldn't believe his eyes. It was a miracle of sorts. His father spoke not a word, and they continued their work.

He would always remember the wisdom of his father and the lesson he learned that day. When a problem presented itself, he wouldn't ask how; he would just do it and that would be the solution. Decide to accomplish something, regardless of the difficulty, and then do it.[596]

Lawrence Joshua Chamberlain was born in 1828 just east of the Penobscot River in Maine. Named after Commodore James Lawrence of the USS Chesapeake who cried his dying words, "Don't give up the ship" during the War of 1812. His father, Joshua Chamberlain Jr., was also a veteran from that war and an independent-minded Yankee

---

[596] Trulock, 33, 52.

who named another son, John Calhoun, in honor of the states' rights, South Carolinian. Lawrence, as he was known to family and friends, began using his middle name to honor his father and the proud family name.[597]

Growing up on a farm, the boy learned the value of hard work and never shied away from it. He helped with the haying, wood chopping, plowing, and clearing the land and quickly packed lean muscle on his thin frame. Recreation was horseback riding, swimming, sailing, and practicing fencing with broadswords with his father. This work ethic and masculine pursuits along with sagely fatherly advice instilled in him a determination which benefited him in all his future pursuits. Rising from mere student to professor of languages at Bowdoin College, he secured a comfortable living and soon married Fannie Adams.[598]

As the national debate over slavery heated up, Joshua gave his opinion of the issue. "The fathers of the Republic found slavery an existing fact and had to deal with it. Some long-recognized property rights were involved in it, and relative wrong would be done by its immediate abolition." He went on to describe slavery as "repugnant to justice and freedom," and should be "limited, not extended—repress[ed], not encouraged." He did believe "some way should be found to satisfy equitable rights of property, and wipe the blot off from our escutcheon."[599]

His religious beliefs told him everything worked for the will of God, even stuck wagon wheels and slavery. If God intended the wagon to move, through his elect children, it would move. If he intended an end to slavery, through his elect, it would end. "I believe that God is over all things and that he will put me where he wants me and where I ought to be." His purpose was God's choosing, not his own.[600]

---

[597] Ibid., 26.
[598] Ibid., 32, 37.
[599] Ibid., 59.
[600] Ibid., 52.

Just do it was genius, and the seemingly simplistic view was the true answer to man-made complexities of life. This had helped him overcome his speech impediment and to excel in college and was the maxim he lived by. The belief that God directed his steps as he followed his father's advice would one day prove critical in the future of that nation he hoped to "wipe the blot off from our escutcheon."

* * * * *

Abraham Lincoln idolized Henry Clay and wanted to follow his example, but just like Clay, he would not compromise his core principles. When slavery became front and center, he made sure his views were crystal clear.

Senator Stephen A. Douglas of Illinois became the new star in Congress and in 1854, introduced the Kansas-Nebraska Bill, pushing it through both houses. This law allowed new states to determine their own course concerning slavery, and the Missouri Compromise was essentially voided, many supporters of the new bill claimed. This popular sovereignty coined by Douglas and other Democrats said the people in the states decided their own course, not the federal government. Lincoln felt this was absurd. The founders did everything they could to halt the spread of slavery and compromised, but they wanted it contained. They knew marginalizing it would cause the institution to die of his own accord. He believed the Democrats were attempting to expand it to the young states to gain new votes. One senator from Indiana proclaimed that "all men are created equal" as a "self-evident lie."[601] It seemed no one would defend the Declaration anymore, but Lincoln made his case.

Making the biggest speech of his life in Peoria, Illinois, on October 16, 1854, Lincoln meticulously peeled back the demagoguery to the logic why the spread of slavery was contrary to the American founding.

Douglas countered this with "all men were created equal, they meant all white men." This contradicted the previous defense on the

---

[601] Burlingame, Vol. 1, 386.

grounds of law. If slaves were considered property, not human as many proslavery advocates claimed, then how could the Declaration only consider white men? Douglas boxed himself in when he jumped on the skin color bandwagon and changed slavery from an issue of legality to one of race. "All men" proclaimed universal equality at birth, from God, without concern for race, and if slaves were men, then they were created equal as well. Some abolitionists felt slavery was inherent in the Constitution and was tainted from the founding, but Lincoln made the case that the founders purposely constructed the government to guarantee the eventual end to all human bondage.

He pointed to the Northwest Territory, which denied slavery, the Missouri Compromise, which banned it north of Missouri's southern border, and the Compromise of 1850, which upheld the Missouri Compromise. He said the Kansas-Nebraska Bill repealed eighty years of this containment of slavery, and in one law, was allowed everywhere. He explained his sole reason for despising the institution:

> I hate it because of the monstrous injustice of slavery itself. I hate it because it deprives our republican example of its just influence in the world: enables the enemies of free institutions with plausibility to taunt us as hypocrites; causes the real friends of freedom to doubt its sincerity; and especially because it forces so many good men among ourselves into an open war with the very fundamental principles of civil liberty, criticizing the Declaration of Independence, and insisting that there is no right principle of action but self-interest.

He went on to say he possessed no prejudice against southerners and understood they were merely protecting their own interests, just as northerners would if roles were reversed. "If slavery did not now exist among them, they would not introduce it. If it did now exist among us, we should not instantly give it up." It wasn't purely sectional, because people from both North and South supported and opposed slavery. He agreed with those who said the South was not responsible for slavery, and getting rid of it would be difficult. "I surely will not blame them for not doing what I should not know how to do myself... My first impulse would be to free all the slaves, and send them to Liberia, to their own native land."[602]

Appealing to southern humanity, he pointed out clear differences between property and men. They treated their own slaves different than their livestock in most cases but now were telling the North to see them the same:

> When the white man governs himself, that is self-government; but when he governs himself and also governs another man, that is more than self-government—that is despotism. If the negro is a man, why then my ancient faith teaches me that "all men are created equal" and there can be no moral right in connection with one man's making a slave of another...What I do say is that no man is good enough to govern another man without that other's consent. I say this is the leading principle, the sheet anchor of American republicanism.[603]

Slavery was counter to American freedom and human nature. The corruption in man was the source of the problem. "Slavery is founded in the selfishness of man's nature—opposition to it, in his love of justice. These principles are an eternal antagonism, and when brought into collision so fiercely as slavery extension brings them, shocks and throws and convulsions must ceaselessly follow. Repeal the Missouri Compromise, repeal all compromises, repeal the Declaration of Independence, repeal all the past history, you cannot

---

[602] Lincoln, *Works*, Vol. 2, 205–206 (Speech at Peoria, Illinois, October 16, 1854); Burlingame, Vol. 1, 379–380.
[603] Ibid., 227–228.

repeal human nature. It still will be the abundance of his heart that slavery extension is wrong and out of the abundance of his heart his mouth will continue to speak."[604]

By quoting Matthew 12:34 and Luke 6:45, he used the Bible to lend holy sanction and cited it to affirm equality of all men as a sacred right since some were now claiming slavery as one. He also used Matthew 6:24 to remind them that one couldn't serve two masters. "These principles cannot stand together. They are as opposite as God and Mammon; and whoever holds to the one must despise the other."[605] He compared the "sacred right" claim to the "divine right" of kings in the past. His Peoria speech was a hit throughout the North but cost him his latest bid to the Senate because of proslavery southerners in Illinois.[606]

Lincoln still considered himself a Whig then, even though the party was now extinct. The new Republican Party was still too radical for him at the time of his Peoria speech, but he eventually became a Republican and helped strengthen it in Illinois.

By 1856, Democrat James Buchanan was elected president over the Republican candidate, John C. Fremont. Buchanan was an old Jackson Democrat from Pennsylvania but supported popular sovereignty. In March of 1857, the Supreme Court handed down the Dred Scott decision—the repudiation of Lincoln's Peoria speech—which said blacks were not included in the Declaration's claim of "all men are created equal." The decision said Congress had no power to prohibit slavery in the new states, and to prohibit slaves, which were property, violated the Fifth Amendment by depriving property without due process. This decision made the Missouri Compromise unconstitutional as well. Seven Democrat justices concurred, while two Whig/Republicans dissented, making it a sectional and political decision.

Lincoln warned in 1858, "In my opinion, it will not cease until a crisis shall have been reached and passed. 'A house divided against

---

[604] Ibid., 238.
[605] Ibid., 246–247.
[606] Ibid., 253.

itself cannot stand.' I believe the government cannot endure permanently half slave and half free." This famous quote were the words of Jesus in Matthew 12:25 and found their mark. He continued, "I do not expect the Union to be dissolved—I do not expect the house to fall—but I do expect it will cease to be divided. It will become all one thing, or all the other."[607]

He refused to accept the Supreme Court's decision as the law of the land. Just because it handed down an opinion didn't make it right. Clearly along ideological lines, the decision didn't change the moral issue at stake simply because seven justices tried to change it. He would not alter his own beliefs and would fight against it until it was overturned by reason or divine justice.

Running for the Senate against Douglas in 1858, he won many supporters nationally among his party with the popular debates running up to the election. Though losing in the end, he was approached the following year about being a candidate for president of the United States. Another apparent failure resulted in a greater opportunity.

Thinking the suggestion lunacy, he thought they were pulling his leg. How could he compete with icons like William H. Seward of New York or Salmon P. Chase of Ohio? They were established men with years of experience in politics, and he was Abe Lincoln, a nobody from Illinois. He had failed in business, politics, and life, and all he had to show for it was a brief time in Congress, a small law practice, and a few well-received speeches. To him, everything he touched seemed to fall apart, but it seemed providence thrust him into the arena to be the most unlikely candidate for some larger purpose. Had all his failures been preparation for this?

In February of 1860, Lincoln travelled to New York and gave a riveting speech at Cooper Union. This kick-off to his candidacy was simply a summation of former speeches but garnered needed support. He called for a return to the original principles of the founding fathers, the majority of which opposed slavery and its extension.

---

[607] Ibid., Vol. 3, 2 (Springfield Speech, June 16, 1858); Burlingame, Vol. 1, 459.

Addressing those who called Republicans radical and the true radicalism of their own "sacred right" claim, he said:

> But you say you are conservative—eminently conservative—while we are revolutionary, destructive, or something of the sort. What is conservatism? Is it not adherence to the old and tried, against the new and untried? We stick to, contend for, the identical old policy on the point in controversy which was adopted by "our fathers who framed the government under which we live," while you with one accord reject, and scout, and spit upon substituting something new.[608]

Some were calling for war and violence to end the attempt to extend slavery, but he said this wasn't the answer. He did, however, call for patience and eventual victory over the scourge regardless.

In May, Lincoln read a telegram about the presidential nomination results at the Republican Convention in Chicago. Staring at the message for three minutes, he couldn't believe the words: "To Lincoln, you are nominated."

When he finally regained his composure, he said, "Well...we've got it."

In November, the national election appeared miraculous, and Lincoln won with only forty percent of the vote as Democrats divided their votes among two candidates. The northern Democrats nominated Stephen Douglas while southern Democrats nominated Vice President John C. Breckinridge of Kentucky, and a third party siphoned votes from both. Lincoln beat Douglas by less than 500,000 votes, and Breckinridge received 849,781 to deny Douglas victory.[609]

His election was an anomaly, a freak occurrence that happened once in a hundred years, and as if by chance, he'd lost previous elections to win this one.

---

[608] Ibid., Vol. 5, 313 (Cooper Union Speech, February 27, 1860).
[609] Oates, 194; Donald, 256; Burlingame, Vol. 1, 679–680.

The day before he left for Washington, he told his law partner, William Herndon, to keep his name on the sign outside. "If I live, I'm coming back some time, and then we'll go on practicing law as if nothing ever happened."[610]

The next day was February 11, one day shy of his fifty-second birthday. Lincoln boarded a train bound for his inauguration, and a crowd seeing him off called for a speech, but he hadn't prepared one. This was home for much of his life and where all his friends lived. From the gray sky, rain fell and added a somber mood to the celebratory event.

Going to the rear of the platform, Lincoln prepared to speak as the crowd cheered. Six southern states had already left the Union since his election, and he grimaced, unsure what to say. Was Mary's interpretation of the two faces in the mirror true? Was this the last time he would see home?

Standing straight, he removed his stove-pipe hat and was silent a few seconds gathering his thoughts. Those in the crowd removed their hats as the rain wet their bare heads. Lincoln began, "My friends—no one, not in my situation, can appreciate my feeling of sadness at this parting. To this place, and the kindness of these people, I owe everything. Here I have lived a quarter of a century, and have passed from a young man to an old man. Here my children have been born...and one is buried." He thought of Anne, the Clary Grove boys, and little Eddie:

> I now leave, not knowing when, or whether ever, I may return, with a task before me greater than that which rested upon Washington. Without the assistance of that Divine Being who ever attended him, I cannot succeed. With that assistance...I cannot fail. Trusting in Him who can go with me, and remain with you, and be everywhere for good, let us confidently hope that all will yet be well. To His care commending you, as

---

[610] Donald, 272; Oates, 224.

I hope in your prayers you will commend me, I
bid you an affectionate farewell.[611]

He stepped inside the train car, and a roar of cheers followed.
As the train departed, he was unsure where it would take him, but
he knew he must go with confidence. The country would need this
if it was to survive. On February 22, standing in Independence Hall
in Philadelphia on Washington's birthday, the very place where the
Declaration of Independence was signed, what was supposed to be a
flag raising ceremony, turned into another call for a speech. Knowing
he must remind them where they came from and where they must
go, he offered hope with his courage:

> I have often pondered over the dangers which
> were incurred by the men who assembled here
> and framed and adopted that Declaration. I have
> pondered over the toils that were endured by the
> officers and soldiers of the army who achieved
> that independence. I have often inquired of
> myself what great principle or idea it was that
> kept this Confederacy so long together. It was
> not the mere matter of separation of the colonies
> from the motherland, but that sentiment in the
> Declaration of Independence which gave liberty
> not alone to people of this country, but hope
> to all the world, for all future time...Now, my
> friends, can this country be saved on that basis? If
> it can, I will consider myself one of the happiest
> men in the world if I can help to save it...But if
> this country cannot be saved without giving that
> principle, I was about to say I would rather be
> assassinated on this spot than surrender it. But I
> have said nothing but what I am willing to live

---

[611] Lincoln, *Works*, Vol. 6, 110–111 (Farewell Address at Springfield, Illinois,
February 11, 1861); Sandburg, 195–196.

by, and, if it be the pleasure of the Almighty God, to die by.[612]

On March 4, 1861, he was inaugurated the sixteenth president of the United States. With the South seceding, a United States military fort in Charleston, South Carolina, was surrounded and told to surrender. A place called Fort Sumter became the powder keg threatening to ignite civil war as Lincoln assumed the presidency.

He tried to find a way to convince his countrymen to reverse their course without portraying weakness. His First Inaugural speech attempted to calm tempers and make them realize the catastrophe they were ushering in. Secession was illegal, he said, just as Daniel Webster claimed thirty years before, but he felt no ill will toward the South and appealed to their common spirit. "Intelligence, patriotism, Christianity, and a firm reliance on Him who has never yet forsaken this favored land, are still competent to adjust in the best way all our present difficulty." Placing the responsibility of further disunion on them, he added:

> In your hands, my dissatisfied fellow countrymen, and not in mine, is the momentous issue of civil war. The government will not assail you. You can have no conflict, without being yourselves the aggressors. You have no oath registered in Heaven to destroy the government, while I shall have the most solemn one to preserve, protect, and defend it.

He ended by pleading for reconciliation:

> We are not enemies, but friends. We must not be enemies. Though passion may have strained it must not break our bonds of affection. The mys-

---

[612] Ibid., 157–158 (Address in Independence Hall, Philadelphia, February 22, 1861).

tic chords of memory, stretching from every battlefield and patriot grave to every living heart and
hearthstone all over this broad land, will yet swell
the chorus of the Union when again touched, as
surely they will be, by the better angels of our
nature.[613]

Abraham Lincoln hoped for a peaceful solution, but the coming fury appeared unstoppable, and it sprinted forward, regardless of
those who tried to avert it. It was in God's hands now.

* * * * *

Throughout the 1850s the debate over slavery grew more
polarized and divisive. In 1856, Senator Charles Sumner, a radical
Republican from Massachusetts, insinuated that Senator Andrew
Butler of South Carolina kept slave mistresses. Butler's cousin,
Congressman Preston Brooks, heard about Sumner's accusations and
approached him on the Senate floor intent on defending Butler's
honor. "It is libel on South Carolina, and Mr. Butler, who is a relative
of mine," Brooks proclaimed.

As Sumner tried to stand, the South Carolinian proceeded to
beat him repeatedly with his wooden cane. Most of the blows landed
on Sumner's head, and he fell to the floor while Brooks continued his
onslaught. Sumner would suffer from headaches and post-traumatic
stress from the assault and was absent from the Senate for nearly
three years recovering. Brooks broke his cane in the process and
received hundreds of new ones as gifts from Southerners in support.
Northerners saw validation that Southerners were barbarians, and
Southerners validated that Yankees were weak. Many Congressmen
came to the Capitol armed after Sumner's beating, and tension continued to mount.[614]

---

[613] Ibid., 173, 184–185 (First Inaugural Address, March 4, 1861).
[614] McPherson, James M. *Battle Cry of Freedom: The Civil War Era.* (New York:
Oxford University Press, 1988), 150–152; Foote, Vol. 1, 15.

The Kansas-Nebraska Bill soon left states the right to determine their own constitutions, and Secretary of State Jefferson Davis was integral in influencing President Pierce to sign the bill. Now, Kansas territory was experiencing its own civil war. Called "Bleeding Kansas," the anti-slavery and states' rights factions were killing each other and burning towns. Each side attempted to ratify their own agenda-driven state constitutions and caused more disunion.

Armed bands from slave state Missouri raided the anti-slavery town of Lawrence, Kansas, in 1856 and burned, looted, and killed one man. Jesse James's future outlaw gang cut their teeth with pro-Southern guerilla raider William Quantrill in Kansas. In an act of revenge, fanatical abolitionist John Brown and his sons decided to murder five supporters of popular sovereignty at Pottawatomie Creek. Small battles and senseless killings continued through 1857 and peaked in 1858 when President James Buchanan appointed a territorial governor who returned order for a time.[615]

By 1857, Jeff Davis was a senator from Mississippi, and though certain about his beliefs, talk of secession was one issue he refused to entertain. Developing a serious eye problem described as metaherpetic keratitis, an inflammation of the cornea believed to be a result of his bout with malaria, covered his left eye with a cloudy film, and pus caused an abscess from the accumulated iris tissue. This painful swelling and hypersensitivity were debilitating and, by 1858, had him bedridden. Visited by Senator William H. Seward, Jeff relished his political opponent's friendship and mutual respect. Seward visited him an hour every day and informed him of the latest news of Congress and tried to keep his spirits up.

For two months, Davis suffered from the infection. Blind in his left eye, he returned to the Senate floor but would need surgery on the eye twice over the next few years and lost most of the sight in it. In 1859, his doctor suggested a cooler climate might help, so he and Varina took a vacation through New England. It would serve two purposes—helping his eye, and to convince the northerners of the South's desire for peace and brotherhood. This talk of war was

---

[615] Ibid., 152–153; Oates, 135–136.

crazy, and only fanatics on both sides spoke of killing their fellow countrymen.[616]

While in New England, he gave several speeches defending states' rights and the Union, and called for both sections to remember their common interests, not their differences. Referring to slavery, he asked why the abolitionists in the Republican party called it un-Christian because it brought more blacks to Christianity than all the missionaries or "do-gooders" could. He focused mostly on the positive hope of peace and unity and criticized those causing sectional prejudices.

Returning home to Mississippi, he once again made a case for states' rights and Union. The South, he said, wasn't excusing the problems away, but the Republicans claimed Seward's "higher law" guided their actions, not the Constitution. Jeff called this "higher law" the same law the serpent tempted Eve with in the Garden. This anarchy of men deciding to become gods themselves to judge the world led to greater sin and the loss of paradise, which led to death. They had a garden in America—why be tempted by the serpent's promise and lose it all? Perhaps thinking of Brierfield and his own rose garden, he wondered why men always succumbed to the promise of greener pastures.

He also disagreed with Lincoln and other abolitionists that slavery degraded free labor. Most in the South didn't own slaves and worked their own farms. This insinuation was an insult to hardworking southerners. Besides, slavery didn't promote laziness as they claimed, but the industrialists of the North did pay slave wages to freemen. Many abolitionists separated the two by claiming the freeman made the choice to better himself, but the slave had no choice. Davis claimed most slaves lived better than free blacks in the North, and slavery, he said, wasn't really the issue at hand, but the real target was the constitutional rights of slave owners. The abolitionists

---

[616] Cooper, 309–312; Eye condition details: http://civilwarmed.blogspot.com/2009/07/medical_department_26_turning_blindeye.html.

were causing division, not slavery, because it was legally protected by law.[617]

In October 1859, John Brown tried to incite a slave insurrection at Harper's Ferry, Virginia. Seizing the federal arsenal there, his armed band killed five townspeople, including the mayor and a free black man. After the raid failed, order was restored, but a Pandora's box was opened throughout the nation. Many in the North saw John Brown as a modern-day Moses coming to free the children in bondage, and a popular song was composed, making him into a savior-like crusader who laid his life down for the sin of slavery. The South suspected Brown had not acted alone and, in time, it was discovered that many northern abolitionists financed it.

Davis was convinced that it had been a conspiracy to violently overthrow the Constitution and force the South to give up its slaves. It had never been about stopping the extension of slavery as they claimed and was really about ending it. John Brown was a martyr to the abolitionists and a terrorist criminal to the South.[618]

This pushed the South closer to secession. Abolitionists had hijacked the Republican party and were evil despots bent on usurping constitutional rights in the South. With the election of Lincoln a year later, they opted to secede rather than wait to see what the abolitionist president would do. He couldn't be trusted, even though he denounced John Brown's actions; his words meant nothing. Jeff hoped the North would see the seriousness of the situation and make some sort of concession to hold the Union together but soon realized the divide could never be crossed.[619]

In December 1860, South Carolina seceded.

Serving in committee in the Senate, he tried to negotiate a compromise to avoid secession, but the Republicans would not budge when it came to slavery extension and said concessions by threat would only encourage future threats. Many in the previous generation tried to avert war but were often scoffed at as remnants of a

[617] Ibid., 322–324; DiLorenzo, 113–116.
[618] Foote, Vol. 1, 31–32: McPherson, 204–206.
[619] Cooper, 343–345; McPherson, 234.

bygone age. Sam Houston, Governor of Texas and strong Union man in a slave state, warned his secession-minded colleagues:

> Some of you laugh to scorn the idea of bloodshed as a result of secession, and jocularly propose to drink all the blood that will ever flow in consequence of it. But let me tell you what is coming on the heels of secession. The time will come when your fathers and husbands, your sons and brothers, will be herded like sheep and cattle at the point of the bayonet; and your mothers and wives, and sisters and daughters, will ask, 'Where are they?' You may, after the sacrifice of countless millions of treasure and hundreds of thousands of precious lives…win Southern independence, if God be not against you; but I doubt it.

The listening crowd respected him, but he was a sixty-seven-year-old symbol of the Jacksonian age, and nearly every old man was against the break-up of the Union. The old were always reluctant to change some thought, but Houston warned them:

> The North is determined to preserve this Union. They are not a fiery, impulsive people as you are, for they live in colder climates. But when they begin to move in a given direction…they move with a steady momentum and perseverance of a mighty avalanche; and what I fear is, they will overwhelm the South with ignoble defeat…

Texas seceded in March of 1861 and each night, he prayed "Dear Heavenly Father, I beseech thee cast out of my mind the dark forebodings of the coming conflict…"[620] Refusing to take the oath to

---

[620] Wisehart, 593–595.

the Confederacy, he resigned. Addressing the people of the state he'd
fought to make free, he said:

> Think not that I complain at the lot which
> Providence has now assigned me. It is perhaps
> but meet that my career should close thus. I have
> seen the patriots and statesmen of my youth, one
> by one, gathered to their fathers, and the govern-
> ment which they had created, rent in twain; and
> none like them are left to unite it once again. I
> stand the last almost of a race, who learned from
> their lips the lessons of human freedom. I am
> stricken down now, because I will not yield those
> principles, which I have fought for and struggled
> to maintain. The severest pang is that the blow
> comes in the name of the State of Texas.[621]

The old hero couldn't believe he had lived to see all he and
others fought and bled for be destroyed. Some accused him of siding with Lincoln, but nothing could be further from the truth. He
understood the South's complaints, but secession and war weren't
the answer. He had seen war firsthand, and it wasn't a game. Sam
Houston died in July of 1863, and the last of his kind were gone. The
next generation would have to learn "the lessons of human freedom"
themselves.

Seeing the end of his blessed Union as inevitable, Jeff Davis
waited for instructions from Mississippi. His first allegiance was to
his state, and she would decide her own course and his own. Like a
spreading brushfire, in January 1861, Mississippi seceded, but not
before appointing him major general of the army of Mississippi.
Dispirited, he gave his last speech as members of both houses of
Congress packed the Senate. Some of the capital's most influential
from both parties came to see the adored statesmen say goodbye.

---

[621] Houston, *Writings,* Vol. 8, 277 (To the People of Texas, March 16, 1861);
Wisehart, 610.

After explaining Mississippi's decision to secede and his duty to its wishes, he said, "We but tread in the path of our fathers when we proclaim our independence, and take the hazard…we will invoke the God of our fathers who delivered us from the power of the lion, to protect us from the ravages of the bear; and thus putting our trust in God, and in our own firm hearts and strong arms, we will vindicate the right…" He ended by assuring his fellow Senators his resignation was not in anger:

> I see now around me some with whom I have served long; there have been points of collision; but whatever of offense there has been to me, I leave here; I carry with me no hostile remembrance. Whatever offense I have given which has not been redressed, or which satisfaction has not been demanded, I have Senators, in this hour of our parting, to offer you my apology for any pain which, in the heat of discussion, I have inflicted. I go hence unencumbered of the remembrance of any injury received, and having discharged the duty of making the only reparation in my power for any injury offered.

Taking his seat, he covered his face with both hands, and some said he wept. A silence fell over the Senate chamber as others sniffled and searched for handkerchiefs. Seconds later, the room erupted into an earsplitting applause. The revered statesman remained seated.[622]

A month later, Jeff was the president of the Confederate States of America, and in his inaugural address, he still hoped for a peaceful separation without war. But events escalated, and at Fort Sumter, Union troops still occupied the fort off the coast of Charleston, South Carolina. When Confederates demanded they surrender, Major Robert Anderson refused. By April 12, 1861, President Davis ordered General Beauregard to demand the surrender of the fort after

---

[622] Cooper, 347–348; Tate, 10–11.

Lincoln's attempt to resupply it failed. Anderson once again refused, and at 4:30 a.m., Beauregard's cannons opened a barrage. Anderson, though stubborn, had no choice now but to surrender. Lincoln then called up 75,000 volunteers to put down the rebellion and there was no turning back.[623]

Jeff Davis wasn't naïve about their predicament. They were facing an uphill struggle. They had fewer men, rifles, ammunition, wagons, shoes, etc., and their industrial capacity was nonexistent. Their challenge, he believed, was much like the founders who won their struggle by sheer spirit and divine providence. The South was now responsible for continuing the spirit of 1776, and God would bless their cause because he was on their side, and if they leaned on him for guidance, they couldn't lose. Eighty-five years ago, George Washington led a ragtag army to victory against the mighty British Empire and won. They could do the same if they stayed true to their principles and faith.

By the middle of July, Union troops crossed into Virginia and were threatening the town of Manassas. Davis wrote to Varina back at Brierfield, two days after his inauguration, "The audience was large and brilliant. Upon my weary heart were showered smiles, plaudits, and flowers…" Perhaps thinking again of the rose garden left behind, he continued, "but beyond them, I saw troubles and thorns innumerable."

His garden was no longer all roses, but the thorns no longer deterred him in his duties.[624]

* * * * *

[623] Swanberg, W. A. *First Blood: The Story of Fort Sumter*. (New York: Charles Scribner's Sons, 1957), 296–298; Cooper, 362–364; Catton, William & Bruce. *Two Roads to Sumter*. (New York: McGraw-Hill Book Co. Inc., 1963), 278–280; Foote, Vol. 1, 48–50.

[624] Foote, Vol. 1, 41; Tate, 83.

II.
A Fiery Trial

Thomas Jackson travelled through Europe in the summer of 1856 and returned a new man. He was determined to remarry and start a family. His charity work, faith, and prayers seemed to cleanse his sorrow and renew his spirit.

Remembering a young lady his friend from West Point, Daniel Harvey Hill, introduced him to, he decided to write a letter to strike up a correspondence. Recalling her as an awkward teenager, he wasn't sure she was right for him but was eager to try again. Receiving an amiable reply from the girl, he paid her a visit and was surprised to see she had grown into an attractive mature woman.

Mary Anna Morrison, called Anna, was destined to be his wife, and the two were engaged by the time he returned to Lexington. They were married in July of 1857, and Anna was quickly pregnant. She had a little girl they christened Mary, and Thomas was elated. God had blessed him with another wonderful wife and child, but three weeks later, the baby died, and Thomas, now a veteran of losing loved ones, seemed to make it through the grief a bit easier once the initial shock of it wore off. He was grateful to still have his wife and appreciated others' children because of his loss. Anna took the death harder, and Tom made it his mission to help her through the grief.

Their marriage was a blessing, and the stoic Jackson was a different man alone with his wife. He would "beam with happiness" on his return home and would shower her with affection every day. Anna explained her husband's behavior and views on maintaining a happy marriage. "No man could be more demonstrative and he was almost invariably playful and cheerful and as confiding as possible. He commenced educating me (if I may so speak) to be as demonstrative as soon as we were married, thought it added quality to happiness and we rarely ever met alone without caresses and endearing epithets." He also had a playful side and would hide behind doors, surprising her with kisses and hugs, making her laugh, and enjoyed dancing polkas with her and gave her pet names like "my sunshine" and "esposita," Spanish for "little wife." He was finally content with a loving wife, a respectable job teaching at the military institute, and a Christian faith that gave him a sense of purpose, but providence would intercede again.[625]

After John Brown's raid at Harper Ferry, the governor of Virginia called on the Virginia Military Institute to supply troops to guard against a possible rescue attempt before Brown's execution. Jackson was to lead the artillery attachment and was there to witness the hanging. On December 2, 1859, John Brown was marched to the gallows, and Thomas described the event:

> Brown rode on the head of his coffin, from his prison to the place of execution... The jailer and high sheriff and several others rode in the wagon with the prisoner. Brown had his arms tied behind him, and ascended the scaffold with apparent cheerfulness. After reaching the top of the platform, he shook hands with several who were standing around him. The sheriff placed the rope around his neck, threw a white cap over his head...the rope was cut by a single blow and Brown fell through about 25 inches... With the fall of his arms below the elbow flew up, hands clenched, and his arms gradually fell by spasmodic motions...the wind blew his lifeless body to and fro... I was much impressed with the thought that before me stood a man, in the full vigor of health, who must in a few minutes be in eternity. I sent up a petition that he might be saved.[626]

He believed Brown didn't want forgiveness for his murders, and his soul would probably not be saved, but he still prayed for his salvation. He also prayed for some sort of compromise between

---

[625] Jackson, 108; Robertson, 191.
[626] Ibid., 130–131 (To Anna Jackson, December 2, 1859).

North and South but felt it was in God's hands now. "Why should Christians be disturbed about the dissolution of the Union? It can come only by God's permission, and will only be permitted if for His people's good; for does He not say, 'All things work together for good to them that love God?'"[627] He also said if the North invaded the South, they should fight to win and take no prisoners if they attempted to deny them:

> Rights guaranteed to us by the Constitution of our Country, Should endeavor to subjugate us, and thus excite our slaves to servile insurrection in which our families will be murdered, without quarter or mercy, it becomes us to wage such a war as will bring hostilities to a speedy close. People who are anxious to bring on war don't know what they are bargaining for; they don't see all the horrors that must accompany such an event.[628]

He supported the Union and peace until Lincoln called for 75,000 troops, and when Virginia seceded, he was wholeheartedly a Confederate. Shortly after, he was commissioned a colonel in the Virginian Army. After training troops for the next few months, Tom and his men were stationed at Harper's Ferry in July of 1861. Quickly promoted to brigadier general, he fought his first battle at Martinsburg. It was no more than a skirmish, but it mentally reinstated his mind for battle.[629]

Union soldiers were now concentrating near the town of Manassas along Bull Run Creek. The North were perceived as invaders, and the South was itching to fight. Major General Joseph E. Johnston of Virginia commanded Confederate troops near the town of Winchester, and Jackson's troops awaited orders. General P. G. T.

---

[627] Ibid., 142; Robertson, 205.
[628] Robertson, 207; Davis, Burke, *Stonewall*, 133.
[629] Jackson, 166–167.

Beauregard held the town of Manassas and would send for reinforcements if the Yankees attacked.

By July 17, Johnston received that message and used his cavalry, commanded by J. E. B. Stuart as a ruse to distract Union scouts from his movement of men by train from Winchester to Manassas.

On Sunday, July 21, 1861, the First Battle of Manassas (also known as Bull Run) opened with Union troops under General Irvin McDowell smashing into Beauregard's left flank. The Union believed it would be a quick and easy war. They simply had to cross into Virginia and spank the South, and it would all be over. Many of the reputable citizens of Washington enjoyed carriage rides and packed picnic baskets to enjoy the festivities of the opening battle. To them, war was a story of glory and heroism, but the carnage and cost of it hadn't affected this generation yet.

Early in the day, the fight seemed to go McDowell's way as Beauregard's left began to weaken. Though reinforcements soon strengthened the Confederate flank, pushing McDowell's army back, the sheer number of Union forces reversed Beauregard's brief advantage. This was the moment Jackson's Virginians were ordered to defend a place called Henry Hill and halt the reverse on the left, where General Bernard Bee was unsuccessful so far. Bee had been a friendly acquaintance of Jackson's at West Point, and was even more eager to assist. If they could hold Henry Hill, they would keep the left flank from being turned and possibly losing the battle. They had to hold that hill at all costs.[630]

Galloping to the crest of the hill, sweat dripping into his eyes, Jackson could still make out the reverse slope as the best advantage. His men were thirsty and hot, and the enemy had twenty-four cannons against his eight, but he had God's will to lead the way. Riding back and forth in front of his men with fire in his eyes and no regard for his own safety, he said, "Steady, men, steady! All's well!" This strange professor from VMI no longer appeared odd or eccentric to

---

[630] Catton, Bruce. *The Coming Fury*. (Garden City: Doubleday & Co. Inc., 1961), 443-444; Robertson, 256, 262–263; Foote, Vol. 1, 76–78; Davis, Burke, *Stonewall*, 144–147.

them. He looked almost comfortable as bullets and shells zinged past him, and though he rode his horse leaning forward in the saddle and wore too small a cap, he had the gritty look of a true warrior. His long auburn beard fluttered from his movements, but his eyes remained steady and his men felt calmer.

General Thomas J. "Stonewall" Jackson

He held up his left arm and a bullet or shrapnel struck his middle finger, and a nearby captain informed him, "General, you are wounded."

Jackson wrapped a handkerchief around it and calmly said, "Only a scratch, a mere scratch."

The Confederate line on Henry Hill was about to break when General Bee approached him and said, "General, they are driving us!"

He replied confidently, "Sir, we will give them the bayonet."

Emboldened by his certainty, Bee rode back to his troops and pointed at Jackson with his sword and yelled, "Look, men, there is Jackson standing like a stone wall! Let us determine to die here, and we will conquer! Follow me!"

Jackson shouted to his men, "Reserve your fire until they come within fifty yards! Then fire and give them the bayonet! And when you charge, yell like furies!" And thus the rebel yell was born, and when the men charged, the northerners broke and ran. The civilian spectators were caught in the melee of the retreat and the advancing southerners. The tide of battle turned, and a panic caused a general retreat of McDowell's forces, leaving behind rifles, cannons, and wagons. It was a total rout, and Union troops didn't stop until they were safely back in Washington.

General Bee was killed soon after he gave Jackson one of the most famous nicknames in history, but "Stonewall" Jackson stuck like glue, though he never liked the name. His fellow officers and men liked "Old Jack" better, but Bee's was immortal.[631]

While having his finger attended to at headquarters, Jackson saw President Davis at the aid station. The president rode up on a horse, ready to do battle. "I am President Davis! All of you who are able to follow me, back to the field!"

Tom took off his cap and boisterously said, "Three cheers for the president!" Speaking directly to Davis he said, "We have whipped them! They ran like dogs! Give me ten thousand men, and I will take Washington tomorrow!"

Even though the feisty general saw an opportunity to win the war, Davis preferred to keep the war defensive in nature. To ensure European support, he had to convince the world that the South wasn't the aggressor, and after Fort Sumter, he needed a clear example of northern aggression. Now he had one, and victory was the icing on the cake.[632]

Jackson gave homage for his performance in battle to the one who kept him safe. Writing Anna the next day, he said, "Yesterday we fought a great battle and gained a great victory, for which all the glory is due to God alone."[633]

---

[631] Jackson, 177–179; Foote, Vol. 1, 78-80; Davis, William C. *Battle at Bull Run*. (Baton Rouge: Louisiana State University Press, 1977), 196–197; Robertson, 263–266.

[632] Robertson, 268–269; Catton, *Fury*, 456-459; Foote, Vol. 1, 83.

[633] Jackson, 177 (To Anna Jackson, July 22, 1861); Robertson, 270.

His brigade afterward was known as the Stonewall Brigade, and the strange cadet who pulled himself up by the bootstraps became a legend.

How could the Union win this war with "Stonewall" Jackson in their way?

* * * * *

Returning east, Ulysses S. Grant continued to make bad decisions, like giving his money away to those down on their luck and ending up broke in New York. An old friend from West Point, Simon Bolivar Buckner, even lent him some money until he received a loan from his father.

Making it back to St. Louis, Julia's father gave them a plot of land to make their home and raise their boys. Sam would raise crops to make a living but had a problem with putting his own concerns over others. Always the good Samaritan, he would do without to help someone else.

Once, an ex-soldier's wife living nearby asked Sam to help her with her drunk husband, who was threatening to sell the cow and run off to Texas. Agreeing with the woman's plea, he found the inebriated man and struck up a conversation, asking the man if he wanted to trade the saddled horse he was planning to leave on. Interested in Sam's offer, the drunk man sat with him and discussed the deal while whittling wood until dark. Around dinner, the sobering ex-soldier returned home to his wife and cried for forgiveness. Sam had convinced him to give up drinking, and he stayed sober the rest of his days.

Another time, he bought a farmer's mule at an auction and returned it to him. So as not to embarrass the man, he agreed to rent it to him but never asked for a penny. Any money made, he gave to neighbors, and once when asked to contribute to the building of a new church, he said, "I don't attend as much as I should, but Julia and the children do. We ought also have a Sabbath school in the neighborhood."[634]

---

[634] Smith, Jean, *Grant*, 89; Lewis, 344–346.

Trying farming again, his crops rarely survived or made a profit. He would end up cutting wood, hauling it to St. Louis, and selling it on the street just to feed his family. It was embarrassing, and sometimes old army friends would recognize him. They never said a word, but it was obvious they felt sorry for him.

This was how he found himself three years later, pawning his gold watch for Christmas presents. He was always scraping by, and it was getting old. After a brief period working as an insurance agent in St. Louis, he finally took his father up on the offer to work at the tannery in Illinois.[635]

In 1860, he moved his family to Galena, Illinois, and left behind their farm. Luckily, the new job was an office job and not in the tannery itself. Now he had a little security but never felt comfortable in the position. He had enough money to live on, but his job felt more like a cage than a job, and this cage had him trapped. As long as he could be with his family and not scraping by to survive, he acquiesced.

With the coming conflict, Sam's war veteran status presented him with the opportunity to train and organize the Illinois volunteers. Agreeing to train the men, he did a competent job and whipped an undisciplined rowdy group into a fighting force.

Once war broke out in 1861, he tried to get an appointment with General George B. McClellan's staff, but the drunk tag remained, and McClellan refused to see him. After being snubbed by the army commander, he resumed command of the 21st Illinois Volunteers with the rank of colonel. Congressman Elihu Washburne saw his potential and pulled some strings to get him appointed brigadier general.[636]

After fighting at the Battle of Belmont, which ended in a retreat, he was again labeled a drunk. After he took Fort Henry, Tennessee, with the help of the naval force's bombardment, he devised a plan to take the greater prize to the east, Fort Donelson. His plan was simple—surround the fort and attack while closing all escape routes.

---

[635] Ibid., 91–92; Lewis, 354–357.
[636] Grant, Vol. 1, 241–243; Smith, Jean, *Grant*, 104–107.

The commanders inside Fort Donelson, General Gideon Pillow and General John B. Floyd, were afraid they would be hanged as traitors and spies for the South, so they escaped before Grant closed in. They left behind General Simon Buckner to take the fall, and seeing the mess the two scattering generals created, he quickly asked for terms. Responding to one of his old friends, "No terms except unconditional and immediate surrender can be accepted. I propose to move upon your works. I am sir, very respectfully, your obedient servant US Grant Brigadier General." If he wouldn't even give lenient terms to an old friend who lent him money, what would he demand of strangers?

On February 16, 1862, Buckner surrendered Fort Donelson, and after a friendly chat with Buckner, Sam didn't forget to see if his old friend needed a loan. Once the fighting was over, he accepted Buckner as an old friend and not the enemy. US Grant became known as Unconditional Surrender Grant throughout the nation, but the brass in the Washington said it was luck.[637]

With all his toughness, Sam had a compassionate side. Right before the surrender of Fort Donelson, he saw two wounded soldiers, one a Union lieutenant and the other a Confederate private. The lieutenant was trying to share his canteen with the private unsuccessfully when Sam noticed and was compelled to help. Asking one of his staff for a brandy flask, he got off his horse and gave each man a swig from it.

"Thank you, General," the private said. The lieutenant was too weak to speak but saluted him.

"Send for stretchers. Send for stretchers at once for these men," he ordered.

When the stretchers arrived, only the Union lieutenant was laid on one. Seeing this, Sam said, "Take this Confederate, too. Take them both together. The war is over between them." Looking around, the dead and wounded of both sides were everywhere. "Let's get away from this dreadful place," he said. This was insanity—fellow coun-

---

[637] Ibid., 292, 310–312; Catton, Bruce. *Grant Moves South.* (Boston: Little, Brown and Co., 1960), 143, 175–177; Foote, Vol. 1, 211–213.

trymen killing each other. "I suppose this work is part of the devil that is left in us all."[638]

Though he pulled no punches in battle, he showed compassion after it, and some portrayals of him as a butcher are unwarranted. He knew war meant killing, and many of his men would die to achieve victory, but it would save lives in the end. The sooner the war was over, the sooner the killing would end. This truth didn't make him insensitive to the suffering on both sides, and he felt it deeply but also had a job to do. The South was not going to give up after one fight. They were a stubborn determined foe and you had to lose men to beat them.

A machine in battle, he would push until the enemy retreated, and never thought of loss until after the fight, because he learned throughout his life that perseverance mattered more than skill. Many generals possessed skill, but when plans went awry, they crumbled. He would keep hitting the enemy, even when it appeared he was losing.

After Donelson fell, the Confederate commander, General Albert Sidney Johnston, pulled his army back to the Tennessee-Mississippi border to regroup. Sam saw an opening to crush the retreating force but continued to fight a greater threat in his rear—his fellow commanders.

General Henry W. Halleck was the overall commander in the west and was also ambitious. He was willing to undercut anyone who got in his way. "Old Brains" as he was called, was a skillful tactician and strategist, not to mention a genius with logistics and organization, but he was no fighting general. This unknown drunk, Sam Grant, was outperforming him, and he couldn't allow it. It began with Halleck's backstabbing him to his chief, General McClellan, claiming Grant didn't follow orders and refused to send his reports. "Old Brains" wrote McClellan, "Satisfied with his victory, he sits down and enjoys it without any regard to the future. I am worn out and tired with this neglect and inefficiency."

---

[638] Catton, *Grant Moves South*, 173.

Sam was doing no such thing and was busy trying to crush the Confederate Army, but McClellan had his own prejudices about him and replied to Halleck's message, "A rumor has just reached me that since the taking of Fort Donelson General Grant has resumed his former bad habit."[639] Suggesting he was drinking and it affected his command was groundless as rumors were mostly officers trying to undercut him to receive his command. He was winning and had the enemy on the run.

Ambition and jealousy saw his success as a threat, and many jumped on the smear bandwagon. How dare the drunk have more success than "Old Brains" who wrote two books on army training or McClellan, the wonder boy who was first in his class at West Point? Even less accomplished commanders thought they deserved a spot over this farmer alcoholic, and some regional officers used him as a scapegoat for their own failures. When someone screwed up in Sam's vicinity, he received the blame, and old labels never died. Defending himself to Halleck on one occasion, he respectfully and confidently caused his superior to back off, and President Lincoln also intervened on his behalf.

Like Washington, Andrew Jackson, and Houston, Grant was fighting a war on two fronts. One against the South and one against his own chain of command. Career soldiers and opportunists saw Sam as something which must be controlled or destroyed. Only a certain breed of men put duty above self, and he was one of those.[640]

Outside Shiloh, Tennessee, in April 1862, Sam was facing Johnston's Confederate army.

On April 4, Sam, who was just recovering from a bout of diarrhea, injured his ankle when his horse slipped in a rainstorm and fell on his leg. The ankle swelled, and he relied on crutches for a few days and of course, the whispers of the general's "bad habit" circulated. Ignoring the attacks, he had a job to do.

On Sunday, April 6, he was eating breakfast on the river a few miles from Shiloh when he heard cannon shots. Frozen in place

---

[639] Ibid., 196–197.
[640] Ibid., 206–208; Grant, Vol. 1, 327-329; Foote, Vol. 1, 317–319.

with a cup of coffee in his hand, Sam sat the cup down and stood. "Gentlemen, the ball is in motion. Let's be off." Within fifteen minutes, the general and his staff were on a steamship heading for Shiloh.

General Albert Johnston attacked at dawn, intending a surprise to push the Union force back. Expecting to crush them with their backs to the river, he planned to reverse any success the Union had in the west thus far, and sent 30,000 men in a massive assault on Grant's frontline.

General William Tecumseh, Sherman's men, were the frontline that got hit, driven back, and overwhelmed. Sherman was in his own battle with the army hierarchy over the past year and was hoping to prove himself here. Accused of being crazy because of a nervous breakdown, he redeemed himself with his performance in the field. Sherman and Grant became fast friends because they both had to prove themselves without the benefit of clout. Both were maligned and underestimated.[641]

At Shiloh, Sam was everywhere on the battlefield. He moved men, encouraged others to return to the fight, all while maintaining his steady calm which made them feel okay if General Grant was there. Many soldiers remembered how this assuredness gave them confidence in battle. If the general was this calm, everything had to be fine, and smoking his cigar like he would any other day, made them relax.[642]

Johnston's army was beating Grant's all over the field, and many Union troops ran to the river in panic. Backed against the Tennessee River according to the Confederate general's plans, Sam's worst fear was unfolding. If his men would just turn and fight, they would give General Buell time to arrive with reinforcements. One point of promise was a spot called the "Hornet's Nest," because of the buzzing bullets stinging all around, and this one pocket of resistance continued to hold out. Sam visited the area earlier in the day and told the

[641] Ibid., 218; Grant, Vol. 1, 335.
[642] Ibid., 218–222; Grant, Vol. 1, 335–337.

commanding officer to hold the ground at all costs, and the young officer was certainly following orders.[643]

Everywhere the battle seemed a Union loss, but an odd event occurred. General Johnston was on the field that day, making decisions, like Grant and Sherman. Sitting atop his horse, he was sending and receiving reports when he suddenly tumbled to the ground. Bleeding from the back of his knee, the wound seemed to be serious but not fatal, and his aides sighed and attempted to attend to him. Realizing he was losing too much blood for a leg wound, his aides sat him by a tree, helpless, and within minutes, Johnston was dead. The bullet had severed the femoral artery and he bled to death. A simple tourniquet might have saved him.

With Johnston's death, command went to General Beauregard who had left the east for a command in the west, but he had difficulty taking the reins of another general's plan. This was Johnston's grand design and he had to save the army to live to fight another day. So he took a cautious attitude and never liked Johnston's reckless strategy to begin with. Instead of pushing the attack, Beauregard maintained his present line.

Grant knew if he held until Buell arrived, they could counterattack and win. Then, the "Hornet's Nest" surrendered, and Sam contemplated his next move when another strange event happened. The Confederates halted and loitered in the previous Union camp, drinking, eating, and looting the area, behaving as if the battle was over.[644]

This pause was just enough for Grant to entrench over fifty cannons to keep the enemy at bay. He opened with a cannonade late into the night, and Beauregard was done for the day.

Just then, one of Sam's staff officers was killed by a cannon shot as he sat calmly on his horse. When asked if the battle was going well, he replied, "Oh no. They can't break our lines tonight, it is too late. Tomorrow we shall attack them with fresh troops and drive them, of course!" One of his generals asked if they should retreat, and he

---

[643] Ibid., 232–234; Grant, Vol. 1, 339=340; Foote, Vol. 1, 335–339.
[644] Foote, Vol. 1, 339–341.

responded with, "Retreat? No. I propose to attack at daylight and whip them." With Grant, it wasn't over until it was over.

The cries of the wounded, like banshees, haunted the battlefield as screams of the dying and thirsty called out for help in the pitch-black night. There was no light except the explosions of cannon and its shells, and the soldiers in the field were so thirsty from the day's fight, they often drank from the streams running red with the blood of the fallen. An eerie presence engulfed the battlefield.

Sherman found Grant later that night standing under a tree, seeking shelter from a spring rain shower. Puffing a cigar and holding a lantern, Sam dripped of rainwater and resolution. Sherman contemplated asking if he should order a retreat, but the expression on the commander's face told him to forget it. When he spoke, he asked instead, "Well, Grant, we've had the devil's own day, haven't we?"

"Yes," Sam said, inhaling the cigar again. "Yes, Lick 'em tomorrow, though."[645]

At dawn, the cannonade continued, and after more deadly fighting; Beauregard called a retreat. His men were exhausted, outnumbered, and Buell's reinforcements, which arrived, demoralized them of any hope of victory.

A few coincidences caused the momentum of the battle to turn back in Grant's advantage. Johnston's strange death, the hold out of the "Hornet's Nest," and the loitering of the southern troops at the Union camp all contributed to the turnaround, but Sam's refusal to give up was the biggest factor.

The Battle of Shiloh was the bloodiest and costliest fight of the war so far. The Union lost more than 13,000 casualties, and the Confederates 10,000. These 23,000 killed, wounded, captured, and missing had a humbling effect on the nation, and hope in a quick or bloodless war was gone. This would take years and possibly thousands of lives. The flamboyant speeches were over, and the picnics were never entertained again. The flag-waving celebrations watching

---

[645] Catton, *Grant Moves South*, 237–242.

loved ones go to war lost their fervor, and the real cost of the war was felt.[646]

In the west, flashy generals with booming voices but no substance were out. When your father, brother, husband, or son's life was at risk, generals who acted and got results were now in heavy demand and would take longer for the eastern theater to realize this. What the North and South needed now were men of action. Tough determined fighters who got the job done were necessary.

They needed generals like Sam Grant, but unfortunately for the North, he was considered a drunk who lacked military genius. Fortunately for the South, many in the Union high command believed it.

* * * * *

Caring for his invalid wife was not the source of Robert E. Lee's stress. Distributing her father's estate and emancipating his slaves was his current worry. The Arlington property was his now but he had to turn the dilapidated plantation into some sort of productive form to dispense of his father-in-law's $10,000 of debt and have something for Mary to inherit. The task was time-consuming, and he asked for an extended leave from service to attend to it. With Mary ill and the plantation needing management, he was a busy man.

Emancipating G. W. P. Custis's slaves was the most difficult part of the old man's dying wishes. Not because Lee supported slavery; no, he never liked the institution, but freeing them wasn't as easy as just letting them go. For slaves to be emancipated, they required some means of support, and without preparing them, it would be tantamount to sentencing them to a life of suffering. From a theoretical position, freeing them was the right and just thing to do, but in Virginia in 1861, it was a major problem. Lee's views on slavery were well-known:

> In this enlightened age, there are few I believe,
> but what will acknowledge, that slavery as an

---

[646] Grant, Vol. 1, 367; Foote, Vol. 1, 350.

institution is a moral and political evil in any
Country. It is useless to expatiate on its disad-
vantages. I think it however a greater evil to the
white than to the black race, and while my feelings are strongly enlisted in behalf of the latter,
my sympathies are more strong for the former.

Admitting the evils of slavery, he acknowledged the malevolent
practice but felt it his duty to try and save the slave owner rather
than the slave. He continued, "The blacks are immeasurably better
off here than in Africa, morally, socially, and physically. The painful
discipline they are undergoing, is necessary for their instruction as a
race and I hope will prepare and lead them to better things."

Lee wasn't justifying slavery. He was submitting to God's will
that it had happened for some greater purpose. The blacks enslaved
were in America for a reason, he believed, and like ancient Israel,
enslaved by Egypt, he felt they would rise from their chains even
stronger. Recognizing it as no mere accident, but providence, he pitied the whites who promoted it, for they were losing their very souls.
He believed the slaves would prevail and overcome their bondage,
but it was the whites who would enter a new era of struggle. "How
long their subjugation may be necessary is known and ordered by a
wise Merciful Providence."

For some, providence has been attributed to deism, Masons,
Gnostics, Illuminati, and other secret societies, but Lee was precise
on what providence he trusted:

Their emancipation will sooner result from the
mild and melting influence of Christianity than
the storms and tempests of fiery Controversy.
This influence though slow, is sure. The doctrines
and miracles of our Saviour have required nearly
two thousand years, to Convert but a small part
of the human race, and even among Christian
nations, what gross errors still exist. While we
see the Course of the final abolition of human

Slavery is onward, and we give it the aid of our prayers and all justifiable means in our power, we must leave progress as well as the result in his hands who sees the end; who Chooses to work by slow influences; and with whom two thousand years are but as a single day.

He did, however, denounce radical abolitionists who called for immediate emancipation and violence. God's will would free the slaves, and choosing force would result in evil and suffering "that although he (the abolitionist) may not approve of the mode by which it pleases Providence to accomplish its purposes, the result will nevertheless be the same..."

Opposing slavery like Washington, Jefferson, Madison, and even Lincoln, he believed it would only end when enough people were convinced it conflicted with Christian principles. Loving your neighbor as yourself conflicted with enslaving them, but he did oppose the self-righteous who instigated violence and pushed the nation closer to civil strife. Questioning those Christians of the North, he wondered, "Is it not strange that the descendants of those pilgrim fathers who Crossed the Atlantic to preserve their own freedom of opinion, have always proved themselves intolerant of the Spiritual liberty of others?"[647]

Lee saw emancipation as a question for Christians on both sides and favored gradual emancipation, not the kind abolitionists were demanding. He hoped for peace and prayed that civil war could be averted, but his hope was betrayed.

In October of 1859, John Brown's raid on Harper's Ferry brought this belief home. While busy with Arlington and Mary, Robert received a message from a young J. E. B. Stuart ordering him at once to the town to restore order. Brown was attempting to

---

[647] Lee, Fitzhugh. *General Lee.* (New York: D. Appleton and Co., 1895), 64; Freeman, *Lee*, 92–93; Davis, Burke, *Gray Fox*, 6–7; Whipple, Wayne. *The Heart of Lee.* (Philadelphia: George W. Jacobs & Co., 1918), 85–86; Lee Family Digital Archive, https://www.encyclopediavirgia.org/Letter_from_Robert_E_Lee_to_Mary_Randolph_Custis_Lee_December_27_1856.

start a slave revolt by inciting one himself. His group of armed men assaulted the town and killed and wounded half a dozen. Now they were holding hostages in a firehouse near the armory. The leader of the raid went by Smith, but everyone knew it was the notorious John Brown of the infamous Pottawatomie Massacre who refused to surrender, even though he was surrounded.

When Colonel Lee arrived, he gave Stuart a message to deliver to Brown under a flag of truce. The note demanded the surrender and their ensured safety, but force would be used if they refused. He told Stuart if Brown refused, he should signal and they would storm the firehouse. Lee told the marines to charge the armory with fixed bayonets to prevent shooting one of the hostages. When Stuart delivered the message to the old bearded man with fire in his eyes, he refused the offer. Stuart waved his hat in the air, and it took only three minutes to capture the raiders and secure the hostages.

A month later, Lee returned to Harper's Ferry to ensure Brown's execution was carried out and guard against any rescue attempt. The governor of Virginia and President Buchanan feared resistance, but Lee kept order, and Brown was executed with no interruptions.[648]

He returned to Texas the following year, but Lincoln's election led Texas to secession against Governor Houston's warnings. Though a southerner, Lee refused to resign from the United States Army, and many in Texas and some fellow officers saw him as a traitor. Writing to his son, he hoped "the wisdom and patriotism of the country will devise some way of saving it, and that a kind Providence has not yet turned the current of His blessings from us."[649] In January of 1861, he wrote a friend, "I wish to live under no other government, and there is no sacrifice I am not ready to make for the preservation of the Union save that of honor…I wish for no other flag than the 'star spangled banner'…I still hope that the wisdom and patriotism of the nation will yet save it."[650]

---

[648] Ibid., 75–77; Freeman, *Lee*, 100–103.

[649] Lee, Robert, 119.

[650] Freeman, *Lee*, 106–107 (To Martha Custis Williams Carter, January 22, 1861); Lee Family Digital Archive, https://leefamilyarchive.org/family-papers/

His allegiance was not to Texas but Virginia, and until it seceded, he would remain in the Union. Writing of the coming conflict, "May God rescue us from the folly of our own acts, save us from selfishness and teach us to love our neighbors as ourselves."[651]

Ordered to the war department in Washington, he reported to his old mentor, General Winfield Scott. Then he met with an official representing the Lincoln administration who offered him command of the United States Army. Lee politely refused, saying if he owned the "four million slaves at the South, I would sacrifice them to the preservation of the Union…but to lift my hand against my own State is impossible."[652] Scott was disappointed he couldn't convince the best officer in the United States Army to take command of it.

After Virginia seceded, Lee prayed intensely for guidance, then wrote his resignation and a separate response to General Scott:

> I therefore tender my resignation, which I request you will recommend for acceptance. It would have been presented at once but for the struggle it has cost me to separate myself from the service to which I have devoted the best years of my life, and all the ability I possessed. During the whole of that time—more than a quarter of a century—I have experienced nothing but kindness from my superiors and a most cordial friendship from my comrades. To no one, General, have I been as much indebted as to yourself for uniform kindness and consideration, and it has always been my ardent desire to merit your approbation. I shall carry to the grave the most grateful recollections of your kind consideration, and your name and fame shall always be dear to me. Save

letters/letters-1861/9-family-papers/1188_robert_e_lee_to_marthacustiscarter_1861_Jan.

[651] Lee, Robert, 122 (January 30, 1861); Freeman, *Lee*, 107.

[652] Whipple, 105–106; Davis, Burke, *Gray Fox*, 13.

in defense of my native State, I never desire again
to draw my sword.[653]

Scott never responded, but it needed to be said, and his character wouldn't allow him to let Scott think he didn't appreciate his
kindness through the years.

After his resignation, he was offered command of the Army
of Virginia. His home state was threatened by Lincoln's call up of
75,000 volunteers to put down the rebellion. Virginia would face
invasion, and Lee vowed not to draw his sword, except in defense of
his state. So he accepted command. Some called him a traitor, but he
resigned and believed the United States to be a Union between states,
not one central power in Washington. States were in this Union, he
believed, by agreement, not force, and if Lincoln wanted to use the
federal power to invade and subjugate Virginia, he would defend her.

After accepting the commission, he addressed the convention
convened to join the Confederacy. "I accept the position your par-
tiality has assigned me, though I would greatly have preferred your
choice should have fallen on one more capable. Trusting in Almighty
God, an approving conscience, and the aid of my fellow-citizens, I
devote myself to the service of my native State, in whose behalf alone
will I ever again draw my sword."[654] With nearly the same words
Washington used upon his commission to command the army of the
rebellious colonies, Lee was following in his hero's footsteps.

Once Virginia joined the Confederacy, Lee was sent to build
up the naval defenses off the Virginia coast. Later, he was promoted
to brigadier general, then major general, and commanded forces in
western Virginia with little success in that theater. His subordinates
were incompetent, and he was not a general who forced his will on
his officers. He was often called "Granny" the same way General
Horatio Gates was during the Revolution. His meekness in building
defenses and cautious maneuvers in western Virginia led some to say
this showed weak leadership.

---

[653] Lee, Robert, 132–133 (April 20, 1861); Davis, Burke, *Gray Fox*, 15–16.
[654] Ibid., 135; Davis, Burke, *Gray Fox*, 21–22.

His humility often conflicted with commanding obedience from his fellow officers, and he never believed he was in control of events, though he had free will to make decisions. He trusted in providence to determine outcomes. He had acquired more important assets to his leadership style, which many with egos lacked, like compassion for both sides, freedom for officers to adapt and improvise to conditions on the field instead of strict adherence to a battle plan, and garnered mutual respect from many. His temperament was indispensable for soothing personal feuds and squabbles within the Confederate Army, and like Washington before, he bridged the gap between President Davis's abrasive personality and his vain generals.

Davis saw this capacity in Lee and snatched him from the field making him his military advisor. Davis liked to micromanage his administration, and Lee was a perfect fit. He wasn't happy with the passive role but accepted it as God's will.

In April of 1862, Union general George B. McClellan positioned his massive Army of the Potomac on the outskirts of the Confederate capital Richmond, Virginia, with a bold plan to end the war quickly. General Joseph E. Johnston was between the northern army and Richmond and evacuated troops out of Williamsburg and Yorktown to concentrate his forces. He essentially gave McClellan the outlying towns instead of fighting several small battles piecemeal. The Union general was emboldened by this and attacked at Seven Pines (Fair Oaks), five miles from the southern capital and the two armies clashed on May 31.

President Davis rode to the battlefield to find Johnston and follow the progress of the fight, and Lee joined him along the way. Seeing Johnston mount his horse and ride away, the same moment they arrived, they felt he was avoiding them and likely afraid they would interfere with his strategy. As the battle quickly deteriorated, Davis tried to rally men into battle but was prevented by their fast retreat. Though the Battle of Seven Pines was inconclusive, it ended with a Confederate recoil.[655]

---

[655] Sears, Stephen W. *To the Gates of Richmond: The Peninsula Campaign.* (Boston: Houghton Mifflin Co., 1992), 134–135; Davis, Burke, *Gray Fox*, 73–75;

Word that General Johnston was wounded reached Davis. A flesh wound in his shoulder and a more serious one from shrapnel to the chest toppled him from his horse, and the Confederate president knew he would be incapacitated for some time. He needed to find a replacement quickly, for McClellan's entire force was across the way, threatening the capital of the Confederacy. Riding through the hordes of his wounded soldiers, Davis turned to Lee and said, "General Lee, I shall assign you to command of this army."[656]

And just like that, Robert E. Lee was made commanding general of the entire army of Northern Virginia which was the main Confederate army in the east. One day, he was shuffling papers, and the next, he had command of the eastern theater of war.

Feeling grateful for such an opportunity, he also felt the weight of the responsibility. Many believed his experience was based on building defenses and scouting for Scott in Mexico. So far in this war, he had failed to impress, and "Granny" Lee now faced a successful general who was first, not second, in his class at West Point. Lee was a good man, but could he fight and win against a prodigy general, a massive army, and superior equipment with no experience leading an entire army?

During the Seven Days battle which soon followed, Lee fought tenaciously and earned the respect of many who doubted him. In the four major battles on the Peninsula, he experienced communication breakdown and missed opportunities but ordered the army at McClellan repeatedly. What Lee lacked in perfection, he made up with energy and caused the Union general to overestimate the enemy and afraid to counterattack. The northern army retreated to the James River, ending the Peninsula Campaign and would soon evacuate back to Washington. Lee's miscalculations showed him how not to command an army. A quick learner, he recognized the mistakes and adjusted to them. He wasn't going to sit back and wait for another invasion and quickly formed a plan to take the fight directly to the heart of the Union. After the Seven Days, he wrote Mary, "I

Freeman, *Lee*, 182–184.
[656] Lee, Robert, 169–170; Freeman, *Lee*, 182–185.

have returned to my old quarters and am filled with gratitude to our Heavenly Father for all the mercies He has extended to us. Our success has not been so great or complete as we could have descried, but God knows what is best for us."[657]

Turning to his new lieutenant, General Stonewall Jackson, for his next move, he targeted General John Pope, whose army was moving near the Manassas battlefield to threaten Richmond again from the north to cover McClellan's evacuation. Pompous and brash, Pope regarded the Virginian civilian population as combatants, and neither respected private property nor civil rights. To Lee, this was unbecoming of an officer to behave this way, and he personally wanted to whip the barbarian. Most of McClellan's army was still near Richmond and could attack if it got word the southern commander moved north to attack Pope. In fact, Pope might be a ruse to draw him away, and he must cover both possibilities. A mere instrument to fulfill a divine purpose, he would do what his heart and instinct guided him to do.

What it guided him to do next would make history.

* * * * *

The White House, February 20, 1862

How could it be happening again? His son was dead. Poor Willie was gone, just like Eddie. Mary fell on the boy's bed, weeping uncontrollably, and Lincoln couldn't seem to comfort her. A nurse, Elizabeth Keckley, helped her to her feet and led her to her room. Mary favored Willie, and this would probably drive her mad from despair. He was such a good boy and smart as a whip.

At the age of eleven, William Wallace Lincoln was much like his father in temperament, with a serious reflective side and a love of reading, and wrote poetry and collected historic news clippings of current events. He was also a very affectionate child, and his mother

---

[657] Lee, Fitzhugh, 171; Davis, Burke, *Gray Fox*, 104.

loved him so. It would kill her, he thought. Tad was ill as well but seemed to be recovering.

Lincoln spoiled his younger sons and was the opposite of his own father when it came to discipline. He believed in letting them be children and wouldn't make them grow up too fast. They would enjoy their childhood while they could. He felt guilty for working too much. His oldest son, Robert, barely had a relationship with him because he was gone so much of his childhood riding the legal circuit. This guilt led him to spoil them. Another reason for spoiling them was the memory of Eddie because children were a gift and could be gone in a blink of an eye, so he never took them for granted.

Now he had lost two sons, and his own grief nearly overwhelmed him. It was like losing everyone he had lost all over again. Why did they all have to die? His mother, sister, Anne, Eddie, and now Willie. The hardest part of living was watching loved ones die.

He was tired and barely slept while Willie was suffering the illness. Sitting by his bed night after night, he watched his small body wither without a way to save him. Why did God want him to suffer so much? Providence made things happen for a reason, but this made no sense. Why take another of his sons?

Looking down at his son's body, he saw his face covered with a sheet and lifted it to see him one more time, "My poor boy, he was too good for this earth. God has called him home. I know that he is much better off in heaven, but then we loved him so. It is hard, hard to have him die."[658] God's will was hard to accept sometimes. Visiting his secretary's office, the president said, "Well, Nicolay, my boy is gone—he is actually gone." This realization finally brought him to tears. Later, he told Tad of his brother's death as he laid next to the sick boy, and they cried together.

* * * * *

---

[658] Keckley, Elizabeth. *Behind the Scenes or, Thirty Years a Slave, and Four Years in the White House.* (New York: G.W. Carleton & Co., Publishers, 1868), 102–104; Oates, 313–315; Donald, 336; Sandburg, 290–291.

On the day of Willie's funeral, one of the nurses told Lincoln many were praying for him, and he replied, tearfully, "I am glad to hear that. I want them to pray for me. I need their prayers." A few days later, the same nurse asked him if he could trust in God that his son was in a better place, and he answered, "I think I can, and I will try. I wish I had that childlike faith you speak of, and I trust He will give it to me." Thinking of his mother, he said, "I had a good Christian mother and her prayers have followed me thus far through life."[659]

He sank into a deep depression and began having vivid dreams, often dreaming of Willie, alive again and playing on the lawn of the White House. Calling out to him, he would always wake to face the truth.

Mary controlled her own emotion long enough to recognize her husband's pain and asked the pastor of Trinity Church in New York, Dr. Francis Vinton, to pay him a visit. When the minister arrived, he assured the president, "Your son is alive in paradise. Do you remember that passage in the Gospels, 'God is not a God of the dead, but of the living: for all live unto him?'"

Lincoln asked, "Alive! Alive! Surely you mock me?"

Rising and moving closer, Vinton said, "No, sir. Believe me, it is a most comforting doctrine of the church, founded upon the words of Christ himself."

Grasping the pastor's neck in a hug, the president placed his head on his chest and, through tears, said, "Alive? Alive?"[660]

Over the next few months, he found meaning in the death of his son and comfort in the promise of salvation. He realized faith was more important than his own understanding and developed a personal relationship with God that profoundly changed him.

---

[659] Johnson, *Lincoln*, 80–81 (from *Lincoln Scrapbook*, Library of Congress, Washington, Letter of Mrs. Rebecca R. Pomeroy, 54); Barton, William E. *The Soul of Abraham Lincoln*. (New York: George H. Doran Co., 1920), 205.

[660] Carpenter, Frank B. *Six Months at the White House with Abraham Lincoln: The Story of a Picture*. (New York: Hurd and Houghton, 1866), 117–119; Barton, 206–207; Oates, 317.

News from the frontline was all bleak that year. McClellan was slow to move and unsuccessful when he did, and on the Virginian peninsula, his grand battle plan failed as the rebels watched him evacuate.

In the west, news was a bit brighter with General Grant's captures of Fort Henry and Donelson, but his technical victory at Shiloh cost so many casualties; it felt like a defeat. Thirteen thousand Union casualties in two days was a hard pill to swallow.

So much defeat was more than any president could bear, and he turned to his newfound faith. When he was informed that Americans were praying for him, he was comforted by it and said if he could choose to go home and live a peaceful life, he would, but "it has pleased Almighty God to place me in my present position and, looking to Him for wisdom and divine guidance, I must work out my destiny as best I can."[661]

On April 10, he issued a First Proclamation for Thanksgiving and asked Americans to "acknowledge and render thanks to our Heavenly Father for these inestimable blessings."[662] These blessings were a new optimism born out of the understanding that God's plan would unfold according to His will, not any man's will.

In June, he was visited by a group of influential men who discussed the progress of the war and the issue of slavery. After some small talk and debate, the president sat quietly, listening to their concerns without interrupting. As they finished their words, springing to his feet, Lincoln pointed at them, his face shining like someone possessed, and said:

> My faith is greater than yours. I will not only believe that Providence is not unmindful of the struggle in which this nation is engaged, that if

---

[661] Johnson, *Lincoln*, 85–86 (from *Lincoln Scrapbook*, Library of Congress, Washington, Reverend N.W. Miner, August 1, 1871, p. 52, relating an encounter from April 1862).

[662] Lincoln, *Works*, Vol. 7, 144 (Proclamation Recommending Thanksgiving for Victories, April 10, 1862).

we do not do right, God will let us go our own way to ruin; and that if we do right, He will lead us safely out of this wilderness, crown our arms with victory, and restore our dissevered Union, as you have expressed your belief…

The room was silent as every man beamed with pride at him. He seemed different to them somehow and continued:

But I also believe He will compel us to do right, in order that He may do these things, not so much because we desire them as that they accord with His plans of dealing with this nation, in the midst of which He means to establish justice. I think that He means that we shall do more than we have yet done in the furtherance of His plans and He will open the way for our doing it.

With holy conviction, he proclaimed, "I have felt His hand upon me in great trials and submitted to His guidance, and I trust that as He shall farther open the way, I will be ready to walk therein, relying on His help and trusting in His goodness and wisdom."[663]

Dealing with the death of Willie, McClellan's continued inaction, and a fear Great Britain and France would become allies of the Confederacy, he leaned on his faith for strength. General John Pope was his next trial, and maybe the general's bragging of prowess in battle would translate to action. McClellan had failed, so he ordered Pope to find the enemy and engage them.

On August 28–30, Pope fell for "Stonewall" Jackson's feint as the rest of Lee's army soundly defeated him at the Second Battle of Manassas (Bull Run). The one-sided battle caused Lincoln disappointment, but he did not waver. "I have done the best I could. I

---

[663] Johnson, *Lincoln*, 88–89 (from *North American Review*, December 1896, "*Some Memories of Lincoln*," p. 667, by James F. Wilson).

have asked God to guide me, and now I must leave the result with Him."[664]

He was ready to change this struggle from one of preserving the Union to one of morality. It could never be just about the Union. Britain and France watched as the Confederacy mauled their armies, and he knew the war had to be about something more. It should be about the liberty God granted them as a nation. It was always about this, regardless of what any of them said. God had willed it, and they were his instruments.

Secretary of State William Seward advised him to wait for victory to announce his new purpose, and to do so now would appear desperate. One single victory could present an opportunity, so they patiently waited for one as Confederates moved closer to Washington.

When asked if God was on his and the Union's side, Lincoln answered, "I am not at all concerned about that, for I know that the Lord is always on the side of right; but it is my constant anxiety and prayer that I and this nation should be on the Lord's side."[665]

* * * * *

Frederick, Maryland, September 11, 1862

Confederate general Daniel Harvey Hill skimmed over the two identical copies of General Lee's Special Order Number 19, detailing plans on invading the North. The first copy was the original, and the duplicate was from General Jackson who always made duplicates of Lee's orders. Hill handed these to his staff officer and finished prepping his men.

The staff officer felt that two identical orders were unwarranted and decided to use the extra copy to wrap three cigars in to keep

---

[664] Ibid., 91 (from *Lincoln Scrapbook*, Library of Congress, Washington, Mrs. Rebecca R. Pomeroy, p. 54).

[665] Carpenter, 282; Wheeler, Joe. *Abraham Lincoln: A Man of Faith and Courage.* (New York: Howard Books/Simon & Schuster, 2008), 183.

them dry. He stuffed this in his pocket, mounted his horse, and rode away with Lee's army as it left Frederick in pursuit of final victory.

After Pope was defeated at Second Manassas, Lincoln fired him and reinstated McClellan. Washington was now vulnerable with nothing between it and Lee's oncoming army, except McClellan. His army had recently completed its evacuation from the Peninsula Campaign, and Lee saw an opportunity to end the war with his return. The Union army was demoralized from their string of defeats, and their commander was still overcautious. If Lee brought the war to northern doorsteps, they might sue for peace, or Britain and France might make an alliance with the South.

The only issue for Lee's army was numbers and supplies. The Confederate army's numbers had dwindled, and food, shoes, and ammunition were scarce. The plan was to enter Maryland and use it as a base to invade Pennsylvania, thus surrounding Washington and the Union army. Maryland, not officially in the Confederacy, had a large population of southern sympathizers, and many believed fresh recruits from this would swell his ranks.

One small problem Lee faced was the Union troops still at Harper's Ferry, Virginia, in his rear. Like General Scott in Mexico, he divided his undermanned army. One force under Jackson would strike Harper's Ferry while the second force continued the main attack. Once Harper's Ferry was taken, Jackson's army would rejoin the main force, hopefully in time for the battle. Lee knew it was a gamble, but because of its audacity, McClellan would never suspect it. McClellan always assumed Confederates had a larger army than they did, and this presumption worked to Lee's advantage. The southern commander was certain this bold move would succeed. This was when he wrote Special Order Number 19 with every detail of his strategy and sent it to his commanders. When Hill's staff officer used a copy of this for his cigars, it seemed as if providence moved.

On the way out of camp at Frederick, Maryland, the cigars wrapped in the order fell unknown from the careless rider's pocket.

On September 13, the Union army moved into Frederick to counter the threat. An Indiana regiment camped near a grove and, stretched out on the ground. Private B. W. Mitchell spotted a wad of crumpled paper lying near a wood pile and decided to investigate. Inspecting it, he showed it to Sergeant J. M. Bloss the bounty of three cigars, and the two soldiers quickly searched for a light, but before discarding the paper, Mitchell noticed writing on it. It described some troop movements and clearly showed the signature of General Robert E. Lee. The two men thought it might be of some importance and gave it to their commander.

Now if only someone would see the importance of it and get it to McClellan.[666]

* * * * *

On September 14, General McClellan attacked Lee's army at South Mountain, Maryland. This massive assault pushed D. H. Hill's forward force back to the small town of Sharpsburg, near Antietam Creek.

Somehow, McClellan took the offensive and he never made risky movements. Lee had to react to him instead of taking his own initiative, and his outnumbered army at Sharpsburg badly needed Jackson's troops who were still at Harper's Ferry. Lee sent an urgent message, ordering him to hurry as fast as possible to Sharpsburg. Jackson had already invested Harper's Ferry and rushed his men to Lee's aid. General A. P. Hill's force brought up the rear and would be the last to arrive.

McClellan had 90,000 men against Lee's 18,000, but his caution returned and he believed he was facing six times this number. This over calculation kept the Union commander from fully committing his entire army and ordered segmented assaults out of fear of being surrounded. His original plan was to send General Joseph Hooker around Lee's left flank and General Ambrose Burnside over a bridge on the creek to hit his right. Once the two attacked, McClellan's force in the center would complete the envelopment.

---

[666] Freeman, *Lee*, 250–251; Sears, Stephen. *Landscape Turned Red: The Battle of Antietam.* (New Haven: Ticknor & Fields, 1983), 349–352 (Appendix 1: The Lost Order); Davis, Burke, *Gray Fox*, 138–140.

On September 17, Hooker attacked but ran into Jackson's army near a church. Exhausted from their forced march, "Stonewall's" army fought tenaciously before they were pushed back and inflicted a heavy toll on Hooker's men. In the center, most of the action took place in a cornfield and near a sunken road where most of the casualties happened. Burnside's men paid a hefty price, trying to cross the bridge, and failed in the attempt. All day, both sides battled back and forth without gaining an advantage. Lee saw his army wearing down while McClellan just fed men into the meat grinder and wondered where A. P. Hill's men were. They still hadn't arrived, and were desperately needed.

As the southerners recoiled further, an unknown force was spotted across the field. Unable to use his spyglass because both hands were wrapped after a fall from his horse, Lee asked a nearby officer to identify them. He recognized them as Confederate soldiers but wasn't sure what regiment. Lee was confident it was A. P. Hill's men arriving at just the right time. Hill's forces struck McClellan's army with renewed energy and seemed to take the fight out of the bluecoats. As the sun set over the field, the battle ended.

Lee regrouped and prepared for new attacks come morning. Surely, "Little Mac" would resume them at dawn. Lee's own casualty count surprised everyone—10,000 in one day. McClellan's casualties were over 12,000, and Antietam was the single bloodiest day in American history with over 22,000 dead or wounded. Both armies were exhausted, and Lee lacked the ability to continue. McClellan, like always, was overcautious.[667]

The next day, there was no resumption of hostilities, and Lee used the lull to evacuate his army back to Virginia. Even though he held his ground, he couldn't continue. The invasion was stopped in its tracks, his supply line was stretched, and his smaller force was at their breaking point. When McClellan attacked, it snatched the offensive from him. The North interpreted Lee's evacuation as a victory, which it was in a technical sense because McClellan still held the ground as Lee abandoned it.

---

[667] Foote, Vol. 1, 677–679, 688; Freeman, *Lee*, 258–261; Catton, Bruce. *Terrible Swift Sword*. (Garden City: Doubleday & Co. Inc., 1963), 453–456.

Though McClellan outperformed his earlier disasters on the peninsula, Lincoln fired him again for failing to chase and destroy Lee's army. It was another missed opportunity, and the president was done with him, and though frustrated by McClellan's failure, he remained optimistic.

Lee's army returned to Virginia in high spirits and were convinced they had beaten the Yankees but were outnumbered and out-supplied. This would continue to haunt them for the rest of the war, and the Battle of Antietam (Sharpsburg) was a failed invasion. Lee's plan was ruined, and McClellan somehow knew where and when to attack.

Lincoln and others criticized McClellan because he had the greatest opportunity of the war and failed to take advantage of it. He had Lee's entire battle plan in his hands and still couldn't deliver a knock-out blow. The lost order found its way to the general and prompted him to strike Lee at South Mountain, halting the invasion. Providence provided detailed plans of the enemy, and he still choked.

When providence moved, it mattered who was at the helm. Lincoln understood this and vowed to never let it happen again. He just needed to find the right general, and appointed General Ambrose Burnside commander of the army because of his courageous performance at Antietam. His actions at the bridge may have been the key to keeping Lee from concentrating his forces on the center, and because Lincoln had no one else.

The miracle at Antietam prevented Lee from possibly winning the war. The discovered order made the difference, and Lincoln saw this an obvious message from God. He had to trust in providence to send him the right commander at the right moment, and until then, he would persevere, certain of eventual victory.

To Robert E. Lee, the failed invasion and lost order was part of God's will, and his purpose would be revealed in time. He was merely a participant in how it would end.[668]

* * * * *

---

[668] Davis, Burke, *Gray Fox*, 154; Donald, 389–390.

The White House, September 22, 1862

The president sat behind his desk, anxiously awaiting the Cabinet. He was going to do it. The time was now, and he was ready to fulfill his purpose. Some would think it reckless and would harm army recruitment, but he felt it was right.

This whole affair was unexplainable with basic logic. He was a simple Illinois lawyer without a college education and essentially no experience governing. His clothes never fit right, and he was a dyed-in-the-wool hick from the sticks. He had a face only a mother could love, and here he was—president of the United States—embroiled in a civil war.

Thinking back on a story his father told him once, he wondered if there was something to it. Way before he was born, Thomas Lincoln had a dream of walking into a new house with his future wife inside coring apples, and swore he somehow knew the unknown woman was his betrothed. Later, when he moved to Kentucky, he walked inside his newly built home, and sitting there, coring apples was Nancy Hanks, just like his dream. The couple were soon married, and Abraham was born. This was one of his father's favorite yarns, yet it never seemed important to Lincoln until now. Maybe it was destiny, and his parents were purposely brought together to conceive him for this very moment. He believed God had a purpose for each person and moved them toward preordained paths with His providence, and maybe it was no accident but the miracle of God's will. He never entertained he would be an instrument for his will, but maybe he had been all along. Praying on it, he felt God had answered.[669]

As the Cabinet members arrived and found their seats, he waited deep in thought. After they settled in and niceties were exchanged, they turned to him with enquiring expressions. He tried to lighten the mood first with a bit of humor, but the joke missed its mark, so he proceeded to the business at hand. "The time for the annunciation of the emancipation policy can be no longer delayed. Public

---

[669] Wheeler, 37–38.

sentiment will sustain it, many of my warmest friends and supporters demand it…" His voice lowered with an air of humility. "And I have promised my God that I will do it."

Secretary of the Treasury, Salmon P. Chase, wanted clarification of his last few words, and he responded with greater confidence in his voice, "I made a solemn vow before God, that if General Lee were driven back from Pennsylvania, I would crown the result by the declaration of freedom to the slaves." God had answered his prayers. This war was never about the Union and had always been about slavery–to God.[670]

The document he wrote for this occasion, the *Emancipation Proclamation*, said that all states in rebellion must end hostilities and rejoin the Union by January 1, 1863, or their slaves would be set free. It wouldn't free the slaves in the border states not in rebellion, but it would throughout the Confederacy. This war measure would work several ways. Politically, it would appease the abolitionists, encourage runaway slaves, and allow the Union army and navy to confiscate any slaves found in conquered territory. These slaves could be used against their former masters in the war effort or enlist in the colored regiments being raised.

It also made a bold statement to the world, and changed the aim of the war from the right of secession to slavery. Since Britain and France had banned slavery years before, this made an alliance with the South impossible. Politically, it was brilliant, but Lincoln's main purpose was explained by his actions and words.

A few days after this Cabinet meeting, answering a letter about this change in purpose, he wrote:

> We are indeed going through a great trial—a fiery trial. In the very responsible position in which I happen to be placed, being a humble instrument in the hands of our Heavenly Father, as I am, and as we all are, to work out His great purposes, I

[670] Welles, Gideon. *Diary of Gideon Welles, Vol. 1 1861–March 30, 1864*. (Boston: Houghton Mifflin Co, 1911), 143 (September 22, 1862 Cabinet Meeting); Carpenter, 89–90; Johnson, *Lincoln*, 96.

have desired that all my works and acts may be according to His will, and that it might be so, I have sought His aid; but if after endeavoring to do my best in the light which He affords me, I find my efforts fail, I must believe that for some purpose unknown to me, He wills it otherwise. If I had my way, this war would have never commenced. If I had been allowed my way, this war would have ended before this; but we find it still continues, and we must believe that He permits it for some wise purpose of His own, mysterious and unknown to us; and though with our limited understandings we may not be able to comprehend it, yet we cannot believe that He who made the world still governs it.[671]

Of course, some said he wrote this merely to placate a religious supporter, but his words and actions in private didn't contradict those in public. Some historians equate Lincoln with modern politicians, but how could he be "Honest Abe" and a compulsive liar collectively? His behavior before and after says otherwise. He believed he was "a humble instrument" of providence and subject to the control of a higher will. He also knew both sides in this war were Christians praying to the very same God for victory, but only one side could be on God's side. God's will and mercy would determine the outcome.

Near the end of September that year, his secretary, John Hay, came across a private paper on Lincoln's desk. It wasn't intended for public consumption, but Hay couldn't resist copying it for his own records. Only after Lincoln's death did Hay reveal it to the public. Titled "Meditation of the Divine Will," it uncovered the president's deepest beliefs. "The will of God prevails. In great contests each party claims to act in accordance with the will of God. Both may be, and one must be, wrong. God cannot be for and against the same thing

---

[671] Lincoln, *Works,* Vol. 8, 50–51 (Reply to an Address by Mrs. Gurney, September, [28?], 1862).

at the same time." Like his borrowing from Christ's own words in "a house divided against itself cannot stand," he drew a precise distinction between good and evil. The will of God and the will of Satan could not stand together as well, and shouldn't:

> In the present civil war, it is quite possible that God's purpose is something different from the purpose of either party; and yet the human instrumentalities, working just as they do, are of the best adaptation to affect His purpose. I am almost ready to say this is probably true; that God wills this contest, and wills that it shall not end yet. By His mere great power on the minds of the now contestants, he could have either saved or destroyed the Union without a human contest. Yet the contest began. And, having begun, He could give the final victory to either side any day. Yet the contest proceeds.[672]

On November 15, 1862, he sent an order for the military to observe the Sabbath. "The importance for man and beast of the prescribed weekly rest, the sacred rights of Christian soldiers and sailors, a becoming deference to the best sentiment of a Christian people, and due regard for the Divine Will." Why issue an order for the Christian Sabbath if he wasn't a Christian as some claim? He also invoked the spirit of George Washington in this order:

> At this time of public distress—adopting the words of Washington in 1776—"men may find enough to do in the service of God and their country without abandoning themselves to vice and immorality." The first general order issued by the Father of the Country after the Declaration of Independence indicates the spirit in which

---

[672] Ibid., 52–53 (Meditation on the Divine Will, September [30?], 1862).

our institutions were founded and should ever be defended. "The General hopes and trusts that every officer and man will endeavor to live and act as becomes a Christian soldier, defending the dearest rights and liberties of his country.[673]

In his second annual message to Congress in December, he restated his new war aim by suggesting constitutional amendments to free every slave. He even suggested monetary compensation to the slave owners to heal the divisions and restore the nation. Summing up, he said:

> The fiery trial through which we pass will light us down, in honor or dishonor, to the latest genera-tion. We say we are for the Union. The world will not forget that we say this. We know how to save the Union. The world knows we do know how to save it. We—even we here—hold the power and bear the responsibility. In giving freedom to the slave, we assure freedom to the free—honorable alike in what we give and what we preserve.

While there were people enslaved anywhere, slavery was accepted as a reality. Abolishing it would proclaim it a sin for all humanity and safeguard liberty to all people everywhere. He continued, "We shall nobly save or meanly lose the last, best hope of earth. Other means may succeed; this could not fail. The way is plain, peaceful, generous, just—a way which, if followed, the world will forever applaud and God must forever bless."[674]

Some said he used God to further his own political aims, while others said he talked of ending slavery as a last desperate act, but these accusations make little sense. So soon after Willie's death and his own soaring faith, why would he be disingenuous? When he was

---

[673] Ibid., 76–77 (Order for Sabbath Observance, November 15, 1862).
[674] Ibid., 131 (Annual Message to Congress, December 1, 1862).

only a clerk at the general store back in Illinois, he travelled miles to deliver money and goods when he discovered his customers had been overcharged. His own political enemies knew him to be incorruptible, and this honesty often hurt him politically. Should a man's past actions and words be judged unworthy of measuring his character? And if so, then what should we measure it by?

Some want Lincoln, the "Great Emancipator," to conform to their own expectations. They want him to be both irreligious and moral but point to immoral behavior to explain away his professed religious beliefs. Clearly to him, he was now doing the will of God, and his new faith was strengthening his purpose. To the end of his life, he spoke of God, Christianity, and the Scriptures in most of his speeches and writings.

God had saved the Union at Antietam, and Lee returned to Virginia, just like he asked in prayers. He had to change the purpose of the struggle to be in harmony with God's will.

The South was winning everywhere, it seemed. From First to Second Manassas and everything in between, they were being outgeneraled and outfought in the East, and Grant was failing to take Vicksburg in the West. All they really could claim at this point in the war was two draws at Shiloh and Antietam, which cost over twenty thousand casualties. Lincoln could see the obvious—their purpose was wrong. The Union had never been God's ultimate purpose; it had always been the freedom it promised to everyone.

General Burnside was moving against Lee at Fredericksburg. Was he the general needed to turn it around? The president would keep praying and asking for the answers. Staying the course and keeping the faith was all he could do for now.

* * * * *

Fredericksburg, Virginia, December 13, 1862

The sight was horrifying. Whole columns of men dead and wounded, then the next row would climb over them and take their turn.

Joshua Chamberlain could only look on anxious and frustrated. Instead of feeding segments into the carnage one at a time, he thought General Burnside should attack with his whole army in one massive assault. Their sheer numbers would overwhelm the rebels, but he knew he had little clout when it came to strategy, although it seemed so obvious.

Lee's army was across the Rappahannock River on the heights above the town. At the bottom of these heights was a sunken road and a stonewall facing the Union army. Twenty-four hundred Confederate riflemen crouched behind this wall while behind them, artillery was ready to open up again.

General Jackson was sporting the new uniform Jeb Stuart gave him and hadn't had one since the war began. General Longstreet teasingly asked him, "Ain't you frightened?"

Jackson answered, "Perhaps, I'll frighten them after a while."

Longstreet smiled but continued to question him, "Jackson, what are you going to do with all those people over there?"

Staring across the river, "Stonewall's" eyes narrowed, and he simply said, "Sir, we will give them the bayonet."

Longstreet stared back across the river and was sure the enemy would never get close enough for that.[675]

General Burnside ordered pontoon bridges built across the river to storm the heights on the right. On the left, Jackson's men and artillery were holding back each successive wave attempting to cross and still, the bloodbath continued.

Chamberlain's temper was getting the best of him, and he slowed his breathing. *Damn it—let us in there! Let the 20th Maine give it a try.* They would make them pay. His adrenaline was pumping, but his judgment remained steady. This was from years of discipline his father taught him. "Do it—that's how," he could still hear the old man's stern voice. Watching this massacre wasn't how you "do it." The rebels were killing them as fast as Burnside could move more units in front of the stone wall to try again.

---

[675] Davis, Burke, *Gray Fox*, 166.

General Joshua L. Chamberlain

The 20th was called later that day, and Chamberlain, on foot, led them forward. Snow had covered the entire landscape, and the temperature plummeted. If they could keep moving, the cold was no problem for these Maine men.

As they approached the plain in front of the town, they saw the horror. The ground was covered with dead and dying blue-coated men. A few of these wounded yelled encouragement to them, but others warned of the impending doom. Arms, legs, heads, and torsos lay everywhere, and the snowy mud-trampled ground was covered in blood.

Straight ahead, Lee's men fired from the protection of the wall as the cannon unleashed canister and grapeshot directly into the 20th Maine. The barrage was so intense, they couldn't continue. They dropped and hugged the ground.[676]

Chamberlain used a nearby dead soldier as his cover, and as day drifted to night, the cold became a factor because he had left his cover and overcoat behind. Using the tail of the dead man's overcoat, he covered his face and huddled closer to the body. General Burnside had blundered on this. To take an entrenched army, one

---

[676] Trulock, 94–97; Foote, Shelby. *The Civil War: A Narrative, Vol. 2 Fredericksburg to Meridian.* (New York: Vintage Books, 1963, 1986), 35–36.

had to use overwhelming force, and even an amateur knew this. With his face covered and laying between two of his dead country-men, Chamberlain waited and dozed.[677]

On the other side, General Lee observed this pointless slaugh-ter. He nearly lost his life twice that day from exploding cannon and knew his life was in the hands of God. He didn't reflect on things beyond his control. Sending a message to General Jackson, remind-ing him to keep his men's ammunition supplied, he said, "I am truly grateful to the Giver of all victory for having blessed us thus far in our terrible struggle. I pray He may continue it."[678]

Chamberlain awoke near dawn, cold and exhausted. A light doze was the most he could hope for among the moans of the wounded and dying. An orderly mistook him for dead at first, but he made his way back to the rear. He asked his commander, Colonel Ames, what the next move would be, but there were no orders.

The 20th pulled back, and Burnside called retreat. He evac-uated his 100,000 men all the way back across the Potomac, and Chamberlain was outraged. Why would they sacrifice 14,000 men for nothing? They just needed to keep trying. Maybe try an assault with overwhelming force? If they were determined to do it, they would.

Burnside decide he had lost too many men while Lee only lost a third of his casualties. To Ambrose Burnside, this meant defeat. Retreat and your army will live to fight another day; so he retreated.[679]

The day of the battle, General Lee watched the total rout of Burnside's army as thousands of Union troops lay dead and wounded across the field. Turning to his officers, he said, "It is well that war is so terrible…we should grow too fond of it."[680]

General Burnside, Lieutenant-Colonel Chamberlain, and President Lincoln saw nothing to grow fond of now. After the disaster

---

[677] Ibid., 97–98.

[678] Davis, Burke, *Gray Fox*, 171.

[679] Trulock, 98–101; Foote, Vol. 2, 40–41; Catton, Bruce. *Glory Road: The Bloody Route from Fredericksburg to Gettysburg*. (Garden City: Doubleday & Co. Inc., 1952), 55–57.

[680] Lee, Robert, 208; Freeman, *Lee*, 278; Foote, Vol. 2, 37.

at Fredericksburg and another failed attempt by Burnside, Lincoln relieved his fourth commander.

The winter lull in the fighting gave his fifth general breathing room to regroup. Hotheaded and arrogant, General Joseph Hooker was appointed to replace Burnside, and Lincoln hoped the fifth time was the charm. Many thought Hooker was dangerous, and he had once called for a military dictatorship to win the war, but Lincoln wasn't worried about the blustery officer. He just wondered if his big talk would translate to victories. Since he'd tried every other personality, maybe some bravado was what was needed. General Hooker's nickname was "Fighting Joe," and the president prayed he would live up to his name.

Calling for a second National Fast-day, he asked the people to pray for God's aid. He knew it would come in God's time, not his own, but maybe more prayers would help.

Now if he could just find a general who would fight.

* * * * *

Headquarters of General Grant, May 1862

Grant puffed on his cigar and continued writing:

> To say that I have not been distressed at these attacks upon me would be false, for I have a father, mother, wife, & children who read them and are distressed by them and I necessarily share with them in it. Then too all subject to my orders read these charges and it is calculated to weaken their confidence in me and weaken my ability to render efficient service in our present.[681]

After Shiloh, the northern newspapers criticized Grant, and rumors of him drinking again during battle damaged his credibil-

---

[681] Catton, *Grant Moves South*, 262 (To E. B. Washburne, May 14, 1862).

ity. Once branded a drunk, it was hard to shake, and now he could play defense or offense. Being removed from command by General Halleck was insulting, to say the least. Even though Halleck gave him second place in order to take command himself, Grant was disgusted that a rumor could cause this much injustice. Second place was an advisory role, and he was ready to resign. If the cause didn't want him, he wasn't going to force the issue. He had to be in the field commanding or he would go home. He would be happier with Julia and the children anyway, and maybe it was for the best.

Telling Sherman of his intention to quit, his friend tried to persuade him to rethink the decision. When Sherman was called crazy, he nearly quit, but Grant convinced him to stay. Now he had his own division, and he told Sam things would turn around for him too. When Grant wrote his memoirs two decades later, his preface began with the quote, "Man proposes and God disposes. There are but few important events in the affairs of men brought about by their own choice."[682]

This was one of those moments. If he quit, he would never know, and besides, quitting wasn't in his nature. He'd been through too much to give up just because it got tough. Selling wood on the streets of St. Louis for food or pawning his favorite watch was harder to swallow than this. Losing your entire crop year after year was even worse. Having a stigma of incompetence hanging over you because of one mistake you made in the past was nothing compared to Mexico, Panama, or Shiloh. Not getting what he thought he deserved, when he wanted it, was routine to him.

He knew this truth, but it took a trusted friend to wake him up. Things would work out; they always had before. General Washington faced criticism and cabal, but he trusted in providence, and General Taylor was removed from command in Mexico because of his popularity and was president of the United States within two years. If he did what was right and kept moving forward, it would work out; he was certain. He'd "lick 'em tomorrow, though" and decided to stay.

---

[682] Grant, Vol. 1, 7 (Preface); Catton, *Grant Moves South*, 274.

Meanwhile in Washington, President Lincoln was visited by the Pennsylvania politician, A. K. McClure. McClure told him that Grant must go because he failed to destroy the Confederates at Shiloh. He pointed at his drunkenness as the culprit, and if the president continued to support him, it would erode support for the war.

Listening as always, Lincoln considered McClure's advice. Shiloh was by no means the victory he wanted, and the newspapers accused Grant of being drunk, but he possessed something other generals were missing. There was something in this man which was indispensable, and the war wasn't going to end by hemming and hawing over an officer's moral perfection. The only way to victory was finding the enemy and destroying it, and they needed generals who understood this. Grant was one of the few who did, and Lincoln liked his pugnacious spirit. He frowned upon the drunk label, and it was rumored the president asked what brand of whisky he drank so he could buy him an entire barrel. If this man was a drunk, he was outperforming his other generals, including the teetotaler ones. Turning to McClure, Lincoln replied, "I can't spare this man: he fights."[683]

* * * * *

Vicksburg, Mississippi, was the South's Gibraltar. Set on high bluffs overlooking the Mississippi River, it was the last obstacle in the way of the Union's complete control of its waterways. New Orleans was already retaken earlier that year, and with the fall of Fort Donelson, Fort Henry, and Shiloh, West Tennessee was now in Union hands. Missouri, Arkansas, and most of Louisiana was as well, but only Vicksburg still stood in the way.

The Union grand strategy to victory was similar to Britain's during the War of 1812. The goal was to split the Confederacy in two and defeat each section separately. Cutting off the Mississippi would cut off supply from the heart of the Confederacy and keep weapons and men from Texas, Louisiana, Arkansas, and Mississippi

---

[683] Donald, 349; Oates, 326; Foote, Vol. 1, 760; Foote, Vol. 2, 217.

from getting to the east. It would also reestablish the North's trade along the river.

General William S. Rosecrans in eastern Tennessee was expected to push General Braxton Bragg's army out of the state, but he was overly cautious, much as McClellan had been in the east. General Halleck was directed to Washington to direct all the Union armies as general-in-chief after McClellan was relieved. Grant was restored to command and was now busy on Vicksburg. Much like the rest of his life, it wasn't going to be easy, but providence had restored his command. It would show him how to capture Vicksburg, and no matter how long or difficult, he would find a way.

Inside the city, General John Pemberton and thirty thousand Confederates had the river covered by heavy artillery. Grant had help from the navy, but getting their vessels past Vicksburg was a huge obstacle. Cannonading the city wasn't an option, because it was out of range high on the bluffs. Grant saw the only possible solution from the east, over land.

First, he sent Sherman from the north through the Yazoo River valley, but Pemberton's men were so dug in, Sherman had to fight his way out at Chickasaw Bluffs. Then Grant had a canal dug south of the city to create a passage for his naval transports to bypass Vicksburg's cannon, but in March of 1863, he gave up the idea when it flooded.

Another canal dug from the Mississippi aptly named Lake Providence, north of the city, failed when it was impractical to accomplish. Then he purposely flooded the Yazoo Pass and sent transports up the river in another attempt to get behind the city. Debris in the river caused delays, and Fort Pemberton was impassable. The transports were forced back in reverse. A subsequent attempt to bypass Fort Pemberton failed as well, and Grant was stopped cold in every attempt to breach Vicksburg.[684]

The Lincoln administration had lost big in the midterm elections in November of 1862, and the humiliating defeat at Fredericksburg darkened the war effort. Halleck was pressured by Secretary of War

---

[684] Foote, Vol. 1, 202–205; Catton, *Grant Moves South*, 378–382.

Stanton to make progress in the west, and he, in turn, put more pressure on Grant for results.

Grant was in the process of learning how to beat the enemy by trial and error. Unknown to him at this time, racking up failures was teaching him and the army lessons for the challenges ahead. Rising above these failures, Grant concocted a new plan in April of 1863.

He marched his army southeast, over land on the Louisiana side, down to an easy crossing on the river. He had Admiral David Porter sneak his transports past Vicksburg in the dark, and it worked. Once past the city, the transports carried the army across to the Mississippi side.

Confederate General Joseph Johnston commanded an army east of Vicksburg to be a threat to Grant's rear, and had to be removed along with the railroad which supplied the city.

He sent Sherman to the city of Jackson, and this caused Johnston to pull back while the Union army captured the railroad. By May, General Pemberton made a determined stand at Champion Hill and the Big Black River, but these encounters only delayed the inevitable, and the Confederates were driven back into the city. Emboldened by his success, Grant ordered an attack on Vicksburg, but after repeated bloody repulses, he realized that taking the city by force would waste too many lives, so he decided to wait and starve them out. The army surrounded the city while Porter's ships closed the ring from the river bombarding the city relentlessly day and night.[685]

Vicksburg's food quickly dwindled. When Pemberton retreated into the city, his fate was sealed. Unless Johnston hit Grant from the rear, his army couldn't escape, and it would be just a matter of days before he'd have to capitulate. Johnston wasn't eager to come to the rescue, so the Confederate general inside Vicksburg had little hope.

Grant was the perfect man for a siege. He had acquired the patience of Job through his life, and especially the last year. He had the southern army right where he wanted and knew if he just kept

[685] Catton, *Grant Moves South*, 455–457; Foote, Vol. 2, 375–378; Catton, Bruce. *Never Call Retreat.* (New York: Washington Square Press/Pocket Books, 1965,1967), 191–195.

at it long enough he would find something that worked. Feeling a certain sense of satisfaction, Sam had proved all the naysayers wrong. They underestimated him, and he showed them all. He wasn't one to tout his success and accepted it humbly.

He had pawned his watch just three years before and now was on the verge of the greatest Union victory of the war thus far. Providence sure was mysterious, he thought. "Man proposes and God disposes. There are but few important events in the affairs of men brought about by their own choice."

Grant would act, but God, like he always did, would determine the outcome.

* * * * *

Richmond, Virginia, May 1863

Jeff Davis arrived back in the Confederate capital from his western trip to bolster morale with much to brag about. With the bloody repulse at Fredericksburg and Burnside's retreat and removal, and Sherman's failed attack at Chickasaw Bluffs in Vicksburg, the war appeared to still be in their favor. Even in Tennessee, Bragg had Rosecrans beat until he decided to retreat.

Everything looked bright for the Confederacy, and Davis still believed Britain and France might intervene. On the trip west, he reestablished the justness of their cause and praised the soldiers' tenacity. He pressed the importance of support and sacrifice of those on the home front. Davis, by nature, wasn't a braggart, but he did have a stubborn unwillingness to see anything other than his own opinion. This rigidity was both attractive and annoying, and once he set his jaw, all other options were out of the question. He believed the Southern army was unstoppable and even invincible. Using his confidence to pump up the crowds with pride for their cause, he still credited their blessings to God.

He countered the Emancipation Proclamation by defending slavery instead of pointing to federal tyranny and the right to secede.

Lincoln had changed the northern war aim from restoring the Union to fighting the national sin of slavery.

Davis accommodated him by allowing him to change the subject, though he never saw the war to preserve slavery as an institution, but only as a right of states to determine, not the federal government. Lincoln took the offense as Davis played defense, and would have global ramifications regardless. Britain wanted southern cotton, but not at the price of supporting slavery and by appearing to defend slavery, Davis seemed to make it the reason for the war.

In the North, the Emancipation was a war measure and a political tool to change the narrative. They believed they were justified banning slavery, because it violated natural law and God-given rights, which the nation was founded upon. Davis played into Lincoln's hands and new purpose for the war.[686]

Even though most Confederate soldiers weren't fighting and dying to maintain slavery,—it now appeared they were by Davis's opposition to ending it. In war, appearances mattered more than the truth, and providence had its own divine purpose.

* * * * *

Fredericksburg, Virginia, May 7, 1863

General Lee had his single greatest victory at the Battle of Chancellorsville but lost his best general. Jackson was recuperating at a safe house after having an arm amputated and would be out of the war for a while. When Lee was briefed on the seriousness of Jackson and that his condition worsened, he relayed a message for the victor of Chancellorsville, "Give Jackson my affectionate regards, and tell him to make haste and get well, and come back to me as soon as he can. He has lost his left arm, but I have lost my right."[687] Jackson lay

---

[686] Cooper, 452–454; Donald, 378; Tate, 166–167; Davis, Jefferson, *Rise*, Vol. 1, Ch. 6–12.

[687] Lee, Robert, 94; Jackson, 468; Freeman, *Lee*, 301–302.

in a house twenty-seven miles from the frontlines and had contracted pneumonia. Speaking to the chaplain a few days before, he said:

> You find me severely wounded, but not unhappy or depressed. I believe that it has been done according to the will of God, and I acquiesce entirely in His holy will. It may seem strange, but you never saw me more perfectly contented than I am today, for I am sure that my Heavenly Father designs this affliction for my good.

Expressing no fear of death, he credited the "the providence of God" with the success in battle. Come what may, "Stonewall" Jackson was a rock in his faith and knew everything happened for a greater purpose. He had little control over events, other than doing what he believed was right and would continue to trust in God's will.[688]

Now he lay delirious from a high fever and the laudanum (mixture of whisky and opium) he was given to manage his pain. Anna Jackson rushed to be by his side, and she was shocked by his appearance. Thinking she would greet a wounded but recuperating husband, she instead found him weak and sick. A week before, she had left him vibrant and full of life, and now, she saw a missing arm, labored breathing, and the shadow of death on his face. Her face sank, and Jackson noticed, and softly said, "You are one of the most precious little wives in the world." She managed a smile, if only to please him.[689]

After a couple more days, Anna was told by the doctor her husband's end was near and knew she must tell him. He always said he wanted to know before he died, if possible, to prepare properly.

She sat next to his bed and calmly said, "Do you know the doctors say you must very soon be in Heaven?" Jackson looked up at her

---

[688] Jackson, 456; Robertson, 740.
[689] Ibid., 465.

as she repeated the question, then she asked, "Do you not feel willing to acquiesce in God's allotment if He wills you to go today?"

He answered, "I prefer it," then louder, "I prefer it."

With her eyes filling with tears, she smiled and said, "Well, before this day closes, you will be with the blessed Savior in His glory."

Jackson drifted in and out of consciousness all day, and at one point, he was determined to live, but Anna told him it wasn't to be. He called for the doctor and said, "Doctor, Anna informs me that you have told her I am to die today...is it so?"

The physician replied that nothing more could be done.

Jackson gazed up at the ceiling, and silence blanketed the room. "Very good, very good," he said, "It is all right."

Later that day, Anna brought their newborn baby, Julia, to see her father. Smiling, he stroked the infant's head and said, "Little darling! Sweet one!" Just as his own mother had died when he was so young, his daughter would never know him.

On Sunday, May 10, Jackson continued to decline. Deliriousness overtook him, and he started shouting commands to his troops in bygone battles. In a moment of clarity, the doctor tried to give him a little brandy, but he refused, saying, "It will only delay my departure, and do me no good. I want to preserve my mind if possible, to the end." It was just like "Stonewall" Jackson to keep his discipline to the end.[690]

At 3:15 p.m., he called out, lost somewhere in his memories. He'd beat the odds and overcame every stumbling block in his path to become one of the greatest generals in history. He'd worked harder than others to achieve greatness, and in his thirty-nine years, he'd accomplished so much.

Perhaps visions of his youth passed before him and the carefree summer days with his sister by the river returned as he shouted with his last breath, "Let us cross over the river and rest under the shade of the trees."[691]

---

[690] Ibid., 469–470; Robertson, 750–752.
[691] Ibid., 471; Robertson, 752–754.

Stonewall Jackson had crossed over the river.

* * * * *

General Lee prayed for Jackson's recovery. Speaking to the same chaplain the wounded general exchanged words with days before, Lee said, "When you return I trust you will find him better. When a suitable occasion offers, give him my love, and tell him that I wrestled in prayer for him last night, as I never prayed, I believe, for myself."[692] Receiving the news of his death the following day, he wrote to Mary, "Any victory would be dear at such a price...I know not how to replace him. God's will be done! I trust He will raise up some one in his place."[693] Telling his brother Carter, "I am grateful to Almighty God for having given us such a man."[694] When he tried to discuss the death, tears trickled down his cheeks.

Writing a general order to his troops, he broke the bad news to the army:

> With deep grief, the commanding general announces to the army the death of Lieutenant General T. J. Jackson... The daring, skill, and energy, of this great and good soldier are now, by the decree of an all-wise Providence, lost to us. But while we mourn his death we feel that his spirit still lives, and will inspire the whole army with indomitable courage and unshaken confidence in God as our hope and strength. Let his name be a watchword to his corps...[695]

---

[692] Ibid., 468; Lee, Robert, 94; Davis, Burke, *Gray Fox*, 205.

[693] Lee, Robert, 94 (To Mary Lee, May 11, 1863); Jones, 242

[694] *Confederate Veteran*, Vol. 31, S.A. Cunningham. (Nashville, 1923), 287 (To Charles Carter Lee, May 24, 1863).

[695] Long, Armistead L. *Memoirs of Robert E. Lee: His Military and Personal History.* (New York: J.M. Stoddart & Co., 1886), 262–263; Jones, 242; Davis, Burke, *Gray Fox*, 206.

Lee was about to launch a second invasion of the North without his best general, and tried to inspire his men to fight because of Jackson's death. The blow was felt all over the South. Thomas Jackson was a unique character who came out of nowhere and left just as fast. The South was dominating the eastern theater with his generalship, and Lee knew First and Second Manassas, the Valley Campaign, Harper's Ferry, and Chancellorsville were all victories because of Jackson. Now he was gone, and the southern army would never be the same without him.

Was Jackson's death an unfortunate accident? Did a freak shooting by his own men, leading to pneumonia and death, seem accidental? Was the providence Jackson put his faith in intervening? He was never afraid in battle, because he believed if God's will intended him to die, he couldn't do anything to prevent it.

After losing his arm, Jackson remained upbeat and described his wounding as "one of the blessings of my life."

One of his lieutenants standing nearby repeated Jackson's favorite verse. "And we know that all things work together for good to them that love God, to them who are the called according to his purpose."

Jackson answered, "Yes, that's it, that's it."[696] Did providence take him home to accomplish its will? His death appeared to be one of those things working for God's purpose. Meanwhile, General Lee was on his way to a small Pennsylvania town named Gettysburg to find out.

* * * * *

The White House, July 1863

The president knew he was in a bind. Hooker had already been relieved of command for the disastrous defeat at Chancellorsville, and General George Meade was his new replacement. Six generals and still not one victory. McClellan's missed opportunity at Antietam

---

[696] Jackson, 454.

was the closest when providence handed them Lee's plans, but still they couldn't win.

With the rout at Chancellorsville, they faced invasion once again, and Lee's army was already in Pennsylvania, outside the hamlet called Gettysburg. If his army beat Meade to Washington, it would be theirs for the taking. If the Union lost the battle, the war would likely be as well. Lincoln knew they needed a miracle.

Going to his room and shutting the door, the president of the United States got down on his knees and prayed for one.[697]

* * * * *

Maryland countryside, June 26, 1863

Lee understood victory was a necessity. The South was losing on every front to the North, except in bravery and victories on the battlefield. They had less men to recruit, and desertion was a major drain on his numbers. Ammo, rifles, clothes, and food were never adequate, and the men fought battles deprived of weapons and calories. Shoes and clothing were another serious worry, and many of the men went barefoot, or ragged clothing barely covered their nakedness. He knew he must move them north again to take advantage of the bounty there, and needed something to divert manpower from Vicksburg as a last attempt to save the western army.

If they succeeded, it would be a colossal victory and possibly ensure the Union's surrender. If they failed, it would mean playing defense for the rest of the war. They had to win, and the fate of the Confederacy depended on this single battle. Gettysburg, Pennsylvania, was up ahead, and so was Meade's army, and in General Lee's opinion, it was all up to God now. In a letter to Mary, he wrote of the impending battle. "I pray that our merciful Father in

---

[697] Collis, 18–19; Rusling, 15.

Heaven may protect and direct us. In that case I fear no odds and no numbers."[698]

* * * * *

Little Round Top, Gettysburg, Pennsylvania, July 2, 1863

Colonel Joshua Chamberlain understood the meaning of his orders, "Hold that ground at all hazards." It wasn't vague or open to discussion but precise.

Like his father's advice—"Do it—that's how!"—Chamberlain knew when determination and providence culminated; miracles seemed to happen, and he was determined to hold Little Round Top at all costs.

The Union had been pushed back the first day of July, but when Lee ordered General Richard Ewell, Jackson's replacement, to turn the Union flank, he failed. Ewell, after all, wasn't the mighty "Stonewall." Where Jackson was daring and hit hard and fast, Ewell was cautious and waited for an advantage in battle. He never saw one that day and never attacked, and lost the only chance to send Meade's first troops into retreat.[699]

The following day, Chamberlain found himself defending a hill as Lee sensed an opportunity. He ordered an attack all along the front and would try to crush the right or left flank to turn the Meade's army. The Union commander positioned his army along a rise known as Cemetery Ridge with his right anchored on a hill called Culp's Hill and his left on two hills—Big Roundtop and Little Roundtop. His army was situated like a fishhook shape with the shaft starting at Culp's Hill and running across the ridge to the two round tops.

Lee recognized it was a strong position, but he had little choice. He would push the fight now. Learning that Meade was the new commander, he said, "General Meade will make no blunder on my

---

[698] Lee, Robert, 95 (To Mary Lee, May 31, 1863); Long, 265–266, 272; Jones, 248-249 (To Jefferson Davis, June 10, 1863); Davis, Burke, *Gray Fox*, 210.
[699] Trulock, 133; Foote, Vol. 2, 478–480.

front." Lee gave General John Bell Hood, attached to A. P. Hill's troops, the responsibility for assaulting the two round tops. General James Longstreet cautioned Lee of the strength of Meade's position, but he responded with, "No, they are there in position, and I am going to whip them or they are going to whip me." He had his feet in the fire and had to act.[700]

Chamberlain's job was holding Little Roundtop at all costs, and if he failed, the southern army would turn Meade's left flank and strike the Union rear from the high ground. It would be a crucial defeat for the North, and Lee could take Philadelphia, Baltimore, or Washington as the Union army retreated. This threat to the capital was also a threat to the surrounding countryside and would provide adequate forage for Lee's deficient army.

The entire fate of the Union may possibly rest on holding this small hill, and it was Chamberlain's charge to hold it. He wasn't a career soldier and spent most of his life with his nose in a book, but he was a quick study, and his time at Fredericksburg taught him much about defeat. To accomplish any objective, one simply had to do it.

General Burnside sent men in piecemeal, then retreated, but he would use his entire force together and refuse to retreat. His father's words echoed in his head, and he remembered the wagon wheel. That's all this was—Lee's army was just a big wagon wheel stuck between two tree stumps called Little and Big Roundtop. All he had to do was rock the wagon enough to dislodge it.

Growing up a Chamberlain taught him about perseverance and how to use his mind to find solutions on his own. His father never did anything for him and let him figure it out for himself. Another memory drifted into Joshua's head. Once when he couldn't move a massive rock from the fields, his father simply said, "Move it!" After some figuring and use of his intellect, he recalled lessons about levers and used a fence rail to move it.[701]

---

[700] Foote, Vol. 2, 480; Freeman, *Lee*, 328-332; Catton, *Never Call Retreat*, 176–178.
[701] Trulock, 32–33; Foote, Vol. 2, 498–502.

If the 20th Maine was responsible for Meade's left and possibly the fate of the Union, so be it. The men under his charge were about to face a battle-hardened foe, and the 20th were sons of farmers and lumberjacks who were as tough and stubborn as their colonel. He had faith in them, and they believed they could hold. Less than four hundred men of the 20th opposed General Hood and General Lafayette McLaws.

Like a swarm of locusts, the Confederates rushed through a rocky area called the Devil's Den and forced Union troops off Big Roundtop. They charged up Little Roundtop, next heading directly into the 20th Maine, and the only thing standing between Lee's victory and defeat was Chamberlain's four hundred. On paper, it seemed an obvious rout, but providence had a way of turning logic on its ear.

The southerners fought like demons, charging and shrieking the rebel yell in all its terrifying aura. The 20th held its ground, even though many were dead and wounded. Chamberlain recognized one of these wounded as Private George Washington Buck who previously lost his sergeant stripes. Kneeling to inspect the twenty-one-year-old, Chamberlain knew the wound was mortal. Private Buck looked at his commander and requested that his mother would know he hadn't died a coward. Amazed by the dying man's selfless concern, Chamberlain immediately promoted him to sergeant for "honor and bravery." Buck died soon after, his honor restored.

The fight descended into close and personal brutality, and one Confederate later claimed he had a bead on Chamberlain but couldn't pull the trigger. An unusual feeling overcame him, so he held back. Trying again, the feeling returned, and he abandoned his target. It seemed as if something protected the northern officer.[702]

Nearly out of ammo and a third of the 20th out of the fight, Chamberlain shouted, "*Bayonet! Forward!*" He raised his sword as his troops yelled like wild men and charged down the hill right into the superior force. For the first time, Lee's men felt real terror from their northern enemy and were now on the receiving end of the "Yankee yell." Some of them surrendered while others fled. One Confederate

---

[702] Ibid., 144–146; Foote, Vol. 2, 504–505; Catton, *Glory Road*, 312–313.

tried to shoot the colonel in the face, but his weapon misfired, and Chamberlain stuck his sword to the man's throat, took the misfired pistol, and made him prisoner. The 20th captured nearly four hundred prisoners while Hood and McLaws retreated back to Big Roundtop. Later that night, Chamberlain and his men forced them off it as well.

The Union left was secure, and Lee's attack had failed because of the 20th Maine. This repulse forced the Confederate commander to try again the following day.

Without Colonel Joshua Chamberlain's leadership and his unwillingness to give up, the Battle of Gettysburg might have ended in total defeat for the Union that day.[703]

"Do it—that's how!" was just what he did.

* * * * *

Gettysburg, Pennsylvania, General Lee's Headquarters, July 3, 1863

Lee believed a strike at Meade's center might turn the tide. The enemy had shown a weakness there the previous day, and their flanks were anchored on good defensive ground. To try there again was futile. He would send Ewell to hit Culp's Hill, Longstreet to strike the two round tops as diversions, and then send General George E. Pickett and his fifteen thousand fresh troops into the center to deliver the crushing blow. Known as "Pickett's Charge," it would go down as the bravest waste of men in American history. Union General Winfield Scott Hancock and his division easily mowed down Pickett's men as they crossed nearly a mile-long field.

Lee sat on his famous gray stallion, Traveler, and spoke to Pickett's men returning from the charge, "Don't be discouraged. It was my fault this time. All good men must hold together now. All this will come right in the end." He told the British observer, Colonel

---

[703] Ibid., 147–149; Catton, *Glory Road*, 314–315.

Freemantle. "This has been a sad day for us, Colonel—a sad day. But we can't always expect to gain victories."

A wounded Union soldier laying on the ground saw General Lee approaching. Weak from blood loss and exposure, the soldier raised his hands at the famous general and managed to say, "Hurrah for the Union!" Dismounting, the southern commander quickly approached the defiant man, and thinking the general was about to kill him, the wounded blue coat recoiled in fear. Grabbing the soldier's hand tightly, Lee stared deeply into his eyes with sorrow and said, "My son, I hope you will soon be well."

The Union soldier's fear left him when he realized the Confederate general was genuinely concerned about him. The wounded man said he would never forget Lee's face that day. The northerner was impressed that such an important man would take time in a moment of defeat to wish him well, especially when he himself acted so obnoxious about the victory. The soldier admitted after General Lee left, he cried himself to sleep from such a show of benevolence.[704]

---

[704] Lee, Fitzhugh, 298–300; Bruce, Philip Alexander. *Robert E. Lee*. (Philadelphia: George W. Jacobs & Co., 1907), 359–360; Davis, Burke, *Gray Fox*, 244–246; Johnson, *Lee*, 113–114.

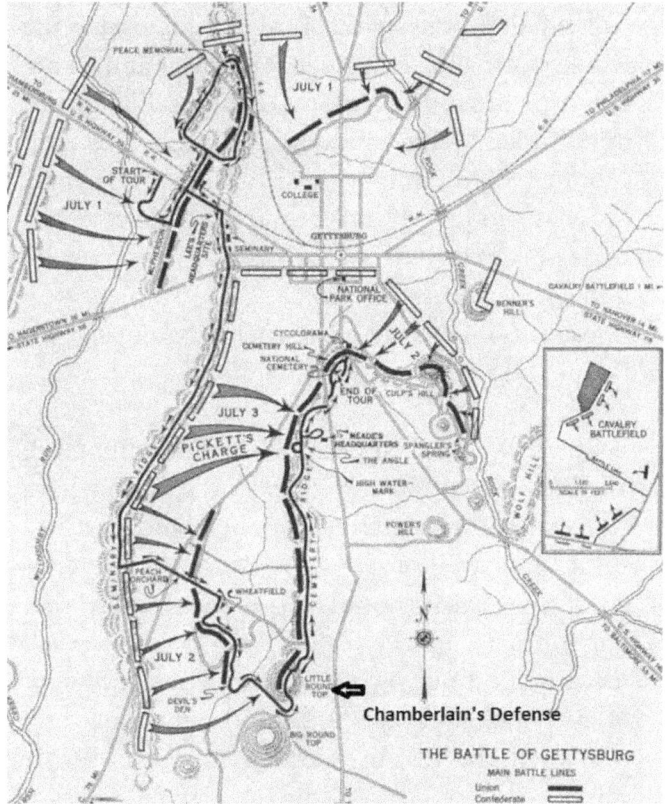

Battle of Gettysburg July 1863

Lee encountered General Pickett on his return from battle and said, "General Pickett, place your division in the rear of this hill, and be ready to repel the advance of the enemy should they follow up."

Pickett looked at Lee with tears in his eyes and said, "General Lee, I have no division now."[705]

Lee called for a retreat and prayed Meade wouldn't attack until he had his army over the river and back into Virginia.

Writing to Mary on July 12, he said:

> I trust that a merciful God, our only hope and
> refuge, will not desert us in this hour of need,

---

[705] Foote, Vol. 2, 567–568; Freeman, *Lee*, 340.

and will deliver us by His almighty hand, that the whole world may recognize His power and all the hearts be lifted up in adoration and praise of His unbounded loving-kindness. We must, however, submit to His almighty will, whatever that may be. May God guide and protect us all is my constant prayer.[706]

By August 1863, Lee issued an order proclaiming "a day of fasting, humiliation, and prayer:"

Soldiers! We have sinned against Almighty God. We have forgotten his signal mercies and have cultivated a revengeful, haughty, and boastful spirit. We have not remembered that the defenders of a just cause should be sure in His eyes; "that our times are in His hands," and we have relied too much on our own arms for the achievement of our independence. God is our only refuge and our strength. Let us humble ourselves before Him.[707]

Robert E. Lee asked God to save the southern cause from itself. Their overwhelming victories throughout the first half of the war created overconfidence, which eventually backfired at Gettysburg.

He blamed himself first, and desperation caused him to misjudge the Union army. The entire war was up to God now. After Gettysburg, he was doubtful the outcome would ever be in their favor again, but duty committed him to see it through.

* * * * *

---

[706] Lee, Robert, 102 (To Mary Lee, July 12, 1863); Davis, Burke, *Gray Fox*, 254.
[707] Ibid., 105–106 (Order, August 13, 1863).

Vicksburg, Mississippi, July 3, 1863, U. S. Grant's Headquarters

As Pickett made his disastrous charge, General Grant was busy writing a return letter to Confederate General John Pemberton who asked for terms of surrender.

Inside Vicksburg, the food was gone, and mule steaks and peas were now the menu. The thirty thousand soldiers and the city's inhabitants were starving and exhausted. Grant wrote "the useless effusion of blood you propose stopping by this course can be ended at any time you may choose, by the unconditional surrender of the city and the garrison." He explained that the brave soldiers defending Vicksburg would be treated humanely, but his only terms were unconditional surrender.

When Pemberton read the message, he wasn't happy. Agreeing to meet with Grant, the two generals met under a neutral tree, and Pemberton tried for better terms, but Grant restated unconditional surrender. Irate, the Confederate general couldn't believe Grant's refusal to budge. President Davis supported Pemberton, even when most southerners didn't trust him because he was a northerner, but he knew he would be blamed for losing Vicksburg. He told Grant if they couldn't negotiate terms, the conference should end. Grant agreed.

Pemberton turned to leave, when Grant or possibly one of his aides, suggested their staffs discuss the terms while the two generals spoke alone. Within a short time, the Union general agreed to send new terms by 10:00 p.m. the same night.[708]

Meanwhile during this truce, the two lines relaxed and swapped stories. Cousins and brothers on both sides reunited, and there were no vengeful attitudes. They had shared in the suffering and understood one another.

Grant had a similar feeling for the Confederates. These were their fellow Americans, not some foreign foe, though they had rebelled. This would be over soon, and they would once again be

---

[708] Grant, Vol. 1, 557–560; Catton, *Grant Moves South*, 471.

countrymen. Pemberton refused unconditional surrender, and Grant realized taking Vicksburg meant more than the southern army. He agreed to parole Pemberton's men instead of making them prisoners. They could keep personal property, minus their slaves, and they would receive medical aid and food.

Pemberton accepted Grant's new terms, and on July 4, 1863, Vicksburg surrendered. After Lincoln heard of the surrender on the heels of Gettysburg, he wrote to Grant, admitting he had doubted his plan but was wrong. "I feared it was a mistake. I now wish to make the personal acknowledgment that you were right, and I was wrong."[709]

After the fall of Vicksburg, Grant was the most popular man in the Union. He was slated for promotion to lieutenant-general, the same rank as George Washington, and would be transferred to Tennessee to finish off Bragg.

He learned to succeed by failing and making mistakes and perseverance was the key to overcome anything.

The sleight forgettable man labelled a drunk, a butcher, and an incompetent now outranked all those who had underestimated him. He didn't know much about army politics, but he knew how to win.

* * * * *

Recovery room of General Daniel E. Sickles Sunday, July 5, 1863

General Daniel Sickles was in the heat of battle, defending Chamberlain's right flank, when a shell shattered his leg. While recuperating in a Washington hospital, the president paid the general a visit.

After some innocent banter with Sickles and General James F. Rusling, the wounded man looked at Lincoln and asked, "Was you anxious about the battle, Mr. President?"

---

[709] Lincoln, *Works*, Vol 9, 26 (Letter to General Grant, July 13, 1863).

Assuming a serious posture, the commander-in-chief answered, "No, I was not. Some of my Cabinet and many others in Washington were, but I had no fears."

The stricken general was surprised by the president's faith in the army but just had to know why he was so sure of victory and inquired. Silent as he mulled over the question, Lincoln delayed only seconds before replying, "Well, I will tell you how it was. In the pinch of your campaign up there, when everybody seemed panic-stricken, and nobody could tell what was going to happen, oppressed by the gravity of our affairs, I went to my room one day, and locked the door, and got down on my knees before Almighty God, and prayed to Him mightily for victory at Gettysburg."

Sickles and General Rusling said nothing, entranced by Lincoln's words.

He continued, "I told Him that this was His war and our cause His cause, but we couldn't stand another Fredericksburg or Chancellorsville. And I then and there made a solemn vow to Almighty God, that if He would stand by you boys, and I will stand by Him."

The two generals were amazed by such faith. Speaking from the heart, the president continued:

> And He did stand by you boys, and I will stand
> by him. And after that—I don't know how it
> was, and I can't explain it—soon a sweet comfort
> crept into my soul that God Almighty had taken
> the whole business into His own hands and that
> things would go all right at Gettysburg. And that
> is why I had no fears about you.

"What's your feelings on Vicksburg, sir?" Sickles asked, but Lincoln still hadn't heard from Grant or Halleck.

He replied, "I have been praying for Vicksburg also, and believe our Heavenly Father is going to give us a victory there, too."[710]

---

[710] Collis, 17–19; Rusling, 13–17.

Within days of the visit, the president received word of Vicksburg's surrender, and on July 15, he issued a second proclamation for thanksgiving:

> It has pleased Almighty God to hearken to the supplications and prayers of an afflicted people... I invite the people of the United States to assemble on that occasion in their customary places of worship, and in the forms approved by their own consciences, render the homage due to the Divine Majesty for the wonderful things He has done in the nations behalf, and invoke the influence of His Holy Spirit to subdue the anger which has produced and so long sustained a needless and cruel rebellion, to guide the counsels of the government with wisdom adequate to so great a national emergency, and to visit with tender care and consolation throughout the length and breadth of our land all those who through the vicissitudes of marches, voyages, battles, and sieges, have been brought to suffer in mind, body, or estate, and finally to lead the whole nation through the paths of repentance and submission to the Divine Will back to the perfect enjoyment of Union and fraternal peace.[711]

Again, on October 3, he called for the first national observance of Thanksgiving Day. "I do, therefore, invite my fellow citizens...to set apart and observe the last Thursday of November next as a day of thanksgiving and praise to our beneficent Father...and fervently implore the interposition of the Almighty Hand to heal the wounds of the nation..."[712]

---

[711] Lincoln, *Works,* Vol. 9, 32–33 (Proclamation for Thanksgiving, July 15, 1863).
[712] Ibid., 152–153 (Proclamation for Thanksgiving, October 3, 1863).

Then in November, he gave a speech at the Gettysburg battle-field to dedicate it as a national cemetery. Following the great orator Edward Everett's two-hour speech, his words were short but on target:

> Fourscore and seven years ago our fathers brought forth on this continent, a new nation, conceived in Liberty, and dedicated to the proposition that all men are created equal...we cannot dedicate—we cannot consecrate—we cannot hallow—this ground. The brave men, living and dead, who struggled here have consecrated it, far above our poor power to add or detract. The world will little note, nor long remember, what we say here, but it can never forget what they did here. It is for us the living, rather, to be dedicated here to the unfinished work which they who fought here have thus far so nobly advanced...that from these honored dead we take increased devotion to that cause for which they gave the last full measure of devotion; that we here highly resolve that these dead shall not have died in vain; that this nation, under God, shall have a new birth of freedom; and that government of the people, by the people, for the people, shall not perish from the earth.[713]

Abraham Lincoln and the Union had turned the corner. More fighting and destruction would follow, but after Gettysburg and Vicksburg, it seemed a matter of time. In the president's view, it would end when God, through his providence, willed it to end.

* * * * *

---

[713] Ibid., 209–210 (Address at the Dedication of the Gettysburg National Cemetery, November 19, 1863).

III.
Out of the Ashes

Richmond, Virginia, Confederate President's Office,
April 30, 1864

"Mr. President," the servant's urgency brought Jeff Davis's attention away from his wife. "You must go home immediately, sir, there's been an accident!"

The president and a very pregnant Varina were enjoying a pleasant lunch together in his office. This intimate setting was a respite from the dreary reports from the front—all of them.

"What is it?" Davis asked.

"Joseph has had an accident, sir."

Varina shrieked in horror as Davis grimaced. Putting his arm around his wife, he said, "There, there—I'm sure everything is fine."

Spending too much time working late, he knew he had neglected his family, but his wife and children were his most prized possessions. They never wondered about his affection for them, but lately, he had been preoccupied by the war. After Gettysburg and Vicksburg, the war seemed to shift from one extreme to the next. No longer was the South devising aggressive tactics to bring the North to the peace table. Now they were fighting a defensive war of attrition and just trying to survive. The Confederacy was no match to the Union's ability to produce supplies and men. Their population was dramatically smaller than the North's, and they possessed few factories to produce weapons for their lack of hands to use them, and it appeared the days of Lee's bold strikes were over.

Lee retreated to Virginia after Gettysburg and Bragg failed to hold Chattanooga once Vicksburg fell. Pulling back into Georgia, he fought a running battle south toward Atlanta. Missouri, Kentucky, Tennessee, Mississippi, and Alabama were gone, victims of Grant's newfound success. Davis felt if they could simply inflict enough damage on the Union, Lincoln might lose his upcoming election in November. Maybe something would turn it around, and he still had faith God was on their side.

But now, he had to find out about little Joe. He was only five and had wandered from the nurse-maid to the piazza where he fell over the side. The piazza was twelve-feet high, and he broke both his legs and fractured his skull. When Davis and Varina arrived, the doctors were shaking their heads, and there wasn't much they could do for him. All Davis and Varina could do now was tell their son goodbye.

When he died, Varina collapsed, inconsolable in her grief, and Jeff cried out, "Not mine, oh Lord, but thine."

A messenger attempted to give the president a dispatch, but he said, "I must have this day with my little child." Spending the entire night pacing the bedroom, he knew he didn't have the luxury of a long grieving period. He was commander-in-chief of the Confederacy and must attend to the war at this crucial time.[714]

* * * * *

Grant, now in the east leading the Army of the Potomac, crossed the Rappahannock River near Chancellorsville. Lee was about to strike the victor of Vicksburg at the very same spot where Jackson was shot the year before.

In the west, General Joseph Johnston retreated toward Atlanta, but Davis still believed the South would prevail if the people would pull together. If deserters would return, no questions would be asked, but there was too much bickering and backstabbing among them. Governor Brown of Georgia and Vice President Alexander Stephens were endlessly criticizing him, and he failed to understand why they couldn't just back him. The cause was all that mattered, not individual concerns.

The Confederacy's nature was its Achille's heel, because each state represented its own interests, independent of the national government. Davis had to secure supplies and get them to the troops

---

[714] Davis, Varina Howell. *Jefferson Davis, Ex-President of the Confederate States of America: A Memoir by his Wife.* (New York: Belford Company, Publishers, 1890), 496–497; Cooper, 515–516.

while maintaining the morale of the army and people without violating states' rights. There were many who had sacrificed for the cause of independence, but there were also many who used the war for profit. The North had similar problems, but the South couldn't bear them because of limited manpower and resources.

Davis was committed to the cause and knew the tenacity of the southern people. Lee was the greatest general since Taylor and Scott. He stopped the enemy at the Battle of the Wilderness in May 1864, but Grant simply marched his army around him and headed for Richmond. At Spotsylvania Courthouse a few days later, Lee whipped him again, but Grant again went around his army, focused on the Confederate capital. At the North Anna, he sidled again, and at Cold Harbor a few weeks later, Lee soundly defeated the Union army again, but victory wasn't Grant's goal. Wearing down the southern army, cutting its rail lines, and taking Richmond was his aim. Winning battles meant nothing to the Union commander; outlasting Lee's army would bring victory.

After Cold Harbor, the northern army was in position to attack Petersburg, the key to Richmond. If Petersburg fell, so would the capital of the Confederacy. Grant attempted the same strategy as Vicksburg, and tried to take it by force, but when this failed, he circled the city and settled for a siege.

General John Bell Hood had recently replaced Johnston in the west but was unsuccessful keeping Sherman from taking Atlanta and marching to the sea. Grant's grand design was to have his and Sherman's armies meet in a pincers movement to crush Lee and bring the war to an end. Sherman marched quickly through South Carolina and was nearly in North Carolina, and Johnston's smaller force barely slowed his progress.

Davis supported Lee's strategy to hurt Grant's army until Lincoln, hopefully, lost the election. The massive casualties the Union army incurred chipped away at northern morale. It was a small chance, but Lee, ever the warrior, was determined to make Grant pay for every acre of ground he gained.

President Davis doubled-down. "I believe that a just God looks upon our cause as holy, and that of our enemy as iniquitous and that

He may chastise us for our offenses, but in so doing He is preparing us and in His good Providence will assist us, and never desert the right."[715]

He would go down fighting, confident he was right and sure in faith that God was on their side.

* * * * *

City Point, Virginia, aboard the River Queen, March 28, 1865

"We will have to fight one more bloody battle before this ends," Grant said.

Lincoln shook his head as his face grew long. "There has been enough bloodshed already!"

Sherman's eyes darted to Grant's as both men chomped on cigars.

Lincoln asked, "Another battle can't be avoided?"

"Mr. President, we can't control that from happening," Grant answered.

Sherman hesitated but knew he must ask the president an important question, "Are you ready for the end of the war, sir?"

Lincoln replied, "Yes."

"What is to be done with the rebel armies when they are defeated and their leaders?"

"Just get the men of the Confederate armies back to their homes, at work on their farms, and in their shops." Lincoln paused, looked at his two generals and reluctantly said, "As to Jeff Davis—he ought to escape the country if he could, but I am not at liberty to say such a thing openly." He just wanted the war over and the country united, and didn't want revenge or harsh terms.

---

[715] Cooper, 516–519, 532; Catton, *Never Call Retreat*, 339–342, 344–345; Oates, 419–421.

Standing, the president shook their hands, certain his two commanders would do what was right, and the three men parted ways, each with their individual paths to follow.[716]

Three weeks before, Lincoln, after being reelected, laid out post-war intentions in his second inaugural with his own path in mind. "Both read the same Bible, and pray to the same God; and each invokes his aid against the other. It may seem strange that any men should dare to ask a just God's assistance in wringing their bread from the sweat of other men's faces; but let us judge not, that we be not judged." After referencing Matthew 7:1, he cited Matthew 18:7 and Psalms 19:9:

> The prayers of both could not be answered—that of neither has been answered fully. The Almighty has his own purposes. "Woe unto the world because of offenses! For it must needs be that offenses come; but woe to that man by whom the offense cometh." If we shall suppose that American slavery is one of those offenses which, in the providence of God, must needs come, but which, having continued through His appointed time. He now wills to remove, and that He gives both North and South this terrible war, as the woe due to those by whom the offense came, shall we discern therein any departure from those divine attributes which the believers in a living God always ascribe to Him? Fondly do we hope—fervently do we pray—that this mighty scourge of war may speedily pass away. Yet, if God wills that it continue until all the wealth piled by the bondsman's two hundred and fifty years of unrequited toil shall be sunk, and until every drop of blood drawn with the lash shall be

---

[716] Sandburg, 679–680; Donald, 574; Catton, Bruce. *A Stillness at Appomattox.* (Garden City: Doubleday & Co., 1953), 340.

paid by another drawn with the sword as was said three thousand years ago, so still it must be said, "The judgments of the Lord are true and righteous altogether."

Then he humbly stated that mercy and forgiveness was the route they must take:

With malice toward none; with charity for all; with firmness in the right, as God gives us to see the right, let us strive on to finish the work we are in; to bind up the nation's wounds; to care for him who shall have borne the battle, and for his widow, and his orphan—to do all which may achieve and cherish a just and lasting peace among ourselves, and with all nations.[717]

Laying his hand on the Bible, he ended the oath with, "So help me God," and kissed the holy book just as George Washington did over seventy years before.[718] In an address of seven hundred and one words, he referred to God fourteen times, quoted or paraphrased scripture four times, and mentioned prayer three times. One Civil War historian claimed, "Lincoln had become convinced that the Almighty had His own purposes in this war and southerners had been forced to conclude that He did not favor a Confederate victory."[719]

A week later, he described the speech's reception. "I believe it is not immediate popular. Men are not flattered by being shown that there has been a difference of purpose between the Almighty and them. To deny it however, in this case, is to deny that there is a God governing the world. It is a truth which I thought needed to be

---

[717] Lincoln, *Works*, Vol. 11, 45–47 (Second Inaugural Address, March 4, 1865).

[718] Donald, 568; Oates, 446–447; Sandburg, 665.

[719] *Religion and the American Civil War*, ed. Randall M. Miller, Harry S. Stout and Charles R. Wilson. (New York: Oxford University Press, 1998), 411 (Afterword by James M. McPherson).

told."[720] He believed the fate of the nation was in God's hands and was dependent on his purpose.

After the meeting with Grant and Sherman, he headed back to the White House, confident of the outcome of his own purpose.

* * * * *

Outside Petersburg, Virginia, the Battle of the Quaker Road, March 29, 1865

The attack on Petersburg by Grant had failed, and Brigadier General Joshua L. Chamberlain lay dying in a field hospital after surgeons did everything they could. Writing his last words to his family, he accepted his fate as the will of God.

Two weeks later, his letter arrived in Maine, and his wife, Fannie, rushed to be by his side, hoping she wasn't too late. When she arrived at the hospital, she found her husband in critical condition, but still alive. He eventually pulled through and had enough strength to write his mother a letter explaining his new beliefs:

> Not for selfish ambition...for these terrible wounds must cast a shadow over the remainder of my days, even though I should apparently recover. But what it is, I can't tell you. I haven't a particle of fanaticism in me. But I plead guilty to a sort of fatalism. I believe in a destiny—one, I mean, divinely appointed, and to which we are carried forward by a perfect trust in God. I do this, and I believe in it. I have laid plans, in my day, and good ones I thought. But they never succeeded. Something else better, did, and I could see it plain as day, that God had done it, and for my good.[721]

---

[720] Lincoln, *Works,* Vol. 11, 54 (To Thurlow Weed, March 15, 1865).
[721] Trulock, 219.

Chamberlain not only survived, he even returned to the fight. At the Battle of the Quaker Road, he was at the front with his men leading them into battle, but was shot once again. This time, the bullet pierced his horse's neck, went through his arm, and struck him in the heart. Falling forward in the saddle unconscious, it appeared his luck had finally run out. A fellow officer grabbed him around the waist and said, "General, you are gone."

Suddenly peering up, Chamberlain watched the Confederate counterattack and said, "Yes, General, I am gone." Raising his sword and calling encouragement to his men, he rode toward the battle very much alive.

The bullet missed his heart because of a thick stack of orders and a brass mirror in his breast pocket. It had deflected the slug and miraculously saved his life.[722] The day before returning to duty in February 1865, he wrote:

> I owe the Country three years' service. It is a time when every man should stand by his guns. And I am not scared or hurt enough to be willing to face the rear when other men are marching to the front. It is true my incomplete recovery from my wounds would make a more quiet life desirable, and when I think of young and dependent family the whole strength of that motive to make the most of my life comes over me. But there is no promise of life in peace, and no decree of death in war. And I am so confident of the sincerity of my motives that I can trust my own life and the welfare of my family in the hands of Providence.[723]

God had spared him again and again for some greater purpose, and he would continue to let him direct his path. He had

---

[722] Ibid., 234–236.
[723] Ibid., 225.

an entire life before him and was determined not to live as a mere spectator.

* * * * *

Petersburg, Virginia, March 1865

Even though Lee's army outfought Grant's man for man, he couldn't overcome the inevitable. It wasn't because he lacked the same tenacity as Grant, but it was the Confederacy's inability to match the Union's numbers and production.

After the Battle of the Wilderness, Lee knew if Grant got to Petersburg first, it would be over. "We must destroy this army of Grant's before he gets to the James River. If he gets there, it will become a siege, and then it will be a mere question of time."[724] The southern commander's personality wouldn't allow him to give up, so he continued to try to hurt the Union army enough to make them recoil.

Once Petersburg was under siege, it was like poking an angry bear, and all he could hope for now was a breakout. His manpower had dwindled from sickness, casualties, and desertion, and the siege forced Lee to extend his lines. Confederate troop numbers made it impossible to defend the city at all points, and taking advantage of this, Grant periodically attacked, keeping the lines busy. Lee attempted to draw away some of the massive northern army by sending General Jubal Early into the Shenandoah Valley to threaten Washington. Grant didn't fall for the bait and sent General Philip Sheridan to confront Early. Sheridan soundly beat him, and Lee ran out of options.[725]

In the west, General Hood failed to stop Sherman's destructive march to the sea, and Sherman was now in North Carolina, swatting Joseph E. Johnston's undermanned army out of his way. Hood's army made a valiant effort against General George H. Thomas's force in Tennessee but to no avail. It was all on Lee, and he had one shot to

---

[724] Davis, Burke, *Gray Fox*, 332; Bruce, 281.

[725] Foote, Shelby. *The Civil War: A Narrative, Vol 3, Red River to Appomattox.* (New York: Vintage Books, 1974, 1986), 553–556.

break out of Petersburg. If he moved south, he might link up with Johnston and dispose of Sherman. Then the two armies could turn north and finish off Grant. It had little chance of success, Lee knew, but if it was God's will, it was possible. He would do his duty no matter the result, and do his best. How could he pull off one of the greatest turnarounds in history if his men had no provisions or ammunition?[726]

Lee revealed some of his deeper concerns to his son, Custis, and his nephew George Taylor Lee at his Richmond quarters. Pacing back and forth, glaring at the floor, the scene was much like the one he found himself in at the start of the war. Turning to Custis, he said, "Well, Mr. Custis, I have been up to Congress and they don't seem to be able to do anything except eat peanuts and chew tobacco, while my army is starving." He paused for a moment, then continued, "I told them the condition we were in, and that something must be done at once, but I can't get them to do anything." Remembering his feelings before the war started, he said, "Mr. Custis, when this war began I was opposed to it, bitterly opposed to it, and I told these people that unless every man should do his whole duty, they would repent it." Pausing as if not wanting to see the obvious, he finished with, "And now they will repent."[727]

President Davis gave him permission to write the Union commander about peace terms, but Grant's response wasn't promising. He said he had no authority to talk of peace and only the president could do this. "Unconstitutional Surrender" Grant, they called him, and he had more men and endless provisions to outlast four confederacies if need be.

Lee decided to try one more offensive against the northern lines to break the siege, but it failed, losing five thousand men he couldn't afford to lose. Sheridan's army then rejoined Grant's, and he now faced even worse odds. Writing to Mary in Richmond, he said:

> I think General Grant will move against us soon…
> and no man can tell what may be the result; but

---

[726] Ibid., 617–620; Catton, *Never Call Retreat*, 365–368.
[727] Freeman, *Lee*, 447; Davis, Burke, *Gray Fox*, 355.

> trusting to a merciful God, who does not always
> give the battle to the strong, I pray we may not
> be overwhelmed. I shall, however, endeavor to do
> my duty and fight to the last. Should it be nec-
> essary to abandon our position to prevent being
> surrounded, what will you do? Will you remain,
> or leave the city? You must consider the question
> and make up your mind. It is a fearful condition,
> and we must rely for guidance and protection
> upon a kind Providence.[728]

By April 2, Grant attacked the city as Lee began his retreat to the west. He abandoned Petersburg and Richmond, then sent an urgent message to President Davis, warning that he could no longer protect the capital. Davis, who was at church when he received the message, believed he could conduct the war from anywhere and prepared to leave the capital.

As Grant moved into Petersburg, another of Lee's best generals, A. P. Hill, was shot and killed when he rode to the front and ran into the enemy. Lee said, "He is at rest now, and we who are left are the ones to suffer." J.E.B. Stuart was killed the previous year, and he had fewer reliable generals to lean on. He evacuated the city, and soon after, Grant captured the capital of the Confederacy.

Mary Lee decided to stay in Richmond because she had faith her husband would turn it all around. Until this happened, she would have a tray of food sent to that nice young man in blue appointed to guard her property and person.[729]

* * * * *

---

[728] Lee, Robert, 146 (To Mary Lee, February 23, 1865); Lee, Fitzhugh, 370.

[729] Freeman, *Lee,* 464; Davis, Burke. *To Appomattox: Nine April Days, 1865.* (New York: Rinehart & Co., Inc., 1959), 207; Davis, Burke, *Gray Fox,* 371.

Richmond, Virginia, April 4, 1865

A week after leaving City Point and his meeting with Grant and Sherman, Lincoln returned to tour the fallen Confederate capital. As he walked through the streets of the city, many of the freed slaves gathered around him. One elderly man dropped to his knees and exclaimed, "Bless the Lord, there is the great Messiah! I knowed him soon as I seen him. He's been in my heart four long years. Come to free his children from bondage. Glory hallelujah!" Others fell to their knees and shouted praise while the old man tried to kiss the president's feet.

Embarrassed by this, Lincoln quickly said, "Don't kneel to me. That is not right. You must kneel to God only, and thank Him for the liberty you will hereafter enjoy." Examining the grateful crowd, he continued:

> My poor friends, you are free—free as air. You can cast off the name of slave and trample upon it; it will come to you no more. Liberty is your birthright. God gave it to you as He gave it to others, and it is a sin that you have been deprived of it for so many years. You must try to deserve this priceless boon. Let the world see that you merit it, and are able to maintain it by your good works.

Beaming like a holy man, he kindly cautioned them, "Don't let your joy carry you into excesses. Learn the laws and obey them; obey God's commandments and thank Him for giving you liberty, for to Him you owe all things." The people were silent as Lincoln continued down the street.

A former slave woman saw him from her doorway and yelled, "Thank you, Jesus, for this! Thank you, Jesus!"[730]

---

[730] Porter, David D. *Incidents and Anecdotes of the Civil War.* (New York: D. Appleton and Co., 1886), 295-298; Donald, 576; Foote, Vol. 3, 897; McPherson, 846–

Making his way to the president's house, he sat a while at Davis's former desk. General Weitzel asked him what was to be done about the people of the city, and he said, "I don't want to give any orders on that General, but if I were in your place, I'd let 'em up easy. Let 'em up easy."[731]

The next day, as Lincoln rode his transport back to City Point, a barge loaded with over a thousand rebel prisoners passed by. One of them shouted, "There's Old Abe, give that old fellow three cheers."

Another clutching his allotted ration yelled, "Your bread and meat's better than popcorn." After weeks of eating popcorn defending Petersburg, he was grateful for a full stomach.

Observing the motley group of haggard soldiers in gray and butternut, Lincoln said, "They will never shoulder a musket in anger again. And if Grant is wise he will leave them their guns to shoot crows with, and their horses to plow with." Perhaps remembering his own early years on the frontier behind a plow, he ended his thoughts with, "It would do no harm."[732]

President Abraham Lincoln

847; Oates, 457; Sandburg, 684; Davis, Burke, *To Appomattox*, 184–186.

[731] Sandburg, 685; Foote, Vol. 3, 899.

[732] Porter, 311–312; Davis, Burke, *To Appomattox*, 213.

Three times during his visit to Richmond, he spoke of praising God and forgiveness. During his inaugural address, he didn't mince words, and yet, many radical Republicans in Congress passed a bill of punitive measures against their defeated foe regardless. He unashamedly vetoed the bill. After four years of war, the nation needed forgiveness, not revenge.

General Sumner overheard Mary Lincoln suggest to the president that Jefferson Davis should be hanged, but he corrected her by citing Matthew 7:1 again. "Judge not, lest ye be judged."[733]

Abraham Lincoln was ready to help heal the broken nation as soon as the war was over, and out of the ashes, they would rise again.

* * * * *

Palm Sunday, Lee's Headquarters near Appomattox Courthouse, Virginia, April 9, 1865

His men were exhausted and hungry. Lee knew they hadn't been beaten by the Union army, but they couldn't compete with it. These men deserved better than this, and he dreaded the decision of what was best for them.

General John B. Gordon attempted a breakout through the Union lines, but it had failed, and hearing this, Lee said, "Then there is nothing for me to do but go and see General Grant, and I would rather die a thousand deaths."

One of his officers asked, "Oh, General, what will history say of the surrender of this army in the field?"

Lee replied, "Yes. Yes, I know they will say hard things of us. They will not understand how we were overwhelmed by numbers. But that is not the question, Colonel. The question is, is it right to surrender this army? If it is right, then I will take all the responsibility."[734] In a rare moment of despair, he said, "How easily I could be rid of this and be at rest! I have only to ride along the line and all

---

[733] Sandburg, 686–687; Foote, Vol. 3, 903.
[734] Lee, Robert, 151–152; Freeman, *Lee*, 483–484.

will be over." Death would be easier than surrender to him, but he regained his composure and sighed, "But it is our duty to live. What will become of the women and children of the South if we are not here to protect them?"[735]

After consulting General Longstreet and Mahone and they agreed, he then met with his artillery commander, E. P. Alexander. The two sat on a fallen tree and discussed the situation. Alexander said, "Then we have only a choice of two courses. Either to surrender, or take to the woods and bushes…"

Lee knew this meant guerrilla war and waited to respond. The artillery officer continued, "If we surrender this army, every other army will have to follow suit. All will go like a row of bricks."

Listening quietly, Alexander sought any other option, but surrender and reminded Lee that the Union general was nicknamed "Unconditional Surrender" Grant. He had offered those terms to Buckner at Donelson and Pemberton at Vicksburg, and did he think they would be exempt? Addressing first Alexander's suggestion of guerrilla war, he said:

> Then, General, you and I as Christian men have no right to consider only how this would affect us. We must consider its effect on the country as a whole. Already it is demoralized by four years of war. If I took your advice, the men would be without rations and under no control of officers. They would be compelled to rob and steal in order to live. They would become mere bands of marauders…We would bring on a state of affairs it would take the country years to recover from. And, as for myself, you young fellows might go to bushwhacking, but the only dignified course for me would be, to go to General Grant and surrender myself and take the consequences of my acts.

---

[735] Davis, Burke, *To Appomattox*, 350.

Pausing a minute, he tried to ease the officer's fear. "But I will tell you one thing for your comfort. Grant will not demand unconditional surrender. He will give us as good terms as this army has the right to demand, and I am going to meet him in the rear at ten a.m. and surrender the army on the condition of not fighting again until exchanged."

Alexander was quiet now and felt ashamed for even suggesting guerrilla war. Grant's reply for a meeting finally arrived, and Longstreet reminded Lee, "I know Grant well enough to say that the terms will be about what you would demand under the circumstances." The commander looked grave, so Longstreet assured him, "If he won't give you honorable terms, break it off, and tell him to do his worst." Lee straightened and seemed inspired by these words, if only momentarily.

Dressed in his newest uniform, complete with gold spurs, the general of the Army of Northern Virginia tied a sash around his waist and fastened on his best sword. It was the right thing to do for the men. It was God's will, not his own, and his hand had guided events.[736]

Mounting Traveler, Lee rode toward a meeting with Grant and his destiny.

* * * * *

The White House, first week of April 1865

President Lincoln, Mary, Ward Hill Lamon, and others were enjoying an evening at the White House when the subject of dreams came up. Lincoln knew this subject well. He'd dreamed of a drifting boat right before every major Union victory and had the vision back in Springfield of the two faces; and after Willie's death, he dreamed of him playing on the lawn. But in the past week, he described macabre dreams.

---

[736] Alexander, E.P. *Military Memoirs of a Confederate, a Critical Narrative.* (New York: Charles Scribner and Sons, 1907), 604-606.

"Why, you look dreadfully solemn." Mary seemed surprised by her husband's words. "Do you believe in dreams?"

"I can't say that I do, but I had one the other night which has haunted me ever since." Mary looked into her husband's eyes and let him speak.

> After it occurred, the first time I opened the Bible, strange as it may appear, it was at the twenty-eighth chapter of Genesis, which relates to the wonderful dream Jacob had. I turned to other passages, and seemed to encounter a dream or vision wherever I looked. I kept turning the leaves of the old book, and everywhere my eye fell upon passages recording matters strangely in keeping with my own thoughts—supernatural visitations, dreams, visions, etc.

He was serious and grim, so the First Lady said, "You frighten me! What is the matter?"

Seeing she was scared, Lincoln said, "I am afraid I have done wrong to mention the subject at all, but somehow the thing has got possession of me..."[737]

Though afraid, she pressed him to tell them about his dream.

Pausing, his face obscured by shadows, he seemed to be recounting a scary tale. "About ten days ago, I retired very late. I had been up waiting for important dispatches from the front. I could not have been long in bed when I fell into a slumber for I was weary. I soon began to dream." The eyes of the listeners widened in anticipation. "There seemed to be a death-like stillness about me. Then I heard subdued sobs, as if a number of people were weeping. I thought I left my bed and wandered downstairs. There the silence was broken by

---

[737] Lamon, 114-115; Oates, 462; Sandburg, 697.

the same pitiful sobbing, but the mourners were invisible." His face grew paler as he continued:

> I went from room to room; no living person was in sight, but the same mournful sounds of distress met me as I passed along. It was light in all the rooms; every object was familiar to me; but where were all the people who were grieving as if their hearts would break? I was puzzled and alarmed. What could be the meaning of all this? Determined to find the cause of a state of things so mysterious and so shocking, I kept on until I arrived in the East Room, which I entered. There I met with a sickening surprise.

Everyone was on edge, and impending doom covered every face. "Before me was a catafalque on which rested a corpse wrapped in funeral vestments. Around it were stationed soldiers who were acting as guards; and there was a throng of people, some gazing mournfully upon the corpse, whose face was covered, others weeping, pitifully. 'Who is dead in the White House?' I demanded of one of the soldiers."

Those in the room held their breath, waiting for the answer as his demeanor darkened. "'The President,' was his answer, 'he was killed by an assassin.' Then came a loud burst of grief from the crowd, which awoke me from my dream. I slept no more that night and although it was only a dream, I have been strangely annoyed by it ever since."

Mary replied, "That is horrid! I wish you had not told it. I am glad I don't believe in dreams, or I should be in terror from this time forth."

"Well," Lincoln assured her, "it is only a dream, Mary. Let us say no more about it, and try to forget it."

Lamon then pressed the issue of the president's personal security, but Lincoln just laughed it off and assured his audience the dead man wasn't him, "but some other fellow." Joking about it, he grinned but returned to a serious tone. He said, "Well, let it go. I think the Lord in His own good time and way will work this out all right. God knows what is best."[738]

He sighed, knowing this was his burden to bear, not theirs; and it was in God's hands now.

* * * * *

Appomattox Courthouse, Wilmer McLean House, 1:30 p.m., April 9, 1865

"Is Lee over there?" Grant asked.

"Yes. He's in that brick house," General Sheridan answered.

"Very well. Let's go up."

After some back and forth, the two commanding generals decided to meet and discuss a surrender. Grant knew Lee would seek favorable terms for his army and knew he would negotiate from a position of power. It's what he would do if the situation was reversed, and Lee still had an army which could cause serious damage before it was destroyed. They could disperse and carry out guerrilla war, but the aim was to end the bloodshed, not continue it.

General Sheridan thought it was a trick to stall so Lee's army could escape, but Grant knew better. Writing later about it, he said, "But I had no doubt the good faith of Lee." Most Americans understood the code of honor Lee followed.[739]

After a truce was called, the two armies stood staring across at each other, unsure if they were about to start killing one another again or if the war would end. General Joshua Chamberlain faced the remnants of Lee's army and almost attacked before word of the truce reached him. The gray and butternut lines stood stoically, and

---

[738] Ibid., 116–118; Sandburg, 698; Oates, 463.

[739] Foote, Vol. 3, 945; Davis, Burke, *To Appomattox*, 371; Grant, Vol. 2, 486; Catton, Bruce. *Grant Takes Command*. (Boston: Little, Brown and Co., 1968, 1969), 462–463.

the only sound was their red, white, and blue battle flags fluttering in a gentle breeze.

The tense moment soon changed to a hopeful amity, and the men shook hands and patted shoulders. Many prayed this was the day the carnage would end. Chamberlain and other officers from both sides gathered near the McLean House and shared swigs of whisky and old memories. Many had been classmates at West Point or served in the Mexican War and chatted amicably, but the southerners held back their emotions while the northerners restrained celebrating.

When General Lee rode up to the house, it was a surreal moment for Chamberlain and others. The Confederate leader showed an inner strength and dignity in his face as well as a touch of sadness. The gold-trimmed uniform and salt-and-peppered short-cropped beard stood out atop the famous horse and turned the heads of everyone as he rode through the lines of the two armies. A short time after Lee arrived, General Grant rode up, and Chamberlain noticed the striking contrast of the two men. The red-haired man's pants and boots were mud-splattered, and his coat had dulled from the wear. He was short and carried himself much like a private without an ounce of an air of superiority. Chamberlain recognized humility and strength in his commander. "He seemed greater than I had ever seen him—a look of another would about him. No wonder I forgot to salute him. Anything like that would have been too little." This small unassuming man became the Union's best general.[740]

Grant stood on the McLean house porch and worried about his uniform. He was about to meet General Lee, General Scott's chief-of-staff in Mexico, and knew he would be dressed immaculately. The Union commander went inside.

Now the two representatives of the North and South were face-to-face. The owner of the house was Wilmer McLean, a farmer who moved to Appomattox after his first home was at the center of the First Battle of Manassas. He wanted to find somewhere peaceful to escape the war, so he relocated to Appomattox, but for some reason,

---

[740] Trulock, 295–297; Grant, Vol. 2, 486–488; Davis, Burke, *To Appomattox*, 378–380.

the war found him anyway, and his houses were destined to be at the opening battle and the final act of the Civil War.

The two generals stood and shook hands. "I met you once before, General Lee, while we were serving in Mexico, when you came over from General Scott's headquarters to visit Garland's brigade. I have always remembered your appearance and I think I would have recognized you anywhere."

"Yes," Lee replied, "I know I met you on that occasion and have often tried to recollect how you looked, but I have never been able to recall a single feature."

Grant didn't expect him to remember an unknown lieutenant, though Lee was an icon, even then, and left an indelible impression on him. The two engaged in casual conversation while Sheridan and a dozen other curious Union officers surrounded them. Lee finally brought up the subject of their meeting, and Grant wrote later the pleasant chat made him almost forget why they were there.

Lee began, "I suppose, General Grant, that the object of our meeting is fully understood. I asked to see you to ascertain upon what terms you would receive the surrender of my army?"

Grant replied, "The terms I propose are those stated substantially in my letter of yesterday—that is, the officers and men surrendered to be paroled and disqualified from taking up arms again until properly exchanged, and all arms, ammunition, and supplies to be delivered up as captured property."

"Those are about the conditions I expected," the southern general said.

"Yes, I think our correspondence indicated pretty clearly the action that would be taken, I hope it will lead to a cessation of hostilities—preventing further loss of life," Grant replied.

Lee suggested that the terms be written out, so the Union commander scribbled them down. As he wrote, he noticed the Confederate commander's sword and included in the terms that the officers could keep their sidearms. When he finished, he handed the terms to Lee.

The dashing Virginian placed the paper on the table nearby and slowly retrieved a pair of glasses from his pocket. Wiping them with a handkerchief before placing them on his face, he, like his hero Washington, had grown gray and blind in the service of his country too. He read Grant's terms:

> General: In accordance with the substance of my letter to you of the 8th inst., I propose to receive the surrender of the Army of Northern Virginia on the following terms, to wit: Rolls of all the officers and men to be made in duplicate, one copy to be given to an officer designated by me, the other to be retained by such officer or officers as you may designate. The officers to give their individual paroles not to take up arms against the Government of the United States until properly, and each company or regimental commander to sign a like parole for the men of their commands. The arms, artillery, and public property to be parked, and stacked, and turned over to the officers appointed by me to receive them. This will not embrace the side arms of the officers, nor their private horses or baggage. This done, each officer and man will be allowed to return to his home, not to be disturbed by the United States authorities so long as they observe their paroles, and the laws in force where they may reside. Very respectfully. U. S. Grant, Lieutenant-General

Lee noticed the word *exchanged* was missing after "until properly" and assumed he intended to add it. Grant replied, "Why, yes, I thought I had put it in."

"With your permission, I will mark where it should be inserted."

"Certainly," Grant said.

The southern general searched unsuccessfully in his coat for a pencil, then one of Grant's staff handed him one. "This will have a very happy effect upon my army." Allowing officers to keep their sidearms was another generous term the Union commander added.

"Unless you have some suggestions to make in regard to the form, I will have a copy made in ink and sign it," Grant said.

Pausing a moment, Lee said, "There is one thing I would like to mention. The cavalrymen and artillerymen in our army own their own horses. Our organization differs from yours. I would like to understand whether these men will be permitted to retain their horses."

"You will find that the terms as written do not allow it. Only the officers are allowed to take their private property," Grant replied.

"No, I see the terms do not allow it. That is clear." Lee's countenance changed and he was about to speak again, when Grant spoke first:

> Well, the subject is quite new to me. Of course, I didn't know that any private soldiers owned their animals, but I think this will be the last battle of the war—I sincerely hope so and…I take it most of the men in the ranks are small farmers, and it is doubtful whether they will be able to put in a crop and carry themselves and their families through the next winter without their horses. I will arrange it in this way. I will not change the terms as they are written, but I will instruct the officers to let all the men who claim to own a horse or mule take the animals home with them to work their little farms.

Grant may have remembered his own experience as a farmer or possibly realized the goodwill it could impress on southerners. Lincoln's wishes of forgiveness were his own as well.

"This will have the best possible effect upon my men. It will be very gratifying and will do much toward conciliating our people," Lee replied and ordered his own aide to write up a response. This was put into a sealed envelope that the Union general didn't open until later that night. He felt Lee's word was good enough for him.[741]

---

[741] Freeman, *Lee*, 489–492; Grant, Vol. 2, 491–493; Catton, *Grant Takes Command*, 467.

The southern general was then introduced to Grant's officers. Colonel Ely Parker, a full-blooded American Indian, approached Lee and noticed him studying his face. Reaching out to shake Parker's hand, he noticed the dark complexion and genetic features and said, "I am glad to see one real American here."

Parker replied, "We are all Americans." Now, they were again.

Lee then explained that his troops were without rations, so Grant asked how many he needed to feed them. He estimated 25,000 would be enough, and the Union commander ordered it done.

Stepping out onto the porch of the McLean House, Lee prepared to face his men. The Union officers stood at attention and saluted as he returned the courtesy. Standing at the top of the porch steps, he peered toward his army. Then, as if resolved to do his duty, he slipped on his gloves and punched his fist into each hand. Mounting Traveler, he slowly rode out of the McLean yard.[742]

Grant stepped down from the porch and looked up at Lee, then waved. Lee returned the wave and went to meet his army. Grant's own thoughts of the surrender were unexpected. "But my own feelings, which had been quite jubilant on the receipt of his letter were sad and depressed. I felt like anything rather than rejoicing at the downfall of a foe who had fought so long and valiantly and had suffered so much for a cause…"[743]

Lee rode among his men, and they removed their hats, some cried, but most shouted praise. Some kissed his hand or brushed against his horse to show affection for their noble general. "Men, we have fought through the war together. I have done my best for you. My heart is too full to say more." Taking off his hat, tears in his eyes, he rode to his headquarter, prepared to write his final address.[744]

The next day, his farewell address explained his reasons for surrendering, and it was clear that it wasn't because of any "distrust of them." To continue would only sacrifice needless lives and would "accomplish nothing." They could return to their homes and had

---

[742] McPherson, 849–850; Davis, Burke, *To Appomattox*, 386–388.

[743] Grant, Vol. 2, 489.

[744] Lee, Robert, 153; Foote, Vol. 3, 951; Davis, Burke, *To Appomattox*, 394–395.

fulfilled their honorable service. Then he shared his own wishes for them. "I earnestly pray that a merciful God will extend to you his blessing and protection. With an unceasing admiration of your constancy and devotion to your country, and a grateful remembrance of your kind and generous consideration of myself, I bid you an affectionate farewell."[745]

He later said, "I have fought against the people of the North because I believed they were seeking to wrest from the South dearest rights. But I have never cherished toward them bitter or vindictive feelings and have never seen the day when I did not pray for them."[746]

General Robert E. Lee

Grant and Lee were men of character, and this was what determined the terms of surrender. Grant handled it with respect and even felt sad at his victory, while Lee showed humility and mutual respect in his defeat.

The war was nearly over, but one more casualty was only six days away, and it had the potential to wipe out the example the two

---

[745] Ibid., 153–154 (General Orders No. 9, April 10, 1865); Foote, Vol. 3, 955-956; Freeman, *Lee*, 496–497.

[746] Jones, William J. *Personal Reminiscences, Anecdotes, and Letters of General Robert E. Lee.* (New York: D. Appleton & Co., 1875), 196.

military leaders set at Appomattox and Lincoln's desire for forgiveness and mercy.

* * * * *

Good Friday, The White House, April 14, 1865

Word of Lee's surrender revived the president's spirit, and the fresh spring day seemed to symbolize the nation's rebirth. He recently brokered the Thirteenth Amendment with Congress, and slavery would soon be abolished.

At breakfast, his son, Robert, who served on Grant's staff by his request, was back from the front, and father and son shared breakfast together. Lincoln asked him about his plans for the future and other small talk, then Robert showed him a portrait of General Lee. Staring at the image of the man who gave him such a hard time on the battlefield required reflection. Sitting the picture down, he studied it for some time. Finally, he said, "It is a good face. I am glad the war is over at last."[747]

During the morning's scheduled Cabinet meeting, Grant reported, in person, on the state of things and said he expected word from Sherman about the fate of Johnston's army soon. Lincoln confidently said good news was on its way without a doubt. He had that same recurring dream the night before, which always preceded "every great and important event of the War."

The secretary of the navy, Gideon Welles, asked him to describe the dream, and the president said he was always onboard an "indescribable vessel" moving swiftly on the water toward "an indefinite shore." This was the same dream he had before Fort Sumter, Bull Run, Antietam, Gettysburg, Stones River, Vicksburg, and other events of the war. He was certain another "great and important event" was on its way.

Grant added that Stone's River was no victory, but Lincoln said though this may be, he assured him, "I had this strange dream again

---

[747] Sandburg, 700.

last night and we shall; judging from the past, have great news very soon." Smiling, he continued, "I think it must be from Sherman. My thoughts are in that direction, as are most of yours."[748] The discussion then turned to what to do about the southern states.

The president said:

> I think it providential that this great rebellion is crushed just as Congress has adjourned and there are none of the disturbing elements of that body to hinder or embarrass us. If we are wise and discreet we shall reanimate the States and get their governments in successful operation, with order prevailing and the Union reestablished before Congress comes together.

He repeated his wish for mercy. "I hope there will be no persecution, no bloody work after the war is over. No one need expect me to take any part in hanging or killing those men, even the worst of them. Frighten them out of the country, open the gates, let down the bars, scare them off." Moving his arms as if swatting away a fly, he added, "Enough lives have been sacrificed. We must extinguish our resentments if we ever expect harmony and union."[749] Many in Congress wanted trials and executions, but he had seen enough bloodshed to last a lifetime.

In the afternoon, he and Mary enjoyed a carriage ride, and they talked of their future after the presidency. He wanted to travel to the Holy Land, then return to Springfield, buy a small farm, and practice law.

Mary noticed he was unusually cheerful, and it made her uneasy because it was so unlike him. She told him this peculiarity and how he had been the same right before Willie's death. He replied, "As well might I be, I consider this day the war has come to a close." Speaking gently of their trials, he said, "We must both be more cheerful in the

---

[748] Welles, Vol. 2, April 1864–December 31, 1865, 282–283 (April 14).
[749] Sandburg, 701–702; Oates, 465.

future; between the war and the loss of our darling Willie, we have been very miserable." Later that day, he told his bodyguard he was aware men wanted him dead, but, "I know no one could do it and escape alive. But if it is to be done, it is impossible to prevent it."[750]

After dinner, he had second thoughts about attending the theater but knew he was expected. The play was *Our American Cousin,* and he enjoyed the comedies almost as much as Shakespeare.

The president's party arrived at Ford's Theater to a packed audience. A standing ovation while the band played "Hail to the Chief" accompanied them to their balcony box seats. The presidential box was draped with a large American flag and a portrait of George Washington for the occasion. As the excitement died down and the play began, Lincoln enjoyed himself, heartily laughing at many of the scenes. At one point, he felt a chill and stood to put on his overcoat. Returning to his chair, Mary grabbed his hand and snuggled closer. Their companions that night were Major Henry B. Rathbone and his fiancé, Clara Harris, and Mary teased Lincoln, "What will Miss Harris think of my hanging on to you so?"

"She won't think anything about it," he said. It had been a long time since he had been in such a good mood. He and Mary were getting along, and the war was over. All the endless slaughter was at an end, and he could finally relax with his wife enjoying laughter.[751]

During a popular scene in the play, the crowd cheered just as the actor John Wilkes Boothe walked up behind the president and fired a bullet into the back of his head.

Slumping forward, Mary kept him from falling and screamed hysterically.

Boothe turned on Major Rathbone, slashed his arm with a knife, and jumped over the balcony rail. Snagging his spur on the draped American flag, the assassin dropped to the stage, fracturing his leg. Limping to center stage, he shouted, "Sic semper tyrannus!" or Latin for "Thus be it ever to tyrants."

---

[750] Ibid., 704; Donald, 593; Oates, 466.
[751] Oates, 467–468; Donald, 595.

For a moment, the audience thought it was part of the play and Boothe was playing a part. Then, Major Rathbone shouted, "*Stop that man!*" But Boothe escaped out a stage door where a getaway horse was waiting.

Clara Harris screamed, "*Won't somebody stop that man? The president is shot!*"

An army doctor at the theater laid Lincoln on the floor and found the hole just behind his left ear. Sticking his finger into the hole, he removed the clotted blood to relieve the pressure building on the brain. The bullet went through Lincoln's brain and was lodged behind his right eye. He was barely breathing, and the doctor failed to find a pulse, so he gave the president mouth-to-mouth resuscitation. Shaking his head, the physician said in a hushed tone, "His wound is mortal, it is impossible for him to recover."

Lincoln was carried across the street to the Petersen House (where a war secretary clerk roomed) and laid on the bed. Mary ran to him, knelt on the floor, and pleaded he speak to her. She was led out of the bedroom to the parlor where she broke down and wailed uncontrollably.

Word of the attack put the capital in a state of fear. Secretary Seward had been viciously assaulted by another assassin but miraculously survived, and the city was afraid they were under attack. Secretary of War Stanton arrived to represent the government and called for Vice President Johnson. Stanton took testimony from witnesses who identified the assassin as the actor, John Wilkes Boothe. The First Lady still wept on a couch in the parlor and cried, "His dream was prophetic." A heavy rain engulfed the city as April 15 arrived.

Senator Charles Sumner held the president's hand as Mary kissed her husband and whispered, "Love, live but one moment to speak to me once—to speak to our children." She pleaded to the man who could accomplish anything. He had tolerated her moods and frivolity and loved her for who she was. He never tried to change her; he just loved her. Who could replace him? First Eddie, then Willie, now him. "Oh my God, and have I given my husband to die?" she asked.

As the room changed from shock and horror to sadness, silence was all that remained. Only Lincoln's shallow breathing and Mary's quiet sobs broke that silence. Gathered around the four-post bed were his friends and family. Even a former opponent was there as Robert cried on Senator Sumner's shoulder. At 7:22 a.m., the president stopped breathing.

Coins were placed on his eyes, and a sheet was draped over him. One of his favorite pastors said a prayer for his family and the nation. Secretary Stanton, the man who showed little emotion, other than anger, was on the verge of tears when he said, "Now he belongs to the ages."[752]

Now he belonged to every American. He would no longer be afraid of losing those he loved. He was now one of those lost. The poor boy from Kentucky who fought the Civil War was now its final casualty. His character and faith guided him down the path to his purpose, and he changed the nation forever. Both traits made him part of the fabric of the nation he loved and inevitably saved.

* * * * *

Irwinville, Georgia, May 10, 1865

The sound of rifles split the quiet as Jeff and Varina Davis woke inside the tent. He quickly dressed. Reaching for his rain cape, he accidently grabbed his wife's. Fumbling for his hat, she threw her shawl over his head to hide his face. Outside the tent, a Union soldier blocked his escape as Varina tried to lure him away, but he grew suspicious.

Davis left the tent and headed for the surrounding woods, and Varina sent her servant, Helen, with a bucket to her husband, hoping to look like they were merely fetching water. Fifty feet from the tent, a Union horse soldier aimed his rifle at Davis and shouted, "Halt!"

---

[752] Welles, Vol. 2, 286–288; Donald, 597–599; Oates, 469–471; Sandburg, 713–716.

Tossing his coat and cover to the ground, he yelled at the mounted man and rushed toward him. He was intending to use an old Indian trick by tossing the rider from his horse and escaping, but as he closed in on the man, Varina threw her arms around her husband and said, "Shoot me if you wish!" Davis was now a prisoner of the Union Army.[753]

Later, his escape attempt would become a yarn of him dressing in a hoop dress and bonnet to allude capture. The press turned his wife's raincoat and shawl into a dress, and much like the false report of Lincoln's arrival in Washington in 1861, it appeared to be fabricated, but the northern media felt vindicated by the tale. Jefferson Davis was not only the most notorious Confederate, but he was also suspected in conspiring with Lincoln's assassins. Upon hearing the news of his murder, Davis said, "I am sorry. We have lost our best friend in the court of the enemy." He knew Johnson had always despised him and accepted that he would be the sacrificial lamb for the cause. He was informed he would be transported to Virginia for prosecution.

Davis sighed and said, "God's will be done."[754] The Confederacy had fallen.

* * * * *

Soon after Lincoln's assassination, John Wilkes Boothe was killed after refusing to surrender. He claimed to have murdered the president to avenge the South, but he only made matters worse. The Union blamed the Confederates for the conspiracy and were out for blood even more. The radical Republicans and Johnson searched for evidence of collusion to implicate Davis. After subsequent trials and the hangings of Boothe's conspirators, no other connection to the Confederacy was ever discovered. Though some proof of conspir-

---

[753] Davis, Burke. *The Long Surrender.* (New York: Vintage Books, 1985, 1989), 143–144; Cooper, 574–575; Tate, 283–284.
[754] Ibid., 86, 145–146; Tate, 279.

acy to commit sabotage and incite dissent in the North occurred in Canada, no assassination plot was unearthed.

After General Joseph Johnston, Secretary of War John Breckinridge, and other trusted officers of the South surrendered, Secretary Stanton and others called for trials and executions. All of Lincoln's words were being ignored now, and his murder was about to undermine his hopes.

Charges were suggested against General Lee and other high-ranking officers who already signed surrender terms.[755] The terms agreed upon decided the surrender, and now, the victor was reneging on a signed agreement, and Grant was outraged. He was the most popular man in the North and most likely the next president of the United States, and his word and honor were now at stake. He honored the president's wishes and wrote of Lincoln:

> I knew the greatness of his heart, his generosity, his yielding disposition, his desire to see all the people of the United States enter upon the full privileges of citizenship with equality among all. I knew the feeling that Mr. Johnson had expressed in speech against the Southern people and I feared that his course toward them would be such as to repel, and make them unwilling citizens.[756]

Even Sherman, who left a path of destruction through the South, wanted healing, not revenge. His initial surrender terms to Johnston were even more generous than Grant's to Lee but were rejected by Johnson's administration.

Lee wrote Grant shortly after being charged with treason against the United States and asked if his agreement at Appomattox was final. Grant assured him that he would personally guarantee the terms were honored. He had brokered the end of the war with Lee and would

---

[755] Ibid., 203–206; Cooper, 601–603.
[756] Grant, Vol. 2, 509.

use his popularity to uphold these terms. President Johnson needed Grant's popular support, so he agreed to drop the charges against Lee and other high-ranking Confederates. Only Jefferson Davis remained in prison with the shadow of retribution hanging over his head.[757]

The American Civil War was over for the rest of the nation.

* * * * *

On Christmas Day, 1868, two years of prison came to an end for the Confederate president when Johnson finally granted amnesty to all Confederates, including Davis.

Davis refused to ever admit wrongdoing and would remain a rebel until he addressed a crowd of admiring Georgians a year before his death by the same malaria which took his first wife:

> The past is dead; let it bury its dead, its hopes and its aspirations. Before you lies the future—a future of golden promise; a future of expanding national glory, before which all the world shall stand amazed. Let me beseech you to lay aside all rancor, and all bitter sectional feeling, and take your places in the ranks of those who will bring about a consummation devoutly to be wished—a reunited country.[758]

The North and the South forgave each other and became Americans once again. Ulysses S. Grant was elected two terms as president and died in 1885 of throat cancer at the age of sixty-three. Cigars apparently were the only thing that could lick him.

Robert E. Lee died in 1870, and for the last five years of his life, he preached forgiveness and reunion. He never allowed his defeat to change who he was as a man. To him, everything happened for a reason, including his failure in the war.

[757] Freeman, *Lee*, 516–518.
[758] Davis, Burke, *Surrender*, 262–263; Cooper, 700–702; Foote, Vol. 3, 1058.

Anna Jackson never remarried, and she preserved her husband's memory until her death in 1915. Jackson is still revered as one of the greatest generals of all time, and his victory at Chancellorsville is studied at West Point still today.

Mary Todd Lincoln lost her third son, Tad, in 1871 at the age of eighteen. She was committed to a mental hospital soon after and released into the custody of her sister. She died in 1882.

Robert Lincoln outlived his entire family and served as Secretary of War under Presidents James Garfield and Chester Arthur and minister to Great Britain under Presidents Benjamin Harrison and Grover Cleveland. He lived long enough to see the dedication of the Lincoln Memorial before his death in 1926.

Joshua L. Chamberlain became Governor of Maine from 1866–1870, president of Bowdoin College, and received the Medal of Honor for his bravery at Petersburg. The wound he received there would cause him problems the rest of his life and eventually claimed him in 1914. He accomplished much with his father's wisdom. "Do it, that's how" was his motto—and he certainly did.

There were 620,000 Americans killed in the Civil War, and another half million were wounded or maimed. Over a million casualties was the price paid for the war, but slavery was abolished in the process, and the nation eventually healed. It would take another century before segregation ended in the South, but the scourge of slavery was purchased in blood during the four years of war.[759]

Lee, Jackson, Grant, Chamberlain, Davis, and Lincoln all believed that God's will was carried out, regardless of their own, and their struggles and failures forged them into the men they became. They were six shades of blue and gray at the mercy of an artist who determined his own masterpiece. Thankfully, he knew better.

---

[759] Foote, Vol. 3, 1040; McPherson, 854.

In 1869, Lee spoke of his surrender, seemingly defining his own and the nation's struggles. "We failed, we failed, but in the good providence of God apparent failure often proves a blessing."[760]

* * * * *

The American Civil War was unique, because the victors and the vanquished both believed in the Christian principles of forgiveness and mercy. The individual was valued above all else. Lee persuaded his officers against guerrilla war and all its horrors because he was guided by these principles. Lincoln, Grant, and Sherman called for leniency and reconciliation, instead of revenge, guided by their own principles.

Those who fought the war put aside their differences to become countrymen again. They tamed the West, grew into a world power, and ushered in historic prosperity and freedom. Their children and grandchildren won two world wars and built the most powerful nation on earth. Individuals set the standard, and together, they found a way to become one nation under God once again.

In 1975, citizenship was restored to General Lee and signed into law by President Ford, and three years later, Jefferson Davis was as well by President Carter. The American faith of Christianity taught forgiveness, so they forgave each other.[761]

Forged in the fires of adversity, Americans overcame starvation and war, revolution and invasion, the frontier and civil war, and through it all, individuals relied on divine providence and purpose. They possessed the will to persevere through impossible odds and chose to determine their own path and, in the end, shaped a nation. Every step down this path from Jamestown to Ford's Theater seemed interconnected and by design. In their darkest hours, God's hand of providence protected them and showed the way. When they relied on him, they were blessed.

---

[760] Freeman, *Lee*, 559.
[761] Davis, Burke, *Surrender*, 285.

Visiting Richmond after its fall, Lincoln's advice to the newly freed slaves still rings true for future generations as well as our own:

> Liberty is your birthright. God gave you as he gave it to others… You must try to deserve this priceless boon. Let the world see that you merit it, and are able to maintain it by your good works. Don't let your joy carry you into excesses. Learn the laws and obey them; obey God's commandments and thank Him for giving you liberty, for Him you owe all things.[762]

Do we merit our blessings by our good works? Do we forget those blessings in our joy and make excuses in our excess? Can we ask ourselves if we deserve our birthright? And have we earned it? Have we been forged in the fires like those before us? Does providence, purpose, and perseverance determine our path? Do we consider what Lincoln challenged the freed slaves to consider—do we deserve our freedom?

These answers will come in God's time, not our own.

---

[762] See note 758.

About the Author

E. Paul Yarbro is a writer and historian with over fifteen years' research of the historical records, diaries, correspondence, and eye-witness accounts of early Americans. He lives in Missouri with his wife, Jennifer, and son, Jacob.

CPSIA information can be obtained
at www.ICGtesting.com
Printed in the USA
LVHW091439190220
647490LV00001B/1

9 781098 025328